Exceptional Lives

Special Education in Today's Schools

Fifth Edition

Ann Turnbull
University of Kansas

Rud Turnbull
University of Kansas

Michael L. Wehmeyer
University of Kansas

PEARSON

Merrill
Prentice Hall

Upper Saddle River, New Jersey
Columbus, Ohio

W9-BPJ-615

Library of Congress Cataloging in Publication Data
Turnbull, Ann P.
  Exceptional lives: special education in today's schools / Ann Turnbull,
Rud Turnbull, Michael L. Wehmeyer.—5th ed.
    p. cm.
  Includes bibliographical references and index.
  ISBN 0-13-170869-4 (paper)
  1. Children with disabilities—Education—United States—Case studies. 2. Special
education—United States—Case studies. 3. Inclusive education—United States—Case studies.
I. Turnbull, Rud. II. Wehmeyer, Michael L. III. Title.

LC4031.T878 2007
371.9073–dc22

                                                                    2005054645

Vice President and Executive Publisher: Jeffery W. Johnston
Senior Editor: Allyson P. Sharp
Development Editor: Linda K. Kauffman
Editorial Assistant: Kathleen S. Burk
Production Editor: Sheryl Glicker Langner
Design Coordinator: Diane C. Lorenzo
Cover Design: Ali Mohrman
Photo Coordinator: Lori Whitley
Production Manager: Laura Messerly
Director of Marketing: David Gesell
Marketing Manager: Autumn Purdy
Marketing Coordinator: Brian Mounts

This book was set in Goudy and Americana by Carlisle Publishing Services. It was printed and bound by R.R.
Donnelley & Sons Company. The cover was printed by Phoenix Color Corp.

Photo Credits: Photo Credits are on page xxix.

Pearson Prentice Hall™ is a trademark of Pearson Education, Inc.
Pearson® is a registered trademark of Pearson plc
Prentice Hall® is a registered trademark of Pearson Education, Inc.
Merrill® is a registered trademark of Pearson Education, Inc.

Pearson Education Ltd.   Pearson Education Australia Pty. Limited
Pearson Education Singapore Pte. Ltd.   Pearson Education North Asia Ltd.
Pearson Education Canada, Ltd.   Pearson Educación de Mexico, S.A. de C.V.
Pearson Education–Japan   Pearson Education Malaysia Pte. Ltd.

10 9 8 7 6 5 4 3 2 1
ISBN: 0-13-170869-4

Ann and Rud dedicate this book to their family: Jay, Amy, Kate, Rahul, and Dylan.

Michael dedicates this book to his family: Kathy, Geoff, and Graham.

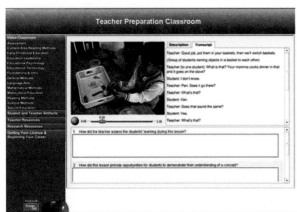

Preface

New Laws and Greater Opportunities for All Students

The great English jurist Lord Coke once famously declared that *if the reason for a rule of law ceases to exist, the rule of law itself should cease to exist*. His axiom applies forcefully to the federal and state laws governing the education of students with disabilities and those who are unusually talented. It does so for two reasons.

First, the federal law applying to all students, the No Child Left Behind Act (NCLB), establishes six principles for the education of all students, including those with disabilities:

- Accountability for outcomes, based on assessment of student progress.
- Use of evidence-based methods of instruction, to secure those outcomes.
- Employment of highly qualified teachers, for the same purpose.
- Authority for school administrators to use federal and state funds flexibly, also for the same purpose.
- Assurances that schools will be safe environments for teaching and learning.
- Grants of power to parents to remove their children from unsafe or "failing" schools.

Second, Congress reauthorized and amended the federal law applying to students with disabilities, the Individuals with Disabilities Education ACT, in 2004. It did so under a law called the "Individuals with Disabilities Education Improvement Act" (IDEIA). But that law still uses the same "short title" that it has used for more than a decade, the "Individuals with Disabilities Education Act" (IDEA), and its six principles also are the same as before:

- Zero reject, or the education of *all* children with disabilities.
- Non-discriminatory evaluation, or the fair assessment of each student's needs and strengths.
- Appropriate education, or an individualized opportunity to benefit from the education offered under NCLB and IDEA.
- Least restrictive environment, or the education of each student with a disability, to the maximum extent appropriate, in the general curriculum.
- Procedural due process, or the opportunity for schools and families to hold each other accountable for the student's education.
- Parent participation, or the opportunity for educators and families to be trusted and trustworthy partners in educating the student.

These two laws, NCLB and IDEA, assert that the reasons for the old rules of law have changed, and so too should the laws. The reason for federal assistance in education used to be to assist the states to continue to do what they had been doing for many years (since the 1960s in general education and since the mid-1970's in special education). Now, however, the reasons have changed, so the laws changed. The current need is to improve the outcomes for students by improving educators' capacities.

Special educators have responded to NCLB and the reauthorized and amended IDEA in several ways, as we point out in this book.

- Special educators are becoming more capable of teaching students with disabilities and being partners with general educators, other professionals, parents, and students.
- They are integrating themselves and their students into the general curriculum more powerfully than ever before.
- They are using the principles of universal design for learning when they teach students with disabilities and collaborate with general educators.
- They seek to develop students' capacities to perform the skills that the curriculum covers, but especially to be self-determined, autonomous individuals.
- They are becoming more competent to educate students from culturally and linguistically diverse backgrounds.
- They are building stronger partnerships with parents and students and building trusted and trustworthy relationships with them and with general educators.

Our Vision and Our Values

Our vision is that the two laws, NCLB and IDEA, will be more than the foundations on which educators, students, and families will rely. Our vision is also that a deep sense of values will permeate every action that every educator takes.

 Envision great expectations for all students. Create an enviable life for all students.

 Encourage students' positive contributions. Recognize that every student has gifts to bestow on other students and all communities.

 Build on students' strengths. By all means acknowledge and address student needs, but abandon the "fix it" approach in education and adopt a strengths-based one instead.

 Enable students to become self-determined. Dare to let go of them and their lives, develop their abilities to know what they want and how to realize their dreams, and do so on the basis of a powerful curriculum taught universally in all aspects of the general curriculum.

 Expand students' relationships with their peers without disabilities, as well as their peers with disabilities and with all educators and relevant community members.

 Ensure students' full citizenship. Less able does not mean less worthy. Build your students' capacities to exercise their rights and responsibilities in this country.

Throughout the book, we refer to these values in margin notes, each identified with its own icon. These margin notes reinforce our vision—to connect educational actions to the values.

Our Book's Organization

Chapters 1 through 4 lay the foundation for the rest of the book. In this new edition, we have created a separate chapter on diversity in today's schools. In addition, because of our commitment to families, we now have a chapter fully devoted to the role of families and the strengths they bring to the education of their children.

- Chapter 1 describes today's students and educators and other professionals; the six principles and basic provisions of IDEA (as reauthorized and amended in 2004) and NCLB, the two federal laws that prohibit discrimination based on disability (Section 504 and Americans with Disabilities Act); and the outcomes of special education (and, implicitly, why Lord Coke's axiom applies today to special and general education).
- Chapter 2 focuses on why and how to educate students with disabilities in the general curriculum, emphasizing universal design for learning and self-determination.

- Chapter 3 addresses the cultural and linguistic diversity of students with disabilities and how educators can become more culturally competent.

- Chapter 4 describes how educators and families can be partners with each other, why trust is the essential ingredient of their relationships with each other, and how the six principles of partnerships can result in trust.

Chapters 5 through 15 comprehensively describe the most research-based, state-of-the-art techniques for evaluating and teaching students with different types of disability, and for doing so in the context of the general curriculum. Chapter 16 devotes itself to the education of students with unusual gifts and talents. Each of these chapters encompasses a similar organization and focus.

Chapter Format

Chapters 5 through 16 have the same "flavor" and format. Their similar flavor comes from the themes that we weave throughout each chapter: universal design, inclusion, multicultural competence, and professional-parent-student partnerships. To reinforce the process of implementing effective education for all students, we present the content of these chapters in a proactive manner, beginning with appropriate evaluation procedures, continuing through developing Individualized Education Programs (IEPs), designing curriculum, and assessing student progress. The similar chapter format comes from the way we present our information. Each chapter follows this order in its presentation of content:

Vignettes. We begin each chapter with a vignette, a short portrait of real students, real families, and real educators—the people in today's schools. These people represent a wide range of cultural and linguistic groups, and they live in a wide variety of geographic locations across the country.

Categorical information. Next, we define the exceptionality, describe its characteristics, and identify its prevalence and causes. At the beginning of each chapter, you get a sharp picture of the exceptionality, framed in its most basic dimensions.

Evaluation procedures. After a presentation of the exceptionalities in each chapter, we take you into teachers' working environments. We explain how and why educators evaluate students and then how educators provide special education and related services. The process of evaluation is the same for all students with disabilities, no matter what the student's "category" is. This is because the IDEA sets out a standardized process. The tools used, however—the evaluation instruments—vary by category. We describe two evaluation tools for each category. First, we describe a research-based, state-of-the-art evaluation instrument for determining whether a student is exceptional. Second, we describe the evaluation tool for determining the nature and extent of the special education that the schools should offer. Many of these evaluation tools, however, are suitable for students across various categories, as we often point out.

Designing an appropriate Individualized Education Program. In the overall process of delivering appropriate education, evaluation leads to services. So we next describe how professionals can be partners with other professionals, parents, and students to provide an appropriate education in the general curriculum. This team of partners designs an IEP, determining what supplementary aids and services a student needs to participate in the general curriculum, how to plan and deliver universally designed education, and how to respond to the students' other educational needs.

Using effective instructional strategies. Because students' needs vary by age, we next describe the research-based effective educational strategies for early childhood, elementary and middle school, and secondary and transition programs. Every categorical chapter presents strategies for each of these grade-level designations to give all prospective teachers real-life examples. These strategies represent the best of the best from teachers and programs across the country.

Including students. Because IDEA commands that students be educated, to the maximum extent appropriate, in the general curriculum, we describe how the strategies lead to students' inclusion in the general curriculum. In this section we also include our *Inclusion Tips* feature that provides practical guidance for the classroom.

Assessing students' progress. Because both NCLB and IDEA seek better student outcomes, we describe how to assess students' progress. Sometimes this includes making accommodations in and for assessment, so we also include practical aspects to consider in assessing the progress of students.

Looking to the future. At the end of every chapter, we then return to the student whom we featured in the vignette, projecting a future that can occur when teachers use the approaches we have described in each chapter. The future, of course, depends, in great respect, on how well educators, families, and other professionals come together to provide the most effective education for all children . . . a lofty goal that we hope you will hold as dear to you as we do.

Summing up the chapter. We end the chapters by summarizing the main points, in concise, bulleted form, for ease of review. We also include a set of activities that help you make connections to the professional standards for the field of special education. Two sets of standards are referenced in these activities, and they appear in Appendix A at the end of the book. The Council for Exceptional Children (CEC) promotes ten professional standards (of the CEC Common Core) that we ask you to relate to the content in the book. We also link the end-of-chapter activities to the Special Education: Knowledge-Based Core Principles standards for special education that provide the basis for the PRAXIS™ exams for teacher certification (also in Appendix A). These activities help you see how the book's content relates to your future professional educational behaviors and dispositions.

Special Chapter Features

Real Students, Real Educators, Real Families, Real Issues

This is not a book of fiction. There are no imagined characters here. Every student, every teacher, every parent, every friend is real. To tell their stories serves a powerful didactic purpose: to describe, in their own words and through these snapshots of their lives, how special education benefits each and every one of them. These students, educators, family members, and friends show you what can happen—how exceptional lives can be made all the more exceptional—when you approach them on the basis of principles and state-of-the-art teaching techniques.

Chapter vignettes. These opening narratives tell the stories of students and their families, friends, teachers, and other educators and service providers. We refer to these vignettes throughout each chapter to exemplify our key points and content. We augment the vignettes and our summaries of research-based, state-of-the-art techniques by highlighting many strategies and tips for educators throughout the chapter.

Vignettes open each chapter and personalize the content—these real students and their families provide insight into the lives of individuals who live with exceptionalities every day of their lives.

Your Own Voice. This feature is a new one to this edition and continues our focus on connecting in personal ways to the content of the book. These features present situations—maybe a dilemma, maybe a particular perspective, maybe a challenge. We ask you to think about the situation, investigate some possible resources, and take a position: How do you feel? What do you believe? How would you handle it? In "your own voice," we want you to reflect on the impact you and others can make. More than that, it challenges you to think hard about what you should, could, and would do as a teacher using the techniques we have described, under the laws that govern you, and pursuant to the values that we recommend should guide you.

Your Own Voice ~ Crossing Boundaries or Not? — Box 4-1

You have just begun your first year as a teacher. Consistent with the practices you have learned in this book, you want to establish a trusting partnership with the parents of the students in your class, especially those who have disabilities or are at risk for disabilities, because you think that they and their parents will need more from you this year. You are willing to give whatever it takes, and you plan to tell the parents that when you meet with them at the beginning of the school year.

But then a veteran teacher cautions you not to invest too much in the parents. "The kids, not the parents, are your first concern," she reminds you. "And if you think the kids are tough," she says, "wait till you encounter some of their parents. You'll need all the recovery time you can get for yourself."

Her admonition causes you to ponder your choices. At one end of your range of choices is being "strictly professional" in working with the families, depersonalizing and keeping a distance and rigidly adhering to doing only the job of teaching the students. In the middle range of your choices is enlarging your obligations by doing some of the extras, such as telephoning other professionals who work with the child or family to advocate for certain evaluations or services or making home visits. At the other end of your range of choices is being "like family," establishing a relationship outside the professional context by attending their family gatherings and inviting them to your family and social events.

You seek guidance from the National Education Association and the Council for Exceptional Children but find that neither organization answers your question in its codes of ethics. You want to practice the seven partnership principles—communication, commitment, equality, professional skills, respect, advocacy, and trust—so you are inclined to disregard the veteran teacher's advice.

But you know that she has a good point: you have always needed your own time and space, even within the confines of your own family and friendship networks. Your solitude refreshes and harmonizes you; it allows you to synchronize your mind and emotions. In turn, you are more compatible with your family, friends, professional peers, and students. Yes, you are committed to enhancing your students' quality of life and their families'. But you've also got to look after your own quality of life.

Take a position on what you think the appropriate boundaries are between parents and professionals. Previously you read about a continuum of choice. Which choice is right for you?

For guidance, read the National Education Association's code of ethics, found at www.nea.org/aboutnea/faq.html. Also read the Council for Exceptional Children's code of ethics, found at www.cec.sped.org/ps/code/html. Finally, read Lord-Nelson, L. G., Summers, J. A., & Turnbull, A. P. (2004). Boundaries in family-professional relationships: Implications for special education. *Remedial and Special Education*, 25(3).

These features help readers formulate personal perspectives, positions, and beliefs regarding their professional responses to situations they might encounter in classrooms, working with other professionals, administrators, and family members.

Observation	**Medical personnel observe:** The student does not attain appropriate developmental milestones or has characteristics of a particular syndrome associated with mental retardation. **Teacher and parents observe:** The student (1) does not learn as quickly as peers, (2) has difficulty retaining and generalizing learned skills, (3) has low motivation, and (4) has more limitations in adaptive behaviors than peers in the general education classroom.
Screening	**Assessment measures:** **Medical screening:** The student may be identified through a physician's use of various tests before the child enters school. **Classroom work products:** The student has difficulty in academic areas in the general education classroom; reading comprehension and mathematical reasoning/application are limited.
Prereferral	**Teacher implements suggestions from school-based team:** The student still performs poorly in academics or continues to manifest impairments in adaptive behavior despite interventions. If the student has been identified before entering school, this step is omitted.
Referral	If, in spite of interventions, the student still performs poorly in academics or continues to manifest impairments in adaptive behaviors, the child is referred to a multidisciplinary team.
Nondiscriminatory evaluation procedures and standards	**Assessment measures:** **Individualized intelligence test:** The student has significantly subaverage intellectual functioning (bottom 2 to 3% of population) with IQ standard score of 70 to 75 or below. The nondiscriminatory evaluation team makes sure the test is not culturally biased. **Adaptive behavior scales:** The student scores significantly below average in two or more adaptive skill domains, indicating deficits in skill areas such as communication, home living, self-direction, and leisure. **Anecdotal records:** The student's learning problems cannot be explained by cultural or linguistic differences. **Curriculum-based assessment:** The student experiences difficulty in making progress in the general curriculum used by the local school district. **Direct obser...** ...nt experiences difficult...

The Non-Discriminatory Evaluation figures in Chapters 5 through 16 outline the process prescribed by IDEA for appropriate evaluation and identification.

Non-discriminatory evaluation process. In Chapters 5 through 16, we summarize the evaluation process as it is established by the Individuals with Disabilities Education Act. This process is outlined in a figure that relates information specific to each exceptionality. This **Non-Discriminatory Evaluation** figure provides succinct guidelines for appropriate evaluation and identification.

Strategies and Tips for Special Education Teachers

The majority of students with disabilities can progress in the general education curriculum if educators will apply the techniques we have described and use the strategies and tips we highlight.

Margin notes. Throughout the chapters we include margin notes that help link content with a practical focus. Some notes link content to the values discussed above; some notes link content to CEC or PRAXIS™ standards; some notes refer readers to the Companion Website. All these additional references help integrate the content in meaningful, professional contexts.

PRAXIS
Standard: When you recognize the needs of families and support them, you are addressing PRAXIS™ Standard 2, Legal and Societal Issues.

Inclusion Tips. This favorite feature highlights one of the major themes of the book. The information in the feature provides helpful advice and strategies for including students in the general curriculum. We address student behaviors, social interactions, educational performance, and classroom attitudes in relation to what teachers may see in the classroom, what they may be tempted to do, other responses, and best practices for including the student's peers in the process. We supplement each highlighted **Inclusion Tips** with information about universally designed learning and self-determination.

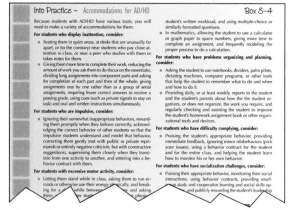

Applying these tips in the classroom assures more effective inclusion of students with exceptionalities.

Creating partnerships makes a critical difference in helping students develop and maintain progress toward goals in and outside of the school environment.

Partnership Tips. To reflect the focus on families and partnerships that guides the book, this feature provides practical, workable ways to develop and maintain effective partnerships between professionals in and out of school, families, and educators. This critical collaboration process makes the difference between effective learning and progress toward goals and unsuccessful attempts.

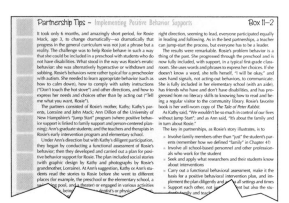

Into Practice. In every chapter, this feature describes practical, step-by-step examples of how to use universal design, secure inclusion, respond to the multicultural nature of American schools, and practice collaboration and partnerships.

Practical, everyday tips for the classroom give students hands-on ways to implement appropriate strategies.

Diversity Tips. These tips help prepare teachers to consider students' diverse backgrounds (their language, gender, ethnicity, race, socioeconomic status, geography, and exceptionality/ability) when planning curriculum, instruction, and evaluation and when collaborating with families and other service providers.

These features are guided by the need for sensitivity to our diverse populations and critical issues in addressing appropriate educational strategies. Maximizing learning and progress in the general curriculum is the ultimate goal for every student.

Samples of technology—software, websites, adaptive equipment—provide up-to-date resources to assist with learning and classroom instruction.

Technology Tips. This resourceful feature highlights a technology that teachers can use in the classroom (or one that supports classroom instruction) to help meet the educational needs of students with disabilities. The technology featured can be anything from a software program to an assistive or adaptive technology, or even specific educational websites.

Supplements

This fifth edition of *Exceptional Lives: Special Education in Today's Schools* boasts the most comprehensive and integrated collection of supplements to date. A number of items assist students and professors alike in maximizing learning and instruction. This book has always tried to immerse the student in its content, and students and instructors who embrace this approach benefit from a deeper and more meaningful learning experience. All of the supplements were designed and updated to reflect first-hand experiences with the content and the individuals in the book and its supplements. The supplements also embrace universal design by using multiple ways of presenting material, multiple ways of engaging the students, and multiple ways of allowing students to respond.

Real Lives and Exceptionalities DVD

Accompanying this edition, we have a new DVD that includes video footage of individuals from the chapter-opening vignettes. Heather and Star Morgan from Chapter 2, George Wedge from Chapter 6, Ryan Frisella from Chapter 12, and Briana Hoskins from Chapter 16 are featured in five segments that cover aspects of school, families, and community. In addition, an extraordinary segment, "Beyond School," highlights nine individuals as they pursue life outside of school, in the workplace, enjoying hobbies, and engaging in community interests, demonstrating the lifelong goal of purposeful and productive lives. These individuals represent a successful transitioning into adulthood and show the myriad ways that individuals with exceptionalities live active, exciting lives. Activities for classroom use, student investigations, and end-of-chapter questions all integrate the use of the DVD for professors and students. Margin notes within the text also guide readers to relevant segments of the DVD for viewing. This DVD is also available on VHS.

Companion Website

Located at *www.prenhall.com/turnbull*, the Companion Website, a valuable resource for both the professor and the student, has several new, exciting features to accompany the text:

■ Brief video clips can accompany any presentation or be used for added enrichment. They include "Focus on Adults" videos that illustrate how adults with disabilities are vital members of our communities.

■ Updated computer activities supplement the chapters, and teaching modules from Special Connections from the University of Kansas and Vanderbilt's Iris Center give extensive interactive case study-based learning opportunities.

■ Additional written case study examples have been added from the Clearinghouse of Special Education Cases from the University of Florida. These online activities can be great supplements or instructional tools for online or online supported classes.

There are several features that appear in the current website that have been retained to help students gauge their understanding of the chapter contents and to explore areas beyond the pages of the text:

- Options for self-assessment
- Chapter overview
- Additional artifacts to match the case studies
- Margin note links that contain important resources from each chapter
- An extensive resources section
- Video Activities to broaden focus of use for instructors
- Activities for students
- Collaboration Activities
- Your Own Voice links
- Partnership Tips
- Inclusion Tips
- Technology Tips
- Into Practice Strategies
- Diversity Tips

OneKey Course Management System

OneKey is Prentice Hall's exclusive new online resource for students and instructors. OneKey is an integrated online course management resource featuring everything students and instructors need for work in or outside of the classroom. It is available in the nationally hosted CourseCompass platform, as well as WebCT and Blackboard. For more information about OneKey, please contact your local Merrill representative prior to placing your textbook order.

For the Professor

Instructor's Manual. The Instructor's Manual helps to synthesize all of the resources available for each chapter, but also helps to sift through the materials to match the delivery method (e.g., semester, quarter) and areas of emphasis for the course. These materials can be used for traditional courses as well as online or online supported courses. The Instructor's Manual includes the following resources for the professor:

- Sample syllabi for semester, and quarter courses
- Chapter objectives
- Chapter outline/PowerPoint slides to guide chapter coverage
- CEC and PRAXIS™ standards linked to chapter content
- Projects and assignments suitable for students, some of which come with scoring rubrics to assist with grading
- Short activities that reflect chapter content
- DVD activities and suggestions for viewing
- Directions for successful classroom activities that have worked with small and large groups will be included, as well as handouts or materials to implement the activities

Test Bank and TestGen software. Students learn better when they are held accountable for what they have learned. That is why we have developed a bank of over 50 test questions per chapter in a variety of formats (including true-false, multiple choice, short answer, and essay) that match the issues, questions, and activities that we set out in each chapter. The Test Bank is available in hard copy and electronic formats for ease of use. Questions have been updated and cross-referenced to match the content of this new edition:

- Questions are now each aligned with the PRAXIS™ and the CEC standards.
- Additional case study–style questions similar to the PRAXIS™ have been added for each chapter.

PowerPoint slides/Transparency Masters. These visual aids display, summarize, and help explain core information presented in each chapter. They can be downloaded from our Companion Website (*http://www.prenhall.com/turnbull*), and they are also available in transparency format for professors. All PowerPoint slides have been updated for consistency and to reflect current content in this new edition. Additionally, these improvements have been added:

- The slides now have updated links to Internet sites that can be used during presentations.
- The slides have been animated for live presentations or online instruction.
- The presentations can also be printed out as transparencies, and the outline option can be used as study guides to accompany the presentations.
- The slide outline is also included in the Student Study Guide so students can take notes effectively.

Presentation Manager Software. The Presentation Manager Software helps to create a valuable multimedia classroom by utilizing the PowerPoint slides, videos, and instructional materials that the book has to offer. Having these supplements together allows the instructor to modify and adapt the ancillaries to create the most optimal learning environment for his or her students.

For the Student

Student Study Guide. The Student Study Guide allows students to practice their learning on a variety of levels. The most important features will lead students to reflect on the connection of what they have learned to incidents in their own life and apply the knowledge to real-world scenarios. The Student Study Guide includes the following:

- Chapter objectives
- Introduction to some special education vocabulary to provide a working knowledge of some commonly used terms
- Replications of PowerPoint slide outlines to allow for ease of note-taking
- Graphic organizers to assist with chapter content
- Hands-on activities to engage students in active learning of chapter content
- Links to the DVD encourage students to engage in the content first-hand.
- Self-assessment items (multiple choice) reflect questions similar to some test bank items to encourage students to use the guide.
- A complete table of the CEC Standards for Special Education is included for reference when answering questions and making content connections.
- Activities that lead to online, DVD and other resources for additional information about the topics in the text
- Students will be given opportunities to utilize the multimedia ancillaries to increase their understanding of the concepts.
- Many concepts will be presented in different formats to accommodate different learning strengths. Students will be asked to respond in a variety of ways to illustrate how response formats can be varied for their students as well—e.g., writing letters, preparing for an IEP meeting. Opportunities for students to reflect on what they learned will be provided.

Acknowledgments

Many people have contributed to this book. From the Turnbulls' perspective, their son, Jay, who is now 38 years old and was one of the students who first benefited from IDEA (when it was enacted in 1975 as Education of All Handicapped Children Act), has been their best professor, teaching them time and again how and why to respond to his very self-determined ways, his great expectations, and his insistence on living as a full citizen. He's their best professor, but he often gives them the final examination before giving them the class. That's not bad; it makes them better educators and advocates and (they hope) better authors of this book. Amy Turnbull Khare and Kate Turnbull, the Turnbulls' two daughters, Rahul Khare, their son-in-law, and Dylan Khare, their grandson, offered the solace of a loving family and the sanctuary of their homes when both solace and sanctuary were the necessary antidotes to the pressures of producing this book.

Michael Wehmeyer would like to acknowledge the ongoing support of his wife Kathy and sons Geoff and Graham in all his professional activities, as well as his colleagues in the University of Kansas Department of Special Education, at the Beach Center on Disability, and in the Kansas University Center on Developmental Disabilities.

Of course, the families, students, and teachers featured in the vignettes are indispensable to this book. Unless they opened their lives to us, we could not have written about them. In every way, they are your professors, and ours, too. Our gratitude to them is unbounded.

This book is the product of a collaboration among many different talented professionals. At the Beach Center on Disability at the University of Kansas, where we work, we have had the immeasurable benefit of Lois Weldon's many skills. She never flinched when presented with yet another draft of a chapter, with still another request to create figures and boxes, and with unexpected deadlines. We could not do what we do daily without her calm, cool, and composed work ethic. Also at the Beach Center, Mary-Margaret Simpson, herself an author, and Ray Pence, a promising young scholar in the new field called disability studies, helped edit our text before we dared send it to our publisher, and they were veritable Sherlock Holmeses in helping us track down all of our references and permissions. They made our work more readable and more precise, and for that we are most grateful.

Stan Trent, a professor at The University of Virginia, and Alfredo Artilles, who had been on the faculty there but finds his home at Arizona State University, added great value by writing the chapter on cultural and linguistic diversity and providing a framework that we track in the *Diversity Tips* throughout the book.

Jane Wegner, of the Schiefelbusch speech-language-hearing clinic at the University of Kansas, and Evette Edmister, a speech-language pathologist in Des Moines, Iowa (who trained with Jane at the University of Kansas), once again contributed a superb chapter on communication impairment.

Sally Roberts, associate professor in the Department of Special Education at the University of Kansas, did likewise with respect to the chapter on hearing impairment. Sandy Lewis at Florida State University once again wrote the chapter on visual impairment and helped us all understand how to educate students with that disability.

Two extramural collaborators were helpful in different ways. Linda Kauffman, our development editor, assisted greatly by developing a comprehensive guide for all authors, editing chapters, advising each author, drafting captions, and coordinating our work with the publisher.

Lori Kauffman Faison, Linda's sister, made it possible for us to meet several families in the San Diego area and to feature them in vignettes. She also contributed materials for the extraordinary DVD, the website, and ancillaries that help bring our book to life, and ancillaries that accompany this book. These two professionals, these two sisters, greatly strengthened the book and its utility.

The book alone does not suffice to teach you all you need to know. That is why we have the ancillaries, and that is why Janna Siegel Robertson, at the University of Memphis, Department of Curriculum and Instruction, plays such an important role in preparing you to be an effective teacher. As a professor who uses this book to teach special education courses, she knows firsthand what best supports learning in the college classroom. She prepared all of the ancillary materials, and she did that job with unsurpassed skill.

At Merrill/Prentice Hall, our publisher, we benefited (again) from the executive leadership of our foresighted editors, Jeff Johnston and Allyson Sharp, who gave us firm direction, ample support, and enduring encouragement. Sheryl Langner reprised her role as our production editor; no authors could have a more cheerful and eagle-eyed colleague than Sheryl. Kathy Burk assisted Allyson, but she also assisted us efficiently and promptly; she moved us off of dead center on many logistical issues.

Our copy editor Dawn Potter returned to the team and, as is her wont, sleuthed every line of the text, found and corrected errors, and rendered the book much more accessible.

This is the fifth edition of *Exceptional Lives*. It still reflects the vision that our former editor, Ann Davis, had for this book—a vision that we would faithfully depict the real lives of the students, teachers, other professionals, and families involved in special education. This edition also mirrors some of the contributions that former co-authors Sean Smith and Marilyn Shank made to previous editions. Memory is the gratitude of the heart; we remember Ann, Sean, and Marilyn with respect.

We also gratefully acknowledge the input and insight of several reviewers who helped us keep our book current and in step with their classrooms and students: Ellyn Arwood, University of Portland; Monica Brown, University of Kansas; Martha A. Cocchiarella, Arizona State University; Sheila Drake, MidAmerica Nazarene University; Helen Hammond, University of Texas at El Paso; Jack Hourcade, Boise State University; Mickie Mathes, Brenau University; Craig Miner, California State University, Fresno; Mary O'Brian, Illinois State University; Wayne Swanger, University of Wisconsin–Oshkosh; and Donna Wandry, West Chester University.

Brief Contents

Contents

Chapter 6
Understanding Students with Communication Disorders   130

Chapter 7
Understanding Students with Emotional or Behavioral Disorders   156

Chapter 11
Understanding Students with Autism   258

Chapter 12
Understanding Students with Physical Disabilities and Other Health Impairments   284

Note: Every effort has been made to provide accurate and current Internet information in this book. However, the Internet and information posted on it are constantly changing, and it is inevitable that some of the Internet addresses listed in this textbook will change.

Special Features

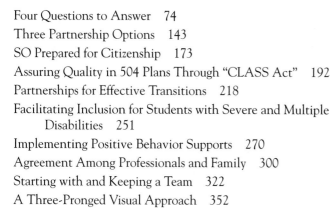 Partnership Tips

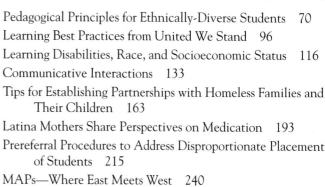 Diversity Tips

Photo Credits

Chapter 1
Courtesy of the Ellenson family, pp. 2, 3, 11, 22, 26; © Ariel Skelley/Corbis, p. 7; Ellen Senisi/The Image Works, p. 17

Chapter 2
Courtesy of the Morgan family, pp. 30, 31, 33, 34, 42, 43; Laima Druskis/PH College, p. 36

Chapter 3
Courtesy of the Cortes family, pp. 56, 57; Will Hart/PhotoEdit, p. 58; © Bettmann/Corbis, p. 61; Tom Watson/Merrill, p. 63; Laima Druskis, /PH College, p. 65; © Ariel Skelley/Corbis, p. 71

Chapter 4
Courtesy of the Holley family, pp. 80, 81; Jonathan Nourok/PhotoEdit, p. 82; Jose Carrillo/PhotoEdit, p. 84; Alan S. Weiner/Getty Images, Inc. – Liaison, p. 91; Robin L. Sachs/PhotoEdit, p. 98

Chapter 5
Courtesy of the Marsh family, pp. 104, 105, 109, 111, 118, 122; Anthony Magnacca/Merrill, p. 107; Michael Newman/PhotoEdit, p. 115

Chapter 6
Courtesy of the Wedge family, pp. 130, 131; PH College, p. 132; Will & Deni McIntyre/Photo Researchers, Inc., p. 135; Courtesy of Ann & Rud Turnbull, p. 142; David Roth/Getty Images, Inc. – Stone Allstock, p. 144; Anthony Magnacca/Merrill, p. 147

Chapter 7
Courtesy of the Ackinclose family, pp. 156, 157; Barbara Schwartz/Merrill, p. 159; Tom Watson/Merrill, p. 162; Nathan Benn/Corbis/Bettmann, p. 163; Tony Freeman/PhotoEdit, p. 172; Mary Kate Denny/PhotoEdit, p. 173

Chapter 8
Courtesy of the Blankenship family, pp. 180, 181; Bill Aron/PhotoEdit, p. 184; Courtesy of Chris Fraser, p. 185; Aaron Haupt/Photo Researchers, Inc., p. 197; Will Hart/PhotoEdit, p. 198

Chapter 9
Courtesy of the Scott family, pp. 206, 207, 210, 212, 220, 224

Chapter 10
Courtesy of the Smith family, pp. 230, 231, 243; Scott Cunningham/Merrill, p. 232; Courtesy of the Spoor family, p. 234 (top); Will & Deni McIntyre/Photo Researchers, Inc., p. 234 (bottom); Michael Newman/PhotoEdit, p. 239; Anthony Magnacca/Merrill, p. 244 (Figure 10–3)

Chapter 11
Courtesy of the Jones family, pp. 258, 259, 276; Peter Buckley/PH College, p. 262; Anthony Magnacca/Merrill, pp. 265, 279

Chapter 12
Courtesy of the Frisella family, pp. 285, 287, 297, 303, 304; Courtesy of the Drayton family, pp. 286, 289, 292, 298, 299

Chapter 13
Courtesy of the Garner family, pp. 312, 313, 317; Michal Heron/Michal Heron Photography, p. 316; The Image Bank/Getty Images, p. 319; Victoria Arocho/AP Wide World Photos, p. 324; Carl D. Walsh/Aurora & Quanta Productions Inc., p. 328

Chapter 14
Courtesy of the Thomas family, pp. 336, 337; David Young-Wolff/PhotoEdit, p. 341; Mark Lewis/Getty Images Inc. – Stone Allstock, p. 344; CC Studio/Photo Researchers, Inc., p. 349; Michael Newman/PhotoEdit, pp. 351, 361; © Gabe Palmer/Corbis, p. 353

Chapter 15
Courtesy of the Sumner family, pp. 368, 369; Lori Whitley/Merrill, p. 371; Todd Yarrington/Merrill, p. 372; Scott Cunningham/Merrill, pp. 374, 389, 391; David Young-Wolff/Getty Images Inc. – Stone Allstock, p. 388; Bob Rowan/Corbis/Bettmann, p. 392

Chapter 16
Courtesy of the Hoskins family, pp. 398, 399; AP Wide World Photos, p. 405; EyeWire Collection/Getty Images–Photodisc, p. 406; Will Hart/PhotoEdit, p. 410; Keith Weller/USDA Natural Resources Conservation Service, p. 412; Rex Perry/AP Wide World Photos, p. 416

Chapter 1

"Easy magic."

"That's the key," says Richard Ellenson, the father of young Thomas, a 7-year-old boy who, along with his teachers and the administrators of his school in New York City, was profiled in the *New York Times Sunday Magazine* (September 12, 2004).

The key to what? To being with Thomas, to entering into his life, and to educating him, especially to including him in school and in life outside school.

And why does Thomas need a key? The answer is obvious. Thomas has cerebral palsy. That condition makes it extremely difficult for him to move from place to place. It also greatly impedes his ability to speak.

So what is the way for a typical person to understand Thomas, to access his obviously good mind, to communicate with him, to hear what is in his head? Without mobility and reciprocity in communication, Thomas could be nearly entirely cut off from others, whether in school or elsewhere.

Richard looked at his son's life from a unique perspective: as a successful New York advertising executive. To be an effective ad man, he tries to understand how prospective buyers will quickly respond to his ads and the products he is helping sell.

Richard asks us to look at Thomas in the same way. Take a look at him from an outsider's point of view, from the perspective of people who are not directly affected by a disability. To do so, you need to see Thomas globally, from society's point of view. But you also need to see Thomas individually, from the perspective of the person with whom Thomas, or any person with a disability, needs to interact. In all of this, regard Thomas for who he is, but also regard him as a surrogate for others with a disability. From an ad man's perspective, that is an enormous load. So Richard looked for ways to communicate his son's easy magic.

Knowing that people will be curious about disability, Richard worked with an all-star creative team he knew from his advertising circles to produce an advertising campaign for United Cerebral Palsy of New York City. It consisted of four simple words: "See me. Not CP."

Look at Thomas. What do you see? Richard does not hesitate to answer, "The killer smile." When people see it, "they get that moment of personality."

A killer smile. That's the easy magic. And it is invaluable. Richard believes that when people understand a killer smile, or any engaging characteristic, as an indicator of ability or personality, they don't simply feel sympathy or, at best, empathy for a person's disability. Instead, they see the light that shines from inside it.

"You can't expect the world to always work to find the less obvious magic," he says. "You need to find the easy magic that will

Overview of Today's Special Education

open that door for people quickly. After that, people will do the work for themselves. Once people have taken an interest, building a relationship is much easier."

The Ellensons' world has hardly been easy. Richard and Lora (a physician and research scientist at New York–Presbyterian Hospital Weill Medical College of Cornell University) redesigned their city home so that it is accessible for Thomas. Fortuitously, they encountered New York's mayor, Michael Bloomberg, at a restaurant. Richard approached him and persuaded him to connect them with the city school officials who would help build an innovative new program that did not exist within the current school system.

Their advocacy then took them to school administrators, teachers, therapists of all kinds, designers of assistive technologies, and, of course, the parents of children who have disabilities and the parents of children who do not. And their advocacy caused them to become experts about education in their own right, not just for Thomas but for all students.

"It's very fair to ask the questions that a typical parent is going to ask about including Thomas in the same school and same program as the typical child of a typical parent," Richard said. Parents of nondisabled students may well ask, "Will Thomas or other students with disabilities take valuable teacher time away from my child?"

When addressing that point, Richard begins to use lawyers' language. "You have to give all those kids [with disabilities] the benefit of the doubt. Frankly, when you do that, you will be developing techniques for better teaching for everyone. You will be gaining insights into delivering curriculum to an increasingly broad group of students. That's benefiting everyone. In short, the benefit of the doubt benefits everybody."

Now Richard's focus changes from law to philosophy, from benefit of the doubt to creating the greatest good for the greatest number. And then it shifts from enhancing someone's cognitive and mobility capacities to something much more ephemeral. "The joy of all of this is that we don't have to convince people. Thomas convinces the kids and the kids convince everyone else."

Joy quotients enter the world of general and special education. Now they become an essential element of the profession and of the partnerships that the Ellensons have with Thomas's educators.

"The fact is, you always need to learn how to best communicate with a person," says Richard. "If you become sensitive to that, your life will open up and, you know, that's the joy."

Richard and Lora will be the first to admit that there are hard and difficult aspects about Thomas's disability. Refusing to use some typical techniques to help Thomas communicate is hard. Knowing that Thomas will not be a ballplayer entails some sadness. Their compensation comes in knowing that Thomas is developing patience with himself and others and that he can still appreciate the times he must be a spectator in life, even as he is a player in many others. And having a goal in mind—teaching Thomas to become all he can be and wanting for him whatever he wants in life for himself—sustains them and, truth be told, Thomas's teachers.

Infusing joy into their lives, into Thomas's, and into the educators'—well, the killer smile is the easy magic. It is a small gesture. But it opens into an enormous and glittering world.

Special education involves advocacy, inclusion, universal design of places and curriculum, self-determination, the law's presumptions against segregation and in favor of inclusion, and utilitarianism—finding the greatest good for the greatest number and then making sure that schools practice what is good.

As you listen to Richard and look at Thomas, you'll also find that there's an easy magic in it, too. As Richard puts it, "Find that one thing that is simple now and just build on it."

Building on a student's strengths. It makes sense. It's what education is all about.

PROFILE OF SPECIAL EDUCATION STUDENTS AND PERSONNEL IN TODAY'S SCHOOLS

Perhaps you have heard these lines, which were written in 1624 by poet and minister John Donne: "Never send to know for whom the bell tolls; It tolls for thee" (from *Devotions upon Emergent Occasions*, Meditation 17).

Disability affects approximately 9 percent of all infants, toddlers, children, and adolescents; it eventually affects most of us as we age. For you, then, the disability bell could toll at least twice: once as you teach, and once as you age. For some of you, the bell peals more frequently because you have a family member or close friend with a disability or because you yourself have special needs.

When the bell tolls, it tolls not only for people with the disability but also for their families, friends, teachers, school administrators, and communities. That is why we recite stories about real families, real children, and real educators. But stories alone are not enough to introduce you to the field of special education, so we also review the most recent research data, combining the real-life personal face of exceptionality with evidence-based practice approaches in special education. Accordingly, we merge the up-front and personal portrayal of real students and their families with extensive reviews of the most current and relevant theory, research, and state-of-the-art practice. As we introduce you to special education and its families, children, and educators, we discuss four themes: universal design for learning, inclusion, family-professional relationships, and being responsive to the multicultural diversity of students.

Exemplary special education occurs when values guide practices. And when value-guided practices are as state-of-the-art as the ones you will read about in this book, no challenge that students and their families or schools and their teaching staff face will be too daunting. Figure 1–1 identifies these values. The margin notes explain why and how these values form the foundation for special education and relate to best practices.

Who Are the Students?

To answer the question "Who are the students in special education?" we describe (1) the total number of students with disabilities, (2) gender of students, (3) provision of gifted education, (4) the categories of disabilities, and (5) issues about labels and language.

Figure 1–1   Values to guide teaching

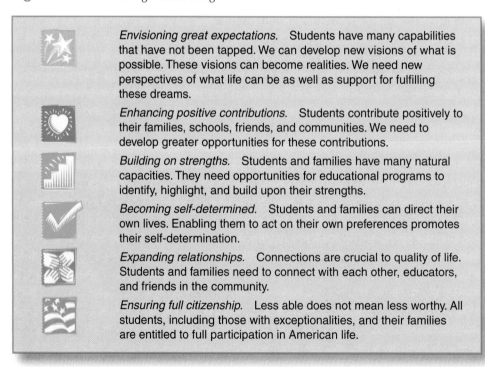

Envisioning great expectations.   Students have many capabilities that have not been tapped. We can develop new visions of what is possible. These visions can become realities. We need new perspectives of what life can be as well as support for fulfilling these dreams.

Enhancing positive contributions.   Students contribute positively to their families, schools, friends, and communities. We need to develop greater opportunities for these contributions.

Building on strengths.   Students and families have many natural capacities. They need opportunities for educational programs to identify, highlight, and build upon their strengths.

Becoming self-determined.   Students and families can direct their own lives. Enabling them to act on their own preferences promotes their self-determination.

Expanding relationships.   Connections are crucial to quality of life. Students and families need to connect with each other, educators, and friends in the community.

Ensuring full citizenship.   Less able does not mean less worthy. All students, including those with exceptionalities, and their families are entitled to full participation in American life.

Total number of students served. In the 2003–2004 school year, 272,454 infants and toddlers (ages birth–2), or 2.2 percent of U.S. infants and toddlers, received early intervention services; and 680,142 preschool children (ages 3–5), or approximately 6 percent of the preschool population, received early childhood services (U.S. Department of Education, 2005). Slightly more than 6 million students, ages 6 to 21, received some form of special education. Here's another way to think about that statistic: 9.05 percent of the schools' enrolled students (ages 6–21) received special education services that year. That percentage reflects a huge growth in special education. Although the population of students ages 6 through 21 grew only 12 percent from 1990–1999, the number of students in the same age range with disabilities grew by 30 percent (U.S. Department of Education, 2001).

Gender of students. In the general education school population, males and females are enrolled in equal proportion, but in special education the male-to-female ratio varies between 1.5 to 1 and 3.5 to 1 (Coutinho & Oswald, 2005). The two categories of disability that have the greatest discrepancy are learning disabilities and emotional and behavioral disorders. Researchers documented substantial variation across states in these two categories. For example, the category of emotional and behavioral disorders was reported to have the greatest male-to-female variation, ranging from 2.2 to 1 to almost 6 to 1. Possible reasons for gender-disproportionate representation throughout special education include (1) physiological/maturational differences—girls mature earlier than boys, (2) education bias—there are more female teachers than male teachers referring students to special education, and (3) assessment bias—the tests that determine who has a disability tend to select boys rather than girls (U.S. Department of Education, 1998).

Provision of gifted education. Special education also serves students who have unusual gifts and talents (see Chapter 16). Although these students are not included in the federal law related to students with disabilities, slightly less than two-thirds of the states have mandates (including legislation and administrative rules or policy) requiring services for gifted education (Council of State Directors of Programs for the Gifted and National Association for Gifted Children, 2003).

Disability categories. The U.S. Department of Education collects data from the states according to students' type or category of disability. Figure 1–2 sets out the numbers and percentages of students associated with each category. Slightly more than two-thirds of all students with disabilities are classified into two categories: specific learning disabilities (47.4 percent) and speech or language impairments (18.7 percent). These two categories, when combined with the categories of mental retardation (9.6 percent) and emotional disturbance (8 percent), account for 84 percent of all students with disabilities. In each chapter, you will meet students who have disabilities, just as you have been introduced to Thomas. You will read about their characteristics, their families, and the education they receive. But before you read about educational characteristics, a word of caution is in order.

Labels and language. How would you feel if you were known only by your disability and not according to your abilities? Devalued? Probably. Indeed, that is precisely how many families and special educators respond when a child with disabilities is labeled as a "disabled person" first and foremost.

There is controversy about labeling and its consequences, which include classification in schools—specifically, classification into special education. Some students may benefit if a label qualifies them to receive services because those services can outweigh the stigma that accompanies some labels (Mesibov, Adams, & Klinger, 1997). Indeed, some people with hearing and visual impairments (see Chapters 14 and 15) welcome the labels.

On the other hand, labeling can lead educators to regard a student as a broken person whom they must "fix" (Obiakor, 1999; Patton, 1998; Reschly, 1996). Labeling also can segregate students with disabilities from their classmates without disabilities (Kliewer & Biklin, 1996). Also, labeling can reflect biases against students' cultural and linguistic backgrounds (Obiakor, 1999; Patton, 1998).

So we ask you to be cautious about using labels. Let Thomas be Thomas, not a youngster with a label. If you or other educators must use labels, avoid those that demean and stigmatize, for they always separate and devalue people, in and outside school (Goffman, 1963; Norwich,

Values: Negative labeling can inhibit students', families', and teachers' *great expectations.*

PRAXIS

Standard: When you learn about the impact of labeling, you are addressing PRAXIS™ Standard 1.

Figure 1-2   Categories of disabilities and corresponding numbers and percentages of students ages 6 to 21 served in the 2003–2004 school year

Disability	IDEA, Part B	
	Number	Percentage
Specific learning disabilities	2,858,260	47.4
Speech or language impairments	1,127,551	18.7
Mental retardation	581,706	9.6
Emotional disturbance	483,805	8.0
Multiple disabilities	132,333	2.2
Hearing impairments	71,903	1.2
Orthopedic impairments	68,188	1.1
Other health impairments	452,045	7.5
Autism	140,920	2.3
Visual impairments	25,814	0.43
Traumatic brain injury	22,534	0.37
Developmental delay	65,921	1.09
Deaf-blindness	1,667	0.03

Source: U.S. Department of Education, Office of Special Education Programs. (2005). *IDEA data* (http://www.ideadata.org/).

Values: Expect Thomas and others with a disability to have or to develop (with the assistance of general and special educators, their peers, and their families) their inherent *strengths* and to make *positive contributions* to others and their communities.

1999), and they impair students' self-esteem (Lapadat, 1998). Instead, use esteeming ones and emphasize your students' strengths. Box 1–1 returns you to Richard and Thomas and asks you to don a stigmatizing label and then shed it.

To show esteem for their students, most educators use "people-first" language. For example, instead of using phrases such as "physically handicapped" or "physically handicapped children," they prefer "students with physical disabilities." Even better, you might consider decreasing the use of labels. Why not just say "students"? Better yet, just "Thomas."

Who Are Special Education Personnel?

If you are considering a career in special education, your job prospects are quite good. According to the most recent data from the U.S. Department of Education (2005), approximately 401,705 special education teachers were employed in 2003–2004 to teach students ages 6 through 21. But for the 1999–2000 school year, approximately 7,000 job openings existed for special education teachers (U.S. Department of Education, 2001). At least one special education teacher vacancy was present in almost 97 percent of school districts.

A large number of special education teachers have received **alternative teacher certification** to teach. They hold emergency certifications (so-called because the school district where they teach has an emergency in the sense of a shortage of regularly certified teachers), they may have attended specialized programs for people who have a college degree other than from a school of education, or they may have been recruited as returning Peace Corps volunteers (Stoddart & Floden, 1995). Almost twice as many special education teachers have alternative certifications than do general educators (Katsiyannis, Zhang, & Conroy, 2003). The area of special education that has the highest percentage of teachers who are not fully certified is in the area of teaching children with emotional or behavioral disorders. Later in the chapter you will learn about the principles and requirements of the No Child Left Behind Act (NCLB) pertaining to qualified teachers and about NCLB's significance for special education teaching positions.

Your Own Voice ~ Labels and Values   Box 1–1

Let us assume that you are Thomas Ellenson, whom you met at the beginning of this chapter. You already have an anti-label advocate, your father. His campaign to remove a stigmatizing label from you is straightforward and short: "See me. Not CP."

Now let's assume that you are Erica Scott, the student with mental retardation whom you will meet in Chapter 8. She carries two labels: African American and "mentally retarded" (or worse). How does this campaign suit you: "It's all about my JQ, not my IQ." Erica's campaign plays down her IQ, her intelligence quotient, and plays up her JQ, her "joy quotient," giving people a chance to find that special attribute—that easy magic—that brings them into her life.

Here's your challenge. Put on any label that you have used to demean another person. (It's okay to admit that you've done that; we've all done that at some point in our lives.) Imagine how it would be to go to school with that label. (That should not be too hard for anyone.) Remember this: stigmatizing labels devalue; affirmative labels ascribe value.

Now take off that stigmatizing label, find its opposite, emphasize that, and then develop your own anti-labeling campaign. Accentuate the positive. Eliminate the negative. Reverse society's expectations. Turn a perceived limitation into a valued attribute.

Start with your race, culture, or ethnicity. Then your gender. Then your academic talents. Then your athletic ones. Then your social ones. And so on.

In your own voice, proclaim how you want others to regard you. Where's your own easy magic? It's hidden behind some label that you want to shed. So relabel yourself.

After you do, start relabeling students and their families. Pretty soon you'll find that you think about yourself and them in a much different way. Now you've got a head start on teaching children with exceptional needs. You've just made them exceptional in a different way than others have made them.

A national study of special education teachers reported the following demographics (Carlson, Brauen, Klein, Schroll, & Willig, 2002):

- Females constitute 85 percent of the workforce.
- White teachers represent 86 percent of the workforce.
- Based on self-report, 14 percent of teachers have a disability.
- Their average age is 43 years.
- Fifty-nine percent of special education teachers have a master's degree.
- Teachers have an average of about 14 years of teaching experience.

The profession of special education offers you many career paths.

Not all special education professionals are teachers. Other educational personnel include school social workers, occupational therapists, physical therapists, recreation and therapeutic specialists, paraprofessionals, physical education teachers, supervisors/adminstrators, psychologists, diagnostic/evaluation staff, audiologists, work-study coordinators, vocational education teachers, counselors, rehabilitation counselors, interpreters, and speech pathologists. The number of certified nonteaching personnel in these roles during the 2001–2002 school year totaled 577,476. Paraprofessionals accounted for about 87 percent of these positions.

The typical paraprofessional working in special education is a white female who is 44 years old (Carlson et al., 2002). This typical paraprofessional serves 21 students, with 15 of those students having disabilities. Paraprofessionals are twice as likely to be proficient in the languages of non-English-speaking students who are receiving special education services. Approximately one-third of paraprofessionals are fluent or almost fluent in the languages other than English that are spoken by their students.

You know now that there is a shortage of both special education teachers and some related-service professionals. What you may not know is how rewarding it can be to be a special educator and how federal law provides a structure for that rewarding career.

For more information about special education teachers and paraprofessionals, go to the Companion Website, *www.prenhall.com/turnbull*, for a link to the website that reports research on personnel needs in special education *(http://ferdig.coe.ufl.edu/spense)*.

OVERVIEW OF THE LAW AND SPECIAL EDUCATION

For more than 30 years now, the education of students with disabilities has been governed by a law that Congress enacted in 1975. That law is called the Individuals with Disabilities Education Act and is known as IDEA. Whatever role you play in American schools, you almost certainly will have to know about this law, the rights it gives to students, and the duties it imposes on schools. Let's begin with a bit of its history.

Two Types of Discrimination

During the early and middle decades of the 20th century, schools discriminated against students with disabilities in two significant ways (Turnbull, Turnbull, Stowe, & Wilcox, 2000). First, they completely excluded many students with disabilities. Or if they did admit students with disabilities, they did not always provide the students with an effective or appropriate education. Second, schools often classified students as having disabilities when they in fact did not have disabilities. Frequently, these students were members of culturally- and linguistically-diverse groups. In addition, schools sometimes labeled students with one kind of disability when the students really had other kinds of disabilities.

Beginning in the early 1970s, advocates for students with disabilities—primarily their families, parent advocacy organizations, and civil rights lawyers—began to sue state and local school officials, claiming that exclusion and misclassification violated the students' rights to an equal education opportunity under the U.S. Constitution (Turnbull et al., 2000; Yell, 1998). Relying on the Supreme Court's decision in the school race-desegregation case (*Brown v. Board of Education*, 1954), they argued that, because *Brown* held that schools may not segregate by race, schools also may not segregate or otherwise discriminate by ability and disability. Students are students, regardless of their race or disability.

Judicial Decisions and Legislation

The advocates were successful. In 1972, federal courts ordered the Commonwealth of Pennsylvania and the District of Columbia to (1) provide a free appropriate public education to all students with disabilities, (2) educate students with disabilities in the same schools and basically the same programs as students without disabilities, and (3) put into place certain procedural safeguards so that students with disabilities can challenge schools that do not live up to the courts' orders (*Mills v. Washington, DC, Board of Education*, 1972; *Pennsylvania Association for Retarded Citizens [PARC] v. Commonwealth of Pennsylvania*, 1972).

In 1975, Congress enacted IDEA (then called the Education of All Handicapped Students Act, or Public Law [PL] 94–142). In enacting the federal law in 1975, Congress intended to open up the schools to all students with disabilities and make sure that they had the chance to benefit from special education. Nowadays the challenge is not to provide access only but to assure that the students really do benefit. Educators and policymakers are determined to secure favorable results for students; they are focused on four outcomes: equality of opportunity, full participation, independent living, and economic self-sufficiency. Later in this chapter you will read about these outcomes and the benefits and results of special education, but now you need to know about the basic components of IDEA.

When Congress reauthorized IDEA in 2004, it enacted the "Individuals with Disabilities Education Improvement Act." Sometimes you will hear people (such as your professor) refer to the law by that name or its abbreviation "IDEIA".

But Congress recognized that people are familiar with the law's former name (before the 2004 reauthorization). So it provided that the "short title" of the reauthorized law is "Individuals with Disabilities Education Act" (abbreviated as "IDEA").

Therefore, in every place where we refer to the 2004 law, we call it "Individuals with Disabilities Education Act" and abbreviate it "IDEA." Thus, this book is entirely correct and current when it cites the 2004 law as IDEA.

The Span of Special Education: Birth Through Age 21

Over the course of the years since it first enacted IDEA in 1975, Congress has expanded the group of students who have a right to special education. At first, the group consisted of students ages 6 to 18, but now it includes the very young (infants and toddlers from birth through age 2), young children (ages 3–5), and older students (ages 6–21). Because the needs of and services provided to the very young (ages birth–2) are so different from needs and services for older children (ages 3–21), IDEA consists of two parts—Part B and Part C. (Part A sets out Congress's intent and national policy to provide a free appropriate public education to all students, ages birth–21.)

Part B. **Part B** benefits students who are ages 3 through 21, each inclusive. It combines a categorical approach (that is, it describes the categories of disabilities) with a functional approach (that is, it provides that student must be unable to function successfully in the general curriculum) to define which students qualify for special education. Figure 1–2 lists the IDEA categories for children ages 6 through 21; one of the chapters in this book discusses the education of students in each of those categories.

These same categories apply to children ages 3 to 9 (those in early childhood special education), but each state may also provide special education to children who meet only the functional approach to disability—namely, those who

- Are experiencing developmental delays in one or more of the following areas—physical development, cognitive development, communication development, social or emotional development, or adaptive behavior and development—and
- Because of these delays, need special education and related services

IDEA gives the states discretion whether to serve children ages 3 through 5 (early education). As of early 2002, all states do so.

Part C. IDEA also gives the states discretion about whether to serve infants and toddlers (ages birth–2, also known as 0–3); and as of early 2002, all states do. **Part C** benefits any child under age 3 who (1) needs early intervention services because of developmental delays in one or more of the areas of cognitive development, physical development, social or emotional development, or adaptive development; or (2) has a diagnosed physical or mental condition that has a high probability of resulting in a developmental delay.

Part C does more than benefit the children who have identified delays. It also gives each state the option of serving at-risk infants and toddlers: those who would be at risk of experiencing a substantial developmental delay if they did not receive early intervention services. Note the difference: a child with a diagnosed condition that has a "high probability" of resulting in a developmental delay is not the same as a child who is "at risk" of having a delay.

Special Education and Students' Eligibility

Eligibility based on need. IDEA defines special education as specially designed instruction, at no cost to the child's parents, to meet the unique needs of a student with a disability. A student with a disability is one who has certain disabilities (which we identify later in the chapter) and who, because of the disability, needs special education and related services. Special education is reserved for students who need it because of their disabilities and whose needs cannot be satisfied in general education.

Where special education is provided. Special education occurs in classrooms (where Thomas receives his), students' homes, hospitals and institutions, and other settings. Special education is provided wherever there are students with exceptionalities.

Components of Special Education

Special education is individualized to the student; that is the meaning of "to meet the unique needs" of the student in the definition of special education that you previously learned. To meet a student's needs, it is usually necessary to provide more than individualized instruction. Educators and other professionals in special education do this by supplementing their instruction with "related services"—namely, services that are necessary to assist the student to benefit from special education. Figure 1–3 identifies and defines related services.

Values: IDEA implements the U.S. Constitution's guarantee that everyone will be treated equally under the law. Equal opportunity is a pathway to *full citizenship* in America.

Standard: CEC Standard 1 incorporates knowledge and skill related to IDEA and its requirements.

Figure 1–3   Definitions of related services in IDEA

The related services apply to Part B and students ages 3 to 21 unless we note that they belong to Part C only and thus to children ages birth to 3.

- *Audiology:* determining the range, nature, and degree of hearing loss and operating programs for treatment and prevention of hearing loss.
- *Counseling services:* counseling by social workers, psychologists, guidance counselors, and rehabilitation specialists.
- *Early identification:* identifying a disability as early as possible in a child's life.
- *Family training, counseling, and home visits:* assisting families to enhance their child's development (Part C only).
- *Health services:* enabling a child to benefit from other early intervention services (Part C only).
- *Medical services:* determining a child's medically related disability that results in the child's need for special education and related services.
- *Nursing services:* assessing health status, preventing health problems, and administering medications, treatments, and regimens prescribed by a licensed physician (Part C only).
- *Nutrition services:* conducting individual assessments to address the nutritional needs of children (Part C only).
- *Occupational therapy:* improving, developing, or restoring functions impaired or lost through illness, injury, or deprivation.
- *Orientation and mobility services:* assisting a student to get around within various environments.
- *Parent counseling and training:* providing parents with information about child development.
- *Physical therapy:* screening, referral, and service provision for therapy regarding bone and muscle capacity.
- *Psychological services:* administering and interpreting psychological and educational tests and other assessment procedures and managing a program of psychological services, including psychological counseling for children and parents.
- *Recreation and therapeutic recreation:* assessing leisure function, recreation programs in schools and community agencies, and leisure education.
- *Rehabilitative counseling services:* planning for career development, employment preparation, achieving independence, and integration in the workplace and community.
- *School health services:* attending to educationally related health needs through services provided by a school nurse.
- *Service coordination services:* assistance and services by a service coordinator to a child and family (Part C only).
- *Social work services in schools:* preparing a social or developmental history on a child, counseling groups and individuals, and mobilizing school and community resources.
- *Speech pathology and speech-language pathology:* diagnosing specific speech or language impairments and giving guidance regarding speech and language impairments.
- *Transportation and related costs:* providing travel to and from services and schools, travel in and around school buildings, and specialized equipment (e.g., special or adapted buses, lifts, and ramps).
- *Assistive technology and services:* acquiring and using devices and services to restore lost capacities or improve impaired capacities.

Categorical and Functional Approaches to Eligibility

As you have just read, a student is eligible for special education and related services if the student has a disability and, because of the disability, needs specially designed instruction. Note the two-part standard for eligibility: (1) there is a categorical element—the student must have a disability, and (2) there is a functional element—the disability must cause the student to need specially designed instruction.

IDEA: SIX PRINCIPLES

It is not enough for IDEA simply to identify the eligible students and to specify the services they have a right to receive. Because of the schools' past discrimination through exclusion and misclassification, IDEA also establishes six principles that govern students' education (Turnbull et al., 2000). Figure 1–4 describes those six principles. Because IDEA is complex and contains general rules, exceptions to the general rules, and even exceptions to the exceptions, we will describe only the general rule and sometimes some detail about it, the exceptions, or both.

Go to the Companion Website, *www. prenhall.com/turnbull*, for a link to a comprehensive website on IDEA statutes, regulations, litigation, and related resources *(www.cec.sped.org/law_res/doc/).*

Zero Reject

The **zero-reject** principle prohibits schools from excluding any student with a disability from a free appropriate public education. The purpose of the zero-reject principle is to ensure that all children and youth (ages 3–21), no matter how severe their disabilities, have an appropriate education provided at public expense. To carry out this purpose, the zero-reject rule applies to the state and all of its school districts and to private schools, state-operated programs such as schools for students with visual or hearing impairments, psychiatric hospitals, and institutions for people with other disabilities.

Educability. In essence, the zero-reject rule means what it says: no student may be excluded from an education because of a disability. To carry out the zero-reject rule, courts have ordered state and local education agencies to provide services to children who traditionally have been regarded as ineducable (not able to learn) because of the profound extent of their disabilities. The courts are saying that "all" means "all"—Congress was very clear that it intends IDEA to benefit *all* children with disabilities, no matter how disabled they are.

The zero-reject rule means that all students are provided with a free appropriate public education.

Figure I-4   Six principles governing the education of students with disabilities

- *Zero reject:* a rule against excluding any student.
- *Nondiscriminatory evaluation:* a rule requiring schools to evaluate students fairly to determine if they have a disability and, if so, what kind and how extensive.
- *Appropriate education:* a rule requiring schools to provide individually tailored education for each student based on evaluation and augmented by related services and supplementary aids and services.
- *Least restrictive environment:* a rule requiring schools to educate students with disabilities with students without disabilities to the maximum extent appropriate for the students with disabilities.
- *Procedural due process:* a rule providing safeguards for students against schools' actions, including a right to sue in court.
- *Parental and student participation:* a rule requiring schools to collaborate with parents and adolescent students in designing and carrying out special education programs.

As we have said, states have discretion about whether to serve children ages 3 through 5. If they do, and if the parents of those children want them to be served under Part B (ages 6–21), the students will have the benefit of the zero-reject principle. Parents and local educational agencies may agree, however, to serve children under Part C (0–3), in which case none of Part B's six principles apply to the same degree as if the child were 6 years old or older.

Discipline. To assure that all students with a disability receive an appropriate education but also to assure that the schools are safe places for teaching and learning, IDEA regulates how schools may discipline students who qualify for IDEA's protection. The principles of the IDEA discipline amendments are simple, but their details are complex. The principles are as follows:

- *Equal treatment.* The school may discipline a student with a disability in the same way and to the same extent as it may discipline a student without a disability, for the same offense, subject to the special provisions set out as follows.

- *No cessation.* No matter what the student does to violate a school code, the school may not expel or suspend the student for more than 10 school days in any one school year.

- *Special circumstances.* The school may take into account any special circumstances related to the student and the student's behavior in deciding whether to discipline the student and, if so, how.

- *Short-term removals.* The school may suspend the student for not more than 10 school days in any one school year.

- *Manifestation determinations.* When the school proposes to change the student's placement for more than 10 days, it must determine whether the student's behavior is a manifestation of the student's disability.

- *Response to no manifestation.* If the school determines that the student's behavior is not a manifestation of the disability, it may discipline the student in the same way as it disciplines students without disabilities except that it may not terminate the student's education (the "no cessation" rule). It may place the student in an interim alternative educational setting.

- *Response to manifestation.* When a school determines that the student's behavior is a manifestation of the disability, the school must conduct a functional behavioral assessment and develop a behavioral intervention plan to address the student's behavior. Unless the school and parents agree otherwise, the student then returns to the student's previous school placement.

- *Services in interim alternative educational settings.* When in such a setting, the student still must have education that assures that the student will make progress according to the student's Individualized Education Program (discussed later in this chapter).

- *Weapons, drugs, and injury.* When a student has weapons or illegal drugs in school or seriously injures another person, the school may place the student in an interim alternative educational setting, without first making any manifestation determination, for up to 45 days.

Nondiscriminatory Evaluation

The effect of the zero-reject rule is to guarantee all students with a disability access to school. Once in school, they are entitled to a **nondiscriminatory evaluation.**

Two purposes. The nondiscriminatory evaluation has two purposes. The first is to determine whether a student has a disability. If the student does not have a disability, then he or she does not receive special education under IDEA or any further evaluation related to special education under IDEA.

If the evaluation reveals that the student has a disability, the evaluation process continues in order to accomplish its second purpose: to specify special education and related services the student will receive. This information is necessary to plan an appropriate education for the student and determine where the student will be educated.

Nondiscriminatory evaluation requirements. Because evaluation has such a significant impact on students and their families, IDEA surrounds the evaluation process with procedural safeguards. Figure 1–5 highlights procedural safeguards related to assessment procedures as well as parent notice and consent. To determine whether a student has a disability and then decide the nature of the special education and related services the student needs, educators typically follow a four-step process: screening, prereferral, referral, and nondiscriminatory evaluation. The first three steps are not required by IDEA but are put into place by educators as a matter of good practice or state or local policy. Picture these four steps as a funnel (see Figure 1–6).

- *Screening:* administering tests to all students to identify which students seem to need further testing to determine whether they qualify for special education.

- *Prereferral:* providing immediate and necessary help to teachers who are experiencing challenges in teaching students and thereby prevent the need for a referral, a full

Figure 1–5   Nondiscriminatory evaluation safeguards

Assessment Procedures

- They should include more than one assessment since no single procedure may be used as the sole basis of evaluation.
- They use a variety of assessment tools and strategies to gather relevant functional, developmental, and academic information, including information provided by the student's parent that may enable the team to determine if the student has a disability and the nature of specially designed instruction needed.
- They may be requested by a parent, the state education agency, another state agency, or the local education agency (initial evaluations).
- They are selected and administered so as to not be discriminatory on a racial or cultural basis.
- They must be used for the purposes for which the assessments are valid and reliable.
- They are administered in a language and form likely to produce accurate information about the student's current levels of academic, developmental, and functional performance, unless such provision is not feasible.
- They are administered by trained and knowledgeable personnel and in conformance with instructions by the producer of the tests of material.

Parent Notice and Consent

- Inform parents fully and secure their written consent before the initial evaluation and each reevaluation.
- If the parents do not consent to the initial evaluation, use mediation or due process procedures to secure approval to proceed with the evaluation or reevaluation.
- Obtain parents' consent before any reevaluation unless the school can demonstrate that it has taken reasonable measures to obtain their consent and parents have failed to respond.
- Fully explain to the parents all due process rights, a description of what the school proposes or refuses to do, a description of each evaluation procedure that was used, a statement of how the parents may obtain a copy of their procedural safeguards and sources that they can contact to obtain assistance in understanding the provisions of the notice, a description of any other options considered, and any other factors that influenced the educators' decisions.
- Do not treat the parents' consent for evaluation as their consent for placement into or out of a special education program; secure separate parental consent for placement.
- Provide the parents with a copy of the evaluation report and the documentation for determining eligibility for special education.

Figure 1-6 Nondiscriminatory evaluation: A funneling process

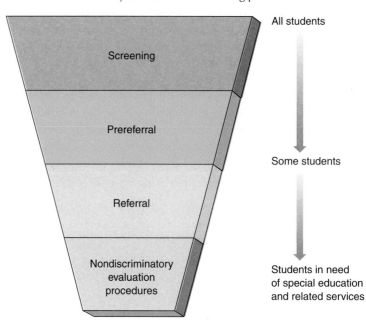

nondiscriminatory evaluation, and possible placement in special education (Bahr, Fuchs, & Fuchs, 1999; Bahr, Whitten, Dieker, Kocarek, & Manson, 1999).

- *Referral:* submitting a formal written request for a student to receive a full nondiscriminatory evaluation.

- *Nondiscriminatory evaluation:* adhering to the safeguards of the full evaluation process in Figure 1–4.

Once the evaluation team has determined that a student has a disability (or is gifted) and the special education and related services the student needs, then educators must provide the student with that kind of education and those services, describing them in the student's Individualized Education Program (IEP), which we discuss in the next section. In short, the nondiscriminatory evaluation leads to, and is the very foundation of, the student's appropriate education.

IDEA does not specify who the members of the evaluation team are. It simply says that a local educational agency must ensure that qualified personnel and the student's parents are part of the evaluation team. The team must follow the procedures we described in Figure 1–4. But because one of the members of the student's IEP team must be a person qualified to interpret the evaluation results, it usually is the case that at least one member of the evaluation team will be a member of the IEP team. To the greatest extent possible, it is helpful to have overlap between the members of the multidisciplinary evaluation team and the members of the IEP team. Regardless of the precise team membership, the result is the same: the evaluation leads to IEP decisions about program (appropriate education) and placement (least restrictive environment).

Appropriate Education

Simply enrolling students (zero reject) and evaluating their strengths and needs (nondiscriminatory evaluation) do not ensure that their education will be appropriate and beneficial. That is why Congress has given each student in special education the right to an **appropriate education** and related services.

The key to an appropriate special education is *individualization*, which is achieved through a planning process and written into a plan. The plan for each student, ages 3 through 21, is the student's **Individualized Education Program (IEP).** The plan for each student from birth through age 2 is the student's and family's **Individualized Family Services Plan (IFSP).** To guide you through IDEA's appropriate education requirements, we will discuss (1) the contents of IEPs/IFSPs; (2) age-specific provisions, including early intervention and transitions to adulthood; (3) the participants who develop the IFSP/IEP; and (4) time lines.

The IEP is based on the student's evaluation and is outcome-oriented. IDEA specifies the content of each IEP, as shown in Figure 1–7. Taken as a whole, the IEP's content is the foundation for the student's appropriate education; it is the assurance that the student will benefit from special education and have real opportunities for equality of opportunity, full participation, independent living, and economic self-sufficiency.

The IFSP describes the services that both the infant-toddler and the family will receive. Like the IEP, the IFSP is based on the child's development and needs; it specifies outcomes for the child. Unlike the IEP, however, the IFSP also provides the option for families to identify their resources, priorities, and concerns related to enhancing their child's development. Furthermore, the IFSP must include outcomes and services for families so long as a family wants to achieve specific outcomes related to the child's development.

Participants who develop the IEP/IFSP. Because the nondiscriminatory evaluation lays the foundation for the student's individualized plan (IFSP or IEP), the IEP team must include at least one person who can link the evaluation to the IEP. IDEA specifies that the following people should be part of the IEP team:

- The parents
- At least one general education teacher with expertise related to the child's educational level
- At least one special education teacher
- A representative of the school system who is qualified to provide or supervise special education and is also knowledgeable about the general education curriculum and the availability of school resources
- An individual who can interpret the evaluation results
- At the discretion of the parent or agency, other individuals with expertise regarding the student's educational needs, including related-service personnel
- When appropriate, the student with the disability

Other people may be included in the IEP or IFSP conference. For example, a parent might wish to bring a friend who knows about the special education process. In addition, some of the student's friends can provide suggestions and support for inclusion (Turnbull, Turnbull, Erwin, & Soodak, 2006).

IDEA requires an IEP to be developed for all students, ages 3 through 21, and to be in effect at the beginning of each school year. Educators and parents may make changes in the IEP either through a team meeting or by developing a written document to amend or change the current IEP. Also, the team must review and, if appropriate, revise the student's IEP at least once a year.

Time lines. IDEA requires an IFSP to be developed within "a reasonable time" after the child has been assessed for early intervention services. The IFSP must be evaluated at least once annually, and families have the right to a semi-annual review or a more frequent review based on the needs of the family, infant, and/or toddler.

IEP/IFSP conferences. IDEA does not have detailed requirements about the process that must be followed at IEP/IFSP conferences. Ideally, those conferences are conducted to help ensure partnerships among educators and parents. Research on the IEP/IFSP, however, has generally reported that the traditional process tends to involve legal compliance—a paperwork process—rather than problem-solving, dynamic teamwork (Turnbull et al., 2006). To ensure that the conference is characterized by partnerships, we recommend that conferences incorporate these 10 components (Turnbull et al., 2006):

1. Prepare in advance.
2. Connect and get started.

Figure 1-7   Required content of the IEP

The IEP is a written statement for each student, ages 3 to 21. Whenever it is developed or revised, it must contain the following statements:

- The student's present levels of academic achievement and optional performance, including
  - How the student's disability affects the student's involvement and progress in the general curriculum (for students 6–21)
  - How a preschooler's disability affects the child's participation in appropriate activities (for children 3–5)
- A description of the benchmarks or short-term objectives for students who take alternate assessments that are aligned to alternate achievement standards
- Measurable annual goals, including academic and functional goals, designed to
  - Meet each of the student's needs resulting from the disability in order to enable the student to be involved in and progress in the general curriculum
  - Meet each of the student's other educational needs that arise from the disability
- How the student's progress toward annual goals will be measured and when periodic reports on the student's progress and meeting annual goals will be provided
- The special education and related services and supplementary aids and services, based on peer-reviewed research to the extent practicable, that will be provided to the student or on the student's behalf and the program modifications or supports for school personnel that will be provided for the student to
  - Advance appropriately toward attaining the annual goals
  - Be involved in and make progress through the general curriculum and participate in extracurricular and other nonacademic activities
  - Be educated and participate with other students with disabilities and with students who do not have disabilities in those three types of activities
- An explanation of the extent, if any, to which the student will not participate with students who do not have disabilities in the regular class and in extracurricular and other nonacademic activities
- Any individual appropriate accommodations that are necessary to measure the student's academic and functional performance on state- and district-wide assessments; if the IEP team determines that the student will not participate in a regular state- or district-wide assessment or any part of an assessment, an explanation of why the student cannot participate and the particular alternate assessment that the team selects as appropriate for the student
- The projected date for beginning the assessment services and modifications and the anticipated frequency, location, and duration of each
- Beginning no later than the first IEP that will be in effect after the student becomes 16, and then updated annually, a transition plan that must include
  - Appropriate measurable goals for postsecondary life that are based on appropriate transition assessments related to training, education, employment, and, where appropriate, independent living skills
  - A statement of needed transition services, including courses of study, needed to assist the student to reach those postsecondary goals
  - Beginning no later than one year before the student reaches the age of majority under state law (usually at age 18), a statement that the student has been informed of those rights under IDEA that will transfer to the student from the parents when the student comes of age

3. Review formal evaluation and current levels of performance.

4. Share resources, priorities, and concerns.

5. Share visions and great expectations.

6. Consider interaction of proposed student goals, placement, and services.

7. Translate student priorities into written goals (or outcomes).

8. Determine placement, supplementary aids/services, and related services.

9. Address assessment modifications and special factors.

10. Conclude the conference.

Mandatory review conferences have one principal reason: to determine whether the student's annual goals (IEP) or outcomes (IFSP) are being achieved. Accordingly, IDEA requires the IEP team to review the student's IEP and revise it as appropriate. A review may cause a reevaluation and even change of placement.

Least Restrictive Environment

Once the schools have enrolled a student (the zero-reject principle), fairly evaluated the student (the nondiscriminatory evaluation principle), and provided an IFSP/IEP (the appropriate education principle), they must contribute one more element to the student's education—namely, education with students who do not have disabilities. This is the principle of the **least restrictive environment (LRE),** formerly known as the mainstreaming or integration rule and now known as the inclusion principle. In early intervention (ages 0–3), IDEA favors education in the student's "natural environment," which could be home or an out-of-home center. In all other education (ages 3–21), IDEA favors placement in general education. The term *general education* has three dimensions: the academic curriculum, extracurricular activities, and other nonacademic activities (for example, recess, transportation, mealtimes, dances, and sports activities).

The rule: a presumption in favor of inclusion. IDEA creates a presumption in favor of educating students with disabilities with those who do not have disabilities. It does this by requiring that (1) a school must educate a student with a disability with students who do not have disabilities to the maximum extent appropriate for the student; and (2) the school may not remove the student from the regular education environment unless, because of the nature or severity of the student's disability, he or she cannot be educated there successfully (appropriately, in the sense that the student will benefit), even after the school provides supplementary aids and support services for the student.

Access to general education curriculum. IDEA specifically states that the education of children with disabilities can be made more effective by "having high expectations" for them and by ensuring their access to the general education curriculum in the regular classroom, to the maximum extent possible, in order to meet their developmental goals and, to the maximum extent possible, the challenging expectations that have been established for all children.

Setting aside the presumption. The school may set aside this presumption in favor of inclusion only if the student cannot benefit from being educated with students who do not have disabilities and only after the school has provided the student with supplementary aids and

In situations requiring educational intervention, IDEA favors education in the general education classroom.

Council for Exceptional Children

Standard: Developing knowledge and skills related to the continuum of services ties to CEC Standard 5.

Companion Website

On the Companion Website, *www.prenhall.com/turnbull*, you will find a link to a consortium that focuses on appropriate dispute resolution through mediation and due process hearings (*http:// www.directionservice.org/cadre*).

services. In that event, the school may place the student in a less typical, more specialized, less inclusive program.

The continuum of services. Schools must offer a continuum, or range, of services from more to less typical and inclusive—that is, from less to more restrictive or separate. The most typical and inclusive setting is general education, followed by resource rooms, special classes, special schools, homebound services, and hospitals and institutions (also called residential or long-term care facilities). You will learn more about these different settings in Chapter 2.

Extracurricular and nonacademic inclusion. Schools also have to ensure that students with disabilities may participate in extracurricular and other nonacademic activities such as meals, recess periods, and other services such as counseling, athletics, transportation, health services, recreational activities, special interest groups or clubs, and referrals to agencies that assist in employment and other aspects of life outside school.

In short, when providing academic, extracurricular, and other nonacademic activities and services to students who do not have disabilities, schools must include students with disabilities to the maximum extent appropriate. That is because, as Congress said in 1997, special education is a service for children rather than a place where they are sent.

Procedural Due Process

Schools do not always carry out IDEA's first four principles: zero reject, nondiscriminatory evaluation, appropriate education, and least restrictive environment. What's a parent to do? Or what if a school believes that one type of special education is appropriate, but a parent disagrees and believes that the proposed placement will not benefit the student? The answer lies in the **procedural due process** principle, which basically seeks to make schools and parents accountable to each other for carrying out the student's IDEA rights.

When parents and state or local educational agencies disagree, IDEA provides each with an opportunity to meet face to face in a "resolution" session to try to settle their differences. If they cannot do so, then the parent has a right to a due process hearing (a mini-trial) before an impartial hearing officer. If the parent is still dissatisfied, he or she may sue the school in federal or state courts. Because lawsuits are expensive, take up time and educational resources, and exacerbate parent-school disagreements, IDEA provides that the parents and school may engage in mediation before the due process hearing. IDEA does not require mediation, and mediation may not be used to deny or delay the right to a due process hearing. But IDEA strongly encourages mediation and requires states to set up a process for it and to compel a parent who rejects mediation to have a meeting with a disinterested party concerning the benefits of mediation.

The due process hearing is an administrative, quasi-judicial hearing similar to a regular courtroom trial. At the hearing, the parents and schools are entitled to be represented by lawyers, present evidence, and cross-examine each other's witnesses.

Parent-Student Participation

Although due process hearings and other procedural safeguards can provide a system of checks and balances between schools and families, IDEA also offers another, less adversarial accountability technique: the parent-student participation principle. You have already learned about many parent rights associated with the first five IDEA principles. These rights include, for example, being members of the IEP team and receiving notice before the school does anything about the student's right to a free appropriate public education.

In addition, parents have the right to have access to school records concerning the student and to control who has access to those records. And parents must be invited to participate on state and local special education advisory committees to ensure that their perspectives are incorporated into policy and program decisions.

Finally, one year before a student reaches the age of majority (usually age 18), the school must advise the student that all of the IDEA rights that belonged to the parent will transfer to the student when the student attains the age of majority. The only exception to this transfer-of-rights

Figure 1-8 The relationships among the six principles of IDEA

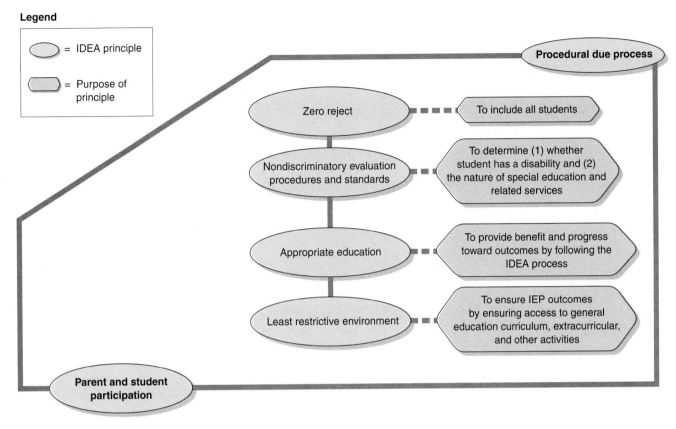

rule is that the parents' rights will not transfer to the student if the student has been determined, under state law, to be incompetent. In that event, the rights transfer to the student's legally appointed guardian.

Bringing the Six Principles Together

How do the six principles really work together to form a process of ensuring an appropriate education for students with disabilities? Figure 1–8 highlights the fact that the first four principles—zero reject, nondiscriminatory evaluation, appropriate education, and least restrictive environment—are the *inputs* into a student's education. The other two principles—procedural due process and parent-student participation—are *accountability techniques,* ways to make sure that the other four principles are implemented correctly. The figure identifies the principles and their purposes and shows their relationships.

FEDERAL FUNDING OF IDEA

Rights run with revenues. Accordingly, Congress grants federal money to state and local educational agencies (school districts) to assist them in educating students ages birth to 21. The state and local agencies, however, must agree to comply with IDEA's principles, or else they will not receive the federal money.

   The state and local agencies may not simply substitute the federal money for the funds that they themselves raise and spend on special education; they may not supplant state and local money with federal money. The federal money supplements state and local contributions.

There is no doubt about this fact: special education is expensive, as the following facts reveal (Chambers, Shkolnik, & Pérez, 2003; Parrish et al., 2004):

- The federal investment in special education was $7.5 billion in the 2002–2003 school year; the federal investment in the first year of IDEA's implementation (1977–1978) was $252 million. Although IDEA authorizes the federal government to cover the access cost of special education up to 40 percent, federal aid in 2002–2003 was only 15.5 percent.

- Although there has been a 109 percent increase for special education students between 1968–1969 and 1999–2000, the rate of increase for general education students has grown at a faster pace.

- It cost approximately $6.7 billion annually for all students with disabilites to go through the processes of referral, nondiscriminatory evaluation, and IEP development. That is a cost of $1,086 for each special education student.

- The average annual expenditure for a student with a disability ($12,525) (excluding students who are homebound) is 1.91 times greater than for a student in general education ($6,556).

- The two largest categories of disability represent the categories of least spending: students with a specific learning disability and with a communication disorder have per-student costs of approximately $10,750. Students with multiple disabilities have the highest of any disability category, with an annual average of about $20,000 per student.

As states seek to make education more cost-efficient, will they sacrifice effectiveness? Will cost cutting be undertaken at the expense of appropriate services? And how can schools be made more accountable for producing the results that Congress wants—equality of opportunity, full participation, independent living, and economic self-sufficiency—in light of the fact that the demand for services may be larger than the resources available to meet the demand?

Those are good questions. But consider them in this light: each state has taken upon itself, usually in its constitution, the obligation to educate all children, including those with disabilities. Thus, IDEA assists the states to do what they would have to do in any event—educate all children with disabilities. IDEA suplements state and local school budgets. The real question is this: do the expenditures result in good outcomes for the students? Before we get to that question and its answers, let's consider a few other laws that apply to students with disabilities.

NO CHILD LEFT BEHIND ACT: SIX PRINCIPLES

The No Child Left Behind Act (NCLB) of 2001 seeks to improve educational outcomes for all students—those with and without disabilities. President George W. Bush justified NCLB in these words: "Too many children in America are segregated by low expectations, illiteracy, and self-doubt. In a consistently changing world that is demanding increasingly complex skills from its work force, children are literally being left behind" (Bush, 2001a). He also observed that there are uneven educational outcomes for students, declaring: "We have a genuine national crisis. More and more, we are divided into two nations. One that reads, and one that doesn't. One that dreams, and one that doesn't" (Bush, 2001b).

Figure 1–9 identifies NCLB's six principles and highlights two requirements associated with each. Addressing NCLB requirements and implications in detail is beyond the scope of this book. For now, the simple point is that IDEA is aligned with NCLB: these two federal laws complement each other, and both seek improved outcomes for students with disabilities.

OTHER FEDERAL LAWS: ENTITLEMENTS AND ANTIDISCRIMINATION

Other federal laws affect special education and students in those programs. There are two types of these laws: (1) some create an entitlement for students or authorize services for them, and (2) others prohibit students from being discriminated against because of their disabilities.

On the Companion Website, *www. prenhall.com/turnbull,* you will find a link to the U.S. Department of Education's website on NCLB (*http://www.ed.gov/ nclb/landing.jhtml?src=tb/*).

Figure 1-9 Principles and implementing activities of the No Child Left Behind Act

1. *Accountability for results.*   Schools should sufficiently educate all students so that they demonstrate proficiency in certain core academic subjects (English, mathematics, and others). School districts that achieve student outcomes will be rewarded, and those that do not will be reformed.
   - By the 2005–2006 school year, each state must test students annually in grades 3 through 8 in reading and math and students in grades 10–12 at least once in reading and math.
   - Every student will be assessed in each state standard in reading/language arts, math, and science with proficiency by the end of the 2013–2014 school year.

2. *School safety.*   Because all students need a safe environment in which to learn and achieve outcomes, schools are required to establish a plan for keeping schools safe and drug-free.
   - States must establish a uniform procedure for reporting data to parents and other citizens regarding school safety and drug-free schools.
   - When a state identifies a school as being persistently dangerous, the state must notify parents of every student and offer them opportunities to transfer to a safe school.

3. *Parental choice.*   Parents of all students should have the opportunity to stay informed in a full and accurate manner about achievement and safety so that they will be in a position to be full partners in their child's education.
   - Parents must receive a report about the overall achievement of students and the particular school their child attends, the qualifications of their child's teacher, and school safety.
   - Parents must be notified if their child is eligible to move to another school or district when their child's school is not making adequate progress in student outcomes, the school is considered to be "persistently dangerous," or the student has been a victim of a violent crime while on school grounds.

4. *Teacher quality.*   Teachers should be proficient to teach and thus must meet certain federal and state standards before they are certified to teach. States' receipt of federal funds will depend on their record in hiring "highly qualified" teachers.
   - Each state must develop a plan to ensure that all teachers of core academic subjects will be highly qualified by the end of the 2005–2006 school year. ("Highly qualified" means that each teacher has full certification and a bachelor's degree and has passed a state-administered test on core academic subject knowledge.)
   - Paraprofessionals hired after January 2002 must have an associate's degree or higher, or they must have completed two years of postsecondary study at an institution of higher education.

5. *Scientifically based methods of teaching.*   Highly qualified teachers must use research-based curricula and instructional methods in order to ensure students' success with academic outcomes.
   - Each state is responsible for establishing a Reading Leadership Team to ensure that schools that need to improve their reading achievement scores are using scientifically based instructional methods.
   - Schools that fail to meet adequate student achievement goals are required to use scientifically based instructional methods in order to remain open.

6. *Local flexibility.*   State and local educational agencies have some discretion in using federal and state matching funds in order to respond to local problems in particularly local ways.
   - Education funding programs are consolidated so they will be easier to administer at the local level.
   - Money may be transferred from many federal programs to another federal program in order to address local needs (but no transfers of IDEA money are allowed).

Entitlements and Other Services

Rehabilitation Act. The most important of several federal employment-related laws for students with disabilities is the Rehabilitation Act. If a person has a severe disability but, with rehabilitation, is able to work despite the disability, the person is entitled to two types of vocational rehabilitation services under the Rehabilitation Act. First, when people are 16 years old, they can receive work evaluations, financial aid so they can pursue job training, and job locator services, all from their state rehabilitation agency.

Second, persons with severe disabilities, including students, can enroll in the supported employment program. They work with the assistance of a job coach, whose duties include teaching the person with a disability how to do a job and then helping him or her do it independently. The supported worker must be paid at least the minimum wage, work at least 20 hours a week in a typical work setting, and be able, after 18 months of supported employment, to do the job alone without support.

Tech Act. The Technology-Related Assistance to Individuals with Disabilities Act of 1988 (as amended), often called the Tech Act, grants federal funds to the states so that they can help create statewide systems for delivering assistive technology devices and services to people with disabilities, including students with disabilities (Kemp, Hourcade, & Parette, 2000; Lahm, Bausch, Hasselbring, & Blackhurst, 2001). In Chapters 5 through 16, we describe how technology benefits students.

In summary, IDEA and the Rehabilitation Act create personal entitlements; they provide direct services to eligible people. By contrast, the Tech Act creates a statewide capacity to serve people with disabilities; instead of directly benefiting the people themselves, it helps the states meet the people's needs.

Prohibiting Discrimination

Education and rehabilitation are, of course, necessary to ameliorate the effects of a student's disability. But they are not sufficient by themselves to overcome the effects of the disability. IDEA, for example, does not prohibit public or private agencies from discriminating against the student on the basis of the student's disability. Yes, a student may receive special education; but that service might not create opportunities for the student to use the skills he or she has acquired through special education. Prejudice against people with disabilities may still foreclose opportunities for the student to show that, although he or she has a disability, the student is nonetheless still able.

How can society attack the prejudice? One answer is to use antidiscrimination laws like those that prohibit discrimination based on race or gender. The first such law, enacted in 1975 as an amendment to the Rehabilitation Act, is known as Section 504 (29 U.S.C., Sec. 794) (deBettencourt, 2002; Denbo, 2003). The second, enacted in 1990, is the Americans with Disabilities Act (ADA) (42 U.S.C. Sections 12101–12213) (Huber & Jones, 2003; Rea & Davis-Dorsey, 2004; Wall & Sarver, 2003). These are fundamentally similar laws. Section 504 of the Rehabilitation Act and ADA both basically provide that no otherwise qualified individual with a disability shall, solely by reason of his or her disability, be discriminated against in certain realms of American life. Figure 1–10 sets out the meaning of "person with a disability" under Section 504 and ADA. Both laws use basically the same definition.

Section 504 and ADA coverage. Section 504 applies to any program or activity receiving federal financial

Assistive technology substantially increases opportunities for students with disabilities to make progress in the general curriculum.

Figure 1-10 Definition of "person with a disability" in the Rehabilitation Act and ADA

Section 504 of the Rehabilitation Act and ADA define a person with a disability as one who
- Has a physical or mental impairment that substantially limits one or more major life activities (e.g., traumatic brain injury)
- Has a record of such an impairment (history of cancer that is now in remission)
- Is regarded as having such an impairment (a person who is especially creative but simultaneously is chronically "wired" or "high" may be regarded as having some emotional disturbances or attention-deficit/hyperactivity disorders)

Note: A student who has HIV but is not so impaired that he or she needs special education is protected under Section 504 and ADA because the person meets the last two criteria: the person has a history of a disability, and others regard that person as having a disability. The same is true of a person who has attention-deficit/hyperactivity disorder (AD/HD). See Chapters 12 and 8, respectively, for other health impairments and AD/HD students' rights under IDEA, Section 504, and ADA.

assistance. Because state and local education agencies receive federal funds, they may not discriminate against students or other persons with disabilities on account of their disabilities. As you will learn in Chapters 8 and 12, not all students with disabilities are entitled to IDEA benefits. Those who are not, however, are entitled not to be discriminated against because of their disability.

Clearly, Section 504 is limited in scope. What if an individual seeks employment from a company that does not receive any federal funds or wants to participate in state and local government programs that are not federally aided or wants to have access to telecommunications systems such as closed captioning for people with hearing impairments? In none of those domains of life will the person receive any protection from Section 504. Instead, ADA comes to the rescue.

ADA extends its civil rights/nondiscrimination protection to the following sectors of American life: private-sector employment, transportation, state and local government activities and programs, privately operated businesses that are open to the public ("public accommodations"), and telecommunications.

IDEA, Section 504, and ADA: overlapping protections. Basically, IDEA and the Rehabilitation Act authorize federal, state, and local educational agencies to undertake programs in education and employment and provide funds for the state and local agencies to pay for those programs. By contrast, Section 504 and ADA prohibit discrimination solely on the basis of disability in education, employment, and other sectors of American life. Together, these laws support students' transition from school to postschool activities, including work. That is why the transition components of the IEP anticipate outcomes that are largely consistent with those that any student—whether one with a disability or not—typically will want: work, education, and opportunities to participate in the community. Those results cannot be achieved as long as there are barriers erected on the foundation of discrimination. These barriers—the deep roots of discrimination—are the targets of Section 504 and ADA.

SPECIAL EDUCATION RESULTS

After the schools started to implement IDEA in 1977 and until Congress reauthorized (reenacted) it in 1997, the major federal criteria for evaluating special education were primarily numerical. The questions always were "How many more students are being served annually, and in what types of placements are they served?"

Starting with the 1997 reauthorization and continuing with the 2004 reauthorization, however, federal and state policymakers and educators do more than count the number of students being served and tally their placements. Today, the goal of special education is to improve the results for students. Congress reflected this goal when it reauthorized IDEA in 2004 and declared that an "essential element" of the nation's policy of ensuring equal opportunity, full participation, independent living, and economic self-sufficiency is to improve educational results for students with disabilities.

The same task exists for general education: to improve the educational results for students. Under NCLB, Congress allots funds to the states, which in turn allot them to each of their school districts. As a condition of receiving the federal funds and to carry out the NCLB principle of accountability, each state and each of its school districts must set 5-year goals for improving the academic scores of all students, whether in general or special education, on standardized tests. If the students do not meet these goals by obtaining higher scores, the federal government will provide the districts with additional funds to meet the goals. If, however, they still do not meet these goals, the federal government will require the states to allot federal funds so that the parents of the children in the "failing" districts can attend any school of their choice, whether the school is inside or outside the district and whether the school is a public school, a charter public school, or a private school, even one that is a parochial (religiously oriented) private school.

The No Child Left Behind Act, then, emphasizes that outcomes—measured by academic achievement—count for all students. For that reason, each student with a disability will take the state and district assessments—the tests of student achievement—unless the student's IEP team excuses the student because of the extent of the student's disability; in that case, the student takes an alternative assessment (see Chapter 2).

Now let's return to IDEA and its results. What did Congress mean when it spoke about equality of opportunity, full participation, independent living, and economic self-sufficiency as the national goals and thus the appropriate outcomes for students with disabilities? Here are the four terms and general definitions for each:

- *Equality of opportunity.* People with disabilities will have the same chances and opportunities in life as people without disabilities.

- *Full participation.* People with disabilities will have opportunities to be included in all aspects of their community and will be protected from any attempts by people to segregate them solely on the basis of their disability.

- *Independent living.* People with disabilities will have the opportunity to fully participate in decision making and to experience autonomy in making choices about how to live their lives.

- *Economic self-sufficiency.* People with disabilities will be provided with opportunities to engage fully in income-producing work or unpaid work that contributes to a household or community.

What is the evidence related to these results? Unfortunately, research on results for students with disabilities does not provide definitive answers. A number of indicators, however, suggest that substantial tasks lie ahead.

One indicator of equality of opportunity is the extent to which students with disabilities are completing their high school education. A national survey of individuals with disabilities indicated that people with disabilities are twice as likely not to complete high school or college than people without disabilities (21 percent versus 10 percent) (National Organization on Disability, 2004). Males from diverse racial backgrounds (especially from urban communities and low-income homes) have the highest dropout rate (National Center for Education Statistics, 2000).

A second major indicator of the achievement of IDEA's goals relates to the area of postschool employment. Clearly, adults who are employed increase their chances for equal opportunity, full participation, independent living, and especially economic self-sufficiency. Although the rate of being employed full or part time for people without disabilities is 78 percent, the employment rate for individuals with disabilities is only 35 percent—a gap of 43 percentage points (National Organization on Disability, 2004). The employment rate for individuals with more severe disabilities is even lower: only 19 percent of individuals with severe disabilities work either full or part time.

To what extent is diversity a factor in the employment of people with disabilities? Latino and African American individuals with severe disabilities are much less likely to be employed than are European American individuals with severe disabilities (National Council on Disability, 2000).

The final indicator of long-term results relates to the data on overall satisfaction with life. Approximately two-thirds of individuals without disabilities report that they are very satisfied with life in general, whereas approximately one-third of individuals with disabilities report the same satisfaction. People with very severe disabilities are much less satisfied with life in general than are people with somewhat severe, slight, or moderate disabilities. The following trends relate to general life satisfaction (National Organization on Disability, 2004):

- Three times as many individuals with disabilities live in poverty with annual household incomes below $15,000 as compared to individuals without disabilities (26 percent versus 9 percent).
- Individuals with disabilities are twice as likely to have inadequate transportation.
- Individuals with disabilities are less likely to attend religious services, socialize, and eat out in restaurants as compared to people without disabilities.
- People with disabilities are more than twice as likely to go without needed health care.

Here's the question that you have to answer for yourself and that we hope our book helps you answer: given that there is a great deal of room for improvement in achieving results for students with disabilities, what role will you play in making it possible for students to make progress in the special and general curriculum so that their long-term results are as positive as possible?

Looking to Tom's Future

No one is more qualified to write about Tom Ellenson's future than his father and mother, Richard and Lora. This is their view of their son's future. Truth be told, it is a vision that we, the authors of this book and the parents of children with exceptional traits, share wholeheartedly. Please note that, in the remaining chapters, we, the authors, write the "vision statement." For this chapter, however, the Ellensons must speak for themselves.

For us, Tom is best understood through a story that's a bit hard to tell.

When he was 5, Tom went in for a double osteotomy, a surgery needed by many kids with CP. When children don't walk, their hipbones often don't settle in the hip sockets quite right. To fix the problem before it gets worse, the children have an operation during which both femurs are sawed in half, hip sockets are filled out with bone chip, and the bones are bolted back together at a new angle.

Tom came home from the hospital after five days. His entire body was in a cast. It went from the middle of his chest down to his ankles. His legs were spread out in a large "v": a steel bar went from one calf to the other so there could be absolutely no movement.

Tom lay on his side for nearly four weeks, held up by plaster, steel, and a half-dozen pillows. But he never showed sadness. He never showed frustration or anger. He watched *Blues Clues* and *Monty Python*, and every night, as a family, we watched *Emeril Live*. A friend of ours got Tom a Spongebob Squarepants karaoke machine and Tom gurgled and wailed to the CDs we played on it: Beatles and Kidz Bop and Avril Lavigne. Think of that: our friend knew Tom couldn't verbalize; but she also understood that, in Tom's head, that didn't mean he wasn't singing.

During this time, Tom's 13-month-old sister, Taite, would lie and crawl on the floor in front of the TV. And one day as we were all watching, Taite got up and took her first steps. She wobbled from the TV over to where Tom lay, his body held rigid by the steel and cobalt blue gauze, and she plopped forward onto the couch. "Taite!" she warbled. And Tom just giggled and giggled, his face alight with love.

That is our son.

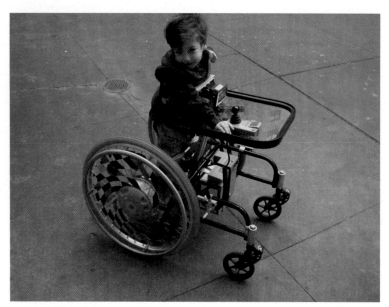

Tom's parents look toward his future and envision him embracing his potential and striving to reach it.

What do we expect for his future? Well, having now met many people in the disabled community, we realize they are filled with many feelings. But among them are so often patience, focus, realism, and optimism. This is not simply the reality we choose to see. It is the way things are. Amid the struggles and the difficulties and, certainly, the moments of sadness and depression we have shared with many people—disabled children, disabled adults, their parents and friends—the overriding emotion in this world is one of happiness. We live within a community that embraces the gift of life.

From a practical perspective, we expect Tom to continue his education and eventually attend college. We expect he will find a job that satisfies him. Like many parents, we do not want to force the specifics of our expectations nor our own backgrounds and interests on him.

Certainly there are many challenges ahead: Tom will need to develop physical access methods so he can work more effectively on the computers with which he already has reasonable proficiency. As he gets older, he will need to develop more consistent and deeper methods of communication. On a very fundamental level, he will need to learn to eat a wider variety of foods.

But although these are certainly significant issues, they are secondary to the broader foundation behind a meaningful life. And as such, what we wish primarily for Tom is that he embraces his potential and then always strives to reach it. We know he will do his share to make that happen. Yet to some degree, it is up to those of us who surround and support the disabilities community to make sure others understand that this is possible.

It must be difficult for people if they cannot verbalize. But it is only tragic if they are not heard. It must be hard to be unable to walk. But it is tragic to be left behind. Our dream for Tom is that he find those individuals who understand these distinctions and who see not the limitations but the person who lives among them, for these will be the people who share Tom's infinite capacity to appreciate life.

SUMMARY

Profile of special education students and personnel in today's schools

- Approximately 9 percent of all students, ages 6 to 21, have disabilities.
- About 1.8 percent of all children, ages birth through 2, received infant-and-toddler early intervention services.
- Nearly 5 percent of all students, ages 3 through 5, received early special education services.
- Most special education students are males.
- Language sensitivity is important, and we recommend the use of people-first language.
- There are teacher and related-service personnel shortages in the special education field all across the United States.

Overview of the law and special education

- The preludes to today's federal special education law were two court cases requiring schools to educate these students.
- The federal law, enacted in 1975, is the Individuals with Disabilities Education Act.
- There are 12 categories of disabilities for children ages 6 through 21.
- The law benefits infants and toddlers (Part C) and students ages 5 through 21 (Part B).

IDEA: Six principles

- IDEA has six principles:
  - Zero reject, a rule of inclusion
  - Nondiscriminatory evaluation, a rule of fair assessments
  - Appropriate education, a rule of individualized benefit
  - Least restrictive placement, a presumption in favor of placement in general education programs
  - Procedural due process, a rule of fair dealing and accountability
  - Parent and student participation, a rule of shared decision making

Federal funding of IDEA

- Special education is funded by federal, state, and local government funds.
- The cost of educating the average student with a disability is almost twice the cost of educating the average student who does not have a disability.

No Child Left Behind Act: Six principles

- NCLB has six principles:
  - Accountability for results, a rule for enhanced student academic outcomes
  - School safety, a rule to keep schools safe and drug-free
  - Parental choice, a rule to provide options to parents to transfer their child
  - Teacher quality, a rule to improve teacher credentials
  - Scientifically based methods of teaching, a rule to increase the delivery of research-based instruction
  - Local flexibility, a rule to increase local decision making

Other federal laws: Entitlements and antidiscrimination

- The Rehabilitation Act provides for work training, especially supported employment.
- The Tech Act makes assistive technology available statewide in each state.
- The Rehabilitation Act, Section 504, and the Americans with Disabilities Act prohibit discrimination solely on the basis of disability in a wide range of services, both in and outside school.

Special education results

- The long-term results are poor in the areas of equal opportunity, full participation, independent living, and economic self-sufficiency.

- Among individuals with disabilities from diverse populations, the results are poor compared to those from majority populations.
- Among individuals with disabilities, the results for those with severe disabilities are poor compared to those with mild/moderate disabilities.

WHAT WOULD YOU RECOMMEND?

Refer to chapter content and the PRAXIS™ and CEC standards in Appendix A to answer the following questions:

1. What labels, if any, should educators use to describe students with disabilities? Which PRAXIS™ and CEC standards are you applying?
2. Go to the Companion Website for this chapter and locate the link to *www.cec.sped.org/law_res/doc/*. Make a list of what basic knowledge about IDEA and NCLB all educators should have. Which CEC standards are you using?
3. Look back over the chapter and outline the particulars of an IEP that all educators should have. Which CEC standards are you applying?
4. What basic knowledge about antidiscrimination laws should all educators have? Which PRAXIS™ standard are you applying?

Who are Heather and Star Morgan?

Travel with us to Independence, Missouri, birthplace of Harry S. Truman and home of Luff Elementary School. Enter the school on a local election day; pass citizens voting—such an American activity, so symbolic of the full citizenship to which Luff's students aspire and toward which their teachers are guiding them. Come into the third-grade classroom of Jean Ann Maloney. There you learn that the class includes Heather Morgan, who has mild mental retardation. You wonder, "How can a student with mild mental retardation be in a third-grade reading class?" You learn from Barbara, Heather's adoptive mother, that Heather is an avid reader. Today she's in a group of four students; she accompanies her three peers in reading aloud from the same book they are using. Significantly, none of the other three students has a disability. It is clear

that the school's administration and faculty have the same expectations for Heather as they have for the other students.

Now you go to a first-grade classroom. You learn about another student who has disabilities. She's Star Morgan. Like her sister Heather, she has been adopted by Barbara. Barbara tells you that Star has many more disabilities than Heather does. Using her hands to sign quotation marks, Barbara explains that Heather has "mild" mental retardation and Star has multiple disabilities, including "severe" mental retardation. In addition, Star does not speak; she can make sounds but not words.

All that aside, you notice aspects of Star that are quite unexpected. She's the student with the brightest eyes; they sparkle, hinting at capacities as yet untapped. She's also very shy except when she's leading her class by signing their favorite book, *Charles Tiger*. Leading the class? Yes, she's in front of her classmates, taking her place with her teacher, Donna Cummings, and her paraprofessional, Pam Eldridge. Her classmates speak the story and sign it simultaneously, following her lead.

By leading, Star signifies that she has an extraordinary relationship with her classmates. It's one in which they learn from her; yes, she's teaching them to become bilingual and multicultural, to enter the culture of those who, like Star, cannot speak unless they sign or like those who have hearing impairments and cannot talk or hear except by signing. Diversity has a language of many tongues and hands.

One more stop is in order: the teacher's lounge. There Peggy Palser, Luff's principal, is meeting with Carrie Hamburg (K–3 special educator), Jackie Browning (4–5 special educator), Dana Pyle (curriculum and instruction specialist for all grades), and Rae Jean Aquero (school counselor for all grades). Jean Ann Maloney (Heather's teacher) and her paraprofessional, Jennifer Genochio, join them.

The topic of conversation is the Missouri Assessment Program (MAP), the annual mandatory assessment of student and school performance. MAP requires students to

Ensuring Progress in the General Education Curriculum Through Universal Design for Learning and Inclusion

demonstrate higher-order skills. They will need prior information (vocabulary and grammar, addition and subtraction) to do well because MAP asks them to solve problems to demonstrate that they can apply what they have learned; MAP asks the students to "show me" (the state's motto) that they grasp the concepts.

Just how Heather will take MAP concerns Luff's faculty. They have the same concerns about Star, who will take the test in 2 years. Should Heather be required to take it in just the same way as her peers without disabilities? Should Star? If not, what accommodations are reasonable? Should either of them be exempted and have the chance to demonstrate mastery through an alternative assessment? After all, just participating in general education is not enough. Progressing in it is the goal, and assessing their progress in such a way that they can truly demonstrate what they have learned is only fair.

If these and all students are going to fully participate in the United States and be as economically self-sufficient as possible, schools such as Luff and states such as Missouri are obliged to reform themselves: to teach content more effectively to all students. Otherwise, independence in Independence will escape far too many students. So Luff's faculty and its principal are meeting. All of them are committed to educating and assessing all students, together—but not without accounting for individual differences.

It takes a large team to make an inclusive school, a team of collaborators committed to inclusion and to a universal, all-students approach to curriculum (what the students learn), in-

struction (how well the teachers teach), and assessment (how teachers know what students have learned). Just as the building is accessible to all students, so is the curriculum. Inclusion is more than a matter of simply being in a school. It involves being there in a significant way, as Star is. And universal design for learning is more than a matter of architecture. It's a matter of combining curriculum, instruction, and assessment for a single purpose: to reach acceptable outcomes for all students.

Consistent with IDEA, we want you to learn how to support students with exceptionalities to make progress in the general education curriculum. Accordingly, we emphasize four themes throughout the book: universal design for learning, inclusion, partnerships, and multicultural diversity.

Use your *Real Lives and Exceptionalities* DVD to "Meet Heather" and "Meet Star."

WHAT IS "PROGRESS IN THE GENERAL EDUCATION CURRICULUM"?

In this chapter, we address universal design and inclusion. In Chapter 3 we discuss multiculturalism, and in Chapter 4 we discuss partnerships. Before learning about universal design and inclusion, you need to know more about the concept of progress in the general education curriculum.

First, progress is what federal law promotes. As you learned from reading Chapter 1, IDEA requires each student's IEP to state how the student will be involved and progress in the general curriculum, how the student's progress will be assessed, and how state- and district-wide assessments will be modified (as appropriate) for the student. The No Child Left Behind Act (NCLB) requires assessment of students' proficiency and exempts no students from assessment. NCLB covers students with disabilities but, like IDEA, allows for appropriate individualized modifications as set out in a student's IEP.

Second, progress in the general education curriculum is achieved by **standards-based reform:** a process that identifies the academic content (reading, mathematics) that students must master, the standards for the student's achievement of content proficiency, a general education curriculum aligned with these standards, assessment of student progress in meeting the general education curriculum and standards, and information from the assessments to improve teaching and learning and to demonstrate that the schools are indeed accountable to the students, their families, and the public.

Third, NCLB requires states to establish challenging academic content and student achievement standards that apply to all students, including students with disabilities. **Academic content standards** define the knowledge, skills, and understanding that students should attain in academic subjects. **Student achievement standards** define the levels of achievement that students must meet to demonstrate their proficiency in the subjects. States may establish **alternate achievement standards** for students with the most significant cognitive disabilities, but even so, those alternate standards must align with the same academic content standards for all students so that these students will be able to make progress in the general education curriculum.

Fourth, a student's IEP team must consider any accommodations in the assessment process the student might need to ensure that his or her achievement is fairly evaluated. Accommodations do not change the content of the assessment; rather, they result in changes in teachers' ways of presenting information (for example, changing the order for taking subtests), in students' ways of responding (for example, using a computer or dictating answers), in timing (for example, having extended time or frequent breaks), and in settings (for example, taking the test in a quiet room or a small group away from the larger class) (Thurlow, 2000).

Fifth, over the past decade, education leaders have asked their peers to raise standards for all students and to assess all students' progress to ensure that everyone meets those standards (American Federation of Teachers, 1999; National Research Council, 1993). With the passage of NCLB, those initiatives have become law.

Last, standards-based reform is not without its problems. One reason is historical. In the past, teachers chose materials, primarily textbooks, from which students could learn grade-level content; then teachers instructed by focusing on the middle range of their students' ability (Pugach & Warger, 2001). This one-size-fits-all approach shortchanged many students. Also, some educators thought that students with disabilities should not be expected to participate in, much less master, the same curriculum as students without disabilities. For students with disabilities, the curriculum was almost always developed from their IEPs, not the general education curriculum standards (Nolet & McLaughlin, 2000). Further, the needs and anticipated results for students with disabilities were often overlooked as states developed their curriculum standards (Erickson, 1998). Only 17 percent of the states included people with disabilities or disability experts in the development of their standards (Thurlow, Ysseldyke, Gutman, & Geenen, 1998). And still further, students with disabilities were not considered when state assessments were first developed and administered and when results were first compiled and reported (Thurlow, 2000). Nevertheless, the states are making progress (Thompson & Thurlow, 2003).

How Does the General Education Curriculum Benefit Students with Disabilities?

Connecting the curriculum to standards. As we just pointed out, the **general education curriculum** for students without disabilities emerges from the academic content and student achievement standards set by each state education agency for students at various grade levels. To learn how the general education curriculum benefits students with disabilities, let's revisit Heather and Star Morgan.

In Missouri, where Heather and Star attend school, the content and achievement standards are set by the state board of education and implemented at the district and school levels. Each district and school is expected to adopt the state curriculum, and all teachers in each school are expected to teach that curriculum. That's why, at Luff Elementary School, Heather and all other third graders will be tested to determine what progress in reading they have made. For example, faculty members at Luff teach language skills to all students through an approach called phonemic awareness. They infuse that approach into all grades. The approach benefits Heather and all other students; phonemic awareness is a whole-school approach to teaching and learning.

The faculty also integrates subjects, such as reading and mathematics. For example, they teach Heather the multiples of 2 and 3 by having her play with a manipulative multiplication chart consisting of windows that open two or three at a time and then having her read about houses, windows, and numbers during her reading lessons. And because she likes to use a computer and has fine-motor difficulties that make her handwriting difficult to read, she uses a computer program with which she can draw and then write a story about an animal using a spell-check program to correct her mistakes . . . all activities linked to the general education curriculum. The difference is in how she is taught and how she shows what she has learned. For example, she recites her multiplication tables with Jennifer Genochi, a paraprofessional, while Mrs. Maloney requires other students to work out story problems at the chalkboard or their tables.

Star Morgan leads her class as they read and she signs a book together.

Star is in her homeroom most of the school week, but because she has educational support needs greater than many other students, she leaves her homeroom for two highly specialized related-service interventions. One involves occupational therapy so Star will learn her shapes, how to grasp a pencil, how to use it to form letters (especially the first letters of her first and last name), and how to fasten her clothes and tie her shoes in sequence. The other involves speech therapy because she has a small mouth, difficulty forming words, and, more problematic, an ability to speak but not to repeat what she says. She amazed her teachers by pointing to the school's Christmas tree and saying the first words they ever heard from her: "Christmas tree." But she has never repeated that phrase or any others she has used.

Ensuring student progress in the general education curriculum does not mean that schools overlook students' individualized needs. IDEA still requires that students with disabilities receive an appropriate education based on both the general education curriculum and the student's unique learning needs. According to IDEA, students with disabilities should be involved with the general education curriculum to the maximum extent appropriate.

Heather Morgan meets with her third-grade faculty, Jennifer Genochio and Jean Ann Maloney, to demonstrate her reading ability.

To learn more about alternate achievement standards in NCLB, go to the Companion Website, *www.prenhall.com/turnbull*, and link to the U.S. Department of Education website, *http://www.ed.gov/nclb/freedom/local/specedfactsheet.html*.

At Luff Elementary School, Star gets plenty of instruction in academics and such matters as being safe in the community. She used to run from the playground whenever she had a chance. With the help of her mother, Barbara, the Luff faculty have devised a system to reward her when she does not run away from school. She also is being taught how to accept changes, even in routine matters such as class schedules; a calendar and advance notice of changes help. And she's learning how to be in the presence of a large number of students, as at school assemblies. Bit by bit, she's including herself in assemblies; if she becomes agitated, she can choose to leave. These are community-living skills that will stand her in good stead as she progresses through school and then works and lives in Independence after graduating from school. So for Star, academics and highly functional training that will help her live independently in the future go hand in hand.

Standard: Using modification, technology, and individualized assessment strategies is an application of CEC Standard 8, Assessment.

Star Morgan follows another student in reading class, but all of the students are signing what they are reading.

Making accommodations in assessments. Currently, all states that administer state-level assessments have written policies or guidelines concerning accommodations in assessments (Thurlow, House, Boys, Scott, & Ysseldyke, 2000). Studies of the five most frequent test accommodations—dictated responses, extended time, large print, braille, and interpretation for instructions—reveal that there is only limited evidence that these accommodations result in more valid responses from students with disabilities (Bolt & Thurlow, 2004).

Under IDEA, a student who (according to the IEP team) cannot learn the same content as same-age peers who do not have disabilities and who cannot take the state assessment even if provided with test accommodations may be exempt from the standard state assessment. But IDEA still requires an assessment of the student's progress, through an **alternate assessment.** States have latitude in developing alternate assessments, but IDEA requires the states to align the alternate assessments with content standards set for all students and to serve the same purpose as standardized assessments—accountability and decision-making. Currently, 40 states align their alternate assessment with state academic content standards or state standards and functional skills, and five assess functional skills only or leave it to the IEP team to determine content (Thompson & Thurlow, 2003). Because of NCLB, states are basing alternate assessments on these alternate achievement standards (Browder et al., 2004).

Let's return to Heather and learn how she is assessed. As a third grader, Heather must take the MAP assessments. Because she has mild mental retardation (as her mother explained) and because she is receiving instruction in the general education curriculum, Heather took the MAP assessment with modifications. She completed the test in a room away from her classmates and was allowed more time to finish it. She was allowed many breaks, and her teachers read the test to her and allowed her to dictate her answers. These are the same modifications that benefit her in her general education reading program; she is assessed as she is taught, all according to her IEP.

It is hard to know exactly what kind of assessments will be administered to Star when she reaches the third grade. Although it now appears that she has severe mental retardation, she is reading the same book as her first-grade peers who do not have cognitive disabilities. She may be able to stay at that level of reading, but then again she may not. If she cannot keep up the pace, she will undergo a reading assessment that is geared to her level. So a change in content is possible. Clearly, a change in her performance requirements is in order because she does not speak but uses only sign language. So she will demonstrate what she can do by signing her answers and perhaps by having a teacher sign the questions to her.

Chapter 4 points out that students from diverse racial and ethnic backgrounds disproportionately receive special education services and that there have been disproportionate results for many students from diverse backgrounds in terms of educational outcomes. You also learned that many students from diverse backgrounds are disadvantaged in the processes of referral and eligibility for special education and for test taking. Do assessments also disadvantage students from racially and ethnically diverse backgrounds? The data seem to suggest so.

The Massachusetts Comprehensive Assessment System (MCAS) is the commonwealth's assessment program. The MCAS-Alt is the alternate assessment for students who cannot take the MCAS even with accommodations. The MCAS-Alt includes products documenting a student's performance on activities related to the standards, called the Curriculum Framework, over the school year. Like students taking the MCAS, students participating in the alternate assessment are assessed on different content each year. Portfolios pertaining to reading and literature are required in 3rd grade; English and language arts in 4th, 7th, and 10th grades; mathematics in 4th, 6th, 8th, and 10th grades; and science and technology in 5th and 8th grades. The MCAS-Alt portfolio involves collection of instructional data, work samples, and other products that document a student's knowledge of concepts, skills, and content outlined in the Curriculum Framework's learning standards. Note how closely the decision-making process in the following figure aligns with the IEP planning process depicted in this chapter. The end result is that assessment results for all students are considered when making decisions about resources and support.

Putting These Strategies to Work for Progress in the General Curriculum

1. For which students is the MCAS-Alt appropriate?

2. What is the purpose of the MCAS-Alt?

3. What documents constitute the MCAS-Alt portfolio?

To learn more about the MCAS-Alt, go to the Into Practice module in Chapter 2 of the Companion Website, www.prenhall.com/turnbull.

Identifying Instructional Goals Through the MCAS-Alt

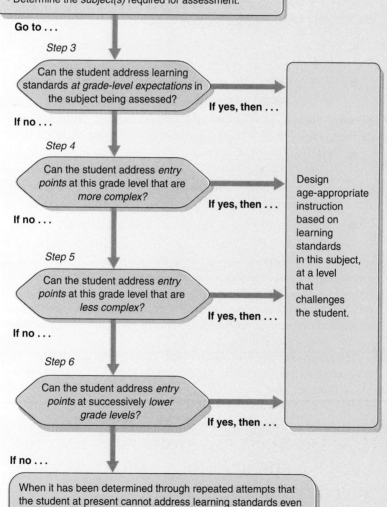

Steps 1 and 2

- Determine the *grade* at which student will be assessed.
- Determine the *subject(s)* required for assessment.

Go to . . .

Step 3

Can the student address learning standards *at grade-level expectations* in the subject being assessed?

If yes, then . . .

If no . . .

Step 4

Can the student address *entry points* at this grade level that are *more complex?*

If yes, then . . .

If no . . .

Step 5

Can the student address *entry points* at this grade level that are *less complex?*

If yes, then . . .

If no . . .

Step 6

Can the student address *entry points* at successively *lower grade levels?*

If yes, then . . .

If no . . .

Design age-appropriate instruction based on learning standards in this subject, at a level that challenges the student.

When it has been determined through repeated attempts that the student at present cannot address learning standards even at the least complex entry point, the student should address *access skills* (social, motor, and communication skills) while participating in academic instruction.

Source: Adapted from Massachusetts Department of Education. (2001). *Resource guide to the Massachusetts Curriculum Framework for students with significant disabilities.* Boston: Author.

High-stakes assessment can prevent some students from graduating from high school, but it can also cause those who do graduate to be better prepared for adult life in college or at work.

- In 2003, European American and Asian/Pacific Islander students scored higher on assessments than did African American, Latino, and American Indian/Alaskan Native students in reading at both grades 4 and 8.
- The average reading scores for fourth and eighth graders who are eligible for free lunch (because of low family income) are lower than the scores for students who are not eligible for free lunch (NCES, 2000).
- In 2000, European American students had higher scores on mathematics than did African American or Latino students.
- Large gaps between European American, African American, and Latino students have remained relatively unchanged since 1990 (National Assessment of Educational Progress, 2005a, 2005b).

Why Is Progress in the General Education Curriculum Valued?

Is it good that students with disabilities are held accountable for progress in the general education curriculum? Is it fair that such progress is determined by accountability for progress toward the same standards? Those who favor the same standards offer two arguments (O'Neill, 2001; Thurlow, 2000):

- Comparable standards will result in higher expectations and higher achievement for students with disabilities.
- By being part of the standards process for assessment, students with disabilities will be part of the reform movement of education.

Opponents argue that the "same standards" approach puts students with disabilities at a disadvantage relative to students without disabilities (Ford, Davern, & Schnorr, 2001; O'Neill, 2001):

- The same-standards approach can conflict with the individualized needs of the students as set out in their IEPs. For example, the focus on academics and passing the state and district assessments will deny students with disabilities adequate instruction in important areas such as vocational education and basic life skills.
- Students will be frustrated, discouraged, and drop out.

Despite the difficulties of involving students with disabilities in standards-based reform, it is important to hold them to high expectations and provide them with access to a challenging curriculum. Underlying high expectations is the value of full citizenship: to deny students the opportunity to benefit from the general education curriculum may actually limit their education and postschool opportunities. Essentially, ensuring progress in the general education curriculum safeguards them against second-class treatment and against being patronized because of their disability (Thurlow, 2000).

How do you provide standards-based education for all students? We will answer that question throughout all chapters in this book. We begin by describing how you can design curriculum, instruction, and assessment to enable students with exceptionalities to progress in the general education curriculum.

Values: For too long, people with disabilities have been denied the opportunity to be *full, participating citizens.* Educational reform efforts that seek to ensure that right for all students must not exclude students with disabilities.

HOW DO SUPPLEMENTARY AIDS AND SERVICES AND UNIVERSAL DESIGN FOR LEARNING SUPPORT PROGRESS?

Under IDEA, a student is entitled to receive supplementary aids and services in order to make progress in the general education curriculum. One aspect of those services is universal design for learning.

What Are Supplementary Aids and Services?

IDEA defines **supplementary aids and services** as "aids, services, and other supports that are provided in general education classes or other education related settings to enable children with disabilities to be educated with non-disabled children to the maximum extent appropriate." These services and aids supplement the student's specially designed instruction and related services that are components of the student's IEP (as you learned in Chapter 1). Thus, they, like the specially designed instruction and related services, ensure that a student receives an appropriate education, and they especially advance the student's participation and progress in the general education curriculum.

Supplementary aids and services are noninstructional modifications and supports. As Figure 2–1 shows, they include modifications to ensure physical and cognitive access to the environment, classroom ecological variables such as seating arrangements or classroom acoustics, educational or assistive technology, assessment or task modifications, and support from other persons.

Although all of these aids and services are important, we will focus on the role of universal design for learning in promoting progress in the general education curriculum.

What Is Universal Design for Learning?

Universal design (UD) is an architectural concept developed to help people with disabilities be fully included in their communities. UD was first applied in architecture to create barrier-free

Figure 2–1   Supplementary aids and services

Domain	Definition	Examples
Universal design for learning	Modifications to how curriculum is presented or represented or to the ways in which students respond to the curriculum	Digital Talking Book formats, advance organizers, video or audio input/output
Access	Modifications to the community, campus, building, or classroom to ensure physical and cognitive access	Curb cuts, wide doors, clear aisles, nonprint signs
Classroom ecology	Modifications to and arrangements of features of the classroom environment that impact learning	Seating arrangement, types of seating, acoustics, lighting
Educational and assistive technology	Technology that reduces the impact of a person's impairment on his or her capacity	Calculator, augmentative communication device, computer
Assessment and task modifications	Modifications to time or task requirements (but not content or material) to assist in participation in assessment or educational task	Extended time, scribe, note taker, oral presentation
Teacher, paraprofessional, or peer support	Support from another person to participate in instructional activities	Peer buddy, paraeducator, teacher

buildings that were accessible to all people. Rather than adding special features such as ramps and elevators to a building so people with disabilities could gain access, architects designed buildings to be universally accessible for all people.

The kitchen in Figure 2–2 features universal design. It is designed so a person using a wheelchair can have access to appliances and includes adjustable cook-top height, an accessible oven for use while seated, and open space under the sink. In addition, a person who has a visual impairment can benefit from the interior-lighted cabinets. Under UD, these features not only provide access for people with disabilities, but they also benefit everyone. Who else, other than a person with a disability, might benefit from this universally designed kitchen? How about an elderly person for whom it might be much easier to load the dishwasher without having to bend over? Or a child who cannot reach the top shelves but could access bread and peanut butter in the lower cabinets? Most UD features make kitchen use easier for all.

This is an important point. UD features ensure accessibility for people with disabilities, but they also benefit all people. For example, the designs of most scissors limit people who have fine-motor difficulties from using them easily. Did you know, however, that most such scissors are also designed for people who are right-handed? People who are left-handed must purchase specially designed scissors. However, scissors like those in Figure 2–3 can be used by people with limited hand strength or fine-motor difficulties as well as by people who are left-handed or right-handed. They are universally designed, consistent with the UD principles set out in Figure 2–2.

So what does universal design have to do with special education services? As schools began to implement standards-based reforms, it became obvious that instructional materials impeded students' progress in the general education curriculum. Students who could not read because of their visual impairments did not have access to the information they needed to learn content. Students who spoke a language other than English experienced barriers for different reasons. In fact, traditional ways of representing content information (written formats such as textbooks), presenting information (whole-class lectures), and having students demonstrate their knowledge and skills (through written papers and examinations) were barriers for a lot of children, not only those with disabilities.

That's where **universal design for learning (UDL)** comes in. UDL refers to the design of instructional materials and activities to make the content information accessible to all children (Orkwis & McLane, 1998, p. 9). UDL achieves that access through technology and adapted instruction.

To learn more about principles of universal design in buildings and devices, go to the Companion Website, *www.prenhall.com/ turnbull*, to link to the Center for Universal Design, at *http://www. design.ncsu.edu/cud/*.

What examples of universal design and assistive technology do you see in Clip 9 (MeMe) under "Beyond School" on the *Real Lives and Exceptionalities* DVD?

Figure 2-2 Features of a universally designed kitchen

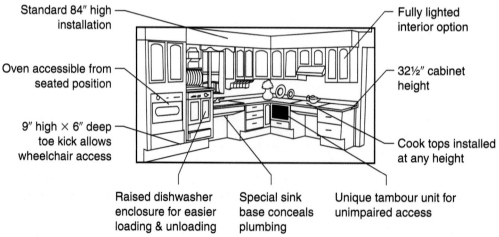

Standard 84″ high installation

Fully lighted interior option

Oven accessible from seated position

32½″ cabinet height

9″ high × 6″ deep toe kick allows wheelchair access

Cook tops installed at any height

Raised dishwasher enclosure for easier loading & unloading

Special sink base conceals plumbing

Unique tambour unit for unimpaired access

Source: http://www.kraftmaid.com

Figure 2-3 Principles of universal design

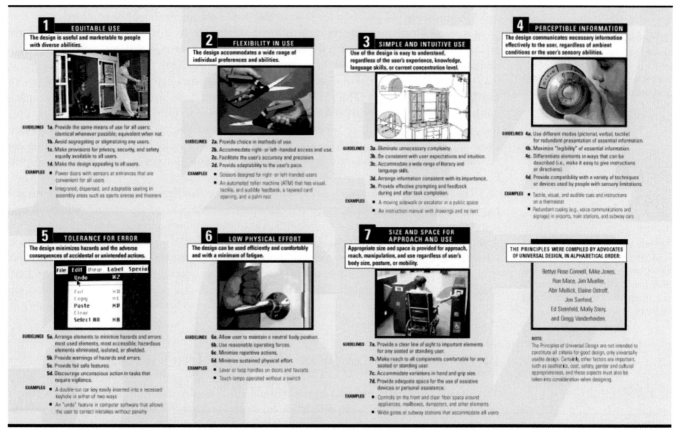

Source: Center for Universal Design. (1997). *The principles of universal design, version 2.0.* Raleigh: North Carolina State University.
Note: The *Principles of Universal Design* were conceived and developed by the Center for Universal Design at North Carolina State University. Use or application of the Principles in any form by an individual or organization is separate and distinct from the Principles and does not constitute or imply acceptance or endorsement by The Center for Universal Design of the use or application.

How Does Universal Design for Learning Facilitate Progress?

UDL contributes to progress in the general education curriculum by ensuring that all students can access academic content information and provide evidence of their learning through more than one means. UDL promotes flexibility in representing content (how instructional materials present the content), presenting content (how educators and materials deliver content), and demonstrating content mastery (how students provide evidence of their learning).

Teachers achieve flexibility in representing and presenting content when they use several different formats, including text, graphics or pictures, digital and other media formats (audio or video, movies), or performance formats (plays, skits) and when they use different means to deliver content information, including lectures, computerized visual presentations such as PowerPoint, role playing, or computer-mediated instruction. Similarly, students can provide evidence of their learning through reports, exams, portfolios, drawings, performances, oral reports, videotaped reports, and other alternative means.

In the "Planning for Universal Design for Learning" sections in Chapters 5 through 16, we describe how UDL principles apply to students with disabilities and how technology and pedagogy enable them to participate and make progress in the general education curriculum. For example, when content information is available in an electronic version, there are many ways to provide access for a wide array of students. Let's illustrate this by discussing the National Instructional Materials Accessibility Standard (NIMAS), which was included in IDEA 2004.

To learn more about Digital Talking Books, go to the Companion Website, *www.prenhall.com/ turnbull*, for a link to the American Foundation for the Blind website, *http://www.afb.org/Section.asp?SectionID=38&DocumentID=2429*.

Values: By focusing on the general education curriculum, students are challenged to "be the best they can be" and, in so doing, focus on their *abilities* and not their disability.

NIMAS establishes the technical specifications for electronic versions of print materials by setting the criteria for the different types of computer language (Extensible Markup Language, or XML, similar to HTML) and for how an electronic document should be prepared.

Once an electronic version of a print product, such as a textbook, complies with the NIMAS standard, students with disabilities may access it through different means. Specially designed readers (similar to web browsers) can convert the XML file to electronic large print, braille for visually impaired readers, virtual sign language for hearing-impaired readers, or Digital Talking Book format. The student can highlight the text, read it at his or her own pace, use hyperlinks to get glossary information in audio or video formats, use animation and photographs to bring the text to life, and obtain audio feedback on word pronunciation. All of these are menu-driven, much like using your web browser. Finally NIMAS-compliant files can be translated by specially designed software into different languages for users who do not speak English.

There also are other ways for presenting information so that a wide range of students will have access to it. For example, advance organizers or concept maps are research-validated ways to present content information to students and improve their academic performance. We will discuss both of these strategies, as well as other pedagogical means of universal design, in Chapters 5 through 16. The bottom line is simply this: universal design for learning tailors instruction to the needs of each student. It focuses on a student's strengths, takes the student's learning capacities into account, and offers each student a full opportunity to benefit from the general education curriculum.

HOW DOES INCLUSION SUPPORT PROGRESS?

You already know that progress in the general education curriculum is one of IDEA's goals, and you know why that is important for students. And you have just started to learn about one way to advance that goal: universal design for learning. There is still a second important way. It is called inclusion. We introduce you to this essential concept here and then elaborate on it in Chapters 5 through 16, where we set out information on how to teach students with exceptionalities.

What Are Student-Placement Trends?

The U.S. Department of Education annually reports on students with disabilities who receive special education and related services in different educational settings. Figure 2–4 lists the department's categories of educational placements and defines each placement (also called "environment").

Figure 2–5 shows the percentage of students with disabilities that is educated in each category and changes in placements in each category. The figure underscores the steady increase in the number of students being included in the general education curriculum.

For example, in 1984–1985 about one-quarter of students with disabilities received their education outside the regular class for less than 21 percent of the school day, but by 1999–2000 this percentage had increased to 45 percent (U.S. Department of Education, 2001).

Clearly, fewer students with disabilities are served outside the general classroom, and the amount of time they spend outside the classroom has decreased. In addition, the number of students in self-contained and separate facilities is gradually decreasing. The number of students in residential facilities and in homebound/hospital placements has remained at a low level over this entire time period.

Not surprisingly, the percentage of students with disabilities in the different placement categories varies according to the age of students and their type of disability. More elementary students than secondary students are served in typical schools with peers who do not have disabilities. Students with milder disabilities (e.g., speech or language impairments and learning disabilities) are more likely to be in general education classrooms for the largest percentage of time compared with students with more severe disabilities (e.g., students with mental retardation

Figure 2–4 Six placement categories designated by the U.S. Department of Education

Special education outside the regular class for less than 21 percent of the day: unduplicated number of children and youth with disabilities receiving special education and related services outside the regular class for less than 21 percent of the school day

Special education outside the regular class for more than 60 percent of the day: unduplicated number of children and youth with disabilities receiving special education and related services outside the regular class for more than 60 percent of the school day

Public separate facility: unduplicated number of children and youth with disabilities receiving special education and related services for greater than 50 percent of the school day in public separate facilities

Private separate facility: unduplicated number of children and youth with disabilities receiving special education and related services for greater than 50 percent of the school day in private separate facilities

Public residential facility: unduplicated number of children and youth with disabilities receiving special education and related services for greater than 50 percent of the school day in public residential facilities

Private residential facility: unduplicated number of children and youth with disabilities receiving special education and related services for greater than 50 percent of the school day in private residential facilities

Figure 2–5 Percentage of students (rounded upward) ages 6–21 in different education environments during the 2003–2004 school year

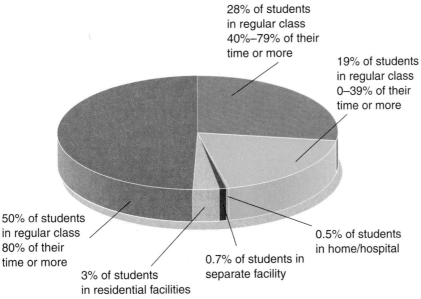

28% of students in regular class 40%–79% of their time or more

19% of students in regular class 0–39% of their time or more

50% of students in regular class 80% of their time or more

3% of students in residential facilities

0.7% of students in separate facility

0.5% of students in home/hospital

Source: U.S. Department of Education, Office of Special Education Programs. (2005). *IDEA data website* (http://www.ideadata.org/aboutThisSite.asp).

or multiple disabilities). In Chapter 4, we point out that students from racially or ethnically diverse backgrounds are disproportionately represented in special education, and we discuss that issue throughout the book.

Issues in residential/home/hospital placements. Settings that have a residential component—special boarding schools and hospitals and students' homes—are generally regarded as the most restrictive placements. Students who attend residential schools often do so because their local schools have not developed the capacity to provide special education services for them. Thus, it is important to distinguish situations in which a student needs a more restrictive environment from those in which schools need to expand their capacity to serve all students.

Yet residential settings can also provide a concentrated group of talented educators and can benefit students, some of whom may prefer to be with other students with the same disability. For instance, students with hearing impairments, visual impairments, and deaf-blindness are most likely to attend residential schools (U.S. Department of Education, 2000). Students with physical disabilities, emotional disorders, and traumatic brain injury are most likely to be educated in a hospital or their home (U.S. Department of Education, 2000). As illustrated in Figure 2–4, however, a low percentage of students are in these settings; this percentage has remained relatively stable over time.

Issues in special-school placements. Separate schools typically congregate students from a specific disability category and provide services related to the characteristics of that disability. Students with emotional or behavioral disorders are most likely to be educated in special schools; the next most likely are students with deaf-blindness and autism (U.S. Department of Education, 2000). Frequently, students, particularly those with emotional disorders and autism, are placed in special schools because of problem behavior that many teachers do not know how to address.

Issues in specialized-settings placements within typical schools. Specialized settings in many schools include resource rooms and self-contained classes. As reflected in Figure 2–4, students who receive 21–60 percent of their education outside the regular classroom typically are served in resource rooms. Resource rooms are staffed by special education teachers who work with students with disabilities for as little as one period or as many as several periods during the school day, depending upon students' needs for specially designed instruction. Students with learning disabilities and other health impairments are most likely to be served in resource rooms (U.S. Department of Education, 2000). There are resource rooms at Luff Elementary because, as principal Peggy Palser notes, the reality is that full-time placement in general education classrooms does not benefit all students all the time.

The second type of specialized setting within typical schools is the special education classroom. Special classrooms usually are provided for students with more intense needs than those students served in resource rooms. Students with mental retardation, autism, multiple disabilities, and emotional disorders are most likely to be served in special classes (U.S. Department of Education, 2000). Traditionally, special education classrooms serve students with more significant disabilities and have a strong focus on functional skills.

In Star Morgan's first-grade classroom, all students become bilingual because all of them learn to sign words.

What Is Inclusion?

Inclusion allows students with disabilities to learn in general education classes and have a sense of belonging in these classes. Inclusion has a long history in the field of special education. Figure 2–6 summarizes that history.

Characteristics of inclusion. Inclusion has four key characteristics: home-school placement, the principle of natural proportions, restructuring teaching and learning, and age- and grade-appropriate placements.

Home-school placement. Within an inclusive model, students attend the same school they would have attended if they did not have an exceptionality. This is the same school other children in the student's neighborhood attend. Heather and Star live in the Luff neighborhood and attend their neighborhood school; by attending Luff, they, like other students with a disability,

Figure 2-6   Four consecutive phases of inclusion

1. *Mainstreaming:* an educational arrangement of returning students from special education classrooms to general education classrooms typically for nonacademic portions of the school day, such as art, music, and physical education (Grosenick & Reynolds, 1978; Turnbull & Schulz, 1979)

2. *Regular Education Initiative:* an attempt to reform general and special education by creating a unified system capable of meeting individual needs in general education classrooms (Gartner & Lipsky, 1987; Reynolds, Wang, & Walberg, 1987; Will, 1986)

3. *Inclusion through accommodations (instructional adaptations):* an additive approach to inclusion that assumes the only viable approach to including students with disabilities in general education classrooms is to add instructional adaptations to the predefined general education teaching and learning approaches (Pugach, 1995)

4. *Inclusion through restructuring:* a design to inclusion that re-creates general and special education by merging resources to develop more flexible learning environments for all students and educators (McGregor & Vogelsberg, 1998; Pugach & Johnson, 2002; Sailor, 2002; Thousand, Villa, & Nevin, 2002)

contribute to a sense of a learning community (Hunt, Hirose-Hatae, Doering, Karasoff, & Goetz, 2000; Schnorr, 1997).

Principle of natural proportions.   The principle of natural proportions holds that students with exceptionalities should be placed in schools and classrooms in natural proportion to the occurrence of exceptionality within the general population (Brown et al., 1991). If, for example, 10 percent of students in a school district receives special education services, the principle of natural proportions holds that, if a classroom has 30 students, not more than three should have a disability. In a modification of this principle, Walther-Thomas and colleagues (1999) suggest that not more than 20 percent of the total classroom should have disabilities. For a classroom of 30 students, this means six students. They also suggest that if some of the students have more severe disabilities and need extensive support, the overall number of students with disabilities in the class should be reduced.

Restructuring teaching and learning.   Inclusion through restructuring involves general and special education educators, working in partnership with related service providers, families, and students, to ensure that supplementary aids and services and special education and related services are provided to support the student in the general education classroom. Tremendous variability exists in how teachers provide special education services within general education classrooms. Just consider the descriptions in Figure 2–6 of inclusion through add-on services and inclusion through restructured services. In state-of-the-art programs that are implementing inclusion through restructuring, the strengths and talents of educators with different types of training and capacities are pooled to provide individualized instruction within the general education classroom.

Age- and grade-appropriate placements.   Finally, inclusion favors educating all students in age- and grade-appropriate placements, just as Heather and Star spend most of their school days at Luff Elementary School with third and first graders, respectively.

These four principles are controversial. Indeed, two major issues are at the heart of the inclusion debate: (1) eliminating the continuum of placements and (2) increasing the amount of time students spend in the general education classroom.

Eliminating the continuum of placements. The concept of a continuum of services has been part of special education ever since Congress enacted

The four characteristics of inclusion guide Luff Elementary School faculty and students when educating Star Morgan.

PRAXIS

Standard: Addressing placement issues and participation in the general education curriculum is one way of addressing PRAXIS™ Standard 3, Delivery of Services to Students.

IDEA in 1975. The continuum refers to services that range from the most typical and most inclusive settings to the most atypical and most segregated settings.

There was a time when accommodating students with disabilities in general education classrooms through supplementary aids and services was not considered an option. That limited perspective caused Taylor (1988) to assert that students with disabilities were "caught in the continuum of services." Unfortunately, once in more restrictive settings, few students ever left them for general education classrooms.

The inclusion movement has tried to limit the need for more restrictive settings by creating a new partnership between special and general educators. This partnership seeks to provide individualized instruction to students in general education classrooms through a universally designed general education curriculum (King-Sears, 2001). Inclusion now rests on the premise that it is not often appropriate or even necessary to remove some students from the general education classroom and to place them in a more specialized and restrictive setting to provide individualized and appropriate education.

To advance this belief, general and special educators partner with each other and with students' parents to promote students' academic success, participation in extracurricular and other school activities, and a sense of belonging (Voltz, Brazil, & Ford, 2001). They also create separate spaces in schools that are used by many students for various purposes: resource centers, study labs, and breakout rooms to enable students to meet together for cooperative learning groups, peer tutoring, and group activities (Voltz et al., 2001). The approach of having separate spaces used by many students contrasts with the approach of having specialized placements used exclusively by students with disabilities.

Increasing the amount of time in general education classrooms. Should educators increase the amount of time a student spends in an age- and grade-appropriate general classroom? How? Inclusion proponents generally agree that placement in general education classrooms does not mean that the student never leaves those classrooms for special services. At Luff, the pullout model is rare. True, some students with disabilities use resource rooms some of the time; true, others leave their general education classrooms from time to time and for very specific instructional purposes. But consistent with the inclusion principle, the two special education teachers and the instruction specialist go into the general education classrooms to work with the general education teachers and their paraprofessionals. All of the Luff faculty regard Star and Heather as authentic members of their classes.

Council for
Exceptional
Children

Standard: As you look at Figure 2–7 and read about teachers' attitudes and behaviors and how they can influence the behavior of students, you are using CEC Standard 5, Learning Environments and Social Interactions.

When supplementary aids and services are readily available within general education classrooms and universal design for learning has been fully implemented, students with disabilities will be more likely to perceive themselves as valued classroom members and will not need to leave the classroom as often to receive an appropriate education.

Educator, parent, and student perspectives on inclusion. The research on inclusion has some limitations. For example, most research studies do not describe the quality of inclusive practices or allow for the amount of time spent in inclusive settings, the impact of universal design, and the extent to which students from culturally- and linguistically-diverse backgrounds have appropriate respect, support, and accommodations. Bear those limitations in mind as you consider Figure 2–7, which identifies the perspectives of educators, parents, and students about inclusive practices.

As you can see, there is a wide range of perspectives about the benefits and drawbacks of inclusion. Clearly, access to in-service training resulted in significantly more teachers feeling successful in inclusive settings. Still, many parents report that they must be vigilant advocates for their children in order to have appropriate supports and services offered in inclusive programs (Erwin, Soodak, Winton, & Turnbull, 2001; Grove & Fisher, 1999). That's certainly part of Barbara Morgan's story, as you can learn by referring to her story (see the Companion Website to this chapter).

Many of the perceptions set out in Figure 2–7 do not take into account the availability of universally designed materials. How might the introduction of such materials change perspectives? As we show in Chapters 5 through 16, the answer is that universal design for learning can enhance the education of all students in inclusive settings and thus can blunt some of the negative perceptions about inclusion.

Figure 2-7 Perspectives of educators, parents, and students about inclusive practices

Perspective	Positive	Studies	Barriers	Studies
Educators	Students with disabilities can be successfully educated in the general education classroom if given adequate supplementary aids and services and specially designed instruction.	Andrews et al. (2000); Sailor (2002); Thousand, Villa, & Nevin (2002); Wehmeyer, Lance, & Bashinski (2002)	Students with disabilities need specialized settings outside the general education classroom to receive the benefit of intensive and individualized instruction.	Kauffman (1995); Kavale & Forness (2000); MacMillan, Gresham, & Forness (1996); Zigmond et al. (1995)
	When given support, most general education teachers feel successful at teaching students with disabilities.	Study of Personnel Needs in Special Education (2002)	Class size is a major obstacle to inclusive practices. Smaller classes contribute to more positive outcomes.	Finn & Achilles (1999); Molnar, Smith, Zahorick, Palmer, & Ehrle (1999)
	Positive experiences with students with disabilities and information about inclusion promote acceptance by principals.	Praisner (2003)	Special education resources have not been sufficiently infused into general education to ensure effective teaching.	Barnett & Monda-Amaya (1998); Boyer & Bandy (1997); Fox & Ysseldyke (1997); Minke, Bear, Deemer, & Griffin (1996)
	The better trained and experienced a teacher is, the more the teacher will know how to practice inclusion and favor it.	McLeskey, Waldron, So, Swanson, & Loveland (2001); Soodak, Podell, & Lehman (1998); Soodak et al. (2002)	Special and general education teachers do not receive adequate time or training to implement inclusion.	Schumm & Vaughn (1995); Scruggs & Mastropieri (1996); Van Reusen, Shoho, & Barker (2000)
Parents	General classrooms do a better job of (1) improving self-concept, (2) promoting friendships, (3) teaching academics, and (4) preparing for the real world.	Duhaney and Salend (2000)	Availability of qualified educators and individualized services are concerns, as are frustrations in getting schools to provide inclusion.	Duhaney and Salend (2000)
	Parents of children without disabilities identified benefits (sensitivity to the needs of others, greater acceptance of diversity, educational benefit) for their children.	Duhaney & Salend (2000); McGregor & Vogelsberg (1998)		

(*continued*)

45

Figure 2-7 *(continued)*

Perspective	Positive	Studies	Barriers	Studies
Students	Students with learning disabilities believe inclusive settings provide more opportunities for making friends and favor having special educators provide assistance to all students in general classrooms rather than only students with exceptionalities.	Vaughn & Klingner (1998)	Students with learning disabilities believe resource rooms provide useful help, a quiet place to work, and less difficult and more enjoyable instructional activities.	Vaughn & Klingner (1998)
	Generally, students without disabilities favor inclusion, usually for equal treatment reasons.	Fisher (1999); Fisher, Pumpian, & Sax (1998); Klingner, Vaughn, Schumm, Cohen, & Forgan (1998)	Students without disabilities express concern about students being teased.	Klingner et al. (1998)

What Student Outcomes Are Associated with Inclusion?

A comprehensive analysis and synthesis of research on the efficacy of special education (Kavale & Forness, 1999) concluded that placement in a special education class resulted in lower achievement for students with mental retardation and students whose IQs are between 75 and 90 but that it benefited students with learning disabilities or emotional and behavioral disorders. The authors concluded: "Features of instruction are probably the major influence on outcomes, but these are not unique to setting. Setting is thus a macrovariable; the real question becomes one of examining what happens in that setting" (p. 70).

It is also true that what school administrators and teachers expect and plan to happen, and what students themselves want to happen, profoundly influence student outcomes. That is one reason why the expectations of the faculty at Luff Elementary School are so important to Heather and Star and why those of their mother, Barbara Morgan, are also so important.

A different research synthesis (McGregor & Vogelsberg, 1998) focused mostly on severe disabilities and reported a number of positive outcomes:

■ With adequate support, students with disabilities demonstrate high levels of social interaction with typical peers in inclusive settings (Fryxell & Kennedy, 1995; Kennedy, Shukla, & Fryxell, 1997; McDonnell, Hardman, Hightower, & Kiefer-O'Donnell, 1991).

■ Social competence, communication skills, and other developmental skills of students with disabilities have improved in inclusive settings (Bennett, DeLuca, & Bruns, 1997; Hunt, Staub, Alwell, & Goetz, 1994; McDougall & Brady, 1998).

■ The presence of students with disabilities does not compromise the performance of typically developing students (Hollowood, Salisbury, Rainforth, & Palombaro, 1994; McDonnell, Thorson, McQuivey, & Kiefer-O' Donnell, 1997; O'Connor & Jenkins, 1996).

■ Some evidence suggests that the costs of inclusive services over time are likely to be less than those of segregated forms of service delivery (in spite of the fact that startup costs may initially increase) (Halvorsen, Neary, Hunt, & Piuma, 1996; McLaughlin & Warren, 1994; Salisbury & Chambers, 1994).

Inclusion Tips

Box 2–2

	What You Might See	What You Might Be Tempted to Do	Alternate Responses	Ways to Include Peers in the Process
Behavior	The student shows an apparently poor attitude toward other students and does not easily cooperate with them during instructional activities.	Discipline him for his poor behavior and separate him from the rest of the class.	Identify his strengths and work together on a list of positive things he can say when responding to other students during instructional activities.	Ask him to identify peers he would like to work with. Then work with this small group to practice verbal responses that would be helpful.
Social interactions	He has few friends and doesn't appear to want any.	Encourage him to take initiative toward others but also allow him to be by himself whenever he chooses.	Collaborate with the school counselor to plan ways to teach him specific social skills.	Work with identified peers to practice the specific social skills with him in and out of the classroom.
Educational performance	Her work is acceptable, but she needs constant supervision.	Assign an aide to work with her and allow her to complete unfinished work at home.	Collaborate with the special education teacher to create step-by-step assignments that she can do on her own. Set up a reward system for each step successfully completed without supervision.	Encourage her to work with her peers to monitor the assignments. Ask peers to work with her to construct a tracking system for class assignments.
Classroom attitudes	She never volunteers answers and is reluctant to participate in class activities.	Carefully choose activities that allow her to work alone.	Together with the special education teacher, work with her ahead of time on content to be covered and plan specific things for her to contribute.	Plan with peers positive contributions that each can make to upcoming class activities.

Clearly, inclusion with support (through individually designed instruction, related services, supplementary aids and services, and universal design in learning) is feasible. Box 2–2 illustrates some effective practices to promote inclusion. We will highlight other inclusion practices in Chapters 5 through 16.

How Does Inclusion Facilitate Progress?

First and foremost, the general education classroom is the place in which the general education curriculum is most likely to be taught to students with disabilities (Wehmeyer, Lattin, Lapp-Rincker, & Agran, 2003). Furthermore, when UDL is implemented and when the four characteristics of inclusion are met, students with disabilities and other exceptionalities can receive individualized and intensive instruction in general education classes that will go beyond simply supporting access but, indeed, promote progress in the general education curriculum.

Until now, the inclusion movement has consisted of two generations of different practices. The first generation focused on moving students with disabilities from segregated settings into the general education classroom. The second generation focused on developing and evaluating practices to support the presence of students with disabilities in the general classroom. Both of these phases focused primarily on the place in which students were educated.

Now, however, standards-based reforms and IDEA's command for access to the general education curriculum have changed the focus from "where" and place to (1) "what" and curriculum mastery—from where a student is educated to what he or she is taught and learns; and (2) "how"—the methods and pedagogy that teachers use. Nothing about the first two generations of inclusive practices is obsolete or unimportant. In fact, as we describe in Chapters 5 through 16, efforts to achieve outcomes associated with first- and second-generation inclusive practices (inclusion in the general education classroom and implementation of high-quality instructional strategies to support students in the general education classroom) continue but with new emphasis on "what" and "how."

HOW DOES A STUDENT'S IEP ASSURE PROGRESS?

You have learned about two initiatives, UDL and inclusion, that promote students' progress in the general education curriculum. We will discuss other practices in Chapters 5 through 16. To lay the foundation for those chapters, however, we turn your attention to other important practices, beginning with student's Individualized Education Programs (IEPs). In this part of the chapter you will learn how a student's IEP team should identify and provide supplementary aids and services, plan and develop specially designed instruction, address the student's other educational needs, and provide related services.

Let's start with a basic proposition—namely, that individualization is a hallmark of special education practices (Turnbull, Turnbull, Wehmeyer, & Park, 2003), and nothing about standards-based reform changes that basic fact. The second is that IDEA requires that a student's IEP take into account the student's right to participate and make progress in the general education curriculum and his or her unique learning needs. This dual focus—the right to the general education curriculum and the relationship of unique learning needs to that right—means that the IEP should do the following:

- Identify the supplementary aids and services that a student needs in order to be educated with nondisabled peers in the general education classroom and to make progress in the general education curriculum.

- Identify the special education services and specially designed instruction that the student needs in order to be educated with nondisabled peers in the general education classroom and to make progress in the general education curriculum.

- Identify the student's other educational needs in order to be educated with nondisabled peers and make progress in the general education curriculum.

- Identify the related services the student needs in order to be educated with nondisabled peers in the general education classroom and to progress in the general education curriculum.

Before we discuss these four "must-have" components of a student's IEP, we introduce you to the process for developing an IEP and remind you that, as you learned in Chapter 1, the team that develops the IEP must be interdisciplinary and consist of the student's parents and the student when appropriate. In Chapter 4 we will discuss the importance of actively involving parents, other family members, and the student in the planning process. Now, however, we describe the process for planning and developing the student's IEP and the components that the IEP team must consider.

Values: Only when educators form meaningful *partnerships* with all stakeholders in the education process can planning occur that ensures student progress in the general education curriculum.

How Do You Design an IEP?

Figure 2–8 is a flow chart of the steps an IEP team should take to ensure that a student participates and makes progress in the general education curriculum. Obviously there are other tasks and decisions that the team must make, but when determining how to ensure student progress in the general education curriculum, the IEP team must consider these specific issues.

Figure 2–8 IEP team decision-making process to promote student progress in the general education curriculum

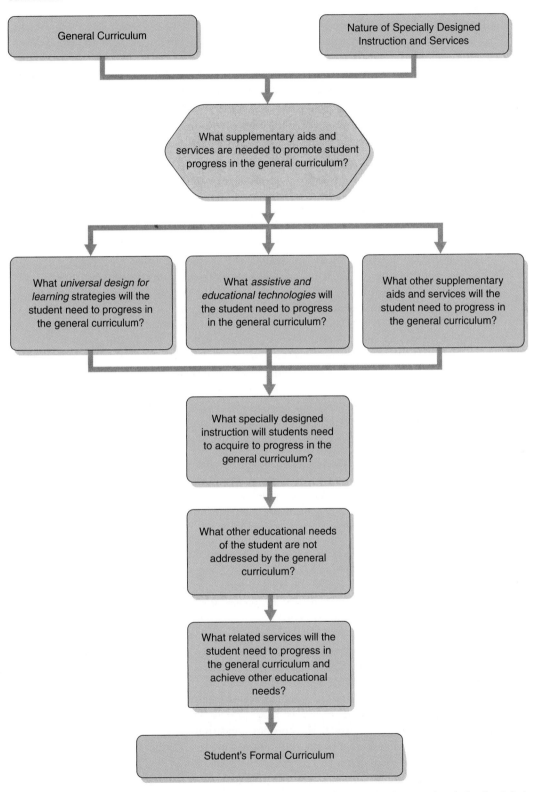

Source: Adapted from Wehmeyer, M. L., Lattin, D., & Agran, M. (2001). Promoting access to the general curriculum for students with mental retardation: A decision-making model. *Education and Training in Mental Retardation and Developmental Disabilities, 36,* 329–344.

PRAXIS

Standard: Learning about and using the process described here for developing an IEP is an application of PRAXIS™ Standard 3, Delivery of Services to Students with Disabilities.

The team begins by taking into account the general education curriculum. Educators need to know what standards, or expectations, exist for students at the same grade level. It may be challenging for educators teaching students with disabilities across multiple ages, grades, and content areas to be familiar with standards across all of these ages, grades, and content areas. That is why it is necessary for general education teachers to be involved in planning and developing the student's IEP.

You learned in Chapter 1 that IDEA defines special education as specially designed instruction. **Specially designed instruction** occurs when educators adapt the content, methodology, or delivery of instruction to address a student's unique needs and ensure that the student can participate and make progress in the general education curriculum. The nondiscriminatory evaluation process that we described in Chapter 1 leads to information about a student's need for and the nature of specially designed instruction.

Determining supplementary aids and services. The IEP team's first step is to determine what supplementary aids and services the student needs. Figure 2–1 lists the areas of the student's needs that the IEP team should consider. The team should begin by considering the student's need for physical and cognitive access in the school, classroom, or community if he or she is receiving community-based instruction.

As you learned in Chapter 1, IDEA requires IEP teams to consider five special factors in developing an IEP for any student: (1) strategies to address a student's behavior that impedes his or other students' learning; (2) the language needs of students with limited English proficiency; (3) instruction in Braille for students who are blind; (4) a student's communication needs, especially when the student is deaf or hard of hearing; and (5) the student's use of assistive technology devices and services.

All of these special factors guide the IEP team to consider supplementary aids and services. Do students need to be seated near the teacher to see or hear the lesson? Does the student work best when seated individually or with other students around a table? What is the role of the paraprofessional in providing supports? What assistive technologies might promote access? Does the student need certain assessment or task modifications to succeed? These are all part of determining needed supplementary aids and supports (Etscheidt & Bartlett, 1999).

Determining specially designed instruction. Once the IEP team has considered these supplementary aids and services, it should identify the specially designed instruction the student needs to ensure participation and progress in the general education curriculum. Ordinarily, the IEP team does not have to identify all possible instructional techniques and strategies a student might need; that is the role of the student's teachers for each course.

Planning to address other educational needs. There are several reasons IEP teams should consider a student's other educational needs. Many students with severe disabilities need functional or life-skills content that other students acquire outside school or at a younger age and that may not be part of the general education curriculum, particularly for older students. For example, Star needs to learn about school and street safety; her tendency to run away endangers her. Most students, whether receiving special education services or not, need instruction related to making the transition from school to the adult world, including instruction in employment and community living; yet these are often not included in the general curriculum standards. Further, some students with disabilities (especially those who have visual impairments) need specialized instruction in areas such as orientation and mobility—namely, how to get from place to place—that other students do not need.

The IEP team should consider the content areas that are not addressed by the general education curriculum and identify the skills and knowledge students may need to acquire to be more productive, independent adults; then the team should develop goals and objectives to address those areas. Historically, the IEPs of students with disabilities began with these alternative or functional curricular content areas. That practice, however, limited students to instruction in only those areas that the IEP team believed were important or possible. In the end, they failed to hold the students to the high expectations of the general education curriculum.

Values: Research shows clearly that students achieve at the level teachers expect them to reach. Historically, many students with disabilities have not been expected to do much. If we are to reverse that trend, students with disabilities must be held to *high expectations.*

Remember that IDEA does not limit a student's educational program to only content in the general education curriculum. IDEA allows educators to address the student's other educational needs, but it also requires them to begin by considering how a student can participate and make progress in the general education curriculum. Thus, the team will consider the other educational needs of a student with disabilities, but it also will begin by asking how the student can participate and make progress in the general education curriculum.

Specifying related services. Finally, the IEP team should consider related services, such as those identified in Chapter 1, that are necessary to enable a student to benefit from special education and to participate and make progress in the general education curriculum.

WHAT SHOULD EDUCATORS DO TO SUPPORT PROGRESS?

Promoting access begins with inclusive practices, UDL, and effective planning, but the heavy lifting occurs day in and day out in the classroom. There are a number of campus- and classroom-level actions that promote student progress. To support students' progress in the general education curriculum, educators should create learning communities, design unit and lesson plans, and implement schoolwide quality instruction.

Creating Learning Communities

Effective instruction begins when educators create learning communities: intentionally created environments in which students learn to respect and value each other and everyone's individual differences, understand their roles and responsibilities, work in a self-directed manner, and participate in setting classroom rules. You can create an effective learning community by discovering the abilities of all your students; developing systematic ways to collect information on student progress for use to plan future lessons; and using collaborative teaching, grouping, and differentiated instructional strategies to individualize student educational experiences. In Chapters 3 and 4 you will learn more about the community and about respecting and valuing diversity, and about creating partnerships with families.

Designing Units and Lessons

Units of study are the "maps" teachers create to organize and plan content and to support student learning and achievement in the general education curriculum. Units of study identify end-of-school-year goals, the standards for determining whether the goals are met, and the knowledge that students will acquire. Once a teacher understands the big picture for the school year, he or she must "backwards-map" to determine what students will need to know and do the middle of the year and then plan for manageable instructional units. When a teacher has an overall idea of what needs to be accomplished by the end of the school year and has chunked that content, skills, and knowledge into midyear and quarterly components, he or she is ready to plan specific units of instruction (Wehmeyer, Sands, Knowlton, & Kozleski, 2002).

Having identified the learning targets, the teacher can plan day-to-day activities to support students in achieving the outcomes of each unit of instruction. Generally, lesson plans identify the theme of a lesson, the purpose of the lesson, how the lesson will be conducted, what students are expected to accomplish, and how those accomplishments will be measured and accounted for.

At both the unit- and lesson-planning level, teachers should identify the skills, processes, or knowledge that *all* students, including students with disabilities, should master and how the teacher and other educators will support all students in doing so. We have mentioned several of these strategies and processes, including UDL, and will introduce you to still others in Chapters 5 through 16.

One such strategy is to identify the big ideas that all students should learn from the lesson or unit. Once you know what you want all students to know, you can develop lesson objectives that allow students to demonstrate, through different means, that they grasp the big ideas.

One way to create those objectives is to use **cognitive taxonomies.** Cognitive taxonomies classify the cognitive demands of learning targets. Perhaps the most familiar cognitive taxonomy is that developed by Bloom and associates. Bloom's taxonomy is a means of categorizing the cognitive skills students use when achieving learning targets. As one ascends Bloom's taxonomy, the cognitive demands from students are more complex. By developing lesson objectives that range from less to more complex cognitive demands, teachers can ensure that all students acquire knowledge about the content and have flexible options for providing evidence of that knowledge.

Implementing Schoolwide Instructional Strategies

In subsequent chapters you will learn more about high-quality instructional strategies that promote student progress in the general education curriculum. These include learning communities, differentiated instruction, positive behavior supports, cooperative learning, collaborative teaming, peer-mediated learning, and many more. It is important for teachers to use these strategies and to enhance their impact by implementing them throughout the entire school, not just in one or more classrooms. As is true in the case of UDL, all students benefit from high-quality instructional strategies, not just those students with exceptionalities. Moreover, by using the principles of UDL, students with disabilities can benefit from high-quality instructional strategies that are not special education services, such as the schoolwide implementation of phonemic awareness strategies at Luff Elementary.

There are two other ways for making it more likely that students with exceptionalities will progress in the general education curriculum. These are multicultural responsiveness and parent/school/community partnerships. We will discuss them in Chapters 3 and 4, respectively, and then revisit them in each of the following chapters.

Council for Exceptional Children

Standard: Understanding how special education relates to the way in which schools and classrooms are organized is an example of CEC Standard 1, Foundations, and will impact your job every day as a teacher of the general education curriculum and of students with disabilities.

Looking to Star's and Heather's Future

If the education that Heather and Star receive at Luff Elementary School continues throughout their school careers, we can expect exactly what Barbara Morgan expects for her children when they are adults. Heather will be living on her own and working in Independence, Missouri; she will have attained her own independence and be at least partly economically self-sufficient. She will have friends in the community, as she does in school; she will have the same opportunities as her friends to participate in life in Independence. Star, whose disabilities require more intense supports than Heather's, will also be living and working in Independence but with a great deal more support. She probably will not live by herself; instead, she may live in a group home with three to five other adults or, better yet, in an apartment with needed supports. Either way, she will need support for the activities of daily living on a 24/7 basis; the support will be in areas of living such as dressing, preparing meals, going from home to work and back again, and participating in her community's recreation and leisure activities. But she also will have friends who have disabilities and who do not have disabilities, so her support will come from paid, formal providers and from unpaid, informal sources.

For Heather and Star to achieve those results, the kind of education they are receiving at Luff will have to continue. They will have access to the general education curriculum; some of the curriculum content will be altered, but the basic core of their education will be comparable to that of students without disabilities. And they will have to continue to receive their education with students who do not have disabilities; whatever is available in the classrooms, extracurricular activities, and other school activities for their peers who do not have disabilities will have to be available to them, sometimes with modifications and supports and sometimes not. Their education in elementary school lays the foundation for the rest of their education; more than that, it is the basis for their lives in Independence—really, for their own independence.

SUMMARY

What is progress in the general education curriculum?

■ IDEA requires each student's IEP to state how the student will be involved and progress in the general education curriculum, how the student's progress will be assessed, and how state- and district-wide assessments will be modified (as appropriate) for the student.

■ NCLB requires states to establish challenging academic content and student achievement standards that apply to all students, including those with disabilities.

■ The general education curriculum refers to the same curriculum as taught to nondisabled students, and IDEA requires that students with disabilities be involved in the general education curriculum to the greatest extent possible.

How do supplementary aids and services and universal design for learning support progress?

■ Supplementary aids and services are aids, services, and other supports that are provided in general education classes or other education-related settings to enable children with disabilities to be educated with nondisabled children to the maximum extent appropriate.

■ Supplementary aids and services are noninstructional modifications and supports such as modifications to ensure physical and cognitive access to the environment, classroom ecological variables such as seating arrangements or classroom acoustics, educational or assistive technology, assessment or task modifications, and support from other persons.

■ Universal design for learning refers to the design of instructional materials and activities to make the content information accessible to all children.

■ Universal design for learning contributes to progress in the general education curriculum by ensuring that all students can access academic content information and can provide evidence of their learning by ensuring flexibility in representing and presenting content information and in demonstrating content mastery.

How does inclusion support progress?

■ Inclusion refers to students with disabilities learning in general education classes and having a sense of belonging in these classes.

■ Inclusion has four key characteristics: home-school placement, the principle of natural proportions, restructuring teaching and learning, and age- and grade-appropriate placements.

■ When supplementary aids and services are readily available within general education classrooms and universal design for learning has been fully implemented, students with disabilities will be more likely to perceive themselves as valued classroom members and will not need to leave the classroom as often to receive an appropriate education.

■ The general education classroom is the place in which the general education curriculum is most likely to be taught to students with disabilities, and inclusion ensures that students will have access to the general education curriculum.

How does a student's IEP ensure progress?

■ A student's IEP, by law, must be determined based on both the general education curriculum and the student's unique learning needs.

■ IEP teams are critical for ensuring that the student's IEP identifies specific supplementary aids and services, related services, and special education services that will promote progress in the general education curriculum.

What should educators do to support progress?

- Teachers can create learning communities that enable students with disabilities to become integrated into their classrooms.
- Creating unit and lesson plans that incorporate universal design features and include goals and objectives that vary in complexity can ensure that all students can show progress.
- Schoolwide strategies such as positive behavior supports promote progress in the general education curriculum.

WHAT WOULD YOU RECOMMEND?

Refer to chapter content and the PRAXIS™ and CEC standards in Appendix A to answer the following questions:

1. How do statewide assessments reflect high expectations for all students? Go to your state's department of education website and find examples of your statewide assessments. Choose a grade level to review and discuss how these tests reflect high expectations for all students but also present challenges for some students. Identify which CEC standard addresses statewide assessments.

2. What five tips have you learned in this chapter about implementing universal design for learning in a special education setting? What PRAXIS™ standard applies to universal design?

3. What answers can you give your colleagues and parents when they ask about inclusion? Refer to Figure 2–8 on perspectives of educators, parents, and students. Then view the DVD segments on Heather and Star Morgan. Taking the perspective of an educator, a parent, or a student, discuss one of the positive aspects and one of the barriers to inclusion. What CEC standard applies to the effective implementation of inclusion?

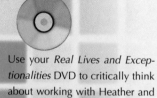

Use your *Real Lives and Exceptionalities* DVD to critically think about working with Heather and Star under "Questions" located below "Meet Star" and "Meet Heather."

Who is Joesian Cortes?

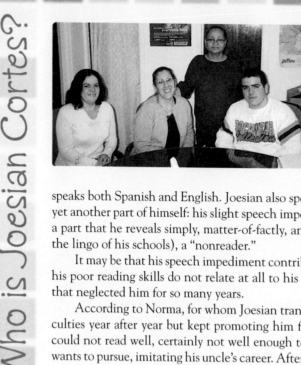

Contributed by Stanley C. Trent, University of Virginia, and Alfredo J. Artilles, Arizona State University

Like any of us, Joesian is a person of many parts. Part of him is obvious: a 17-year-old student enrolled in the 11th grade in Brooklyn, New York. Another part is equally obvious from his name and accent: he is Latino. His parents, Norma and Joaquin, were born in Puerto Rico. She speaks only Spanish; he speaks both Spanish and English. Joesian also speaks both languages. When he does, he displays yet another part of himself: his slight speech impediment. There is still one other part to Joesian, a part that he reveals simply, matter-of-factly, and without embarrassment: he is, he says (using the lingo of his schools), a "nonreader."

It may be that his speech impediment contributes to his nonreader status. It may also be that his poor reading skills do not relate at all to his impediment but derive from the school system that neglected him for so many years.

According to Norma, for whom Joesian translates, his teachers overlooked his reading difficulties year after year but kept promoting him from grade to grade. Norma knew that her son could not read well, certainly not well enough to be able to master the plumber's trade that he wants to pursue, imitating his uncle's career. After all, her daughter Tatiana, age 15, and her other son Juan, age 11, read quite well. And they have attended the same schools as Joesian.

Where, she wondered, was the explanation for his reading difficulty? Did it lie in his speech impediment? Or in the fact that, because of that impediment, his teachers simply ignored him and failed to develop his reading skills? Or in the possibility that, because he is Latino, he was the victim of cultural discrimination?

Norma got an answer when she took Joesian for an evaluation by a specialist not employed by the city board of education. That specialist concluded that Joesian has the ability to read at the 11th-grade level. The discrepancy between his ability and his skill is clear. He can but doesn't read.

The answer to Norma's question—why does Joesian have such a poor ability to read?—seemed to point toward the schools. Either they could not address his speech impediment, or they chose not to do so. In either event, they contributed to his reading difficulty.

It would be entirely defensible for her to conclude that Joesian's teachers chose not to respond to his needs; his speech impediment is slight and barely noticeable. He is soft-spoken, well mannered, and attentive as he shakes hands with others and introduces himself and his mother; switches easily from one language to another while speaking with several individuals or translating for his mother; and displays all of the attributes of an eager, sincere, and kind young man. He defers to his elders and his teachers, he is not a troublemaker, and he is not likely to draw attention to himself or provoke any special remediation or special discipline. With a barely noticeable impediment and an independently evaluated ability to read at the 11th-grade level, were he properly instructed, what else except discrimination can explain Joesian's label as a nonreader?

Discrimination lies in the eye of the beholder. Norma and perhaps Joesian attribute it to his teachers, most of whom have not been Latino. The family's advocates at United We Stand of New York (UWS/NY), a community-based resource center for traditionally underserved and unserved families and students, allege discrimination.

But discrimination has two sides; prejudice never has just one face. There is discrimination that works against a person. And there is discrimination that works for a person. Joesian may well have been the victim of the one and the beneficiary of the other.

That is because, after UWS/NY helped Norma secure the independent evaluation, it also represented her and Joesian in an IDEA due process hearing. One of the school administrators at that hearing was herself a Latina. During the course of the hearing, she learned that she and a member of the UWS/NY staff, Martha, shared a common avocation: church missionary work in the Dominican Republic.

Recessing the hearing for a day, this woman made two singularly significant telephone calls: one to staff at Joesian's school, the other to the city school district's central office. Within a week of that call, Joesian was enrolled in a program for students with learning disabilities in his neighborhood school, in Brooklyn, and in a vocational trade program in the city's best trade school, in Manhattan.

To stand in Joesian's, Norma's, UWS/NY's, and the administrators' place is to know Joesian as a student of many parts and to learn how culture influences behavior. In Joesian's case, it created discrimination. But it also overcame it. Culture is a phenomenon; its meaning and its implications for special education, however, are deeply personal.

Vignette contributed by Rud Turnbull, based on Turnbull, A., Turnbull, R., Erwin, E., and Soodak, L. (2006). *Families, professionals, and exceptionality: Positive outcomes through partnership and trust.* Upper Saddle River, NJ: Merrill/Prentice Hall.

DEFINING CULTURE AND ITS IMPLICATIONS FOR SPECIAL EDUCATION

What is culture? It is "the customary beliefs, social forms, and material traits of a racial, religious, or social group; *also:* the characteristic features of everyday existence (as diversions or a way of life) shared by people in a place and time" (Merriam-Webster's Collegiate Dictionary, 2003, p. 304). Banks and Banks (2001, p. 31) emphasize the "everyday existence" feature of culture: "Culture is in us and all around us, just as is the air we breathe. It is personal, familial, communal, institutional, societal, and global in its scope and distribution." Thus, there are four key points about culture that we will discuss in this chapter:

■ Culture embodies a historical component since it is transmitted over time (Cole, 1996).

■ Culture is a resource for daily life; hence, everything human beings do is influenced by culture.

■ Culture is associated with but not limited to particular locations in which people interact over time.

■ Cultures exist in everyday contexts such as the culture of a family, school district, school, classroom, or team meetings (Gallego, Cole, & LCHC, 2001; Nieto, 2004).

This fourth point is particularly relevant to teachers and other educators because everything they do in their schools reflects cultural assumptions and codes such as rules of student-faculty, family-professional, and student-student partnerships. Accordingly, teachers and other educators need to learn how to unpack their cultural assumptions and codes and be as culturally neutral as possible, especially when evaluating, making placement decisions, and teaching students from diverse backgrounds. In Joesian's case, cultural neutrality would have been preferable to cultural discrimination; in either event, culture has been part of his everyday context in school.

This "everyday-context" view of culture reinforces a central assumption of culture theory and admonishes educators to observe the meanings, value, and influence of cultures in their interactions with students, families, and other educators. This is not an easy task. On the one hand, teachers and other professionals are increasingly expected to understand and respond to the cultural backgrounds and practices of various groups of students. To this end, they might observe and describe cultural practices of students. On the other hand, they may not recognize that their own insights derive from their own culturally based perspectives. It is one thing for a teacher to say, "I'll observe so I can respond," and altogether another to say, "I'll observe and respond only after I examine my own cultural perspectives."

To observe and respond, the teacher focuses on the student. To examine her own cultural perspectives, the teacher holds a mirror up to herself and then, and only then, does she focus on the student. Along with other professionals, school administrators, and the student and his or her parents, the teacher must determine the degree to which, if any, race and ethnicity, social class, education level, exceptionality, and gender has influenced educators' decisions (Rogoff, 2003).

Educators who deliberately adopt the everyday-context understanding of culture will then shine a light on the student and ask, "How should I interpret this student's performance through a cultural lens?" To answer, they need to know and apply the four aspects of culture that we describe in Figure 3–1: the group practices, the group's history, the student's life as set within that history, and the cultural aspects of the school or school district in which the student is enrolled.

The everyday context of culture requires these nondiscriminatory evaluation team members to examine their own cultural perspectives before determining whether a particular student from a diverse background qualifies for special education or for programs for linguistically-diverse students.

Figure 3–1 Using four aspects of culture to interpret students' performance through a cultural lens

When interpreting students' peformance through a cultural lens, educators should consider four aspects of culture, noting that these begin with an overriding, umbrella-like aspect and then become increasingly relevant to a single student:

1. The practices of the cultural group to which the student belongs

2. The group's history, including the forces that have shaped its relationships to a mainstream culture, such as its access to opportunities, societal status, and legacy of discrimination

3. The particular child's history and how it may or may not embody one or more of her group's traditions

4. The culturally expected roles, goals, resources, constraints, tensions, beliefs, and biases of the individuals who have shaped and now participate in the student's community, school, and classroom

These four aspects enable educators to become aware of their own cultural perspectives about important issues such as

- The existence of various societal groups

- These groups' experiences in America

- The differential effect of access and opportunity to quality education on the groups

- The groups' stance toward the dominant European American culture

- Teachers' and other professionals' own cultural vantage points and their effects on their own behavior

We have emphasized that educators must examine themselves and the everyday contexts in which culture affects them. We might well have also emphasized that students themselves must do the same; indeed, as Box 3–1 illustrates, they often do. Culture, then, is a reciprocal phenomenon. Educators transmit it to their students; their students, in turn, respond. But just as

Values: Cultural bias, whether against or for a particular student or group of students, will profoundly affect teachers' *great expectations* of students and the students' own opportunities to capitalize on their strengths, expand their relationships with others, be self-determined, contribute to their schools and communities, and become full citizens.

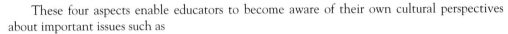

Your Own Voice ~ Transmitting and Receiving Culture   **Box 3–1**

Two boys who recently migrated from the same rural town in Mexico share a common cultural history; it affects how they look at the world and respond to it. They were acculturated to never question adults or their teachers' decisions.

In this country, however, they have become aware of a different culture, one that even second-generation Mexican students have adopted. This culture holds, in part, that resistance to a dominant Anglocentric culture is appropriate.

The boys are assigned to work with other students on a group project. Their teacher scolds them for not making eye contact when he is reprimanding them for using Spanish in the small-group discussion.

One boy, adhering to his culture's respect for adults, stops speaking Spanish in class. The other boy, adopting a culturally resistive posture, continues to speak Spanish in class.

Which boy is right? The first? The second? Both? Neither? Before you answer, bear in mind that each is reproducing and transforming his cultural history.

The first boy perpetuates his cultural history of deference to adults and educators. In doing so, he affirms his heritage but does so by adopting a new language. He learns that language embodies culture but that he can remain faithful to his culture without having to use its language.

The second boy retains his native language but adopts the resistance stance that he learned from other students from diverse backgrounds. In doing so, he learns that he can remain faithful to his culture by using its language but can adopt a new culture of less deference.

Each boy has changed his cultural history. Each reproduces it—the first boy by showing deference, the second by retaining his native language. But each also transforms it—the first by using English, the second by using Spanish.

In your own voice, defend the teacher and his request. And then, in your own voice, justify what each boy did.

To prepare your response, see McLaughlin, M. J., Artiles, A. J., & Pullin, D. (2003). Challenges for the transformation of special education in the 21st century: Rethinking culture in school reform. *Journal of Special Education Leadership, 14*(2), 51–62.

teachers' and professionals' transmission of culture varies according to their own cultures and their own capacities to practice the self-reflection that we have outlined above, so, too, do students' responses vary. Individual nuances from the transmitter to the receiver have the overall effect of producing and then transforming culture.

We have said that, when making decisions about the education of students from diverse backgrounds, teachers and other professionals must understand the concept of culture from an exceptionally broad, four-dimensional perspective. We have also said that they are transmitters of cultural values and that their students are the recipients of those values and in turn the transformers of them.

What we have only hinted at in Box 3–1 is that culture can involve discrimination. It is now appropriate to be explicit about cultural discrimination. In the following section, we provide historical anchors that will help you understand the role that the cultural interactions just described have played and continue to play in education.

Council for Exceptional Children

Standard: When you learn about the history of special education and diversity in special education, you are applying CEC Standard 1, Understanding Foundations of Special Education.

THE SOCIAL CONTEXT OF SPECIAL EDUCATION

To understand the basics about special education for students from diverse backgrounds, it is important to understand current perspectives and practices in the light of history. That history is not altogether benign. Although many educators worked diligently to create effective and equal educational opportunities for all students, especially those from diverse backgrounds, they met resistance because of ingrained sociocultural factors (Obiakor & Ford, 2002). The question nowadays is whether these factors still play a role and, if so, the degree to which they affect the school systems, their teachers and other professionals, and the students and their families. In Joesian's case, the question has an answer: the factors seem to have played a role; how else to explain the discrepancy between his ability and his current nonreader status?

The next question, of course, is what you, a future teacher, can do to mitigate those factors and to fulfill your obligation to the students from diverse backgrounds. Before we address that challenge, let's review the basic elements of the relevant history.

History before the Enactment of IDEA

As Chapters 1 and 2 pointed out, school systems had discriminated against students from diverse backgrounds primarily through the process by which they were evaluated for placement in schools. That is why the second principle of IDEA is nondiscriminatory evaluation. The question is, why did that discrimination occur; what were its origins? In most cases, the student's attributed insufficiencies—what educators regarded as their deficits—and then their predictable academic failure had been linked to their chromosomes and cultures (Deschenes, Cuban, & Tyack, 2001; Skiba, Simmons, Ritter, Kohler, & Wu, 2003).

Theories about genetic and cultural deficits. From the 1700s to contemporary times, pseudoscientists have developed **genetic deficit theories** holding that white people are genetically superior to nonwhite people. For instance, craniologists—professionals who measured people's head size and classified their head shape—were polarized about whether or not whites and nonwhites evolved from the same species. For the most part, however, they agreed that the larger brains of whites rendered them superior to nonwhites. Their theories justified a two-track system of education, one for the "superior" whites and another for other people (McCray, Webb-Johnson, & Neal, 2003).

Other professionals developed a **cultural deficit theory** that blamed the academic failure of students from diverse backgrounds on the inherent disadvantages that existed within their own cultures. These professionals argued that the students' cultural deprivation (e.g., the lack of books in their schools or homes) explained why there were significantly disparate academic and behavioral outcomes between students from racially/ethnically-diverse backgrounds and from poverty backgrounds, on the one hand, and their European American, middle-class counterparts, on the other (McCray et al., 2003).

Interestingly, the genetic and cultural deficit theories reemerged in the early 1990s with the publication of *The Bell Curve* (Herrstein & Murray, 1994). There, the authors reiterated the thesis about the genetic inferiority of particular groups. They also claimed that, in addition to race, socioeconomic status plays a pivotal role in the performance patterns of particular groups and argued that economically poor whites should be included as members of any allegedly genetically inferior groups.

Theories about cultural difference. Proponents of **cultural difference theories** (not cultural "deficit" theory, which we have just discussed) have argued that academic failures of students from diverse backgrounds cannot be attributed solely to their lack of assimilation into the dominant European culture in America. Instead, their school failure is primarily the result of a mismatch between their own cultures and the cultures of the schools themselves (Artiles, Trent, & Palmer, 2004; McCray et al., 2003).

School systems' responses to the genetic/cultural deficit theories and the cultural differences theories. The three theories we have briefly described played important roles in American education. During the early to mid-19th century, for example, advocates of the common school focused on developing educational programs that would provide all children with equal educational opportunities in integrated settings. They believed that an education that focused on basic skills, morality, and citizenship would put immigrant students (those from culturally- and linguistically-diverse backgrounds) on par with the most privileged European American students who were born in the United States.

Inequities in education have existed for centuries in the United States.

Nonetheless, immigrant students still experienced school failure in large numbers and were often blamed for these failures, as though the fault were inherent in them and not in a school system that did not take their cultural diversity into account but remained rigidly Anglocentric. Interestingly, at this same time, some states enacted anti-literacy laws that prohibited educators from teaching free or enslaved African Americans how to read (Span, 2003).

During the last half of the 19th century, school systems "held back" (retained in grade) many second- and third-generation European Americans, immigrant students, and African American students at alarmingly high rates. Only rarely, however, did these same educators entertain the notion that students' poor performance (such as Joesian's) might also be linked to a combination of factors such as inappropriate instruction and racial and ethnic discrimination (Deschenes et al., 2001).

The progressive movement of the first half of the 20th century produced educational reforms designed to promote educational equity for all students, this time through differentiated instruction. Many educators believed that the new technology of standardized testing, when combined with differentiated instruction, would result in school placements that were more aligned with students' abilities and that differentiated placements—"tracking"—would themselves provide the differently placed students with the skills they needed to be successful in life (Safford & Safford, 1998). The unfortunate consequence of differentiated instruction, standardized testing (administered in English), and discriminatory placements was that many immigrant children from Central and Eastern Europe continued to be held back and assigned to remedial and vocational tracks.

The result of the practice of tracking was that many students from diverse backgrounds, especially those from African, Native American, Hispanic, and Asian backgrounds, were segregated from their more "typical," majority-culture peers largely because of their race, socioeconomic status, immigrant status, and language (Safford & Safford, 1998). Predictably, school segregation was a prelude to segregation in nearly all other aspects of life, including schooling (Mickelson, 2003).

In the middle of the 20th century, segregation itself, in all of its forms, received frontal challenges from civil rights activists and their allies. And no greater challenge existed than the challenge to racial segregation in education. It reached its peak during the early 1950s.

For several years, lawyers for African American students had been hammering away at school segregation, arguing that the 14th Amendment to the U.S. Constitution, prohibiting a state from denying equal protection of the laws to anyone in its jurisdiction, required the schools

Values: It is sad that these theories were not integrated to paint a more holistic, contextual view of school success and failure for culturally- and linguistically-diverse students. Failure to assess teaching and learning from a broader sociocultural perspective squelched the opportunity of students from diverse backgrounds to attain *full citizenship* in this country.

to desegregate by race. In what many regard as one of its most far-reaching decisions, the U.S. Supreme Court, in *Brown v. Board of Education* (1954), agreed.

Brown was a case brought against the Topeka, Kansas, Board of Education and was combined with lawsuits against the states of Delaware, South Carolina, and Virginia on the grounds that each of the defendants officially condoned racial segregation and thereby denied African American students an equal opportunity, compared to their European American peers, for an education. The Supreme Court agreed with that theory and ordered those school systems and indeed all others to desegregate, by race, with all due deliberate speed.

One early consequence of the efforts at school racial desegregation was that, as enrollments of culturally- and linguistically-diverse children in previously all-white schools increased, so did their enrollment in self-contained programs for students who allegedly were "mildly mentally retarded" (Dunn, 1968; Mercer 1973; National Research Council, 2002). Given what we have just written about the history of school segregation in America, you should not be surprised to learn that both African American and Hispanic American students were increasingly tracked into programs for students with mental retardation and that their results on standardized tests, usually administered in English and not their native language, justified their placement into separate special education programs (Mercer & Richardson, 1975). Nor should you be surprised to learn that, just as African American students used a theory of equal opportunity and the facts of racial segregation to win their victory in *Brown*, so did Latino students use the same theory and the same kind of data—the demographics of segregated placement—successfully to attack special education classification, in which standardized tests were administered in English to students who were not English-speaking or English language learners and the students' placement into separate and segregated special education programs (*Diana v. Board of Education*, 1973).

Inarguably, *Brown* and other school-classification, school-segregation cases played a huge role when advocates for students with disabilities challenged the classification procedures and standards that many school systems were using and sought the remedy of a free appropriate public education in the least restrictive environment. As we pointed out in Chapter 1, the advocates were successful: Congress enacted P.L. 94–142, the Education for All Handicapped Children Act, in 1975 (and later renamed it the Individuals with Disabilities Act, or IDEA).

Standard: When you learn about assessing English language learners, you are applying CEC Standard 6, Language.

Visit the Companion Website, *www.prenhall.com/turnbull*, to find more information about the history of EHCA/IDEA. Also visit *http://www.thearc.org/education.html* for more information about the law.

Enactment and Implementation of IDEA

As you learned in Chapter 1, IDEA attacked school practices of pure and functional exclusion and discriminatory evaluation and assured a free appropriate public education in the least restrictive environment to all students with disabilities. Did it, however, dismantle the vestiges of discrimination against students from diverse backgrounds?

The students' advocates thought not; they still could document segregation based on diversity of background and they believed that special education was the process and place that permitted segregation. Accordingly, in a suit they brought against the state commissioner of education in California (before Congress enacted P.L. 94–142), they sought to prevent the state's school system from using standardized tests for evaluating students and classifying them into special education (*Larry P. v. Riles*, 1972). Four years after Congress enacted IDEA, they finally persuaded the federal courts in California to limit the schools' use of standardized intelligence tests and to adopt additional means for evaluating and classifying students into special education (*Larry P. v. Riles*, 1979). Indeed, at one point the courts banned schools from using standardized IQ tests to determine where to place African American students, especially limiting their placement into programs for students who (in the language of the day, which we disavow now—see Chapter 1) were "mildly mentally retarded").

Larry P. was not, however, the last word on classification. In *PASE v. Hannon* (1980), a federal court in Chicago held that the standardized IQ tests were only minimally biased and that their administration, coupled with interpretation by qualified experts and supplemented by other evaluation procedures and standards, did not deny students from diverse backgrounds an equal opportunity for an education nor their IDEA rights. Today, as you learned in Chapter 1, schools use standardized tests but must do so in nondiscriminatory ways and must adopt other standards and procedures for nondiscriminatory evaluation of students from diverse backgrounds and indeed from nondiverse backgrounds, too. The question, now, is whether the discrimination that the advocates attacked before Congress enacted IDEA persists. In a word, did that law and the cases make a sufficient difference in education?

Disproportionate overrepresentation. In 1979, mounting controversy about placement of students from diverse backgrounds into special education prompted Congress to ask the National Research Council (1982) to determine whether those students, particularly African Americans, were overrepresented in programs for students with mild mental retardation and to recommend policies to address that issue.

At the national level, the National Research Council found that overrepresentation did exist. In all but four states in its sample, the council found that the average percentage of students from diverse backgrounds in programs for students with mild mental retardation was higher than the average percentage of

Overrepresentation of culturally- and linguistically-diverse students in special education placements remains a problem even today.

European Americans in these same programs. It also concluded that African American students were significantly more likely to be placed in those programs than were students from other diverse backgrounds.

The National Research Council attributed overrepresentation to legal and administrative requirements, the students' characteristics, the quality of the instruction they received, possible biases in schools' evaluation and assessment processes, the characteristics of the students' home and family environments, and broader historical and cultural contexts such as conflicts between minority and dominant cultures (see also Chinn & Hughes, 1987; Losen & Orfield, 2002).

Despite these and numerous other reports and recommendations as well as IDEA's nondiscriminatory evaluation principle, overrepresentation of students from diverse backgrounds in special education persisted, so much so that in 1997, 22 years after first enacting IDEA, Congress amended it to require state educational agencies to do the following:

- Assess the efficacy of educational and transitional services for students with disabilities from diverse backgrounds

- Provide annual data about the number of students from diverse backgrounds who are referred for special education assessment, the number who receive special education, the extent to which they were served, their high school graduation rates, and their performance on state assessments

- Intervene in school districts where there is significant overrepresentation

Congress also asked the National Research Council to reassess overrepresentation, focusing on the overrepresentation of students from diverse backgrounds in special education programs in all three high-incidence categories (learning disabilities, mental retardation, and emotional or behavioral disorders) and their underrepresentation in programs for students who are especially gifted and talented. Had Congress wanted to exemplify its global concerns about overrepresentation, it could have done no better than to point to Joesian and his school system.

Results from these analyses were similar to results found decades earlier. Figure 3–2 shows the percentage of students ages 6 through 21 served under IDEA by disability and race/ethnicity during the 2000–2001 school year.

Data on representation in gifted programs unveiled quite different results. African Americans, Native Americans/Alaskans, and Latinos were underrepresented in programs for students who are gifted and talented, and Asian and Pacific Island students were overrepresented. This finding was consistent across social-class levels and parent education levels for African American and Latino students. Gaps were higher for lower parent education levels. For example, "black 12th graders with parents with college degrees had average scores that were about the same as for

Figure 3-2 Percentage of students ages 6–21 served under IDEA by disability and race/ethnicity during the 2000–2001 school year

Disability	American Indian	Asian/Pacific Islander	Black (non-Latino)	Latino	White (non-Latino)	All Students Served
Specific learning disabilities	56.3	43.2	45.2	60.3	48.9	50.0
Speech/language impairments	17.1	25.2	15.1	17.3	20.8	18.9
Mental retardation	8.5	10.1	18.9	8.6	9.3	10.6
Emotional disturbance	7.5	5.3	10.7	4.5	8.0	8.2
Multiple disabilities	2.5	2.3	1.9	1.8	1.8	2.1
Hearing impairments	1.1	2.9	1.0	1.5	1.2	1.2
Orthopedic impairments	0.8	2.0	0.9	1.4	1.4	1.3
Other health impairments	4.1	3.9	3.7	2.8	5.9	5.1
Visual impairments	0.4	0.8	0.4	0.5	0.5	0.4
Autism	0.6	3.4	1.2	0.9	1.4	1.4
Deaf-blindness	0.0	0.0	0.0	0.0	0.0	0.0
Traumatic brain injury	0.3	0.3	0.2	0.2	0.3	0.3
Developmental delays	0.7	0.7	0.7	0.2	0.6	0.5
All disabilities	100.0	100.0	100.0	100.0	100.0	100.0

Note: Does not include data for New York State.
Source: U.S. Department of Education, Office of Special Education Programs, Data Analysis System (DANS), 2001.

white students with no parent with a high school diploma" (Miller, 2000, pp. 14–15). In addition, the Children's Defense Fund (2004) reported that more than 12 million children (one in six) live in poverty, and millions live just above the official poverty line.

- The poorest one-fifth of households made only 11 percent more in 2002 ($9,990) than they did 30 years ago, after adjusting for inflation.
- An American child is more likely to be poor today than 25 or 30 years ago; more likely to be poor than an American adult; and more likely to be poor than a child living in Canada, Germany, France, Britain, or Spain.
- One in three poor children (35 percent) lives with a full-time year-round worker.
- In 2001, more than 5.1 million children lived in low-income households that spent at least half of their income on housing. (p. 2)

Also, proportionally, a higher percentage of African American and Latino students ages 5 to 17 have consistently lived in poverty compared to their European American peers. More specifically, the U.S. Department of Education (2003) found that 30.5 and 28.2 percent of African American and Latino students lived in poverty, respectively. This is in contrast to 9.7 percent of European American children who lived in poverty.

Into Practice ~ Seven Steps of the Cultural Inquiry Process   Box 3–2

1. *Select a "puzzlement."* Puzzlements are perplexing student social and academic behaviors. These behaviors are incompatible with your world views and actions (your culture). They are not immediately attributable to deficits and weaknesses within students, their families, and their communities. They are just puzzling situations. Identify one puzzlement, such as parents' low participation in their child's evaluation for special education, that you want to understand better.

2. *Collect and summarize existing data about that puzzlement within a broad context.* To understand why parents of students from diverse backgrounds do not participate as much as parents from European American backgrounds in evaluations and multidisciplinary team meetings, you and the team members review and analyze the last year's worth of multidisciplinary team meetings and the parents' participation in them. You and your colleagues conclude that the team simply intimidates and overpowers parents, especially those who are uneducated and economically disadvantaged. You know your behavior is irresponsible, alienates the parents, and prevents you from acquiring information that you can use to evaluate and instruct the child. You choose to change.

3. *Consider alternative cultural influences and select one or more of them to explore.* Together with your colleagues, identify your own cultural perspective. Do you regard yourselves as experts and superior to the parents? Then place yourself in the parents' position. Do this by hosting a focus group—don't call it that; call it a community gathering—so the parents may express their views about how they want to partner with you. Make it clear that they may say anything they want; they don't have to fear that you will retaliate against their children.

4. *Gather and analyze relevant information as needed.* After adjourning the gathering, analyze how the parents' perspectives differ from yours. Consider how social interactions, roles, and hierarchies affect their perspectives and yours, too. Were the parents themselves treated discriminatorily when they were in school? Were any of them evaluated for special education? Did they regard special education as a dead end for their children? Did they think you were simply carrying on a tradition of cultural discrimination?

5. *Develop and implement intervention(s) as needed.* Based on this analysis, address the issue of parent alienation and frustration. Do not focus primarily on deficits and dysfunction within families. Instead, investigate how the students' home and community can contribute information about the students' characteristics (nondiscriminatory evaluation) and about how to instruct them more effectively (appropriate education) (Moll & Gonzalez, 1997). For example, develop a layperson's special education vocabulary glossary, explaining your often-used terms in simple language, both English and the parents' home language. Develop a special education "map" that has flow charts and diagrams illustrating the evaluation process, its purpose, and its consequences. Ask parents to suggest how to improve the glossary and map. Adopt their suggestions.

6. *Monitor the process and results of intervention(s).* Monitor your own behavior. Do the parents participate more? Do you understand them better? Are they more satisfied with the evaluation process? Do they attend meetings more often and are they more candid about their children? What, if any, additional problems have you identified?

7. *Write a report of your cultural inquiry process study.* Document the entire process, from analysis through results. Rely on videotapes and transcripts of community gatherings, interviews with parents, and action plans. Archive these for future use.

Putting These Strategies into Practice in the General Curriculum

1. Identify a puzzlement that you have related to teaching students from culturally- and linguistically-diverse backgrounds. Use the Internet and the library to collect existing data. Summarize that data.

2. Based on your puzzlement and the data you collect, implement steps 3 and 4. (Althogh step 3 suggests that you do this with other colleagues, in answering this question, you should do it by yourself.)

3. Develop a list of questions that you would have for the student's families that would enable you to gain a clear perspective on the family's cultural values.

To answer these questions online, go to the Into Practice module in Chapter 3 of the Companion Website, *www.prenhall.com/turnbull.*

Nondiscriminatory Evaluation

As we pointed out in this chapter when we discussed the history of educational discrimination and as Chapter 1 highlighted, nondiscriminatory evaluation—or, if you prefer, culturally responsive evaluation practice—attempts to ensure that educators do not mistake cultural differences for disabilities. To avoid the mistake of confusing *difference* and *disability*, educators have to challenge the adequacy of the evaluation tools and processes that they now use to identify students from diverse backgrounds for special education eligibility. How can they do that? One obvious way is to adhere to the everyday-context approach and to adopt the several approaches we suggested for prereferral teams. Another is to apply the strategies that we describe in Figure 3–3.

Figure 3–3 Nondiscriminatory evaluation process

1. Comply with IDEA's standards and processes as Chapter 1 explained them and adhere to the nondiscriminatory evaluation figure that appears in Chapters 5 through 15 about each category of exceptionality.

2. Identify assessment tools and measures that are culturally sensitive and less apt to reveal cultural bias.

3. Observe the student in home, school, and community settings. Do not focus primarily on identifying the student's deficits. Instead, seek out individuals in those settings who can give you information about how the student functions in them. What skills does he have? What supports does she use? What supports does she need?

4. Compare the student's development and performance with her same-age peers from her cultural community who are performing satisfactorily in school, especially when English is not their dominant language (Artiles & Ortiz, 2002). Identify any differences and learn why they exist.

5. When the student uses a language or dialect that is not English, consider the developmental stages of that particular language when interpreting test results. For example, when evaluating English-language learners for special education, determine both their basic interpersonal communication skills and their cognitive academic language proficiency (Cummins, 1989). If the students have not reached a level that is more complex and abstract, poor performance on a standardized test may indicate that they have not become proficient in using the language, not that they have a disability.

USING EFFECTIVE INSTRUCTIONAL STRATEGIES

To be effective instructors of students from diverse backgrounds, educators will have to adopt culturally responsive professional practice. That term refers to teaching that uses

> the cultures, experiences, and perspectives of African, Native, Latino, and Asian American students as filters through which to teach them academic knowledge and skills. Other critical elements of culturally responsive professional practice include unpacking unequal distributions of power and privilege, and teaching students of color cultural competence about themselves and each other. (Gay & Kirkland, 2003, p. 181)

Culturally responsive professional practice is more than an application approach; it requires more than the mere application of teaching techniques (Gay, 2000). At its root, culturally responsive professional practice is a multidimensional notion that includes personal, technical (curriculum and instruction), and institutional dimensions (Ladson-Billings, 1995).

Personal Dimension of Culturally Responsive Professional Practice

The personal dimension of culturally responsive practice calls attention to the central role of a teacher's own learning (Richardson, 2001). Aspects that influence someone to learn to teach include the following (Putnam & Borko, 2000):

- The teacher's own biography
- The teacher's beliefs about culture, learning, and teaching
- The school and classroom contexts in which the teacher has learned and practices
- The teacher's professional development activities

If these aspects influence teachers as they learn to teach, what factors should influence them as they develop the personal dimensions of culturally responsive professional practice? Figure 3–4 outlines the culturally responsive educator's characteristics and provides tips on how teachers can be culturally responsive as they teach.

To meet a bilingual teaching volunteer who also has an exceptionality, visit Jael (Clip 1) under "Beyond School" on the *Real Lives and Exceptionalities* DVD.

Figure 3-4 Characteristics of culturally responsive educators

Develop your sociocultural consciousness.   The typical teacher is a white middle-class female with little intercultural experiences (Cochran-Smith, Davis, & Fries, 2004). Whether you fit that profile or not, reflect on how your values, beliefs, and actions are affected by your cultural assumptions and ways of understanding your world—for example, how your race, ethnicity, social class, gender, language background, and religion shape your expectations, forms of interactions, and means for expressing your ideas and feelings. Analyze how, despite the nation's laudable democratic ideals, American schools and other institutions have perpetuated inequalities; ask how privileged access for disparate groups has existed. In a word, connect your analysis of the past with your and our country's present cultures and condition.

Build an affirming attitude toward diverse students.   Acknowledge and confront the negative views about culturally-diverse communities that are part of your education and upbringing. Develop an affirming attitude toward all students, particularly those from diverse backgrounds. Recognize and be able to describe the differences between cultural groups but refrain from overgeneralizing and stereotyping. Although certain groups share similar beliefs and behavior patterns, there are also within-group differences that must not be overlooked. Also refrain from evaluating those differences from narrow-minded cultural perspectives (i.e., what students lack or cannot do) (Valencia, 1997). When in doubt, observe and ask questions. Bear in mind that the distinction between *describing/recognizing* versus *evaluating/judging* is important in developing respect for cultural perspectives different from your own and enhancing your self-awareness as a cultural being (Rogoff, 2003).

Commit and cultivate the skills to become a change agent.   Transcend cultural sensitivity; instead, engage in *praxis* (i.e., critical reflection plus action) with other teachers (Hoffman-Kipp, Artiles, & López-Torres, 2003). Do this to understand better that your work is situated in institutional contexts that are affected by larger (historical and political) forces. Do this to become more aware of the need for schoolwide changes, identify the barriers and obstacles to school change toward progressive models, and experience the role that professional collaboration plays in implementing culturally responsive practices. Teach students from diverse backgrounds the codes and skills they need to function in mainstream society (Delpit, 1988, 1995).

Develop a clear understanding of teaching-learning processes.   Base your work on a solid theoretical foundation about how to orchestrate teaching-learning processes. Follow guiding principles such as believing firmly in the potential of all students, meeting your duty to promote their learning by building on what they already know and have experienced, nurturing and valuing critical thinking and multiple perspectives, and embracing collaboration in solving problems.

Re-present learners' cultures and reimagine their communities.   Understand your and others' culture from the dynamic and complex perspectives we described in this chapter. Adopt an ethnographic stance to understand your students' lives and school life (Mehan, Okamoto, Lintz, & Wills, 2004). Re-present their cultures and reimagine their communities (Moll & Gonzales, 1997). Do this by examining the cultures of classrooms, communities, and households "as strategizing units; [this way, educators will be able to see how families] function as part of a wider economy; how family members obtain and distribute their material and intellectual resources, their funds of knowledge, through social networks or other adaptive arrangements" (Moll & Gonzales, 1997, p. 191). Use the insights from the re-presentation of students' cultures and the reimagining of their communities as you teach.

Cultivate culturally responsive teaching practices.   Integrate these guidelines into your work to assist your students to construct knowledge, build on their personal and cultural strengths, and examine the curriculum from multiple perspectives.

Source: Ladson-Billings, 1992, 1994, 1995; Moll & Gonzales, 1997; Villegas & Lucas, 2002.

Technical Dimension of Culturally Responsive Practice

Teaching occurs in a context, the classroom being the most immediate one. To accommodate their classrooms to students from diverse backgrounds involves a technical dimension of culturally responsive practice. Classrooms in which teachers enact the principles of culturally responsive pedagogy have these characteristics (Ladson-Billings, 1995):

- Teachers deliberately create social environments in which academic success, cultural competence, and critical consciousness are nurtured.

- Teachers are intent on building a community of learners and stimulate collaboration and self-regulation in their students.

- Teachers promote fluid and spontaneous social interactions in classrooms by regarding knowledge as a socially constructed phenomenon and by promoting critical thinking and using a sociocultural view of assessment, teaching, and learning.

Culturally Responsive Pedagogy for Ethnically-Diverse Students

The concept of transformative teaching refers to a culturally responsive pedagogy for ethnically-diverse students. Banks (1995) described transformative teaching and learning as "characterized by a curriculum organized around powerful ideas, highly interactive teaching strategies, active student involvement, and activities that require students to participate in personal, social, and civic action to make their classrooms, schools, and communities more democratic and just" (p. 22) (see also Banks, 1993). Boxes 3–3 and 3–4 exemplify how teachers can establish a classroom that supports students from diverse backgrounds.

Culturally Responsive Pedagogy for Linguistically-Diverse Learners

Who are linguistically-diverse students? According to Garcia (2004):

- They have substantial exposure to a social environment in which English is not the primary language.

- They have acquired the communicative abilities of that social environment.

- They are first exposed to a predominantly English-speaking environment when they begin their formal educational careers.

Teachers can use a variety of approaches to respond to these students' educational needs; indeed, they will have to. That is so because linguistically-diverse students represent a heterogeneous population. Among them, they use more than 100 different languages in America's schools (Garcia, 2004). The largest group of linguistically diverse learners is, like Joesian, of Latino ancestry (more than 70 percent).

A dilemma that general educators often confront (as they must have when educating Joesian) is whether linguistically-diverse students experience academic difficulties because of limited

---

Diversity Tips ~ Pedagogical Principles for Ethnically-Diverse Students   Box 3–3

1. Promote academic rigor with social supports.
   - Facilitate learning by creating opportunities for "experts" to assist performance.
   - Have students work collaboratively in small mixed-ability groups.
2. Demonstrate connectedness with all students.
3. Create student-centered classrooms and discuss organization.
4. Build on students' personal and cultural strengths.

5. Help students access prior knowledge and beliefs.
   - Use examples and analogies from students' lives.
   - Use appropriate instructional materials.
   - Tap community resources.
6. Create different paths to learning by using varied instructional activities.
7. Adapt general principles to local circumstances.

Source: Adapted from Artiles et al., 2004; Mehan et al., 2004; Villegas & Lucas, 2002.

Technology Tips ~ Supporting Students from Diverse Backgrounds   Box 3–4

As you learned in Chapter 2, universal design for learning (UDL) enables all people to have access to typical environments and activities to the fullest extent possible (Scott, McGuire, & Shaw, 2003). One component of UDL, especially in schools, is universal design for instruction (UDI). UDI creates user-friendly instructional tools that give all students access to the general education curriculum.

One of UDI's principles highlights the need for *perceptible information*—namely, the need to communicate information to all students in an effective manner. From a cultural perspective, UDI can provide learning experiences that are relevant and meaningful and are connected to students' lives, enabling them to develop self-regulatory and citizenship skills that they later can use to create a more culture-honoring society (Banks, 1995)—a "just society."

Let us say that you decide to use social justice as a medium to improve your students' reading, writing, research, and critical-thinking skills. The comprehensive website, *www.tolerance.org*, presents a project of the Southern Poverty Law Center; the center and its site can help you accomplish these goals. This website describes Rosa Parks and the Montgomery bus boycott. Links provide readings for students, curriculum kits, and activities to augment the readings. One link identifies 10 ways to fight hate and provides a process to address injustice in local settings. These include (1) act, (2) unite, (3) support the victims, (4) do your homework (research), (5) create an alternative, (6) speak up, (7) lobby leaders, (8) look long range, (9) teach tolerance, and (10) dig deeper. These steps require reading, writing, speaking, research, and collaboration. They also represent skills that will be tested on state assessments emanating from NCLB. Visit the website and investigate what curricular materials are available to you.

English proficiency or because of a disability (Klingner, Artiles, & Méndez Barletta, 2004). Because they are unsure of what causes students' academic difficulties, some teachers often refer disproportionate numbers of linguistically-diverse students to special education. Other teachers, especially those in urban school districts, tend to underrefer these students for support services, fearing that the students may trigger a discrimination lawsuit in response (Artiles, Rueda, Salazar, & Higareda, 2005; Gersten & Woodward, 1994); perhaps underreferral explains what happened to Joesian. Researchers have also reported that at-risk, linguistically-diverse students in general and English-as-a-second language (ESL) classrooms usually have teachers who pay minimal attention to language development issues and that these teachers tend to lecture the whole class most of the instructional time; not surprisingly, these students tend to have low rates of academic engagement (Arreaga-Mayer & Perdomo-Rivera, 1996). So what is an individual teacher to do?

The primary purpose of bilingual special education is to help each individual student achieve a "maximum potential for learning" (Baca & Cervantes, 2004, p. 18). Specialists have designed several bilingual educational programs to serve these students (Garcia, 1993):

- Transitional bilingual education
- Maintenance bilingual education
- English as a second language
- Immersion
- Sheltered English
- Submersion

Each of these models rests on distinct conceptual assumptions and goals. The two most widely used models are the transitional and maintenance approaches, and the majority of bilingual programs in the United States are based on the transitional model (Gollnick & Chinn, 1994). Figure 3–5 describes these two models.

Perhaps one of the most contested issues in bilingual education is related to effective methods for teaching linguistically-diverse students. Instead of analyzing this ongoing debate (see August & Hakuta [1997] for a synthesis of this research), we summarize the instructional guidelines for linguistically-diverse students in Figure 3–6.

Establishing a classroom conducive to learning for culturally- and linguistically-diverse students is important for the success of all children.

Figure 3-5 Transitional and maintenance bilingual programs

Transitional programs. Educators use students' native language until the students are ready to transition into English-only classrooms. Educators still dispute, however, how to determine when is the best time to transition a student and what is the best approach to conduct the transition (Gersten & Jiménez, 1996). A premature or abrupt transition can have negative academic consequences (Artiles et al., 2004).

Maintenance programs. These programs allow linguistically-diverse students to function in both English and their primary language. Maintenance programs nurture bilingualism and biculturalism in students (Correa & Heward, 1996). Researchers have advocated for these programs because they produce positive consequences in students' development (Cummins, 1989).

Figure 3-6 Instructional guidelines for linguistically-diverse students

1. Use a balanced approach in which you emphasize both form (e.g., correct reading and writing skills) and process (e.g., interpretation, relevance, higher-order thinking).
2. Distinguish between language development and academic growth, and enhance both. Language development should target the following:
   - Proficiency and fluency in English, including the ability to communicate socially and academically
   - Competence in the use of standard English grammar
   - Acquisition of new academic content
3. Gradually build and use a relevant and useful vocabulary.
4. Use visuals (e.g., concept maps, graphic organizers) to strengthen vocabulary.
5. Use collaborative learning and peer tutoring strategies.
6. Use learners' primary language during instruction in strategic ways—e.g., use English to review content and primary language to teach complex content that requires the use of higher-order thinking skills.

Source: Adapted from Artiles et al., 2004; Bos & Reyes, 1996; Fletcher, Bos, & Johnson, 1999; Gersten & Baker, 2000; Jiménez, Gersten, & Rivera, 1996; Reyes, 1992.

Institutional Dimension of Culturally Responsive Practice

The institutional dimension is a critical element in any model that claims to be culturally responsive. This dimension calls attention to equity issues as they relate to leadership, programmatic emphases, school climate, governance, and structural supports for students', faculty's, and families' learning. Because Chapter 4 discusses partnerships among professionals, students, and their families, we outline guidelines to address the institutional dimension in Figure 3–7.

INCLUDING STUDENTS FROM CULTURALLY- AND LINGUISTICALLY-DIVERSE BACKGROUNDS

Partnerships in Schools: A Brief History

When educators develop partnerships with each other, they contribute mightily to the success or failure of standards-based general and special education reforms. (As Chapter 4 points out, partnerships among educators and families also powerfully influence student outcomes.) What is a partnership among educators? A *partnership* refers to a relationship that involves joint responsibilities

Council for Exceptional Children

Standard: As you learn about strategies for working with colleagues, parents, and students, you are addressing CEC Standard 10, Effective Collaboration.

Figure 3–7 Guidelines for a culturally-responsive institutional dimension

1. Engage school personnel in the development of collective responsibility for student learning. This way, each teacher's individual responsibility will strengthen a collective vision for students' well-being.
2. Create a discourse at the school level about social justice education and about how subordination and dominance issues permeate the education of culturally- and linguistically-diverse students with and without disabilities. As teachers learn to interpret their work through a social justice lens, they will be able to see their professional practices as mediated by the interaction of local and macro forces.
3. A key topic in the school community's discourse on social justice education ought to be the analysis of individuals' and the school's theories about competence and difference and the consequences for curricula, assessment, instruction, program placement practices, and allocation of resources.
4. Center professional development efforts around the examination of student learning through the creation of communities of practice. Efforts might include teacher study groups or lesson study groups that allow teachers to engage in a sustained and systematic study of their own professional practice. The study of one's own professional practice allows teachers to move constantly from personal experience to theoretical sense-making as a powerful way to develop professionally.
5. Realign school structures (scheduling, teaching assignments) to maximize opportunities for teacher learning in classrooms and communities.
6. Use professional development resources to enhance school personnel's effective use of colleagues, materials, and strategies.

Source: Artiles et al., 2004; Cochran-Smith et al., 2004; Villegas & Lucas, 2002.

(*Merriam-Webster Collegiate Dictionary*, 2003). Thus, a partnership among educators refers to opportunities for educators to collaborate with each other in order to increase the soundness of their decisions. The question is simply this (for the purposes of this chapter): will the partners necessarily take into account the everyday context of their respective cultures? The simple answer is no. Especially when they are from diverse backgrounds, they will find it useful to follow the tips that we present in Box 3–5.

As Box 3–5 indicates, educators will need constantly to consider their personal and collective histories or else put a student's right to a free appropriate public education at risk. On the most fundamental level, they use similar terminology, but because of their individual and group histories, they may act on beliefs, definitions, and mores that may be very different and seemingly mutually incompatible. If, for example, one of Joesian's teachers concludes, simplistically, that he is a nonreader because he just can't learn to read, without asking why that is so, the teacher will ignore Joesian's individual history; the history of discrimination that Puerto Rican students in New York have experienced; and the possibility that discrimination, not an inherent impediment, explains Joesian's nonreader status.

It could be difficult for teachers to make those beliefs, definitions, and mores explicit. It could be even more difficult for them to communicate about them with each other and thereby blunt any discriminatory effects on the student. It could be still more difficult for them to develop their own collective history, one in which their respective beliefs, definitions, and mores are part of that collective history but are subsumed into a new collective history—their own. And it could be most difficult for them to identify, acknowledge, and address the role and history of power in school districts, schools, and classrooms (Artiles, 2003).

To do all this is no simple matter, but neither is it impossible. The cultural inquiry process model that we described previously can benefit them. So, too, can the tips we describe in Box 3–6, especially when the partners are determining how to comply with IDEA's fourth principle, the placement of students with disabilities in the least restrictive (most inclusive) environment.

Values: There is power in numbers. When a school-based team grapples with the issues of culture and discrimination, it becomes more powerful than any one of its members to assure that students from diverse backgrounds have equal opportunity and *full citizenship* within their schools, especially within the inclusive general curriculum.

Partnership Tips ~ Four Questions to Answer   Box 3–5

1. **Who?** "Who" consists of those individuals responsible for meeting student's needs. "Who" includes but is not limited to school personnel. "Who" includes parents, community organizations, and the students themselves. Do you and your school welcome them as partners? How do you know? How can you find the answer?

2. **Why?** "Why" consists of indentifying the goals you wish to accompolish for the students. Include the goals that IDEA and NCLB set out. Be sure that the goals for particular students are based on their capabilities, not stereotypes and overgeneralizations.

3. **How?** "How" refers to the curriculum, instructional approaches, related services, and supplementary aids and services, including assistive technology and universal design, that you will use to promote student outcomes. Call these, collectively, "tools." Develop the tools by considering, among other things, what funds of knowledge you can acquire from the students' home and community cultures (Moll & Gonzales, 1997).

4. **Where?** "Where" focuses on the placement, restrictiveness of the placement, and the degree to which students will be served in special and general education settings. Given the disproportionate representation of students from diverse backgrounds in special education, work with your partners to reduce that unwanted overenrollment

(Fierros & Conroy, 2002). As you respond to a student's needs, vigorously ask whether you are reflecting cultural biases, your own or the system's, against the student.

Putting These Tips to Work for Progress in the General Curriculum

1. Imagine that you have a new student in your classroom who has just immigrated to the United States from Vietnam and does not speak any English. Who are some of the partners that you could pursue to assist you in providing this student with an appropriate education?

2. Consider that you have a student in your class who is from a family who experiences extreme poverty. It is clear to you that this student is malnourished, does not have adequate clothes for the cold weather, and cries a good portion of the day because of gum disease. What impact do you believe such circumstances has on student learning, and what is the role of the school?

3. Prepare a list that describes your own cultural values. For each value, note the impact that you believe it will have on your teaching.

To answer these question online, go to the Partnership Tips module in Chapter 3 of the Companion Website, *www.prenhall.com/turnbull*.

Based on what you have learned about culturally responsive ways to use effective instructional strategies and include students from diverse backgrounds in educational settings, consider how you would apply what you have learned, based on the scenario in Figure 3–8.

ASSESSING STUDENTS' PROGRESS IN A CULTURALLY RESPONSIVE MANNER

Values: Culturally responsive assessment highlights students' *strengths,* not just their needs, and leads to curricular and instructional methods that foster self-determination, especially in students whose cultures may not value self-determination and independence.

PRAXIS

Standard: Learning about culturally responsive assessment practices for minority students is an application of PRAXIS™ Standard 3, Delivering Services to Students with Disabilities and Selecting Assessments.

As Chapter 2 pointed out, the educational outcomes for students with disabilities has not been impressive. That is why IDEA and NCLB both emphasize outcomes—IDEA through its third and fourth principles, appropriate education and least restrictive placement; and NCLB through its principles of accountability, highly qualified teachers, and evidence-based instruction.

To comply with these principles, teachers can use the cultural inquiry process and similar approaches that we have described to assess and monitor their students' progress. They should be cautious, as we have warned, not to allow standardized assessment, which is often used to determine eligibility for special education or pre- and post-tests administered at the beginning and end of the school year, to dominate the assessment process. Instead, they should administer, on an ongoing basis, various tools that are designed to monitor performance on annual goals, short-term objectives, and benchmarks. They should not use these tools solely to document their students' weaknesses but to identify their students' strengths, growth, or lack of growth as well. They also should use these tools to assess the efficacy of their instructional approaches and processes.

In Chapters 5 through 16, you will learn many assessment techniques that enable teachers to accomplish these goals. For example, curriculum-based assessment, which you will learn about in Chapters 5 and 6, involves an outcome measurement tool for evaluating students' performance and the efficacy of teachers' instructional practices. Usually students' performance is graphed to provide a visual representation of their performance over time.

Inclusion Tips   Box 3–6

	What You Might See	What You Might Be Tempted to Do	Alternate Responses	Ways to Include Peers in the Process
Behavior	A student who is an English-language learner and has learning disabilities puts her head on her desk when she does not understand written instructions. She rarely completes assignments.	Tell her that she should go to bed at a reasonable hour so that she can stay awake and complete her classwork.	List steps of the instructions in sequence on the board. Use pictures whenever possible. Ask parents how help is requested and provided in their culture.	Model the skill of asking for help to all students and let them role-play. Also provide reinforcement when they use the skill and encourage their classmates to use it.
Social interactions	She rarely initiates a greeting but usually responds to one appropriately.	Do not push her to initiate because you believe this skill will develop as her English improves.	Have students share greetings from the different languages represented in the classroom, including English.	Have this student and others teach the different greetings and reinforce use of them in and outside the classroom.
Educational performance	The student has strong math skills but performs poorly on word problems when he has to read them.	Request that he have more time in the English-as-a-second-language room for reading support and stop giving him word problems.	Work with English-as-a-second-language and learning disabilities teachers to provide text in the student's primary language whenever possible.	Establish a peer tutoring system within the class: he can tutor students who have problems with computation. Students who share the same primary language can help him read the word problems.
Classroom attitudes	He complains of a head- or stomachache and asks to go to the clinic when assigned to read a children's novel and answer comprehension questions in written form.	Allow him to go to the clinic, hoping that he will grow out of this behavior as his English improves.	Order the novel on tape from Recordings for the Blind and Dyslexic (RFBD) *www.rfbd.org*. Also try to obtain a copy of the book in his native language.	When possible, provide copies of the novel written at lower reading levels and have students partner-read and answer questions during center time.

Ongoing monitoring will not necessarily yield outcomes that are more positive for students from diverse backgrounds if educators do not analyze assessment results in a culturally responsive manner. For example, Trent (1997) and educators in an urban school established a study group to document the implementation of a full-inclusion program for students with high-incidence disabilities. The majority of these students were African American and economically disadvantaged; among them, they were classified as having specific learning disabilities (Chapter 5), emotional or behavioral disorders (Chapter 7), and mental retardation (Chapter 9).

Trent believed that temporal inclusion (that is, merely being *placed* in a general education environment) should not take precedence over the academic performance of students with these high-incidence disabilities. He worked with teachers, paraprofessionals, building-level

To learn more about curriculum-based measurement and performance assessment, go to the Companion Website, *www.prenhall.com/turnbull*, to link to *http://www.nasponline.org/publications/cq276cba.html* and *http://www.performanceassessment.org/performance/index.html*.

75

Figure 3-8 Becoming a culturally responsive teacher

Jeremy is a first-year high school chemistry teacher. Two of the students in his fourth-period chemistry class have a specific learning disability, and four are first-generation Asian American students. The learning disabilities teacher works closely with him to modify the curriculum for the first two students, but Jeremy has major concerns about his Asian American students. They keep to themselves and rarely interact with the other students except during breaks. They also are performing poorly on lab assignments, quizzes, and tests. Jeremy is surprised by this behavior because he grew up thinking that Asians were gifted in science and math. He remembered hearing on the news that Asians were the "model minority." He volunteers to tutor them after school on several occasions, but none of them takes him up on his offer. He is aware that cultural differences, in part, may account for these students' unanticipated behaviors. He reflects about how he can address the situation in a culturally responsive manner. He relies on the cultural inquiry process model. (Can you recommend other approaches to Jeremy?)

1. Reflect on what you believe about cultural groups other than your own; how are they the same as or different from your own? What are the origins of your beliefs?

2. Ask, "Have my past social interactions and beliefs influenced my current thinking and actions toward these students?" If you answer yes, develop strategies to help you be more consciously aware of your thinking and actions when working with these students.

3. Ask the students why they do not ask for help in class or agree to stay after school for extra assistance.

4. Talk with their parents to gain additional insights about students' actions and intentions. Ask about transportation as a problem. Is language an issue? Are there customs, values, and/or mores within their culture that preclude requesting and receiving extra help?

5. Talk with other teachers who teach these students. Find out about the students' social behaviors and academic performance in these classes. If they are successful in other classes, ask your colleagues to identify the instructional strategies they use to produce this success. When possible, observe some of these teachers and have them observe you.

6. Check with your school's ESL staff to determine if the students' English proficiency levels have been determined through formal or informal language assessments. The students may be able to engage in basic conversational English but have not progressed to a point where they can comprehend material written at more abstract levels. If this is the case, you may need to alter presentation formats and procedures that will help concretize instructions and requirements for these students.

7. Attempt to identify patterns across environments that contribute to or detract from student growth.

8. Based on this analysis, develop strategies that may result in more desirable outcomes for these students. Create a process that will allow you to incorporate values and communicative styles that are more consistent with the values and communication styles of these students and their families. For example, you may learn from parents, students, or colleagues that, in some Asian cultures, asking for help from adults outside the family is embarrassing and shameful. Help is accepted more willingly when siblings and other peers mentor and teach. Initially, then, a peer tutoring program may be more effective than ongoing tutoring from the teacher.

9. Seek ongoing support and input from students, parents, and colleagues. Engage in continual monitoring and assessment of the strategies to determine if they are effective, if they need to be modified, or if they have created new problems.

10. Begin this cyclical process anew. Remember that it is best to collaborate with parents, students, and colleagues throughout the process. Moreover, their input must be acknowledged, valued, and incorporated into instructional activities and processes.

administrators, and a central office administrator to develop a curriculum-based measurement system to monitor student and teacher outcomes in an ongoing, systematic, and standardized manner (Marston, 1989).

After several weeks of designing probes parallel to statewide assessments and the district's curriculum, Trent, his colleagues, and the school-based team began collecting math curriculum-based measurement data on a weekly basis. The results from administration of the first probe revealed what was expected: the overwhelming majority of students performed significantly below the expected level of average fifth-grade students.

Instead of using this information to determine specific strengths and weaknesses and design more effective instructional interventions, some but not all of the educators attributed this performance to the students' intellectual deficits. These educators believed, therefore, that there was no need for them to develop alternative instructional approaches—the students' deficits were inherent in the students and not able to be changed. In their estimation, there was little they could do to improve the students' performance.

Trent made the point that transformation of teachers' beliefs, biases, and expectations and a commitment to change along the recommendations set out in this chapter are necessary for schools to create and sustain equitable educational practices for all students. Such equitable practices are a prerequisite in order to improve outcomes for students who are poor, from diverse backgrounds, and classified into special education because of their disabilities.

His work, and that of others, justifies you to pay close attention to the critical sociocultural factors that we have outlined in this chapter. If you do take those factors into account, and if you adopt the practices we have described, you will become a culturally competent teacher, one of many who use the practices to dispel the social reproduction of inequity in education.

Looking to Joesian's Future

Joesian's allies include his teachers in the learning disabilities program in his school in Brooklyn and in the trade school in Manhattan. Other allies include his parents, Norma and Joaqin; his sister, Tatiana, and brother, Juan; and his uncle, the plumber. And, of course, United We Stand of New York and the school administrator who recessed the due process hearing to open doors for Joesian.

Together these people seek the outcome that Joesian himself wants: the opportunity to enter his uncle's trade. Not just that, for, truth be told, Joesian would rather be a firefighter than answer any other calling, despite the tragedy of the 9/11 Twin Towers attack. He wants to enter a trade that helps people. He is an other-directed person, the willing translator, the eager apprentice, and the rejuvenated student. To help others entails practicing a useful trade.

The plumbing trade, however, is publicly licensed. To pass the license examination, the candidate must be able to read. In English.

There it is, at last. "In English." Not in a candidate's native language, such as, for Norma, Spanish. But in the language of commerce in America: English.

Nonreaders can expect not to pass. It is not clear that the licensing board accommodates candidates who have specific learning disabilities, but it is clear that it requires a candidate to read, write, and pass an examination in English.

Is that in itself an act of discrimination? It certainly reflects a cultural norm: business in America traditionally has been conducted in English.

But cultural norms may well reflect discrimination: the English-only examination will screen out candidates who could be good plumbers but who do not use English as their native language.

And thus culture will determine Joesian's future. Not by itself, for his other attributes will affect how he fares in school and in life. But its role is undeniable and large. It always has been, as in his education, and it always will be, as in his future as a worker. The question is always this: how do teachers and licensing-boards use culture and language—as a force for discrimination or not?

SUMMARY

Defining culture and its implications for special education

- Culture is "the customary beliefs, social forms, and material traits of a racial, religious, or social group; also: the characteristic features of everyday existence (as diversions or a way of life) shared by people in a place and time" (*Merriam-Webster's Collegiate Dictionary*, 2003, p. 304).

- In interactions with students, families, and other educators, it is important for teachers to observe the meanings, value, and influence of their own culture and other cultures.

- Educators should follow four aspects of culture in interpreting students' performances: group practices, the group's history, the student's life as set within that history, and the cultural aspects of the school or school district in which the student is enrolled.

- Culture is a reciprocal phenomenon; educators transmit it to their students, and their students, in turn, respond.

The social context of special education

- Before the enactment of IDEA, students' attributed insufficiencies were generally linked to their chromosomes and cultures through theories about genetic/cultural deficits and theories about cultural difference. Early in the 20th century tracking led to segregation as did placements in classrooms for students with mild mental retardation. Court cases (*Brown v. Board of Education* [1954]; *Diana v. Board of Education* [1973]) were instrumental in systemically addressing problems related to segregation. The National Research Council reported that there was disproportionate representation of students from culturally- and linguistically-diverse backgrounds in classes for students with mild mental retardation.

- The disproportionate representation in special education has been a consistent problem over the past couple of decades. The U.S. Department of Education (2003) has consistently found that schools with the highest percentage of limited-English, diverse-background, and low-income students are more likely to hire beginning teachers than are other schools.

- Educators should consider historical factors in order to avoid repeating the past unequal educational opportunity as they serve students with exceptionalities.

- The interactions between and among cultural groups over time has influenced how special education has been implemented in this country. These interactions must be considered when developing, implementing, and evaluating educational programs for minority students from diverse backgrounds.

Evaluating students from culturally- and linguistically-diverse backgrounds

- Prereferral teams should take into account the historical context of a student's background, in addition to the personal histories of team members, when making prereferral decisions for students from diverse backgrounds. One process for doing this is the cultural inquiry process.

Using strategies to help you instruct effectively

- The nondiscriminatory evaluation process should involve using culturally sensitive assessment tools, observing students in multiple settings, comparing the student's performance with same-age peers from the same cultural community, and determining both interpersonal communication skills and cognitive academic language proficiency when evaluating students from diverse linguistic backgrounds. Culturally responsive professional practice is a multidimensional notion that includes personal, technical (curriculum and instruction), and institutional dimensions.

- The personal dimension focuses on the teacher's own learning.
- The technical dimension includes pedagogical practices for ethnically-diverse students and linguistically-diverse students.
- The institutional dimension addresses equity issues as they relate to leadership, programmatic emphases, school climate, governance, and structural supports for learning (students, faculty, and families).

Including students from culturally- and linguistically-diverse backgrounds

- Partnerships among educators and with families are critically important in promoting successful inclusion of students from culturally- and linguistically-diverse backgrounds.
- Evaluation of effective inclusive education practices must take into account all the critical sociocultural factors we have addressed in this chapter.

Assessing students' progress in a culturally responsive manner

- Informal and alternative assessments must be used to monitor teacher and student performance.
- Curriculum-based measurement is an outcome measurement tool for evaluating students' performance in the efficacy of teachers' instructional practices.

WHAT WOULD YOU RECOMMEND?

Refer to chapter content and the PRAXIS™ and CEC standards in Appendix A to answer the following questions:

1. Think about your own teacher education preparation program. What could your program do to help you develop an awareness of cultural and linguistic diversity in ways that move beyond a primary focus on deficit theories of intelligence and learning? What PRAXIS™ or CEC standards are you applying as you answer this question?

2. What do you think would be major differences in instruction developed and implemented by culturally responsive teachers and those who are not? What PRAXIS™ or CEC standards are you applying as you consider your response?

3. View the segment on Briana on your DVD. Assume that you are a teacher who is part of Briana's multidisciplinary team. The team has been charged by your principal to create an assessment process that considers the home culture and parents' knowledge of their child's learning in the evaluation process to determine if special education is needed. How would you go about accomplishing this goal? What PRAXIS™ or CEC standards are you applying?

Use your DVD to answer this question.

There is a slogan within the U.S. Army that derives from the motto at the military academy at West Point: The slogan is "The needs of the Army override the needs of the individual soldier." The motto is "Duty, Honor, Country." Duty first. No quarrel about it.

Major Jamie Holley knows all about duty. He's both a career officer and an "army brat," the son of a career soldier. But he and his wife, Leia, know how hard it can be on a family to answer the call of duty, especially because one son Sean, now 12 years old, has autism and epilepsy, and their other son, JT, now 14 years old, has been classified as having learning disabilities yet is now in gifted education. Without a doubt, Sean's autism presents the greatest challenges to the Holleys and Sean's teachers.

Being a father with military obligations that conflict with parental obligations makes for some hard duty. The extra tours of duty that he has to take outside the United States—a year in Korea without his family, one year at home, and then another year in Europe, also without his family—are Jamie's payback to the Army for its consent that he and his family may stay where Sean and JT are receiving an excellent education, in Bonner Springs, Kansas, just a few miles down the road from Fort Leavenworth. These hardship tours are also his way of demonstrating a father's love for his family: he will forego the comfort of family for a year or more so that his family will reap the benefits of an appropriate education.

Just who are the members of the Holley family? Of course, there are Leia, Jamie, Sean, and JT. Sean's elementary-school teacher, Tierney Thompson, at Bonner Springs Elementary School, is a reliable ally but not quite a family member. And now that Sean has left that school and is enrolled at Robert E. Clark Middle School, Sean's teachers there are becoming closer than "just" professionals, but they are not yet true insiders. They are partners, but they have not been in the crucible that Leia and Tierney occupied together for almost a full school year. They don't have the combat ribbons that Leia and Tierney earned, often in opposition to each other but eventually as comrades in Sean's education.

A crucible is a place or situation in which concentrated forces interact to cause or influence change or development. For Leia and Tierney, the place was Sean's elementary school, and the situation revolved around two issues: first, was Sean receiving an appropriate education; and second, was he surrounded by a staff that was prepared to respond to life-threatening seizures?

Inside that crucible, Leia and Tierney were the concentrated forces. They started as allies, then became adversaries, and finally became partners, close enough to become family. Inside their own particular crucible, trust was broken and then re-created because Leia and Tierney committed themselves to Sean and each other, pledged to communicate with

candor but with civility, learned to respect each other's competence in raising and teaching Sean, agreed to advocate together for Sean and each other, and began to treat each other as equals.

The predictable results of their poor partnership were that Leia's (and the entire Holley family's) quality of life plummeted; so did Tierney's. Not surprisingly, Sean's education suffered, too. The predictable results of their repaired partnership were the opposite: quality of life and effective education soared.

Now that Sean is at Clark Middle School, there is no crucible at school, only the cool assurances from general educators that they want Sean in their classes. Their welcome is manifested through Sean's participation, with accommodations, in choir, science projects, a general education class, and swimming classes. Sean's special education teacher, paraprofessionals, and general education teachers, guided by Leia, now constitute more than the usual school-based team. They are partners, collaborating in planning and delivering an appropriate education; capitalizing on each other's strengths; and witnessing Sean's painfully slow but inevitable progress in communicating what he wants, complying with teacher requests, and making friends and earning the respect of his peers who do not have disabilities.

During Sean's transition from elementary to middle school, Jamie heard the call to duty once again: take another post, bring your family, and stay on the good side of the promotion list from major to colonel. Higher rank, more responsibility, and more money and benefits lay ahead. But to move ahead would be to leave behind the hard but eventually fruitful years at the elementary school and the fulfilling time at the middle school. Called to duty by two forces, "duty, honor, country" on the one hand and fatherhood on the other, Jamie struggled to resolve the conflict by visiting Clark Elementary School.

There, Sean's general education teachers persuaded him that his family simply had to stay put in Bonner Springs. They did not talk about Sean's disability so much as about his strengths; they made accommodations without celebrating themselves for doing so; and they said that Sean had made them better teachers than they had been before they had had him in their classes.

For Jamie, a man whose instincts were always toward duty, honor, and country, there was only one way to act. Accept the hardship tour overseas. Leave his family for another year. And repeat to himself, day after day, what he told Leia about his visit to Clark Elementary School: "I see now why you don't want to move. Sean doesn't have a disability there. We'll do what we have to do. I'll take the hardship post."

Families do hard duty for their children. Their performance of it, however, is easier to bear when their children's teachers and other professionals are their partners.

WHO ARE TODAY'S FAMILIES?

Defining Family

Who is in your family? Before answering, try to define the word *family* as it applies to you. Does it include only your blood relatives? Or in-laws? Or others, such as uncles, aunts, and grandparents? Or does it also include close friends? Even some teachers? In a word, just how nuclear or extended is your family? How much has your family changed in the past 10 years? What changes can you now project for the next 5 years? Answering these questions may prompt you to learn more about how others define *family*.

Many definitions exist. The U.S. Census Bureau defines *family* as a group of two or more people related by birth, marriage, or adoption who reside together (Iceland, 2000). To what extent does this definition fit your own family composition? Do all of the members of your family reside together? If "reside together" is a controlling element of the definition, how do we account for the fact that Major Holley has not resided with his family during some of his international tours of duty? Does "marriage" override "reside" when it comes to the Holleys?

Based on our research with families, we define **family** as two or more people who regard themselves to be a family and who carry out the functions that families typically perform (Poston et al., 2003). This means that people who do not reside together and who may not even be related by birth, marriage, or adoption qualify as family if they and others regard them as family members and if they carry out some of the various family functions that we will describe later in this chapter. Tierney is not a Holley family member; she is not related by blood or marriage and does not live with the Holleys. Yet she has contributed greatly to their emotional, physical, and disability-related quality of life.

Go to the Companion Website, *www.prenhall.com/turnbull,* for a link to the Turnbull's family textbook that also features the Holley family.

As an educator, you will find that your students have families whose composition is very different from your own. Some might have more than four grandparents because their biological grandparents have divorced and remarried. Others might have parents of the same gender or children who have not been adopted but whom they are raising. (**Kinship care** is the technical term.)

Traditionally, educators have communicated primarily with mothers of children with and without disabilities, having parent-teacher conferences, reporting progress, and being involved in school activities. But there may be other family members—even *many* other family members—who are willing and able to be involved in educating your students. It is good practice to ask the family member who is most involved with any student whether there are other family members with whom you should enter into a partnership in educating the student.

Including any interested family member in the partnership to educate students may mean going beyond immediate family members.

Demographics of Today's Families

Families of children with exceptionalities are not all that different from families whose children do not have special needs. A mother of two children, one with multiple disabilities and the other one without any disability, described her family as the universal family:

> I am the universal parent. . . . as such I have many joys, sorrows, fears, and questions. Deep inside I feel that I am "normal." I look around my home, and I observe my family, and I see us to be very "normal." We wake up in the morning, and we rush to get teeth brushed and hair combed in time to inhale Cream of Wheat before the bus arrives. I go about my routine as parent and provider and often momentarily forget that I am a parent of a child . . . [with a disability]. I love to party on Friday night, feel proud when the teacher says my child did well, get angry when the lawn mower won't start, and worry

Values: Family members can make *positive contributions* to students with disabilities. These contributions prepare the students to make their own positive contributions to others.

when I realize that my not-so-long-ago high school days happened 20 years ago (how could time pass so quickly). I have dreams of making a lot of money, fears of having more month than paycheck, and hopes of a brighter tomorrow. (Gerdel, 1986, p. 1)

Like the parents of children who are developing typically, parents of children who have various exceptionalities face the predictable challenges of family life: job changes (such as Jamie's) and loss, financial problems, physical and mental illnesses, substance abuse, child abuse, community violence, and uncertainty about the future. They also experience many of the joys of life: graduations, job promotions, vacations, birthday parties, weddings, and births.

Do not be misled into thinking that families of children with exceptionalities are all that similar to other families; in fact, they differ in many ways. As you learned in Chapter 3, these families, as a group, are disproportionately from racially-, ethnically-, culturally-, and linguistically-diverse populations and from lower socioeconomic subclasses.

Indeed, approximately 35 percent of students with disabilities come from a family where the annual income is less than $25,000; by contrast, only 20 percent of students without disabilities come from families earning less than $25,000 annually (U.S. Department of Education, 2002). Given the disproportionate rate of placement of African American students into special education, it is noteworthy that African Americans have been approximately 2.5 times more likely than European Americans to experience poverty (Fujiura & Yamaki, 2000). Poverty and race clearly correlate with each other.

In addition, approximately 22 percent of youth with disabilities come from a family where the head of the family household has less than a high school education (U.S. Department of Education, 2002). This number drops to approximately 13 percent for youth without disabilities.

Families of children with exceptionalities also differ from other families in terms of household composition. Figure 4–1 compares youth with and without disabilities in terms of parents living within the household, single-parent status, and the average number of children per family.

In Figure 4–1, you will note the discrepancy between youth with and without disabilities in terms of where both biological parents live, at home or not. The percentage of youth with disabilities living in a single-parent household is substantially higher than the percentage for youth without disabilities. Approximately one-third of youth with disabilities live in a single-parent household where the parent is a biological mother. Families headed by single-female parents have a particularly high poverty rate—almost 40 percent when a child in the family has a disability (Fujiura & Yamaki, 2000). Clearly, two characteristics contribute greatly to the likelihood that families will experience poverty: the presence of children (particularly more than one child)

Use your *Real Lives and Exceptionalities* DVD to see Barbara discussing her "forever family" (Clip 4) under "Meet Star." What are the joys and challenges Barbara faces with Star?

Figure 4–1 Household composition of youth with disabilities and youth in the general population

Individual Characteristics	Youth with Disabilities	Youth in the General Population
Percentage of households with		
No biological parents present	19	3
Biological father present	4	3
Biological mother present	35	21
Both biological parents present	42	73
Percentage living in a single-parent household	36	26
Average number of children in the household	3	2

Source: U.S. Department of Education (2002). *To assure the free appropriate public education of all children with disabilities: Twenty-fourth annual report to Congress on the implementation of the Individuals with Disabilities Act.* Washington, DC: Author.

On the Companion Website, *www.prenhall.com/turnbull*, you can find a link to the National Center for Children in Poverty, *http://www. nccp.org/*.

who have a disability and a single female parent as the head of the household. Throughout this chapter, we will point out how poverty and single-parent status can affect families' special challenges and how you and other educators can support families to address their priorities and needs.

WHAT ARE PARTNERSHIPS AND WHY ARE THEY IMPORTANT?

Defining Partnerships

As you learned in Chapter 3, the term *partnership* refers to a relationship involving joint responsibilities (Merriam-Webster, 2003). Jamie's responsibilities were clear to him: do as the Army tells you to do. But the Army's responsibilities to him also were clear: keep a good soldier by accommodating to his family's exceptional needs. Together, Jamie and the Army constituted a partnership.

In Chapter 1, you learned that both IDEA and NCLB set out the rights and responsibilities of educators with respect to other professionals, families, and students. Taken as a whole, these reciprocal rights and responsibilities mean that families and professionals should become partners in making decisions about a student's education.

What do we mean by **family-professional partnerships?** These are relationships in which families and professionals collaborate, capitalizing on each other's judgments and expertise in order to increase the benefits of education for students, families, and professionals (Turnbull, Turnbull, Erwin, & Soodak, 2006).

When Congress enacted the federal special education law in 1975 (the predecessor to IDEA), it gave rights to students and parents and expected parents to hold schools accountable for satisfying the students' and parents' rights (Turnbull, Turnbull, & Wheat, 1982). (We reviewed those rights in Chapter 1.) That is still one of the roles that parents play. But it is by no means the only one, especially nowadays. Partnerships also relate to a culture of trust, such as the connection that has developed between Leia and Sean's teachers, and to educational outcomes, such as Sean's development.

Importance of Partnerships

There are several reasons why partnerships are important. First, schools that foster partnerships among administrators, faculty, families, and students are more likely to have high levels of trust than are schools where partnerships are fragile or nonexistent (Hoy, 2002; Sweetland & Hoy, 2000). When trust exists, morale is better, the school climate is more positive, and problems are easier to solve. Second, student achievement in the elementary grades (Goddard, Sweetland, & Hoy, 2000), middle school grades (Sweetland & Hoy, 2000), and high school grades (Hoy & Tarter, 1997) is likely to be higher than it is in schools where partnerships and trust do not abound.

Student achievement increases when parents are partners with their children's educators. Three decades of research have documented many positive student outcomes associated with family participation in a child's education, including the following (Turnbull et al., 2006, p. 277):

Research tells us that family participation and support result in greater success in school and more positive attitudes in and out of the school environment.

■ Reading achievement (Chavkin, Gonzalez, & Rader, 2002; Faires, Nichols, & Rickelman, 2000; Hara & Burke, 1998; Shaver & Walls, 1998)

- Math achievement (Balli, Demo, & Wedman, 1998; Chavkin et al., 2002; Shaver & Walls, 1998)

- Positive attitudes toward school (Shumow & Miller, 2001)

- Attendance and school retention (Henderson & Berla, 1994)

- Homework completion (Balli, Demo, & Wedman, 1998; Callahan, Rademacher, & Hildreth, 1998)

- Positive behavior at home and school (Comer & Haynes, 1991; Sanders & Herting, 2000)

Third, it may well be that family-professional partnerships enhance families' quality of life. That certainly has been the case for the Holleys: the more they are able to trust Sean's teachers, the less emotional and physical stress they experience and the more their parenting and disability-related support increases. Research bears out the relationship between (on the one hand) early childhood services for children with disabilities that are delivered through quality family-professional partnerships and (on the other hand) enhanced family quality of life (Mannan, 2005). Think about that finding in these terms: you can boost families' quality of life when you are partners with them in educating their children.

Before you learn how you can form partnerships with families, you should learn about how children with exceptionalities affect their families. Learning how families adapt to their children can help you "walk in their shoes." And the more you walk in their shoes, the greater the chances are that you will understand their perspectives and become partners with them.

HOW DO CHILDREN WITH EXCEPTIONALITIES AFFECT THEIR FAMILIES' QUALITY OF LIFE, AND WHAT IS YOUR ROLE AS AN EDUCATOR?

Researchers have been documenting the impact of children with exceptionalities on their families for nearly 50 years. Most of the research has measured mothers' stress and depression (Singer, in press; Turnbull et al., 2006). The findings have been mixed. It does appear that, as compared with mothers of children without disabilities, those who have children with exceptionalities, particularly with problem behavior or intensive caregiving needs related to medical issues, experience greater stress (Baker et al., 2003; Hastings, Daley, Burns, & Beck, in press; Shapiro, Blacher, & Lopez, 1998). A recent comprehensive analysis of many research studies related to maternal depression concluded that approximately one-third of mothers of children with disabilities experienced depression as compared to about 18 percent of mothers who have children without disabilities (Singer, in press). That finding means, however, that approximately two-thirds of the mothers of children with disabilities do not experience depression.

More recently, we and our colleagues at the Beach Center on Disability at the University of Kansas investigated what "quality of life" means to families who have children with and without disabilities (Turnbull, Brown, & Turnbull, 2004). Using the families' descriptions, we concluded that **family quality of life** refers to the extent to which (1) the family's needs are met, (2) family members enjoy their life together, and (3) family members have a chance to do the things that are important to them (Park et al., 2003). Let's apply that definition to the Holley family: their needs are met by the schools and the Army; they enjoy their time together, however interrupted it may be by tours of duty overseas; and they have the chance to do the activities that are important to them—Leia to remain in Kansas as an advocate in the Kansas Parent and Training Center, Sean and JT to remain in effective schools, and Jamie to pursue his career and answer his call to duty.

Through both open-ended interviews with families and national surveys, we identified five **domains of family life** (Park et al., 2003; Poston et al., 2003; Summers et al., in press):

- Emotional well-being

- Parenting

- Family interaction

Using your *Real Lives and Exceptionalities* DVD, view clips, highlighted in orange, of each student's family. How are the families different? How are they the same?

■ Physical/material well-being

■ Disability-related support

We will briefly describe each of these domains in terms of the impact of children with exceptionalities on families and then suggest what you can do to support families through your partnerships with them. We will highlight only one family need in each domain.

Emotional Well-Being

Emotional well-being refers to the feelings or affective considerations within the family. Families experience better emotional well-being when they have the following:

■ Friends or others who provide support

■ The support they need to relieve stress

■ Some time to pursue their own interests

■ Outside help available to take care of the special needs of all family members

Families tend to report lower satisfaction on the domain of emotional well-being than on any of the other four domains (Jackson, 2004; Mannan, 2005). Consider, for example, the element of having "friends or others who provide support." Many families of children with exceptionalities worry because their children are lonely and generally lack friends (Turnbull & Ruef, 1997); that has been one of Leia's major concerns about Sean (Turnbull et al., 2006). In one research study, 40 percent of the mothers were worried that their children would be rejected by peers and that this rejection would cause their children to have problems with self-esteem (Guralnick, Conner, & Hammond, 1995).

Teachers report that they need to know more about fostering positive interactions among children with and without disabilities (Hamre-Nietupski, Henrickson, Nietupski, & Sasso, 1993; Hamre-Nietupski, Henrickson, Nietupski, & Shokoohi-Yekta, 1994). One effective approach is through the technique called **circle of friends,** an approach that worked wonders for Sean at his elementary school and that is still in effect in his middle school (Turnbull et al., 2006). Professionals or parents invite peers to form a support network for a student with a disability so the student will have friends (Falvey, Forest, Pearpoint, & Rosenberg, 2002). Research with elementary school students with emotional and behavior disorders found that the circle-of-friends approach increased their social acceptance within their classrooms (Frederickson & Turner, 2003).

In addition to families wanting their child with an exceptionality to have more friends, parents themselves may feel isolated and stigmatized by their child's disability. The research evidence is that parents of preschool children with disabilities tended to interact with equal frequency with parents of children with and without disabilities. However, parents of children without disabilities in the same classroom were less likely to interact with parents of children with disabilities than they were with parents of children without disabilities (Bailey & Winton, 1989). Moreover, parents of children without disabilities were more satisfied than parents with disabilities with their awareness about other families of children in the classroom.

Research also reveals that children with autism sometimes cause family members to feel embarrassed or isolated in public. One parent described the situation:

> One time I took George to the supermarket, and he kind of jumped up and down and rocked and hummed. He was laughing a lot, and a woman gave me a look. She wouldn't dare say anything, but she gave me a look almost to say, "Why would you bring a boy like that in here?" She didn't have to say anything. Her look told it all. (Turnbull & Ruef, 1996, p. 283)

Many families of children with exceptionalities appreciate it when teachers are available to them outside of regular work hours. Because many parents feel that others do not understand their child's needs, it can be especially helpful to have teachers' support. As one parent described her child's teacher: "She went as far as giving me her home phone number and told me whenever I feel depressed and need to call and just need to talk, I could always call her" (Lord-Nelson, Summers, & Turnbull, 2004, p. 158).

Values: Assisting students with disabilities to expand their *relationships* with their peers without disabilities can be a route toward their full citizenship in their schools and communities.

PRAXIS

Standard: When you recognize the needs of families and support them, you are addressing PRAXIS™ Standard 2, Legal and Societal Issues.

Many parents want educators to carry out their jobs with the attitude that it means more to them than "just a paycheck." Some parents even talked about wanting to have a family-like relationship or friendship with professionals working with their children. That occurs when educators participate in family events such as birthday parties, weddings, and funerals. An early childhood service provider commented:

> A lot of them [parents] do not have other supports. Their own family members, for whatever reasons, and they don't have neighbors that they feel like they can call on. So, I mean, if they see that, for six hours a day that their child is with us, and that yes, we love them and we're going to care for them . . . it's just a bond that we seem to make, not that we really set out to do that, but it just happens. It's just like we're an extension of their family. (Lord-Nelson et al., 2004, p. 160).

Do you think it is appropriate for educators to form family-like relationships, very close friendships, or both with their students' families, especially the families of students with exceptionalities? Box 4–1 provides an opportunity for you to explore both sides of this issue.

Parenting

A second domain of family quality of life is parenting—namely, those activities that adult family members do to help children grow and develop. This domain is strong when families do the following:

- Know how to help their child learn to be independent
- Know how to help their child with schoolwork and activities
- Know how to teach their child to get along with others
- Know how to have time to take care of the individual needs of every child

We will discuss "know[ing] how to help their child learn to be independent."

Your Own Voice ~ Crossing Boundaries or Not?   Box 4–1

You have just begun your first year as a teacher. Consistent with the practices you have learned in this book, you want to establish a trusting partnership with the parents of the students in your class, especially those who have disabilities or are at risk for disabilities, because you think that they and their parents will need more from you this year. You are willing to give whatever it takes, and you plan to tell the parents that when you meet with them at the beginning of the school year.

But then a veteran teacher cautions you not to invest too much in the parents. "The kids, not the parents, are your first concern," she reminds you. "And if you think the kids are tough," she says, "wait till you encounter some of their parents. You'll need all the recovery time you can get for yourself."

Her admonition causes you to ponder your choices. At one end of your range of choices is being "strictly professional" in working with the families, depersonalizing and keeping a distance and rigidly adhering to doing only the job of teaching the students. In the middle range of your choices is enlarging your obligations by doing some of the extras, such as telephoning other professionals who work with the child or family to advocate for certain evaluations or services or making home visits. At the other end of your range of choices is being "like family," establishing a relationship outside the professional context by attending their family gatherings and inviting them to your family-and-friend social events.

You seek guidance from the National Education Association and the Council for Exceptional Children but find that neither organization answers your question in its codes of ethics. You want to practice the seven partnership principles—communication, commitment, equality, professional skills, respect, advocacy, and trust—so you are inclined to disregard the veteran teacher's advice.

But you know that she has a good point: you have always needed your own time and space, even within the confines of your own family and friendship networks. Your solitude refreshes and harmonizes you; it allows you to synchronize your mind and emotions. In turn, you are more compatible with your family, friends, professional peers, and students. Yes, you are committed to enhancing your students' quality of life and their families'. But you've also got to look after your own quality of life.

Take a position on what you think the appropriate boundaries are between parents and professionals. Previously you read about a continuum of choice. Which choice is right for you?

For guidance, read the National Education Association's code of ethics, found at *www.nea.org/aboutnea/faq.html*. Also read the Council for Exceptional Children's code of ethics, found at *www.cec.sped.org/ps/code/html*. Finally, read Lord-Nelson, L. G., Summers, J. A., & Turnbull, A. P. (2004). Boundaries in family-professional relationships: Implications for special education. *Remedial and Special Education, 25*(3), 153–165.

Many children and youth with exceptionalities do not become independent at the same rate as their same-age peers. For example, children and youth with mental retardation, learning disabilities, and traumatic brain injury have a harder time making complex decisions and evaluating the outcomes of those decisions. Children and youth who are deaf will often have a harder time asserting themselves through communication with other family members and family friends. Children and youth with a health impairment may not have the stamina to engage in the same experiences as others of their same age. All of these factors can influence the extent to which these children learn to be independent and direct their own actions. Their delayed independence often causes their parents and other family members to assume more responsibility for them for longer periods of time. The Holleys will likely need to provide support for Sean for his entire life.

Educators can offer an antidote to delayed independence and longer-term family responsibility, and that antidote is education that teaches a child to be self-determined. (You will learn more about self-determination in other chapters, especially Chapter 9.) Teaching self-determination to children with mental retardation leads to long-term positive outcomes such as paid employment after high school, just as teaching it to students with other exceptionalities and to typically developing students makes them more effective adults (Algozzine, Browder, Karvonen, Test, & Wood, 2001).

Self-determination means "acting as the primary causal agent in one's life and making choices and decisions regarding one's quality of life free from undue external influence or interference" (Wehmeyer, 1996, p. 24). There are four characteristics of self-determined behavior:

- The student acts autonomously.

- The student's behavior is self-regulated.

- The student acts in a psychologically empowered manner in initiating and responding to events.

- The student acts in a self-realizing manner.

Self-determined individuals have been described as follows:

> They know what they want and how to get it. From an awareness of personal needs, self-determined individuals achieve goals, and then doggedly pursue them. This involves asserting an individual's presence, making his or her needs known, evaluating progress for meeting goals, adjusting performance, and creating unique approaches to solve problems. (Martin & Marshall, 1995, p. 147)

As you will learn in other chapters, many children and youth with exceptionalities would experience more success inside and outside the classroom if they were more self-determined. Too often, problem behavior in the classroom is caused by students who do not know how to make choices, create and implement their own action plans, and monitor their own performance. In addition, many parents of individuals with exceptionalities experience distress in their homes, neighborhoods, and community settings because their children have problem behaviors associated with a lack of self-determination (Turnbull & Ruef, 1997). Figure 4–2 includes tips you can share with families for supporting their children to be self-determined.

Family Interaction

The quality-of-life domain called family interaction focuses on the relationships among family members. Children with exceptionalities affect every other member of their family—with the emphasis on "every." Their effect on the entire family is interactive, just as a mobile is:

> In a mobile all the pieces, no matter what size or shape, can be grouped together and balanced by shortening or lengthening the strings attached or rearranging the distance between the pieces. So it is with the family. None of the family members is identical to any others; they are all different and at different levels of growth. As in a mobile, you can't arrange one without thinking of the other. (Satir, 1972, pp. 119–120)

Think of the Holleys as a mobile: Jamie's duty to the Army and his family, Leia's duty as an advocate for her children and others, and Sean's and JT's rights to an appropriate education. All of these factors interact among all four members. Families who have high levels of family interaction

On the Companion Website, *www.prenhall.com/turnbull*, you can find a link to many research studies carried out by Dr. Wehmeyer, a national leader in self-determination for students with disabilities: *http://www.beachcenter.org/PBSBlueprint.asp*.

Council for Exceptional Children

Standard: When you teach students to be more self-directed, you are applying CEC Standard 5, Learning Environments and Social Interactions.

Figure 4–2 Tips for families for promoting self-determination

1. **Autonomy:** the process of developing a personal identity and taking action consistent with one's personal identity.
   • Create opportunities for your child to explore different interests related to toys, games, preferred people, and preferred settings.
   • Capitalize upon your child's unique interest in terms of developing one or more hobbies.
2. **Self-regulation:** making decisions or implementing plans about what to do and how to do it and then evaluating the outcomes of one's actions.
   • Develop routines at home (such as mealtimes and getting ready for bed) so that children will know what to anticipate.
   • Ask children questions to encourage them to reflect upon what they want to do, why they want to do it, and what they think the best process will be for accomplishing their goals.
3. **Psychological empowerment:** our own belief that we can take action to get what we want and need.
   • Encourage your child to overcome a particular fear by trying a new experience.
   • Encourage your child to take initiative in planning recreation rather than always relying on others to lead the way.
4. **Self-realization:** a keen understanding of one's preferences, strengths, and limitations.
   • Encourage your child to assist others in areas of his or her strengths.
   • Provide honest and candid feedback to your child to help him or her gain insight into personal strengths and needs.

Source: Adapted from Shogren, K. A., & Turnbull, A. P. (in press). Promoting self-determination in young children with disabilities: The critical role of families. *Infants and Young Children.*

■ Enjoy spending time together

■ Talk openly with each other

■ Solve problems together

■ Show they love and care for each other

A question we posed at the beginning of this chapter bears repeating: who are the members of your students' families? As you answer that question for each family, pay special attention to the effect of exceptionality on the siblings of the child with the exceptionality. Research has documented both negative and positive impacts. In terms of negative impacts, some studies have found that brothers and sisters in a family that has a child with a disability tend to have a higher incidence of their own emotional/behavioral problems (Fisman, Wolf, Ellison, & Freeman, 2000; Orsillo, McCaffrey, & Fisher, 1993). Some sibling problems can include embarrassment, guilt, isolation, resentment, increased responsibility, and increased pressure to achieve. When Kate Turnbull, the younger daughter of two of this book's authors, was in second grade, she shared the following feelings related to embarrassment concerning her older brother, Jay, who has mental retardation, autism, and a bipolar disorder:

Jay embarrasses me sometimes like when he has such a loud voice in movie theatres. He says loudly, "Don't talk, Jay." His voice is so loud that lots of people stare at us. I kinda bend down . . . because I'm really embarrassed that everyone is looking at me. They're probably saying, "What, who said that? Maybe some 'wacko' or something." And it really makes me feel mad when they think my brother is a 'wacko.' I try to teach Jay not to do that. Every time he does, I say, "Jay, be quiet." I kinda elbow him softly and go, "Now, Jay, quiet down, please," and then I feel better. (personal communication, 1985)

But brothers and sisters also often experience positive contributions. They develop problem-solving skills, empathy, the ability to advocate, a capacity for understanding and seeking social justice, and, researchers conclude, a greater sense of self-directedness (Burton & Parks, 1994).

To see an example of a sibling talking about her relationship with her brother Ryan, go to the *Real Lives and Exceptionalities* DVD and view Clip 5 under "Meet Ryan."

Kate, whom we just quoted, also characterized one of her brother's positive contributions, writing in the 11th grade as follows:

> Jay's many accomplishments and my parents' struggle have taught me to have great expectations for *myself*. If Jay, with his problems, can face his challenges with courage and a sense of optimism, then so can I. Jay's lesson is a universal one: we all have the capacity for human greatness. (Turnbull, 1997, pp. 91–92)

Kate's perspectives are typical: the child with a disability offers challenges and benefits to all family members (Turnbull et al., 2006). That is one reason why it is helpful for family members, including siblings, to have opportunities to reflect on their conflicting feelings and to know how to respond to them in the most constructive way. "Sibshops" are helpful resources for brothers and sisters. Sibshops are workshop-based support programs for brothers and sisters of children and youth with exceptionalities (Meyer & Vadasy, 1994), offering them the chance to share their feelings and gather information about the special needs of their brother or sister.

As an educator, you might want to consider how you could provide siblings with information. And you should bear in mind that siblings can give you some good advice about how to provide an appropriate education to their brother or sister, including offering insight into how to include them in school and other activities (Gallagher et al., 2000).

Visit the Companion Website, *www.prenhall.com/turnbull*, for a link to a description of sibshops, *www.thearc.org/siblingsupport/sibshops-about.*

Physical/Material Well-Being

The fourth domain of family quality of life involves physical and material well-being—namely, the resources available to the family to meet its members' needs. Family quality of life is enhanced when families

- Have transportation to get to the places they need to be
- Have a way to take care of expenses
- Feel safe at home, work, and school and in the neighborhood
- Get medical and dental help when needed

Family resources often largely depend upon family income; yet as you learned previously in the chapter, families of children with disabilities are more likely than families of children without disabilities to experience poverty (Fujiura & Yamaki, 2000). The odds that a student will receive special education services are one-and-a-half times greater for children living in poverty than for those whose families avoid poverty. Some educational effects that have been associated with poverty include the following:

- IQ scores are 5–13 points lower for children living in poverty as contrasted with children who do not live in poverty (Kaiser & Delaney, 1996; Korenman, Miller, & Sjaastad, 1995).
- Families living in poverty are more likely to have children who are late to develop their vocabularies and thus to be able to read (Hart & Risley, 1995).
- Families in the top 20 percent of family income have children with a 2 percent high school dropout rate, middle-income families have children with a 5 percent dropout rate, and families from the bottom 20 percent of the income distribution have children with an 11 percent dropout rate—five times higher than families in the top income bracket (Kaufman, Kwon, Klein, & Chapman, 2000).

What does all of this information about poverty have to do with you as a teacher? There are an extensive number of educational impacts related to poverty, but the one we will highlight here is the capacity of families from poverty backgrounds to attend school activities and teacher-parent conferences. A parent described her financial situation as follows:

> If you have no money, it's very difficult to be—to do—to be together, to do fun things, to be at peace, to come home to a haven. . . . Because if you have no money, the bills not paid, you're not gonna rest when you get home. You might have a good family, you know, a good husband, whatever, whatever. But, you don't have money, all that can go down the drain, so. . . . Money provides a way of release. You can go on a vacation,

maybe, once a year, whereas if you don't have the money, you won't be able to do that. And when you can't do those things, you have this feeling of insecurity which floods over into other problems, emotionally. Anger, bitterness, and then it jumps off on the other family members and you got chaos. (Beach Center, 1999)

Consider what it might be like for the mother who shared this perspective to attend school activities and teacher-parent conferences. How might her lack of financial resources affect her opportunity to be at evaluation and IEP meetings, other teacher-parent conferences, and various school events? What about transportation, clothing, child care for their other children at home, self-confidence to interact with educators and other parents, and the ability to get time off from a low-paying job? When parents do not attend school meetings or events, some educators may detect a lack of interest and concern for the child, but the truth is that lack of financial resources is a major barrier.

Families from poverty backgrounds have numerous barriers that interfere with their ability to participate fully in school activities and teacher-parent conferences.

You can help remove barriers by working with other educators in your school, student service clubs at the high school, or other community resources to help arrange child care during school activities and transportation assistance. You might also meet with the family in their home or in a setting in their neighborhood such as a recreational center or a library (Jordan, Reyes-Blanes, Peel, Peel, & Lane, 1998).

When families who experience poverty attend school events, let them know how much you value their presence and show your respect for them, treat them with dignity, and manifest your appreciation. School counselors and social workers can be helpful in making sure that families know about community resources and economic support related to their children's disabilities, including benefits under the Social Security Act such as Supplemental Security Income and Medicaid (Turnbull et al., 2006).

Standard: When you recognize the impact of poverty on opportunities for families and their children, you are addressing CEC Standard 6, Communication.

Council for Exceptional Children

Disability-Related Support

The fifth and final domain of family quality of life is disability-related support—namely, support from family members and others to benefit the person with a disability. Among the aspects of disability-related support are those targeted toward the individual with a disability:

- Achieve goals at school or work
- Make progress at home
- Make friends
- Have a good relationship between the family and service providers

What does it mean to have support to "achieve goals at school and work"? A recent national random-sample survey of more than 500 parents of children in special education reported the following results (Johnson, Duffett, Farkas, & Wilson, 2002, p. 23):

- Forty-five percent of parents believe their child's special education program is failing or needs improvement to prepare him or her for life after high school.
- Thirty-five percent believe their child's special education program is failing or needs improvement to be a reliable source of information about learning problems and disabilities.
- Thirty-five percent report they were frustrated in seeking special education services their child needed.
- Thirty-three percent believe their child's current school is doing a fair or poor job when it comes to giving their child the help that they need.

To meet a university professor with an exceptionality who went through the educational system before PL 94-142, visit "Maxine" (Clip 3, under "Beyond School") on the *Real Lives and Exceptionalities* DVD.

As early as 1972, parents and their skilled civil rights lawyers persuaded federal courts in Pennsylvania and the District of Columbia that their children have a constitutional right to go to school (*Mills. v. DC Board of Education*, 1972; *PARC v. Commonwealth*, 1971, 1972). Armed with these victories, parents then persuaded Congress to put some teeth behind that right to education; the result of their advocacy was, of course, IDEA (Turnbull, Turnbull, Stowe, & Wilcox, 2000).

When state and local educational agencies were reluctant or unable to discharge their duty to educate children with disabilities, parents sued. Sometimes they got what they wanted, such as clean intermittent catheterization (*Irving Independent School District v. Tatro*, 1984) or school nursing services (*Cedar Rapids v. Garrett F.*, 1999). Sometimes they did not get what they wanted (such as an interpreter) but instead benefited from a decision holding that the state and local agencies must provide some benefits to the students and cannot get away with simply opening the schoolhouse doors and admitting them to the building (*Board of Education v. Rowley*, 1982).

One indication that parents are concerned about special education comes from research concluding that approximately 16 percent of parents reported that they have considered legal action because of the lack of quality in their child's special education program (Johnson et al., 2002). Thirty-one percent of parents of children with severe disabilities indicated that they had considered suing, as contrasted with 13 percent of students with mild disabilities. There is no question about the fact that Leia Holley considered suing the Bonner Springs schools when Sean was in elementary school and that her threats caused Sean's teachers to react negatively (Turnbull et al., 2006). Although major system change in special education has often resulted from lawsuits, many parents cannot afford to hire a lawyer. A parent commented about the need for financial resources in order to pursue legal remedies:

> You have no rights actually unless you're wealthy enough to defend yourself in court. That's what it boils down to. If you have the money to challenge the system, they don't care about your complaining; they don't care that you're unhappy. You can sit in the IEP meeting, fine, so what are you gonna do about it? Like, "We're not doing what you want, Ms. C, what ARE you gonna do about it? Unless you take us to court, we're finished talking to you." So, now the laws are only in place to defend the people who are wealthy enough to hire an attorney and take them to court over that. (Beach Center, 1999)

Although the data show that approximately one-third of parents of children with disabilities are dissatisfied with the special education program attended by their child, the data also show that approximately two-thirds of parents are generally satisfied, in large part because of the way teachers become partners with the parents. One parent expressed this perspective:

> The last two years have been like in a dream world. It is like I want to call them up and say, "You do not have nothing negative to say?" This educational system—this school itself has worked wonders with my son. It has taken a lot of stress off ME, so that when I go home, I do not have to get into it with him and say, "Oh, you know, the school called me today about this and that." They will call me, but they have already worked it out. Or they will call me to praise him and tell me how wonderful and how positive a role model he is now, and it's because they have worked with us. It is like I said, it has been a dream world to me. (Beach Center, 2000)

When parents are dissatisfied with their child's education, they, like Leia Holley, often become advocates for their children and for others, too. Indeed, they are more likely to be advocates than are parents of children and youth with typically developing children (Fiedler, 2000). Many families, however, would prefer to be partners with educators, not advocates; like Leia, they would prefer not to have to engage in systems reform, pushing and prodding educators to provide an appropriate education for their child. A recent study of parental perspectives related to advocacy revealed the underlying hostility that comes from dashed expectations and broken partnerships; parents often used words and phrases such as *fighting, ammunition, being armed,* or *gun*. For example, one parent commented:

> Ninety-five percent of the time was a fight. . . . it's the parents who have to, the parents have to prove why they think their child needs the service, and I don't think that's the way it should be. (Wang, Mannan, Poston, Turnbull, & Summers, 2004, p. 148)

Another parent commented, "But, you know, it is really unfortunate that you have to pull out those kinds of guns" (p. 148).

Parents sometimes complain that educators are not adequately trained to deal with the challenges associated with some exceptionalities. For example, a parent described the following situation related to the competence of a paraprofessional:

> Because K's teacher was late or she was coming a half-day, the school is calling me to see if I could pick K up because the "aide is nervous" . . . that's exactly what they said—"the aide is nervous" and [K's teacher] wants to do a lot of work. You know, and I couldn't believe that the school was calling me. And I told them no—first of all I asked them, "Is she okay? Is she ill?" "She's not ill." "Did she hit anybody?" "She didn't hit anybody." "Well, what are you telling me?" She wanted to do a lot of work that the aide could not do. . . . I said, "No, she needs to stay in school." (Wang et al., 2004, p. 150)

To make a positive contribution to a family's quality of life, you can provide such excellent services that parents do not need to become advocates against you or your colleagues. In short, you can become a trusted partner.

Values: When you comply with the IDEA requirements for a free appropriate education, you offer your students an opportunity to be *full citizens* in the sense that they have equal opportunities for an education, to be economically self-sufficient, to live independently, and to fully participate in their communities.

How Can You Form Partnerships with Families?

We have defined a *partnership* as a relationship in which families and professionals collaborate with each other by capitalizing on each other's judgments and expertise in order to increase benefits for students, families, and professionals (Turnbull et al., 2006). We also identified several positive outcomes of partnerships, including a trusting school climate, improved student achievement, and positive influences on family quality-of-life outcomes. And we discussed the challenges facing families in terms of their quality of life and how you can make a difference, minimizing problems and maximizing positive outcomes. So how can you develop and carry out your partnerships with families?

Partnerships build on the strengths, talents, resources, and expertise of educators, families, and others who are committed to making a positive difference in the lives of children and youth with exceptionalities. Figure 4–3 illustrates the seven principles of partnerships, using the structure of an arch (Turnbull et al., 2006). On each side of the arch, there are three partnership principles, and trust, the final partnership principle, is the arch's keystone. A keystone is the wedge-shaped piece in the arch's crown that secures other pieces in place (Merriam-Webster, 1996). Trust is the partnership principle that brings all of the other principles together.

Why is an arch an appropriate illustration of the seven partnership principles that lead to good outcomes for students, families, teachers, and other professionals? The answer lies in the purpose that an arch serves. Think of the students, their families, and the professionals as following a path through an arch; think of Sean Holley and his path, with Leia and Tierney Thompson, through elementary school. The path is education; the arch denotes the school. At the front of the arch is Sean's life before school, under the arch is the time when Sean is in school, and behind the arch is Sean's life after school. Students such as Sean, families such as the Holleys, and professionals such as Tierney Thompson follow the path of education with each other, through the arch and education, to life beyond school. In the illustration, you see them together, on top of the arch, partway through school, for Sean has just started middle school, still working as partners.

In the best of worlds, educators, parents, and students embark on this journey in partnership with each other. And during their journey they learn to trust each other. They know that none of the six other partnership principles is, alone, sufficient to sustain them. They must trust each other throughout the journey.

Without trust, the partnership is weak or may not even exist. With trust, the partnership remains strong and can sustain them; they can move along the path of education, in partnership with each other, to a life beyond school that is shaped by what happens during the school years. They can move together, on parallel paths, through school to outcomes. But they cannot do it well and joyously without trusting each other (Turnbull et al., 2006).

Figure 4-3 The arch and its seven partnership principles

Each of the seven principles has three to five key practices associated with it. We will high-light only one practice for each principle. Our book about families, professionals, and partner-ships will tell you more (Turnbull et al., 2006).

Communication

The first partnership principle is communication—namely, the verbal, nonverbal, or written messages that partners exchange among themselves. Following are five practices for effective communication (Blue-Banning, Summers, Frankland, Nelson, & Beegle, 2004):

- Be friendly
- Listen
- Be clear
- Be honest
- Provide and coordinate information

In terms of providing and coordinating information, families appreciate it when profession-als provide information to them about current services, possible future services, the nature of their child's exceptionality, community resources, and their legal rights (Park, Turnbull, & Park, 2001; Ruef & Turnbull, 2001; Shapiro, Monzo, Rueda, Gomez, & Blacher, 2004). You may believe that you alone do not know all that you need to know about the topics around which families have questions. The good news for families and yourself is that there are three major national networks of parent programs that provide information directly to families and to professionals as well.

Into Practice ~ Parent Training and Information Centers   Box 4–2

When you are a teacher in special or general education, you have some "string" to guide you through the maze of school programs for students, whether they have any exceptional needs or not. That string is your training and your colleagues' assistance.

But if you are a parent of a child with a disability, especially if you are coming into special education for the first time, you have to find your "string" because you almost never have any training or much assistance from other people.

Guiding parents through the maze is exactly what the Kansas Parent Training and Information Center, Families Together, does says its director, Connie Zienkewicz. In that respect, it is nearly identical to the Parent Training and Information Centers that exist in every other state. (Some states have more than one.) "We have families standing by who have the experience and expertise to help other families," Connie proclaims, citing Leia Holley as an example of the PTI staff available to families in eastern Kansas.

Families Together provides statewide coverage, family experience, training by experts (families and professionals, alike), and knowledge of local situations. Like other PTI centers and like the Community Parent Resource Centers exemplified by United We Stand of New York (Box 4–3), Families Together supports parents to understand their children's disabilities and

related needs, communicate more effectively with school and other professionals, participate in evaluation and IEP meetings, and connect with advocacy and professional associations related to their child's disability.

Putting These Strategies to Work for Progress in the General Curriculum

1. Locate the name, address, telephone, fax, website, and e-mail address for your state's Parent Training and Information (PTI) center, for any Community Parent Resource Centers (CPRCs) in your state, and for your state's Protection and Advocacy (P&A) agency.

2. Develop a one-page handout that lists that information. Distribute the handout to your students' families. Keep extra copies for yourself, the school secretary, and other special education staff to distribute.

3. Send an e-mail to your state's PTI and ask them to put your name on their mailing list. When the material comes in the mail, pay special attention to it.

To learn more about PTIs, CPRCs, and P&A agencies, go to the Into Practice module in Chapter 4 of the Companion Website, www.prenhall.com/turnbull.

The first network is Parent Training and Information Centers. There are approximately 107 Parent Training and Information Centers (PTIs) funded by the U.S. Department of Education. These centers support parents to be effective educational decision makers. Leia Holley works for the Kansas Parent Training and Information Center and is responsible for its work in eastern Kansas. Box 4–2 describes the Parent Training and Information Center network and its various resources. We encourage you to sign up for the mailings of your state's PTI and participate in its training activities.

The second national network consists of the Community Parent Resource Centers. These centers, also funded by the U.S. Department of Education, serve communities characterized by cultural and linguistic diversity. They offer one-on-one assistance to families, translate written information into the families' native language, and help professionals be culturally responsive partners with families. Box 4–3 describes one of these programs, United We Stand of New York, and its supports and services for Latino families. Do you recognize this program? It's the one that helped Joesian (from Chapter 3) and his mother, Norma, secure their educational rights by getting an independent evaluation and having a due process hearing.

The third national network consists of Parent to Parent programs, now located in more than two-thirds of the states. Parent to Parent provides a one-to-one match between a veteran parent, a person who has had experience with a challenging issue associated with disability, and a parent who is just beginning to experience the challenge. The supportive veteran parent offers emotional support and information, so the new one learns from an experienced person. A veteran parent has described her journey from being a new, learning parent to being a veteran, supporting parent:

> When our son with Down syndrome was born three years ago, my husband and I were shocked and devastated. We called our Parent to Parent program, which supplied us with invaluable information, as well as sending us a "support couple" to talk with. It was important to us to meet with the couple—not just the mother—since my husband takes as much responsibility for caring for our children as I do. Also important was that we were matched with a couple whose child had also been through open heart surgery (our son had major defects). The couple that our Parent to Parent program sent us were such warm, optimistic, "normal" people, they gave us hope. About a year later, my husband

Visit the Companion Website, *www.prenhall.com/turnbull*, for connection to a map giving the locations of all the Parent Training and Information Centers, *www. taalliance.org*.

On the Companion Website, *www.prenhall.com/turnbull*, you will find a link to the Beach Center's website that has a Parent to Parent map and Parent to Parent research articles, *www. beachcenter.org*.

Diversity Tips ~ Learning Best Practices from United We Stand   Box 4–3

They call it "the Big Apple." They also call it "the Melting Pot of the World." Of course, we're talking about New York City— the five boroughs, including Brooklyn and Manhattan. And what a melting pot New York is. Its white, non-Latino population declined from 43 percent in 1990 to 35 percent in 2000, with Latino and Asian populations increasing the most. In 2000, 48 percent of its population over age 5 spoke a language other than English in their homes, an increase from 41 percent in 1990. Less than 25 percent of all children under age 18 are non-white Latinos; 29 percent are black non-Latinos; and 34 percent are of Latino origin. A large majority of the students receive free lunches, indicating that their families meet federal poverty criteria. And special education enrollment and English-as-a-second-language enrollment rise annually.

United We Stand of New York (UWS/NY) is an ally to the families and students whose culture, language, poverty, and disability create barriers to implementing IDEA's six principles of zero reject, nondiscriminatory evaluations, appropriate education, placement in the least restrictive environment, procedural due process, and parent and student participation. Founded in 1990 by three parents of students with disabilities,

Lourdes Rivera-Putz, Carmen Morales, and Thelma Ragland, UWS/NY staff provide a wide range of services:

- Training and information to parents (in their native languages) about IDEA and NCLB
- Follow-up group training with individualized support and guidance
- Transportation and child-care services so parents can attend trainings or school-called meetings
- Attendance at evaluation and IEP meetings and at mediation and due process hearings
- Referral to professional evaluators and providers who are independent of the public school system
- Advocacy for families to receive other federal and state benefits from health, mental health, social service, and justice-system providers

For additional resources, see Turnbull, A., Turnbull, R., Erwin, E., and Soodak, L. (2006). *Families, professionals, and exceptionality: Positive outcomes through partnership and trust.* Upper Saddle River, NJ: Merrill/Prentice Hall.

and I were trained by our program to be support parents. The Parent to Parent office has many requests for visits from both father and mother. My husband was one of very few men willing to go through formal training. I have also found that support for non-English speaking families is hard to come by. It has been satisfying to me to be able to serve the Spanish-speaking community. (Beach Center, 1999)

We encourage you to find out about state and local Parent to Parent programs near you, refer parents to them, and even attend their conferences and workshops. Indeed, we encourage you to acknowledge that one of your key roles is to be knowledgeable about all sorts of resources so that you can recommend them to families and benefit from them yourself.

Professional Competence

The second partnership principle is professional competence—namely, being highly qualified for one's professional role. There are three practices associated with professional competence within family-professional partnerships (Blue-Banning et al., 2004):

- Providing a quality education
- Continuing to learn
- Setting high expectations

As you learned in Chapter 1, both IDEA and NCLB declare that educators should have high expectations for all students and should hold all students to high standards for their educational, developmental, and functional outcomes. In Chapter 2, you learned about standards-based assessment and the importance of determining just how much progress students with disabilities are making in the general curriculum.

It is never too early to set high expectations for students and convey those expectations to the students themselves and to their families. The sooner you start talking about desirable outcomes, the sooner you will launch the families into developing a vision for the future and plans to make that vision come true. We encourage you to read the perspective of Nina Zuna, now a doctoral candidate in special education at the University of Kansas and formerly a teacher of students with severe disabilities. In Figure 4–4, Nina describes some challenges she faced during her first year of teaching—challenges related to her professional competence and her high expectations for students. What tips for your own first year of teaching do you find in Nina's narrative?

Figure 4–4   Perspectives on professional competence

My first year as a teacher was filled with many learning experiences. I will share with you one of the greatest lessons I learned that year: professional competence is an all-encompassing phenomenon. As I reflect upon my experiences, I now realize it is impossible to be professionally competent unless you believe in your abilities and are a confident decision maker. So much of the success of our students depends upon our own success as teachers. How competent I felt as a teacher had a profound impact on my relationships with both my peers and the parents of the children I served.

While a student teacher and a beginning teaching professional, I taught several students with rare disabilities. At first, I felt very guilty because I had not heard of their disabilities. Several thoughts and questions circulated in my mind. Perhaps I hadn't studied enough while a student. Why hadn't I heard of these disabilities? Would the parents think I was incompetent to teach their child? Admitting lack of knowledge was my first step, and deep down I knew it was the right thing to do. Upon confiding in the parents, I found my fears were unwarranted. I was not chastised for my ignorance, and oftentimes, the parents were still learning about their child too. They appreciated my honesty and were eager to share with me knowledge about their child and also their frustrations about sometimes just not knowing what to do.

Personally, I had to accept that it was unrealistic for me to have a full understanding of all the possible disabilities that exist. While my education degree provided me with a good foundation of best practices, I realized it had not prepared me for every possible teaching opportunity. It was now up to me to continue my professional growth so I could provide the best services for my new students. As a professional, I had to be comfortable with learning as I went along. I had to be confident as I shared information with peers, parents, and paraprofessionals, and I had to trust the decisions I made. What was most important, though, was how the parents made me feel—they valued my judgment and my teaching expertise despite my not knowing about their child's specific disability. I believe this was possible because my outside persona represented confidence.

The partnerships I had with families seemed to click much more easily than those I shared with professionals. I was very comfortable conversing with parents and being an advocate for all of my students, but sometimes this stance negatively impacted my relationships with my peers. I thought of my students as my own children, so my goals, hopes, and dreams were in line with those of their parents. I never gave up hope of progress despite some of the negative research reported, especially the research surrounding autism. My unabashed optimism and willingness to try new things was sometimes met with skepticism from my peers. At times I felt challenged during interchanges to defend my actions, while at other times, I could sense that my peers felt that I challenged their work too. In this mode, we were no longer focused on producing the best educational outcomes for the child but were instead embroiled in a competition of purporting ideas or ideological viewpoints. This situation illustrates just how expansive the concept of professional competence is. Professional competence includes not only knowing your content area but also knowing how to apply good partnership skills. This represented an area of growth for me. I had to work on my interpersonal skills, diplomacy, and patience to ensure that my partnerships with my peers were productive and respectful.

Many individuals immediately associate professional competence with earning continuing education or professional development units, but this alone does not ensure professional competence. Professional competence also entails how you view yourself as a professional and the image you project to others as a professional. Sometimes I think we all get so bogged down with our numerous professional development classes that we forget that one of the simplest ways to improve our performance is to improve our confidence and well-being and the well-being of those around us. There is always something to improve upon, even if it is as simple as smiling at those with whom you work. Ensuring continued professional growth is a daily job. My most valuable learning experience was connecting my academic professional growth with my personal growth. The greatest wisdom is not learned from books alone.

Nina Zuna
Lawrence, Kansas

Source: Adapted from Turnbull, A. P., Turnbull, R., Erwin, E., & Soodak, L. (2006). *Families, professionals, and exceptionality: Positive outcomes through partnerships and trust* (5th ed.). Upper Saddle River, NJ: Merrill/Prentice Hall.

Respect

The third partnership principle is respect—namely, that each partner regards all others with esteem and communicates that esteem through actions and words (Blue-Banning et al., 2004). Professionals who demonstrate respect

- Honor cultural diversity
- Affirm strengths
- Treat students and families with dignity

In Chapter 3, you learned key practices for honoring cultural diversity. We encourage you to recognize the strong link between the material in Chapter 3 and this partnership principle of respect.

A fundamental aspect of demonstrating respect and esteem for others is to recognize, value, and affirm their strengths. A parent describes how painful it is when educators do not affirm her daughter's strengths:

> I often think if [school staff] could do one-on-one instead of [coming] with five people, telling me Susie can't do this, and Susie can't do that, and Susie can't this, and Susie can't that. And I am thinking, What about "Susie *can* do this and Susie *can* do that"? (Lake & Billingsley, 2000, p. 245)

This parent's first recommendation is to think about the numbers that occur in meetings. In her case, there were five professionals and just one of her! It is easy to see how she could feel outnumbered. Her second recommendation is that the teachers not identify her daughter's needs without identifying her strengths. Take the "shoes test" with this parent. Picture yourself in a meeting with five of your current or past teachers; each is highlighting what you are not able to do. How would you feel, and what impact would such a meeting have on your own self-esteem? Although Susie obviously has many needs, certainly she has strengths as well. The more you communicate about strengths, the more you will encourage parents to talk about their children's needs.

Values: When you build on a student's strengths, you enable the student and family to begin to envision great expectations.

Commitment

The fourth partnership principle is commitment. Commitment occurs when partners feel loyalty to each other, but it is hard to achieve when parents and educators believe that the only reason they are working together is because the law compels them to do so. A committed professional will

- Be available and accessible
- Go above and beyond
- Be sensitive to emotional needs

Professionals who are available and accessible seek to arrange their schedule so that students and families can communicate with them. Sometimes this means attending meetings that are important in terms of planning the student's educational program. Although it can be a challenge to schedule parent-teacher conferences and IEP meetings at times when all parties can be available, it can be especially frustrating for families when professionals walk in and out of a meeting (Salembier & Furney, 1997):

Meetings with parents should focus on the student's strengths, not just weaknesses, and support the student's parent.

> I had to leave my job to go to the [IEP] conference. . . . Do you want to know how many educators came in and had me sign something and walked out? And I just, I thought that was so rude. . . . they do not give me or my daughter the respect that we need. . . . It's like you're just being brushed through like an assembly line. Or they were like scanning you through the grocery line. And then, they leave. (Beach Center, 2000)

Obviously, professionals have busy schedules and personal lives outside their workday. Sometimes it takes a great deal of creativity to find times to connect with parents who also have limited time available and work responsibilities. Options include using a dialogue journal, telephone contacts with voice mail, and technology such as e-mail and school websites. Approximately two-thirds of adults have a computer with e-mail or Internet access (Madden, 2003).

Equality

The fifth partnership principle is equality—namely, each partner has roughly equal opportunity and talent to influence the decisions that the partners make. Professionals who seek equality in their partnerships

- Share power
- Foster empowerment
- Provide options

The human service professions traditionally have been characterized by hierarchies, not partnerships. In these hierarchies, professionals have the greatest amount of power, and "patients," "clients," or "consumers" have the least, receiving direction from the professional. Increasingly, however, and especially within special education, policies and practices attempt to avoid hierarchies and instead establish partnerships in which people have equal power. Each partner agrees to defer to the others' judgments and expertise. Sometimes professionals defer to parents' expertise; sometimes parents defer to professionals'. Professional dominance, or having power over others, can be particularly prevalent in situations in which there are many more professionals than parents. Previously you read a quotation from a parent who felt outnumbered when there were five professionals and only herself in a meeting. The same perspective is expressed by another parent, but it is complicated by professionals who are emphasizing their professional degrees:

> I was told that this is a room full of professionals. All the people have college degrees. She told me, there's an MSW, and there's a Ph.D., and I mean she was naming off more initials than I even know what they mean. . . . And I'm just sitting here, nobody looked at me as the professional(s) of knowing how these boys live. (Wang et al., 2004, p. 15)

Power-sharing partnerships are an alternative to power-over hierarchies. In power-sharing partnerships, everyone shares their strengths, talents, resources, and time so that the best possible decisions can be made. A parent describes a power-sharing process as follows:

> It has been WONDERFUL. It has absolutely been the best thing. Not only have there been benefits and services that have come, but all of the people that we deal with have got to where there's relationships there with everybody and there's this bonding and we're getting to where we're on the same page and . . . nobody gets 100% of their way. It's everybody there, you put it in a pile, and it's give and take. (Wang et al., 2004, p. 151)

As you work with families in making decisions, we encourage you to recognize that, ultimately, families must be comfortable with decisions in order to implement them. So professionals should be humble; after all, their roles usually are short term, but the family's role is for a lifetime. One parent reflected on power sharing and roles:

> I said, you intend to do this regardless of what I say. I said, if you made the wrong mistake, what will happen to you? Nothing, I said. I have to live with the outcome of any erroneous decision for the rest of my life because I will be caring for my child until I'm gone from this planet and I have to reap the consequences. . . . I said, I want to make the decisions about my child, and I'll live with the consequences if I happen to make the wrong one. But it's difficult to live with the consequence for the decision you made that I was against. (Beach Center, 2000)

Advocacy

The sixth partnership principle is advocacy—namely, speaking out and taking action to pursue a cause on a personal, organizational, or societal level or on any two or more of those levels. To advocate effectively, professionals should do the following (Blue-Banning et al., 2004; Turnbull et al., 2006):

- Seek win-win solutions
- Prevent problems
- Keep your conscience primed

PRAXIS

Standard: Advocating for students and families addresses PRAXIS™ Standard 2, Legal and Societal Issues.

- Pinpoint and document problems
- Form alliances

We particularly want to emphasize the importance of creating win-win solutions. When a solution is win-win, it satisfies all of the partners; each understands that everyone's perspective was considered by everyone else, even if it was not adopted. A win-win solution differs from a win-lose situation. In the former, all perspectives are valued, and each partner's desired result is maximized to the greatest extent possible. In the latter, not all perspectives are valued, and some perspectives prevail completely over others; there is *my* right way, and it's better than *your* wrong way. Win-win solutions are more likely to occur when the other partnership principles are put into place. For example, good communication, respect, and equality all contribute to win-win solutions.

One strategy for reaching win-win solutions is called **skilled dialogue.** This strategy involves two elements: **anchored understanding** and **third space** (Barrera & Corso, 2002). Anchored understanding occurs when there is a "compassionate understanding of differences" that comes from truly getting to know individual families (Barrera & Corso, 2002, p. 108). You have achieved an anchored understanding when you respect and appreciate the actions, intentions, and beliefs of a particular family, even in situations where you might have acted or thought differently.

Third space refers to a situation in which people creatively reframe each other's diverse perspectives and contradictions so that the perspectives merge to address challenging issues. A third-space perspective is achieved when family members and professionals each reach a new perspective without abandoning their individual points of view. Implementing skilled dialogue during interpersonal interactions encourages you to generate questions such as the following (Turnbull et al., 2006, p. 193):

- What is the meaning of this person's actions?
- How does my behavior influence this interaction?
- What can I learn from this person?

We encourage you to think of your partnerships with families as opportunities to advocate for both their interest and systems change. Families can be some of your most reliable allies in advocating for your and your colleagues' needs.

Trust

The final partnership principle is trust—namely, having confidence in another person's word, judgment, and action and believing that the trusted persons will act in the best interest of the person who trusts them (Baier, 1986; Tschannen-Moran & Hoy, 2000; Turnbull et al., 2006). There are four practices associated with being a trusted partner:

- Being reliable
- Using sound judgment
- Maintaining confidentiality
- Trusting yourself

We will emphasize maintaining confidentiality since there often is a great deal of personal information in students' school records. As you learned in Chapter 1, students must have nondiscriminatory evaluations in order to be identified as having a disability. Those evaluations reveal psychometric and other scores and assessments that characterize a student's performance and provide a portrait of the student's family. In multidisciplinary team meetings related to the evaluation or the IFSP or IEP, often a great deal of personal information is revealed. The Family Educational Rights and Privacy Act (FERPA) and IDEA require that teachers keep all information confidential, disclosing it only when the student's parents consent to the disclosure or when the law compels disclosure. An educator's perspective is revealing:

> It's purely a matter of trust, that they can trust that person so that they can tell them whatever. I have heard all kinds of things ya know, from families and from the children that I work with, and I consider that pretty sacred, actually. It's kind of a compliment, as far as I can see, that they're willing to trust me with those kinds of things. (Blue-Banning et al., 2004, p. 179)

Typically, educators share confidential information about the student in multidisciplinary team meetings in order to make decisions that will enhance the quality of the student's education. This information should not be discussed outside the meeting, such as within the school building, teachers' lounge, or anywhere else. Keeping information confidential will encourage parents and other professionals to trust you.

Looking to Sean's Future

Sean Holley figures prominently in our book *Families, Professionals, and Exceptionality* (Turnbull et al., 2006). There his life is described as consisting of five circles.

The first is the Circle of Tears, the place (like a crucible) where there was only antagonism between Leia and the faculty at Bonner Springs Elementary School. The second is the Circle of Triumph, the place where Leia, Tierney Thompson, and other teachers raised their hands together in victory over antagonism and the challenges of Sean's significant disabilities. The third is the Circle of Transition Terror, the place in which Leia anticipated that Sean's middle school experience would be nothing but a struggle. That circle is misnamed; the word *terror* must be replaced by *continued triumph*. Sean's middle school years are triumphant because of the partnerships that Leia and Sean's teachers are able to forge and because of the partnership that the Army and Major Holley have—each responding to duty, each accommodating the other.

The last two circles represent Sean's life as an adult and then as a man at the edges of life, at the end of his life. No one can say what events will come to pass in those circles or how the circles will be named. One thing is for sure, however: Sean's greatest security for the future—indeed, his family's greatest security for the future—lies in the willingness and ability of his family and various professionals to be trustworthy partners. The past is indeed prologue.

SUMMARY

Who are today's families?

- Families consist of two or more people who regard themselves to be a family and carry out the functions that families typically perform.
- As contrasted with the families of children without exceptionalities, families of children with exceptionalities have a higher rate of poverty and lower educational levels.
- Two characteristics contributing to the likelihood of families experiencing poverty are the presence of children who have a disability and a single female parent as head of household.

What are partnerships and why are they important?

- Family-professional partnerships are relationships in which families and professionals collaborate with each other, capitalizing on each other's judgments and expertise in order to increase benefits for students, families, and professionals.
- Three reasons why family-professional partnerships are important are that (a) schools with strong partnerships are more likely to have high levels of trust, (b) partnerships result in higher student achievement, and (c) positive family quality of life is more likely when families experience positive partnerships with professionals.

How do children with exceptionalities affect their families' quality of life, and what is your role as an educator?

- The five domains of family quality of life are emotional well-being, parenting, family interaction, physical/material well-being, and disability-related support.

- Regarding emotional well-being, students often do not have friendships, and their families sometimes feel isolated.

- Regarding parenting, parents benefit when professionals show them how to support their children to become more independent.

- Regarding family interaction, siblings of children and youth typically experience both positive and negative impacts from their experiences.

- Regarding physical/material well-being, families who experience poverty often need additional supports in order to be able to attend school conferences and school activities.

- Regarding disability-related supports, professionals can positively contribute to families by ensuring that the services that they offer are high quality.

How can you form partnerships with families?

- The seven partnership principles are communication, professional competence, respect, commitment, equality, advocacy, and trust.

- Trust is the key element of partnerships.

- Three national resources for relevant information and caring support for families of children with exceptionalities are Parent Training and Information Centers, Community Parent Resource Centers, and Parent to Parent programs.

WHAT WOULD YOU RECOMMEND?

Refer to chapter content and the PRAXIS™ and CEC standards in Appendix A to answer the following questions:

1. When you interact with parents who have cultural and linguistic characteristics different from your own, make a list of five partnership tips that you would implement and identify the associated CEC standard.

2. Describe a hypothetical situation that could occur in your teaching situation that would cause you to advocate for systems change in order to protect the rights of students and families. What PRAXIS™ standard would you be addressing?

3. Visit at least three websites mentioned in the chapter that provide helpful information about how to communicate with families from diverse backgrounds. As you develop your own competency in communicating with diverse families, what CEC standard are you addressing?

For more information, go to the Web Links module in Chapter 4 of the Companion Website.

Who is Lauren Marsh?

There is a special place in this world for the peacemakers. However much we might worship the victorious warrior, we value still more the person who offers the olive branch and induces opposing parties to accept it. That is one reason why at Bohemia Manor Middle School in Elkton, Maryland, Lauren Marsh is so well respected. She's the one who (in her words) tells her classmates to "calm down, sit down, chill out, and leave it alone" when they get "really hyper" or start crying or fighting. She's the one who (in the words of one of her teachers, Sherry Eichinger) is a candidate for the school-designated role of peer mediator.

There is a special place, too, for the problem solvers. However much we admire a person who acts passionately about issues, we look to the analyst to figure out what the problem is, why something is a problem at all, what the possible solutions are, and how to evaluate whether the solutions are working once they are applied. That is one reason why Lauren is so important in school. She brings her analytical ability to bear as a member of a clique of white and African American girls who are the school's leaders. And it is also one reason why Sherry Eichinger is so important at Bohemia Manor Middle School. As a special educator, she teaches Lauren and other students to use various strategies for learning how to calculate and how to learn to read and read to learn; she also teaches other teachers how to be as effective as possible in educating students who, like Lauren, have a specific learning disability in math or, unlike Lauren, find math or other subjects to be relatively easy. It's all about **differentiated instruction**—teaching strategies, altering some students' tasks, and modifying how they perform those tasks.

As an eighth grader, Lauren takes courses in math, English, science, social studies, fine arts, gym, music, and technology (using computers). If you were to go to Lauren's and Sherry's school, you would find Lauren in class with students who have no disabilities and with those who do. Sometimes you would find Lauren working in a small group with other students, receiving special help from Sherry, or in a small group of students leading as a tutor for her peers. Only once every week would you find Lauren in a group, separate from other groups of students, learning strategies to learn to read and read to learn. But you would find her using those strategies for the books that all eighth graders use, even though, at times, Lauren, like other students, might read somewhat below that grade level. Differentiated instruction promotes Lauren's inclusion in the general curriculum.

If you explore Bohemia Manor Middle School, you would find Sherry being a "Jill of All Trades." Sometimes she collaborates with a general educator to teach math, language arts, and reading, and sometimes she provides consultation for the general educators who teach science or social studies. In these roles, she focuses on differentiated instruction and collaborative teaching. You will learn more about differentiated instruction later in this chapter and about collaborative teaming in Chapter 13.

Understanding Students with Learning Disabilities

You would not find Sherry, however, in Lauren's classes in art, computers, and physical education. Always, you would find her as a member of the team of educators who convene as a student's individualized education team; always you would find her advocating for Lauren to have some extra time to take the math section of the Maryland statewide assessments of student proficiency; and always you would find her following up on what Lauren is learning, how she is learning something, and how her teachers are instructing her. Sherry's a collaborator, a specialist, an advocate, and an accountability-for-progress monitor on behalf of Lauren and the school as a whole. She's also a person who encourages Lauren to advocate for herself; a self-determined student ultimately becomes a more effective adult.

Lauren has two other important allies in her education. Her father, Jeff Moore, is an interstate truck driver who owns his own 18-wheeler and covers the east coast from New Jersey to the South Carolina–Georgia border. Her mother, Florence Moore, has her own job: making sure the Moore household, consisting of Lauren and her five brothers, runs as smoothly as Jeff's tractor-trailer. Whenever Jeff is not on the road, both attend regular teacher-parent meetings with Lauren's teachers, and both attend her IEP meetings. When he is on the road, Florence represents both of them.

Lauren's reliable allies—Sherry and her parents—concur that Lauren brings something extra to her education and her school. It underlies her peacemaking and her happy personality, and perhaps explains both. It's a sense that Lauren can do whatever she chooses to do if she puts her mind to it, learns the strategies for doing it, and applies her problem-solving skills to make her choices come true, whether on her own or with help. Lauren puts it this way: what she most likes about school is "learning new things." Florence describes that sense of great expectations somewhat differently: "I tell Lauren that there is nothing she can't accomplish." And Sherry explains why Lauren's future seems bright. It's because there are "so many positives" in Lauren's life—her leadership capacities; her ability to advocate for herself and others; her willingness to work; her diligent use of the strategies she is learning for mastering her coursework; her circle of friends, both white and African American; and her family's support.

IDENTIFYING STUDENTS WITH LEARNING DISABILITIES

Defining Learning Disabilities

Ever since Sam Kirk first coined the term *learning disabilities* in 1963, legislators, parents, and professionals have debated about how to define the condition (Kavale & Forness, 2000; Lyon et al., 2001). IDEA provides one definition, but even that one is controversial. Let's consider the IDEA definition first and an alternative one later.

IDEA defines the term **specific learning disability** as a "disorder in one or more of the basic psychological processes involved in understanding or in using language, spoken or written (20 U.S.C., Sec. 1400)." IDEA adds that the "disorder may manifest itself in an imperfect ability to listen, think, speak, read, write, spell, or do mathematical calculations."

IDEA also sets the criteria for determining whether a student has a specific learning disability. Under the IDEA, the evaluation team may determine that a student has a specific learning disability under two circumstances, and both must exist. First, the student must have "a disorder in one or more of the basic psychological processes involved in understanding or using written or spoken language." The "disorder may manifest itself in an imperfect ability to listen, think, speak, read, write, spell, or do mathematical calculations." The disorder includes "perceptual disabilities, brain injury, minimal brain dysfunction, dyslexia, and developmental aphasia." This is the **inclusionary standard;** it identifies what conditions are included.

Second, however, the definition does not include "a learning problem that is primarily the result of visual, hearing, or motor disabilities of mental retardation, of emotional disturbance, or of environment, cultural, or economic disadvantage." This is the **exclusionary standard;** it says that primary causal conditions are excluded.

Note that the definition has two special components: the inclusionary criteria and the exclusionary criteria. These criteria both enlarge and constrict students' eligibility to be classified as having a specific learning disability. The inclusionary criteria are those related to listening, thinking, speaking, reading, writing, spelling, and calculating. The exclusionary criteria relate to impairments arising from other disabilities or from socioeconomic conditions. Lauren's specific learning disability relates to "calculating"—her math skills.

Learning disabilities continue to be the most prevalent of all disabilities. Slightly less than half of all students with disabilities served under IDEA have specific learning disabilities (U.S. Department of Education, 2005). This category is rapidly expanding: between the 1990–1991 and the 1999–2000 school years, the percentage of students ages 6 to 21 identified as having learning disabilities increased by 34 percent. And since 1975, the number of students identified with a learning disability has nearly tripled.

Unlike some of the other categories of disability, there have not been particular concerns about the disproportionate representation of African American or Latino students in the category of learning disabilities (National Research Council, 2002). Apparently, that is so because the dramatic increase in learning disabilities has occurred across all racial/ethnic groups, with the exception of Asian/Pacific Islander students. There is a higher-than-expected placement rate for children from low socioeconomic backgrounds in this category (Blair & Scott, 2002). In terms of gender, studies have traditionally reported that boys are 4 to 5 times more likely than girls to be identified as having a learning disability (Shapiro, Church, & Lewis, 2002).

Describing the Characteristics

Individuals with learning disabilities commonly have average or above-average intelligence. Nevertheless, they almost always demonstrate low academic achievement in one or more areas. Approximately 30 percent of students with learning disabilities also have been diagnosed with attention-deficit-hyperactivity disorder (AD/HD) (Kotkin, Forness, & Kavele, 2001; Shaywitz, Fletcher, & Shaywitz, 1995). There is no such thing as a typical student with learning disabilities. One may exhibit strengths in math and nonverbal reasoning but weaknesses in receptive and expressive language skills. Another may be strong in motor skills, reading, and receptive

On the Companion Website, *www.pren-hall.com/turnbull,* you will find a link to the Council for Learning Disabilities, which provides extensive educational resources, *www.cldinternational.org.*

PRAXIS

Standard: Understanding recent legislation and how it impacts services for and identification of students with learning disabilities is an application of PRAXIS™ Standard 2, Legal and Societal Issues.

language but weak in math and expressive language. Lauren, for example, has powerful social skills, quite satisfactory language skills, and average reading skills; math, however, challenges her greatly. In this section we will review the characteristics related to students' academic achievement, memory, meta-cognition, and behavior and social/emotional adjustment.

Academic Achievement

Reading. Reading difficulties are one of the most significant challenges facing students with learning disabilities (Kavale & Reese, 1992; Lyon et al., 2001). This is especially troublesome because reading is so important to performance in most academic domains and to adjustment to most school activities (Chard & Kame'enui, 2000; Fuchs et al., 2001). There are several different types of reading challenges.

Dyslexia refers to the condition of having severe difficulty in learning to read.

Instructional tools like computers can help students with disabilities write more easily.

Dyslexia is a specific learning disability that is neurological in origin. It is characterized by difficulties with accurate and/or fluent word recognition and by poor spelling and decoding abilities. . . . Secondary consequences may include problems in reading comprehension and reduced reading experience that can impede growth of vocabulary and background knowledge (International Dyslexia Association, 2002).

Dyslexia, as well as milder forms of reading problems, is related to deficient language skills, especially phonological awareness (Al Otaiba & Fuchs, 2002; Coyne, Kame'enui, & Simmons, 2001; Torgesen, 2002). Students who lack skills in phonological awareness cannot recognize sound segments in spoken words (e.g., "push" has three sound segments, or phonemes: /p/ /u/ /sh/). Effective readers must use other skills, but phonological skills are especially important in learning to read.

Students with reading disabilities may exhibit word recognition errors. When asked to read orally, they may omit, insert, substitute, and/or reverse words. They also may have difficulty comprehending what they have read because they have limited ability to recall or discern basic facts, sequences, and/or themes. Likewise, they may lose their place while reading; read in a choppy, halting manner; or struggle to comprehend the text they are reading (National Reading Panel, 2000).

Written language. Children and youth with dyslexia frequently also experience problems with spelling and writing (Fletcher et al., 2002). Even students with learning disabilities who also read well often have problems with written language (Graham, Harris, & Larsen, 2001). Their difficulties usually occur in the areas of handwriting, spelling, productivity, text structure, sentence structure, word usage, and composition. They may exhibit the following behaviors:

- Feel overwhelmed by the idea of getting started
- Struggle to organize and use the mechanics of writing
- Struggle to develop their ideas fluently
- Often have difficulties spelling and constructing written products legibly
- Submit written work that is too brief

Handwriting problems are known as **dysgraphia,** a partial inability to remember how to make certain alphabet or arithmetic symbols in handwriting (Meese, 2001). Students' handwriting problems can arise from their lack of fine-motor coordination, failure to attend to task, and inability to perceive and/or remember visual images accurately, or from inadequate handwriting instruction in the classroom (Friend & Bursuck, 2002). Students with dysgraphia may learn much less from an assignment because they must focus on the mechanics of writing instead of the content of their assignment.

Students may also have difficulty with spelling. Common spelling errors include the addition of unneeded letters, the omission of needed letters, reversals of vowels, reversals of syllables, and the phonemic spelling of nonphonemic words.

Mathematics. Students' mathematical difficulties can range from mild to severe; it is likely that Lauren's are mild to moderate. A term commonly associated with math difficulties is **dyscalculia,** which is "characterized by a poor understanding of the number concept and the number system" (Vaidya, 2004, p. 17). Students' difficulties may include the following:

■ **Procedural problems:** frequent errors in understanding math concepts and difficulty sequencing the steps of complex problems.

■ **Semantic memory problems:** difficulty remembering math facts.

■ **Visual-spatial problems:** difficulties in reproducing numerals.

Students with dyslexia frequently also experience challenges with math (Fletcher et al., 2002). It stands to reason that these students would have difficulty with word problems because of the language-processing requirements. Additionally, remembering number facts can be especially challenging for them.

Memory

How are Lauren and Heather's learning disabilities different? How are they the same? View Clip 5 in "Meet Heather" on the *Real Lives and Exceptionalities* DVD and compare it to what you read about Lauren in this chapter.

Many students with learning disabilities have difficulty with short- and long-term memory (Swanson, 2000). Students with short-term memory challenges cannot easily recall information shortly after it is presented to them. Students with long-term memory challenges cannot easily store information permanently for later recall. Research on short- and long-term memory has shown that many students with learning disabilities have poor strategies for memorizing information, insufficient metacognitive skills for recalling information, and limited semantic memory capabilities (O'Shaughnessy & Swanson, 1998; Torgesen & Wagner, 1998). Together or separately, these limitations cause erratic academic performance.

Metacognition

When you study for a test on this chapter, how will you do it? You might review chapter headings, definitions, summaries, and class notes. Or you might use flashcards and/or memory devices, called mnemonics, such as acronyms for lists. (You'll learn more about mnemonics in Chapter 11.) You probably have found an approach to studying that works best for you. If so, you have good skills in the area of metacognition. That term refers to awareness of how you think and how you monitor your thinking (Swanson, 2001). Efficient learners take control and direct their own thinking process, but students with learning disabilities tend to lack these skills and have deficits in the following areas of metacognition (Gersten, 1998):

■ Knowing a large number of strategies for acquiring, storing, and processing information

■ Understanding when, where, and why these strategies are important

■ Selecting and monitoring the use of these strategies wisely and reflectively

These students often tend to deal impulsively with a problem-solving task instead of being reflective in their approach (Shapiro et al., 2002).

Social, Emotional, and Behavioral Characteristics

The processing problems that many students experience can also cause them to have difficulty understanding their own and other persons' social cues and behaving in socially acceptable ways. Note that we said "can," not "will." Lauren, for instance, clearly does not have any such problems; indeed, she is highly skilled in social, emotional, and behavioral dimensions. If you add the frustration that these learning problems cause and the difficulty that can arise when dealing with people who do not understand this poor performance, you have some students at risk for social, emotional, and behavioral problems. The fact that approximately one-half of a sample of more than 200 students with behavior disorders were found to also have a learning disability (Glassberg, Hooper, & Mattison, 1999) drives educators to emphasize social skill training along with academic skill training.

In part because many students with learning disabilities—not Lauren, for sure—lack effective interpersonal skills, have difficulty modeling other students' behavior and reading others' social cues, and misinterpret others' feelings, they are likely to be rejected by their peers (Settle & Milich, 1999; Valas, 1999) and to be regarded by their teachers, parents, and peers as having problems with social relationships. Obviously, that generalization applies to some, not all, students with learning disabilities. It certainly does not apply to Lauren. She "reads" her peers with the maturity of an older woman; she is not typical in this respect.

Research findings on the self-concepts of students with learning disabilities are inconsistent, with some researchers reporting that students with learning disabilities do not think of themselves as having less academic competence or being less intelligent than their classmates without learning disabilities (Bear & Minke, 1996; Meltzer, Roditi, Houser, & Perlman, 1998). Others, however, find that students with learning disabilities do feel worse about their ability and school status as compared to their classmates without disabilities (Gans, Kenny, & Ghany, 2003; Harter, Whitesell, & Junkin, 1998). Interestingly, students with learning disabilities appear to be able to separate their self-concept related to their academic achievement from their global self-concept, which is comparable to that of their peers without learning disabilities (Gans et al., 2003).

Due to her well-honed social skills, Lauren and her teachers feel confident about her inclusion in the general education program.

Research has also focused on the impact of the label *learning disabilities* on students' self-esteem. Paradoxically, students with learning disabilities seem to have higher levels of self-esteem after receiving the diagnosis of learning disabilities than they did before the diagnosis (MacMaster, Donovan, & MacIntyre, 2002). This increase might be due to the students "coming to perceive their disability as limited in scope and manageable through remediation" (p. 101). A 20-year longitudinal research project has documented the perspectives of a group of 41 individuals with learning disabilities (Higgins, Raskind, Goldberg, & Herman, 2002). These authors described distinct stages characterized by the participants in terms of the process that they experienced in coming to terms with their learning disability. Figure 5–1 identifies each of these five stages and provides an illustrative comment. Most research underscored the importance of reframing the disability from being only a negative fact of life to conferring some positive benefits.

Values: Enhancing a student's self-concept and mitigating the effect of a label can help the student have *great expectations* for his progress in the general curriculum and outside school.

Determining the Causes

Neurological mechanisms. Traditionally, most researchers and educators have asserted that learning disabilities result from a central nervous system dysfunction—that is, from an underlying neurological problem (Lyon et al., 2001). New neuroimaging technologies have enhanced scientists' ability to assess brain activity more accurately. These technologies have enabled scientists to pinpoint brain activity associated with reading (Kibby & Hynd, 2001). The left temporal lobe has been identified as the center of phonemic analysis of spoken language (Shapiro et al., 2002). Neuroanatomy research has reported that reading involves a broad neural network of different regions and that reading disabilities can be caused by a defect located at any point in the network (Georgiewa et al., 1999; Shaywitz et al., 1998). Studies of brain structure in adults with dyslexia have identified abnormalities in the connectivity of brain cells that originate during early brain development (Shapiro, 2001).

Genetics. Evidence continues to accumulate that there is a strong genetic contribution to different learning disabilities (Raskind, 2001).

- The risk of having a reading impairment is 75 percent if both parents are affected and 51 percent if one parent is affected (Wolff & Melngailis, 1994).

- More than half of the reading impairments of identical twins have been found to be a result of heredity (DeFries & Alarcon, 1996).

- Learning disability has a recurrence rate of approximately 35 to 45 percent in susceptible families, indicating that a single gene may be involved (Pennington, 1995).

Environmental causes. There are connections between genetic and environmental causes in that parents who experience problems with reading are likely to read less to their children during their

Figure 5-1 Stages of acceptance of a learning disability

Stage	Illustrative Quote
1. Awareness of a difference	"I don't think I really believed I wasn't stupid 'til long, long time after that. You're behind—everybody knows you're behind." (p. 9)
2. Labeling event	"We went to all kinds of people. People thought it was my eyes, to all kind of people who came along. I think a lot of times people are looking for . . . and certainly I think my parents wanted to look for an easy fix, too."
3. Understanding/negotiating the label	"I didn't understand. I thought I was retarded. I thought that someone with a learning disability, because it wasn't explained to me, was second to somebody with Down's Syndrome. That I was doomed to riding the short bus all my life, so to speak. I did not understand and it was very, very difficult." (p. 12)
4. Compartmentalization	"Actually I don't like the term learning disability. I don't like the term dyslexia because it has come to be known as a catch-all. I prefer reading and writing, problems in reading or writing. . . . when you say learning problem, that doesn't mean I have a problem learning. The problem isn't learning. The problem is reading and writing." (pp. 12–13)
5. Transformation	"I have learned . . . the ability to keep going. I have learned to keep going no matter what people said. No matter if it was inspired by anger or revenge, or whatever, still its ability to keep plotting [sic] along. It gives you mental toughness." (p. 13)

Source: Higgins, E. L., Raskind, M. H., Goldberg, R. J., & Herman, K. L. (2002). Stages of acceptance of a learning disability: The impact of labeling. *Learning Disability Quarterly, 25,* 3–18.

children's early years (Lyon et al., 2001). Other environmental causes include pollutants and **teratogens** (aspects of the environment that cause developmental malformations in humans) that can cause learning disabilities. If a child ingests lead-based paint, the child's brain can be impaired; likewise, if a pregnant woman is exposed to lead from other sources, her fetus's brain can be impaired. There also is clear evidence that, if a pregnant woman abuses alcohol or takes crack cocaine, she places her fetus's brain at risk for learning problems (Murphy-Brennan & Oei, 1999).

EVALUATING STUDENTS WITH LEARNING DISABILITIES

The IDEA definition of a specific learning disability has remained constant. The 2004 reauthorization did not change the definition. As we pointed out under the section dealing with identification, the student still must have a disorder that manifests itself in an imperfect ability to listen, think, speak, read, write, spell, or do mathematical calculations. The question facing state and local educational agencies is how to operationalize the definition. Just how "imperfect" must the student's ability be?

To answer that question, the pre-2004 IDEA regulations authorized and nearly required the agencies to apply a discrepancy standard—"severe discrepancy" between the student's ability and performance. A severe discrepancy is one that is statistically significant. During the 1970s and 1980s, 98 percent of the states used the discrepancy standard for identifying students as having a learning disability (Frankenberger & Fronzaglio, 1991).

When Congress reauthorized IDEA in 2004, it adopted a different approach. Instead of requiring an agency to use the discrepancy standard, IDEA now provides that a state or local educational agency may but is not required to take into consideration whether a student has a severe discrepancy between achievement and intellectual ability in oral expression, listening comprehension, written expression, basic reading skill, reading comprehension, mathematical calculation, or mathematical reasoning. Note, however, that an agency *may* use the discrepancy standard; it is simply not required to do so under federal law, and the pressure to do so is no longer part of the law.

When Congress reauthorized IDEA in 2004, it also adopted a different approach to determining whether a student has a disorder related to performing certain academic tasks. An agency now may use a process that determines if the student responds to

At Bohemia Manor Middle School, even the principal, Mr. Buckley, is involved in Lauren's education. A whole-school approach to effective instruction requires leadership from the top.

scientific, research-based intervention. This is the "responsiveness to intervention" approach.

It is far too early to detect what state and local agencies will do. Some may continue to use the discrepancy standard; some may not. Some may use the responsiveness approach; others may not. Some may use both; some may use neither.

Accordingly, we will explain how the agencies have been evaluating a student, using the pre-2004 approach and the discrepancy standard. We will then explain some of the controversy surrounding that standard, clarifying why the 2004 reauthorization made these two changes. Before we explain the evaluation process, however, you ought to read Box 5–1 and imagine a parent's perspective on evaluation and intervention.

Determining the Presence of a Learning Disability

Figure 5–2 shows the traditional nondiscriminatory evaluation procedure for identifying learning disabilities. Generally, students are referred for evaluation because, even after prereferral, they seem to have more ability than their academic performance in one or more subject areas indicates.

The discrepancy model. A nondiscriminatory evaluation to determine whether a student has a specific learning disability traditionally has established a discrepancy between the student's intellectual ability, as measured by an IQ test, and the student's achievement, as measured by a standardized achievement test.

In the field of learning disabilities, educators usually use an intelligence test, such as the Wechsler Intelligence Scale for Children—IV Integrated (WISC-IV). This and other intelligence tests measure a sample of a student's performance on tasks related to reasoning, memory, learning comprehension, and ability to learn academic skills; based on the student's performance, educators infer the student's intellectual capacity. IQ tests yield an intelligence quotient (IQ) that is a ratio of the student's mental age (MA) to his or her chronological age (CA): $IQ = MA \div CA \times 100$. So if a student has a mental age of 12 and a chronological age of 10, the student's IQ would compute at 12 divided by 10 times 100, which equals 120.

Council for Exceptional Children

Standard: As you learn strategies to evaluate students to determine if they have a learning disability, you are addressing CEC Standard 8, Assessment.

Assume that you are one of the parents of Danny, your only child. He's just finished second grade. Early in that school year, his teacher recognized that Danny was having difficulty reading. He was embarrassed when asked to read aloud; his reading was extremely labored and slow when compared to his peers. His teacher, Ms. Montrose, provided Danny with phonics exercises that helped him decode words and make them easier to read and understand and extra time so he could recognize words and use them in his reading. None of her efforts seemed to benefit Danny.

Ms. Montrose has called you and asked for your permission to discuss Danny with the school's referral committee. You consent, hoping that a referral will offer some explanation for why Danny is a slow reader and, more than that, some strategies to help him learn to read, spell, and write.

The committee reports that Danny does better in math than in reading or when he is asked to engage in activities that require him to speak, not to write, what he knows. You ask, "So what's next? Special education?" To which the committee answers, "Not yet; we need to test Danny further."

The further testing—the school calls it a nondiscriminatory evaluation, as required by IDEA—reveals that Danny's IQ is 97, perfectly average, but that his reading quotient is 84. That does not seem too bad to you until the school referral committee tells you that Danny does not qualify for special education.

The reason, the school psychologist explains, is that the discrepancy between Danny's IQ and his reading quotient is only 13 points, not 15, as the state requires in order for him to receive services as a student with a specific learning disability. So Danny will have to stay in general education, cannot receive the full spectrum of special education interventions, and can retain only those few accommodations in general education that he has already been getting.

Exasperated, you say, "So Danny basically has to fail at third-grade reading, having already failed at second-grade reading, in order for him to get some special education help. That's what you're telling me? What sense does that make? Do you wait to get a disease when you know you can prevent it? Do you wait for an auto accident when you know you can prevent it or protect yourself with seat belts? What kind of upside-down world is education, anyway?"

In your own voice, ask yourself:

- Does it make sense to wait to see if response-to-intervention really works?

- Or does it make more sense to intervene early and powerfully?

- Do we really have to wait for your son Danny to fail?

To answer these questions you will need to read the rest of this chapter. But you also may want to read a major article arguing that the discrepancy standard that Danny's school uses and that also governs Lauren Marsh's education in Maryland (as of 2005) shortchanges students with reading difficulties. That article is Stuebing, K. K., Fletcher, J. M., LeDoug, J. M., Lyon, G. R., Shaywitz, S. E., & Shaywitz, B. A. (2002). Validity of IQ-discrepancy classifications of reading disabilities: A meta-analysis. *American Educational Research Journal, 39*(2), 469–518.

The bell-shaped curve in Figure 5–3 shows below-average, average, and above-average ranges of intelligence on the WISC-IV. Note that 50 percent of the students at any particular age average an IQ below 100, and 50 percent average an IQ above 100. Most states identify students with IQs at or above 130 as gifted (Chapter 16) and students with IQs at or below 70 as having mental retardation if they also meet other criteria (Chapters 9 and 10).

The WISC-IV has two scales: performance, which measures skills that relate to mathematics achievement; and verbal, which measures skills that relate to reading and written expression. When combined, performance and verbal scores yield a full-scale IQ score.

In addition to using intelligence tests, educators typically also administer a **norm-referenced** achievement test. A frequently used achievement test is the Wechsler Individualized Achievement Test—Second Edition (WIAT-II). This test reveals the student's academic skills in reading, written language, and mathematics.

One benefit of using these two tests concurrently is that the same group of students (called a **norm group**) took the tests initially to develop standard scores. Both tests have a **mean** (or average) score of 100 and a **standard deviation** (a way to determine how much a particular score differs from the mean) of 15 points. Therefore, with two different scores, evaluators can compare a student's IQ and achievement scores.

Woodcock (1990) has described three types of discrepancies:

- **Aptitude-achievement** (also called ability-achievement): the discrepancy between different abilities and areas of achievement.

- **Intracognitive**: the discrepancy between different abilities (e.g., performance and verbal scores).

- **Intra-achievement**: the discrepancy between different areas of academic achievement.

When educators determine that a student has a severe discrepancy, they nearly always look at the first type: aptitutde-achievement. States have different criteria for defining a severe

Figure 5–2 Nondiscriminatory evaluation process for determining the presence of a learning disability

Observation ↓	**Teacher and parents observe:** Student appears frustrated with academic tasks and may have stopped trying.
Screening ↓	**Assessment measures:** **Classroom work products:** Work is inconsistent or generally poor. Teacher feels student is capable of doing better. **Group intelligence tests:** Usually the tests indicate average or above-average intelligence. However, tests may not reveal true ability because of reading requirements. **Vision and hearing screening:** Results do not explain academic difficulties.
Prereferral ↓	**Teacher implements suggestions from school-based team:** The student still experiences frustration and/or academic difficulty despite interventions. Ineffective instruction is eliminated as the cause for academic difficulty.
Referral ↓	**Multidisciplinary team submits referral.**
Nondiscriminatory evaluation procedures and standards ↓	**Assessment measures:** **Individualized intelligence test:** Student has average or above-average intelligence, so mental retardation is ruled out. Student may also have peaks and valleys in subtests. The multidisciplinary team makes sure that the test used is culturally fair. **Individualized achievement test:** A significant discrepancy (difference) exists between what the student is capable of learning (as measured by the intelligence test) and what the student has actually learned (as measured by the achievement test). The difference exists in one or more of the following areas: listening, thinking, reading, written language, mathematics. The team makes sure the test is culturally fair. **Curriculum-based assessment:** The student is experiencing difficulty in one or more areas of the curriculum used by the local school district. **Behavior rating scale:** The student's learning problems cannot be explained by the presence of emotional or behavioral problems. **Anecdotal records:** The student's academic problems are not of short duration but have been apparent throughout time in school. **Direct observation:** The student is experiencing difficulty and/or frustration in the classroom. **Ecological assessment:** The student's environment does not cause the learning difficulty. **Portfolio assessment:** The student's work is inconsistent and/or poor in specific subjects.
Determination	The nondiscriminatory multidisciplinary evaluation team determines that the student has a learning disability and needs special education and related services.

Figure 5–3 Ranges of intelligence

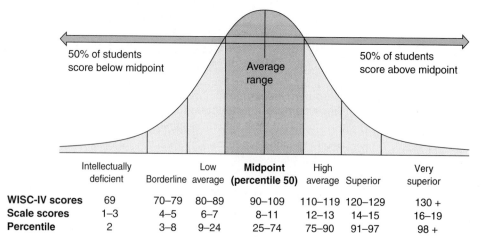

	Intellectually deficient	Borderline	Low average	Midpoint (percentile 50)	High average	Superior	Very superior
WISC-IV scores	69	70–79	80–89	90–109	110–119	120–129	130 +
Scale scores	1–3	4–5	6–7	8–11	12–13	14–15	16–19
Percentile	2	3–8	9–24	25–74	75–90	91–97	98 +

Source: From the WISC–IV Companion (in press) by S. Truch, 2006; Austin, TX: PRO-ED. Copyright 2006 PRO-ED.

discrepancy. Your state might use 1 standard deviation (15 points, as in the hypothetical case in Box 5–1), 1.5 standard deviations (22 or 23 points), or 2 standard deviations (30 points). Regardless of the extent of discrepancy that a particular state specifies, the discrepancy model is based on the premise that students do not achieve at their expected level of ability. Thus, measurement focuses on a comparison and contrast of what a student would be expected to achieve based on IQ and what a student actually achieves based on achievement test scores. Some states change the discrepancy requirement based on age, and others use complicated statistical formulas to determine discrepancy (Mercer & Pullen, 2005).

We will illustrate a severe discrepancy with the hypothetical scores of Joseph (see Figure 5–4). You will notice that he has peaks and valleys in his scores, suggesting the possibility of a severe discrepancy. (By comparison, students with mental retardation typically have flat profiles.) The first obvious discrepancy is intracognitive. He has a difference of 36 points (more than 2 standard deviations) between his verbal and performance IQs. An intra-achievement discrepancy of 2 standard deviations exists between his reading and mathematics scores, so some states would allow him to qualify for services based on this criterion alone.

In addition, Joseph has an IQ achievement discrepancy between his full-scale IQ and his reading and written expression. So he does not qualify for special education services in mathematics based on his full-scale IQ. But if the state in which he lives allows educators to compare

Figure 5–4 Joseph's nondiscriminatory evaluation scores

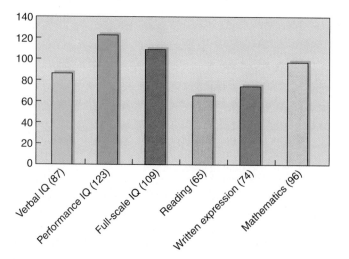

his verbal with his reading and written expression, he could qualify for services in reading but not written expression because of the discrepancy. And he could even qualify for services in mathematics when his math score is compared to his performance IQ, also because of the discrepancy.

A major criticism of the discrepancy formula is that it is biased against students from diverse racial/ethnic backgrounds who score lower on IQ tests (McLeskey, Waldron, & Wornhoff, 1990; Warner, Dede, Garvan, & Conway, 2002). When students have a lower IQ, it is more difficult to establish a discrepancy between their IQ and their achievement in order for them to qualify for a learning disability. Thus, students who are not demonstrating progress in the general education classroom would be excluded from more intensive special education instruction. In Maryland, where Lauren lives, the state and her own school district use the discrepancy standard, so Lauren qualified for the specific learning disability category and, by implication, has only that disability and no other.

Criticism of the **IQ-achievement discrepancy** centers on the fact that a discrepancy between achievement and IQ frequently cannot be reliably assessed until a student is around 9 years old (Shaywitz et al., 1992; Stuebing et al., 2002). Waiting is required because it takes a while for a student's achievement to become delayed enough to show up as a severe discrepancy. Educators must wait for the student to fail before detecting a specific learning disability. This means that early identification of learning disabilities is not possible and the valuable learning opportunities for more intensive instruction do not occur.

In addition to this "wait-to-fail" approach, other problems with the IQ-achievement discrepancy include the fact that discrepancy formulas often vary from state to state, the psychometric accuracy of the discrepancy formula has been called into question, and there has been a lack of relevant information generated for planning instructions that will be successful with the student (Lyon et al., 2001). These criticisms may explain why the reauthorized IDEA allows states to use the discrepancy standard and the reponsiveness standard as well.

In this section about evaluation, we have highlighted some of the criticisms of the discrepancy standard, reviewed issues related to potential bias in testing for learning disability, and said that the student's age and the "wait to fail" model warrant some criticism. There seems to be some connection, then, between classifying a student as having a learning disability and the student's traits other than IQ. Is that so? Box 5–2 suggests that there is a connection, but it also suggests what educators might do for students with certain traits early in their education.

Response-to-intervention model. Researchers have several perspectives about how to determine reliably whether a student responds to scientific, research-based intervention (Fletcher et al., 2002; Fuchs, Mock, Morgan, & Young, 2003; Vaughn & Fuchs, 2003). They tend to agree, however, that the purpose of assessment is to provide information for intervention as well as to determine eligibility for special education services. Although no one precise process has been established for **response-to-intervention** procedures, the general process includes the following steps (Fuchs et al., 2003, p. 159):

1. Students are provided with "generally effective" instruction by their classroom teacher.

2. Their progress is monitored.

3. Those who do not respond get something else, or something more, from their teacher or someone else.

4. Again, their progress is monitored.

5. Those who still do not respond either qualify for special education or for special education evaluation.

Step 1 includes providing "generally effective" instruction. This means that the student receives instruction regarded to be effective and that the instruction occurs in general education classes (Vaughn & Fuchs, 2003). Step 2 involves monitoring the student's progress with this "generally effective" instruction. Step 3 involves enhancing the nature of systematic instruction so that the student

Monitoring student progress by reporting and charting data is critical to the response-to-intervention process.

Diversity Tips ~ Learning Disabilities, Race, and Socioeconomic Status   Box 5–2

There is a theory called the new morbidity that applies to special education. The theory is that a student's race (African American, Latino, or not), family structure (single-parent family or not), place of residence (in a minority school district or not), and family socioeconomic status (poor or not) powerfully influence whether a student will be placed into special education. In short, the more "diverse" a student's race, family structure, place of residence, and socioeconomic status, the more likely it is that he or she will be placed into special education.

The theory certainly holds water when it comes to disabilities such as emotional or behavioral disturbance (Chapter 7) or mental retardation (Chapter 9), as you will read later in this book. Those disabilities, by definition, allow evaluators to use a large degree of judgment, so sometimes, it seems, bias comes into play in classifying a student into one of those categories.

But does the theory of co-morbidity hold water when it comes to students with specific learning disabilities? It seems that it should not. After all, IQ is IQ, and discrepancy between the student's IQ and the student's performance can be measured on standardized tests anywhere in the country. Moreover, the IDEA procedures for evaluating a student for a specific learning disability are constant across the country, and so are the inclusionary and exclusionary criteria. A person either has an average or above-average IQ and a low performance, or not. If not, then the student does not qualify for the specific learning disability category.

Yet some research indicates that risks at birth related to socioeconomic factors also predict a student's placement into specific learning disability programs by the time the student is between the ages of 12 and 14. Specifically, the mother's level of education (under 12 years of schooling), the mother's marital status (unmarried), prenatal care after the first three months of pregnancy (low attention to care), and the child's low birth weight (unacceptably low) all correlate with special education placement into specific learning disability programs.

What should we make of the finding? Certainly, it suggests that educators should do the following:

- Acknowledge the early risk factors.
- Use evidence-based research, especially in reading, as soon as possible to prevent special education placement.
- Be conscious that it's not always bias but often science that explains how risk factors drive special education placements; the bias exists when educators do not intervene early and effectively when they work with a student with these risk factors.

Source: Data from Blair, C., & Scott, K. G. (2002). Proportion of LD placements associated with low socioeconomic status: Evidence for a gradient? *Journal of Special Education, 36*(1), 14–22. See also Lader, M., & Hammons, C. (2001). Special but unequal: Race and special education. In C. E. Finn, A. J. Rotherham, & C. R. Hokanson (Eds.), *Rethinking special education for a new century* (pp. 85–110). New York: Progressive Policy Institute and Fordham Foundation.

who does not respond to typical instruction in general education classes has an opportunity for more explicit, intensive, and/or supportive instruction (Torgesen, 2002).

- More *explicit* instruction involves the systematic teaching of critical skills that enable learners to be more successful in their mastery.

- More *intensive* instruction involves a higher frequency of instructional opportunities per day than is typically provided in general education classrooms.

- More *supportive* instruction involves more precise scaffolding in order to (1) better sequence skills and (2) provide more precise prompts to students on the learning strategies they need to use to be successful with their learning tasks.

Step 4 involves careful monitoring of the student's progress after the instruction is more explicit, intensive, and/or supportive. The results of this monitoring lead to step 5, referral for special education evaluation, or, if an evaluation has already been completed, for special education services.

There are five potential benefits of the response-to-intervention approach (Lyon et al., 2005):

1. Students can begin to receive more explicit, intensive, and supportive instruction in kindergarten. They do not need to wait to fail or document statistical discrepancy between their potential and achievement.

2. Only students who have a genuine learning disability are identified for assistance. Students whose learning needs can be remediated through more systematic instruction do not enter the assisted population.

3. Students do not need to be labeled in order to receive services.

4. Some students with lower IQs who do not achieve the statistical discrepancy between potential and achievement but still have significant learning problems may receive assistance.

5. The IQ test, which some people question as not being relevant to instructional planning, does not have a role in the eligibility process.

Some researchers criticize the responsiveness-to-intervention approach on the grounds that the approach itself has not been scientifically validated (Fuchs et al., 2003). However, with the new IDEA requirement that authorizes state and local education agencies to use a response-to-intervention approach rather than the discrepancy formula, it is very likely that significant research will be done in this area over the next three to five years. Some leaders within the field of learning disabilities predict that the response-to-intervention model provides a foundation for redefining learning disabilities and possibly even considering a noncategorical approach to special education service delivery. Under the noncategorical approach, students who have different disabilities would be educated together if the teachers' curriculum, methods of instruction, and methods of assessment are effective for all of them. Thus, for example, a noncategorical approach would include students with specific learning disabilities, attention-deficit/hyperactivity disorder, and slight degrees of mental retardation and emotional or behavioral disorders. With such a situation looming, some researchers have posed hard questions:

> Are parents, professional organizations, and others ready for a non-categorical approach to service delivery? Are they willing to combine LD with mild mental retardation and behavior disorders into an undifferentiated "high-incidence-disabilities" entity as some have proposed? (Fuchs et al., 2003, p. 168)

Determining the Nature of Specially Designed Instruction and Services

In order for instruction to be more explicit, intensive, and supportive, it must rest on evaluation data (as we point out in this and all subsequent chapters). Educators have relied on general achievement tests, such as the Wechsler Individualized Achievement Test, for evaluating a student. Although the test scores help educators to compute a discrepancy, they do not provide explicit guidance for intervention and instruction. That is so, for example, with respect to reading.

Often students cannot read as young children because they have limitations in **phonological processing,** which refers to the ability to "understand and use the sound system of our language to process written and oral information" (Jorm & Share, 1983; Wagner & Torgesen, 1997; Allor, 2002, pp. 47–48). So evaluation should explicitly identify a student's current level of achievement in phonological awareness, phonological memory, rapid naming of letters, and oral vocabulary (Allor, 2002; Catts et al., 2002; Fletcher et al., 2002; Stuebing et al., 2002).

The Comprehensive Test of Phonological Processing is a valid and reliable way to evaluate a student's current level of performance related to the first three skills—awareness, memory, and rapid naming. The test not only identifies students whose achievement is significantly below their peers, but it also precisely analyzes the students' strengths and weaknesses in those three areas of phonemics. One version of the test is appropriate for children ages 5 and 6, who are at the very beginning stage of reading. Another is appropriate for students ranging in age from 7 through 24. Both versions include core subtests of basic skills. The test requires about 30 minutes for administration. Scores are stated according to percentiles, standard scores, and grade-equivalent scores. Separate scores also are given for each of the three major skills areas—awareness, memory, and rapid letter naming. The test results provide teachers with specific information for planning instruction (Sofie & Riccio, 2002).

DESIGNING AN APPROPRIATE INDIVIDUALIZED EDUCATION PROGRAM

Partnering for Special Education and Related Services

Throughout this book you will learn different ways to become a partner with others who design and implement a student's Individualized Educational Program. Some of these strategies are specific to a student's unique needs resulting from his or her disability, such as partnering to develop a health

On the Companion Website, *www.prenhall.com/turnbull,* you will find two links that will provide you with information about the steps of self-directed IEPs and an assessment form that students can use at the end of meetings, *http://web.uccs.edu/education/ special/self determination/cmcr sdiep.html* and *www.vcu.edu/ rrtcweb/techlink/GEB/hughes/ handouts/431b.PBS.*

Values: Involving students with disabilities in educational planning and decision making tells the student you have *great expectations* and enhances the student's self-determination.

Standard: Using curriculum mapping to identify appropriate instructional support is an application of CEC Standard 7, Instructional Planning.

The results of a successful partnership between Lauren's mother, Florence, and her teacher, Sherry, are—to use an LD word— "manifest" by their perfect smiles.

plan for students with other health impairments (Chapter 12); sometimes the partnerships are important across disability categories. You will learn about partnering with parents and family members, related service providers, medical and rehabilitation professionals, and others. It's important, however, to remember one partner with whom teachers should collaborate in the development of an IEP: the student for whom the program is being developed!

In later chapters you will read about universal design for learning and instructional strategies that emphasize student-directed learning. Active involvement of students begins, however, with the educational planning process. This is often linked with transition planning, discussed in Chapter 9, but, really, actively involving students with disabilities in educational planning across their school career is an important aspect of the process.

Student involvement in educational planning can take many forms, depending on the student's interest and capacity. Several procedures exist to facilitate that involvement. For example, Martin and colleagues (1998) developed a process they call the *self-directed IEP.* The process enables students with learning and emotional/behavioral disorders to learn how to direct their own IEP meeting. Schumaker and Deschler (2003) have developed and validated the *self-advocacy strategy,* which includes a step-by-step process for adolescents with learning disabilities to lead their IEP. Even without these and similar instructional packages, however, students with learning disabilities can be involved in setting goals and solving problems related to their education through instructional strategies such as the *self-determined learning model of instruction* (Wehmeyer, Palmer, Agran, Mithaug, & Martin, 2000), discussed in greater detail in Chapter 9.

Research has shown that student involvement is possible and reaps positive outcomes. Researchers conducted an extensive review of the literature pertaining to student involvement and determined that students across disability categories can be successfully involved in transition planning (Test et al., 2004). Martin, Marshall, and Sale (2004) conducted a three-year study of middle, junior, and senior high school IEP meetings and found that the presence of students at IEP meetings had considerable benefits, including increasing parental involvement and improving the probability that a student's strengths, needs, and interests would be discussed.

Determining Supplementary Aids and Services

In Chapter 2, you learned about the types of supplementary aids and services that enable students with disabilities to gain access to the general curriculum, including the importance of universal design for learning. For most of these aids and services to be effective, however, it is often necessary for teachers, schools, and IEP teams to know the scope and sequence of content being delivered at a given school. They can learn this information by engaging in a curriculum mapping process. While not necessarily a supplementary aid and service in and of itself, the curriculum mapping process helps educators implement those supports and ensure high-quality planning (Udelhofen, 2005).

When educators engage in curriculum mapping, they use the school calendar as an organizer and then collect information about each teacher's curriculum, including descriptions of the content to be taught during the year, the processes and skills emphasized, and the student assessments used. Through a variety of review steps involving all school personnel, they develop a curriculum map for the school, identifying gaps or repetitions in the curriculum content. They then can determine whether they are teaching all parts of the curriculum framework, performance objectives, and other standards at the appropriate grade/course (Jacobs, 2004).

The curriculum mapping process can identify where in the curriculum students with disabilities can receive instruction on content from the general curriculum that is based on the student's unique learning needs. So, for example, Lauren's teacher, Sherry, may be looking for opportunities across the school day to provide Lauren with additional opportunities to learn and practice math skills. If Bohemia Manor Middle School had conducted a curriculum map, she could turn to that document and explore where these additional math opportunities exist—maybe in the math-rich musical notations in band class or through history-related activities that deal with numbers. More important, perhaps, if Sherry were an active participant in the school curriculum mapping team, she could actually make sure that the type of information that would benefit the educational planning for students like Lauren was, in fact, available. Since administrators are part of the IEP team, the team can make sure that special educators like Sherry are represented on school mapping teams and that data from the curriculum mapping process are available to the team in making educational planning decisions for students with learning disabilities.

On the Companion Website, *www.prenhall.com/turnbull*, you will find examples of curriculum maps.

Planning for Universal Design for Learning

As you learned in Chapter 2, teachers can apply the theories of universal design for learning through both technology, such as the use of digital or electronic text (about which you will learn more in Chapter 12), and pedagogical methods.

One commonly used curriculum adaptation for students with learning disabilities involves a pedagogical form of universal design called advance organizers. Advance organizers present information before a learning experience (Lenz, Deshler, & Kissam, 2003). Think of advance organizers as cognitive road maps. Maps tell us where we are and help us determine how to get where we want to go. In the same way, advance organizers help students associate new information with their existing cognitive schemas and to anticipate the relationships between their prior knowledge and the new curriculum they must master (Wehmeyer, Sands, Knowlton, & Kozleski, 2002). Ausubel (1963), who pioneered the use of advance organizers, noted that they help students organize and process new material and activate student participation in traditionally passive instructional activities such as lectures and reading. Other forms of organizing information and activating student participation include lesson organizers, chapter survey routines, unit organizers, and course organizers, some of which you will learn about later in this chapter.

Values: Involving all educators, especially special educators, in the curriculum-mapping process enhances schoolwide collaboration, creates the potential for inclusive practices to emerge, and then increases the potential for *relationships* such as Lauren has with many of her peers with and without disabilities to flourish.

Are advance organizers important for students with learning disabilities? The research is clear that they are. Swanson (2001) conducted a meta-analysis of intervention studies to promote higher-order cognitive processes among adolescents with learning disabilities and found that one factor that significantly increased the effect of the intervention was the use of advance organizers. Swanson and Deshler (2003) found that nearly 35 percent of studies in the Swanson meta-analysis involved an advance organizer component, which included "statements in the treatment description directing adolescents to look over material before instruction, directing adolescents to focus on particular information, providing prior information about the task, or directing the teacher to state the objectives of instruction" (p. 127). So powerful was the implementation of advance organizers in this study that Swanson and Deshler concluded the organizers should be components of most interventions for students with learning disabilities.

Planning for Other Educational Needs

A critical area of concern for many students with learning disabilities is their transition from secondary education to postsecondary education. Despite the fact that during the past decade colleges and universities have increased their support services for individuals with disabilities to assist them in their transition to and through two- or four-year institutions, students with learning disabilities struggle in their postsecondary programs.

One solution to this problem is to ensure that students with learning disabilities acquire the skills they need to advocate on their behalf in college. They also must possess knowledge about how their disability impacts learning. A recent survey by researchers at the Virginia Commonwealth University Rehabilitation Research and Training Center on Workplace Supports asked college students with disabilities to identify the skills they believed are necessary for success in postsecondary education. The students identified these skills in priority order (Thoma & Wehmeyer, in press):

1. Understanding their disability
2. Understanding their strengths and limitations
3. Learning to succeed despite their disability and learning what accommodations facilitate learning

4. Setting goals and learning how to access resources needed to attain those goals

5. Acquiring problem-solving skills

6. Acquiring self-management skills

7. Forming relationships with instructors, university or college disability support staff, friends, and mentors

Values: By providing students with learning disabilities critically important instruction in self-advocacy, you can enhance their potential for success in college while also enhancing student self-determination and choices.

The educational programs of students with learning disabilities should include instruction to learn these types of skills. Materials such as the self-advocacy strategy discussed previously provide a systematic way to do this. Reis, McGuire, and Neu (2000) determined that self-advocacy and self-determination–related skills were among those that successful college students with learning disabilities employed. Izzo, Hertzfeld, and Aaron (2001) conducted focus groups of college students with disabilities and faculty members and found that self-advocacy skills were critical to success in college. Box 5–3 provides information on how to use technology to promote self-advocacy.

USING EFFECTIVE INSTRUCTIONAL STRATEGIES

Early Childhood Students: Embedded Learning Opportunities

For children from birth to age 3 who have or are at risk of having a learning disability or other disabilities, there is literally no substitute for early intervention. Numerous early childhood special educators have recommended incorporating instruction into these children's daily activities by using a strategy called embedded learning opportunities (Davis, Kilgo, & Gamel-McCormick, 1998; Sandall, Schwartz, & Joseph, 2001).

This strategy calls on teachers to "identify the opportunities that are most salient to the individualized learning objectives for each child and embed short, systematic instructional interactions

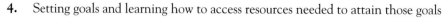

Technology Tips ~ Using Hypermedia to Promote Self-Advocacy   **Box 5–3**

The self-advocacy strategy is one of the instructional strategies developed by researchers at the University of Kansas Center for Research on Learning. You learned about several such strategies in this chapter. The intent of the self-advocacy strategy is to enable students with learning disabilities to participate more fully and meaningfully in educational planning and decision making. One important component of the self-advocacy strategy is the implementation of the I PLAN process. I PLAN is an acronym to assist students to remember the steps in setting goals:

- **I**nventory your strengths, areas of needed improvement, and learning needs.
- **P**rovide your inventory information.
- **L**isten and respond.
- **A**sk questions.
- **N**ame your goals.

Lancaster, Schumaker, and Deshler (2002) evaluated the efficacy of an interactive hypermedia version of the self-advocacy strategy. Interactive hypermedia formats allow the use of video and audio segments, text, and graphics and provide multiple paths for students to follow in a nonlinear fashion as they interact with the material. The most common form of interactive hypermedia format is HTML (hypertext markup language), which is used to design web pages.

The hypermedia version of the self-advocacy strategy allowed students to navigate through the process at their own pace and with minimal teacher supervision. Students can begin and end lessons at any time. The hypermedia version includes video clips of instructors modeling each step in the strategy, including each of the I PLAN steps. At the end of the lesson, students model what they've learned to the teacher.

The hypermedia version of the self-advocacy strategy is available from the Center for Research on Learning (http://www.ku-crl.org/iei/index.html), but creating your own hypermedia materials is relatively simple. There are authoring software packages available that allow you to develop HTML-based materials, such as Microsoft DreamWorks. Even more easy: most word processors have the capacity to save any text document as an HTML file, which then can be viewed with a web browser. Moreover, using a Macintosh platform, it is relatively simple to create hypermedia materials that incorporate video and audio clips that can be burned to a CD.

Is it worth the additional effort? Lancaster and colleagues (2002) found that students with learning disabilities, other health impairments, and behavioral disorders who learned the process taught in the self-advocacy strategy through the hypermedia program were able to run their own IEP conferences!

Source: Adapted from Lancaster, P. E., Schumaker, J. B., & Deshler, D. D. (2002). The development and validation of an interactive hypermedia program teaching a self-advocacy strategy to students with disabilities. *Learning Disability Quarterly, 25*(4), 277–302.

that support the child's goals into existing routines and activities" (Horn, Leiber, & Li, 2000, p. 210). While bathing, for example, children can learn skills to develop their communication (e.g., using words to label bath objects), cognitive (e.g., finding submerged objects), motor (e.g., picking up objects), and adaptive (e.g., washing hands and face) abilities. When teachers, caregivers, and therapists embed children's goals and objectives into daily activities, they build on the children's interest and increase their motivation (Hemmeter & Grisham-Brown, 1997).

The embedded learning approach is a promising intervention strategy because it does the following (Bricker, Pretti-Frontczak, & McComas, 1998):

- Provides children with lots of practice within the context of their daily activities and events
- Can be used in inclusive environments
- Capitalizes on a child's interest and motivation
- Is available to parents, teachers, therapists, and peers
- Is compatible with a wide range of curricular models

One example of an effective embedded learning opportunities program derives from a Nashville child-care program. The program enrolls 12 3- to 4-year-old children and provides them with a single lead teacher. Among the children are several who have learning disabilities, including Alex. Alex is 4 years old and has moderate delays in the areas of expressive language and speech; because he also has cerebral palsy, he has delays in his gross- and fine-motor and cognitive and social development. In his classroom, the children's daily activities include a large-group circle as an opening activity for the day and as a transition between outdoor play and lunch; time focused on dramatic play, preliteracy, and hands-on science and computer; outdoor play; lunch; and self-care and cleanup.

Using this model, Alex's teacher created opportunities for him to place materials in centers (e.g., he placed a pitcher in the snack center). Then she added a task as a requirement for his center participation (e.g., he had to pour paints from one container to another in the art corner) and provided verbal prompts, models, and physical guidance during play (e.g., guided his pouring between containers during water-table play).

In and of themselves, these activities do not guarantee that Alex or other children will make progress on their learning objectives, even when the activities are fun and engaging. Instead, teachers need to pair these learning opportunities with instruction that lets the children know what they need to do, how a correct response looks and feels and what the correct response is, as well as reassurance that a response will result in a positive outcome.

Elementary and Middle School Students: Differentiated Instruction

Council for Exceptional Children

Standard: Learning how to differentiate instruction is a way to apply CEC Standard 4, Instructional Strategies.

Perhaps the most prevalent strategy to promote participation in and progress through the general curriculum has been differentiated instruction. *To differentiate* means to make something different by altering or modifying it. Differentiated instruction modifies traditional instruction.

In differentiated instruction, a teacher uses more than one instructional methodology, increasing students' access to instructional materials in a variety of formats, expanding test-taking and data collection options, and varying the complexity and nature of content presented during the course of a unit of study (Tomlinson, 2001, 2003). Differentiated instruction is a logical companion to universal design for learning. Both attempt to ensure that content or instruction reaches all students, independent of student abilities, disabilities, language, or preparation for school. When working with Lauren, Sherry Eichinger, her teacher, uses the same curriculum as all students in Lauren's class use, but she and Lauren work in a special reading program for about 30 minutes each week so that Sherry can teach Lauren how to anticipate what she will read, how to review and recall what she has already read or will read in class that week, and how to implement other advance-organizer techniques. In addition, Sherry, Jean Clark (an instructional coach at Lauren's school), and Lauren's general education mathematics teacher also make special efforts to break down the word-math problems for Lauren because she

Sherry (left) and Jean (right) team with each other and with other faculty to include Lauren in the general education curriculum and to assure that she makes progress in it.

Values: Differentiating instruction shows that you, as a teacher, are working to ensure that all students have equal opportunities to acquire skills and knowledge critical for life and their *great expectations.*

On the Companion Website, *www.prenhall.com/turnbull,* you will find a link to more information on learning strategies, *www. kucrl.org/sim/lscurriculum.html.*

Use your *Real Lives and Exceptionalities* DVD to meet Ms. Guinn, a fifth-grade teacher discussing differentiated instruction. Click on "Meet Heather" and select "Accommodations" (Clip 2).

not only has to read the problem but also has to solve it. So differentiated reading and math instruction go hand in hand.

Research has demonstrated that teachers can effectively differentiate curricular content, the instructional process, product requirements, and/or assessment practices to facilitate students' access to and success within the general curriculum (Tomlinson, 2003). Examples of curricular content differentiation include reducing the number of math problems assigned to certain students or giving students the option of taking a weekly spelling pre-test to opt out of spelling for that week.

Differentiating the instructional process can be accomplished through a myriad of techniques that themselves should be implemented schoolwide for the benefit of all students. Consider the following, each of which is effective for Lauren when applied by Sherry and Lauren's general education teachers (Janney & Snell, 2004):

- Providing visual or graphic organizers to accompany oral presentations
- Incorporating the use of models, demonstrations, or role play
- Using teacher presentation cues (e.g., gestural, visual, or verbal) to emphasize key points
- Scaffolding key concepts to be learned
- Getting students more actively involved in the learning process through the implementation of every-pupil response techniques (e.g., lecture response cards) or the incorporation of manipulatives for student use

Secondary and Transition Students: Learning Strategies

Deshler and his team of researchers at the University of Kansas Center for Research on Learning have developed a host of strategies for use with students with learning disabilities (Deshler et al., 2001; Lenz et al., 2003). These strategies, called **learning strategies,** help students with learning disabilities to learn independently and to generalize, or transfer, their skills and behaviors to new situations (Hock, Deshler, & Schumaker, 1999; Lenz et al., 2003).

Learning strategies work especially well for students who have learning disabilities in basic skill areas such as reading, language arts, writing, spelling, and math. Similarly, they are effective for specialized school tasks such as test taking, paragraph writing, and lecture comprehension (Lenz et al., 2003). And they are effective in assisting students to comprehend content-oriented classes such as science and social studies. Box 5–4 provides an example of one learning strategy, the sentence writing strategy.

The first step in using a learning strategy in any instructional area is to assess how well a student can perform a skill. The second step is to point out the benefit of using learning strategies—namely, the student will ultimately discover how to learn on her own and succeed in and out of school. And the third step is to explain specifically what a student will be able to accomplish when she has learned the skill. Although it is not possible in this chapter to introduce you to all of the learning strategies, we can give you some examples.

Acquiring information. As we have noted, students with learning disabilities have difficulty acquiring information; they do not have particularly strong meta-cognition skills. The self-questioning strategy is one of six strategies for acquiring information. It requires students to create questions, predict answers to those questions, and search for the answers while they read a passage. Self-questioning is advantageous for four reasons:

Into Practice ~ Sentence Writing Strategy   Box 5-4

As with all the learning strategies developed by the Center for Research on Learning, students need to learn the sentence writing strategy so that they will use it automatically. Just as teachers use repetition to teach beginning readers to master basic sound-symbol relationships, so they instruct older students to master task-specific learning strategies through highly structured practice. Practice, practice, and practice again: that is how teachers help students use the sentence writing strategy automatically.

Teachers instruct students in how to use the strategy by pretesting them to measure each student's sentence-writing skills. Then the teachers deliver the strategy in four parts, over and over again.

Part 1. They teach the skills involved in writing simple sentences.

Part 2. They teach the skills involved in writing compound sentences and require their students to integrate those skills with the previously taught skills for writing simple sentences.

Part 3. They teach their students how to write complex sentences and how to integrate those skills with the previously taught skills for writing simple and compound sentences.

Part 4. They teach their students how to write compound-complex sentences and how to integrate those skills with the three previously taught skills.

Students must reach mastery in the previous part of the sequence before moving to the next. Thus, the instruction is a building process whereby students are required to integrate new skills with previously learned skills.

This four-part instruction can be adapted to a variety of needs. For example, a student can receive instruction in all four parts in a large block of time (e.g., 30 minutes per day for 9 or 10 weeks). Alternatively, teachers can provide instruction in a single part and then shift to other strategies as students master that single part.

At some later time, the student may return to instruction in the sentence writing strategy to learn additional sentence types. For example, some teachers prefer to teach Parts 1 and 2 in the seventh grade, Part 3 in the eighth grade, and Part 4 in the ninth grade.

The strategy will not work unless the teachers use the four parts in sequence. Although students can write simple sentences, they must go through the simple-sentence instruction because it provides them with vocabulary and a knowledge base upon which subsequent parts build. The foundation provided in the simple-sentence instruction is critical for success in the other parts, and each subsequent part logically builds on previous instruction.

Putting These Strategies to Work for Progress in the General Curriculum

1. How might one of Lauren's content-oriented teachers integrate this strategy into her classroom?

2. Search the Internet for information on learning strategies developed by the Center for Research on Learning at the University of Kansas. State three facts that you found on the Internet that expands your knowledge about learning strategies.

3. How can partnerships among special and general education teachers and Lauren's parents assist her in learning this strategy?

To answer these questions online, go to the Into Practice module in Chapter 5 of the Companion Website, www.prenhall.com/turnbull.

- It requires students to actively interact with the material.

- It helps divide the passage into small, manageable units so the students can more easily acquire the information.

- It helps to promote intrinsic motivation for learning by having students identify their own reasons for reading a passage.

- It requires students to verbalize the information that they are learning, thereby enhancing their understanding and later recall of the information.

Council for Exceptional Children

Standard: Selecting and adapting instructional strategies for students with learning disabilities is an application of CEC Standard 4, Instructional Strategies.

Storing information and remembering. Students with learning disabilities also have difficulty recalling what they have read or mastered earlier. To help them, teachers are instructing their students to use organizational strategies. The purpose of these strategies is to help students understand the direction they are taking when they are trying to learn and later recall information. Advanced organizers, as you have learned, are especially helpful (Swanson & Deshler, 2003).

One type of advance organizer is called a graphic organizer. Sometimes referred to as webs, maps, or concept diagrams, graphic organizers assist students to (1) identify key concepts and sub-concepts, (2) compare and contrast information, and (3) relate cause to effect (Friend & Bursuck, 2002). By enabling students to visualize information in an organized fashion, graphic organizers help them grasp key information. The styles of graphic organizers vary depending on concepts being taught and the maturity of the students. Generally, teachers and students brainstorm together to identify one or more effective models.

Figure 5-5 Educational placement of students with specific learning disabilities (2003–2004)

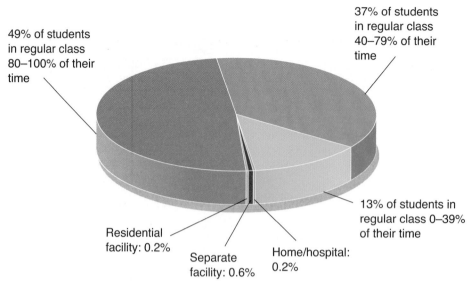

49% of students in regular class 80–100% of their time

37% of students in regular class 40–79% of their time

13% of students in regular class 0–39% of their time

Residential facility: 0.2%

Separate facility: 0.6%

Home/hospital: 0.2%

Source: U.S. Department of Education, Office of Special Education Programs. (2005). *IDEA data website.* (http://www.ideadata.org/aboutThisSite.asp).

INCLUDING STUDENTS WITH LEARNING DISABILITIES

As illustrated in Figure 5–5, students with learning disabilities have the highest rates of inclusion in general education classes when compared to students with other disabilities. Nevertheless, their inclusion cannot be effective unless educators use evidence-based strategies for instructing them. Box 5–5 provides tips for increasing success for students with learning disabilities in the general education classroom.

ASSESSING STUDENTS' PROGRESS

Measuring Students' Progress

Progress in the general curriculum. A frequently used method to track progress in reading, writing, spelling, and math for students with disabilities is **curriculum-based measurement,** which involves direct assessment of a student's skills in the content of the curriculum being taught (Fuchs & Fuchs, 2002). When using curriculum-based measurement, the instructor gives the student brief, timed samples or probes made up of academic material taken from the student's school curriculum. These probes are given under standardized conditions. The child's performance on a curriculum-based measurement probe is scored for speed, fluency, and accuracy of performance. Since curriculum-based measurement probes are quick to administer and simple to score, they can be given repeatedly.

The types of probes vary according to content. Reading probes typically involve two measures: a maze task in which a student reads a passage, aloud or silently, with words deleted, and then selects a word to replace the missing word; or having a student read a passage aloud for a specified duration and counting the correct number of words read (oral reading fluency). Curriculum-based measurement of spelling typically involves having students write words dictated to them for a specified time and counting the correct letter sequences. Applied to math, students answer computational questions for a set time period and then count the number of correct answers (Hosp & Hosp, 2003).

Curriculum-based measurement has been found to be valid in tracking the progress of students with learning disabilities across multiple content areas, including math (Calhoon & Fuchs,

On the Companion Website, *www.prenhall.com/turnbull,* you will find a link to more detailed information about curriculum-based assessment, *www.teacherstoolkit. com/classroom1.htm.*

Inclusion Tips   Box 5–5

	What You Might See	What You Might Be Tempted to Do	Alternate Responses	Ways to Include Peers in the Process
Behavior	She continually disrupts other students when she needs to be working independently on assignments.	Move her away from peers or send her to the principal's office.	Use advance organizers to guide her learning on independent assignments.	Match her with a peer tutor of whom she can ask questions when she is not sure what she is supposed to be doing.
Social interactions	He misinterprets social cues. He misinterprets facial gestures and/or verbal inflections.	Point out the misinterpretation and tell him how to do it "right."	Include him in the IEP conference to plan collaboratively a social skills curriculum.	Establish a peer partnership where the peer can practice specific social cues with him.
Educational performance	His work is inconsistent or generally poor.	Grade him down for poor or incomplete work.	Use differentiated instruction to ensure that his learning strengths and needs are addressed.	Use differentiated instruction with all students.
Classroom attitudes	He easily gives up in areas of weakness to get out of work.	Excuse him from some assignments or reprimand him for his unwillingness to try.	Use curriculum-based measurement to enhance his awareness about the progress he is making.	Give him opportunities to tutor others (peers or younger students) in areas of his success.

2003), reading (Compton, Appleton, & Hosp, 2004), and social studies (Espin, Busch, Shin, & Kruschwitz, 2001).

Progress in addressing other educational needs. As is the case for many students with disabilities, but not Lauren, the biggest barrier to successful inclusion and positive postsecondary outcomes may be their limited social skills (Vaughn, Elbaum, & Boardman, 2001). That is why the strategies for tracking student progress that we will discuss in Chapter 7, including using rating scales and sociometric ratings, will be equally important for students with learning disabilities. There are a few checklists to track progress in the types of self-advocacy skills discussed previously in this chapter, although there are some standardized measures of self-determination that have been used with students with learning disabilities (Wehmeyer, 2002). The Arc's Self-Determination Scale, available from *http://www.beachcenter.org/*, is a student self-report measure of self-determination for students with cognitive disabilities, including students with learning disabilities.

Making Accommodations in Assessment

Perhaps in no other category of disability is the issue of test accommodations as controversial as it is in the area of specific learning disabilities. This is so because many test givers (teachers, local educational agencies, and state educational agencies) are concerned that students who do not require accommodations (so that they will have an authentic opportunity, equal to that of students without disabilities) will seek and obtain the accommodations and be placed at a competitive advantage relative to other students.

The fact remains, however, that students with learning disabilities may need a wide array of accommodations to be able to perform according to their highest level on standardized tests. For example, a research team found that providing a reader (either a person or a computer) on a standardized math test improved student outcomes (Calhoon, Fuchs, & Hamlett, 2000). Weaver

(2000) found that extended time for taking an examination enabled students with learning disabilities to perform more effectively. Other effective test accommodations include the administration of a test via a computer or the use of a calculator (Fuchs et al., 2000).

Looking to Lauren's Future

It is rarely possible to make accurate predictions about any student's future. So many events can intervene between a 14-year-old student's life in middle school and her life as an 18- or 21-year-old high school graduate.

Assuming, however, that the characteristics that mark Lauren's middle school years—her family's support, her eagerness to learn, her mastery of problem-solving strategies, and her instinctive peace-seeking nature and leadership talents—become even more powerful, it is by no means optimistic to see Lauren, at the age of 21 or 22, having finished her IDEA eligibility at age 21 and graduated from high school, enrolling at the Cecil County Community College, studying a variety of office-clerical skills, changing her emphasis to medical technology and health-care administration, and volunteering all the time in her hometown's youth development programs.

Upon her graduation from the community college, Lauren will continue to be a peacemaker, perhaps teaching youngsters how to resolve their disagreements as a volunteer in her town's park and recreation programs and offering programs for teenagers in her church, the Elkton Church of Christ. She may work in the local hospital, assisting medical technicians in procuring blood and urine samples and various X-ray and other images. And she will continue to have a large coterie of loyal friends, boys and girls alike, from all walks of life and all different backgrounds.

It's as though Lauren always carries the olive branch, always proffering it to anyone who comes within the arc of her optimistic personality.

SUMMARY

Identifying students with learning disabilities

- IDEA has inclusionary (severe discrepancy between achievement and intellectual ability in math and reading) and exclusionary (not due to mental retardation or environmental/economic disadvantages) criteria for determining whether a student has a learning disability.

- Learning disabilities is the most prevalent category of exceptionality.

- Students with learning disabilities are a heterogeneous population with varied academic problems related to reading, written language, and math.

- Academic problems relate to challenges with memory and metacognition.

- Students with learning disabilities often have difficulties with social skills; they sometimes have poor self-concepts.

- Research suggests that different neurological regions of the brain are associated with particular learning problems and that learning disabilities have a strong genetic basis.

Evaluating students with learning disabilities

- Nondiscriminatory evaluation includes the use of standardized intelligence and achievement tests to pinpoint a severe discrepancy.

- The most current evaluation focus in the field of learning disabilities is establishing the student's response to intervention in terms of documenting the nature of instruction that will be most advantageous for the student.

Designing an appropriate individualized education program

■ Perhaps the most important partner you can include in educational planning and decision making is the student. Curriculum mapping involves a determination of the scope and sequence of the delivery of content in a school and can be a critical source of data for IEP teams when making decisions about a student's educational program.

■ Advance organizers, which present information to be learned in advance of a student's engagement in the learning activity, have been shown to be very powerful pedagogical tools that enable learners with learning disabilities to perform more effectively.

■ Promoting student self-advocacy skills can enable students with learning disabilities to make the transition from high school to college.

Using effective instructional strategies

■ Embedded learning opportunities involve instruction of key skills that are embedded in other routines or tasks. These strategies have been shown to be very useful with young children with learning disabilities.

■ Differentiated instruction involves the differentiation of content and instructional strategies to ensure that all students in a classroom have the opportunity to learn. This is among the most important strategies to ensure effective inclusive practices.

■ Learning strategies instruction provides the opportunity for students with learning disabilities to acquire "learning-to-learn" strategies that impact knowledge acquisition, information storage and retrieval, and other higher-order cognitive functions.

Including students with learning disabilities

■ Students with learning disabilities have the highest rate of inclusion in general education classes.

Assessing students' progress

■ Curriculum-based measurement involves the use of multiple, frequent probes that collect samples of student progress in content areas, including math, reading, science, and social studies.

■ There are a number of test accommodations, including extended time, oral presentation, computer administration, and calculator use, that have been shown to be effective with students with learning disabilities.

WHAT WOULD YOU RECOMMEND?

Refer to chapter content and the PRAXIS™ and CEC standards in Appendix A to answer the following questions:

1. Select an instructional strategy that is described in this chapter that you believe would be helpful in teaching Lauren. Describe the strategy and explain how you might use it to assist Lauren's progress in the general education classroom. Identify which PRAXIS™ and CEC standards you are applying as you do this research.

2. Go to the Companion Website for Chapter 5, *www.prenhall.com/turnbull*, and find examples of advance organizers. Prepare an advance organizer for the chapter, using the

samples as a model. Share the organizer with your class and explain how it helps you organize the chapter contents. Identify which PRAXIS™ and CEC standards you applied as you prepared your advance organizer.

3. Using the curriculum map on the Companion Website for Chapter 5, *www.prenhall. com/turnbull*, identify areas on the map where a student with learning disabilities in mathematics computation would find opportunities for learning. Identify how you are applying PRAXIS™ and CEC standards as you complete this activity.

Who is George Wedge?

Contributing authors: Jane Wegner, University of Kansas, and Evette Edmister, Des Moines, Iowa

You know that words have many meanings. Take the word *telegraph*. It is a noun (a sent message), an adjective (as in "telegraph machine"), and a verb (to give advance warning). In the lives of George Wedge, age 9, and his parents, Linda and Phil, telegraphing has been a way of life, one that they experienced even before George was born.

Like many women, Linda underwent an ultrasound examination when she was pregnant. The results were alarming: her unborn baby had a congenital malformation of his brain and surely would have a disability upon birth. What a telegraph! And what to do about it?

Step 1: Get help. Where? At the Douglas County, Kansas, Inter-Agency Coordinating Council for Infants and Toddlers (ICC). What kind of help? Information about their baby's speech-limiting condition, called Dandy Walker syndrome, and its likely effects. One potential effect was infant mortality. But even if the baby were to live, he might not walk, talk, or learn to read, and he might have a low IQ.

Step 2: Plan for early intervention. How? Don't give in and don't give up. As soon as George was born, Linda and Phil enrolled him in the county's early intervention program (through the ICC). Enrollment led him into a program for infants and toddlers at the University of Kansas's Sunnyside program (in a building on Sunnyside Avenue, of course). He began attending at the age of 3 months and graduated at the age of 3. Upon his graduation, George continued his education at the university's Hilltop Child Development Center, from which he graduated at the age of 6. George is now in the second grade at Cordley Elementary School.

Step 3: Provide intensive intervention, not just one intervention but many: finger spelling and American Sign Language instruction, surgery to repair a cleft palate and insert a feeding tube

because George has difficulty swallowing, instruction on how to swallow and shape words, a hearing aid for his right ear, and an assistive technology device for augmentative communication (the Tablet Portable IMPACT from Enkidu Research).

Step 4: Assemble a team. Who? Start with the ICC staff; add the Sunnyside and Hilltop staff. Augment with physicians. Corral George's brother, Roy, and other school-age boys and girls. Get instruction on helpful devices from the Capper Foundation in nearby

Understanding Students with Communication Disorders

Topeka. Include the teachers and related service professionals. Give extended family and friends a role. Be sure Linda and Phil are the head coaches. And give the ball to George as often as he can carry it.

Step 5: Expect great results and celebrate them. When? Always, and be grateful—more, be joyful—that George is alive. Applaud him and everyone on his team for the outcomes: his ability to form words and talk to those who know him well or pay close attention to him; his ability to use sign language and finger-spell; his mastery of his assistive technology device; his progress through two early intervention settings that include children with and without disabilities in the same classrooms; his progress through second grade; his ability to walk, ride a horse, take classes at the local art center and museums; his developing talent as a chess player and his love of reading and drama; his ability to make friends; and the composure and wherewithal to summon help by calling 911 during two separate emergencies.

Step 6: Prepare for and face the challenges of today and tomorrow. Acknowledge that George still needs help learning to swallow; that after more palatal and ear surgery he still needs to learn how to shape words; that his teacher, Beverly Hyde, is learning about communication disabilities but still wants to learn more; that George needs extra help in math; that his speech pathologist, Annette Dabney, has to teach not only George but also his teacher and other school staff so they can help George with speech and swallowing at lunchtime; and that the best way for this team to communicate and work together is to have a "playbook" that travels daily between home and school.

Last Step: Take a good hard look at George, Linda, Phil, and Roy Wedge. Why? Reread the first telegraph that Linda and Phil received, the bad-news one. Now send a different one, the good-news one. Let it read as follows: "Past is prologue. Hard work ahead. Nothing that you can't do. See you when George graduates from elementary, middle, and high school. Banking on him moving away for college or on to a satisfying job." Sign it "special educators and related service providers." P. S.: "Speech pathology always available."

Use your *Real Lives and Exceptionalities* DVD to "Meet George."

IDENTIFYING STUDENTS WITH COMMUNICATION DISORDERS

Defining Communication Disorders

Communication entails receiving, understanding, and expressing information, feelings, and ideas. It is also such a natural part of our daily lives that most of us take our ability to communicate for granted. Most of us participate in many communicative interactions each day. For example, we talk with others face to face or on the phone; we e-mail a colleague or friend; we demonstrate social awareness by lowering our voices when we see a raised eyebrow or a frown; we wink at friends over private jokes.

Communication involves speaking as well as a multitude of nonverbal behaviors such as facial expression, gestures, and head and body movements.

Although we usually communicate through speech, we also communicate in many other ways. Some people communicate manually, using sign language and/or gestures. While speaking, others add nonlinguistic cues such as body posture, facial and vocal expression, gestures, eye contact, and head and body movements. Many speakers vary their voices by changing their pitch or rate of speaking. All of these skills make our communication more effective.

Communication is the cornerstone of the teaching and learning process. Teaching and learning are typically carried out via spoken and written language. Although most children come to school able to understand others and express themselves and thus participate in school more easily, many children do not. Imagine the difficulties a student with a communication disorder might encounter with classroom activities, social interactions, instructional discourse exchanges, acquisition of knowledge and language, and the development of literacy skills. Effective communication in school is a complicated and vital process.

Speech and language disorders. Communication disorders relate to the components of the process affected: speech, language, or both (ASHA, 2004b; Stuart, 2002; Hulit & Howard, 2002). A **speech disorder** refers to difficulty producing sounds as well as disorders of voice quality (for example, a hoarse voice) or fluency of speech, often referred to as stuttering. A **language disorder** entails difficulty receiving, understanding, and formulating ideas and information. A **receptive language disorder** is characterized by difficulty receiving or understanding information. An **expressive language disorder** is characterized by difficulty formulating ideas and information. IDEA recognizes that both types of communication disorders can adversely affect a student's educational performance.

Speech and language disorders are often associated with other disorders. Specifically, speech disorders are sometimes associated with a **cleft palate or lip,** a condition in which a person has a split in the upper part of the oral cavity or the upper lip. George's speech difficulties are a result of his cleft palate, so he uses an augmentative and alternative communication (AAC) device called the Tablet to express himself more clearly as he works to improve his speech. Language disorders are sometimes the primary feature through which other disorders are identified. For example, a child with a hearing disorder may initially be referred because she is not talking as well as other children her age.

Cultural diversity in communication. Students from different cultural backgrounds may have speech or language differences that affect their participation in the classroom. Although many individuals have a speech or language *difference,* they do not necessarily have a language or speech *disorder.* Difference does not always mean disorder (Battle, 1998). Box 6–1 provides information relevant to classroom interactions and other cultural differences in communication.

Diversity Tips ~ Communicative Interactions

Box 6-1

Instructors need to remember that students come from varied cultural and linguistic backgrounds. Their interactions at school may be very different from those at home (Allington & Cunningham, 2002; Bunce, 2003; Giangreco, 2000). "Teachers need to be aware of possible causes of communication failure in the school environment in order to circumvent misunderstandings and to facilitate academic achievement and acceptance of the bilingual/bicultural child in the school system" (Bunce, 2003, p. 370). Try some of these strategies to improve interactions:

- Use cooperative group activities to foster multicultural relationships as well as role-playing and team-building exercises.
- Highlight the value of diversity through cultural influence and the contributions of events, celebrations, and people in curricular content.

- Incorporate community activities and speakers who reflect differing cultures.
- Invite parents to visit classes and share information about their culture.

Students in the classroom need information about different cultural practices and reassurance that one cultural communicative practice is not better than another. They are simply different, and these differences need to be respected, understood, and considered when people communicate (Bunce, 2003).

Some children may have a cultural difference combined with a speech and/or language disorder. Others may not have a speech and/or language impairment and do not need support services. However, in all cases teachers need to consider how instruction and assessments may need to be adapted and/or augmented in order to assist students' learning and participation.

Some students are bilingual, while others have dialectical differences or accents. An accent is a phonetic trait carried from a first language to the second (ASHA, 2004a). Every language contains a variety of forms, called dialects. A **dialect** is a language variation that a group of individuals uses and that reflects shared regional, social, or cultural/ethnic factors. Examples of culturally- and linguistically-diverse populations that may use an accent or a social dialect include African Americans, Latinos, Asian/Pacific Islanders, and Native Americans. Accents and dialects are not communication disorders; rather, they are differences (ASHA, 2004a). Nevertheless, although differences in dialects do not necessarily indicate communication disorders, students with dialectical differences may also have communication disorders.

Incidence. Of all the students receiving special education ranging in age from 6 to 21 years old, 18.8 percent have received speech and language services (U.S. Department of Education, 2002). Fifty-five percent of children 3 to 5 years old served under IDEA had speech-language disorders (U.S. Department of Education, 2002). These figures do not include children who have communication disorders secondary to other conditions. Most students with communication disorders spend the majority of their day in the general education classroom.

Describing the Characteristics

For most children, the development of communication is uneventful and follows a typical, predictable pattern and timetable. For others, it does not; these children may have a communication disorder. It is helpful to understand the typical pattern of acquiring speech and language skills so you can recognize instances when communication disorders are present.

Typical development. **Speech** is the oral expression of language. This expression occurs when a person produces sounds and syllables. (Figure 6–1 illustrates the speech mechanism that, through a coordinated effort, allows for sound production.) As a person pushes air from her lungs, the muscles in her larynx move her vocal folds, producing sounds. The larynx sits on top of the trachea and contains the vocal folds (ligaments of the larynx); voice is produced here. A person forms sounds by varying the position of her lips, tongue, and lower jaw as the air passes through her larynx (voice box), pharynx (a space extending from the nasal cavities to the esophagus), mouth, and nose.

Language is a structured, shared, rule-governed, symbolic system for communicating. The five components of our language system are phonology (sound system), morphology (word forms), syntax (word order and sentence structure), semantics (word and sentence meanings), and pragmatics (social use of language). Each dimension works together with the others to create a robust language system.

Council for
Exceptional
Children

Standard: As you learn about typical speech and language development and speech and language impairments, you address CEC Standard 6, Communication.

Figure 6–1   Speech mechanism

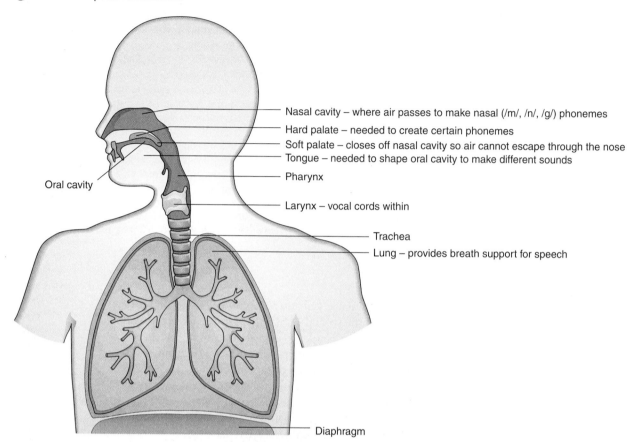

Nasal cavity – where air passes to make nasal (/m/, /n/, /g/) phonemes
Hard palate – needed to create certain phonemes
Soft palate – closes off nasal cavity so air cannot escape through the nose
Tongue – needed to shape oral cavity to make different sounds
Pharynx
Larynx – vocal cords within
Oral cavity
Trachea
Lung – provides breath support for speech
Diaphragm

Phonology is the use of sounds to make meaningful syllables and words. Phonology is a much broader concept than articulation is. Phonology encompasses the rules and sequencing of individual speech sounds (called **phonemes**) and how they are produced, depending on their placement in a syllable or word. For example, consonants at the beginning of syllables or words (e.g., "*t*ap") are produced slightly differently from those in the middle (e.g., "ca*tt*le") or at the end of syllables or words (e.g., "pa*t*"). Phonological use requires correct pronunciation as well as awareness of sound differences as they signal change in meaning. In English, for instance, the word "bill" is different from "pill" by only one phoneme: /b/. By changing one phoneme, a speaker can produce a totally different word. Although English spelling has 26 letters, English speakers use them to produce 45 different sounds. For example, /th/, /sh/, /oy/, and /ou/ are four completely different sounds that are represented in spelling as different combinations of 2 of the 26 letters (Owens, 2001).

Morphology is the system that governs the structure of words (Owens, 2005). Phonemes or single sounds have little meaning on their own, but some can be grouped into syllables or words that have meaning. The smallest meaningful unit of speech is called a morpheme. For instance, when -s is added to "bill," the word becomes plural. Formerly having one **morpheme,** the word now has two: "bill" (a mouth structure on a bird, a written document) and -s (denoting plurality). Morphological rules allow speakers to add plurals, inflection, affixes, and past-tense markers to verbs. For example, correct use of morphological rules allows a child to change "swim" to "swimmed" and then, as the child matures, to "swam," an irregular past-tense verb. Understanding of morphological rules allows us to recognize meaning just by hearing it.

Syntax provides rules for putting together a series of words to form sentences (Owens, 2005). Receptively, a child must be able to note the significance in the order of others' words. For example, "I want that cookie" means that the speaker desires a cookie, whereas "Do I want that cookie?"

indicates a question in which the speaker is determining if he wants a cookie. Expressively, a child must be able to use word order to generate new sentences and to know when sentences are not grammatically correct. Just as phonology provides the rules for putting together strings of phonemes to form words, syntax provides rules for putting together a series of words to construct sentences.

The first three dimensions of language—phonology, morphology, and syntax—all combine to determine the form of language: that is, what the language looks like. The next two dimensions of language—semantics and pragmatics—determine the content and social use of language (Bloom & Lahey, 1978).

Semantics refers to the meaning of what is expressed. Semantic development has both receptive and expressive components. Children first learn to understand the meaning of words and then to verbally or manually use the words and sentences meaningfully. Children start out with a small number of words that represent a large number of objects in their environments; for example, to young children, all men may be "daddy." This is called an overextension and is typical in semantic development (Owens, 2005).

Pragmatics refers to the use of communication in contexts. Pragmatics is the overall organizer for language (Owens, 2005). Caregivers and infants use the rules of pragmatics in their interactions, and children learn to use social communication very early. After using smiles and simple verbalizations, children request objects, actions, or information; protest actions; comment on objects or actions; greet; and acknowledge comments. These skills allow children to use language socially to interact within their environments and with people in those environments more efficiently.

No one knows for sure just how the five dimensions of language come to work together so that children acquire useful language. Theories explaining how children acquire language abound (Loeb, 2003). In the 1950s, Chomsky (1957) proposed that children are born ready to develop language skills because of an inborn language acquisition device. Later behaviorists proposed that the ability to learn and use language is not inborn but happens as children imitate and practice. Today researchers investigate the effects of a child's imitation, practice, and other social interactions on language development. Their research has been compiled into social interaction theories.

It is important that young children learn and practice pragmatics in and outside school.

Social interaction theories emphasize that communication skills are learned through social interactions. Parents and caregivers teach language during their interactions. These theories hold that language development is the outcome of a child's drive for attachment with his or her world; communication develops in order for the child to convey information about the environment to others and is learned through interactions with others.

The belief that social context and interaction within that context influence communicative choice is support by philosopher Lev Vygotsky (1978, 1987). He suggests that children develop by supplementing their independent problem-solving abilities with adult guidance or peer collaboration. Children learn by doing, from interacting with their more experienced partners. Social interactionists agree with Vygotsky's premise that children learn language by interacting either with adults, who naturally have more experience, or with peers, who may have more or different experiences. They are guided through the language learning process (Loeb, 2003).

Children quickly learn to produce speech sounds during their early years. By the age of 8, they have learned to produce nearly all the consonants and vowels that make up the words of the family's native language. Learning these sounds usually proceeds in a fairly consistent sequence, but there may be variation among children in the time of acquisition. Figure 6–2 illustrates the times at which 90 percent of English-speaking children have mastered the consonant sounds needed for speech.

PRAXIS

Standard: Learning about different theories of language development is an application of PRAXIS™ Standard 1, Understanding Exceptionalities.

Figure 6-2 Typical ages for mastery of consonant sounds

By age 3:	/p/, /m/, /h/, /n/, /w/
By age 4	/b/, /k/, /g/, /d/, /f/, /y/
By age 6:	/t/, /ng/, /r/, /l/, /s/
By age 7:	/ch/, /sh/, /j/, /th/ as in "think"
By age 8:	/s/, /z/, /v/, /th/ as in "that"
Even later:	/zh/ as in "measure"

Source: From When Are Speech Sounds Learned? " by B. Sander, 1972, *Journal of Speech and Hearing Disorders, 37,* pp. 55–63. Copyright 1972 by the American Speech-Language-Hearing Association. Adapted with permission.

To learn more about early language development, go to the Web Links module in Chapter 6 of the Companion Website, *www. prenhall.com/turnbull,* for a link to the American Speech-Language-Hearing Association, *http://www. asha.org/public/speech/development/child_hear_talk.htm.*

Children's language development is complex. It begins early and depends on biological preparation, successful nurturance, sensorimotor experiences, and linguistic experiences (McCormick, 2002a). Within the first month, babies begin to respond to human voices and, by 3 months, turn, smile, and coo when spoken to (ASHA, 2005). By their first birthdays, babies make sounds when spoken to, vary vocal pitch and intensity, and experiment with rhythm; they may even say their first words. Within the next year, their spoken vocabularies increase to 200 to 300 words; and the 2-year-old's "no shoe" may become the 3-year-old's "I don't want shoes." Three-year-old toddlers understand simple questions and prepositions such as "in," "on," "under," and "up" and are able to follow two-step directions. They have a vocabulary of 900 to 1,000 words and use three- to four-word sentences. The rapid development continues, and by age 4, preschoolers ask questions using "who," "what," "when," "where," "why," and "how" and have vocabularies of 1,500 to 1,600 words. By age 6, they use irregular verbs such as "be," "go," "run," and "swim" and can verbally share their feelings and thoughts with an expressive vocabulary of 2,600 words (Owens, 2005).

Although most language development takes place in the preschool years, it continues throughout the school years. This later development occurs in the areas of language structure, vocabulary, and language use. During the school years the language skills of reading and writing are also learned (Hulit & Howard, 2002). Though not as rapid as earlier language development, this later progression is equally important.

Speech disorders. Speech disorders include disorders of articulation, voice, and fluency (rate and rhythm of speech). These disorders can occur alone, in combination, or in conjunction with other disorders. For example, students who have hearing losses (Chapter 14) or cerebral palsy (Chapter 12) often have articulation or voice disorders as well as language disorders. Similarly, some students with mental retardation (Chapter 9) may demonstrate no communication delays, while others demonstrate speech delays, language delays, or both speech and language delays.

Articulation disorders. Articulation disorders are one of the most frequent communication disorders in preschool and school-age children. **Articulation** is a speaker's production of individual or sequenced sounds. An articulation disorder occurs when the child cannot correctly produce the various sounds and sound combinations of speech.

Articulation errors may be in the form of substitutions, omissions, additions, and distortions. **Substitutions** are common, as when a child substitutes /d/ for the voiced /th/ ("doze" for "those"), /t/ for /k/ ("tat" for "cat"), or /w/ for /r/ ("wabbit" for "rabbit"). It is common for young children to make sound substitutions that disappear with maturation. It is pervasive and ongoing substitutions that are of concern.

Omissions occur when a child leaves a phoneme out of a word. Children often omit sounds from consonant pairs ("boo" for "blue," "cool" for "school") and from the ends of words ("ap" for "apple"). **Additions** occur when students place a vowel between two consonants, converting "tree" into "tahree."

Distortions are modifications of the production of a phoneme in a word; a listener gets the sense that the sound is being produced, but it seems distorted. Common distortions, called lisps, occur when /s/, /z/, /sh/, and /ch/ are mispronounced.

George substitutes, omits, and distorts speech sounds. His cleft palate has prevented him from moving his tongue against his palate, so he is learning where to place his tongue to make particular speech sounds.

Articulation problems, like all communication disorders, vary. Often children are identified in early childhood settings through school-based speech-language screenings. Many identified children have mild or moderate articulation disorders; their speech is understood by others yet contains sound-production errors. Other children have articulation disorders that have more significant impact on their interactions, making it nearly impossible for others to understand them. When individuals have serious articulation disorders, they usually benefit from evaluation for an AAC device.

There are many reasons for teachers to refer a student with articulation problems to a speech-language pathologist. If a student's articulation problem negatively affects his interactions in your class or his educational performance, referral is in order. Likewise, if a child's sound-production errors make his speech difficult or impossible to understand, referral is warranted. Furthermore, articulation problems resulting from neurological injuries (e.g., cerebral palsy and stroke) typically require therapy. Therapy is also needed to assist students with clefts of the palate or lip if they cannot produce speech sounds or sound combinations correctly. Therapy may also be needed to help a student with a hearing loss who is experiencing difficulty in correctly producing speech sounds because she cannot hear the sounds clearly.

Apraxia of speech. **Apraxia** is a motor speech disorder that affects the way in which a student plans to produce speech. Apraxia can be acquired as the result of a stroke, a tumor, or a head injury. Apraxia can also be developmental. Students with apraxia have difficulty with the voluntary, purposeful movements of speech even though they have no paralysis or weakness of the muscles involved in speech. They have difficulty positioning the articulators and sequencing the sounds. Students with apraxia may be able to say the individual sounds required for speech in isolation or syllables but cannot produce them in longer words and sentences. They may be able to say sounds and words correctly when there is no pressure or request to do so but not when there is.

Some characteristics of apraxia are errors in production of vowels, inconsistent speech errors, more errors as words or sentences get longer, voicing errors (for example, /b/ for /p/ or /g/ for /k/), and stress on the wrong syllables. These types of errors are not usually present in students who have traditional articulation disorders. Students with apraxia need frequent therapy that focuses on repetition, sound sequencing, and movement patterns (Caruso & Strand, 1999).

Voice disorders. Each person has a unique voice. This voice reflects the interactive relationship of pitch, duration, intensity, resonance, and vocal quality. Pitch is determined by the rate of vibration in the vocal folds; men tend to have lower-pitched voices than do women. **Pitch** is affected by the tension and size of the vocal folds, the health of the larynx, and the location of the larynx. **Duration** is the length of time any speech sound requires.

Intensity (loudness or softness) is based on the perception of the listener and is determined by the air pressure coming from the lungs through the vocal folds. Rarely do individuals believe that their voices are too loud. Rather, they may seek professional voice therapy because their voices are too soft.

Resonance, the perceived quality of someone's voice, is determined by the way in which the tone coming from the vocal folds is modified by the spaces of the throat, mouth, and nose. Individuals with an unrepaired cleft palate may experience resonance problems because the opening from the mouth to the nasal cavity may be too large or inappropriately shaped.

Sometimes students without a cleft palate have resonance problems; they may sound as if they have a cold or are holding their noses when speaking. This is called **hyponasality** because air cannot pass through the nose and comes through the mouth instead. Other students have a different trait, **hypernasality,** in which air is allowed to pass through the nasal cavity on sounds other than /m/, /n/, and /ng/. Speech therapy may be needed to teach these students appropriate ways to produce non-nasal sounds.

Council for Exceptional Children

Standard: When you learn to observe and distinguish typical and atypical articulation, you are applying CEC Standard 2, Development and Characteristics of Learners.

The quality of the voice is affected by problems of breath support or vocal-fold functioning as well as resonance. You might have experienced short-term vocal-quality problems after cheering at a football game. Repeated abuse of the vocal folds may cause vocal nodules, growths that result from the rubbing together of the vocal-fold edges. When the folds cannot vibrate properly or come together completely, the sound of your voice will change temporarily until the vocal nodules heal. This short-term problem usually heals because the vocal-fold abuse is not constant. If, however, nodules develop and persist, therapy may be needed to help a student learn to talk in a way that is less abusive to the vocal mechanisms. In most cases, nodules disappear after vocal rest and/or voice therapy. If vocal nodules are the result of an organic problem, therapy alone may not resolve them, and surgery may be required (Pannbacker, 1999).

Fluency disorders. Normal speech requires correct articulation, vocal quality, and **fluency** (rate and rhythm of speaking). Fluent speech is smooth, flows well, and appears to be effortless. Fluency problems are characterized by interruptions in the flow of speaking, such as atypical rate or rhythm as well as repetitions of sounds, syllables, words, and phrases.

All children and adults have difficulties with fluency on occasion. They hesitate, repeat themselves, or use fillers such as "umm" at one time or another. Occasional dysfluency is not considered stuttering, which is frequent repetition and/or prolongation of words or sounds. More males than females stutter.

Language impairments. Students may have language disorders that are receptive, expressive, or both. Their language impairment may be associated with another disability such as autism or mental retardation, or it may be **specific language impairment**—not related to any physical or intellectual disability. Despite the cause, language impairments have a substantial effect on classroom participation and learning.

Phonology. Students with phonological disorders may be unable to discriminate differences in speech sounds or sound segments that signify differences in words. For example, to them the word "pen" may sound no different from "pin." Their inability to differentiate sounds as well as similar, rhyming syllables may cause them to experience reading and/or spelling difficulties (Apel & Swank, 1999; Lombardino, Riccio, Hynd, & Pinheiro, 1997). Phonological difficulties are common in children with language impairments and may affect reading (McCormick & Loeb, 2003). Teachers should be sensitive to these phonological disorders as young children develop early literacy skills.

Morphology. Children with morphological difficulties have problems using the structure of words to get or give information. They may make a variety of errors. For example, they may not use -ed to signal past tense as in "walked" or -s to signal plurality. When a child is unable to use morphological rules appropriately, the average length of her utterances is sometimes shorter than that expected for the child's age because plurals, verb markers, and affixes may be missing from her statements (McCormick & Loeb, 2003). Students with morphological difficulties are unable to be as specific in their communication as others. For example, if they do not use verb markers such as -ed, it is difficult to know if they are referring to past or present tense.

Morphology errors can be associated with differences in dialects as well as with a variety of other conditions, including mental retardation (Chapter 9), autism (Chapter 11), hearing loss or deafness (Chapter 14), and expressive language delay. Incorrect use of morphology is also associated with specific language impairment.

Syntax. Syntactical errors are those involving word order, such as ordering words in a manner that does not convey meaning to the listeners ("Where one them park at?"), using immature structures for a given age or developmental level (e.g., a 4-year-old child using two-word utterances, such as "Him sick"), misusing negatives (a 4-year-old child saying, "Him no go"), or omitting structures (e.g., "He go now"). As with phonology and morphology, differences in syntax sometimes can be associated with dialects and other conditions.

Children who experience difficulty using words singly or together in sentences may have *semantic* disorders. They may have difficulty with multiple-meaning words and have restricted meanings for words (McCormick & Loeb, 2003). Some students with semantic disorders may have problems with words that express time and space (e.g., "night," "tiny"), cause and effect (e.g., "Push button, ball goes"), and inclusion versus exclusion (e.g., "all," "none"). Sometimes students with semantic language disorders rely on words with fairly nonspecific meanings (e.g., "thing," "one," "that") because of their limited knowledge of vocabulary. Difficulty with semantics can impact both understanding and expressing concepts in the classroom.

Pragmatics. Pragmatics focuses on the social use of language—the communication between a speaker and a listener within a shared social environment. Pragmatic skills include adapting communication to varied situations, obtaining and maintaining eye contact, using appropriate body language, maintaining a topic, and taking turns in conversations.

Pragmatic disorders are reflected in many different ways. A student who talks for long periods of time and does not allow anyone else an opportunity to converse may be displaying signs of a pragmatic disorder. Similarly, a student whose comments during class are unrelated to the subject at hand or who asks questions at an inappropriate time may be exhibiting a pragmatic disorder. Students who have difficulty with pragmatics include those with autism (Chapter 10) and traumatic brain injury (Chapter 13).

Determining the Causes

There are two types of speech and language disorders, each classified according to its cause: (1) **organic disorders,** those caused by an identifiable problem in the neuromuscular mechanism of the person; and (2) **functional disorders,** those with no identifiable organic or neurological cause.

The causes of organic disorders are numerous; they may originate in the nervous system, the muscular system, the chromosomes, or the formation of the speech mechanism. They may include hereditary malformations, prenatal injuries, toxic disturbances, tumors, traumas, seizures, infectious diseases, muscular diseases, and vascular impairments (Wang & Baron, 1997). Neuromuscular disabilities may result in difficulties with clear speech-sound production. The speech disorder would then have an organic origin and be classified as an organic speech disorder.

A functional speech and/or language disorder is present when the cause of the impairment is unknown. An articulation disorder with no known physical cause would be considered functional in nature.

Communication disorders can be classified further according to when the problem began. A disorder that occurs at or before birth is referred to as a **congenital disorder.** For instance, George, who was born with Dandy Walker syndrome, has a congenital organic speech disorder. A disorder that occurs well after birth is an **acquired disorder.** For example, a communication disorder may be present after a severe head injury (Chapter 13), which may then be described as an acquired organic speech and/or language disorder. A functional disorder may also be congenital or acquired.

Some causes have both organic and functional origins. In addition, portions of the communication disorder may have been present at birth, and other parts may have been acquired later in life.

EVALUATING STUDENTS WITH COMMUNICATION DISORDERS

Determining the Presence of Communication Disorders

According to IDEA's current regulations, a speech or language impairment is a "communication disorder such as stuttering, articulation/phonology, language, or voice and associated disorders, such as disorders of swallowing or oral function that adversely affects a child's educational performance" (34 C.F.R. Sec. 300.7 [a][11]). Educators, early intervention specialists, and speech-language therapists try to meet the physical, cognitive, communication, social, or emotional and adaptive needs of infants and toddlers, ages birth through 2, and young children, ages 3 through 5, who have communication disorders. They start by conducting a screening, an intervention also called problem solving and prereferral, a referral for evaluation, or both. Many school districts use interventions as the first step to determining if a referral is needed (ASHA, 1999). The emphasis of the intervention or prereferral "is on classroom modifications and supports that, when successful actually prevent the need for special education intervention" (ASHA, 1999). Figure 6–3 describes the evaluation process.

Figure 6–3 Nondiscriminatory evaluation process for determining the presence of communication disorders

Observation	**Medical personnel observe:** The child is not achieving developmental milestones related to communication skills or there is a change in a child's communication skills. **Teacher and parents observe:** The child has difficulty understanding or using language. The child may also have difficulty speaking clearly.
Screening	**Assessment measures:** **Classroom work products:** The child may be hesitant to participate in verbal classroom work. Written classroom projects may reflect errors of verbal communication or, in some instances, be a preferred avenue of expression for the student. **Vision and hearing screening:** The child may have a history of otitis media (middle-ear infection): hearing may be normal, or the student may have hearing loss. Limited vision may impact language skills.
Prereferral	**Teacher implements suggestions from a school-based team:** The teacher models speech sounds, expands language, asks open-ended questions, etc. If the child has been identified before entering school, the parents may implement suggestions from the school-based team.
Referral	If, in spite of interventions, the child still performs poorly in academics or continues to manifest communication impairments, the child is referred to a multidisciplinary team. The team may continue with more in-depth interventions.
Nondiscriminatory evaluation procedures and standards	**Assessment measures:** **Speech and language tests (articulation, phonology, language sample, speech sample, oral motor functioning, receptive language, and expressive language):** The student performs significantly below average in one or more areas. **Anecdotal records:** The student may have genetic or medical factors that contribute to speech or language difficulties. Some students with other disabilities are at risk for having speech and language disorders. **Curriculum-based assessment:** A speech and/or language difficulty may affect progress in the curriculum. **Direct observation:** The student experiences difficulty communicating.
Determination	The nondiscriminatory evaluation team determines that the student has a communication disorder and needs special education and related services. The team proceeds to develop appropriate education options for the child.

During interventions, after a referral for an assessment, or both, the speech-language pathologist gathers information from school records, parent and teacher interviews, hearing and vision screenings, observations, speech samples, language samples, classwork samples/portfolios, checklists, standardized tests, nonstandardized tests, and/or curriculum-based assessments. Having completed the assessment, the speech-language pathologist will evaluate the child to determine if a communication impairment/disorder is present and if it affects the child's learning.

Depending on the area of speech and/or language being assessed, the speech-language pathologist may obtain certain types of information, using the assessment tools described in Figure 6–3, which we describe here.

Speech assessments. Speech assessments determine the presence of articulation, voice, or fluency problems.

Articulation and apraxia. Specifically, articulation assessments evaluate a student's abilities to produce speech sounds in single words, sentences, and conversation. Speech-language pathologists listen, noting the phonemes in error, the pattern of the error, and the frequency of the error. Test items include use of consonants in the initial, middle, and final positions of words (e.g., for /p/, students might name a "pig," a "zipper," and a "cup"). An **oral motor exam,** which is the examination of the appearance, strength, and range of motion of the lips, tongue, palate, teeth, and jaw, is also typically conducted.

Voice. Voice evaluations include information about the onset and course of the voice problem, environmental factors that might affect vocal quality, and typical voice use (Verdolini, 2000), including pitch, intensity, and nasality.

Fluency. When completing a fluency assessment, the speech-language pathologist measures the amount of dysfluency as well as the type and duration of dysfluencies while the student is speaking. The pathologist also notes associated speech and nonspeech behaviors such as eye blinking or head movements (Zebrowski, 2000).

Language assessments. Language assessments focus on specific components of language such as phonology, semantics, morphology, syntax, pragmatics, and overall expressive and/or receptive language. Students who are nonverbal or use nonconventional means of communication require more descriptive than standardized assessment measures (Downing, 2005). The communicative forms (conventional and nonconventional) and the functions these forms serve are documented during observations across environments and communication partners (Downing, 2005). For example, a speech-language pathologist might observe this interaction: John looks at a friend's snack and then at his friend. He repeats this several times. When the friend gives John some of his snack, John smiles. The pathologist then notes the communication functions observed and the form the student used. In this example the student exhibited the following communication functions: initiated a communication interaction, requested an item, and expressed a social interaction (e.g., thank you or please). The following forms of communication were observed: eye contact (to gain attention to initiate communication), eye gaze (to request), and facial expression (a smile as thanks). Then the speech-language pathologist would determine what next steps could shape and expand on the communication forms (e.g., speech, pointing to pictures, voice output, etc.).

Multicultural considerations. Sometimes a student will need specialized speech or language assessment, as when the student is bilingual or multilingual. The speech-language pathologist must be particularly skilled when assessing the communicative capabilities of students for whom English is not the primary language. Fair, unbiased evaluation is difficult for a student who is **bilingual** (one who uses two languages equally well) or **bidialectal** (one who uses two variations of a language) or for whom language dominance (the primary language of the student) is difficult to determine.

To assess such a student, it is not sufficient to simply translate test items into the child's primary language. The speech-language pathologist must determine whether a bilingual student should be tested in the student's first language or in English (ASHA, 1984). Then the speech-language pathologist tests the student in the dominant language with appropriate diagnostic tools to determine whether a language difference or a disability exists. The pathologist

141

Bilingual and bidialectical skills make this speech-language pathologist especially effective, but note that she and her student also communicate by a semi-universal sign.

Council for Exceptional Children

Standard: As you develop an awareness of how to meet the needs of bilingual students, you are using CEC Standard 6, Communication.

Companion Website

See the Companion Website, *www.pren-hall.com/turnbull,* for further information regarding students who are English language learners, *http://www.asha.org/about/leader-ship-projects/multi-cultural/readings/bilingual_lep_esl.htm.*

determines a student's language strengths and preferences using appropriate assessment tools and learns about the student's communicative abilities and needs. If the pathologist observes a communication disorder or disability, she then can plan appropriate therapies, using, whenever possible, culturally sensitive standardized measures.

Determining the Nature of Specifically Designed Instruction and Services

Curriculum-based assessment can allow an educational team to determine the student's entry point within the areas of the educational program and provide information to develop strategies helpful for a student to progress within the curriculum (Losardo & Notari-Syverson, 2001). Language occurs throughout the school day and is the vehicle for teaching the curriculum (Howell & Nolet, 2000; Losardo & Notari-Syverson, 2001). Whether the student is asked to discuss a topic verbally, answer questions, read language, write language, or work with others cooperatively, he or she is practicing language through the entire curriculum.

Within curriculum-based assessment, the team determines the nature of specifically designed instruction by data-based performance modifications and assisted assessment portions of the assessment model (Howard & Nolet, 2000). This portion of the assessment usually begins after the team identifies the student's problem and his degree of discrepancy from peers. The speech-language pathologist then develops theories aimed at decreasing the discrepancy, tests the theories systematically, and monitors the student's performance by collecting data. Since speech and language occurs throughout the day and data collection may need to be taken in multiple settings, the pathologist may need members of the educational team to assist in data collection as well, usually from the classroom teacher because that teacher is generally with the student for more of the day than other educational staff are. The pathologist then analyzes the data and makes decisions about instruction based on the data that reveal the student's best improvement in performance (Howard & Nolet, 2000). This procedure is called data-based performance modification (Howard & Nolet, 2000). Assisted assessment is the process of determining what strategy or supports the student may need to accomplish the task being monitored (Howard & Nolet, 2000). Both of these procedures help define the instruction that best suits a student and the supports that may be needed so that the student will be successful in communicating in school.

DESIGNING AN APPROPRIATE INDIVIDUALIZED EDUCATION PROGRAM

Partnering for Special Education and Related Services

Collaboration is critical when planning and providing services for students with communication disorders. Communication occurs throughout the day, so it is important that everyone who works with the student has a good understanding of how she best understands and/or expresses information. For instance, the lunchroom and recess staff may need to understand strategies to help a student initiate requests from others and take turns. Those staff members also could be an excellent resource for anecdotal information regarding progress toward the student's goals in a natural context with peers. Furthermore, collaboration may help lighten everyone's workload (Giangreco, 2000; Sandall & Schwartz, 2002).

Teachers can expect speech-language pathologists to move away from the more traditional model of individual and group pullout services and to participate in more collaborative consultation, curriculum-based intervention programs, and classroom-based services (ASHA, 2003). Four ways for speech-language pathologists to collaborate with teachers include supportive teaching, complementary teaching, consultation, and team teaching. Each activity cluster requires a high level of collaboration with teachers and families, as exemplified in Box 6–2.

ASHA (2003) has identified four different types of activities (called activity clusters) that speech-language pathologists engage in while working in schools: direct services to students, indirect services to implement students' education programs, indirect services to support students in the general education curriculum, and activities as members of the community of educators. Each requires a high level of collaboration with teachers and families.

Direct service involves individual and/or small group pullout services. Traditional direct services historically have constituted the majority of the speech-language pathologist's workload. By contrast, indirect services consist, for example, of designing and programming a student's augmentative communication device and training paraeducators in how to use it. Indirect activities also include meeting and planning with teachers and paraprofessionals to align the student's IEP goals with the standards for the general curriculum and designing instructional strategies so the student can make progress in the general curriculum. Activities that speech-language pathologists engage in as members of a community of educators include staff meetings, school committees, and other duties expected of all educators. Partnerships between teachers and speech-language pathologists are critical to student success.

PRAXIS

Standard: When you learn about the IEP process and what services a speech-language pathologist can offer, you are engaged in PRAXIS Standard 2, Delivery of Services to Students with Disabilities.

Values: The collaboration and consultation of teachers and speech-language pathologists allows both the opportunity to learn from one another and share their respective expertise, building on each others' *strengths*.

Partnership Tips ~ Three Partnership Options   Box 6–2

There are many ways for teachers and speech-language pathologists to work with each other and other professionals to support access to the curriculum for students receiving special education services. Consultation, supportive teaching, and complementary teaching are possible options (ASHA, 2003). Examples of each are presented here:

Consultation. Cristen is a ninth grader with autism. She loves science, music, and drama. The science curriculum presents many challenges for Cristen, so the speech-language pathologist works with the classroom teacher to adapt text materials, handouts, and tests so that they match Cristen's language abilities. The adapted science handouts are used by many of the students in the class who need more visual presentations of the content.

Supportive teaching. Andrew is a second grader with Down syndrome. His class is studying the life cycle of the frog. The speech-language pathologist and teacher meet to plan for the unit and determine what extra supports Andrew will need to participate. The pathologist works with Andrew individually to preteach vocabulary and then teaches part of the unit to the whole class. She may meet individually with Andrew again to clarify any information he did not understand.

Complementary teaching. Beth is in the fifth grade. She has language learning difficulties that include auditory processing weaknesses. Taking notes for Beth during social studies is hard. The speech-language pathologist takes notes while the teacher teaches. He also prepares study guides, teaches small

groups that need more adaptation, and on occasions teaches organizational skills to the whole class.

Tips for Partnerships with Speech-Language Pathologists

- Remember that speech-language pathologists have a role in helping students succeed in the general education curriculum. There are many ways they can be involved.
- Include speech-language pathologists in curriculum planning and instructional opportunities.
- Define roles and responsibilities of team members. Focus on student outcomes.

Putting Partnership Tips to Work for Progress in the General Curriculum

1. As Cristen's classroom teacher, how might you work to promote her self-determination in her own mastery of the science curriculum as she works with you and the speech-language pathologist?

2. Identify three ways that you believe the speech-language pathologist's work with Andrew would benefit other students in the class.

3. Develop a plan for how the speech-language pathologist might involve Beth's classmates in a cooperative learning activity.

To answer these question online, go to the Partnership Tips module in Chapter 6 of the Companion Website, www.prenhall.com/turnbull.

Determining Supplementary Aids and Services

An augmentative and alternative communication (AAC) system is an example of, in IDEA's terms, an "assistive technology and supplementary aid." AAC systems are integrated groups of components that supplement the communication abilities of individuals who cannot meet their communication needs through gesturing, speaking, and/or writing (Beukelman & Mirenda, 2005). An AAC system may include an AAC device, which is a physical object that transmits or receives messages. Such devices include communication books, communication/language boards, communication charts, mechanical or electronic voice output equipment, and computers.

An AAC device has two components: a symbol set and a means for selecting the symbols. A symbol is "a visual, auditory, and/or tactile representation of conventional concepts" (ASHA, 1991, p. 10). A symbol set includes gestures, photographs, manual sign sets/systems, pictographs (symbols that look like what they represent), ideographs (more abstract symbols), printed words, objects, partial objects, miniature objects, spoken words, braille, textures, or any combination of these symbols.

If educators are concerned about a student's ability to express and/or understand information in the classroom, they should contact the school's speech-language pathologist. A team approach is helpful when determining what assistive technology may be needed because so many areas need to be considered. Input from the parents as well as information regarding the student's vision skills, fine-motor skills, gross-motor skills, hearing, and curriculum requirements all help educators and pathologists determine what features the AAC system should have.

Assistive technology can be as simple and universal as a hand-held personal assistant, and even that device can be specially tailored for a designated user.

Devices can range from low tech, such as line-drawn pictures in a notebook or a wallet, to high tech, such as a computer with a dynamic touch screen that stores pictures and photos and produces a voice output for items selected by the student. Some students may use a device for their primary communication but may supplement it with speech, line drawings, voice-output switches, and gestures. The device, speech, and gestures all comprise the student's AAC system. Chapter 10 provides more information about AAC devices.

Once the student is trying out or using an AAC device, the speech-language pathologist needs to provide the appropriate vocabulary. If the student is using a more low-tech device, such as line-drawn pictures in a notebook, the vocabulary will need to be located and put into the notebook in an organized fashion so the student can find it.

If the student is using a voice-output device, needed vocabulary will have to be programmed into the device so the student can press a button and hear the voice-output expression of the vocabulary. It is possible on most devices to assign a single word, a phrase, or a sentence to a button.

Students, especially those who are still acquiring literacy skills, depend on others to make vocabulary available for them to communicate. For instance, if a student were to participate in a unit about frogs, then vocabulary about frogs (for example, stages of a frog's life cycle, animals that eat frogs, insects frogs eat, possible places frogs may live, and plants in and around a pond) need to be available. Without vocabulary, the student will not be able to express his thoughts or discuss topics being shared in his environments. The selection of a device and its features, the degree of a student's needs and capacities, and the capabilities of the school's staff all figure into the selection of AAC. So does another factor—cost. Box 6–3 challenges you to think as an administrator about these various factors.

Planning for Universal Design for Learning

Values: It is important for students to be able to freely express themselves in order to make *choices* and become *self-advocates*.

When planning universal design for learning for students with communication disorders, a teacher must answer two questions: how can I assure that my student understands what I am teaching? and how can I assure that my student can express what she knows? Remember that universal design for learning includes modifications to how content is presented. When teachers use only one or two

Your Own Voice ~ Weighing All the Factors — Box 6-3

Assume that you are the principal of an elementary school in a rural school district. Your district's school board has decided to send nearly all of its students with disabilities to an interdistrict cooperative. You, however, want to include students with disabilities in your school, and you particularly want to include Sarah, who has communication challenges, in your fifth-grade program. She's new in the district, and you believe it's time to break the precedent of separation.

You and Sarah's parents have secured a complete evaluation of her communication and assistive technology needs from a statewide assistive technology center's staff. The staff has concluded that Sarah has an IQ well above normal; indeed, the staff report said, "Sarah may qualify for the state's gifted-and-talented program if she has the most appropriate AAC device available to her. Otherwise, she would simply make some, but not the most, progress in the general curriculum." The staff recommended full inclusion with the supplementary aid of an AAC and a qualified instructor.

You have presented the staff proposal to your district superintendent, and she in turn has presented it to the board. You have received an e-mail from the board's chairman, asking you to respond to the following questions:

1. Why should we include Sarah when we don't include other students?
2. What's wrong with sending her to the coop program where she can share some of the AAC devices that other students use and where there is staff to train her to use them?
3. Why do we always have to get the most expensive AAC and other devices for these kids with disabilities? Our other kids and our teachers are paying the price for these devices. We've got a limited budget.
4. Why should we try to leapfrog Sarah into the gifted program? Wouldn't that just cost us more money later? When will we ever stop being nickel-and-dimed to death with requests?

To prepare your answers, see Beukelman, D. R., & Mirenda, P. A. (2005). *Augmentative and alternative communication*. Baltimore: Brookes.

methods to teach, especially if they only use verbal methods, some students with communication disorders as well as some students without disabilities are not able to access the material. So teachers can vary the way in which they communicate, such as using audio *and* text formats, visual representations with verbal information, graphics, graphic organizers, and controlled vocabulary. Similarly, teachers can vary the ways that students demonstrate their knowledge, such as by asking a student to convert a written report to a PowerPoint presentation, supplementing a demonstration with visual supports, using a taped oral report, or performing a skit solo or with others. These and the book-access strategies set out in Box 6–4 provide access to the general curriculum.

Planning for Other Educational Needs

Students with communication disorders may need support in building social relationships because they are at greater risk for difficulties in social communication (Rice, 1993). Social interactions

Technology Tips ~ Talking Books — Box 6-4

Talking books can be viewed on the computer and are a great way to engage students of all ages in literacy activities. Books that include photos can be some of the most motivating first books for very young children (Trelease, 1995). Books created with photos of students and their friends and families or of items of interest can also be very motivating for older students who are reading at a lower instructional level. These books also can help supplement the age-appropriate books available at a lower reading level for older students. In addition, books viewed on the computer can be accessed with a switch, so a student who may have difficulty physically holding a book and/or turning the pages can easily access the book by pressing the switch to see the next page. Creating these books in class with the students can also be a great interactive writing activity.

Books that incorporate photos and line drawings can easily be made on the computer using a program by Microsoft called PowerPoint. Many computers have Microsoft Office software already available. The following websites have more information about how to make books using PowerPoint:

- *http://atto.buffalo.edu/registered/Tutorials/talkingBooks/powerpoint.php* for Windows 97 and 2000
- *www.wati.org/Literacy/documents/PwrPnt-1.doc* for Mac Microsoft 97
- *http://www.accintervention.com/tipthre.html#July%202003*

There are other computer programs such as IntelliPics Studio, IntelliTalk, and My Own Bookshelf that also allow one to create these digital books. The books can have sound so the computer can read the story to the student, or the sound can be turned off. The books that are created in the classroom can also be printed to make hardcopies that can be stored in the classroom or sent home. Classroom books can also be saved on a computer disc or CD-ROM and sent home. The following website contains a PowerPoint viewer that can be downloaded for home or school computers, *www.wati.org/Literacy*.

are important; they enlarge classroom participation and build social relationships. Most children learn social skills with no instruction or support. But some students with communication disorders, such as those with autism, will need to be taught specific social skills; while others, such as those with specific language impairments or those using communication devices, will need support to initiate and sustain interactions because of their limited expressive language.

One such support is a *social story*. Social stories (Gray, 2004) help children with autism spectrum disorders carry out various social interactions. A social story describes social concepts, skills, or situations by providing information about the situation and people involved. Social stories have been effective in increasing prosocial behaviors and decreasing inappropriate behaviors (Barry & Burley, 2004; Ivey, Heflin, & Alberto, 2004; Kuoch & Mirenda, 2003). You will learn more about social stories as an instructional strategy in Chapter 10.

Using Effective Instructional Strategies

Early Childhood Students: Facilitative Language Strategies

Given that 55 percent of children 3 to 5 years old served under IDEA have speech and language difficulties and that these figures do not include children who have communication disorders secondary to other conditions (U.S. Department of Education, 2002), facilitating language development is a primary component of most early education programs. Because communication is social in nature and is learned across all parts of a child's day, the child's communication partners should use strategies to promote his or her speech and language development. A set of such strategies, described in Box 6–5, has been developed, researched, and refined in the Language Acquisition Preschool at the University of Kansas (Bunce & Watkins, 1995; Rice & Wilcox, 1995). In the preschool classroom, the adults' interactions provide the intervention with no additional pullout therapy, so children do not receive individual therapy. These strategies rest on several foundations: language intervention is best when provided in a meaningful social context; language facilitation occurs across the preschool curriculum; language begins with the child; language is learned through interaction; valuable teaching occasions can arise in child-to-child interactions; and parents are valuable partners in language intervention programming.

Elementary and Middle School Students: Graphic Organizer Modifications

When children leave early childhood programs, their curriculum begins to focus more on learning to read and write in the early elementary grades and then on reading and writing to learn in the later elementary and middle school years. For students with communication disorders, these transitions are difficult. Graphic organizers are a form of advance organizers, which you learned about in Chapter 5. They can help students with communication disorders develop their literacy skills (Sturm & Rankin-Erickson, 2002).

Graphic organizers are tools that assist students to comprehend and write more effectively (Cunningham & Allington, 2003). They provide a visual representation in an organized framework. Graphic organizers have been especially useful for students with Down syndrome, autism spectrum disorders, and language-learning disabilities (Kumin, 2001; Myles & Simpson, 2003; Nelson & Van Meter, 2004). Graphic organizers can be hand-drawn or computer-generated. When using graphic organizers, it is important to first determine which organizer will best meet the desired curriculum outcome. A teacher might choose a web design, a story map, a feature matrix, or data charts, to name a few.

It is also important to consider how students will participate. Some students find blank forms of the organizer beneficial. Others may indicate that writing or spelling is difficult, that decoding the words written on the organizer is difficult, or that restructuring opportunities are needed. Some students need to group information together and see the grouping to decide if the items go together or if they should be placed somewhere else.

Visit the Companion Website, *www.prenhall.com/turnbull*, for examples of these types of graphic organizers, *www.graphic.org*.

Into Practice ~ Facilitative Language Strategies   Box 6–5

The facilitative language strategies described here have been validated in a variety of preschool settings with children with communication disorders (Bunce & Watkins, 1995; Rice & Wilcox, 1995). They can be implemented in any adult-child interaction in any context and provide many natural teaching and learning opportunities.

Focused contrast. This is a production by an adult that highlights the difference between the child's speech or language and the adult's. This can occur as feedback or a model. During a feedback instance, when the child says, "Otey," for "Okay," the adult could say, "Oh, you said 'Otey,' and I said, 'Okay.'" During a modeled focused contrast, the adult provides many examples for the child. For example, if the focus is on the past-tense marker -ed, the adult, while playing house, may say, "She is walking," while moving the doll and then stop the movement and say, "She walked to the door." This can be repeated with numerous actions during play.

Modeling. Modeling is often used to help a child learn a language or speech structure he doesn't yet use. If the structure is the plural marker -s, the adult may use it to describe the plurals in the ongoing activity, highlighting them with extra emphasis or stress.

Event casts. Event casts provide an ongoing description of an activity, just like a sports broadcaster might. The events described can be what the child or adult is doing. For example, during dress-up play, the adult may say, "You are putting on the hat. Now you are putting on blue shoes."

Open questions. Questions that have a variety of possible answers are open questions. Examples are "What should we do next?" "What do you think happens next?"

Expansions. The adult repeats the child's utterance, filling in the missing components. For example, if the child says, "Two horse," the adult expands with "Two brown horses."

Recasts. When recasting, the adult keeps the child's basic meaning but changes the structure or grammar of the child's utterance. For example, if the child says, "He has juice," the adult can say, "Yes, he is drinking juice now."

Redirects and prompted initiations. These strategies encourage children to interact with each other. When a child approaches an adult and makes a request that could be made to another child, the adult redirects him to ask a classmate: "You could tell Tom, 'I need a blue crayon.'" When a child does not make a request to an adult but has the opportunity to interact with another child, he might be prompted to ask another child to play or request some item.

Putting These Strategies into Practice in the General Curriculum

1. Create a hypothetical example of an articulation error that a second grader and an eighth grader might realistically make. For each error, give an example of a *focused contrast* that you could provide to the student as an opportunity for learning.

2. Assume that you are a speech-language pathologist working with George. From what you have learned in the chapter, specify one instructional objective for his language development. Focusing on this objective, write a script of how you would use (1) expansions and (2) redirects and prompted initiations.

3. As George's teacher, how might you inform his parents about these facilitative language strategies so that they can incorporate them at home?

To answer these questions online, go to the Into Practice module in Chapter 6 of the Companion Website, www.prenhall.com/turnbull.

Organizers can be adapted to allow all students access to them (Foley & Staples, 2000). For some students, teachers provide concepts, facts, ideas, and/or events. Then the student chooses the information and places it in the organizer (Foley & Staples, 2000). Photographs, magazine pictures, commercial line drawings, written words, or any combination of visual symbols can represent the information to be placed in the organizer.

For example, if a student with a receptive language delay or disorder needs to learn and remember information for a science unit on insects, the teacher may provide a web design using pictures to organize the insects' anatomical makeup, what the insects eat, what animals eat insects, habitats the insects live in, and so on. The information in a graphic organizer visually links groups of important information together for the student. Figure 6–4 shows an example of a computer-generated graphic organizer for a second-grade unit on frogs. A student with an expressive language difficulty may find this same web helpful because he could point to the area of the web he wanted to comment on or the web could help him respond to a question.

Graphic organizers are simple yet effective methods for helping students with receptive language disorders remember information.

Figure 6-4 Graphic organizer generated by Kidspiration for a second-grade unit on frogs

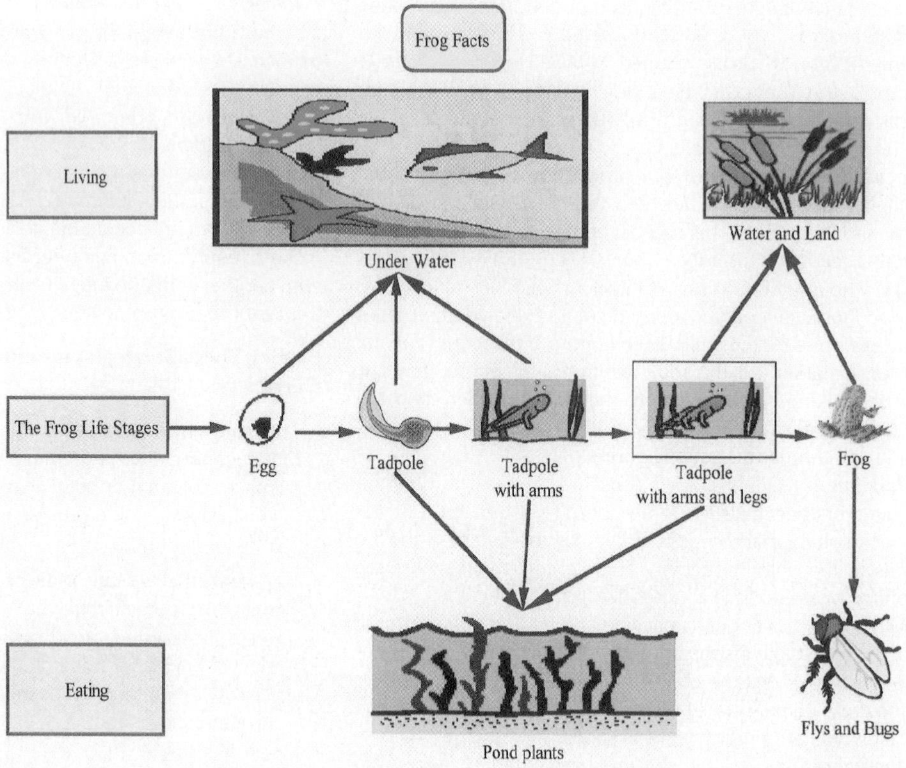

This example graphic organizer was created by Evette Edmister, speech-language pathologist doctoral student at the University of Kansas, using a graphic organizing software program entitled Kidspiration. The pictures within the graphic organizer were generated with Kidspiration and Mayer-Johnson's Boardmaker software.

Secondary and Transitional Students: Augmented Input

AAC systems enable many students to participate in the curriculum. But learning to use these systems takes a team effort, and the student's familiar and frequent communication partners play an important role. AAC instructional strategies should focus on teaching communication rather than teaching the student to use AAC. AAC is simply a means to an end, the end being communication and participation.

As students transition to more community-based instruction, they need to learn new vocabulary and new ways to interact. This is a challenge even for students who have successfully used AAC in the classroom. Participating in social exchanges in the break room with less familiar partners is quite different from participating in more structured interactions with familiar partners in school. Transitioning students will need instruction and support to meaningfully integrate their AAC communication systems into this new communication environment.

One instructional strategy that has been effective is the **System for Augmenting Language (SAL)** (Romski & Sevick, 1988). SAL focuses on augmented input of language. Using SAL, communication partners augment their speech by activating the student's communication device in naturally occurring communication interactions at home and school and in the community, encouraging but not requiring the student to use the device (Romski & Sevcik, 2003). For example, a student enters the bakery with his job coach. The job coach greets the cashier by saying, "Hello, how are you?" while activating the buttons for "hello" and "you" on the student's device. The student not only has a model of the vocabulary to use in that situation but also a model with respect to the use of the vocabulary.

Although the SAL strategy was developed for use with electronic communication devices, augmented input can also be used if students have communication books or boards or sign language. It is sometimes then called *aided language stimulation* (Elder & Goossens, 1994; Goossens, Crain, & Elder, 1992) or, when sign language is used, *total communication*. The SAL strategy is effective with toddlers as well as students between the ages of 6 and 20 (Romski & Sevcik, 1992; Romski & Sevcik, 1996; Romski, Sevcik, & Forrest, 2001).

The SAL instructional strategy depends on the training of frequent and signficant communication partners. Blackstone and Berg (2003) have developed a tool called Social Networks to identify these important partners. Special educators and speech-language pathologists can use this tool to determine who should receive training. Romski and Sevcik (2003) suggest that a student's communication partners should receive instruction about the importance of input with respect to understanding and the physical operation of the device as well as practice in providing input in natural settings and feedback and coaching.

INCLUDING STUDENTS WITH COMMUNICATION DISORDERS

Most students with speech and language impairments spend the majority of their day in the general education classroom (see Figure 6–5). According to the U.S. Department of Education, 88 percent of the children who receive speech and language services spend 80 to 100 percent of their time in the general education classroom for these services. The trend toward receiving services in the general educational classroom and spending more of the school day there has been increasing since 1984 (U.S. Department of Education, 2001). That is so, in part, because effective teachers use some of the tips that you will find in Box 6–6.

It is important for teachers to observe students' speech and language skills and contact the building speech-language pathologist if they have concerns. If a student does not develop speech and language skills early in life, she will have a difficult time acquiring these skills later

How do George's teachers and family include George in daily activities? Use your *Real Lives and Exceptionalities* DVD to view "Accommodation" (Clip 2) and "Collaboration" (Clips 3 & 5) videos.

Figure 6–5 Educational placement of students with speech-language impairments (2003–2004)

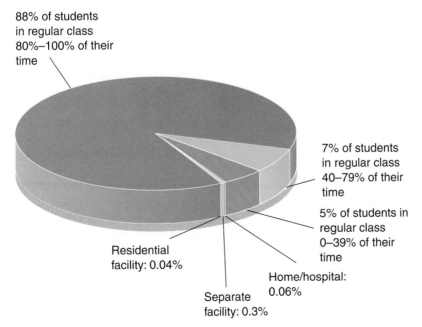

88% of students in regular class 80%–100% of their time

7% of students in regular class 40–79% of their time

5% of students in regular class 0–39% of their time

Residential facility: 0.04%

Home/hospital: 0.06%

Separate facility: 0.3%

Source: U.S. Department of Education, Office of Special Education Programs. (2005). IDEA data website (http://www.ideadata.org/aboutThisSite.asp).

Inclusion Tips   Box 6–6

	What You Might See	What You Might Be Tempted to Do	Alternative Responses	Ways to Include Peers in the Process
Behavior	The student may appear shy and reserved. She may not participate in large-group settings. It may take her time to compose a response when speaking in front of the class.	Tell her to hurry up; the class is waiting. Do not allow her time to complete her idea and move on to another student. Never call on her.	Provide a multiple-choice response option. Provide information in advance for preparation of rehearsed responses. Allow for small-group discussion and reporting.	Provide multiple-choice response options or alternate response options for all students along with other types of question formats.
Social interactions	She may be alone during unstructured times. She does not ask friends to play. She does not join in with other peer interactions.	Assume she is happy alone and let her be.	Demonstrate that you value her contributions. Provide a model and help her learn to interact with the other students.	Encourage a peer buddy to help model and encourage interactions with other children.
Educational performance	She produces syntactically incomplete sentences verbally and in writing. She avoids writing tasks.	Constantly correct her. Decrease the occurrence of writing assignments.	Provide visual and verbal models of complete sentences. Continue to provide lots of opportunities for writing. Provide positive feedback.	Allow small-group interactions with assigned roles that rotate to every student. The students can then provide models for each other.
Classroom attitudes	She might expect the teacher to intercede when having difficulty with other students. She might rely on the teacher to initiate interactions with other students.	Tell her to go play with others. Assume the children will work it out on their own.	Teach all the students ways to interact and solve problems.	Provide opportunities for the students to practice independent interactions with one another, providing assistance where needed.

(Downing, 2005). In addition, if a student does not have a conventional communication system, he may look for unconventional means to meet his needs. These means may be inappropriate, aggressive, or ineffective (Downing, 2005). Some students may become passive when they feel their communication will not be understood. Language is also the basis for reading and writing skills; indeed, 50 percent or more of children with a language impairment in preschool or kindergarten have reading disabilities in primary or secondary grades (Catts & Kamhi, 1999). The communication skills that students learn in school are needed long after they graduate to "assume life in their community as contributing adults" (Downing, 2005).

ASSESSING STUDENTS' PROGRESS

Measuring Students' Progress

Progress in the general curriculum. The reauthorization of IDEA in 2004 (see Chapters 1 and 2) emphasized that educators must measure a student's progress within the general education curriculum. There are many different tools for measuring a student's progress, but curriculum-based assessment, which you learned about in the previous chapter, is a favorite because it focuses on how a student's skills are progressing in the curriculum (Howell & Nolet, 2000; Losardo & Notari-Syverson, 2001). Educators working with students with communication disorders may use the data-based performance modification procedure of curriculum-based assessment that we discussed previously to monitor a student's progress and make decisions about instructional strategies.

With input from the educational team, the speech-language pathologist, working with the student's teachers, will try to reduce the discrepancy between the student's current communication skill level and the curriculum standard against which the student's progress is assessed. For example, if a student exhibits atypical dysfluencies (or stuttering) and if the dysfluencies negatively affect his participation in class, his interaction with other students, or both, the pathologist should set a goal of monitoring the amount of class participation that occurs as a result of the student's improved fluency, give the teacher and the parents suggestions that may be helpful when speaking with someone who stutters, work with the student to teach different fluency strategies, observe in class to monitor the use of the strategies in the classroom and the student's class participation, and ask the teacher to rate the student's fluency during the day and tally her class participation at agreed-upon times.

Visit the Companion Website, *www.prenhall.com/turnbull*, to learn more about stuttering characteristics, fluency strategies, and suggestions to consider when talking with someone who stutters, *http://www.asha.org/public/speech/disorders/stuttering.htm*.

Progress in addressing other educational needs. Ecological inventories are another helpful tool for monitoring communication progress. You will learn more about the ecological inventory process in Chapter 9, but such inventories can also assist in determining the communication expectations that exist in natural environments (Downing, 2005). The first step in using an ecological inventory is for the speech-language pathologist and others to determine what interactions occur within the natural environment. For example, assume that the student is completing a vocational training for waiting on customers. The pathologist and others analyze the steps or components of the job, such as greeting the customer, asking how to help the customer, answering the customer's question, recording the customer's order, clarifying any information not understood, and ending the conversation. The team then observes one of the student's peers complete the task and monitors the degree to which the peer is independent. Was the peer completely independent; did equipment need to be set up first; were verbal cues needed? Now the student completes the task, and the speech-language pathologist and others record the steps that the student needed assistance with or was not yet able to complete. Observers compare those data with the peer's data to determine the student's degree of discrepancy and target the areas of discrepancy for instruction, strategies, and possibly supplementary aids. By reassessing the student's performance in the environment, using the ecological inventory, the pathologist and others can determine whether the instruction, strategies, and/or supplementary aids are helping the student decrease the discrepancy in performance observed. For instance, the student may need additional vocabulary added to an AAC device, picture cues for the steps, pages of pictures of line drawings (called topic boards), or role playing and practice with others.

Values: Helping students succeed within the work environment will increase job opportunities available for the students at a later date and assist the students to be more economically self-sufficient and make *positive contributions* to their communities.

Making Accommodations for Assessment

Many students with communication disorders may not need accommodations for assessment. Other students may need additional time for tests or access to a word processor and computer software when writing. When assessing a student with more significant speech and language impairments, educators should ask, "What is being assessed, how does the student best receive information, and how does the student best express himself?" They should consider the focus of the assessment in order to reduce the chances that the student will be assessed in more than one area at one time. For instance, if the student's augmentative voice-output communication system is new or unfamiliar and she uses it during a science test, then teachers can assess the student's understanding of the communication system as well as her understanding of science. They may find it difficult, however, to determine whether the student did not answer a question correctly because she did not know how to find the answer with the new system or did not know that particular science concept. Similarly, if a student who exhibits difficulty understanding written complex language structures takes a science test but the test format is not adapted for him, then professionals may be assessing the student's ability to read complex sentence structures as well as his knowledge about science. If they want to assess the student's understanding of complex language structures, then they should make sure that the test consists of complex structures. If, however, they are assessing science, they may need to take into account the student's preferred manner of receiving information. When the assessment is isolated, the student may concentrate solely on what he knows about science.

It is important to present information in a manner that assists the student's comprehension of the assessment directions and questions. For instance, if a student finds it difficult to receive written information, she may benefit from having the assessment explained verbally or from having visual supports. If a student has difficulty understanding complex sentence structures, he may benefit from having the language adjusted or from visual supports to assist his comprehension.

If the student has difficulty expressing herself verbally or in written form, she may benefit from an assessment format that does not require long verbal or written output. For example, a multiple-choice or true-false format may be helpful. She may then only need to respond with a one-word answer, a switch activation, or a gesture indicating the correct answer. This change in format may decrease the probability that the student did not provide the answer because of the length of the response needed, her inability to clearly express an answer, or both.

The format should complement the student's most common means of expression. For instance, if the student has begun to explore a new communication system, such as a device using a computer screen, it may be advisable to use the more familiar system for assessment until he has had time to learn the new system.

Values: Communication displays student strengths and helps students be *self-determined,* have friends, and be a *full citizen* of their schools and communities.

Looking to George's Future

Despite a tenuous beginning, George's future looks positive. Where will he be, and what will he be doing when his education in the local school system is complete? His parents would like him to be in college. They would like him to have his own dreams and to achieve them. They want him to be self-determined. Perhaps he will pursue his interests in horses or computers. Professionals collaborating with George and his family expect him to successfully progress through the general education curriculum. Given his outgoing nature and good pragmatic skills, they expect him to have good friends and a wide social network. Communication will likely continue to be a focus for George's educational participation as the complexities of the curriculum increase. Technology may become more important to George to compensate for his fine-motor and communication challenges. Assuming that collaboration and support continue as they have begun, George's future is full of possibilities.

SUMMARY

Identifying students with communication disorders

- Communication disorders include both speech and language impairments.
- A speech disorder is an impairment of one's articulation of speech sounds, fluency, or voice.
- A language disorder reflects problems in receiving information; understanding it; and formulating a spoken, written, or symbolic response.
- Communication differences that are related to the culture of the individual are not considered impairments.
- Language is a shared system of rules and symbols for the exchange of information. It includes rules of phonology, morphology, syntax, semantics, and pragmatics.
- Five to 10 percent of the population has a communication disorder.

- Communication impairments can affect a student's academic, social, and emotional development.

Evaluating students with communication disorders

- The speech-language pathologist is the professional most likely to determine the presence and extent of a speech and/or language impairment.
- Assessments include the use of informal and formal measures. They should occur in settings comfortable and natural for the student.

Designing an appropriate individualized education program

- The collaborative participation of students, their teachers, speech-language pathologists, and parents to enhance communicative development results in students' language objectives being targeted in many settings and situations.
- When planning universal design for learning for students with communication disorders, a teacher must answer two questions: how can I assure that my student understands what I am teaching? and how can I assure that my student can express what she knows?

Using effective instructional strategies

- Early childhood students with communication disorders benefit from language facilitation strategies.
- Graphic organizers and story webs can be helpful for elementary and secondary students with communication disorders.
- Students transitioning to community-based instruction will need instruction and support to meaningfully integrate their AAC communication systems into this new environment.
- One instructional strategy that has been effective is the System for Augmenting Language (SAL).

Including students with communication disorders

- According to the U.S. Department of Education, 88 percent of the children who receive speech and language services spend 21 percent or less of their time outside the general education classroom.

Assessing students' progress with communication disorders

- Curriculum-based assessment can help monitor student's progress in the general education curriculum.
- Ecological inventories can be helpful for assessing and monitoring progress in and outside the classroom.

WHAT DO YOU RECOMMEND?

Refer to chapter content and the PRAXIS™ and CEC standards in Appendix A to answer the following quesitons:

1. Look up Dandy Walker syndrome in Chapter 6 of the Companion Website, *www.prenhall.com/turnbull*. Write a two- to three-paragraph description of the syndrome and identify which PRAXIS™ and/or CEC standards you are putting into practice.

Use your *Real Lives and Exceptionalities* DVD to critically think about working with George under "Questions" located below "Meet George."

2. Go to the DVD section that features George Wedge. Select one or two sections to view. How does the material you viewed affect your attitudes toward George and other students with speech-language dissorders? What PRAXIS™ and/or CEC standards are you addressing as you complete this question?

3. Go to Chapter 6 on the Companion Website, *www.prenhall.com/turnbull*, and find information about typical and atypical speech development. Listen to the samples of speech and see if you can identify which articulation or language disorders the children exhibit. Which PRAXIS™ and/or CEC standards are you using as you engage in this activity?

Who is Matthew Ackinclose?

Matthew Ackinclose has been through some remarkable changes in the past few years. At one time, this 14-year-old eighth grader needed 22 prescriptions to manage his behavior, attended school for only an hour a day, and had conflicts with nearly everyone in school. Now he attends all of his classes, most of which focus on content in the general education curriculum. He also takes only two medications, and one is for occasional migraines. He has good relationships with his school's administrators and faculty and with his peers. He is earning As and Bs in school and has a 99.5-percent average in his general education math class!

Matt's resiliency—his ability to overcome emotional or behavioral challenges—is a result of his determination and the supportive relationships he has with his mother, his therapist/social worker, and a special education teacher, among others. Those relationships and outcomes were hard to come by.

During Matt's early years, professionals routinely told his mother, Laura, to place him in a residential setting, but she refused. She knew in her heart that being separated from Matt was not the answer.

Matt's behavioral challenges began when he was just an infant. One day, when he was 7 months old, his face was bloody when his mother picked him up from daycare. Matt had repeatedly banged his head on the crib and the wall before a teacher could stop him. That was when Laura knew Matt needed help. She began a long search for someone: a psychologist, a physician, a teacher—anyone who could meet her son's needs.

In the meantime, Laura contrived new ways to keep Matt safe at home. Unfortunately, on one Halloween all of her precautionary measures failed. Matt got out of the house when some kids came to the door trick-or-treating. When Laura finally found him, he was standing in a nearby creek. She still remembers fearing that, if she tried to get close to him, he would run, slip under the water, and drown or badly injure himself. At about this time he also threatened to kill Laura and himself; he was only 5 years old. Clearly, Matt was a boy in pain.

Instead of recognizing that Matt and Laura were struggling to overcome a serious disability, professionals criticized Laura's parenting. "They can make you feel like a war criminal!" Laura says of the treatment she received from teachers and other professionals who wanted to blame her for Matt's disability.

Laura saw the strengths in Matt that others were unwilling to see: his intelligence, persistence, and sensitivity. She was alone in her point of view until she made a fortuitous phone call 6 years ago to social worker Rebecca Hall.

Rebecca sensed that what Matt needed most was a caring relationship with someone he could trust, who would connect with him and believe in his potential, not be intimidated by his words or behaviors, give him a sense of personal power by offering him choices; and work with him, not fight against him. She was determined to be that person.

Rather than focusing on Matt's deficits, Rebecca looked for his strengths. To Matt, she asked,

Understanding Students with Emotional or Behavioral Disorders

"What do you do well? When do you feel successful?" She asked Laura about the times when Matt behaved in a way she liked. Then she worked with Matt and Laura to increase those positive behaviors. Rebecca taught Matt how much he had to offer others and also worked with him on problem-solving skills. She would ask, "What's the problem? What can be done to fix it? What would you be willing to do instead?"

Despite the fact that Matt's behaviors improved, he and Laura searched in vain for a teacher who was willing to work with him until they found Charlotte Hott, a special education teacher. Charlotte's history with Matt began on a positive note when Rebecca placed a call to her and asked if Matt could enroll in her class. Charlotte replied without hesitation over the speakerphone, "I would love to have him!" Matt heard her response and realized that this teacher would care about him.

Charlotte welcomed Matt into her classroom. She built on the foundations of trust and strength-based interventions that were already in place, and she encouraged Matt and Laura through consistent, positive communication. Charlotte tailored her teaching approach to Matt's individual needs and realized, as Rebecca did, that a cooperative relationship with Matt was the key. "It's about respect," Charlotte says. "To get respect you must give respect."

When confronted by a tough lesson or a challenging social task, Matt frequently asked Charlotte, "Why are you doing this?"

"I always explained my reasons," Charlotte says. "I never said, 'Because I'm the teacher.' " She realized Matt was really asking if he could trust her.

Charlotte is the hub of a team consisting of Laura and Matt's general education teachers. Her role varies. For instance, Charlotte talked to Matt's physical education teacher and asked that he be allowed to participate in his school clothes rather than shorts and a T-shirt. This simple accommodation has made it easier for him to participate fully. Although he does not require any accommodations in his math, science, and social studies classes, he sometimes has difficulty expressing himself in papers and reports in his language arts class, so Charlotte spends extra time with him to help him with these assignments.

"You can be trained to do this job," Charlotte says, "but you have to want to do this job. It has to be genuine with Matt." The results of this mutual respect are clear: Matt can regulate his behavior, he takes fewer medications, he is making academic and social progress, he has better self-esteem, and he and others know about his strengths.

Matt is ultimately responsible for the positive changes in his life, but he acknowledges that, because people care about him and teach him effectively, he wants to change and has learned how. These changes aren't going unnoticed. When Rebecca told Matt how excited she was that he was going to be featured in this textbook, Matt said, "Well, it's not like I won the principal's Pride Award or anything." What Matt didn't know at the time was that he would receive that award a few weeks later, an acknowledgment and a celebration of all of his hard work.

IDENTIFYING STUDENTS WITH EMOTIONAL OR BEHAVIORAL DISORDERS

Defining Emotional or Behavioral Disorders

IDEA uses the term *emotional disturbance*, not *emotional or behavioral disorders*, which is the term that educators use. According to IDEA, emotional disturbance is a condition that is accompanied by one or more of the following characteristics over a long time and to a marked degree and that adversely affects a child's educational performance:

- An inability to learn that cannot be explained by intellectual, sensory, or health factors
- An inability to build or maintain satisfactory interpersonal relationships with peers and teachers
- Inappropriate types of behavior or feelings under normal circumstances
- A general pervasive mood of unhappiness or depression
- A tendency to develop physical symptoms or fears associated with personal or school problems

The term *emotional disturbance* includes schizophrenia but does not apply to children who are socially maladjusted unless they also meet the other criteria for having an emotional disturbance.

Educators and parents alike generally have not used the term *emotional disturbance*, preferring *emotional or behavioral disorders*. Having a "disorder" is generally perceived as being less stigmatizing than having a "disturbance."

In 2003–2004, approximately 0.7 percent (483,805) of all students in all of the nation's schools received special education because they had emotional or behavioral disorders (U.S. Department of Education, 2005). Experts disagree about whether the 0.7 figure accurately reflects the number of students with the disorder. Some believe that a more accurate identification rate is 9 to 10 percent of the school population (Walker et al., 1999). Still others conclude that 0.7 is an accurate figure (Coutinho, Oswald, Best, & Forness, 2002).

Gender, ethnic, and socioeconomic factors influence the prevalence of emotional or behavioral disorders. The interaction of gender and ethnicity is clear:

> White males were 3.8 times as likely as White females to be identified as ED while Black females were 1.4 times as likely as White females to be so identified. . . . Black males displayed the largest disproportionality, with an odds ratio of 5.5. These data starkly represent the extent of the problem of disproportionality in ED identification across gender and ethnic groups. (Coutinho et al., 2002, p. 116)

Moreover, a family's low-income status correlates with emotional or behavioral disorders in their children (Coutinho et al., 2002; Qi & Kaiser, 2003). Thus, acting out and aggression have been identified in up to one-third of preschool Head Start children from low-income backgrounds. Moreover, poverty is associated with risk factors such as toxic environments, poor nutrition, poor health care, and increased neighborhood/community violence (Brooks-Gunn & Duncan, 1997; Park, Turnbull, & Turnbull, 2002). Box 7–1 considers an educator's duty to these children.

Describing the Characteristics

Not all students who have emotional or behavioral disorders receive services under IDEA; that is because their disorders do not interfere with their educational progress. A student with phobia of heights, for instance, may not need special education services or specially designed instruction. But a student who has phobia of school may need special education services under IDEA.

There is no single profile of students with emotional or behavioral disorders. Males and females differ; females, for example, more frequently have physical symptoms or fears (Cullinan, Evans, Epstein, & Ryser, 2003). The students' profiles vary across gender and races/ethnicities (Cullinan, Osborne, & Epstein, 2004). European American females have been found to have greater difficulties with depression, but African American females tend to have greater difficulty with problem behavior. Thus, given how heterogeneous these students are, we will highlight only three of their principal characteristics: emotional traits, behavioral traits, and cognitive/academic traits.

Emotional characteristics. The *Diagnostic and Statistical Manual of Mental Disorders* (DSM-IV-TR) (American Psychiatric Association, 2000) is the standard classification system for mental illness and emotional-behavioral disorders. Under it, the conditions of childhood and adolescence that cause some children to be classified as having emotional or behavioral disorders are (1) anxiety disorder, (2) mood disorder, (3) oppositional defiant disorder, (4) conduct disorder, and (5) schizophrenia.

Anxiety disorder. **Anxiety disorder** is the most common childhood disorder (Albano, Chorpita, & Barlow, 2003). It is characterized by excessive fear, worry, or uneasiness and includes the following:

- **Separation anxiety disorder:** excessive and intense fear associated with separating from home, family, and others with whom a child has a close attachment.

- **Generalized anxiety disorder:** excessive, overwhelming worry not caused by any recent experience.

Each student with emotional or behavioral disorders has a unique combination of strengths and needs, and each teacher should seek out and build on those strengths.

- **Phobia:** unrealistic, overwhelming fear of an object or situation.

- **Panic disorder:** overwhelming panic attacks resulting in rapid heartbeat, dizziness, and/or other physical symptoms.

- **Obsessive-compulsive disorder:** obsessions manifesting as repetitive, persistent, and intrusive impulses, images, or thoughts (i.e., repetitive thoughts about death or illness) and/or compulsions manifesting as repetitive, stereotypical behaviors (i.e., handwashing or counting).

- **Post-traumatic stress disorder:** flashbacks and other recurrent symptoms following exposure to an extremely distressing and dangerous event such as witnessing violence or a hurricane.

Anxiety disorders can impair a student's academic and social functioning (Adams, 2004; Langley, Bergman, & Piacentini, 2002; Saavedra & Silverman, 2002). These disorders are often treated with medication that is prescribed by a physician and sometimes administered at school.

Mood disorder. A **mood disorder** involves an extreme deviation in either a depressed or an elevated direction or sometimes in both directions at different times (Forness, Walker, & Kavale, 2003; Hammen & Rudolph, 2003). Depression can occur at any age, including childhood. Students having a major depression may experience these changes:

- *Emotion:* feeling sad and worthless, crying often, or appearing tearful.

- *Motivation:* losing interest in play, friends, and schoolwork, with a resulting decline in grades.

Visit the Companion Website, *www.prenhall.com/turnbull*, for a link to the National Mental Health Association's fact sheets on childhood depression, *www.nmha.org/children*.

Visit the Companion Website, *www.prenhall.com/turnbull* for a link to American Association of Suicidology. Read their Youth Suicide Fact Sheet, *www.suicidology.org*.

- *Physical well-being:* eating or sleeping too much or too little, disregarding hygiene, or making vague physical complaints.
- *Thoughts:* perhaps believing he or she is ugly and unable to do anything right and that life is hopeless.

The prevalence of depression has increased over the past several decades; the highest rate occurs in adolescent females (Hammen & Rudolph, 2003). Major depressive episodes typically last 7 to 9 months (Kovacs, 1996), and the vast majority of children have recurrences within 5 to 7 years after their first episode (Emslie et al., 1997).

Tragically, depression sometimes leads to suicide. Annually, approximately 750,000 young people between the ages of 10 and 24 will attempt suicide (McIntosh & Guest, 2000). After accidents and homicides, suicide is the third leading cause of death for youth and young adults ages 15 to 24. In 2002, 3,932 young people in this age range committed suicide (Kochanek & Smith, 2004). Females are more likely to try to commit suicide, but males succeed at a much higher rate. For example, among 15- to 24-year-olds who committed suicide in 2001, 86 percent were male and 14 percent were female (Anderson & Smith, 2003). Four factors are strongly associated with an increased suicide risk: hopelessness, hostility, negative self-concept, and isolation (Rutter & Behrendt, 2004).

There are two actions you can take to try to prevent your students from attempting suicide. First, bearing in mind that children typically know the meaning of suicide by the third grade (Mishara, 1999) and that young children usually get their information about suicide from other children or television, you can work with school counselors and social workers to give children an accurate understanding of suicide and reassure them that they should confide in a trusted adult when they, their friends, or their family make suicidal statements. Second, whenever you believe that one of your students may be even casually considering suicide, you should act as though your student were having an emergency at that very moment and put him and his family in immediate touch with professional experts (Bostic, Rustuccia, & Schlozman, 2001).

A **bipolar disorder,** also referred to as manic depression, occurs in children and adolescents as well as adults (Hammen & Rudolph, 2003). Approximately one-fourth of individuals who are bipolar experience the condition before they are 20 years old (Faedda et al., 1995). Exaggerated mood swings characterize the condition. At times, the student experiences depression; at other times, she experiences manic or excited phases, increased activity and even agitation, racing thoughts, decreased need for sleep, and an exaggerated sense of strength. Experiencing mania has been described as living on fast-forward speed (Miklowitz & Goldstein, 1997). Often a student's heightened mood phase has characteristics associated with attention-deficit/hyperactivity disorder (AD/HD) (Geller et al., 1998).

Oppositional defiant disorder. **Oppositional defiant disorder** causes a pattern of negativistic, hostile, disobedient, and defiant behaviors (American Psychiatric Association, 2000). Your students' symptoms may include loss of temper, arguments with adults, irritability, vindictiveness, swearing and using obscenities, blaming others for mistakes and misbehavior, and low self-esteem. These symptoms may be exacerbated if the students believe that they have no control over an important life situation, such as their parents' divorce or a move (Hewitt, 1999). The students may also abuse drugs and alcohol. Appropriate interventions may prevent a student's oppositional-defiant disorder from escalating to the more serious level known as conduct disorder (Loeber et al., 2000). One effective intervention is "tagging"—telling a student, "I'd like to discuss this at a later time when both of us are clam," and ending the discussion, thus interrupting the student's oppositional cycle (Milne, Edwards, & Murchie, 2001, p. 24). Additional suggestions for encouraging compliance from students with oppositional defiant disorders include providing choices, encouraging physical activity, anticipating and preventing problems, and referring new students for counseling or therapy (Knowlton, 1995).

Conduct disorder. **Conduct disorder** consists of a persistent pattern of antisocial behavior that significantly interferes with others' rights or with schools' and communities' behavioral expectations (American Psychiatric Association, 2000; Hinshaw & Lee, 2003). The American Psychiatric Association (2000) has identified four categories of conduct disorders: (1) aggressive conduct, resulting in physical harm to people or animals; (2) property destruction; (3) deceitfulness or theft; and (4) serious rule violations, such as truancy and running away.

Students who exhibit conduct disorders usually have little empathy for others. Their self-esteem is low or overly inflated. And approximately 50 percent of all teenagers with oppositional defiant disorder or conduct disorder also have ADHD (Hinshaw & Lee, 2003). The most frequent types of interventions for conduct disorder include rewarding positive behavior and training in social skills (Kavale, Forness, & Walker, 1999).

Students with conduct disorders usually manifest the same bio-behavioral characteristics as students with oppositional defiant behavior; but various psychosocial factors also are linked to conduct disorders, including being abused as a child, living in neighborhoods characterized by poverty, and experiencing conflictual relationships with adults (Burke, Loeber, & Birmaher, 2002).

Schizophrenia. **Schizophrenia** is a disorder in which people typically have two or more of the following symptoms: hallucinations, withdrawal, delusions, inability to experience pleasure, loss of contact with reality, and disorganized speech (American Psychiatric Association, 2000; Asarnow & Asarnow, 2003). Schizophrenia is rarer than most other types of emotional or behavioral disorders, and sometimes diagnostic confusion exists between schizophrenia and mood disorders (Calderoni, 2001). Although schizophrenia generally begins in late adolescence or early adulthood, some children have the condition. Schizophrenia is often treated with a combination of medication and behavioral and social-skills interventions (Asarnow & Asarnow, 2003; Forness et al., 2003).

Behavioral characteristics. Students with emotional or behavioral disorders have one or both of two easily identifiable behavioral patterns: externalizing or internalizing (Gresham, Lane, MacMillan, & Bocian, 1999).

Externalizing behavior. **Externalizing behaviors**—those that are persistently aggressive or involve acting-out and noncompliant behaviors—often are characteristics of conduct and oppositional defiant disorders (Walker, Colvin, & Ramsey, 1995). Sometimes teachers do not recognize that teenagers and children who are depressed may exhibit externalizing, acting-out behaviors rather than the typical internalizing, withdrawal behavior more common in adults. Students with externalizing behaviors are more likely than their peers to exhibit high-intensity but low-frequency behavioral events such as setting fires, assaulting someone, or exhibiting cruelty (Gresham et al., 1999). Teachers tend to refer students with externalizing behavioral characteristics for special education services because they disrupt classrooms (Rubin et al., 1995). Additionally, students with externalizing behavior, especially aggression toward peers, tend to be frequently referred for office discipline, suspensions (in and out of school), detentions, and expulsions (Nelson, Gonzalez, Epstein, & Benner, 2003).

Children who display early externalizing behavior may experience either increases or decreases in problem behavior as they grow older. The risk factors associated with an escalation of externalizing behavior include reduced verbal ability, more behavioral impulsiveness, more stringent discipline from parents, a greater likelihood that parents experience emotional maladjustment (Ackerman, Brown, & Izard, 2003), and family poverty (McCulloch, Wiggins, Joshi, & Sachdev, 2000).

Like all other students, students with externalizing behaviors are subject to zero tolerance policies that allow educators to expel a student who exhibits violent behavior or brings drugs or weapons to school. However, IDEA protects them against total cessation of their education if they have been evaluated and receive special education services under IDEA (see Chapter 1).

Internalizing behavior. **Internalizing behavior** includes withdrawal, depression, anxiety, obsessions, and compulsions. Students with internalizing behavior have poorer social skills and are less accepted than their typical peers (Gresham et al., 1999). They often tend to blend into the background to the point that teachers forget they are in the classroom. Because their behaviors are not as disruptive as externalizing behaviors, these students are less likely to be identified for special education services. Educators sometimes assume that internalizing problems do not pose the same or similar long-term risks as those associated with externalizing problems. However, the level of social withdrawal of second-grade students predicted their low self-regard and loneliness when they were in ninth grade (Rubin et al., 1995).

One of the students in this classroom experiences depression and anxiety. Both conditions can affect the student's performance in class and extracurricular activities.

Externalizing and internalizing behavior can occur simultaneously (Hinshaw & Lee, 2003). For example, a student may have an internalizing disorder such as depression that occurs alongside problems with externalizing behavior such as aggression (conduct disorder). These and other dissimilar emotional or behavioral disorders do not occur in isolation.

Cognitive and academic characteristics. Students with emotional or behavioral disorders may be gifted or have mental retardation, but most have IQs in the low average range (Duncan, Forness, & Hartsough, 1995). More than half have concurrent learning disabilities (Glassberg, Hooper, & Mattison, 1999). The relationship between academic and social behaviors seems to be reciprocal: students who experience failure in one area also tend to experience failure in the other (Jolivette, 2000):

- Students tend to achieve below grade level in reading, math, and written expression (Trout, Nordness, Pierce, & Epstein, 2003).

- They drop out of school at a higher rate than other students with disabilities, with more than half of students in this category dropping out annually (Osher, Quinn, & Hanley, 2002).

- They have a mean achievement level at the 25th percentile, their greatest academic challenges being in the areas of math and spelling (Reid et al., 2004).

- They are more likely to have problems with academic achievement when externalizing behaviors are present than when internalizing behaviors exist (Mattison, Spitznagel, & Felix, 1998; Nelson, Benner, Lane, & Smith, 2004).

- They are less likely than most students with other types of disabilities to attend postsecondary school (Bullis & Cheney, 1999; Kauffman, 2001).

Most students with emotional or behavioral disorders (71 percent) have expressive and/or receptive language disorders (Benner, Nelson, & Epstein, 2002), and many have undiagnosed language deficits (Cohen et al., 1998). Predictably, slightly more than half of children identified as having language deficits also have emotional or behavioral disabilities. Language can be a key factor in students with either externalizing or internalizing behavior; these students are more apt than others to engage in aggressive behavior and less apt to use verbal communication to address their interpersonal problems. In addition, students who do not comply with teachers' or others' directions after repeated requests may have receptive language impairments that interfere with their ability to conform to the behavioral expectations of their classrooms (Fujiki, Brinton, Morgan, & Hart, 1999). Remember the vignette? You may want to know that Laura noticed Matt's language delay early; he began intervention for his speech problems at age 2.

Determining the Causes

Although it is difficult to determine with absolute confidence the causes of students' emotional or behavioral disorders (Sternberg & Grigorenko, 1999), it is clear that the major causes are biological and environmental.

Biological causes. "There are far-reaching biological and physical influences on mental health and mental illness" (U.S. Surgeon General, 2000, p. 52). Only recently has it become clear that genetics also influence children's behavioral characteristics, including anxiety disorder, depression, schizophrenia, oppositional defiant disorder, and conduct disorder (Bassarath, 2001; Burke et al., 2002; Kumra et al., 2001). Hallowell (1996) concluded, "All behavior and all personality are in some way genetically influenced, and to a greater degree than most of us take into account" (p. 62).

Environmental stressors. Biological factors do not exist in a vacuum. There is a dynamic interplay between biological and environmental factors (Mash & Dozois, 2003; Van Der Valk, Van Den Oord, Verhulst, & Boomsma, 2003). Three environmental stressors that can contribute to emotional or behavioral disorders are (1) stressful living conditions, (2) child maltreatment, and (3) school factors.

Standard: Understanding the various influences that affect students with emotional or behavioral disorders applies to CEC Standard 3, Individual Learning Differences.

Stressful living conditions. Although many families who live in poverty are emotionally healthy, a student who lives in poverty is more likely to develop emotional or behavioral disorders than one who lives in abundant circumstances (Yeung, Linver, & Brooks-Gunn, 2002; Qi & Kaiser, 2003). Indeed, 38 percent of all youth with emotional or behavioral disorders come from households with an annual income of under $12,000, and another 32 percent come from households with an income of $12,000 to $24,999 (Fujiura & Yamaki, 2000). Further, 44 percent come from single-parent households. Significantly, low income and single-parent status are highly correlated (Fujiura & Yamaki, 2000). Finally, half to three-quarters of school-age children in foster care have emotional or behavioral disorders (Clausen et al., 1998; Leslie et al., 2000).

Poverty adds stress to people's lives and can contribute to a student's having emotional or behavioral disorders.

IDEA pays particular attention to one group of students that experiences particular complications associated with poverty: homeless students. The 2004 law requires state and local educational agencies to cooperate with social service agencies in reaching out to and enrolling these students and then assuring that they have all of IDEA's benefits if they qualify. Children and youth who are homeless often move from shelter to shelter, which disrupts both their school attendance and their social relationships (Institute for Children and Poverty, 2001). Homeless students experience emotional or behavioral disorders three to four times more frequently than do children in the general school population (Kelly, Buehlman, & Caldwell, 2000). It can be especially challenging to form partnerships with the parents of students who are homeless and with the students themselves. Box 7–2 provides tips, based on a successful program in Tennessee, for meeting the needs of this special population.

Diversity Tips ~ Tips for Establishing Partnerships with Homeless Families and Their Children

Box 7–2

The Home, Educator, Readiness, and Opportunity (HERO) program in Nashville, Tennessee, operates out of the school district's social work and school attendance division. The HERO program addresses the diverse needs of families and children who do not have a stable home. Following are tips based on this successful program:

- Track school attendance of children who are admitted to a city's homeless shelters to identify students who are truant and to learn why a student is not attending school.
- Inform parents about the rights of their children to remain in their school of origin and not be moved to a different school within the district when the family moves to a different shelter.
- Help arrange or pay for transportation so students can go from any shelter to their school of origin.
- Provide after-school tutoring in the shelters.

- Provide recreational opportunities during weekends, holidays, and summers.
- Create opportunities to collect donated school supplies and clothing and deliver them to the students and families.
- Model for parents how they can support their children to do homework as well as address their social and emotional needs.
- Partner with parents to follow up on their children's school performance and increase attendance rates.
- Coordinate services across different human service agencies so that families have an opportunity to address their comprehensive needs.

Source: Adapted from Davey, T. L., Penuel, W. R., Allison-Tant, E., & Rosner, A. M. (2000). The HERO program: A case for school social work services. *Social Work in Education 22*(3), 177–190. Copyright 2000, National Association of Social Workers, Inc., Social Work in Education.

Go to the Companion Website, *www.prenhall.com/turnbull*, for a link to the National Advocacy Organization working on behalf of families who have children and youth with emotional and behavioral disorders, *www.ffcmh.org*.

In the vignette, you learned that Matt's mother, Laura, who worked so hard to help her son, felt she was being treated like a war criminal. As you discovered in the section on causes, researchers are beginning to discover genetic and other biomedical bases for emotional or behavioral disorders. Blaming parents may give teachers an excuse to give up on a child, but placing blame does nothing to solve problems. "One of the most important things I learned going through school," Charlotte says, "is 'always remember that parents believe that their child is a direct reflection of them.' So when you say, 'That kid's a bad kid,' they're thinking, 'I'm a bad parent.' That's why I always try to be upbeat. Communication comes down to this: It's daily; it's immediate; it's positive." A strength-based perspective carries over to the family, building on what members do right and responding to their needs as well as the student's.

Child maltreatment. There are four specific types of **child maltreatment:**

- *Neglect:* failure to provide for the child's basic physical, educational, and emotional needs.
- *Physical abuse:* a physical injury to the child, regardless of whether or not the caretaker intended to hurt the child.
- *Sexual abuse:* activities including incest, rape, sodomy, indecent exposure, fondling a child's genitals, vaginal or anal penetration, and commercial exploitation through prostitution or pornographic materials.
- *Emotional abuse:* any behavior such as constant criticism, threats, or rejection that impedes a child's self-esteem and emotional development.

The shocking news is that, on every day in 2001, approximately 2,500 children were victims of child abuse (Administration for Children and Families, 2004).

Click on our Companion Website, *www.prenhall.com/turnbull*, for a link to Prevent Child Abuse America and What You Can Do to Prevent Child Abuse, *www.preventchildabuse. org*.

In a national survey, 556 teachers of students with emotional or behavioral disorders reported that approximately 38 percent of their students had been abused physically or sexually, 41 percent had been neglected, 51 percent had been abused emotionally, and some had suffered more than one kind of maltreatment (Oseroff, Oseroff, Westling, & Gessner, 1999). Eighty-two percent of the teachers reported evidence of their students' maltreatment, usually to school administrators but less often to a child abuse hotline run by state or local child protective service agencies. As a teacher, you are legally responsible to report suspected child abuse.

PRAXIS

Standard: Understanding your legal responsibilities in regard to child maltreatment is an application of PRAXIS™ Standard 2, Legal and Societal Issues.

Students who have experienced abuse may display (1) low self-image, (2) aggression toward others, (3) sudden change in activities or personality, (4) sexual acting out or age-inappropriate interest in sex, (5) nervousness around adults, and (6) frequent or unexplained injuries or bruises (Administration for Children and Families, 2004). Some, however, may conceal the abuse; they may even be popular, straight-A students. In Figure 7–1, you will find short answers to common questions about child abuse.

School factors. As is true across all disabilities, educators have been effective in educating students with emotional or behavioral disabilities, and as is true across all disabilities, they continue to be challenged by their students' unique needs. In the field of emotional or behavioral disabilities, for example, some specialists believe that students' reading instruction is not based on research-validated procedures (Levy & Vaughn, 2002), offers limited opportunities for them to respond and limited delivery of new content (Gunter, Hummel, & Venn, 1998), and consists of few data-collection procedures (Gunter, Callicott, & Denny, 2003). Other specialists think that it is difficult to meet NCLB's requirements related to the provision of scientifically based practices for these students (Mooney, Denny, & Gunter, 2004). Unhappily, students' academic underachievement tends to spawn behavior problems and academic failure (Gunter, Coutinho, & Cade, 2002; Pierce, Reid, & Epstein, 2004).

In addition, there is an insufficient number of highly qualified teachers of these students; approximately two-thirds of the teachers begin teaching without being fully certified (Billingsley, 2001). These teachers also tend to experience job stress and burnout at a higher rate than do teachers in other areas of special and general education (George, George, Gersten, & Grosenick, 1995). All too often, teacher training programs focus only on preparing teachers to deal with externalizing behavior, not how to deliver academic instruction (Mooney et al., 2004; Wehby, Lane, & Falk, 2003).

Values: You can help support students by helping them to develop *relationships,* make friends, and minimize the stigma and rejection that their peers without disabilities might impose on them.

Figure 7–1 Questions and answers about child abuse

What is child abuse? Child abuse and neglect include actions or inaction creating an imminent risk of death, serious physical or emotional harm, sexual abuse, or exploitation by a parent or caretaker who is responsible for the child's welfare.

How common is it? The National Clearinghouse on Child Abuse and Neglect reported that 879,000 children were identified as victims of abuse and neglect in 2000. Children who have disabilities are at 1.7 times higher risk of abuse and neglect than are children without disabilities.

How do I know if it is occurring? Physical indicators may include skin or bone injuries, evidence of neglect such as malnutrition, failure to meet medical needs, or lack of warm clothing in cold weather. Behavioral indicators may include a demonstration of sexual knowledge that is not developmentally or age appropriate.

What do I do if I think a child is being abused? Is this really my business? It *is* your business. Abuse and neglect impede learning. Under most state laws, educators are "mandated reporters." You must report to a state or local child protection agency. Mandated reporters who fail to report may be penalized, but they also are immune from civil or criminal liability if they act in good faith. Many school systems have their own policies concerning child abuse and neglect. To learn your state's hotline number, call 1-800-4-A-CHILD, which will direct you to your state's agency.

You must report suspected abuse, but it is not your responsibility to investigate whether a child is being abused. Your child protection agency must do that. No state requires that the person reporting has proof—only that the person has reasonable cause to believe that abuse is occurring.

What kind of information will they want when I make a report? The child's name, age, address, and telephone number; the parent's or other caretaker's name, address, and telephone number; and the reason for your call.

What should I do when a student confides in me about abuse?

- Do not promise that you will not tell. Say that you will inform the student about the nature or identity of the persons you may need to tell and why you need to tell them.
- Encourage the student to talk freely; avoid judgment.
- Take the student seriously. Students who are listened to and understood fare better in therapy than do those who are not.
- Emphasize that the student did the right thing by telling.
- Tell the student that she is not at fault but avoid making derogatory comments about the abuser. The abuser may be someone the student cares for deeply, and such comments might cause the student to retract what was said.
- Promise that you will continue to be there for the student and will take steps to try to stop the abuse.

Source: National Clearinghouse on Child Abuse and Neglect. (2002, April). *National child abuse and neglect data system (NCANDS): Summary of key findings from calendar year 2000* (http://www.calib.com/nccanch/pubs/factsheets/canstats.cfm); American Academy of Child and Adolescent Psychiatry. (1997). *Child abuse: The hidden bruises* (http://www.aacap.org/publications/factsFam/Chldabus2.htm).

EVALUATING STUDENTS WITH EMOTIONAL OR BEHAVIORAL DISORDERS

Determining the Presence of Emotional or Behavioral Disorders

Figure 7–2 describes the nondiscriminatory evaluation process. A wide variety of measures helps teachers and other professionals identify students with emotional or behavioral disorders. The measures include behavior rating scales and personality inventories (Collett, Ohan, & Myers, 2003; Wingenfeld, 2002). Many of these measures, however, do not align with or take into

Figure 7–2 Nondiscriminatory evaluation procedures for students with emotional or behavioral disabilities

Observation	*Teacher and parents observe:* The student may be unable to build and maintain satisfactory interpersonal relationships, may engage in aggressive behaviors, or may have a pervasive mood of unhappiness or depression. The student acts out or withdraws during classroom instruction and independent activities. Problematic behavior occurs in more than one setting.
Screening	*Assessment measures:* **Classroom work products:** The student may require one-to-one assistance to stay on task. The student has difficulty following basic classroom behavioral expectations during instruction or assigments, resulting in incomplete or unsatisfactory work products. **Group intelligence tests:** Most students perform in the low-average to slow-learner range. Performance may not accurately reflect ability because the emotional/behavioral disorder can prevent the student from staying on task. **Group achievement tests:** The student performs below peers or scores lower than would be expected according to group intelligence tests. Performance may not be a true reflection of achievement because the student has difficulty staying on task as a result of the emotional/behavioral disorder. **Vision and hearing screening:** Results do not explain behavior.
Prereferral	*Teacher implements suggestions from school-based team:* The student is not responsive to reasonable adaptations of the curriculum and positive behavior-support techniques.
Referral	
Nondiscriminatory evaluation procedures and standards	*Assessment measures:* **Individualized intelligence test:** Intelligence is usually, but not always, in the low average to slow learner range. The multidisciplinary team makes sure that the results do not reflect cultural difference rather than ability. **Scale for assessing emotional disturbance:** As described in the chapter, this scale is specifically tailored to IDEA's definition of emotional or behavioral disorders and is especially helpful in diagnosis in this area. **Individualized achievement test:** Usually, but not always, the student scores below average across academic areas in comparison to peers. The evaluator may notice acting-out or withdrawal behaviors that affect results. **Behavior rating scale:** The student scores in the significant range on specific behavioral excesses or deficiencies when compared with others of the same culture and developmental stage. **Assessment of strengths:** Using the Behavioral and Emotional Rating Scale (as described in the text) enables evaluators to identify student strengths. **Assessment measures of social skills, self-esteem, personality, and/or adjustment:** The student's performance indicates significant difficulties in one or more areas according to the criteria established by test and in comparison with others of the same culture and developmental stage. **Anecdotal records:** The student's problem behavior is not of short duration but has been apparent throughout time in school. Also, records indicate that behaviors have been observed in more than one setting and are adversely affecting the student's educational progress. **Curriculum-based assessment:** The student often is experiencing difficulty in one or more areas of the general curriculum. **Direct observation:** The student is experiencing difficulty relating to peers or adults and in adjusting to school or classroom structure or routine.
Determination	The nondiscriminatory evaluation team determines that the student has emotional or behavioral disorders and needs special education and related services.

account IDEA's description of the five characteristics of emotional or behavioral disorders. As you will recall from the discussion at the beginning of the chapter, these five elements include inability to learn, inability to build or maintain satisfactory relationships, inappropriate behavior, unhappiness or depression, and physical symptoms or fears.

To address this problem, researchers have developed and proven the reliability and validity of a scale that specifically measures these five elements—the Scale for Assessing Emotional

Disturbance (Cullinan, Evans, Epstein, & Ryser, 2003; Epstein, Cullinan, Ryser, & Pearson, 2002; Epstein, Nordness, Cullinan, & Hertzog, 2002). This norm-referenced scale contains five subscales, each of which corresponds directly to one of the five elements in the IDEA definition, and 45 items, each of which is a 4-point scale ranging from 3 to 0 (3 equals severe problem; 0 equals no problem). For example, three of the items on the relationship subscale ask the evaluator (who should know the student well and can be a teacher, parent, or other adult) whether any of the following applies to the student:

- Does not work well in group activities

- Feels picked on or persecuted

- Avoids interacting with people

Having completed the scale, the evaluator sums the subscale scores and converts them to percentiles, thereby attaining an overall indication of the student's emotional or behavioral functioning. The scale takes only about 10 minutes to complete and includes items to help identify a student's resources, competencies, and other assets (for example, family support).

Determining the Nature of Specially Designed Instruction and Services

Determining that a student qualifies for IDEA services precedes an evaluation that identifies his areas of strengths and needs and then uses them to develop his IEP. Although educators may have a tendency to be deficit-oriented in working with students, they can avail themselves of a tool developed specifically for identifying a student's strengths.

The Behavioral and Emotional Rating Scale (Epstein, 1999; Epstein & Sharma, 1998) is a companion to the Scale for Assessing Emotional Disturbance and is based on four assumptions related to strengths, influences of significant others, and the need for opportunities to learn (Rudolph & Epstein, 2000).

This tool consists of five subscales, containing a total of 52 items. Each item is scored on a 4-point scale ranging from "not at all like the child" to "very much like the child." Teachers, parents, or other adults who know the student well can complete the Behavioral and Emotional Rating Scale in approximately 10 minutes. Research on the scale's reliability and validity shows that it has strong psychometric properties for measuring students' emotional or behavioral strengths (Epstein, Hertzog, & Reid, 2001; Epstein, Nordness, Nelson, & Hertzog, 2002; Reid, Epstein, Pastor, & Ryser, 2000).

A second way to evaluate students' strengths is to talk with them about their interests, their preferences, and the experiences that give them a sense of excitement about their life. Imagine having a conversation with Matt Ackinclose, the student in the opening vignette. What questions would you ask to learn about his strengths, and how do you think he would react to a teacher who is genuinely interested in listening to what is working well for him in his life? Prominent Harvard psychiatrist Robert Coles (1989) describes the advice that one of his mentors gave to him: "Why don't you chuck the word 'interview,' call yourself a friend, call your exchanges 'conversations!'" (p. 32). Having conversations with students and listening carefully to their life stories can open the door to learning about their strengths. "Their personal narratives help us detect exceptions to their problems . . . because it is often in these exceptions that possibilities for solution construction lie and the leverage to bounce back from life's hardships can be found" (Laursen, 2000, p. 70).

Values: Strengths-based assessment ensures that you will build on your students' *strengths* in evaluating them and then providing them with an appropriate education.

DESIGNING AN APPROPRIATE INDIVIDUALIZED EDUCATION PROGRAM

Partnering for Special Education and Related Services

Best practice involves the use of a collaborative process known as **wraparound.** The term refers to "a philosophy of care that includes a definable planning process involving the child and family

Standard: Participating in the wraparound process is an example of applying CEC Standard 10, Collaboration.

For more information about the National Wraparound Initiative, visit our Companion Website, *www.pren-hall.com/turnbull*, for a link to *http://www.rtc.pdx.edu/nwi/*.

Values: The wraparound process focuses on your students' *strengths* and abilities and ensures that they and their family members have an opportunity to make choices about their education and related services.

that results in a unique set of community services and natural supports individualized for that child and family to achieve a positive set of outcomes" (Burns & Goldman, 1999, p. 13). Wraparound is family-driven, collaborative, individualized, culturally competent, and community- and strengths-based (Walker & Schutte, 2004). Just as the word itself suggests, school, community, mental health, and other services are "wrapped around" the student instead of being compartmentalized by field or agency. You saw this at work as Matt's mother, teachers, and therapist wrapped school and mental health services around him so he could move from homebound services to inclusion in the general education classroom.

The National Wraparound Initiative Advisory Group recommends that professionals should do the following (Bruns et al., 2004; Walker et al., 2004):

- Stabilize any immediate crisis so the student and family members can pay full attention to the planning process. Ask family members and the student about their concerns related to the crisis and, if warranted, respond with temporary relief from the crisis.

- Orient family members and the student to the wraparound process.

- Develop a support and planning team that includes the student, family members, educators, agency representatives, and other key stakeholders.

- Identify the student's and family's strengths, needs, culture, and vision, always including the student and family members in those discussions and in planning wraparound services.

- Create a team mission and ground rules.

- Prioritize interventions and goals and indicators for each goal.

- Identify strength-based and culturally competent strategies to achieve the goals.

- Develop a crisis and safety plan for everyone's benefit.

- Ensure fidelity to treatment; implement and track the plan's progress.

The Wraparound Fidelity Index "assesses the services and supports a family receives with respect to adherence to the essential elements of the wraparound approach" (Bruns et al., 2004, p. 81). It is completed by interviewing family members, the student, and the primary case manager or facilitator to obtain information about fidelity in 11 elements of wraparound.

The wraparound model repeats themes relevant to students with other types of disabilities, such as involving the student, family members, and others. It also focuses on strengths and abilities and uses community and inclusive settings for intervention and treatment.

Determining Supplementary Aids and Services

Problem behavior and negative interactions with peers impede inclusion, so each student's IEP team needs to consider what types of supplementary aids and services the student needs to succeed in the general education classroom. One that can lead to more positive behavior outcomes is classwide, peer-assisted self-management (Mitchem, 2001). This practice combines peer-mediated learning with self-management strategies to help students learn to manage their own behavior.

There are several steps in this process. First, as a group, students learn how to define self-management and why it is effective generally and to decide how it might benefit them. Next, they learn the relationship among antecedents (the triggers of their behaviors), their specific behaviors, and the consequences of those behaviors. They also discuss how to respond appropriately and inappropriately to the triggers, and they identify positive consequences for appropriate behaviors.

The teacher then reviews the school and classroom rules and two social skills: how to follow instructions and how to get the teacher's attention. Using an instruction given by the teacher as an antecedent, the students can identify appropriate and inappropriate responses and consequences for those responses.

The teacher instructs students on how to use a rating scale of "honors, satisfactory, needs improvement, and unsatisfactory" in terms of classroom expectations (e.g., following the teacher's directions). After asking students for the names of three students they would like to work with, the teacher pairs them and then groups them into two teams. Students then practice rating their partner's behavior according to a scale on a card. When cued, the students mark their and their partner's behavior and reflect on how their ratings compare with their partner's. Perfect matches earn bonus points. At the end of class, they report their partner's totals and then tally those with the totals of other members of their team. Both teams receive praise for their efforts, and the team with the highest points for the week becomes the winning team.

The success of classwide, peer-assisted treatment demonstrates how important it is for teachers to plan carefully how they will address their students' problem behavior. These behaviors usually require interventions that have multiple components. In this case those components were peer tutoring and self-management strategies. Tournaki and Criscitiello (2003) found that **reverse-role tutoring**—that is, using students with emotional or behavioral disorders as tutors for nondisabled peers—not only resulted in benefits for the nondisabled peers but also improved the behavior and writing skills of the tutors. Similarly, Kamps and colleagues (2000) combined social-skills training, peer tutoring, and classroom-management techniques to improve outcomes for youth with emotional or behavioral disorders. Whatever the actual intervention, it is critical that planning teams, such as those involved in wraparound, consider a wide array of supplementary aids and services and instructional strategies.

Planning for Universal Design for Learning

Modifications are almost always necessary to make it possible for students with emotional or behavioral disorders to demonstrate mastery (Gunter, Denny, & Venn, 2000). Allowing your students to use a computer with word processing software is one such modification; it can minimize their frustration by making it easier for them to revise their work and produce clean, legible products (Hasselbring & Glaser, 2000). Indeed, students who use standard word processing software programs may be more willing to edit and correct their work than if they have to hand-write original and revised products. Moreover, many affordable word processing programs include features such as word prediction and spelling correction that enable students who are struggling writers to identify the areas they need to improve. Box 7–3 provides information about word processing programs that might benefit not only your students with emotional or behavioral disabilities but also students with other disabilities.

Technology Tips ~ Talking Word Processors: Using Technology to Improve Writing Performance

Box 7–3

Schools rely heavily on written student products as a way to evaluate student progress. However, many students with disabilities, including those with emotional or behavioral disabilities, have barely legible handwriting or cannot write at all. In addition, students often have difficulty with spelling and sentence structure. There are a number of software and assistive technology products that enable students with disabilities to use the computer to improve their writing performance.

The simplest such modifications involve changes to how students input information on a computer. Students with emotional or behavioral disorders may benefit from a keyboard on which the letters are arranged alphabetically. The typical keyboard is called a QWERTY layout (those are the first six letters on the top row from the left). The alphabetically arranged keyboard is called, logically, the ABCDEF layout!

Of more potential benefit to students with emotional or behavioral disorders may be word processing software programs that make writing easier or more efficient. Perhaps the most common modified word processing program involves the use of "talking word processors." These software programs are similar to typical word processing packages, except that as students type in words, they are "read" back to them. In addition to this basic feature, various software programs incorporate other features that make writing more effective for students with disabilities. Like common word processing packages, most of the available programs include a spell-checking capacity. Some link the synthesized voice capacity to spell checking and can read out suggestions for spelling or sentence structure from which students can choose. Some packages have word prediction capacity. When a student types in the start of a word but can't remember the rest, the word prediction capacity makes suggestions for finishing the word.

Some commercially available talking word processors include Write:Outloud, available from Don Johnstone, Inc. (*http://www.donjohnstone.com/catalog/writecover/writecoverfrm.htm*); IntelliTalk 3, available from Intellitools (*http://www.intellitools.com/products/intellitalk/home.php*); and eReader from CAST (*http://www.cast.org/udl/index.cfm?i=211&option=Introduction*).

Planning for Other Educational Needs

Values: If your students are to achieve *full citizenship,* they have to stay in school. Do all you can to prevent them from dropping out.

Dropping out of school is almost always sure to create, not solve, students' problems. A 2002 report from the U.S. Department of Education determined that more than half of students served under the category of emotional disturbance dropped out of school before graduating, and only 41.9 percent graduated. Some students aged out of school; that is, they did not drop out, but neither did they earn enough credits to graduate with a diploma. What are the consequences of dropping out? Two years after they dropped out, only 36 percent to 42 percent of all dropout students were employed, compared to 53 percent to 63 percent of their peers with emotional or behavioral disorders who graduated (Sitlington & Neubert, 2004). These data give teachers a very strong message: try to prevent your students from dropping out.

Students with emotional or behavioral disorders leave school for many reasons, generally because they are not interested in what is being taught and feel negative about school in general (Scanlon & Mellard, 2002). According to a study by the Oregon Department of Education (Martin, Tobin, & Sugai, 2002, p. 11), there are 10 specific reasons why students drop out:

1. Insufficient credits to graduate.
2. Lack of parental support for education.
3. Problematic home lives.
4. Student work schedule (greater than 15 hours per week).
5. Substance abuse.
6. Frequent discipline problems and referrals.
7. Student perceptions that he or she does not "fit in."
8. Student pregnancy or caring for a small child.
9. Peer pressure to leave school.
10. Frequent moves between schools (attending three or more high schools.)

Several universal and student-based interventions can reduce dropout rates (Martin et al., 2002). Universal interventions involve district- or campuswide interventions, the wraparound process, and schoolwide positive behavior support (discussed in Chapter 11). They also include the following interventions (Martin et al., 2002):

- *Establish a student advisory program* linking students to an adult mentor in the school.
- *Establish and involve students in extracurricular activities,* including sports, music, vocational activities, or other extracurriculars.
- *Systematically monitor risk factors associated with dropout,* tracking student attendance, tardiness, grades, and referrals for discipline.
- *Develop "schools within schools"* or smaller units.
- *Establish school-to-work programs,* demonstrating how school relates to work.
- *Engage in community-based learning,* making school more relevant and learning more practical.
- *Use the "check and connect" strategy,* linking an adult monitor with a student to track risk factors and work with the student and family to reduce them.
- *Provide vocational education,* attempting to forestall poor employment outcomes.

Combining the "check and connect" strategy with self-management and problem-solving skills engages students in school and reduces the chance that they will drop out (Christenson, Evelo, & Hurley, 1998). So do vocational education (Corbett, Sanders, Clark, & Blank, 2002), involvement in extracurricular activities (Mahoney, 2000), and instruction in conflict-resolution skills (Hunt et al., 2002).

As we have pointed out, a student's ethnicity and the student's family make a difference in whether he or she is classified as having an emotional or behavioral disorder and how you work with the student's family as a partner. Being an effective partner with families from diverse backgrounds requires you to be culturally competent, as you learned in Chapter 3.

USING EFFECTIVE INSTRUCTIONAL STRATEGIES

Early Childhood Students: Multicomponent Interventions to Prevent Conduct Disorders

As early as first grade, a student's learning problems often predict depression; likewise aggression predicts "antisocial behavior, criminality, and early substance abuse" (Ialongo, Poduska, Werthamer, & Sheppard, 2001, p. 147). That is why early intervention to prevent or counteract these challenges is essential. Complex behavioral problems require complex solutions. Two rules of thumb are particularly important: begin early, and use all the tools available. Two models of early intervention illustrate this approach.

Researchers at Johns Hopkins University have created strategies to intervene against poor academic achievement and aggressive and shy behavior (Ialongo et al., 2001). Referred to as the **classroom-centered intervention,** the first intervention combined mastery learning and a good-behavior game (which we describe later in this section). The second strategy involved a family-school partnership intervention to improve parent-teacher communication and parents' behavior management strategies. Three first-grade classes in each of nine schools participated. One class received classroom-centered intervention, the second received the family-school partnership intervention, and the third received no special intervention.

The classroom-centered, mastery-learning intervention program enhanced the curriculum, applied specific behavior management strategies, and provided additional supports for students who were not performing adequately. The enhanced curriculum consisted of critical thinking, composition, listening, and comprehension skills. The behavior management strategies included once-weekly class meetings to develop social problem-solving skills and opportunities to play the good-behavior game. The class was divided into three groups; points were given to each group for precisely defined appropriate behavior, and points were taken away when a member of the group was shy or aggressive. Students could exchange points for tangible rewards that gradually were replaced by social reinforcers.

In the family-school partnership intervention, teachers and other school staff received training on communicating with parents. The parents themselves received weekly home-learning and communication activities from teachers and behavior management training from a school psychologist or social worker who was teamed with the first-grade teacher. Each school also provided a voicemail system to allow parents to communicate easily with school personnel.

The Johns Hopkins researchers knew that their interventions might increase short-term gains in academic achievement and appropriate behaviors, but they did not know whether these gains could be maintained. They learned, however, that, by the end of sixth grade, students in the classroom-centered intervention, when compared to students who received no intervention, were significantly less likely to receive a diagnosis of conduct disorder, to have been suspended, or to need or appear to need mental health intervention.

Although the classroom-centered intervention resulted in the most significant changes, students in the family-school partnership program also improved when compared to those children who received no treatment. The researchers speculate that combining the two interventions might result in even greater benefits for students. It is significant that even one year full of effective interventions can make such a huge difference in a child's life.

Elementary and Middle School Students: Service Learning

Strength-based interventions emphasize the spirit of generosity: sharing gifts and talents with others. "Young people cannot develop a sense of their own value unless they have an opportunity to be of value to others" (Brendtro, Brokenleg, & Van Bockern, 1991, cited in Panico, 1998, p. 37).

One of the most effective ways for students to serve others is through **service learning,** a method for students to develop newly acquired skills by active participation and structured reflection in organized opportunities to meet community needs (Muscott, 2000). Students who participate in service learning are less likely to rebel or be delinquents and more likely to cope

Standard: Using research-validated teaching methods with children with emotional or behavior disorders is an application of CEC Standard 9, Professional and Ethical Practice.

Service learning helps students with emotional or behavioral disorders develop positive character traits.

Values: Service learning allows your students to contribute to others in their community and, at the same time, lets community members see that students with disabilities make *positive contributions* to that community.

Use your *Real Lives and Exceptionalities* DVD to view *Project Success*, a service learning program. Click on, "Beyond School," to meet "Karen," (Clip 4) the *Project Success* Director as well as "Jamie" (Clip 5) and "Jonathan," (Clip 6) who participate in the program.

effectively with life challenges (Laursen, 2000). Service learning creates partnerships for learning and can be as diverse as working with pets or participating in a community cleanup. It prepares students to make a living and allows people in the community to discover that students with emotional or behavioral disorders can contribute positively in a work environment.

Frey (2003) developed a service-learning model in which middle school students with emotional or behavioral disorders engaged in service activities associated with a senior citizens apartment complex near the school. The service-learning activities required the students to beautify the complex's grounds. Students met with residents to identify their preferences, measured the area for landscaping needs, developed architectural and landscaping plans, met with a local nursery owner to discuss cost and delivery issues, made decisions about types of shrubs and bushes based on cost and need, developed a budget, purchased the materials, and landscaped the grounds.

Did you notice a lot of measuring, calculating, developing, and deciding going on there? That's part of the point of service learning: students learn skills they need! The students who participated in the project had increased attendance at school and were more positive about school as a result of being involved in the project.

Matt Ackinclose is fortunate to participate in a Work to Life program developed by Picaway Ross Vocational Center. Among other things, the service learning incorporated into this program helps prepare students for good citizenship. Currently, Matt is writing to a soldier to thank him for serving our country. Charlotte and Matt are baking cookies to send with the letter. In Box 7–4, we describe how a program called SO Prepared for Citizenship benefits elementary, secondary, and college students as well as the community.

Secondary and Transition Students: Conflict Resolution

Unfortunately, conflict between youth with emotional or behavioral disorders and peers, family members, educators, and other authority figures is all too common. In Chapter 11, you will learn about using positive behavior supports, which involve changing the environmental circumstances that contribute to problem behavior. Through conflict-resolution instruction, however, students can learn three skills for resolving conflicts in a positive way: effective communication, anger management, and taking another's perspective (Daunic et al., 2000). The benefits include "(a) providing students with a framework for resolving conflicts, (b) giving students an opportunity to assume responsibility for their behavior, (c) lowering teacher stress by reducing the number of student conflicts they have to handle, (d) increasing instructional time, and (e) helping students understand how cultural diversity can affect interpersonal communication and human interactions" (p. 95). Conflict resolution instruction is best infused into classes such as social studies or literature, in which conflicts between people and cultures can serve as examples of conflict and resolution (Daunic et al., 2000).

Students need to learn that conflicts can be gentle, tough, or solution seeking (Addison & Westmoreland, 2000). When two students are friends and wish to continue to be friends, their conflict is gentle: they may prefer to yield or withdraw by avoiding, ignoring, or denying the conflict. In tough conflicts, one student verbally or physically threatens another. When seeking solutions, the students negotiate to find a consensus that satisfies both of them and preserves their friendship.

Conflicts usually originate because of three major issues: resources, needs, or goals. Helping students identify the origins of the issues they face can help them resolve their conflicts peacefully. Students also need to understand that anger is normal and provides important information; the person who is angry believes that a want or need is not being met. However, anger can be either constructive or destructive, and students need to discuss the differences.

Partnership Tips ~ SO Prepared for Citizenship   Box 7–4

How can students with emotional or behavioral disorders develop friendships with peers; learn important character, academic, and prevocational skills; establish resilience-building relationships with older teens and adults in their communities; and develop a sense of significance, purpose, and accomplishment?

In Nashua, New Hampshire, a partnership among faculty and students at Riviera College and local elementary and secondary schools found the answer through the college's Service-Learning Opportunities (SO) Prepared for Citizenship. Together, they did the following:

- Identified their students' citizenship needs, such as
  Reducing the incidents of cursing, bullying, and fighting
  Increasing understanding and compassion
  Offering leadership training, team building, tolerance, and civic responsibility opportunities
- Created a planning, implementation, and assessment team consisting of students and faculty from the college and the elementary and secondary schools
- Awarded curriculum credits to the college students who helped coordinate the curriculum at the college and in the schools
- Developed a curriculum that taught the traits of respect and appreciation for diversity, caring and compassion, trustworthiness, and fairness and justice
- Implemented the curriculum by having a college student, a high school student, and an elementary school student become co-teachers at the college and in the schools
- Participated in community activities, such as food drives, that put into practice the classroom-based curriculum
- Regularly assessed what students were learning and doing in response to the curriculum

- Held an awards ceremony that featured all of the participating students, their faculty, and community members

The strategies that SO Prepared for Citizenship used apply to nearly every other kind of partnership activity that educators may want to undertake:

- Identify a common interest (in SO's case, student citizenship training).
- Identify who has the same interest, and recruit that stakeholder into partnership.
- Identify the goals and strategies to respond to the interest.
- Develop a plan for carrying out the goals and strategies.
- Implement the plan.
- Assess its effectiveness and incorporate the feedback into the action plans.
- Celebrate its success.

Putting Partnership into the Context of Student Progress in the General Curriculum

1. How could community mentors be helpful in teaching character traits to students with emotional and behavior disorders?

2. How could you embed literacy learning into a service-learning project such as voter registration?

3. How could you partner with parents in the implementation of a service-learning curriculum?

To answer these question online, go to the Partnership Tips module in Chapter 7 of the Companion Website, www.prenhall.com/turnbull.

Source: Adapted from Muscott, H. (2001). Fostering learning, fun, and friendship among students with emotional and behavioral disorders and their peers: The SO Prepared for Citizenship program. *Beyond Behavior,* *10*(3) 36–47.

Problem solving and successful decision making are important conflict-resolution skills (Bullock & Foegen, 2002). Students need to identify the problem specifically, brainstorm and evaluate the pros and cons of solutions, decide which is the best solution, and make a plan to carry it out. In addition, they need to find solutions that will help both parties save face (Addison & Westmoreland, 2000). Students also benefit from learning to negotiate to make sure their needs are met rather than backing down when conflict occurs.

There are several ways for teachers to use conflict-resolution training to reduce conflicts on a schoolwide level. For example, they can offer high school students who previously would have been suspended for violent behavior the option to enroll in a conflict-resolution program that teaches social problem-solving skills, negotiation skills, and anger-management skills. Students who were involved with one particular conflict-resolution training program were four times less likely to receive another suspension for violent behavior than were students who were not involved in the training (Breunlin, Cimmarusti, Bryant-Edwards, & Hetherington, 2002). Box 7–5 provides tips about how to teach conflict-resolution skills.

Conflict resolution skills can help students resolve problems with their peers.

Into Practice ~ Activities for Teaching Conflict Resolution

Box 7–5

Several strategies are helpful in resolving conflict (Addison & Westmoreland, 2000). The first is active listening, a nonjudgmental approach in which the listener paraphrases the content of what is said and reflects the feelings of the speaker: "I'm hearing you say that you are tired of having to do all this work and feel angry that I'm asking you to do it. Is that correct?" Another important strategy is behavior examination: learning to express feelings without aggression. Finally, students need to learn tolerance: accepting others' differences. Teaching students to resolve conflicts can be integrated into the everyday curriculum and does not have to be stressful. Addison and Westmoreland suggest the following games and activities.

Active Listening: Listening Mirror

Hold up a hand mirror and ask your students what they see. When they say they see themselves, explain that they see a reflection of themselves. Let the students discuss the difference. After telling the students that they are going to learn about another type of reflection, let them decorate a "hand mirror" made out of construction paper. Laminate the papers and provide the students with washable markers. Tell the students they are going to learn to listen to other people very carefully and make a reflection of their words. Have each student listen to a partner tell about something that happened to her in the last week and write down the partner's words. Have the partners trade roles and then share what they wrote. Ask them how they felt when in the roles of speaker and listener. Then discuss how being a listening mirror might help resolve conflicts.

Reflecting on Conversation

Divide students into groups of three: a facilitator and recorder, a listener, and a talker. At the facilitator's signal, the listener closes his or her eyes and the talker speaks on any subject. The listener needs to be aware of changes in voice patterns and tone as well as the content. After 3 to 5 minutes, the listener shares what the speaker has said, seems to feel, and why. Have the students exchange roles until they have experienced each role.

Behavior Examination: Angry Shakes

You will need a blender, vanilla ice cream, milk, and strawberry-flavored drink. As you add ice cream to the blender, ask students to share how they would feel if a younger brother or sister borrowed their favorite CD without permission and lost it. Let them talk about what they would do. Add the strawberry drink and start the blender. Ask students what color the shake is now (pink). Explain that when they express anger inappropriately through yelling or hitting, they change the color of the conflict into violence. Pour out the shake, rinse the blender, and add more vanilla ice cream. Add milk and blend as you talk about how the situation will stay calm if they talk quietly to the younger brother or sister about their feelings and help the sibling understand the importance of not borrowing without permission. Let the students sample the shakes as they talk about their own examples of conflict and whether the conflict was strawberry or vanilla.

Tolerance: Wizards and Frogs

Have the students discuss characters from J. K. Rowlings's Harry Potter series and note how Harry Potter's uncle, aunt, and cousin are not tolerant of his being a wizard. Playing the Peter, Paul, and Mary song "I'm in Love with a Big Blue Frog" can generate a discussion of intolerance among secondary students.

Problem Solving and Decision Making: Choose Your Own Ending

Read a story to students and stop at the point of conflict. Have the students brainstorm solutions that would provide a win-win solution.

Creative Negotiating: Harmony

Have the students role-play a scenario that is age-appropriate. Elementary students might negotiate computer time with a sibling; secondary students might negotiate school cafeteria changes with the principal. Have them divide into groups of four to six members. Have half the members take one point of view and the other half the other person's point of view.

Putting These Strategies to Work for Progress in the General Curriculum

1. What other activities can you think of to help students learn these strategies?

2. Which strategies do you believe will be most challenging for students to learn? Why?

3. How will you handle conflict that occurs in the classroom? How can you be an effective role model? What could you do to improve your own conflict-resolution skills?

4. How could you help students apply these skills in everyday conflicts that occur in the classroom?

To answer these questions online, go to the Into Practice module in Chapter 7 of the Companion Website, www.prenhall.com/turnbull.

Source: Adapted from Addison, M. M., & Westmoreland, D. A. (2000). Over the net: Encouraging win-win solutions through conflict resolution. *Reaching Today's Youth,* 5(1), 53–54.

INCLUDING STUDENTS WITH EMOTIONAL OR BEHAVIORAL DISORDERS

In Figure 7–3, you will find the percentage of students with emotional or behavioral disorders in each of several educational placements. Approximately three times as many students with emotional or behavioral disorders as all other students with disabilities are served in residential settings, hospitals, or homes (U.S. Department of Education, 1998). Nevertheless, inclusion is entirely feasible, consistent with IDEA, as Box 7–6 shows.

Figure 7–3 Percentage of students with emotional or behavioral disorders in educational placement (2003–2004)

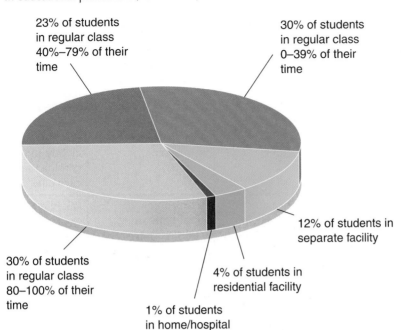

23% of students in regular class 40%–79% of their time

30% of students in regular class 0–39% of their time

12% of students in separate facility

30% of students in regular class 80–100% of their time

4% of students in residential facility

1% of students in home/hospital

Source: U.S. Department of Education, Office of Special Education Programs. (2005). *IDEA data website.* (http://www.ideadata.org/aboutThisSite.asp).

More than 134,000 teenagers are in juvenile correctional facilities (Sickmund, 2002), and estimates vary from 30 to 70 percent in terms of the numbers of those youth who have disabilities (Leone, Meisel, & Drakeford, 2002). Typically, these teenagers are boys from a culturally- and linguistically-diverse background, are members of families who are poor, and have substantial learning and/or behavior problems (Leone et al., 2002). Although incarcerated youth have been reported to have academic achievement one to several years below grade level, the extent of their special education services in correctional facilities tends to be about two-thirds less than that offered in public schools (Foley, 2001).

ASSESSING STUDENTS' PROGRESS

Measuring Students' Progress

Progress in the general curriculum. In "mastery learning" or "mastery training" instruction, teachers frequently assess their students' mastery of content, determining whether it is timely to move to the next concept or activity. They offer more instruction to those students who do not show mastery, and then they assess these students again. In all of this, teachers intend to make it possible for all of their students to master the content, even if they do so at different rates. Mastery training has been used with students with disabilities, including those with emotional or behavioral disabilities (Lee, Belfiore, & Toro-Zambrana, 2001), and is a useful means of ensuring student progress in the general curriculum. To monitor their students' progress toward mastery, effective teachers will do the following (King-Sears & Mooney, 2004):

■ *Ask questions of the whole class.* Ask all of the students in the class to indicate what they think the correct answer is. Ask them to raise their hands to answer a question. Some students will feel intimidated and will not participate. But technology-based response systems allow greater anonymity. There, students have remote-control devices and respond by pressing a button to represent a particular answer. The responses, when presented on the screen through the software that accompanies the program, are anonymous so far as all other students are concerned, but the teacher obtains data on the response from each student.

Inclusion Tips

Box 7–6

	What You Might See	What You Might Be Tempted to Do	Alternate Responses	Ways to Include Peers in the Process
Behavior	The student refuses to follow directions and uses inappropriate language.	Respond in anger and send him out of the classroom. Place him in time out for extended periods.	Include him in conflict-resolution instruction and seek to capitalize on his strengths in this instruction.	Involve classmates in the conflict-resolution instruction so that all students have an opportunity to work closely and constructively with each other.
Social interactions	He fights with other students and is always on the defensive	Seat him as far away as possible from the students with whom he is fighting.	Teach appropriate social skills, using modeling, videos, and social skills programs.	Pair him with different students who can model and help him practice social skills and responses.
Educational performance	She is rarely on task and appears to have an inability to learn.	Give poor grades and require her to remain after school until all her work is done.	Based on her interests, create the opportunity to engage in service learning that will enable her to make contributions to others.	Develop a buddy system in implementing service learning so that students work together collaboratively.
Classroom attitudes	She is sad all the time and does not speak or interact with others.	Discipline her for nonparticipation, and instruct her to cheer up.	Recognize the warning signs of depression. Partner with the school counselor to get professional help.	Encourage all students to affirm each others' strengths by giving positive feedback to each other.

- *Use a cooperative learning strategy such as "think-pair-share"* (King-Sears & Mooney, 2004, p. 249). You will learn more about cooperative learning in Chapter 13. It consists of students teaching each other. Applying that approach to assessment, the teacher will create small groups of students, ask each group to *think* about a question, *pair* with a peer in the group, and *share* their responses. Teachers need to be sure that at least one student has the correct responses.

Progress in addressing other educational needs. Students with emotional or behavioral disorders often also need to learn social skills, and teachers need to know how to chart their students' progress in learning those skills. A commonly used social skills rating scale, validated for use by students with emotional or behavioral disorders, is the Social Skills Rating System (Gresham & Elliott, 1990; Wright & Torrey, 2001). It has three rating forms (teacher, parent, and student forms) and two scales (the Social Skills Scale and the Problem Behaviors Scale) that allow students to report both the frequency and importance of the skill and how well they are learning it.

In addition to this commercially available measure, Algozzine, Serna, and Patton (2001) identified three strategies for tracking students' progress in which teachers can use sociometric ratings for rankings. They can ask their students to identify classmates with whom they play and would like to play; tally the number of times any particular student is identified; and then determine who is popular and who is not, based on frequency counts of peer nominations. This is a measure of student acceptance by class members; so if students with emotional or behavioral disorders are not frequently identified by peers, the teacher can infer that those students may need instruction in social skills. By extension, a teacher can also use the entire process to track, over time, how social skills instruction affects students' acceptance by their peers.

Making Accommodations for Assessment

As you have already learned in this chapter, students with emotional or behavioral disorders are more likely than other students with disabilities to be served in alternative schools. Does this mean that those schools are no longer accountable for these students' performance? Certainly not. Gagnon and McLaughlin (2004) conducted a survey of private and public day treatment and residential schools for elementary school students with emotional or behavioral disorders to evaluate whether the students were being given the opportunity to progress in the general curriculum and to participate in district accountability systems. The students need those opportunities because, when they return to their neighborhood schools, they will be behind other students if they have not been provided with instruction in the same curriculum. These researchers investigated whether these alternative schools offered accommodations in the state and district assessments. Nearly 20 percent of the schools had no accommodation policy. Of the 80 percent that did have such a policy, most simply adopted the school district's policy.

Among the factors that a growing number of states are using to determine the need for accommodations is "student emotional anxiety" (Thurlow et al., 2002). Students with emotional or behavioral disorders may have more difficulties completing tests than other students do because of their heightened anxiety problems. Accommodations to address this difference include extended time to take the tests, individual administration of the tests, and testing with breaks.

PRAXIS

Standard: Making accommodations in assessment reflects PRAXIS™ Standard 3, Delivery of Services to Students with Disabilities and Using Appropriate Assessments.

Looking to Matthew's Future

A strength-based approach emphasizes that students are potential victors, not victims (Laursen, 2000). Matthew Ackinclose exemplifies the power of that belief. Rebecca remembers fondly the first day that Matt called her to say he was too busy to see her. She knew then that Matt was beginning to stand on his own without her support. Next year, Matt will be in high school, his first experience away from Charlotte's support after several years in her class. She is beginning to prepare him for that transition. And Matt is still working on refining some of his social skills and developing a more positive relationship with his family. Rebecca believes that high school will be Matt's chance to shine.

Beginning in his junior year, Matt will have a work placement through Picaway Ross Vocational Center, perhaps in auto mechanics. The program has a 95 percent post–high school job-placement rate. Although Matt thinks he might be interested in auto mechanics, he also thinks he might become a professional golfer. Rebecca hopes he will try out for his school's golf team "to show himself off a little bit." Matt certainly has the intelligence to continue his education after high school, if he chooses. Several years ago, his prospects for the future were dismal; now his options seem limitless. Matt can have a productive, happy life, thanks to the caring of some important people in his life and his own determination.

When Rebecca and Charlotte talked to Matt about sharing his story in this textbook for teachers, he told them why he chose to do so—his vision for *your* future: "They need to know that you need to care and not give up. Keep trying."

SUMMARY

Identifying students with emotional or behavioral disorders

- Students with emotional or behavioral disorders manifest emotional, behavioral, social, and/or academic characteristics that are chronic and severe and adversely affects their educational performance.

- Students may exhibit disorders including, but not limited to, anxiety disorder, mood disorder, oppositional defiant disorder, conduct disorder, or schizophrenia.
- Two broad categories of emotional or behavioral disorders include externalizing (aggressive, acting-out, noncompliant) behaviors and internalizing (withdrawn, depressed, anxious, obsessive, compulsive) behaviors.
- Prevalence estimates vary from 3 to 6 percent of all students. However, fewer than 1 percent are identified for IDEA benefits. Many of the identified students are from minority populations.

Evaluating students with emotional or behavioral disorders

- The Scale for Assessing Emotional Disturbance is a norm-referenced scale tied directly to the five elements of the IDEA definition.
- The Behavioral and Emotional Rating Scale, a norm-referenced tool with strong psychometric properties, is designed to identify students' strengths and needs as the basis for educational planning.

Designing an appropriate individualized education program

- The wraparound planning model is a process linking school, community, and mental health services to provide a family-driven, collaborative, individualized, culturally competent and strengths-based planning approach.
- Complex problems require thoughtful planning and multicomponent interventions, such as the classwide, peer-assisted, self-management approach described in the chapter.
- An important universal design feature for all students, including those with emotional or behavioral disorders, involves modifications to the ways in which students respond to the curriculum content and provide evidence of their knowledge, either orally or through multimedia presentations.
- It is important to implement multiple dropout prevention strategies, such as linking youth with a mentor or involving them in extracurricular activities.

Using effective instructional strategies

- Two rules of thumb need to be in place for preventing conduct disorders: begin early, and use all the tools available.
- Service-learning strategies provide a means for students with emotional or behavioral disorders both to learn important skills and to contribute to their communities.
- Students with emotional to behavioral disorders need to acquire conflict-resolution skills, including negotiation skills, compromising, problem solving, and decision making, if they are to succeed as adults.

Including students with emotional or behavioral disorders

- Students with emotional or behavioral disorders have one of the lowest rates of inclusion in general education classrooms.
- Approximately three times as many students with emotional or behavioral disorders as all other students with disabilities are served in residential settings, hospitals, or homes.

Assessing students' progress

- Mastery evaluation takes a different approach to evaluation and is intended to provide information on student progress that teachers can use to modify instruction.

- Interventions to promote social skills are important for students with emotional or behavioral disorders, and teachers can use a commercially available scale to measure progress or can use sociometric ratings techniques.

- Students with emotional or behavioral disorders need access to the general curriculum. A critical component of that is the provision of accommodations, such as extended time, individual administration, and testing with breaks.

WHAT WOULD YOU RECOMMEND?

Refer to chapter content and the PRAXIS™ and CEC standards in Appendix A to answer the following questions:

1. If you are a general education teacher and you refer a student in your class to be evaluated for an emotional or behavior disorder, what role do you anticipate you would assume for the multidisciplinary evaluating? Identify what CEC standard you would be applying.

2. How might you partner with a school counselor or school social worker in developing and implementing a training program on conflict-resolution skills? What PRAXIS™ standard would you be applying?

3. Using websites in the module for this chapter, conduct Internet research on the use of service-learning strategies with high school students. What are six tips that could guide your implementation of service learning, and to what CEC standard does service-learning instruction apply?

Visit the Companion Website to find links to Chapter 7.

Who is Kelsey Blankenship?

Imagine being 9 years old and acting in front of thousands of people. Kelsey Blankenship, a fourth grader from rural Ohio, performed twice to an audience of 6,000 in a Cincinnati competition, receiving a superior rating for both performances.

Superior acting abilities are remarkable for any child, but they are even more so for Kelsey. These performances represent a dramatic change in her because she has attention-deficit/hyperactivity disorder (AD/HD). According to her grandmother, Yvonne, a few years ago Kelsey would have "been all over the church" instead of learning her lines. Kelsey's second-grade teacher, Barb Tootle, remembers those days well:

> You would always know where Kelsey was: There would always be some commotion. I would have students saying, "Kelsey did this to me; Kelsey did that to me." Kelsey never walked slowly through the classroom. It was more like pushing her way through. She would raise her hand, but she wouldn't have anything to say or would make something up.

But these days, Kelsey is a different child. Barb describes the change that occurred during second grade:

> Kelsey always came in with a smile. She would sharpen her pencil, hand in her homework, and do an activity that was on the board. She kept her hands to herself, not hitting people or taking their things; and she would pay attention. We would have good discussions, and Kelsey would be a part of them. She stayed on task. And her grades improved! She was happier.

Yvonne is also quick to comment on Kelsey's strengths:

> One thing I like about her is her homework schedule. She does it immediately when she gets home. There's no fighting or fussing or anything. You wouldn't want a better kid. She'll do anything for you she can. She's a people person.

Kelsey still struggles with being patient and attentive. Now, however, she has friends and recently made the honor roll for the first time. She is focused enough to enjoy dramatics, art, music, cheerleading, and animals.

As her therapist, Chris Fraser, points out, the difference in Kelsey occurred primarily because Kelsey wanted to change and worked hard enough to make change happen. She was open to a treatment plan developed by her teacher, her therapist, and her psychiatrist as well as the two most important people on her team: Yvonne and Bill, the grandparents who adopted her. Kelsey calls them Mom and Dad.

Understanding Students with Attention-Deficit/ Hyperactivity Disorder

Kelsey's journey toward change began when Barb Tootle contacted Yvonne. Yvonne remembers, "Kelsey was having problems in Mrs. Tootle's class, and I would always stop by and ask her how she was doing. Mrs. Tootle started talking about this AD/HD problem she thought Kelsey might have. So I talked to a couple of her other teachers, and they agreed we should check it out."

The evaluation confirmed that Kelsey has AD/HD. She and her parents began seeing Chris regularly. Chris helped the family interact in new ways. One difficult issue the family faced was homework; so Chris brought Kelsey's teacher, Barb, into one of the sessions. He recalls:

Kelsey's parents were getting frustrated because every night they were fighting her about sitting still and doing her homework. So Barb told them, "This is Kelsey's homework. She has to do it. And if she doesn't do it, she has to be accountable to me. Don't fight the war with her at home." Then we had Kelsey come in, and we explained, "Kelsey, this is your responsibility. If you don't get it done, that's okay. But you will face the consequences at school." That allowed her parents to back off. She started doing better because there was less parent-child conflict.

Chris also worked with Kelsey on problem solving. When some of the other students teased her about living with her grandparents, Chris encouraged Kelsey to think of ways to respond appropriately. Her creative, three-page list included "So?" "Whatever," and "I already knew that."

Yvonne and Bill work hard as a team to help Kelsey. Yvonne says, "Bill has been a big help. Sometimes I have a little temper, and he reminds me that she's just a little girl. We both help her with her homework. If there's something I don't understand, and Bill understands it, he'll help her."

Another important factor in Kelsey's change is medication. Her psychiatrist prescribed the stimulant Adderall. Yvonne says:

I was scared about the medication. I had heard all these things about what it causes you to do. Then I heard that, when they get older, they turn into addicts because they've been on all this medicine. I was scared to death to even put her on it. It was a hard decision to make.

Despite Yvonne's concerns, the change resulting from the medication was positive and dramatic. Barb remembers, "I can't tell you the total difference in the way she related to the other students in the classroom, on the playground, walking in the hallway and to the principal and the other teachers. Everyone noticed a difference."

Chris explains the key to making a multimodal treatment plan such as Kelsey's work: "Everybody needs to be pulled in. I think continuity is the most important part."

IDENTIFYING STUDENTS WITH AD/HD

Defining Attention-Deficit/Hyperactivity Disorder

Instead of listing AD/HD as a separate disability category, IDEA includes it as a subcategory under the general category "other health impairments" (see Chapter 12). Under the IDEA definition, a student with other health impairments has limited strength, vitality, or alertness, including a heightened alertness with respect to the educational environment, that

Go to the Companion Website, *www.prenhall.com/turnbull*, for a link to the American Psychiatric Association, where you can learn more about their classification manual.

You can find out more about CHADD, the largest ADHD organization advocating for individuals with AD/HD, by visiting the Web Links module in Chapter 8 of our Companion Website, *www.prenhall.com/turnbull*.

■ is due to chronic or acute health problems such as asthma, attention deficit disorder or attention deficit hyperactivity disorder, diabetes, epilepsy, a heart condition, hemophilia, lead poisoning, leukemia, nephritis, rheumatic fever, and sickle cell anemia; and

■ adversely affects a child's educational performance. (34 Code of Federal Regulations § 300.7[c][9])

Because IDEA does not specifically define AD/HD, most professionals abide by the definition offered by the American Psychiatric Association (2000) as set out in the APA's *Diagnostic and Statistical Manual of Mental Disorders* (DSM-IV):

> The essential feature of Attention-Deficit/Hyperactivity Disorder is a persistent pattern of inattention and/or hyperactivity-impulsivity that is more frequently displayed and severe than is typically observed in individuals at a comparable level of development. (p. 85)

The limiting criteria of persistence, frequency, and severity are important. Everyone is forgetful and absentminded at times, especially during periods of stress. Also, some people are simply more or less energetic than others. But unless those characteristics are persistent, frequent, and severe and interfere with a person's daily ability to function, the person does not meet the APA criteria. A student whose educational performance is not adversely affected will not qualify for IDEA services. The APA criteria also require that the student must manifest the symptoms before age 7 and that the symptoms must persist for at least 6 months, be present in at least two settings, and not be attributable to another disability.

Approximately 2 percent to 9 percent of all children are identified as having AD/HD (Spencer, Biederman, Wilens, & Faraone, 2002; Wolraich et al., 1996). The percentage of children and youth with AD/HD has been increasing significantly, not only in the United States but worldwide as well (Robison, Sclar, Skaer, & Galin, 1999). The prevalence of AD/HD varies from country to country (Dodson, 2002).

The prevalence of AD/HD also varies according to gender, age, and ethnicity. Approximately three times as many boys as girls have AD/HD (Barkley, 2003). Elementary teachers tend to refer boys more frequently than girls for evaluation, particularly when the boys are hyperactive (Sciutto, Nolfi, & Bluhm, 2004). Prevalence rates tend to be higher at the preschool level, taper off slightly at the elementary level, and decrease yet again at adolescence (Breton et al., 1999; Nolan, Gadow, & Sprafkin, 2001; Romano et al., 2001). Indeed, some children "recover" from AD/HD as they get older (Biederman et al., 1996); by contrast, some people do not receive an AD/HD label until they are adults (Willoughby, Curran, Costello, & Angold, 2000). Even though some individuals do "recover," approximately 70 percent of the children who are diagnosed with AD/HD during early childhood years continue to have the diagnosis in their adolescence.

AD/HD is present in all ethnic groups, but prevalence varies across groups (Barkley, 2003). Latino students are less likely than other students to receive an AD/HD diagnosis (Stevens, Harman, & Kelleher, 2004).

Describing the Characteristics

Diagnostic criteria for AD/HD. Under the APA's DSM-IV diagnostic criteria, there are three subtypes of AD/HD: predominately inattentive type, predominately hyperactive-impulsive type, and combined type. Accordingly, the acronym AD/HD features a slash, indicating inclusion of all three subtypes: attention-deficit disorder, hyperactivity disorder, or a combination.

Predominately inattentive type. A student must exhibit six (or more) of the following characteristics to be classified as having the predominately inattentive type (APA, 2000, p. 92):

(a) Often fails to give close attention to details or makes mistakes in schoolwork, work, or other activities.

(b) Often has difficulty sustaining attention in tasks or play activities.

(c) Often does not seem to listen when spoken to directly.

(d) Often does not follow through on instructions and fails to finish schoolwork, chores, or duties in the workplace (not due to oppositional behavior or failure to understand instructions).

(e) Often has difficulty organizing tasks and activities.

(f) Often avoids, dislikes, or is reluctant to engage in tasks that require sustained mental effort (such as schoolwork or homework).

(g) Often loses things necessary for tasks or activities (e.g., toys, school assignments, pencils, books, or tools).

(h) Is often easily distracted by extraneous stimuli.

(i) Is often forgetful in daily activities.

Because students with the inattentive type of AD/HD usually are not as disruptive as those with hyperactivity-impulsivity, their needs may be overlooked. Without a specific diagnosis and appropriate interventions, these students are at risk for long-term academic, social, and emotional difficulties (Solanto, 2002). Students with the inattentive type of AD/HD usually have difficulty working in a distracting environment, absorbing large amounts of new information, shifting flexibly from one task to another, or linearly linking a series of cognitive operations (Weiler, Bernstein, Bellinger, & Waber, 2002). That is why you should (1) make sure that your students with inattentive-type AD/HD have enough time to shift from one activity to another, (2) teach them techniques for organizing their thoughts and materials, (3) offer them flexible time limits for finishing their assignments or examinations, and (4) simplify tasks that have multiple steps. As you will learn, planning for and implementing supplementary aids to support your students' organizational skills can help them be successful in school.

Predominately hyperactive-impulsive type. A student must have six (or more) of the following characteristics to be classified as having the predominately hyperactive-impulsive type of AD/HD. These characteristics must have been present for at least 6 months and be present to the extent that the student is recognized as falling outside the range of adaptive behavior (APA, 2000, p. 92):

Hyperactivity

(a) Often fidgets with hands or feet or squirms in seat.

(b) Often leaves seat in classroom or in other situations in which remaining seated is expected.

(c) Often runs about or climbs excessively in situations in which it is inappropriate (in adolescents or adults, may be limited to subjective feelings of restlessness).

(d) Often has difficulty playing or engaging in leisure activities quietly.

(e) Is often "on the go" or often acts as if "driven by a motor."

(f) Often talks excessively.

Impulsivity

(g) Often blurts out answers before questions have been completed.

(h) Often has difficulty awaiting turn.

(i) Often interrupts or intrudes on others (e.g., butts into conversations or games).

Standard: When you learn the characteristics of students with AD/HD, you are addressing CEC Standard 2, Understanding the Development and Characteristics of Learners.

Problems associated with hyperactivity and impulsivity typically start when a child is 3 or 4 years old—several years before problems with the inattentive type of AD/HD emerge (Barkley, 2003).

Combined type. The third classification describes students who have features of both inattention and hyperactivity-impulsivity; the literature refers to the combined type as ADHD (without the slash). Most students with AD/HD have combined ADHD (Barkley, 1998).

Deficits in executive functioning. **Executive functioning** includes being able to process information to make decisions, take actions, and solve problems. Most students with AD/HD, regardless of the specific type of AD/HD they experience, have deficits in their executive functioning (Barkley, 2003; Biederman et al., 2004; Kourakis, Katachanakis, Vlahonikolis, & Paritsis, 2004). Students with AD/HD usually have impairments in four types of executive functioning (Barkley, 2003).

The first executive function is **nonverbal working memory.** This is the ability to retrieve auditory, visual, and other sensory images of the past. Students with this deficit have difficulty learning from their experience. For example, Joshua, one of your students, is repeatedly disciplined (by in-school suspension—that is, exclusion from some aspects of school) for the same behavior. Is he sorry he committed the offense the first time? Yes. Does he dislike being disciplined, again and again? Yes. But he cannot associate his present inappropriate behavior with his past discipline.

Internalization of speech is also an important executive function. Most people talk to themselves, planning what they will do and say, and recognizing when it is appropriate to speak their thoughts. They also think about social rules when deciding on their behaviors. That's not so for students with AD/HD; they often blurt out whatever comes to their minds and do not recognize that their behavior is socially inappropriate and irritates others. For example, Julia is unable to inhibit an inappropriate comment ("What a crock!") while you are teaching. Other students might think the same thought, but they hold their tongues; not Julia, however—she says what she thinks whenever she thinks it, much to your chagrin and much to her peers' amusement. Because she does not anticipate any consequences, she is surprised when you reprimand her and ask her to raise her hand to be recognized. A few minutes later, she blurts out another similar comment, clearly unable to learn from her first experience.

Many children with AD/HD have difficulty learning from their experiences and cannot remember routines and procedures so they often are corrected.

The third executive function is **self-regulation of affect, motivation, and arousal.** Students with AD/HD who experience difficulty with this function are often less objective and more emotional in responding to events, have difficulty understanding the effect of their behavior on others, and often cannot generate the energy and enthusiasm to carry out their behavior (Barkley, 2003). For example, assume you are giving a test in your high school history class tomorrow. Juanita needs the history credit to graduate. While doing her homework to prepare for your test, her best friend calls her and tells her about a party that everybody is going to. Because she is more motivated by the immediate rewards of going to the party than the long-term rewards of passing history, Juanita grabs her coat and heads to the party. The goal-setting strategies that you will learn about later in the chapter can help students with AD/HD forego their immediate gratification for longer-term benefits.

The fourth executive function is **reconstitution,** the skill of analyzing and synthesizing behaviors. In Chapter 5, we noted that many students with a learning disability have difficulty breaking words into individual sounds. Likewise, students with AD/HD have difficulty breaking their behaviors and thoughts into steps or individual tasks. Barkley (2003) described this characteristic as a reduced "capacity to mentally visualize, manipulate, and then generate multiple plans of action (option) in the service of goal-directed behavior, and to select from among them those with the greatest likelihood of succeeding" (p. 86). For example, Eva has had 2 months to write a term paper for your English class. Rather than breaking the assignment down into individual tasks (e.g., gathering resources, reading the information and writing notecards, developing an outline, etc.) and sticking to a schedule to complete those tasks, she suddenly remembers the day before the due date that she needs to write the report and frantically tries to throw something together at the last minute.

Given impairments in these four areas of executive function—nonverbal working memory; internalization of speech; self-regulation of affect, motivation, and arousal; and reconstitution—AD/HD is a disability of performance (Barkley, 1998). Students with AD/HD know what to do; their challenge, from deficits in their executive functions, is to do what they know to do. Knowing provides "little consolation to them, little influence over their behavior, and often much irritation to others" (Barkley, 1998, p. 249).

Intellectual functioning and academic achievement. Experts disagree concerning the extent to which students with AD/HD have typical or reduced levels of intelligence. One research team gave IQ tests to a group of children with AD/HD, another group with reading difficulties, and a third group with AD/HD plus reading difficulties. The researchers found that the IQ scores of all three groups were normally distributed, with a majority of them being in the average range (Kaplan, Crawford, Dewey, & Fisher, 2000). Barkley (2003), however, reported that IQ ranges of students with AD/HD tend to be 7 to 10 points below the norm (IQ 100).

Whether they do or do not have typical intelligence, students with AD/HD frequently have problems achieving academically; the impairments to their executive function capacities contribute to their academic problems. Research related to the academic achievement of students with AD/HD reveals the following:

- Ten to 40 percent have a learning disability (Stein, Efron, Schiff, & Glanzman, 2002).

- Thirty percent have a reading disability (Fletcher, Shaywitz, & Shaywitz, 1999).

- Students with more severe AD/HD typically have more severe impairments in academic functioning (Barry, Lyman, & Klinger, 2002).

- These students are 3–7 times more likely than their classmates to repeat a grade, be expelled or suspended, and receive special education (LeFever, Villers, Morrow, & Vaughn, 2002).

Despite their academic challenges, these students also have a variety of strengths. In Figure 8–1, Chris Fraser, an adult who has experienced both personal and professional success and who also has grown up with AD/HD, shares his perspectives on ways to capitalize on strengths.

The three defining characteristics of AD/HD—inattention, hyperactivity, and impulsivity—are "also key descriptors in the biographies of highly creative individuals" (Cramond, 1995). That often is because they can **hyperfocus:** demonstrate intense levels of concentration and attention in completing tasks (Dodson, 2002; Wells, Dahl, & Snyder, 2000).

As many as 40 percent of adolescents and adults with AD/HD can enter what appears to be an altered state of consciousness while doing activities which they consider particularly intriguing. During a hyperfocus the person performs at almost 100 percent efficiency, does not notice the passage of time, does not become tired or hungry, and has virtually 100 percent comprehension and retention of what he reads. (Dodson, 2002, p. 18)

Novelty, interest, or the sudden awareness of a crisis related to an approaching deadline can cause some individuals with AD/HD to lock onto a task, completely oblivious to everything else going on around them. Parents and teachers often wonder how children can have AD/HD when they can sit for hours, hyperfocused on a hobby. This trait helps many people with

As in Chris Fraser's family, AD/HD is often multigenerational, suggesting a genetic link. Enjoying a family ski trip, Chris Fraser, a master's level licensed independent social worker, is pictured here with his father, J. Scott Fraser, a full professor at Wright State University.

Figure 8–1 Perspectives on strengths: Chris Fraser

One of my life's greatest assets and greatest teachers has been growing up and living with attention-deficit disorder paired with a learning disability, and I've been waiting to have my voice heard for many years. As you can imagine, I obviously haven't felt this way for the majority of my life. Rather, this has been a gradual realization that I have felt growing in my heart ever since I was a young child. My personal perception of AD/HD is that describing it as a "disorder" is a matter of perspective.

As an adult, I work as a therapist in a community mental health center and share with children and their families an empowering and hopeful perspective about AD/HD: that it is a collection of adaptive mechanisms and temperament traits that are more suited to some societies and tasks than to others. I enjoy looking at AD/HD as an inherited set of skills, abilities, and personality tendencies that I can use to my benefit. For me, this has been a very healing and empowering perspective. I would like to share a number of tips about how people with AD/HD can survive in a world that doesn't automatically accommodate some of our personality characteristics:

- *Use your resources and advocate for your needs.* I was very sensitive about other people thinking I was not intelligent, and I didn't want to be seen as different in any way. Therefore, I was embarrassed to go to the resource room each day in elementary school, and in high school I didn't even use available resources. I didn't learn that it was okay and smart to use those resources until after I suffered my way through high school.

- *Find your joy or bliss and follow it.* In college I found that, like other students with AD/HD, I have the ability to hyperfocus and excel in subjects I have a passion for. These interests gave meaning to the frustrations I endured in academia and gave me a sense of hope for the future.

- *Work on acknowledging your growth areas and develop your own special ways of dealing with them.* In college I also found out that the real world was not going to accommodate to me, so I needed my own bag of tricks to survive in it. I confess that I still am disorganized occasionally and that I still have difficulty managing time. But I deal with this growth area by making lists. I find that even if I don't refer back to the list, the process of writing things down helps me to remember them better.

- *Never give up on your dreams, and view your mistakes as learning opportunities rather than personal failures.* To this day, I am still developing my own tips for learning how to use my capabilities as a person with AD/HD.

Overall, my family has made all the difference in the way I view my challenges. My father also grew up with AD/HD traits and was told that he was not college material. He went on to get a bachelor's degree, a master's degree, and a doctorate in psychology. My mother was always a strong student and is a remedial reading and gifted teacher. I was doubly fortunate to have parents who posessed both personal and professional knowledge about AD/HD. They were great models for how to be an effective advocate.

My journey as a person with AD/HD has involved continuous learning, struggle, toil, frustration, realization, and finally peace. Along the way I obtained a bachelor's degree in social work and sociology with a psychology minor and a master's degree in social work. But most important, I am now in a position to pass on this information and help others who live with AD/HD.

AD/HD to be highly successful, but sometimes at a cost to their families, friends, and personal health.

Behavioral, social, and emotional characteristics. Many students with AD/HD face behavioral, social, and emotional challenges, including mood disorder, anxiety disorder, bipolar disorder, or obsessive-compulsive disorder (Broitman, Robb, & Stein, 1999; Brown, 2000; Pliszka, Carlson, & Swanson, 1999). Indeed, approximately one-quarter of the children and youth diagnosed with AD/HD also have an anxiety disorder (Pliszka et al., 1999). Typically, their behavioral, social, and emotional challenges consist of the following:

- Conflicts with parents (Johnston & Mash, 2001; Klassen, Miller, & Fine, 2004).
- Conflicts with teachers and peers (DuPaul, McGoey, Eckert, & VanBrakle, 2001; Gresham et al., 1998).
- Low self-esteem (Klassen et al., 2004).
- Frequent rejection, low peer regard, and difficulties making and keeping friends (Hinshaw et al., 1997).

■ Higher rates of using alcohol and tobacco (Milberger et al., 1997; Whalen et al., 2002).

■ Higher rates of substance dependence (Gordon, Tulak, & Troncale, 2004).

It is encouraging that childhood AD/HD is not a predictor of adolescent delinquency (Lahey, McBurnett, & Loeber, 2000; Lee & Hinshaw, 2004).

What do children with AD/HD think about their own behavior? This was a question addressed in a small research study that included elementary-age children with and without a diagnosis of AD/HD (Kaider, Wiener, & Tannock, 2003). As compared to children without AD/HD, children with AD/HD said they were less likely to be able to control their problem behavior, believed their problem behavior was more likely to persist into the future, and were more likely to report that their problem behavior occurred almost all the time. Interestingly, the children with AD/HD reported similar perceptions to children without AD/HD in terms of the extent to which parents, teachers, and peers were bothered by their behavior. As you have learned, children and youth with AD/HD have a difficult time understanding the perceptions of others. Thus, even though they felt their behavior was more of a problem, they did not perceive this was a concern to others.

Determining the Causes

Do you agree or disagree with each of these statements (Harman & Barkley, 2000)?

■ AD/HD stems from a lack of will or any effort at self-control.

■ AD/HD is caused by parents who don't discipline their children.

■ AD/HD results from children watching too much television or playing too many video games.

■ Dietary issues such as too much sugar cause AD/HD.

■ AD/HD results from living in a fast-paced, stressful culture.

We hope you disagreed with each statement because each reflects a misconception. So what does cause AD/HD? To answer, start by learning what does not cause it. Research has discounted many environmental explanations, including these popular myths: too much sugar, too little sugar, aspartame, food sensitivity, food additives/coloring, lack of vitamins, television, video games, yeast, lightning, fluorescent lighting, and allergies (Baren, 1994; Barkley, 2000; Hoover & Milich, 1994). Research has also discounted poor parenting as a cause (Stein et al., 2002). Have you ever heard somebody say, "Why doesn't that parent just get control of that kid?" One study related to parenting as a cause revealed that "the negative behavior of mothers [toward their child with AD/HD] seemed to be in response to the difficult behavior of these children and not the cause of it" (Barkley, 2000, p. 80).

There are three well-identified biological causes: heredity, structural differences in the brain, and other biological causes.

Heredity. Genetic factors cause AD/HD in about 80 percent of the children and youth who experience it (Cook, 1999). Children who have a parent with AD/HD have a greater than 50 percent chance of having AD/HD, and siblings of children with AD/HD are five to seven times more likely to have AD/HD than children whose siblings do not (Biederman et al., 1995; Kuntsi & Stevenson, 1998). Research on genetic factors in twins found that identical twins have AD/HD in 55 percent to 92 percent of cases (Cook, 1999). Similarly, a recent study of approximately 1,500 twins found that they had highly stable AD/HD symptoms during elementary and secondary years and that the stability and similarity of their characteristics was mainly genetically based (Larsson, Larsson, & Lichtenstein, 2004). Current research is focusing on genes related to **dopamine,** which is one of the brain's **neurotransmitters,** carrying signals between neurons (Tannock & Martinussen, 2001).

Structural differences in the brain. The frontal lobe of the brain (see Figure 8–2) is the area that is likely to be compromised in its role of controlling executive functions (Stein et al., 2002). Other areas of the brain that appear to have a critical role related to motivation, behavioral inhibition, and movement include the cerebellum and basal ganglia (Corkum, Tannock, & Moldofsky, 1998). Researchers are using **neuroimaging**—producing images of the

Figure 8-2 Areas of the brain associated with AD/HD

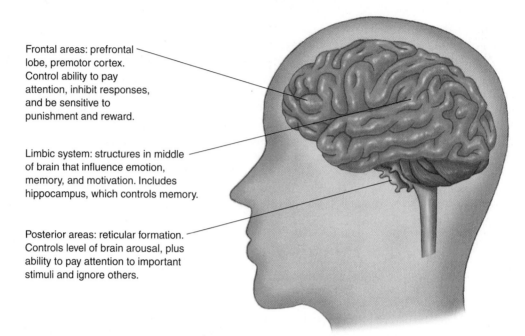

Frontal areas: prefrontal lobe, premotor cortex. Control ability to pay attention, inhibit responses, and be sensitive to punishment and reward.

Limbic system: structures in middle of brain that influence emotion, memory, and motivation. Includes hippocampus, which controls memory.

Posterior areas: reticular formation. Controls level of brain arousal, plus ability to pay attention to important stimuli and ignore others.

Source: From "The Human Brain," in *Teenagers with ADD: A Parent's Guide* (p. 12), by C. A. Z. Dendy, 1995, Bethesda, MD: Woodbine House. Copyright 1995 by Woodbine House. Reprinted with permission.

On the Companion Website, *www.prenhall.com/turnbull,* you will find a link to information about the neurobiology of AD/HD, *www.adhd. org.nz.*

brain using noninvasive techniques—to study the structure of the frontal lobe, cerebellum, and basal ganglia of individuals with AD/HD. They are finding that these parts of the brain are less well developed and less active in people who have AD/HD than in people who do not (Mostofsky et al., 2002; Semrud-Clikeman et al., 2000; Sowell et al., 2003). Although this research has been criticized because some of the participants were taking medication (Cohen & Leo, 2004; Leo & Cohen, 2003), this line of research seems likely to provide still further evidence of the biological cause of AD/HD (Stein et al., 2002).

Researchers have also linked areas of the brain, dopamine, and the benefits of stimulate medication. These brain regions, which are rich in dopamine, are known to regulate attention, working memory (the ability to retain, associate, and manipulate information "online" over brief time intervals), impulsiveness, and motor control. Recent studies have shown that stimulate medication, widely used to treat AD/HD, is effective because it increases the levels of dopamine in the brain and thus improves executive functions (Tannock & Martinussen, 2001).

Other biological causes. Prenatal factors (e.g., prenatal exposure to cigarette smoking, lead, and alcohol), perinatal factors (e.g., complications with labor and delivery), and postnatal causes (e.g., brain infections) also can cause AD/HD (Barkley, 2003; Stein et al., 2002).

EVALUATING STUDENTS WITH AD/HD

Determining the Presence of AD/HD

Some students may receive a diagnosis of AD/HD before they enroll in school; others, such as Kelsey, are referred for IDEA's nondiscriminatory evaluation because their teachers or school psychologists suspect they have AD/HD. School psychologists typically refer students who seem to have AD/HD to a variety of professionals, including pediatricians, family doctors, psychiatrists, clinical psychologists, and neurologists (Demaray, Schaefer, & DeLong, 2003). The purpose of these referrals is to receive expert assistance in performing IDEA's mandatory nondiscriminatory evaluation (see Figure 8–3).

Figure 8-3 Process for the nondiscriminatory evaluation of students with AD/HD

Observation	**Teacher and parents observe:**
	Predominantly inattentive type: The student makes careless mistakes, has difficulty sustaining attention, doesn't seem to be listening, fails to follow through on tasks, has difficulty organizing, often loses things, is easily distracted, or is forgetful.
	Predominantly hyperactive-impulsive type: The student is fidgety, leaves seat when expected to be seated, runs or climbs excessively or inappropriately, has difficulty playing quietly, talks excessively, blurts out answers or comments, has difficulty taking turns, or acts as if always on the go.
	Combined type: Characteristics of both are observed.
Screening	**Assessment measures:**
	Classroom work products: Work is consistently or generally poor. The student has difficulty staying on task, so work may be incomplete or completed haphazardly.
	Group intelligence tests: Tests may not reveal true ability because student has difficulty staying on task.
	Group achievement tests: Performance may not be a true reflection of achievement because the student has difficulty staying on task.
	Medical screening: Physician does not find physical condition that could cause inattention or hyperactivity-impulsivity. Medication may be prescribed.
	Vision and hearing screening: Results do not explain academic difficulties.
Prereferral	**Teacher implements suggestions from school-based team:** The student still experiences frustration, inattention, or hyperactivity despite reasonable curricular and behavioral accommodations.
Referral	The child should be referred to a multidisciplinary team for a complete evaluation if prereferral intervention is not successful.
Nondiscriminatory evaluation procedures and standards	**Assessment measures:**
	Psychological evaluation: Psychiatrist or psychologist determines that the student meets DSM-IV criteria for AD/HD.
	Individualized intelligence tests: The student's intelligence may range from below-average to gifted.
	Individualized achievement tests: Performance on achievement tests may suggest that the student's educational performance has been adversely affected by the condition.
	Behavior rating scales: The student scores in the significant range on measures of inattention or hyperactivity-impulsivity.
	Teacher observation: The student's educational performance has been adversely affected by the condition. The behaviors have been present in more than one setting, were first observed before age 7, and have lasted for more than 6 months.
	Curriculum-based assessment: The student may be experiencing difficulty in one or more areas of the curriculum used by the local school district because the behaviors have caused the student to miss important skills.
	Direct observation: The student exhibits inattention or hyperactivity-impulsivity during the observation.
Determination	The nondiscriminatory evaluation team determines that the student has AD/HD and needs special education and related services. The team develops appropriate education options for the student.

How do you talk to parents about referring their child for AD/HD evaluation? Kelsey's therapist, Chris Fraser, has a suggestion:

> It's a very touchy subject with parents, and some of them take it as a personal assault on their family. I would take a very nonaccusatory manner. If I were a teacher, I would recommend saying, "You know, it's always good to rule things out. For example, you take them to the doctor and rule out that the child doesn't have measles by having tests. Your child seems to be showing some symptoms of AD/HD, but I'm not a doctor; I'm not a counselor or psychologist. There's a good chance that your child doesn't have AD/HD. But then we'll know one way or the other." It helps parents let their guard down and allows them to align with you instead of against you. If more people got that message, there would be a lot more compliance with going to a psychologist or psychiatrist.

After the student's parent(s) agrees to the referral for nondiscriminatory evaluation, the process described in Figure 8–3 begins. When a medical evaluation is warranted as part of the AD/HD evaluation, the school district is responsible for paying the physician. If you suspect that a student has AD/HD, you will want to make a record of the student's behavior, referring (in your record) to the characteristics that we discussed when we defined AD/HD.

The nondiscriminatory evaluation seeks to answer three questions: (1) does the student have AD/HD and can the evaluators rule out other disabilities, (2) what should the student's IEP contain, and (3) do other disabilities exist simultaneously with AD/HD (Barkley, 1998)? Typically, evaluations involve rating scales, interviews, observations, and psychological and educational testing. Approximately 84 percent of school psychologists conduct classroom observations, 90 percent use rating scales with parents and teachers, and 80 percent interview parents and teachers (Demaray, Schaefer, & DeLong, 2003). Because rating scales are easy and efficient to administer, they are the assessment of choice. For an initial evaluation of whether a student has AD/HD, many psychologists use the Conners' Rating Scales—Revised (Conners, 1997). The Conners' Rating Scales (CRS-R) are available in long and short versions. The long version contains 13 subscales (for example, Oppositional, Hyperactivity, Social Problems) and takes 15 to 20 minutes to complete. The short version contains only four subscales and requires 5 to 10 minutes to complete. Both the long and short versions are completed by parents (for ages 3 to 17), teachers (for ages 3 to 17), and the students themselves (for ages 12 to 17).

The technical manual describes the standardization that involved developing norms for the scales. Based on a thorough review of this and four other frequently used rating scales, researchers came to the following conclusions (Demaray, Schaefer, & DeLong, 2003, p. 359):

> The CRS-R possesses strong psychometric properties and has been found to be instrumental in a variety of arenas (screening, assessment, treatment monitoring, and research). Thus, use of the CRS-R is recommended for assessment of ADHD.

In comparing five frequently used rating scales, the authors indicated that the Connors' is substantially more comprehensive than the other four. A national survey of school psychologists reported that the Connors' is the most frequently used rating scale that particularly focuses on AD/HD. Approximately 80 percent of school psychologists use it (Demaray, Schaefer, & DeLong, 2003).

Determining the Nature and Extent of Specially Designed Instruction and Services

After determining that the student has AD/HD, the evaluation team must decide whether he or she needs special education and related services. Many teams use the Attention Deficit Disorders Evaluation Scale (ADDES) because it prescribes interventions more often than any other available rating scales do (Demaray, Elting, & Schaefer, 2003). The ADDES has three main scales:

- Attention Deficit Disorders Evaluation Scale—Second Edition (ADDES-2)
- Early Childhood Attention Deficit Disorders Evaluation Scale
- Attention Deficit Disorders Evaluation Scale—Secondary-Age Student

On the Companion Website, *www.prenhall.com/turnbull*, you will find a link that will give you more information about the Conners' Rating Scales, *www.pearsonassessments.com/tests/crs-r.htm.*

PRAXIS

Standard: When you develop competency related to evaluating students with AD/HD, you are incorporating PRAXIS™ Standard 3, Delivering Services to Students with Disabilities.

Each scale has a subscale that addresses the inattentive type of AD/HD and the hyperactive-impulsive type. The ADDES-2 is suitable for evaluating students who are between 4 and 18 years old. It has both a home and a school version for parents and teachers, respectively. The ADDES-2 is supplemented by the following:

- A technical manual

- Prereferral checklists

- Prereferral documentation forms for intervention strategies

- A diagnostic tool for comparing the student's ADDES-2 score with DSM-IV eligibility criteria

- Norms that include only students with AD/HD as well as norms that include a random population of students

- Intervention manuals for teachers and guidebooks for parents that are specifically geared to each of the items on the scale

Researchers who evaluated the ADDES-2 and compared it to four other rating scales described the intervention manual (Demaray, Schaefer, & DeLong, 2003):

Each manual is outlined in a clear, comprehensive manner and provides helpful goal, objective, and intervention information, relevant to each of the specific behaviors described on its corresponding rating form. These manuals were defined to assist educators and parents in the development of programs to assist children and youth identified as ADHD. Although the addition of these intervention tools is an advantage for the ADDES, it should be noted that the intervention manuals are presented in a "cookbook" approach to intervention.

A national survey of school psychologists concluded that nearly half of them use the ADDES-2 (Demaray, Schaefer, & DeLong, 2003).

DESIGNING AN APPROPRIATE INDIVIDUALIZED EDUCATION PROGRAM

Partnering for Special Education and Related Services

Not every student with AD/HD qualifies for IDEA services. That is so because, as we explained at the beginning of this chapter, their AD/HD must adversely affect their educational performance. Many students with AD/HD, especially when they begin a treatment regimen that includes medication, can function well in a general classroom with modifications and accommodations like those discussed in this chapter.

If a student does not qualify for special education and related services under IDEA, does that mean he or she cannot get the types of modifications and accommodations that are effective? No; in fact, another option is to develop what is called a 504 plan. Section 504 of the Rehabilitation Act Amendments of 1973 and the Americans with Disabilities Act (ADA) both prohibit discrimination against students with AD/HD or other disabilities if their disabilities substantially limit one or more major life activities. To comply with these laws, states offer 504 plans to students who are not classified into the "other health impairments" category and provided with IDEA benefits. A school team (typically, the student's teacher, the principal or principal's designee, and someone who is knowledgeable about the disability) decides what accommodations are necessary (CHADD, 2005). Parent and student participation is not mandated but, as you've learned throughout this book, is very important.

One of the roles of either the 504 or IEP team is to plan educational supports that can accompany the use of medication for students with AD/HD. Educators and other members of 504 or IEP teams should never suggest to parents that their child needs to be on or off medication. Only a physician can make that determination. Educators may suggest to parents that they may

On the Companion Website, *www.prenhall.com/turnbull*, you will find a link to information about 504 plans at *www.chadd. org.*

Values: Although not every student is eligible for IDEA services, many more may be eligible for Section 504 services that increase their opportunities to succeed in school and in life as *full citizens.*

Partnership Tips ~ Assuring Quality in 504 Plans Through "CLASS Act"   Box 8-1

How does a grossly underfunded school district meet the needs of students with AD/HD? In the Davis, Utah, County School District, collaboration helps (Harman, 2000). As you will recall from Chapter 1, students who qualify for IEPs under IDEA make their schools eligible for federal dollars, but students who have Section 504 plans (under the Rehabilitation Act) do not draw in federal financial support. So how can a poor school district meet the needs of Section 504 students?

Linda Smith and Linda Stover, who started a local chapter of Children and Adults with Attention Deficit Disorder (CHADD) in 1994, had already been collaborating with the director of student services, Katie Davis, by providing her with updated information on federal policy for serving students with AD/HD. During the 1994–1995 school year, the three of them began educating school personnel and parents about the rights of students with AD/HD under Section 504.

By 1995, the district had a full-time director of Section 504 services, David Turner, who worked with parents to form Collaborative Learning Accommodation Services for Students, nicknamed "CLASS Act." CLASS Act consisted of 20 teachers. The group planned in-service meetings for teachers, parents, and administrators; obtained teaching materials and developed a budget; and developed an effective communication network. "The district wanted every teacher to know about CLASS Act," says Linda Sorensen, a member of the group (Harman, 2000, p. 27). Each CLASS Act teacher was assigned to seven schools,

and each offered in-service training at those schools. Sorensen says they told teachers they were bringing information on a new mandatory exercise program for teachers that involved running up stairs and on a track. After teachers learned about the real reason for the in-service, they were ready to hear that "'one size doesn't fit all' and to relate to the situation the kids [with AD/HD] are in" (Harman, 2000, p. 29).

CLASS Act teachers provide consultation services from in-house trainers, teachers, a nurse, a social worker, a parent representative, and a psychologist. They also provide training brochures for parents, teachers, and students. David Turner, director of 504 services, comments, "The 504 Plan should be a roadmap to help kids be successful in school. After all, teaching is about people helping people" (Harman, 2000, p. 29).

Putting Partnerships into the Context of Student Progress in the General Curriculum

1. What advantages would CLASS Act provide for teachers, parents, and students?

2. Explain the difference between educational rates afforded through Section 504 of the Rehabilitation Act and IDEA.

3. What are five tips you should remember when you serve on a 504 team?

To answer these questions online, go to the Partnership Tips module in Chapter 8 of the Companion Website, www.prenhall.com/turnbull.

want to secure a medical evaluation because, as you have learned, AD/HD is linked to physiological conditions. However, IDEA prohibits educators from requiring a student to take medication as a condition of attending school. That's all the more reason why partnerships among educators and parents are important, as you will read in Box 8–1, which describes model partnership practices that school districts can put into place to ensure that 504 plans are developed in a quality fashion.

Research indicates the benefits of medication for many students with AD/HD (Volkow et al., 2002). The National Institute of Mental Health's (NIMH) "Multimodal Treatment Study of Children with Attention Deficit Hyperactivity Disorder" (MTA), the longest and most thorough study yet completed on AD/HD (MTA Cooperative Group, 1999a, 1999b), concluded that medication alone is superior to behavioral therapy alone but that a combined approach adds to medication's effectiveness, sometimes even reducing the amount of medication needed. The NIMH report also emphasized that each student's treatment needs must be considered individually; some students will not tolerate medications well, but others may actually experience brain maturation as a result of medication (NIMH, 2002, p. 1). Nevertheless, despite the undoubted benefits of medication, not all parents want their children to take medication for AD/HD. Sometimes their opposition is culturally based, as you will learn from reading Box 8–2.

What do students think about taking medication? Box 8–3 asks you to stand in the shoes of a student with AD/HD who is considering whether or not taking medication is appropriate. When you "take the shoes test," what are your perspectives?

Determining Supplementary Aids and Services

Many classroom factors influence learning and may need to be considered when you are designing the educational programs of students receiving special education services. You will recall from Chapter 2 that supplementary aids and services involve modifications to aspects of the classroom environment. These include student seating arrangements, classroom furniture arrangement, or lighting and auditory features. For example, a student who is deaf and reads lips will need to be

Diversity Tips ~ Latina Mothers Share Perspectives on Medication   Box 8–2

Here is an allegedly indisputable fact about AD/HD and medication: many parents, educators, and physicians favor using medication to treat AD/HD. "Allegedly indisputable" is the moving phrase in this sentence because it appears that some Latina mothers may believe that they know what is best for their children with AD/HD, even when the evidence contradicts their beliefs.

In a research study, mothers from Cuba, Puerto Rico, and the Dominican Republic who have children with AD/HD overwhelmingly reported that they do not regard medication as a desirable treatment for their children's behavior. They avoid physicians' help, they do not regularly comply with medication regimens, and they disagree with educators who want their children to take medication. The mothers in this study, it is important to say, were both new and long-time residents of the United States; some had postgraduate degrees, while others had barely finished the sixth grade; some were single heads of household, while others were not; some were receiving Medicaid benefits because they were low-income and had children with disabilities; and some used psychotropic medications themselves. So socioeconomic and other differences existed among the mothers, but still the general finding was consistent: resistance.

What explains the resistance? As a group, the mothers believed that the medication would dull or slow down their children's minds; they wanted their children to be active and not to be considered as incapable of facing life. They regarded their children as specially vulnerable because of their age, and they believed that their children should learn to be in willful control of their lives, not in an altered state. They favored talk therapy to deal with what they believed were behavioral or personality quirks, not medication to address organic causes of behavior. They listened to the children's grandparents, who were skeptical about medication, more than to physicians, educators, and popular-media reports about the benefits of medication.

Who can overcome the resistance, and how? Physicians, educators, and even other Latina mothers or Latino fathers whose children regularly use and benefit from medication are good sources. Speaking in Spanish is important when that is the family's principal language. Explaining that AD/HD is biologically caused, not a personality quirk, will help. So, too, will describing the benefits of the medication. And offering additional interventions, information, and support—all the while being nonjudgmental—is important.

Source: Adapted from Arcia, E., Fernandez, M. C., & Jaquez, M. (2004). Latina mothers' stances on stimulant medication: Complexity, conflict, and compromise. *Journal of Developmental and Behavioral Pediatrics, 25*(5), 311–318.

Your Own Voice ~ Altered States   Box 8–3

If there is any one word destined to stir controversy among school-age children, their parents, and their teachers, it has to be "drugs." Its derivations frighten: "drugged," "druggie," "drugging." Steroid-boosted athletic performances are both condemned and often overlooked. "Shooting," "smoking," and "toking" are illegal. "Just say no" is a simplistic and insufficient antidote. And often wrong.

Wrong? Yes. Let's look at the other side of the controversy. Let's start by taking into account that nearly everyone uses drugs. Some use only the simplest pain reliever for a mild headache, whereas others use powerful psychotropics and polypharmaceutical regimens to alleviate the debilitating effects of mental illness.

So "drugs" conjures various responses; our perspectives depend on our experience with medication and the context in which we or others use that powerful word.

Let's set the context. Imagine a hypothetical scene in which you are a student ending your middle school years and headed to secondary school and all of its academic and social pressures. You have had the devil's own time in middle school; "concentrate," "pay attention," "sit down," "stop fidgeting," and comparable commands from your teachers seem to constitute your entire school day.

You have picked up the street talk from your peers about how they take prescription medication and benefit from it; even in middle school, getting an edge in academic competition seems to come from taking drugs. Your peers make it seem that taking medication is a good thing.

But they also have added to your distress; some bring prescription drugs to school and sell them in exchange for money or favors. That's wrong, and you know it, and you don't want to be any part of that business.

So you ask yourself, is an altered state—one that is induced by drugs—better or worse than your usual state? To ask that is to take you to an answer that consists simply of more questions. What do you know about AD/HD that leads you to want to ask your parents, teachers, and physician about taking medication so that "sit down" and the like are bygone phrases replaced by "excellent behavior," "close attention to detail," and "strong work products"? Where can you find out more about AD/HD, its organic and behavioral aspects, the research about drugs, and support groups?

Questions upon questions. Several meanings for a simple four-letter word. It's not as confusing as facing school in your unaltered state, is it? Or is it?

For some answers, go to *www.CHADD.org,* the website of Children and Adults with Attention Deficit/Hyperactivity Disorder. You will find information about the use of medication with students with AD/HD.

seated where she has a clear view of the teacher's face. A student with a physical disability who uses a wheelchair will need to have the classroom furniture arranged to allow physical access, and so on.

Box 8–4 sets out various classroom and educational program modifications that might benefit students with AD/HD. If a student has the predominately hyperactive-impulsive type, for

Into Practice ~ Accommodations for AD/HD

Box 8–4

Because students with AD/HD have various traits, you will need to make a variety of accommodations for them.

For students who display inattention, consider:

- Seating them in quiet areas, at desks that are unusually far apart, or (to the contrary) near students who pay close attention in class, or near a peer who studies with them or takes notes for them.
- Giving them more time to complete their work, reducing the amount of work you ask them to do (focus on the essentials), dividing long assignments into component parts and asking for completion of each part and then of the whole, giving assignments one by one rather than as a group of serial assignments, requiring fewer correct answers to receive a passing grade, using cues (such as private signals to stay on task) and oral and written instructions simultaneously.

For students who are impulsive, consider:

- Ignoring their somewhat inappropriate behaviors, rewarding them promptly when they behave correctly, acknowledging the correct behavior of other students so that the impulsive students understand and model that behavior, correcting them gently (not with public or private reprimands or entirely negative criticism, but with constructive suggestions), supervising them closely when they transition from one activity to another, and entering into a behavior contract with them.

For students with excessive motor activity, consider:

- Letting them stand while in class, asking them to run errands or otherwise use their energy physically, and breaking for a short while between assignments and asking them and the other students to do something physical ("stretch break").

For students who have mood characteristics, consider:

- Reassuring and encouraging them, speaking gently, and reviewing your assignments so they truly understand them.
- Meeting with their parents and asking how their parents want to communicate with you and you with them.
- Being on the alert for unusual moods, especially frustration or anger, and modify your expectations at those times and also provide support and contact the student's parents.
- Helping the student learn anger-control strategies, or referring the student to professionals who can teach those strategies.

For students who have academic challenges, consider:

- In reading, offering more time for the student to complete reading assignments, reducing the amount of reading, using texts that are less "dense" (number of words on a page), and not having the student read aloud in front of peers.
- In speaking, accepting nearly every spoken response so as to encourage the student to speak out, allowing the student to develop a poster or other type of display of what the student has read and learned, and asking the student to speak about topics that interest the student.
- In writing, accepting displays or oral projects as substitutes for some written work, allowing the student to use a keyboarded form of writing or a tape recorder, reducing the student's written workload, and using multiple-choice or similarly formatted questions.
- In mathematics, allowing the student to use a calculator or graph paper to space numbers, giving more time to complete an assignment, and frequently modeling the proper process to do a calculation.

For students who have problems organizing and planning, consider:

- Asking the student to use notebooks, dividers, palm pilots, dictating machines, computer programs, or other tools that help the student to remember what to do and when and how to do it.
- Providing daily, or at least weekly, reports to the student and the student's parents about how the the student organizes, or does not organize, the work you require, and regularly checking and assisting the student to improve the student's homework assignment book or other organizational tools and devices.

For students who have difficulty complying, consider:

- Praising the student's appropriate behavior, providing immediate feedback, ignoring minor misbehaviors (pick your issues), using a behavior contract for the student and for the entire class, and helping the student learn how to monitor his or her own behavior.

For students who have socialization challenges, consider:

- Praising their appropriate behavior, monitoring their social interactions, using behavior contracts, providing small-group study and cooperative learning and social skills opportunities, and publicly rewarding the student's leadership or participation.

Putting These Strategies to Work for Progress in the General Curriculum

1. Can you think of at least one more adaptation or modification in each area that is not on the list?

2. Sharise is a fifth grader with the combined type of AD/HD. She has difficulty staying on task and frequently blurts out comments and talks to others when she should be working. She has a wonderful sense of humor, so sometimes you have a hard time not laughing at her comments, however inappropriately timed they may be. Which adaptations or modifications might be helpful for her?

3. Jonathan is a compassionate tenth grader with the inattentive type of AD/HD and who is well liked by peers. He has difficulty getting to classes on time because he can't remember his locker combination. When he finally does get his locker open, everything spills onto the floor. He usually doesn't have the necessary supplies when he does make it to class. What adaptations or modifications would you recommend?

To answer these questions online, go to the Into Practice module in Chapter 8 of the Companion Website, www.prenhall.com/turnbull.

Source: Adapted from Parker, H. C. (1996). Adapt: Accommodations help students with attention deficit disorders. *ADD Warehouse Articles on ADD* (*http://www.addwarehouse.com*).

example, he or she will have difficulty sitting for long periods of time and may need some classroom modifications to address these issues. Those modifications may be as simple as allowing the student to stand during work periods rather than sit or to get up from the chair every 5 or 10 minutes. Classroom arrangements that minimize the distraction associated with student movement and support more frequent instructional activities involving movement, like role plays and strategies derived from multiple intelligences theory (see Chapter 16), accommodate students with AD/HD. Carbone (2001) has suggested several classroom arrangement features that minimize disruption related to hyperactivity-impulsivity:

Values: By arranging the learning environment to ensure that students with AD/HD can succeed, teachers build on their *strengths*.

- Arrange the classroom in a consistent manner to maximize predictability.

- Although all students benefit from collaborative learning techniques (discussed in Chapter 13), it is not always best to seat students with hyperactivity-impulsivity with peers because they can be distracted and become a distraction.

- Seat the student in close proximity to the teacher, possibly the front row of a row of desks.

- Do not seat students with hyperactivity-impulsivity too near highly distracting areas, such as a window, an open door looking into a hallway or another room, or any area with movement and potential distractions.

- To address issues of impulsivity, clearly post the daily and weekly schedules where students can see and consult them to provide prompts to students to engage in scheduled activities.

- Keep the schedule consistent to provide greater predictability and reduce impulsive behavior; reduce unstructured time for the same reasons.

- Minimize potentially distracting classroom decorations that are superfluous to learning.

- Arrange the classroom to facilitate smooth transitions between classroom activities.

Another characteristic of many learners with AD/HD is their lack of organization skills. In the next section you'll learn about curriculum augmentations related to goal setting and organizational skills that can enable students with AD/HD to be more organized and engage with the general curriculum more effectively.

There are also classroom ecological features that can assist in this. Teachers can establish clearly marked locations for students to store materials. Sometimes color-coding those areas can help students remember where materials belong. Similarly, teachers can provide clearly marked locations for students to store personal items, such as coats, backpacks, lunchboxes, and athletic gear. Minimizing the amount of clutter in a classroom can reduce student confusion about where materials and personal effects belong. Carbone (2001) suggestes setting up student mailboxes in which students can retrieve handouts and homework papers and can turn them in.

Planning for Universal Design for Learning

Classroom modifications such as student mailboxes and storage bins are only the first steps to enabling students with AD/HD to succeed in the general education classroom. Teaching students organizational and goal-setting skills augments the curriculum and can help students engage effectively with the general curriculum. As you learned in Chapter 2, curriculum augmentations involve expanding or adding to the general curriculum to teach students learning-to-learn or self-regulation strategies that, in turn, enable them to learn more effectively.

Students who are more organized are more likely to know what tasks they need to accomplish and what homework needs to be completed or has been submitted. Moreover, students can apply those organizational skills to improve their study habits. A component of effective study and academic skills involves setting goals related to the completion of academic work. Whether it is setting a goal to study for a set amount of time each night or to get a certain percentage of problems right on a quiz, students who set goals perform more effectively.

Classroom modifications such as those listed in the previous section help students learn organizing skills. Teaching students to think about their own environmental modifications can be helpful—for example, organizing their notebooks by folders marked by different colors, with each color indicating a different course or topic.

Values: Teaching students goal setting and attainment skills enhances their *self-determination*.

Many students have organizational problems. Use your *Real Lives and Exceptionalities* DVD to review an organizational solution George's teacher implemented to help him find his materials faster. Click on, "Meet George," and then select "Accommodations" (Clip 2).

Because they are easily distracted, students with AD/HD may also have difficulty with neatness. This is a common problem for many students, certainly, but it can be particularly problematic for students with AD/HD. Students can be taught effective work skills (for example, making sure numbers in a math equation are lined up appropriately) and note-taking skills. Using strategies like self-instruction and self-monitoring (described in Chapter 11), they can develop the habit of checking their work to make sure it has been completed and meets the standard set by the teacher.

Goal-setting and organization skills go hand in hand to promote better outcomes. Goals specify what a person wishes to achieve and, as such, act as regulators of human action (Locke & Latham, 2002). Simply put, if a student sets a goal, it increases the likelihood that he or she will perform behaviors related to that goal. The value of teaching goal-setting skills cannot always be measured only in terms of goal achievement. People do not reach every goal they set. The process of setting and working toward that goal, however, improves the person's goal-setting and attainment skills and increases the probability of reaching subsequent goals.

Within educational settings, the process of promoting goal-setting skills involves helping students to learn to do the following:

1. Identify and define a goal clearly and concretely
2. Develop a series of objectives or tasks to achieve the goal
3. Specify the actions necessary to achieve the desired outcome

At each step, students must make choices and decisions about what goals they wish to pursue and what actions they wish to take to achieve their goals. Goal-setting activities can be easily incorporated into a variety of educational activities and instructional areas as well as in educational planning. Involving a student in his or her IEP or transition-planning meetings or simply in planning for educational activities can provide multiple opportunities to practice setting goals and also can give the student a sense of involvement in and control over his or her educational experiences.

Research has suggested some general strategies to follow to make goals both meaningful and attainable for students with disabilities. Goals should be challenging for the student. They should not be so challenging that the student cannot attain them, as this will lead to frustration, but they must provide enough motivation for the student to work to attain them. If goals are too easy, there is no motivation to engage in the work necessary to attain them nor is there a feeling of accomplishment after achieving them. Finally, while it is preferable for students to participate in setting their own goals, at whatever level is appropriate given the nature of their disability, if this is not possible and goals need to be set by teachers, then the student's preferences and interests should be incorporated into the goal to increase his motivation to pursue the goal. Goals that have personal meaning are more likely to be attained (Sands & Doll, in press).

Students with AD/HD may have a difficult time attending to multiple goals. Several strategies are available to address this challenge. For example, complex goals should be broken down into smaller subgoals that the student can complete in a shorter amount of time with fewer steps. Students should make a list of their goals so they have a concrete, easy-to-find visual reminder of their goals. And the strategies to promote student-directed learning that we discuss in Chapter 11 can enable students with AD/HD to self-monitor their progress toward their goals (Wehmeyer & Shogren, in press).

Planning for Other Educational Needs

As you saw in the vignette about Kelsey, medication is often an important component of a student's multimodal educational program. (You'll learn more about multimodal treatments in the next section.) In addition, medication becomes an area of educational need for students with AD/HD.

Teachers working with students who are taking medicine to treat AD/HD should be familiar with the types, effects, and side effects of medications frequently used to treat AD/HD, such as Ritalin, Dexedrine, and Adderall. Side effects of these types of medications include sleep and appetite disruption, stomachaches, headaches, dizziness, irritability, anxiety, and sadness/unhappiness (Kollins, Barkley, & DuPaul, 2001). Although many parents favor the administration of medication, others are opposed to this approach. Obviously, it is important for teachers to contribute to efforts to monitor the impact of medications on the child. Students who are drowsy may present less of a problem in the classroom, but trading hyperactivity or impulsivity for drowsiness does not ensure the student's educational progress. The IEP should stipulate what teacher training needs to occur to ensure an appropriate education program. Thus, it is important that teachers have knowledge about medications and medication use (Snider, Busch, & Arrowood, 2003).

It is also important to assess systematically the effects of medication for students with AD/HD. The IEP team should consider how teachers and students can contribute to that assessment and recognize that parental observations and a physician's assessment yield information about the student's functioning (Kollins et al., 2001). Simple checklists of student behavior patterns and behavior states through the day also can provide useful information. Indeed, pediatri-

Consistent administration of medication, even at school, helps some children manage the symptoms of AD/HD.

cians indicate that they prefer to have this type of information when they make prescription and medication decisions (HaileMariam, Bradley-Johnson, & Johnson, 2002). Furthermore, students can learn to self-monitor and self-evaluate their own behaviors and feelings by using student-directed learning strategies such as those we discuss in Chapter 11. Finally, the IEP team should consider teaching students to self-manage their medication process, increasing the likelihood that they will take their medicine as prescribed.

USING EFFECTIVE INSTRUCTIONAL STRATEGIES

Early Childhood Students: Multidisciplinary Diagnostic and Training Program

The strategies most effective for young children with AD/HD, and indeed for students with AD/HD throughout their life spans, involve the use of multimodal treatments. Multimodal treatments are more than just the use of multiple intervention components, such as the multicomponent interventions you learned about in Chapter 5. **Multimodal treatments** involve multiple interventions or treatments across modes or types of therapies. Multimodal treatments for young children with AD/HD typically involve medication and other behaviorally oriented treatments (dosReis, Owens, Puccia, & Leaf, 2004). McGoey, Eckert, and DuPaul (2002) conducted a review of early interventions for preschool students with AD/HD and found that three primary treatment approaches were most effective: medication, parent training, and classroom behavior management interventions.

The University of Florida Multidisciplinary Diagnostic and Training Program (MDTP) (Travis, Diehl, Trickel, & Webb, 1999) focuses on increasing the academic progress and social success of children in early intervention classes by using multimodal treatments. Initially, the children attend a diagnostic classroom to receive individualized interventions based on their learning characteristics. They then transition back to the general classroom with the ongoing support of AD/HD project teachers, who continue to collaborate with general educators and parents to maintain the positive effects of the initial training. The interventions include the following (Travis et al., 1999, p. 2):

- Comprehensive academic, behavioral, and medical evaluation at a multidisciplinary diagnostic clinic
- A data-based classroom that tracks the child's progress
- Educational interventions based on the child's learning characteristics

PRAXIS

Standard: When you build competency in understanding medications related to the treatment of AD/HD, you address PRAXIS™ Standard 3, Delivering Services to Students with Disabilities.

Values: Teaching students self-regulation and self-medication skills decreases their dependency on others and enhances their capacity to be more *self-determined*.

Values: Partnerships based on multimodal treatments build students' capacity for *relationships*.

After receiving individualized instruction in a diagnostic classroom, children transition back to a general classroom with the support of a teacher with AD/HD specialization.

Standard: CEC Standard 4, Instructional Strategies, is reflected in developing your competency related to the delivery of instructional strategies such as errorless learning.

■ A structured classroom environment with a consistent routine and clear, concrete expectations and consequences

■ Appropriate medication, if necessary, with systematic documentation of effects on academics and behavior

■ Ongoing support for classroom teachers

■ Follow-up of children transitioning into general education settings

■ Ongoing research on children's attention to advance the understanding and treatment of attention disorders

Elementary and Middle School Students: Errorless Learning

Errorless learning refers to a procedure that presents the discriminative stimuli and arranges the delivery of prompts in a learning situation in such a way as to ensure that the student gives only correct responses (or only a few incorrect responses) (Alberto & Troutman, 2003). The discriminative stimulus, called the S^D, is a specific event or environmental condition that elicits a desired response. This stimulus acquires control over the desired response when the response is paired with a reinforcer. Prompts are any additional stimuli that increase the chances that the S^D will elicit the desired response.

These are technical terms for some fairly simple concepts that provide powerful teaching strategies. When a teacher asks a student to perform a task, he or she is providing an S^D. The instruction itself is intended to elicit a particular response from the student. For example, a teacher might ask a third-grade student to "tell what time it is." That S^D ("tell what time it is") should result in the student's telling the time (the response). Let's say, though, that the student does not provide the correct response, no matter how many times the teacher repeats the instruction. Once the teacher knows this, she might again ask the student to "tell what time it is" and then point to the clock on the wall. The pointing gesture is a prompt; it is an additional stimulus intended to increase the chance that the S^D will elicit the desired response.

There are several kinds of prompts, including physical, verbal, and visual prompts. Taking a student's hand to help him shape a piece of clay is a physical prompt. Verbal prompts can be questions ("Does this have four sides?" in response to the S^D to "Find the square"), instructions, or hints. Visual prompts include pictures or gestures to provide information to students but also can include written instructions (a list of the classroom rules posted on the wall) or even the way a room or furniture is arranged.

The basic idea behind errorless learning is that learning that occurs without mistakes is stronger and lasts longer. With trial-and-error learning, students run the risk of learning something that is wrong or learning to do something incorrectly; they then have to unlearn and relearn the correct information or process.

Errorless learning begins by identifying a task the student can reasonably perform with a prompt. Let's say you are teaching a third-grade student with AD/HD how to add fractions. Unless that student has mastered basic addition skills, there is no reason to believe she will be ready for three-digit subtraction. If, however, she knows basic addition skills, it is likely she can learn to add simple fractions.

Having identified the task, the teacher then must determine how best to present the S^D, what level of prompt to use, and when to present the prompt. All of these decisions should be made based on what it will take to ensure that the student can give the correct response. If the student has never added fractions, for example, the probability that she will respond correctly may increase if the problem is written instead of just given verbally. Once the S^D is presented, the next step is to determine what level of prompt to use and when to deliver that prompt.

In errorless learning, teachers typically use a most-to-least prompting strategy. That is, they begin with prompts that are, on a continuum, more intrusive but more likely to ensure the correct response. Physical prompts are the most intrusive, followed by visual and then verbal prompts. Sometimes teachers combine types of prompts as well, delivering both a visual and a verbal prompt, for example. Finally, teachers determine how soon to deliver the prompt. Prompts that are delivered almost immediately following the delivery of the S^D and that are of sufficient intensity to ensure that the response will occur tend to ensure errorless learning.

Let's consider the examples we've presented. In the case of the student responding to the S^D to "tell me what time it is," the teacher might have provided the visual prompt (pointing at the clock) immediately following the instruction. In teaching addition of fractions, the teacher might present the S^D ("add these fractions") and then immediately present the problem visually, using an overhead projector, and provide a verbal prompt ("if the bottom numbers in each fraction are the same, just add the top numbers"). Once students begin to master the tasks, teachers should begin to fade the prompting, moving from more intrusive to less, doing the same for the way the S^D is presented, and lengthening the time between the presentation of the S^D and the prompt.

Secondary and Transition Students: Cognitive Behavioral and Self-Control Strategies

Instructional strategies such as errorless learning and discrete trial training (Chapter 10) grew out of the discipline of applied behavior analysis (ABA). ABA emphasizes the manipulation of environmental variables, such as the discriminative stimulus, prompts, and reinforcers, to change behavior. Other behavior change strategies derive more from the discipline of cognitive psychology and emphasize the role of a person's cognition on changing behavior. These strategies, including cognitive behavioral strategies and self-control strategies, can be useful for students with AD/HD and other disabilities.

Smith (2002) defined **cognitive behavioral therapies** as "teaching the use of inner speech ('self-talk') to modify underlying cognitions that affect overt behavior" (p. 1). As indicated by the phrase "cognitive behavioral," these strategies draw from behaviorally oriented procedures but add a cognitive component. Smith (2002) noted that cognitive behavioral strategies have been used to address problem behavior for a wide array of students with disabilities, including hyperactivity and impulsive behavior.

One difference between cognitive behavioral strategies and the self-instruction strategies that we describe in Chapter 10 is that the purpose of cognitive behavioral strategies is to modify behavior and thinking patterns. As such, the self-instructions used in cognitive behavior strategies are less task-specific and may be more focused on self-talk to modify thoughts or feelings as well as actions.

Teachers implement cognitive behavioral interventions through a number of steps. First, teachers should talk with students about the connection between negative thoughts and outcomes. Students can learn that the way they think about themselves or a situation may be self-defeating; these ways of thinking are described as congnitive distortions. Cognitive distortions may include dichotomous or all-or-nothing thinking (outcomes in only one way or another), magnifying or minimizing a problem or issue, overgeneralizing from one circumstance to another, filtering (picking out only negative aspects of a situation), and "should statements" (e.g., overly punishing oneself for an action or inaction).

The actual self-talk statements vary according to the student, his or her needs, and the context. Often, these self-talk statements include both thoughts to counter the types of cognitive distortions identified previously as well as problem-solving thinking. For example, Miranda and Presentacion (2000) taught students with AD/HD to think through problem-solving steps ("What do I need to do? What are my options? What is the best option?") along with thoughts to counter negative thinking (e.g., "I need to concentrate on this and not let other thoughts disrupt my thinking. I have considered all my options and this seems to be the best one.")

Technology Tips ~ Captain's Log and Play Attention   Box 8–5

In one elementary school, Anishra, age 8, is playing a specially designed Bingo game on the computer. Todd, age 18, is playing the same game in his high school computer lab. Anishra and Todd share three features in common, along with AD/HD: they find the game enjoyable, stimulating, and age-appropriate.

Captain's Log (BrainTrain, 2000), a "complete mental gym," incorporates software that helps students and adults with AD/HD improve cognitive skills through exercises to enhance "attention, concentration, memory, eye-hand coordination, basic numeric concepts, and problem solving/reasoning skills" (p. 1). In addition, the game seeks to build self-esteem and self-control. Thirty-five games, arranged in five modules, make up Captain's Log.

Students wear a cool-looking helmet while using another cognitive skill builder, Play Attention (Play Attention, 2001). The program's purpose is to train students with AD/HD to focus

and "enhance attention, visual tracking, time-on-task, data sequencing, and discriminatory processing" (p. 1).

The system actually processes brain output, allowing students to use only their mind to control the action on a video game. As their attention wavers, the game changes. For example, in an early game, students watch a bird flying across the computer screen. As their attention wavers, the bird begins to fall. They must refocus their attention to help the bird maintain its flight pattern. One student says, "I learned being focused and on task was the way to be. My grades went from Cs and Ds to As and Bs after using Play Attention."

You can use this software in your classroom to help students learn to focus their attention. The Captain's Log website is *http://www.mindfitness.com/smart/caplog.htm*, while the website for Play Attention is *http://www.playattention.com/*.

Children with AD/HD involved in this study clearly benefited from the intervention and increased their capacity to self-control and self-regulate behavior. Because impaired self-regulatory ability is one characteristic of students with AD/HD, these types of cognitive behavioral treatments to increase self-control and self-regulation are important.

In addition to these strategies, students across the age range with AD/HD may acquire enhanced self-regulatory skills by using technology, particularly computer-based technologies. Box 8–5 provides examples of two computer programs that address issues relevant to students with AD/HD.

INCLUDING STUDENTS WITH AD/HD

Because AD/HD is not a separately identified category under IDEA, the U.S. Department of Education does not provide data on the extent to which students with AD/HD participate in general education classrooms. Box 8–6 provides some inclusion tips useful for students with AD/HD.

Although Kelsey has friends and many opportunities to enjoy her friendships through dramatics, art, music, and cheerleading, many students with AD/HD face particular challenges in making friends. An especially helpful guide in supporting girls with AD/HD to make friends is entitled *The Girls' Guide to AD/HD* (Walker, 2004). Even though this book is written especially for girls, many of the helpful suggestions apply to boys as well. Figure 8–4 is an excerpt from that book that focuses on the conversation among three girls with AD/HD describing issues associated with how they deal with their disorder within the context of friendships. As you will see, they have their individual preferences about what works best.

ASSESSING STUDENTS' PROGRESS

Measuring Students' Progress

Progress in the general curriculum. In Chapter 5 you learned about curriculum-based measurement as a means of tracking progress in the general curriculum. One of the advantages of CBM over standard pencil-paper measurements is that data are collected on an ongoing basis and information gathered from CBM can be used to modify instruction.

Another potentially beneficial means of determining student progress within the general curriculum involves the use of the goal attainment scaling process. Most students with AD/HD

Inclusion Tips   Box 8–6

	What You Might See	What You Might Be Tempted to Do	Alternate Responses	Ways to Include Peers in the Process
Behavior	*Inattentive type:* The student is inattentive, withdrawn, forgetful, a daydreamer, and/or lethargic. *Hyperactive-impulsive type:* He is restless, talkative, impulsive, and/or easily distracted. *Combined type:* The student has features of both.	*Inattentive type:* Overlook him. *Hyperactive-impulsive type:* Be critical and punitive.	*Inattentive type:* Consider changing the student's seating arrangement and providing daily schedules of activities. *Hyperactive-impulsive and combined types:* Teach the student organization and goal-setting skills.	Model acceptance and appreciation for him. Then peers are more likely to do the same.
Social interactions	*Inattentive type:* He withdraws from social situations. *Hyperactive-impulsive type:* He bursts into social situations and may be gregarious or inappropriate and annoying.	*Inattentive type:* Call attention to his isolation in front of other students; try to force him to play. *Hyperactive-impulsive type:* Pull him out of social situations for inappropriate behavior.	Role-play friendship skills. Help students discover their strengths, and encourage group participation in those activities. Start with small groups. Encourage membership in a support group for students with AD/HD.	For projects, pair him with another student who has similar interests and tends to be accepting. The initial goal is achieving one close friend.
Educational performance	Work is incomplete, full of errors, and sloppy.	Assign failing grades to the student.	Use errorless learning procedures to present the discriminative stimuli and to arrange prompts that will enable the student to be successful.	Model for peers good prompting strategies that they can also use in peer-tutoring interactions.
Classroom attitudes	Her motivation is inconsistent or lacking.	Send frequent notes to parents about your disappointment in their daughter's motivation.	Use goal attainment scaling (discussed later in this chapter) as a way for the student to see her progress. Provide rewards on a periodic basis when goals are accomplished.	Enable the student to teach another member of the class how to document his or her progress through goal attainment scaling.

and other disabilities have educational goals pertaining to all aspects of their educational program, including general curriculum content areas. Unfortunately, comparing goals among students or even comparing among goals for an individual student is not very helpful. Some goals are simpler to reach than others, and some goals address areas that are very different from other educational areas.

The **goal attainment scaling** process allows teachers to compare goals and to quantify student goal attainment. This process begins by identifying a goal (Roach & Elliott, 2005). Once a goal is set, the teacher must identify five potential outcomes of instruction to address it. These five outcomes range from a least-effective outcome to a highly effective outcome. Thus, the first outcome would quantify what the least-positive outcome would be, usually indicating

Figure 8–4 Perspectives on friendships: three girls with AD/HD speaking out

Maddy: I used to not want to talk about having AD/HD, but after a while, I realized it was hopeless to try to explain myself any other way, so I've become AD/HD Girl. I need a cape and a few superpowers, and I'll be ready to go. Maybe I'll get a tattoo that says AD/HD Girl!

Or not.

Anyway, if I find myself in a situation where I just know AD/HD is going to make for trouble (like working with other kids on a big project), I just tell the other kids that I have AD/HD. And mostly that works okay. It's amazing how people open up when you tell them something like that about yourself. I've learned that lots of people have lots of stuff going on. One of my best friends, Karla, and I together agree that Karla has AD/HD, even though she hasn't been diagnosed. We think Karla also has obsessive compulsive disorder (OCD). Then I tell her I wish I had some of her OCD, and she says fine, you can have it, but she won't take any of my depression, sheesh. Because I am willing to talk about having AD/HD, I've found out a lot about other kids in my classes. One of my friends is a superb artist and she has bipolar disorder. And a lot of the girls I know have either taken antidepressants or talked to a counselor at some time or other.

Sometimes, it is clear that the person I'm talking to thinks I'm faking it or that AD/HD isn't real or something equally supportive (NOT). So I just change the subject. If the person keeps bugging me about it, I tell the truth—that it doesn't do any good to talk to somebody about something when they won't listen. Because usually they just want to argue and say it isn't real or that I'm just lazy or whatever.

Eventually, I shrug my shoulders and walk away. I've learned that I don't have to take any abuse from anybody about it.

Like I said, most people start talking to you about their lives if you start talking openly about yours. It helps if you are matter-of-fact, I think, because it makes it easy for the other person to be nonjudgmental and matter-of-fact. People are sometimes afraid of emotions, even though I think that is silly. Anyway, I have found that if I stay calm and just bring AD/HD up without making a big deal, people seem okay with it most of the time. I also make jokes—most people appreciate a sense of humor, especially when you gently poke fun at yourself. They see that you aren't taking yourself that seriously, even if you have brought up a serious topic like AD/HD.

My favorite AD/HD joke is this one, that I made up:
Question: How many AD/HDers does it take to change a light bulb?
Answer: Want to go for a bike ride?
Get it? Zero attention span.

Bo: I don't talk about AD/HD. It's nobody's business. Once I get to know someone and trust them, I might talk about it. Until then, forget it. I don't say anything.

I'm not matter-of-fact, though. I go home and sweat and worry about what I said. Sometimes the person I'm talking to acts like she doesn't want to hear it. Even worse, she might act like AD/HD is fake. So I clam up. Which is easy.

Helen: Me? I don't care. I'll talk about it. Or not. Depends on if it comes up. I talk a lot, so it just dribbles out of my mouth.

Bo: I wish, I think it's plain hard. Sometimes I feel like I walk around labeled. Other times I forget that I have AD/HD. Then it feels like it's my fault that I mess up. I feel like a failure. Then I might remember I have AD/HD. Even so, it feels like a lame excuse.

Helen: You should hang around me, then! I'll remind you, at least when I remember, and I'll talk about it so you don't have to.

Bo: Actually, that sounds great.

Source: From *The girls' guide to AD/HD* by Beth Walker, pp. 127–128. Copyright 2004 by Woodbine House. Reprinted with permission.

no progress toward the goal. The second outcome would be better but still less than expected. The third outcome reflects what the teacher would consider an acceptable outcome, one that she would be satisfied to have the student achieve. The fourth outcome stipulates an outcome that is better than expected, and the fifth outcome identifies an outcome that far exceeds expectations.

Once these outcomes are set, instruction to achieve the goal can proceed. When the student has completed the educational program, the teacher then returns to the rubric of outcomes created at the start and circles the outcome closest to what the student actually achieved. From least to most effective, outcomes are awarded scores ranging from -2 to $+2$, with 0 being the middle outcome (the one that was viewed as an acceptable outcome).

Teachers can simply graph these scores across multiple goals to determine student progress or can transform the raw scores into a standardized t-score (which ranges from 0 to 100, with 50 as the middle or acceptable point), using tables published by Kiersuk, Smith, and Cardillo (1994). In most cases, however, simply graphing the goal attainment will suffice. It allows a teacher to compare a student's progress on widely varying goals and to compare goals across multiple students so as to determine the effectiveness of an intervention. Wehmeyer and colleagues (Palmer, Wehmeyer, Gibson, & Agran, 2004; Wehmeyer et al., 2000) have used the goal attainment scaling process to evaluate the impact of teaching students with disabilities a wide array of skills, including evaluating progress on goals linked to the general curriculum.

Progress in addressing other educational needs. Sometimes tracking progress in areas like social skills, self-control, or medication management (areas important to students with AD/HD) can be accomplished simply by using T-Charts or checklists. A **T-Chart** is simply a chart that is laid out in the form of a capital letter *T*. The chart allows teachers to track two aspects of a behavior together. Stanford and Reeves (2005) created a T-Chart to help students figure out what appropriate behavior "looks like and sounds like" (p. 20), listing visual cues that reflect appropriate behavior on the left side and the auditory sounds on the right (e.g., sounds like using "please" and "thank you").

Checklists are even easier to design and simply involve breaking down the task into discrete steps, listing them, and then identifying ways of marking or quantifying progress, often using check boxes. While T-Charts and checklists cannot be quantified easily, they can be an important tool in collecting a wide array of data pertaining to student progress in areas of other educational needs.

Making Accommodations for Assessment

The most common areas of accommodations for students with AD/HD pertain to attention and concentration problems. Students with AD/HD who have a difficult time sitting still and concentrating for longer periods of time may qualify for an accommodation to take extra breaks. Students for whom such extra break times, which allow them to stretch, are not sufficient may request multiple testing sessions instead of a single session. Another possibility would be for students to request a reduced-distraction testing environment.

Looking to Kelsey's Future

Kelsey dreams of being a veterinarian. She loves animals, and everyone on her team is supporting her dream to be a veterinarian. "I'd love to see her get good grades in school and get the opportunity to go on to college," Yvonne says.

"I want Kelsey to be happy," Barb adds. "I think she is now. And if she wants to be a vet, I hope she is a vet."

"First, small steps toward her goal begin today," says Chris. "Her work at school, volunteering at the pound, walking a dog—making it real for her. I would like her to learn to advocate for her needs, to blossom into a woman who is self-confident—who knows what she needs to be successful. I hope she learns how to articulate needs with teachers and professors and get better and better until she reaches her goal."

Sidebar

Go to the Companion Website, *www.prenhall.com/turnbull*, for a link to information about and examples of goal attainment scales, *www.2.uta.edu/sswmindel/s6324/Classpercent20Materials/measurement/goalpercent20Attainmentpercent20Scalingpercent20presentation.pdf.*

On the Companion Website, *www.prenhall.com/turnbull*, you will find a link to a website that provides an illustration of a T-Chart, *www.readwritethink.org/lesson_images/lesson390/t-chart.pdf.*

SUMMARY

Identifying students with AD/HD

- AD/HD is defined by criteria in the *Diagnostic and Statistical Manual of the American Psychiatric Association*, 4th ed. (DSM-IV) (American Psychiatric Association, 2000).

- Under IDEA, students with AD/HD are served under the "other health impairments" category.

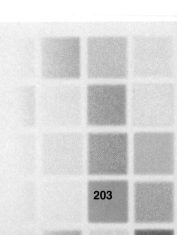

- There are three types of AD/HD: (1) predominately inattentive type, (2) predominately hyperactive-impulsive type, and (3) combined type.

- Although prevalence of AD/HD varies according to gender, age, and ethnicity, approximately 2 to 9 percent of all children are identified as having AD/HD.

- In addition to the characteristics of AD/HD associated with the three types, other characteristics include deficits in executive functioning; intellectual functioning in the average range; impaired academic achievement; and challenges associated with behavioral, social, and emotional functioning.

- AD/HD has multiple biological causes associated with heredity, structural differences in the brain, and other biological causes.

Evaluating students with AD/HD

- Diagnosis of AD/HD by a psychologist, a psychiatrist, or a physician often occurs outside the school system. The person who makes the diagnosis becomes part of the evaluation team.

- A frequently used evaluation tool to identify AD/HD is the Conners' Rating Scales—Revised, which come in both long and short versions.

- A particularly helpful evaluation tool for determining the nature and extent of specially designed instruction is the Attention Deficit Disorders Evaluation Scale because it prescribes interventions more often than any other available rating scale does.

Designing an appropriate individualized education program

- Students with AD/HD who may not qualify for special education services might still benefit from a Section 504 plan that enables them to receive some of the supports they might need to succeed in school.

- There are a number of classroom ecological variables that can benefit students with AD/HD, including arranging student seats to take distractability into account, posting daily schedules, and arranging the classroom to facilitate smooth transitions.

- Teaching students with AD/HD organization and goal-setting and attainment skills gives them strategies to better interact with the general curriculum.

- Many students with AD/HD take medicines so it is important for the IEP team to address additional programmatic areas, including teacher knowledge about medicine use and potential side effects as well as student self-medication strategies.

Using effective instructional strategies

- Young children with AD/HD can benefit from multimodal treatments—namely, multiple treatments across multiple fields or disciplines (e.g., medicine and behavioral programming).

- Errorless learning involves arranging the presentation of stimuli and the provision of prompts to ensure that students acquire new skills without the traditional errors associated with trial-and-error learning.

- Cognitive behavioral strategies can enable students with AD/HD to learn self-control strategies and to compensate for impairments in self-regulation.

Including students with AD/HD

- The U.S. Department of Education does not provide data on the extent to which students with AD/HD participate in general education classrooms.

- A particular challenge associated with inclusive placements for many students with AD/HD is making friends.

Assessing students' progress

- Goal attainment scaling allows teachers to compare student progress in the general curriculum by tracking goal attainment and can be used to compare among students and, for a particular student, among goals.

- Simple T-charts or checklists can be excellent ways to supplement more standardized data collection and to document progress in areas of other educational needs.

- Students with AD/HD may need test accommodations to address problems with attention and concentration that include extra breaks, multiple sessions, or distraction-free testing environments.

WHAT WOULD YOU RECOMMEND?

Refer to chapter content and the PRAXIS™ and CEC standards in Appendix A to answer the following questions:

1. If you were Kelsey's teacher, what could you do to enrich her curriculum by capitalizing on her love for animals? Which CEC standard relates to enriching a student's curriculum?

2. Design a lesson plan that you could use to teach content to Kelsey in one of the core academic subjects using the instructional strategy of errorless learning. What five tips would you be sure to incorporate in the lesson related to errorless learning? Which CEC standards are you addressing?

3. Visit the Companion Website for this chapter and locate the link to *www.readwritethink.org*. Based on the lesson plan you developed in Question 2 above, design a T-chart (with information from the website) as a way to collect data on Kelsey's performance. In which CEC standard does attention to this competency appear?

Chapter

9

Who is Erica Scott?

- "She's going to be more than a greeter at a department store."

- "The real barrier facing Erica is the stigma of mental retardation and how so many people underestimate her."

- "I want her to be aware of a lot of things and what she can be able to do herself if something were to happen to me. She's got to learn how to do these things because I'm not going to be here forever. She's going to need help regardless, but I want her to be able to depend on herself more than depending on someone else because, as I explained to her, no one's going to do the things for you that I do. When you help yourself, then others will help you as well."

Who made those statements about Erica Scott, and why are they remarkable? Let's answer the last question first.

They are remarkable not just because Erica, now 18, has mental retardation but also because she has cerebral palsy (which makes it difficult for her to walk without a motorized walker), is completely blind in her left eye, and is partially deaf in one ear. Her disabilities resulted from being born prematurely and from having had oxygen twice after she was born, to keep her alive. The paradox is that the oxygen kept her alive but also impaired her sight and hearing.

Now let's answer the first question. The first two statements express the great expectations and dedicated intent of the two teachers, Teresa Pena and Kristen Zajicek, who have Erica and nearly a dozen other students with disabilities in their special education resource room. The third expresses her mother's commitment to Erica's future as a full citizen in Temple, Texas. Abby Williams knows what she wants for her daughter and how to go about getting it by being a partner with Teresa and Kristen. Undoubtedly, if Erica's father, Sergeant First Class Nelson Williams, were available to speak with us instead of serving with the First Calvary Infantry in Iraq, he, too, would say something that makes us question what we have assumed about students with mental retardation.

Great expectations are good; in IDEA, Congress said that one of the barriers to the education and postschool outcomes of students with disabilities is that so many people have low expectations for them. But expectations alone will not make that much of a difference in Erica's life. They must be linked to effective teaching and research-based practices; that, too, is another one of IDEA's lessons.

And so it is reassuring that Teresa and Kristen partner with each other in educating Erica. They are not alone, however: three paraprofessionals and one functional academics teacher, Lynne McMurtry, constitute the school-based team, and Erica's mother, Abby, is the other principal member of Erica's team.

Together, these seven people, and Erica, have decided that she will remain in school until she is

Understanding Students with Mental Retardation

21 and that she will indeed graduate to a job, perhaps in Abby's beauty parlor or perhaps in the hospital or plastics-manufacturing plant where she has interned under her school's work-training program. But she will work; of that, no one has any doubts, including Erica.

To work, of course, Erica needs skills; so her curriculum consists of functional academics—reading (obtaining information out of written texts, such as about places, names, titles), mathematics (counting change), geography (knowing where you are at any one time and how you got there and how to return to a designated place), personal health (grooming, dressing, taking care of your body's normal functions), social skills (greeting people and remembering their names, setting boundaries with boys), and independent-living skills (cooking, taking care of your living space).

With so much learning packed into one school day, it's no surprise that Erica spends half the day at her school and half the day on a community-based vocational site off campus. Whatever she learns at school, she can apply at work and home; she learns to generalize.

And she learns how to behave and remember the prompts she gives herself about her behavior. She knows it is wrong to have a temper tantrum, pull her own hair, throw her eyeglasses onto the floor, pretend she is crying, or flail her arms when something or someone upsets her. Erica may want predictability in her life, but she cannot "lose it" every time one of her paraprofessionals cannot be with her or she cannot have what she wants when she wants it. So learning how to accommodate to change is part of her curriculum, and functional behavioral assessments and positive behavior support are the state-of-the-art interventions that determine why she

becomes distressed and how she can learn to remain calm.

Likewise, opportunities to be with peers who do not have disabilities are part of Erica's curriculum—not being with them in the academic programs at Temple High School because of her age and community-based program, but in extracurricular and other school activities: the school's Valentine's Day cake-bake sales, Thanksgiving-week meals for the students and staff at school, football spirit rallies and games, homecoming "mums and garters" sales, and a myriad of other ordinary events in this large high school located between Austin and Waco, near Fort Hood, Texas.

There are a few other ingredients that bode well for Erica's future. One is her mother's insistence that Erica become a full citizen, a responsible adult who is as independent as she possibly can be, but who also has the support of her family and professionals to be that way. A second is her teachers' instruction to promote self-determination. And yet another is Erica's own personality. She may be "all about control," to quote her mother Abby, and about getting her way, but she rarely forgets a person's name or birthday, smiles broadly at everyone, is outgoing for a good 90 percent of her days at school, and, like her mother Abby, is a strong-willed woman.

Don't underestimate Erica, her parents, or her teachers. Great expectations, state-of-the-art instruction, and determination constitute a winning combination.

IDENTIFYING STUDENTS WITH MENTAL RETARDATION

Defining Students with Mental Retardation

The U.S. Department of Education defines mental retardation as "significantly subaverage general intellectual functioning existing concurrently with deficits in adaptive behavior and manifested during the developmental period that adversely affects a child's educational performance" (34 C.F.R., Sec. 300.7 [b] [5]). The American Association on Mental Retardation (AAMR), the nation's oldest and largest professional association concerned with individuals who have mental retardation, defines it similarly: "Mental retardation is a disability characterized by significant limitations both in intellectual functioning and in adaptive behavior as expressed in conceptual, social, and practical adaptive skills. This disability originates before age 18" (AAMR, 2002). Figure 9–1 lists the five assumptions of the AAMR definition and shows how they apply to Erica. Note that items 4 and 5 call for teachers, other professionals, and family and community members to support people with mental retardation to function more competently in everyday environments. Supports are the services, resources, and personal assistance for enabling a person to develop, learn, and live effectively (AAMR, 2002). They can be intermittent (provided from time to time) or pervasive (constant), as Figure 9–2 describes.

Note that neither IDEA nor AAMR defines mental retardation as an inherent trait but as a state of functioning that describes the fit between an individual's capabilities and the structure

Go to the Web Links module in our Companion Website, *www. prenhall.com/turnbull*, for a link to the AAMR website.

Figure 9–1 Assumptions regarding the definition of mental retardation and their applications to Erica

Five Assumptions	Applications to Erica
1. Limitations in present functioning must be considered within the context of community environments typical of the individual's age, peers, and culture.	Since Erica is interested in the high school's social scene, wheelchair accessibility is a limitation that requires advocacy and creative planning.
2. Valid assessment considers cultural and linguistic diversity as well as differences in communication, sensory, motor, and behavioral factors.	Appropriate assessments for Erica must be racially/culturally nonbiased.
3. Within an individual, limitations often coexist with strengths.	Even though Erica has some challenges with memory associated with her cognitive function, she still remembers every birthday of everyone she meets and even knows what day their birthday falls on.
4. An important purpose of describing limitations is to develop a profile of needed supports.	By describing Erica's limitations in math, it is possible to focus on functional skills such as counting money and measuring for recipes, which will be important to her future independent living.
5. With appropriate personalized supports over a sustained period, the life functioning of the person with mental retardation generally will improve.	As the curriculum is individualized for Erica to maximize long-term outcomes, Erica will continue to increase her capacity to experience a quality of opportunity, full participation, independent living, and economic self-sufficiency.

Source: Adapted from American Association on Mental Retardation (AAMR). (2002). *Mental retardation: Definition, classification, and systems of supports.* Washington, DC: Author.

Figure 9-2 Definitions of intensities of support

Intermittent
    Supports on an "as-needed" basis. Characterized by episodic nature, person not always needing the support(s), or short-term supports needed during life-span transitions (e.g., job loss or an acute medical crisis). Intermittent supports may be high or low intensity when provided.

Limited
    An intensity of supports characterized by consistency over time, time-limited but not of an intermittent nature, may require fewer staff members and less cost than more intense levels of support (e.g., time-limited employment training or transitional supports during the school to adult provided period).

Extensive
    Supports characterized by regular involvement (e.g., daily) in at least some environments (such as work or home) and not time-limited (e.g., long-term support and long-term home living support).

Pervasive
    Supports characterized by their constancy, high intensity; provided across environments; potential life-sustaining nature. Pervasive supports typically involve more staff members and intrusiveness than do extensive or time-limited supports.

Source: From *Mental Retardation: Definition, Classification, and Systems of Supports,* by R. Luckasson, D. L. Coulter, E. A. Polloway, S. Reiss, R. L. Schalock, M. E. Snell, D. M. Spitalnik, and J. A. Stark, 1992, Washington, DC: American Association on Mental Retardation. Copyright 1992 by the American Association on Mental Retardation. Reprinted with permission.

and expectations of the individual's personal and social environment (AAMR, 2002). Whether a person such as Erica has mental retardation, then, depends in large part on how she functions in the settings (environments) that are typical for people without disabilities. For example, Erica receives positive behavior support (see Chapter 11) in school to help her avoid having tantrums when she is frustrated, and she receives training in functional mathematics and experiences in shopping and counting change so that she will learn about the value of money.

It is difficult to obtain an accurate prevalence rate for mental retardation. Reported rates are inconsistent and range from less than 1 percent up to 3 percent of the general population (Fujiura, 2003; Larson et al., 2001; MacMillan, Siperstein, Gresham, & Bocian, 1997). Perhaps most useful for educational purposes is the 0.9 percent rate reported by the U.S. Department of Education (2001). During the 2003–2004 school year, 581,706 students with mental retardation, ages 6 to 21, received special education services.

Describing the Characteristics

The two major characteristics of mental retardation are limitations in intellectual functioning and limitations in adaptive behavior.

Limitations in intellectual functioning. Intelligence refers to a student's general mental capability for solving problems, paying attention to relevant information, thinking abstractly, remembering important information and skills, learning from everyday experiences, and generalizing knowledge from one setting to another. Educators measure intelligence by administering tests such as the Wechsler Intelligence Scale for Children—III, which you learned about in Chapter 5. Students are classified as having mental retardation when they have an IQ score approximately two standard deviations below the mean—namely, an IQ of 70 or below on the Wechsler scale. Regardless of their IQ score, students with mental retardation have impaired intellectual functioning, including memory, generalization, and decreased motivation.

Memory. For many years, professionals thought that individuals with mental retardation had impairments in memory, especially short-term memory (Ellis, 1970). **Short-term memory** is the

Council for Exceptional Children

Standard: When you learn about the characteristics of students with mental retardation, you are applying CEC Standard 2, Understanding the Development and Characteristics of Learners.

mental ability to recall information that has been stored for a few seconds to a few hours, such as the step-by-step instructions teachers give to their students.

Happily, however, many students, including Erica, can use strategies to improve their memory (Bray, Fletcher, & Turner, 1997; Bray, Huffman, & Fletcher, 1999). Indeed, when provided with verbal and physical prompts, 17-year-old students with mental retardation have used memory strategies at a rate comparable to 17-year-olds without mental retardation (Fletcher, Huffman, & Bray, 2003). Examples of strategies that you might teach your students to use are learning to repeat silent instructions to themselves, listening to tape-recorded instructions, and moving objects in a particular order as aids to remembering a sequence of activities they need to perform.

Generalization. **Generalization** refers to the ability to transfer knowledge or behavior learned for doing one task to another task and to make that transfer across different settings or environments (Horner, Dunlap, & Koegel, 1988; Stokes & Baer, 1977). Individuals with mental retardation typically have difficulty generalizing the skills they have learned in school to their home and community settings; that is because the cues, expectations, people, and environmental arrangements of one setting usually do not exist in other settings (Bebko & McPherson, 1997; Mechling, Gast, & Langone, 2002).

Home and community settings often have greater complexity, more distractions, and more irrelevant stimuli than classrooms do (Bebko & Luhaorg, 1998). Outside the classroom, the cognitive demands on the students increase greatly, yet they receive most of their instruction in classrooms, not community settings. As you will learn later in the chapter, one way to increase their ability to generalize is to provide community-based instruction (Mechling & Gast, 2003). Erica receives both school-based and community-based instruction, the former in functional mathematics and reading and in socialization and daily living skills, the latter in being an effective employee in various types of jobs.

Motivation. No single profile of motivation applies to all people with mental retardation, any more than any single profile applies to all people without mental retardation (Switzky, 2004). The experiences of people with mental retardation, however, are more likely to explain why their motivation differs from that of people who do not have mental retardation than to explain anything about mental retardation itself. People with mental retardation are often externally oriented (Switzky, 2001). They tend to wait for other people to prompt them before acting, and they believe that they have little control over their lives (Wehmeyer, 2003b). Further, most students with mental retardation are not highly motivated because they experience failure whenever they choose to act. That is not true of Erica; she is all about control and expressing her preferences.

Your students' low motivation leads them to use a problem-solving style called **outer-directedness**—distrusting their own solutions and depending on others to guide them. This fact is troublesome (Zigler, 2001) because outer-directedness can make them especially vulnerable to control by others. As you will learn later in this chapter, however, even very young students can benefit from your instruction in how to become more self-determined.

Limitations in adaptive behavior. **Adaptive behavior** refers to the typical performance of individuals without disabilities in meeting the expectations of their various environments (Demchak & Drinkwater, 1998; Widaman & McGrew, 1996). People with mental retardation also have "significant limitations . . . in adaptive behavior as expressed in conceptual, social, and practical adaptive skills" (AAMR, 2002, p. 1). The adaptive behavior of your students with mental retardation will almost always fall below the norm of their typical peers (Kraijer, 2000). For example, Erica becomes frustrated and sometimes has a tantrum whenever the paraprofessional who works with her regularly is unable to be with her; so Teresa and Kristen, her teachers, tell her in advance that there will be a change in the paraprofessionals, and they

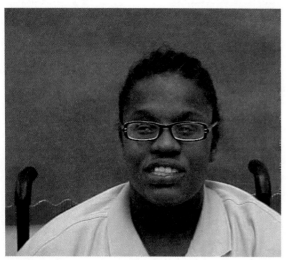

Erica Scott relies on such common devices as eyeglasses and a wheelchair, as well as a powerful curriculum, to benefit from school.

deliberately plan other changes in Erica's routine so she will learn how to anticipate and adapt to changes. A person's age, cultural expectations, and environmental demands influence adaptive behaviors. The older Erica becomes and the more she understands that change is normal, the more she should be able to adapt to the expectations of her school, work, home, and community environments.

Adaptive behavior consists of three domains (AAMR, 2002):

■ Conceptual skills, such as self-determination, reading, and writing

■ Social skills, such as taking responsibility and following rules

■ Practical skills, such as daily living and employment skills

A student may have a combination of strengths and needs in one or more of these domains; Erica has some strengths related to the first two but needs a good deal of training in the third. Later in the chapter you will learn about how to assess your students' adaptive behavior. For now, let's look at self-determination and its relationship to your student's conceptual skills.

Self-determination refers to "acting as the primary causal agent in one's life and making choices and decisions regarding one's quality of life free from undue external influence or interference" (Wehmeyer, 2001, p. 30). Being a causal agent means that an individual is able to take action to cause things to happen in his or her life (Wehmeyer, Abery, Mithaug, & Stancliffe, 2003). Self-determined people try to shape their future; they tend not to rely on chance (Wehmeyer et al., 2000). Self-determined behavior incorporates many skills, including choice making, decision making, problem solving, and goal setting (Wehmeyer, 2001).

Teachers can make a huge difference in their students' lives by teaching them the skills they need to be more self-determined and to meet the normal expectations of everyday environments, including the general curriculum. Self-determined students are more likely to achieve more positive adult outcomes, such as having a job and earning more money, than are peers who are less self-determined (Wehmeyer & Schwartz, 1997). They also are more likely to have a savings or checking account, to live outside their family's home, and to hold a job with health care and vacation-leave benefits (Wehmeyer & Palmer, 2003). Also, students at the secondary level who are self-determined are more likely than their less self-determined peers to join their teachers and families in making important decisions about their classes, curriculum, and extracurricular activities (Test et al., 2004).

Erica herself is involved in a research study aimed at enhancing her ability to become more self-determined. In the study, she has numerous opportunities throughout the school year to make choices and decisions concerning her work and her inclusion activities. As a result of participating in the study, she has drastically increased her ability to voice her likes and dislikes about her duties and even her job sites. At the beginning of the school year, she "just went to work." Work was something she did because she was asked to do it; she simply complied. Now she is distinguishing between her likes and dislikes and the level of difficulty of various duties and sites. Participation in research has produced progress for Erica.

Determining the Causes

There are two categories of causes of mental retardation: those that refer to timing and those that refer to type (AAMR, 2002).

Causes by timing. Timing refers to time of onset of the disability.

■ Prenatal (before birth)

■ Perinatal (during the birth process)

■ Postnatal (after birth)

A comprehensive study of a large number of school-age children with mental retardation revealed that 12 percent of them had a prenatal cause, 6 percent had a perinatal cause, and 4 percent had a postnatal cause. A probable cause could not be determined for 78 percent of the children (Yeargin-Allsopp et al., 1997).

Values: When you enhance your students' *self-determination,* you increase the likelihood that they will be able to make and act on their *choices.*

Causes by type. There are four categories of causes (AAMR, 2002, p. 126):

- Biomedical factors relate to biologic processes, such as genetic disorders or nutrition.

- Social factors relate to social and family interaction, such as stimulation and adult responsiveness.

- Behavioral factors relate to potentially causal behaviors, such as dangerous activities or maternal substance abuse.

- Educational factors relate to the availability of educational supports that promote mental development of adaptive skills.

Biomedical causes. Biomedical causes develop within the individual. They are inherent in the person. Typically, they originate early in a child's development and require extensive supports. A biomedical cause can be identified in about two-thirds of the children with mental retardation who have more severe cognitive impairments and therefore require extensive and pervasive supports (Batshaw & Shapiro, 2002). The cause of Erica's mental retardation is that she was born approximately 12 weeks prematurely.

Chromosomal disorders occur at or soon after conception in the prenatal period. When the egg and sperm unite during conception, they bring together genes from the mother and father. These genes determine the personal characteristics of the developing embryo and are found on threadlike structures called **chromosomes.** Chromosomes direct each cell's activity. Humans have 23 pairs of chromosomes in each cell, with one chromosome in each pair coming from the mother and one from the father. A chromosomal disorder occurs when a parent contributes either too much (an extra chromosome is added) or too little (all or part of a chromosome is missing) genetic material. Chromosomal disorders cause mental retardation for approximately 30 percent of individuals who require extensive and pervasive support and for 4 to 8 percent of the individuals who need less intensive support (Murphy et al., 1998).

Chromosomal disorders are verified through a procedure called **karyotyping,** which involves arranging the chromosomes under a microscope so that they can be counted and grouped according to size, shape, and pattern (Schonberg & Tifft, 2002). Down syndrome, one of the most common chromosomal disorders, accounts for the largest number of children and youth who have mental retardation as a result of a chromosomal condition. Down syndrome occurs when there is an extra 21st chromosome. Thus, an individual with Down syndrome has 47 individual chromosomes rather than 46.

Social, behavioral, and educational causes. We consider these three causes together because their boundaries often overlap, making it difficult to distinguish among them. The majority of individuals who have mental retardation experience adverse influences related to social, behavioral, and educational factors (Batshaw & Shapiro, 2002).

- Reading success can be predicted by the size of a student's vocabulary; families from lower socioeconomic backgrounds are much more likely to have children whose vocabulary is underdeveloped (Hart & Risley, 1995).

- The high school dropout rate is approximately 2 percent for students in the top 20 percent of family income, 5 percent for students from middle-income families, and approximately 11 percent for students whose families' incomes are in the bottom 20 percent distribution (Kaufman, Kwon, Klein, & Chapman, 2000).

- Younger mothers with 12 years of education or less are more likely to have children with mental retardation than are other mothers (Chapman, Scott, & Mason, 2002).

In Chapter 3 you learned about the strong association between poverty and disability. Poverty is much more associated with mental retardation

To learn more about Down syndrome, go to the Web Links module in our Companion Website, *www.prenhall.com/turnbull.*

Erica's curriculum includes functional academic and adaptive behavior skills.

than with other disabilities (Feldman & Walton-Allen, 1997; Fujiura, 2003; Fujiura & Yamaki, 2000; National Research Council, 2002). Moreover, African American students are more than twice as likely to be identified as having mental retardation than are European American students (National Research Council, 2002). Interestingly, poverty among African Americans is three times as high as poverty among European Americans (Blank, 2001).

EVALUATING STUDENTS WITH MENTAL RETARDATION

Determining the Presence of Mental Retardation

To determine whether a student has mental retardation, teachers and other professionals evaluate his or her intellectual functioning and adaptive skills. As you have learned, these are the two major traits of mental retardation. The evaluation process includes observation, screening, and the IDEA nondiscriminatory evaluation process (see Figure 9–3). Because poverty, race, and mental retardation are associated with each other, some professionals who evaluate students to determine whether they have mental retardation may be inclined to "find" mental retardation when, in fact, what they "find" is the consequence of an impoverished environment. Box 9–1 offers tips on how to guard against wrongly identifying students as having mental retardation.

As we have noted above, a student should not be classified as having mental retardation unless he or she has significant limitations in both intellectual functioning and adaptive behavior. Evaluators frequently use the tests we described in Chapter 5 (learning disabilities), particularly the Wechsler Intelligence Scale for Children—III (Wechsler, 1991), to determine whether a student's intellectual functioning is two standard deviations below that mean (that is, the student meets the cutoff point for "significant limitation" in intellectual functioning).

In addition to using intelligence tests for identification, evaluators must also assess a student's adaptive behavior. To date, 49 states require educators to evaluate a student's adaptive behavior when classifying the student as having mental retardation (Denning, Chamberlain, & Polloway, 2000).

Evaluators need to know whether a student has conceptual, social, and practical adaptive skills appropriate to his age and the environments typical of his community. Accordingly, they rely on adaptive behavior scales that have been normed on individuals with and without disabilities. Unlike intelligence tests, which are given directly to the student who is being evaluated, most adaptive behavior scales require the evaluator to rely on information provided by an individual who is familiar with the student's daily activities, such as one of the student's teachers, one or both of the student's parents, or other individuals (Gordon, Saklofske, & Hildebrand, 1998).

The AAMR Adaptive Behavior Scale—School is appropriate for evaluating students ranging in age from 3 to 18 (Lambert, Nihira, & Leland, 1993) and has scientifically adequate reliability and validity (Stinnett, Fuqua, & Coombs, 1999). Part 1 of the scale assesses personal independence in daily living and includes 9 behavior domains: physical development, economic activity, language development, numbers and time, prevocational/vocational activity, self-direction, responsibility, and socialization. Part 2 concentrates on social behaviors in 7 domains: social behavior, conformity, trustworthiness, stereotyped and hyperactive behavior, self-abusive behavior, social engagement, and disturbing interpersonal behavior.

The score for each domain is norm-referenced, enabling the evaluator to compare the student's performance with the performance of other students of the same age and thus to determine whether the student has mental retardation because of low adaptive behavior. Although the majority of the items on the scale are not racially biased, approximately one-third of the items in the scale's section on community allegedly reflect racial bias, with 10 of the items being biased in favor of European Americans and four being biased in terms of races other than European American (Bryant, Bryant, & Chamberlain, 1999).

The domains of the Adaptive Behavior Scale—School were developed before AAMR categorized adaptive behavior into the three domains of conceptual, social, and practical. Currently,

On our Companion Website, *www.prenhall.com/turnbull*, you will find information about risk factors associated with the causes of mental retardation according to timing and type.

PRAXIS

Standard: When you learn about and use these assessments you apply PRAXIS™ Standard 3, Delivering Services to Students with Disabilities and Selecting Assessments.

Values: When you evaluate and remediate your students' adaptive behavior, you can help them be more successful in their *relationships* with peers.

213

Figure 9–3   Nondiscriminatory evaluation process for determining the presence of mental retardation

Observation	***Medical personnel observe:*** The student does not attain appropriate developmental milestones or has characteristics of a particular syndrome associated with mental retardation.
	Teacher and parents observe: The student (1) does not learn as quickly as peers, (2) has difficulty retaining and generalizing learned skills, (3) has low motivation, and (4) has more limitations in adaptive behaviors than peers in the general education classroom.
Screening	***Assessment measures:*** **Medical screening:** The student may be identified through a physician's use of various tests before the child enters school.
	Classroom work products: The student has difficulty in academic areas in the general education classroom; reading comprehension and mathematical reasoning/application are limited.
Prereferral	***Teacher implements suggestions from school-based team:*** The student still performs poorly in academics or continues to manifest impairments in adaptive behavior despite interventions. If the student has been identified before entering school, this step is omitted.
Referral	If, in spite of interventions, the student still performs poorly in academics or continues to manifest impairments in adaptive behaviors, the child is referred to a multidisciplinary team.
Nondiscriminatory evaluation procedures and standards	***Assessment measures:*** **Individualized intelligence test:** The student has significantly subaverage intellectual functioning (bottom 2 to 3% of population) with IQ standard score of 70 to 75 or below. The nondiscriminatory evaluation team makes sure the test is not culturally biased.
	Adaptive behavior scales: The student scores significantly below average in two or more adaptive skill domains, indicating deficits in skill areas such as communication, home living, self-direction, and leisure.
	Anecdotal records: The student's learning problems cannot be explained by cultural or linguistic differences.
	Curriculum-based assessment: The student experiences difficulty in making progress in the general curriculum used by the local school district.
	Direct observation: The student experiences difficulty or frustration in the general classroom.
Determination	The nondiscriminatory evaluation team determines that the student has mental retardation and needs special education and related services. The team proceeds to develop appropriate education options for the child.

AAMR experts are developing an adaptive behavior scale for identifying significant limitations in adaptive behavior in people ages 3 to 85 years old. The new instrument, expected to be available in 2006, will provide a complete assessment of conceptual, practical, and social skills in a culturally fair manner.

Diversity Tips ~ Prereferral Procedures to Address Disproportionate Placement of Students — Box 9–1

Students from diverse backgrounds are overrepresented in special education. In particular, African American students are overrepresented in programs for students with mental retardation.

To reduce the risk of classifying African American students as having mental retardation and placing them into special education, teachers and administrators can develop a prereferral process that consists of three elements.

- Support teachers to keep a student in general education if at all possible.
  - Create a prereferral team for students (general education teacher; school psychologist or educational assessor; school counselor; reading and math specialists; grade-level or clusters of teachers; specialists in vision, hearing, and health; parents or other close family members).
  - Document students' difficulties and why they occur.
  - Modify the classroom or instructional strategies (differentiated instruction; culturally competent teachers providing culturally relevant and appropriate instruction; individualized interventions; home-school-community partnership).

- Apply the modifications and strategies for a long period of time.
  - Evaluate whether the modifications and strategies work.
- Create an effective school climate.
  - Determine whether bias exists and try to eliminate it.
  - Ensure that your school has culturally competent teachers and administrators.
- Partner with the student's family.
  - Communicate with families about the students' educational needs.
  - Involve families in prereferral discussions and interventions.

For further information, see the National Alliance of Black School Educators and ILIAD Project. (2002). *Addressing overrepresentation of African American students in special education: The pre-referral intervention process—an administrator's guide.* Arlington, VA: Council for Exceptional Children, and Washignton, DC: National Alliance of Black School Educators (*www.nasbse.org*).

Determining the Nature of Specially Designed Instruction and Services

Many other procedures also help members of the student's nondiscriminatory evaluation team determine what kind of special education services are appropriate to meet a student's educational and other needs and what kinds of related services the student requires in order to benefit from general and special education. A useful procedure for determining the strengths and needs of all older students with disabilities and for planning educational services and supports for them, especially **transition services,** is the Transition Planning Inventory (Clark & Patton, 1997). Instruction in transition teaches students the skills they need to be successful at work and in their community as adults. (You will learn more about transition services later in this chapter.) The inventory is appropriate for students who range in age from 14 to 25. It consists of 46 transition planning statements organized into nine areas: employment, further education/training, daily living, living arrangements, leisure activities, community participation, health, self-determination, communication, and personal relationships. Each area has three or more items related to knowledge, skills, or behaviors that are associated with successful postsecondary outcomes.

The inventory consists of four forms: student, home, and school forms as well as a form used for profiles and further assessment recommendations. Students, parents (or other family members or guardians), and a school representative independently complete a five-point rating scale (strong disagreement to strong agreement) for each item.

The Transition Planning Inventory is available in either a print or a computer version. To supplement the inventory, the authors have published a manual titled *Informal Assessments for Transition Planning* (Clark, Patton, & Moulton, 2000). This publication subdivides the 46 competency items on the Transition Planning Inventory into more than 600 items. It also provides 45 additional informal instruments that relate to each of the nine areas of the inventory.

All of the information that the evaluation team acquires, whether from standardized tests or scales or from the student, parents, and teachers, forms the basis for the student's IEP. Before you learn about the IEP, however, you should be aware that, in evaluating whether a student has mental retardation, most states continue to use the AAMR's 1983 classification system, not the current 2002 definition of mental retardation (Denning et al., 2000).

Visit our Companion Website, *www.prenhall.com/turnbull*, to see sample items from the Transition Planning Inventory.

Figure 9–4 AAMR 1983 classification system

AAMR 1983 Classification	IQ Range	Educational Classification
Mild mental retardation	50–55 to 70	Educable mental retardation
Moderate mental retardation	35–40 to 50–55	Trainable mental retardation
Severe mental retardation	20–25 to 35–40	Severely/multiply handicapped
Profound mental retardation	Below 20 or 25	Severely/multiply handicapped

Source: From Grossman, H. J. (Ed.). (1993). *Classification in mental retardation.* Washington, DC: American Association on Mental Deficiency.

The 1983 system categorized mental retardation as existing at mild, moderate, severe, and profound levels. Figure 9–4 shows the 1983 AAMR classification system in the first two columns and the resulting special education classification terminology in the third column (MacMillan, 1982). Many school systems still maintain special classes for students with mental retardation according to this classification system, and today you may still hear terms such as "EMR" or "TMR" classrooms. As a general rule, "EMR" refers to a classroom for students with mild mental retardation, sometimes known as "educable students," while "TMR" refers to "trainable students," or those with moderate mental retardation. However, all these terms are outdated. Even the terms "mild, moderate, severe, and profound" have lost favor under the new definition of mental retardation. It is more appropriate for professionals and families to focus instead on how much support the student requires. Refer back to Figure 9–2, which presents the four levels of support—intermittent, limited, extensive, or pervasive.

Furthermore, it is inappropriate to use separate classrooms for any student or group of students where the placement decision is based solely on a student's disability category. (Erica's classroom is separate, but her activities often are integrated with students who do not have disabilities, as we have pointed out. Her placement is determined by the level of her need, not simply by the nature of her disability.) There are two reasons for this. First, as you learned in Chapter 2, IDEA requires schools to provide students access to the general curriculum to the maximum extent appropriate for each student. Second, the focus on the relationship between a student's limitations and the environment in which he or she functions makes it even more important that students are included (Wehmeyer, 2003a). The focus on universal design for learning emphasizes changing the school environment, not the person, by improving the person's ability to function in the general curriculum.

DESIGNING AN APPROPRIATE INDIVIDUALIZED EDUCATION PROGRAM

Partnering for Special Education and Related Services

Despite the availability of tools such as the Transition Planning Inventory and the importance of a curriculum that takes into account a student's age and transition and vocational needs (Turnbull, Turnbull, Wehmeyer, & Park, 2003), schools rarely are held accountable for students' transition-related outcomes (Kochhar-Bryant & Bassett, 2002). Transition services, however, are particularly important for students with mental retardation and, under IDEA, must be included in a student's IEP. These transition services enable students to become more successful as adults in employment, independent living, community inclusion, recreation and leisure, and postsecondary education.

Transition planning requires IEP-based partnerships among the student, parents and family members, educators, and adult support providers (Thoma & Sax, 2002). The student, of course, is at the center of the transition planning process because IDEA requires the IEP team to take into account the student's needs, preferences, and interests. Getting the student actively involved in transition planning means having her attend and even be the chairperson of her own transition planning meeting, thus giving her the opportunity to communicate her preferences and interests and teaching and reinforcing skills such as goal setting, decision making, and problem solving, all of which lead to enhanced self-determination.

The student's parents also can help ensure successful transition planning (Morningstar & Wehmeyer, 2005). As is the case with Abby and Erica, parents know a great deal about their child; and they not only have a stake in the outcomes of transition planning, but they also are often the primary means of support for their son or daughter.

Of course, school personnel, including special educators, general education teachers, transition specialists, vocational specialists, and administrators, are important members of the student's IEP and transition-planning team. In addition, the team should consist of representatives of agencies that provide adult supports, vocational rehabilitation counselors, employment support providers, residential support providers, case managers or brokers, and even potential employers. Debbie Wilkes is someone who knows how to use partnership to create successful transition planning; in Box 9–2, we describe her work as an example to you.

Determining Supplementary Aids and Services

Paraprofessionals are important IEP team members because, as is the case with Erica, they are so intimately involved with the students; their membership on the team is a "supplementary aid and service" under IDEA (Carroll, 2001; French, 2001; Giangreco, Edelman, Broer, & Doyle, 2001; Riggs & Mueller, 2001). Approximately 280,000 paraprofessionals provide special education supports and services to students with exceptionalities (ages 3 to 21) who are being served in general and special education classrooms (U.S. Department of Education, 1999). More than 3,300 paraprofessionals provide services to children from birth through age 2.

Some educators and researchers have expressed concerns about how paraprofessionals support students in general education classrooms. Although the presence of paraprofessionals can add appropriate and meaningful support for students with disabilities as well as their classmates, often the added-on paraprofessional results in the "protective bubble" effect:

> During the years of our research, my colleagues and I saw students walking through hallways with clipboard-bearing adults "attached" to them or sitting apart in classrooms with an adult hovering over them showing them how to use books and papers unlike any others in the class. Often these "Velcroed" adults were easily identifiable as "special education" teachers because the students called them by their first names while using the more formal Ms. or Mr. to refer to the general education teacher. (Ferguson, 1995, p. 284)

Here is how a student without a disability described the "Velcroed" situation of one of her classmates:

> Whenever you try to talk to her you can't because her aides are there and they just help her say what she's trying to say and you want to hear it from her. They do it for her, and then they say, "Is that right?" It's like you're having a three-way conversation and [the aide] is the interpreter and it is not right that way. . . . It just doesn't work. (Martin, Jorgensen, & Klein, 1998, p. 157)

Appropriate partnership roles for paraprofessionals include providing individualized instruction to groups of students with and without disabilities, facilitating friendships among students with and without disabilities, supporting peer tutors, using state-of-the-art technology, teaching in community settings, and assisting students with personal care (e.g., bathroom care and feeding). Significantly, most paraprofessionals provide direct instruction to students for at least three-quarters of the time they are on the job (Riggs & Mueller, 2001). That role certainly

Partnership Tips ~ Partnerships for Effective Transitions   Box 9-2

Let's test a pair of assumptions about teachers. First, teachers teach in classrooms, right? Wrong. Or at least with respect to Debbie Wilkes in the Richardson, Texas, schools. Second, most collaboration happens among educators, right? Wrong. Or at least wrong when it comes to—yes, you guessed it—Debbie Wilkes.

For Debbie, now the special education supervisor in Richardson and a former classroom teacher in what was called the "mental retardation program," partnership takes many forms and requires her to perform many roles. What are these roles?

Debbie leaves the school grounds and becomes an active member of her community. With the support of the district's administrators, she attends the regular weekly or monthly meeting of eight different community and state organizations during her workdays. Especially when working with local business leaders, Debbie gives a single, consistent message: the schools are producing students who are ready to work; some do not have disabilities, and some do. At these meetings, she learns about market demand: how many employees the businesses need, what skills the employees need, and so on. Only then does she begin to advocate for the businesses to hire students. There's a second benefit to listening: Debbie takes that information back to the schools so the faculty can teach those skills and brings that information to the transition-planning process. Not only does Debbie have information about what job possibilities exist in the Richardson area, but she also has built relationships with employers and adult support providers, including vocational rehabilitation counselors, so that when she asks them to participate in a transition-planning meeting, they understand the mutual benefit to their participation.

Debbie sums up her partnership for successful transition tips in a few well-chosen sentences: "It's all about connecting; it's all about community. If we want our students to be full citizens and participating and contributing members of their communities, we educators have to connect with our communities. If we don't, our students won't." So Debbie connects with general educators, school administrators, business leaders, parents, professional agencies, adult support providers, and parent-support organizations. She extends her circles of partnerships wider and wider, connecting herself and the circles so that her students will also be connected. "Building partnerships means knowing what another person wants, how she is evaluated, and what will persuade her to work with you. You can't listen and learn if you're doing all the talking and teaching." Partnerships consist of listening, responding, and then asking—and making sure that the asking is inclusive, that it benefits all students, whether or not they have disabilities.

Of course, the students and their parents are inside the circle. Debbie helps them think broadly about the kind of life they want to lead (dreams), be candid about their worries about their present and future lives (nightmares), and begin to take a series of logical steps that will help them fulfill their dreams (action steps). This kind of planning also takes place with the students' other teachers, family friends, and even, from time to time, the business leaders. Debbie is quick to note that these partnerships take a lot of time.

Debbie has established a listserve that connects veteran parents (those whose children were her students many years ago and are still not living as full citizens in the community) with new parents (those whose children are just beginning to think about transition from school to work and independent living in the community). Debbie's listserve does double duty: it makes it possible for her to reach a large audience with a great deal of efficiency, and it helps her and the veteran parents share a powerful message with the new parents—namely, a good future lies ahead for those who plan ahead.

Tips for transition partnerships:

- Form strong school-employer partnerships by getting to know local employers, what their personnel needs are, and how graduating students can satisfy their needs.
- Work with providers of other adult service agencies to coordinate services for the students' and their families' benefit.
- When you are having a transition-planning meeting, include people who can help future visions come true — employers, community leaders, adult service providers, and friends.
- Encourage families whose sons and daughters have already made successful transitions to provide emotional support and information to families whose children are in transition.

Putting Partnerships into the Context of Student Progress in the General Curriculum

1. If you were a secondary teacher in Richardson, Texas, how would your own partnership with Debbie benefit your students and their families?

2. When you first move to a community, what steps can you take to learn about resources available in the community to support young adults after they transition from high school to adulthood?

3. Would you like to have a position similar to Debbie's? What appeals to you about it, and what concerns would you have if you had a role like this?

To answer these question online, go to the Partnership Tips module in Chapter 9 of the Companion Website, www.prenhall.com/turnbull.

---

assists students to progress in the general curriculum. It also enables general educators and special educators to concentrate on other students—those with and without disabilities—and on their progress in the general curriculum.

Planning for Universal Design for Learning

Exciting new technologies can help students with mental retardation learn more effectively. One such technology is the universally designed literacy software discussed in Box 9–3. The software was developed by researchers at CAST, Inc., and embodies many of the principles of universal design.

Values: When you support your students, you increase the likelihood that they will have equal opportunities—a way to achieve *full citizenship.*

Technology Tips ~ Literacy by Design: Teaching Students with Mental Retardation to Read

Box 9-3

Researchers at CAST, Inc., are developing universally designed instructional materials. Their project, Learning by Design, led by researchers David Rose, Bridget Dalton, and Margaret Coyne from CAST and Lucille Zeph at the University of Maine, investigates the effects of the universally designed approach to literacy on the reading achievement of students with mental retardation. The project rests on research in literacy that suggests that, like all students, students with mental retardation benefit from literacy instruction that focuses on reading for meaning and that also provides direct instruction in the skills and strategies needed to decode and understand print in meaningful contexts. To provide those learning opportunities, these researchers developed software that incorporates universal design features to enable young children with mental retardation to learn to read.

Students begin by selecting the level of interaction they want with the material (reading for understanding or reading aloud). They also select the book they want to read from a menu of several options. Students then use simple arrow icons to navigate the book, using button-driven options to access features such as having the text read to them. If they get stuck on a particular word, they can select a vocabulary button that takes them to a video- and audio-based menu that allows them to play a clip of the word in action.

Project director Bridget Dalton, chief education officer at CAST, says, "This project demonstrates that when we integrate research based literacy instruction, the principles of Universal Design for Learning, and technology, it is possible to create learning environments that unlock the potential for students with significant cognitive disabilities." Researcher and project director Peggy Coyne notes, "Teachers view CAST's Universally Designed Picture Book as a powerful tool because it supports the challenging task of customizing curriculum materials for their students. After using it, one teacher said to me, 'I like Picture Book better because it has everything right in it.'"

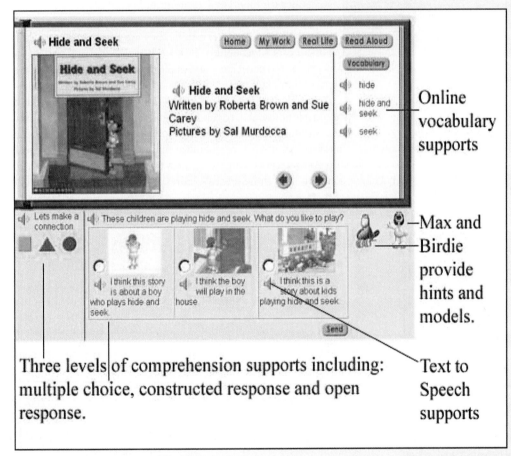

This screen shot from CAST's Universally Designed Picture Book illustrates scaffolded vocabulary, word recognition, and comprehension supports (Dalton & Coyne, 2003).

Erica's teachers, Kristen Zajicek and Teresa Pena, clearly enjoy being with her.

The software presents an audio- and video-based curriculum, includes an audio-based glossary that defines a word, and gives an example of how to use it and a video illustrating that use. Thus, teachers can tailor the content to the student's capacities (flexible use, cognitive taxonomies), and attention-grabbing cartoons help deliver the curriculum content.

Planning for Other Educational Needs

To address students' limitations in intellectual functioning and challenges associated with memory, generalization, and motivation, to develop their behavior in conceptual, social, and practical adaptive-skill areas, and to teach them to function successfully in their community, teachers need to support students to master skills that are sometimes more functional than the content of the general curriculum. These skills include applied money concepts, applied time concepts, community mobility and access, grooming and self-care, leisure activities, health and safety, and career education (Wehmeyer, Sands, Knowlton, & Kozleski, 2002). Erica's teachers, Teresa Pena and Kristen Zajicek, and her functional academic instructor, Lynne McMurtry, are making sure that Erica develops all of those skills. Like Erica's teachers, educators who use best-practice approaches provide their students with functional content and apply the concept of generalization and memory development by teaching in the settings in which their students will have to use the skills they are learning (Kluth, 2000; Langone, Langone, & McLaughlin, 2000). They also ensure that their students have access to and participate and make progress in the general curriculum to the maximum extent appropriate to each student. There are, however, objections to community-based instruction, as you will discover in Box 9–4.

To what extent should a functional curriculum be taught to students with mental retardation in typical community environments rather than classroom settings? The answer is that when students with mental retardation are unable to generalize skills to typical community settings such as home, places of worship and recreation, and work sites (as is the case with Erica), their instruction should occur in some or all of those settings (Bates, Quvo, Miner, & Korabek, 2001; Test &

Your Own Voice ~ Inclusive Community-Based Instruction   **Box 9–4**

Imagine that you are a teacher of students with disabilities. Under IDEA, you owe them an appropriate education in inclusive settings. You know that community-based instruction is a technique for an appropriate education. It rests on the principle of generalization: students learn best where they will have to practice the skills they are learning. You also know that students in general education benefit from community-based instruction, especially for learning some of the core subjects, such as English and math, on which they will be assessed under NCLB.

You ask the principal of your school to endorse inclusive community-based instruction for your students; they will take some of their instruction with students without disabilities in the community or neighborhood where they go to school.

"No way," says the principal. Her reasons are clear. Inclusive community-based education costs more than educating all students in the school; transportation costs—the schoolbus and a driver, or city bus and subway fares—have to be met. Additional teachers or other staff are necessary to supervise the students. Just being in the community creates

risks for the students and potential liabilities for the school. Local businesses and public accommodations, such as libraries, don't want to have students learning on site. Scheduling classes and teacher assignments becomes more difficult. Finally, the school has to teach to the statewide assessments, as required by NCLB.

As the teacher, how do you answer your principal, or do you concede that she has the better case?

To prepare your answer, see the following:

■ Braham, R. S., Collins, B. C., Shuster, J. W., and Kleinert, H. (1999). Teaching community skills to students with moderate disabilities: Comparing combined techniques of classroom simulation, videotape modeling, and community-based instruction. *Education and Training in Mental Retardation and Developmental Disabilities, 34*(2), 170–181.

■ Kluth, P. (2000). Community-referenced learning and the inclusive classroom. *Remedial and Special Education, 21*(1), 19–26.

Spooner, 2005). Further, students improve in their intellectual and adaptive behaviors when they learn in community settings (Agran, Snow, & Swaner, 1999; Langone et al., 2000).

USING EFFECTIVE INSTRUCTIONAL STRATEGIES

Early Childhood Students: Prelinguistic Milieu Teaching

All preschool-age children need to acquire language, but children with mental retardation obviously are limited in doing so (Abbeduto, 2003). Prelinguistic milieu teaching (PMT), developed by Warren and colleagues, is an effective language-acquisition instructional strategy for these children (Brady & Warren, 2003; Warren & Yoder, 1998; Yoder & Warren, 2001).

Prelinguistic milieu teaching is consistent with the concept of self-determination because its philosophy is that children will learn if their instruction matches their interests and abilities. Accordingly, PMT teaches children with mental retardation who do not speak to make frequent, clear requests or comments with gestures or sounds while looking at the person with whom they are communicating.

The steps in prelinguistic milieu teaching are simple and straightforward, as Box 9–5 depicts. While following these steps, teachers should keep in mind a few basic principles. First, follow the child's lead. Children focus best on things in which they are interested. The teacher observes the child and begins a session only when she sees what the child is interacting or playing with. Face to face, at eye level with the child, she talks about that object.

Second, set the stage for communication. By putting a favorite toy in the room but out of reach, the teacher encourages the child to ask for it. By putting objects out of order in a room, the teacher may elicit a comment from the child.

Third, be strategic when using games like Pat-a-Cake and Peek-a-Boo. Children learn the game ritual; when the teacher interrupts or changes the ritual, the child will communicate in order to keep playing. Pat-a-Cake and Peek-a-Boo also reinforce face-to-face contact; they entail give and take, like a conversation. As researcher and prelinguistic milieu teaching developer Steve Warren notes, "A substantial body of research has shown Prelinguistic Milieu Teaching to be the most effective approach to enhancing the communication development of young children with developmental delays and disorders" (personal communication, October 2004).

Elementary and Middle School Students: The Self-Determined Learning Model of Instruction

As you have learned, students with mental retardation face challenges related to motivation; they tend to be outer-directed, not inner-directed. Happily, instructional strategies help teachers overcome this challenge. Erica's teachers are using one of those strategies, the self-determined learning model of instruction. That model builds on the principles of self-determination (Wehmeyer et al., 1999, 2003) and promotes middle school students' progress in achieving the goals of the general curriculum (Palmer, Wehmeyer, Gibson, & Agran, 2004) and other goals as well (Agran, Blanchard, & Wehmeyer, 2000; Wehmeyer et al., 2001, 2003).

The model involves three phases. In each phase, the teacher presents the student with a problem that the student must solve. In phase 1, the problem is "What is my goal?" In phase 2, it is "What is my plan?" In phase 3, it is "What have I learned?" The student learns to solve the problem by answering a series of four student questions in each phase. Although they vary within each phase, each question represents one of four steps in a typical problem-solving process: (1) identify the problem, (2) identify potential solutions to the problem, (3) identify barriers to solving the problem, and (4) identify consequences of each solution. Figure 9–5 shows each of the 12 questions.

These questions in turn connect to a set of teacher objectives. In each phase, the student is the person who makes the choices and takes various actions, even when the teacher eventually remains in charge of the teaching. Each phase in the objectives includes a list of educational supports that teachers can use to enable students to direct their own learning.

Standard: As you learn about successful strategies used with students with mental retardation, you are addressing CEC Standard 4, Learning Instructional Strategies.

Values: The 12 guided *self-determination* questions can enable your students to identify their *strengths* and build on them.

Want more information on the self-determined learning model of instruction? Go to the Web Links module in our Companion Website, *www.prenhall.com/turnbull*.

Into Practice ~ Steps to Prelinguistic Milieu Teaching

Box 9–5

Prelinguistic milieu teaching is a research-validated, early intervention strategy for teaching young children with mental retardation and other disabilities such important prelinguistic skills as gesturing, vocalizing, and making eye contact that serve as the foundation for language development. PMT has several advantages. It is implemented in children's natural environments; involves activities and routines that are based on the child's preferences and interests; involves the child's natural communication partners, including parents and teachers; and creates opportunities for teachers and speech and language pathologists to be partners.

Prelinguistic milieu teaching improves language acquisition outcomes for children with mental retardation, but it requires educators to follow these steps in carrying it out (Yoder & Warren, 2001):

Step 1: Prompt the child to communicate. To begin the training session, the trainer, whether a teacher or the child's parent, conveys through verbal, gestural, or nonverbal means of communication an expectation that the child should communicate or use a particular communicative behavior to obtain a preferred object or engage in a preferred activity. The trainer might ask, for example, "What do you want?" or say, "Look at me," or provide a gesture, such as upturned or extended palms to indicate a question and request. These prompts are contextually specific to the child's preferred object or activity.

Step 2: Prompt the child to initiate. Next, the trainer provides a verbal prompt to the child to imitate a sign or a word, such as "Say, 'Ball,'" with reference to a preferred activity (playing with a ball) or "Do this," while modeling the sign for "more" (obtaining more of something the child likes).

Step 3: Vocally imitate the child's resultant vocalizations. When the child responds to the prior prompt, the trainer provides an exact, reduced, or expanded imitation immediately following the child's vocalization. So, for example, if the child responds to the "Say, 'Ball,'" prompt in Step 2 with the vocalization "Aba," the trainer immediately imitates the vocalization, saying, "Aba." When the child repeats the "Aba" vocalization, the trainer expands that, saying, "Abada."

Step 4: Comply with the child's request. The child's vocalizations in Step 3 were the result of prompts in Steps 1 and 2 related to a preferred object or activity. In this step, the trainer complies with the intended or apparent request by the child ("Aba" to play with the ball, imitating the "more" sign to get more of an item). So when the child says, "Aba," the trainer repeats the vocalization and gives the child the ball.

Step 5: Recode the child's communication act. In the context of complying with the child's apparent request, the trainer recodes or interprets the child's communication in the form of a question or statement. Thus, as the child is reaching for the ball and looking at the trainer, he or she says, "Ball," or "Do you want the ball?"

Step 6: Acknowledge the child's communicative act. In a reinforcing manner, the trainer tells the child he or she did what was required. So when the child obtains the ball, the trainer should say, "You asked for the ball!"

Step 7: Talk to the child. To continue the interaction and further reinforce the child, the trainer should continue to talk to the child, saying things like "Good, you are playing with the ball," and "You asked for the ball!"

Putting These Strategies to Work for Progress in the General Curriculum

1. Conduct an online search of prelinguistic milieu teaching and summarize five tips that you learn from this search.

2. Imagine that you have a child in your classroom who could benefit from prelinguistic milieu teaching. How might you and a speech and language pathologist partner in order to provide instruction?

3. What do you see as the advantages of teaching communication within natural environments and typical routines as contrasted to having language instruction in specialized therapy sessions?

To answer these questions online, go to the Into Practice module in Chapter 9 of the Companion Website, www.prenhall.com/turnbull.

Source: Adapted from Yoder, P. J., and Warren, S. F (2001). Relative treatment effects of two prelinguistic communication interventions on language development in toddlers with developmental delays vary by maternal characteristics. *Journal of Speech, Language, and Hearing Research, 44,* 224–237.

Some students will learn and use all 12 questions exactly as they are written. Other students will need to have the teacher reword the questions. And still other students will need to have the teacher explain what the questions mean and give examples of each question.

The outcome of phase 1 is that students set an instructional goal based on their preferences, interests, abilities, and learning needs. The outcome of phase 2 is that they design a plan for achieving their goal and self-monitor to track their progress toward the goal. The outcome of phase 3 is that they evaluate data from their self-monitoring process and, if necessary, alter their action plans or change their goal.

Are students successful in setting and attaining their goals? Yes. Palmer and colleagues (2004) examined the effect of the model on the progress of 22 middle school students with mental retardation on goals linked to the general curriculum (e.g., science, social studies, or language arts). The students received support to implement the model by addressing a goal based on a standard that had a self-determination focus (e.g., learn to solve a problem, set a goal, or create a study plan). Students who received intervention on self-determination skills (problem solving and study planning)

Figure 9–5   Student questions in the self-determination learning model of instruction

Phase 1 Problem: What Is My Goal?	
Student question 1	What do I want to learn?
Student question 2	What do I know about it now?
Student question 3	What must change for me to learn what I don't know?
Student question 4	What can I do to make this happen?
Phase 2 Problem: What Is My Plan?	
Student question 5	What can I do to learn what I don't know?
Student question 6	What could keep me from taking action?
Student question 7	What can I do to remove these barriers?
Student question 8	When will I take action?
Phase 3 Problem: What Have I Learned?	
Student question 9	What actions have I taken?
Student question 10	What barriers have been removed?
Student question 11	What has changed about what I don't know?
Student question 12	Do I know what I want to know?

Source: Wehmeyer, M. L., Agran, M., Palmer, S. B., & Mithaug, D. (1999). *A teacher's guide to implementing the self-determined learning model of instruction (adolescent version).* Lawrence: University of Kansas, Beach Center.

significantly improved their knowledge and skills in these areas, achieving educationally relevant goals tied to district-level standards at expected or greater-than-expected levels and thereby showing that instruction in self-determination can serve as an entry point to the general curriculum.

Secondary and Transition Students: Community-Based Instruction

"Learn it where you'll need to do it." That's good advice for any student, especially students like Erica, who have mental retardation and for that reason are challenged to remember and generalize their education to the community and to adapt to community expectations.

"Teach it where you want your students to practice it." That, too, is good advice for teachers, especially those whose students have mental retardation and thus memory and generalization challenges.

Shelby, North Carolina, is the seat of a largely rural county. Its school system consists of approximately 3,000 students in grades K through 12, of whom approximately 250 have disabilities. In Shelby, students with mental retardation are graduating from high school with a regular diploma. They are taking local jobs for good pay and benefits, and they are receiving positive work evaluations. At the heart of their success is the practice of providing effective community-based instruction in teaching a functional curriculum related to employment and independent living. Community-based instruction involves teaching students transition-related skills in the actual community settings in which they will be used.

One hundred and twenty students ages 14 to 18, more than half of whom have mental retardation, are involved in the district's Project TASSEL and are provided individualized, functional, community-based instruction. Consistent with IDEA's requirements, educators in the Shelby schools create a school-level, community-referenced, interagency transition team by the time each student reaches transition age (which is now age 16).

Use your *Real Lives and Exceptionalities* DVD to view Rachel, a career woman with Down syndrome. Click on "Beyond School," and then select, "Rachel."

Erica learns employment and independent living skills such as doing laundry.

Values: When your students have opportunities for competitive employment during high school, they begin to have *great expectations* for successful employment after they graduate.

PRAXIS

Standard: Using the self-determination model reflects PRAXIS™ Standard 2, Legal and Societal Issues That Relate to School, Family, and/or Community.

The teams consist of students, parents, teachers, vocational rehabilitation specialists, technical college administrators, and residential service providers. Each team focuses on a student's strengths and needs, particularly in the adaptive skill areas of work, community use, and self-direction/self-determination.

The "self-determination" motto is simple and clear, one the students learn and practice with the help of school and community teams: "Nothing about me without me." The students, with support from their teams, identify their future quality-of-life goals, especially those related to work. The curriculum for the community-based instruction is tied to everyday life experiences. To begin, the students simulate the challenges in the community that they are likely to encounter (you are sick and can't go to work, or you can't use your usual method of transportation this morning) and then apply the problem-solving skills that they would use in the community (what do you do, and whom do you call?). Over the course of their high school career, the students increasingly move off campus for their instruction. In this way, they learn skills that will generalize to the world of work; and they increase their adaptive skills, learning what it takes to adapt to and have a good quality of life in Shelby. By the end of their senior year, they must also have 360 class hours of competitive employment (work in an inclusive setting for at least the minimum wage, with or without a job coach—a person who shares the job with them and teaches them how to do it on their own or with only a little help).

The students benefit from the cooperation of 50 local businesses that provide job-shadowing sites, paid community-based contracts, and individual job placements. This kind of school-industry collaboration means that, when a student graduates with a diploma in the occupational curriculum, local employers know the student is well prepared. You should recall that one aspect of mental retardation is the need for supports; now you see how schools and community businesses collaborate to provide employment supports.

The challenge comes in aligning these community-based instructional approaches with the goals of inclusion. If students with disabilities are in the community but not at school, how can they also be included in the general curriculum with students who do not have disabilities? The answer is that, increasingly, models of reformed and effective high schools indicate that community-based learning is an important part of the curriculum for all students (Wehmeyer & Sailor, 2003). Like universally designed learning, community-based instruction is good for all students, not just students with mental retardation.

INCLUDING STUDENTS WITH MENTAL RETARDATION

To what extent are students with mental retardation included in general education classes? Figure 9–6 illustrates the percentage who were educated in the entire continuum of educational environments during the 2003–2004 school year. You will observe that students with mental retardation are more than twice as likely to spend the majority of their school time outside the general education classroom than are all other students with disabilities combined. Nevertheless, progress toward inclusion is happening.

Students with mental retardation spend more time in general education classes and less time in special education classes than they did a decade ago (Katsiyannis, Zhang, & Archawamety, 2002). That is the case with Erica, who takes two classes with Mr. Hilley in functional academics (mathematics and reading) and a class with Kristen Zajicek and Teresa Pena in community-living skills and then spends three class periods receiving community-based job training.

Figure 9–6   Educational placement of students with mental retardation (2003–2004)

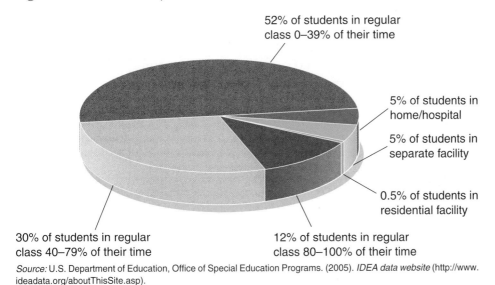

52% of students in regular
class 0–39% of their time

5% of students in
home/hospital

5% of students in
separate facility

0.5% of students in
residential facility

30% of students in regular
class 40–79% of their time

12% of students in regular
class 80–100% of their time

Source: U.S. Department of Education, Office of Special Education Programs. (2005). *IDEA data website* (http://www.ideadata.org/aboutThisSite.asp).

Yet the percentage of students with mental retardation who have earned a diploma and/or certificate has decreased over the past decade, even as their inclusive placements have increased (Katsiyannis et al., 2002). Furthermore, there are substantial regional differences: students in the northeast experience more inclusion and attain higher graduation rates than do students from other regions. The causes for this finding are not clear, but it is likely that state assessments of students' academic proficiency have negatively affected the graduation rates for students with mental retardation. Box 9–6 provides tips for increasing students' success in inclusive settings.

Assessing Students' Progress

Measuring Students' Progress

Progress in the general curriculum. An important and time-tested means for monitoring a student's progress is for teachers to observe how well he or she has mastered certain skills and then to record those observations (Belfiore & Browder, 1992; Browder & Spooner, 2005; Farlow & Snell, 2005). Figure 9–7 illustrates the steps in this type of data-based decision making.

Data-based monitoring requires teachers regularly to collect different types of data, including the following (Farlow & Snell, 2005):

At school, Erica contributes by helping keep exercise mats clean.

1. *Response-by-response data.*   How well has a student learned a task that has been broken down into discrete steps or subtasks?

2. *Instructional and test data.*   How well does a student perform under teaching and non-teaching conditions? Instead of collecting data strictly on each step in a task, data are collected on the student's independent performance on the task as a whole.

3. *Error data.*   How many and what kinds of errors does a student make, and how often, in performing a task?

4. *Anecdotal data.*   What other student performance information has the teacher acquired?

As Figure 9–6 points out, teachers must collect data continuously and systematically; otherwise, the data will not yield particularly helpful information about the student's progress.

Inclusion Tips   Box 9–6

	What You Might See	What You Might Be Tempted to Do	Alternate Responses	Ways to Include Peers in the Process
Behavior	The student demonstrates potentially distracting behavior such as loud laughter.	Tell her to stop the behavior (laughter) and be quiet or leave the room.	Teach skills to enable students to self-regulate their behavior.	Encourage peers to ignore inappropriate behavior and praise classmates when they regulate their behavior.
Social interactions	On her job-training sites, she feels very shy around co-workers.	Tell her she will never get a job unless she learns to interact with others on the job.	Include social skills as an important component of transition planning.	Gather information from co-workers about preferences for social interactions at work.
Educational performance	She shows an apparent lack of interest and boredom with class activities.	Discipline her for lack of cooperation.	Create opportunities for community-based instruction of relevant skills.	Include other class members as part of the community-based instruction.
Classroom attitudes	She demonstrates learned helplessness with new activities.	Let her be excused from the activity.	Encourage her to identify motivational strategies that have worked in the past and incorporate them into the class.	Pair her with a partner who needs help in an area of her strength (e.g., music).

Figure 9–7 Guidelines for making data-based instructional decisions

1. Collect response-by-response data.
2. Collect instructional and test data.
3. Collect error data and anecdotal data.
4. When a program is new, collect data daily. If instruction does not take place at least daily, collect data at each session.
5. When the student is making progress, collect data at least once a week.
6. Collect data more often and in more detail—at least twice a week—when the student is not making progress.
7. Draw a red line on graph paper showing the progress you want the student to make across time. This is called an aim line.
8. Plot student data points on the graph paper and connect those points with black lines. This is the student progress line.
9. Review the data at least once a week, comparing the progress line with the aim line and decide whether to continue the program or to make a change.

Source: Farlow, L., & Snell, M. (2005). Making the most of student performance data. In M. Wehmeyer & M. Agran (Eds.), *Mental retardation and intellectual disabilities: Teaching students with innovative and research-based strategies.* Upper Saddle River, NJ: Merrill/Prentice Hall.

Progress in addressing other educational needs. Teachers can assess a student's progress in community-based instruction by using an ecological inventory process (Snell & Brown, 2001; Test & Spooner, 2005). This process begins before teachers design and implement community-based instruction. Teachers collect two kinds of data: first, baseline data about how well a student functions in certain community settings; next, information about the student's current environments and prospective environments for community-based instruction. This whole process is called the **life space analysis.**

The first step in a life space analysis is for teachers to gather information about the student's daily environments, such as home and living, employment, school and education, recreation and leisure, and community integration. Who is present with the student, what activities are involved in those environments, and what skills does the student need to be successful in them? Teachers, family members, and others use the answers to these questions to determine how many subenvironments a student is involved in, the choices the students are making or can make to be involved in various activities common to all of the environments, the skills the students need to succeed in these environments, and who the students interact with. They then use this information to determine what other environments the students might access and what unaccessed environments might be appropriate for community-based instruction.

The second step in the life space analysis involves conducting **ecological inventories** in each of the environments where teaching will occur and comparing those inventories with ecological inventories for peers who are the same age as the student but do not have a disability. These ecological inventories identify the subenvironments in which students function, the activities involved in them, and the skills needed in them. For example, a student may have a preferred fast-food restaurant (environment) in which community-based instruction might occur. Within that restaurant, there are several subenvironments (for example, the counter where food is ordered, the dining area, and the restrooms) in which a student needs a different set of skills.

Having completed ecological inventories for the student and her nondisabled peers, the evaluation team members then conduct a **discrepancy analysis,** examining where and how the two ecological inventories differ and whether the points of difference can be the basis for instruction or can be addressed through other means, such as assistive technology.

Once they have identified the specific activities and the skills the student needs to function in each of the natural environments, team members perform an **activity task analysis,** identifying each step the student needs to master and the goals for community-based instruction.

At this point, the activity task analysis ceases to be a planning tool and becomes a means for measuring the student's progress. The team members will use data-based decision-making procedures to measure the frequency of the student's behavior, percent correct, level of prompts necessary, duration information, and error data and then to determine just how effective they have been in teaching the student to master the skills she needs in those environments.

Making Accommodations for Assessments

To demonstrate their competencies through statewide or district-wide assessments, most students will require one or more assessment accommodations. IDEA requires a student's IEP team to set out in the student's IEP the accommodations the student will receive. The accommodations for students with mental retardation typically include the following (Thurlow & Bolt, 2001):

- Dictating responses to a scribe
- Having extended time to complete an assessment
- Having test items read to them
- Securing clarification of test items

Looking to Erica's Future

Some aspects of Erica's life are fixed, or at least as certain as anything can be about life. Her mother Abby and her father Sergeant Williams are her reliable allies. Her teachers Teresa and Kristen are, too, but they will not be her teachers after she leaves school in three years.

Some aspects of Erica's life are changing and will continue to change. Her schooling will end, but her involvement with a vocational rehabilitation agency might start when she is in school or soon after she graduates. Her abilities to learn and work are growing; so, too, are her capacities for appropriate behavior and knowing what she wants and how to get it.

So let's look down the road a few years after Erica leaves school. It is the fall after she graduates, and Erica has confounded everyone by refusing to go to work. It's not that she does not love her mother and the beauty salon or that the other job placements she has had while in school are not entirely satisfactory as places to work. It's that Erica has been listening to what her classmates without disabilities have been saying about going to a 4-year college, a junior college, or a technical school. After all, she's been a senior for three years (students with mental retardation often stay in school until they are 21), so the notion of continuing education is not foreign to her. Indeed, some of her classmates without disabilities, as well as some who have disabilities, have left school and headed off to a nearby junior college. So, thinks Erica, why shouldn't I do the same?

It's not a pipe dream, though it does confound everyone. No one except Erica had that great expectation for her. Indeed, few people have expectations for postsecondary education for anyone with mental retardation. Yet it's not so far-fetched after all. Postsecondary options must make reasonable accommodations; that's the law under Section 504 of the Rehabilitation Act and the Americans with Disabilities Act (as you learned in Chapter 1).

So Erica capitalized upon her academic curriculum, her job training, and her training to promote self-determination. She set a goal for herself based on what she learned at school and used the planning steps she mastered in the self-determination research project. And now she is enrolling in "juco" (the local community college), taking classes in computer skills (she can spell and type, using the right kind of computer technology) and cosmetology. The support system she cultivated in school still exists; some of her schoolmates are at the junior college, others work in the community, and they all encourage her as she attends classes and provide various other kinds of support as she asks for it.

Her mother's beauty salon awaits her; but first, Erica needs further preparation for life as an adult. Not much different from most high school graduates, is she?

SUMMARY

Identifying students with mental retardation

- Mental retardation consists of significant limitations in both intellectual functioning (memory and generalization) and adaptive behavior (motivation and the ability to conform to the norm within a given situation). It originates before age 18.
- AAMR identifies three adaptive-behavior skill areas: conceptual, social, and practical.
- The causes of mental retardation relate to timing and type. Timing includes prenatal, perinatal, and postnatal. Type includes biomedical, social, behavioral, and educational.

Evaluating students with mental retardation

- AAMR proposes a comprehensive assessment that involves diagnosing mental retardation, classifying and describing the student's strengths and weaknesses as well as the need for supports, and developing a profile that includes intensities of needed supports.
- The AAMR Adaptive Behavior Scale—School assesses school-age children's adaptive behavior.
- The Transition Planning Inventory assesses nine knowledge, skill, and behavior areas to provide a level of performance information related to transition needs.

Including students with mental retardation

- Students are not often included in general education programs.
- But students achieve higher academic and social gains when they are included in general education classes.

Designing an appropriate individualized education program

- It is especially important to form partnerships among students, parents, educators, and adult support providers in planning for the transition needs of students with disabilities.

- Paraprofessionals can be a valuable resource in enabling students with mental retardation to make progress in the general curriculum.

- CAST has created software that provides audio and video resources for students to advance in literacy skills.

- A functional curriculum is important for students with mental retardation to ensure that they learn relevant skills for independent living.

Using effective instructional strategies

- Preschool and early-education students benefit from prelinguistic milieu teaching to elicit communication and language from them.

- Elementary and secondary students develop their abilities to function effectively in school and postschool environments by using the self-determined learning model.

- Students in transition programs benefit from community-based instruction.

Assessing students' progress

- Data-based decision-making strategies document students' progress in the general curriculum.

- The ecological inventory process is useful for both planning community-based instruction and assessing students' attainment of community-based instructional goals.

- Students' IEPs must describe the accommodations to which they are entitled, such as dictating responses, having questions read to them, having more time, and having items clarified for them.

WHAT WOULD YOU RECOMMEND?

Refer to chapter content and the PRAXIS™ and CEC standards in Appendix A to answer the following questions:

1. Visit the Companion Website module for Chapter 9, and locate the link to *www.transition.org*. Using information from this site, discuss how transition planning would benefit Erica. What PRAXIS™ and CEC standards are you applying when you consider a transition plan for a student?

2. If you were Erica's teacher, what other types of community-based instruction might be appropriate? Identify which PRAXIS™ and CEC standards apply to your ideas or suggestions.

3. What types of assessment accommodations might Erica need to participate in the Texas state assessment? What CEC or PRAXIS™ standards are you applying?

Use your *Real Lives and Exceptionalities* DVD to critically think about Rachel's success. Click on the questions following, "Beyond School" and answer questions 3 and 4.

Chapter 10

Sierra Smith, age 6, is a rarity and a paradox. Why a rarity? Because she is the only child in all of New Mexico, and one of only about 500 in the entire world, who has a documented case of Smith-Magenis syndrome (SMS). The incidence of SMS is estimated at 1 in 25,000 children.

Why a paradox? Because she has seemingly contradictory qualities. Let's begin with her mental facilities. Her parents, Denise and David, describe her as a bookworm, always absorbing information from the printed page or her computer-assisted toys; and her teachers, Maureen Torres and Kreg McCune, say that she is on grade-level with her kindergarten nondisabled peers, has made progress in the general curriculum, and should be retained in an inclusion program rather than placed in an intensive supports program for first grade.

Sierra's other traits, however, create the paradox. She has self-injurious behaviors that include head banging, hand biting, and picking at her skin and sores. She experiences temper tantrums and emotional meltdowns. She is constantly mouthing objects, hands, clothing, toys, or small rubbery objects that don't belong in her mouth. She is not yet toilet-trained; that's because her bladder and bowels do not send signals to her that she needs to use the toilet. She demands the attention of adults (often to the exclusion of nondisabled peers in her kindergarten class and her brother and two sisters). At school, she experiences daytime sleepiness and requires frequent short naps and a few longer ones because she does not have a great deal of stamina and because, like other children with SMS, her sleep cycle is opposite that of children without SMS. She has an inverted circadian rhythm of melatonin. She awakens frequently during the night, usually four to five times, and she almost always awakens at 5:00 A.M. She is tiny for her age yet powerful enough to hurt herself and to cling like Velcro to adults. Her gross- and fine-motor challenges require several accommodations from her teachers, her one-on-one educational aide, and physical, occupational, and speech therapists at school.

A rarity? Yes. Who would have expected Sierra to have SMS, given how unusual the condition is and that there is no obvious reason why she has it? Like other people with SMS, her genes went awry. Her parents say that her condition is a random occurrence, a fluke.

A paradox? Yes. Who would have expected her to have made such progress in school, to have earned the pro-inclusion support of her general education teacher, special education teacher, and their principal, Bea Harris, and to have won the affection of her peers? All this despite her many challenges.

There's another aspect to Sierra that commands attention. It is her appearance—not her size, but her cherubic face, also typical of children with SMS. She is, beyond argument, an appealing-looking child.

Given Sierra's abilities and her angelic appearance, it is understandable why Maureen, Kreg, and Bea are committed to her. The paradox is that their commitment simply reinforces her behaviors—those that demand adults' attention and result in meltdowns when she does not get her way. They are drawn to her, and she in turn absorbs them, producing even more attention from them.

This circular, symbiotic, paradoxical relationship—this co-dependency—itself is challenging. Sierra needs to learn to be more independent, not just for her own sake, looking ahead to her future in school and then as an adult, but also for her teachers' sake, so that they can attend to other students.

To teach Sierra how to become more independent, Kreg and Maureen had to learn how to depend on each other, for both of them have responsibilities in Sierra's classroom of 17 students without disabilities and 2 (including Sierra) who have disabilities. Here, too, is another paradox:

Understanding Students with Severe and Multiple Disabilities

two highly qualified teachers, expert in general early childhood education (Maureen) and early childhood special education (Kreg), have to learn to be partners, depending on each other, in order to teach a student to depend less on them.

To include Sierra in a regular education program, given her disabilities, is itself a rarity in her school district in Albuquerque, New Mexico. There, district administrators have created an intensive supports program that operates separately from other special education and general education programs and that contains a critical mass of students with high needs and professionals with high talents. Some of those administrators wanted Sierra to start that program in first grade. Yet Sierra benefits from being in an inclusion program. Indeed, she has made so much progress in her kindergarten year that Maureen, Kreg, and Bea, together with Denise and David, have refused the separate program and arranged for Sierra to be included again next year and perhaps thereafter. The collaboration among Sierra's teachers and their principal on the one hand and her parents on the other may not be rare, but it is essential to her education.

Besides a commitment to inclusion and collaboration, one other facet of Sierra's education is worth mentioning: it is relatively easy to teach her to be independent when highly qualified teachers such as Kreg bolster the general educators and supplement their general education curriculum. Kreg's long-term task of developing Sierra into a more independent person, less Velcroed to adults and less prone to self-injury and behavioral meltdowns, began with a simple, immediate strategy: the picture book. That strategy derives from Kreg's and Maureen's, and Denise's and David's, analysis of why Sierra acts out.

Sierra needs consistency and predictability in her life, and she has trouble communicating, which is part of why she acts out. She can acquire consistency and predictability, each day at school and home, when she sees what she will be doing that day, is prepped by the pictures for those activities, and can absorb both the pictures and then her teachers' and parents' directions and supports. There was a time when Sierra would melt down whenever an adult asked her to do something she did not want to do. Yet it is in the nature of education itself that adults do and should direct students. So the challenge was to provide Sierra with consistency and predictability in her life, direct her without causing her to melt down, and teach her how to secure consistency and predictability by acting on her own.

The picture book does all that, but it is also no substitute for consistent behavior from Kreg, Maureen,

Denise, and David. (Sierra's education is a 24-hour enterprise. She needs to practice at home what she learns at school. And that in turn requires her teacher and parents to follow through on each other's instruction and to communicate, by a communication log, regularly.)

Sierra's picture book illustrates the activities of her school day; because she is, as Denise says, a bookworm, always absorbing information through the printed page, a book is an ideal mode of communication. In a word, a simple response to a complex challenge, based on Sierra's own strengths and preferences and on adults' analysis of why she behaves as she does, becomes a powerful and effective form of intervention. Here, too, a paradox arises, at least for Sierra: simple often is better in situations fraught with complexity.

Let's return to the question "Who is Sierra Smith?" She is a rarity, in larger part because she has a rare syndrome and in lesser part because she is among the smallest population of special education students. She is a paradox because her gifts and challenges are so seemingly contradictory and because the ways in which Kreg, Maureen, Bea, Denise, and David respond—including her in the general education program, collaborating when specialization might create barriers, and using simple methods to address complex needs—seem to be contra-indicated.

Yet in Albuquerque in the spring of 2005, educators' response to rarity and paradox produced a result that IDEA seeks—education that benefits, is inclusive, and leads to the outcome of independence.

IDENTIFYING STUDENTS WITH SEVERE AND MULTIPLE DISABILITIES

Defining Severe and Multiple Disabilities

No single definition covers all the conditions associated with severe and multiple disabilities. Schools usually link the two areas (severe disabilities and multiple disabilities) into a single category for students who have the most significant cognitive, physical, or communication impairments. These impairments often occur in combination with each other. Some of these students may have average or above-average intelligence, although their physical and communication limitations may mask it. That seems to be the case for Sierra: intelligent but challenged physically, communicatively, and behaviorally.

One current regulation implementing IDEA defines multiple disabilities (but not severe disabilities) as follows:

> Multiple disabilities means concomitant impairments (such as mental retardation–blindness, mental retardation–orthopedic impairment, etc.), the combination of which causes such severe educational problems that they cannot be accommodated in special education programs solely for one of the impairments. The term does not include deaf-blindness. (34 C.F.R., sec. 300[b] [6])

Another regulation defines severe disabilities as follows:

> The term "children with severe disabilities" refers to children with disabilities who, because of the intensity of their physical, mental, or emotional problems, need highly specialized education, social, psychological, and medical services in order to maximize their full potential for useful and meaningful participation in society and for self-fulfillment. The term includes those children . . . who have two or more serious disabilities such as deaf-blindness, mental retardation and blindness, and cerebral palsy and deafness. (34 C.F.R., sec. 315. 4 [d])

Students with severe and multiple disabilities have complex needs that frequently involve cognitive, motor, and sensory functions.

These different definitions have common elements: the extent of supports required by students across all adaptive-skill areas is usually extensive or pervasive, and two or more disabilities typically occur simultaneously. Sierra exemplifies the definition: she needs extensive and pervasive supports and has more than one disability.

The U.S. Department of Education (2005) reported that 132,333 students, ages 6 to 21, were served in 2003–2004 under the category of multiple disabilities. This number represents 0.2 percent of all students, ages 6 to 21, receiving special education services. Because IDEA does not regard "severe disabilities" as a separate category, there are no federal data on the number of students with severe disabilities served.

Describing the Characteristics

Just as it is difficult to find a single definition of severe and multiple disabilities, so it is also difficult to accurately describe all characteristics of all students with those disabilities. Collectively, they are a widely heterogeneous group in terms of their characteristics, capabilities, and educational needs. Their nondisability characteristics (e.g., interests, preferences, personalities, socioeconomic levels, cultural heritage) are as diverse as the general population (Giangreco, 2006). Nevertheless, these students share five characteristics involving intellectual functioning, adaptive skills, motor development, sensory functioning, and communication skills.

Intellectual functioning. Most of the students have significant impairments in intellectual functioning, yet they are capable of learning (Giangreco, 2006). No one yet knows exactly what Sierra's intellectual capacity is; she reads and is progressing in kindergarten, yet she also has been found to have mental retardation.

But determining just how capable students like Sierra are is not easy. As you have already learned, schools typically measure a student's intellectual functioning by administering an intelligence test. Yet these traditional methods are inappropriate for many students with severe and multiple disabilities (Brown, Snell, & Lehr, 2006). This is so because, first, students with severe disabilities typically are not included in the normative samples of standard intelligence tests; the information generated from these tests is not useful in designing appropriate educational programs. Second, these students have not been exposed to some of the academic content on the test that is used to measure basic cognitive abilities. Third, most intelligence tests rely primarily on verbal abilities, and many students with severe disabilities have language and communication impairments that limit their capacity to respond verbally, as Sierra does.

Students with severe and multiple disabilities vary widely in their academic abilities. Some students develop functional academic skills such as how to count money, find items in a grocery store, and read basic vocabulary (Browder, Ahlgrim-Delzell, Courtade-Little, & Snell, 2006). It seems that Sierra is one of these students. Other students have such extensive support needs that their educational programs may focus on learning to make eye contact, track objects with their eyes, and respond to stimuli around them (Forney & Wolff Heller, 2004; Guess, Roberts, & Rues, 2000).

Adaptive skills. As you learned in Chapter 9, adaptive skills include conceptual, social, and practical competencies for functioning in typical community settings in an age-consistent way. With respect to social competencies, Sierra sometimes gives the "Bronx cheer" (also known as a "raspberry cheer") to her classmates. They laugh, thereby reinforcing a behavior that Sierra should not practice. So who needs to be taught? All of these students, not just Sierra.

With respect to practical competencies, parents often place a high priority on their child's self-care skills (Hamre-Nietupski, 1993). That's true for Denise and David; they, together with Kreg and Maureen, want Sierra to understand when she should go to the bathroom and how to take care of herself there. Most students and adults with severe and multiple disabilities can attain some level of independence in caring for their own needs (Farlow & Snell, 2006). School programs typically include instruction in self-care skills such as dressing, personal hygiene, toileting, feeding, and simple household chores. All of these skills promote school and community inclusion.

Motor development. Students with severe and multiple disabilities usually have significant motor-development impairment (Campbell, 2006; Szczepanski, 2004). Again, Sierra is typical; her petite size and low stamina impede her ability to get around in school as quickly as other students or to use a pencil without tiring quickly. Students with severe and multiple disabilities usually have sensorimotor impairments that produce abnormal muscle tone. Some students have underdeveloped muscle tone; they often have difficulty sitting and moving from a sitting to a standing position. Other students have increased muscle tension and extremely tight muscles, causing spasticity. Any abnormal muscle tone can interfere with a student's ability to perform functional tasks such as eating, dressing, using the bathroom, and playing with toys (Szczepanski, 2004). Nevertheless, many of these students learn to walk with assistance from canes, crutches, or strollers.

Sensory functioning. Hearing and vision impairments are common among individuals with severe and multiple disabilities (Silberman, Bruce, & Nelson, 2004). Although we include deaf-blindness

Standard: When you learn about the characteristics of students with severe and multiple disabilities, you are addressing CEC Standard 2, Development and Characteristics of Learners.

Values: If you teach your students to master self-care skills such as dressing and personal hygiene, you can make it easier for them to have *relationships* that can bloom into friendships in school and the community.

Joshua Spoor, from upstate New York, uses a computer and its "steering wheel" to help him communicate; he also uses a customized wheelchair. Both of these assistive technologies minimize the effects of his physical limitations.

To learn more about the characteristics and support needs of students who experience deaf-blindness, go to the Web Links module in Chapter 10 of our Companion Website, *www.prenhall.com/turnbull*.

in the category of "severe and multiple disabilities," IDEA currently regards it as a separate category of disability and defines it as follows:

> Concomitant hearing and visual impairments, the combination of which causes such severe communication and other developmental and educational needs that they cannot be accommodated in special education programs for children with deafness or children with blindness (34 C.F.R., sec. 300. 7[c][2])

It is wrong to assume that students classified as deaf-blind are completely unable to hear or see. They have various combinations of vision and hearing impairments. Their impairments in both of these senses, however, are so severe that they need specially designed instruction, especially in developing meaningful communication, including how to recognize and respond to tactile and gestural cues (Rowland & Schweighert, 2003). For example, a student might learn a simple touch cue such as a classmate waving good-bye just in front of the student's face so that the hand movement and the air movement it generates signal the student and elicits a response (Engleman, Griffin, Griffin, & Maddox, 1999).

Communication skills. Almost all students with severe and multiple disabilities, not just those who are deaf-blind, have communication impairments (Kaiser & Grim, 2006). Typically, they have difficulty objecting to others' action, drawing attention to their needs (especially their pain), and otherwise communicating (Stephenson & Dowrick, 2000). Kreg, Maureen, Denise, and David believe that many of Sierra's behaviors occur because she can speak only a few words and cannot sufficiently express herself. So behavior becomes her mode of communication.

Determining the Causes

Sometimes the cause of a student's disability is simply unknown; Sierra's appears to be a fluke. Often, however, the cause can be pinpointed. Approximately three-quarters of all children who have severe levels of mental retardation have that condition because of a biological cause—typically, a prenatal biomedical factor (Batshaw & Shapiro, 2002). For example, recent research found that severe mental retardation was caused by genetic factors in 22 percent of the population, chromosomal disorders in 21 percent, developmental brain abnormalities in 9 percent, and inborn errors of metabolism and neuro-degenerative disorders in 8 percent (Batshaw & Shapiro, 2002; Stromme & Hagberg, 2000). Complications during birth (perinatal causes) and after birth (postnatal causes) also account for many of these disabilities (Luckasson et al., 2002).

In 2003, the International Human Genome Sequencing Consortium, led in the United States by the National Human Genome Research Institute and the Department of Energy, announced the completion of the Human Genome Project (HGP) more than two years ahead of schedule and on the 50th anniversary of the discovery of DNA. The completion of the HGP provided information about the order of the genes and their general location in the DNA of all 24 human chromosomes.

Genes are biological units that can determine or influence what traits we inherit from our parents. By mapping the location of human genes, the HGP pro-

By using an augmentative communication device, students with communication impairments are able to "talk" with other people. This device consists of icons, words, and alphabet letters that the student touches to activate a sound or voice.

vided a foundation for determining the function of each gene and its role in causing or influencing human characteristics, including disability.

This information may assist professionals in identifying the precise cause of disabilities and whether biomedical interventions to treat impairments, before or after a child is born, are warranted. As you might imagine, the HGP raises many ethical and legal questions, including those we describe in Box 10–1. Does DNA knowledge pose any dangers; and if so, which ones? Or does the knowledge outweigh the dangers and provide an overall benefit to humankind? After you read Box 10–1, do your own Internet search and grapple with the promises and problems of our society's knowledge about DNA.

Parents of children with Sierra's disability, Smith-Magenis Syndrome, have created a website that connects them with each other and provides them with information. Go to *www.PRISMS.org*.

EVALUATING STUDENTS WITH SEVERE AND MULTIPLE DISABILITIES

As you have already learned, IDEA's nondiscriminatory evaluation process determines whether the student has a disability and requires specially designed instruction and, if so, what the student's special education and related-service needs are. Figure 10–1 describes this process for students with severe and multiple disabilities.

Determining the Presence of Severe and Multiple Disabilities

The **Apgar test** is a traditional way to screen for the detection of a disability in a newborn (Ward & McCune, 2002). When using this test, a physician ranks the child on five physical traits (heart rate, respiratory effort, muscle tone, gag reflex, and skin color) at 1 minute and 5 minutes after birth. The newborn receives a score of 0, 1, or 2 for each trait. A low Apgar score (less than 5 on a scale of 10) provides evidence that the infant has or is at risk of having a disability (Ward & McCune, 2002, p. 72).

Figure 10–1   Nondiscriminatory evaluation process for determining the presence of severe and multiple disabilities

Observation	***Physician/medical professionals observe:*** The newborn may have noticeable disabilities associated with a syndrome or may have medical complications that are often associated with severe disabilities.
	Parents observe: The child has difficulties nursing, sleeping, or attaining developmental milestones.
Screening	***Screening measures:*** Apgar scores are below 4, indicating the possibility of severe disabilities.
Prereferral	Prereferral is typically not used with this population because the severity of the disability indicates a need for special education and related services.
Referral	Children with severe and multiple disabilities should be referred by medical personnel or parents for early intervention during the infancy/preschool years. Many states have Child Find organizations to make sure these children receive services. The child is referred upon reaching school age.
Nondiscriminatory evaluation procedures and standards	***Assessment measures:***
	Genetic evaluations: Evaluation leads to identification of a genetic cause.
	Physical examinations: Medical procedures, including vision and hearing tests, blood work, metabolic tests, spinal tests, etc., reveal the presence of a disabling condition.
	Individualized intelligence test: The student scores at least two standard deviations below the mean (70 to 75 or lower), indicating that mental retardation exists. Most students with severe and multiple disabilities have IQ scores that are significantly below 70, indicating severe cognitive impairment.
	Adaptive behavior scales: The student scores significantly below average in two or more areas of adaptive behaviors, indicating severe deficits in skills such as communication, daily living, socialization, gross- and fine-motor coordination, and behavior.
	Assistive technology assessment: The student receives a comprehensive assessment for assistive technology needs in all of the environments in which the student particularly participates. This evaluation should be consistent with IDEA's definition of assistive technology device and assistive technology service.

Following an Apgar screening and assuming that the infant's Apgar score reveals present or potential disability-related complications, professionals conduct more precise and thorough tests to identify the nature of the disability, its possible causes, and the extent of the disabling conditions. They use neuro-behavioral assessments, brain imaging studies, and other examinations to determine the extent of the child's neurological impairments, sensory deficits, concurrent medical needs, and motor involvement (Batshaw, 2002). As infants and toddlers get older, evaluators typically administer IQ and adaptive behavior scales. This is particularly true when students have mental retardation. Sierra's evaluations include educators', related service providers', and physicians' assessments of her intelligence, behavior, speech-language, hearing, vision, cardiovascular (heart-lung), and renal (kidney), function.

Determining the Nature of Specially Designed Instruction and Services

Standard: You address CEC Standard 8, Assessment, when you are able to determine the nature of specially designed instruction and services for students with severe and multiple disabilities.

Students with severe and multiple disabilities are prime candidates for assistive technology—the use of existing, modified, or specially created technology to improve how a student functions. That is because assistive technologies can help students overcome any functional limitations they may have. Sierra uses a laptop computer and its software toys and games to supplement her classroom instruction. To determine whether a student needs assistive technologies, the student's evaluation team should ensure that assistive technology devices

- Are necessary for the student to make progress in the general curriculum
- Meet the IDEA definition, which defines an assistive technology device as any commercial or noncommercial item, piece of equipment, or product system that is used with the student to increase, maintain, or improve functional capabilities
- Are considered appropriate for the environments in which the student participates
- Are examined through procedures that lead to potentially effective interventions

Assistive technology evaluations typically are multidisciplinary. An assistive technology evaluation team should include assistive technology specialists, speech and language pathologists, orientation and mobility specialists, and occupational and physical therapists. The team should consider the student's educational, medical, and behavioral records and provide the following assessments, each of which constitutes part of an overall assistive technology evaluation:

- A speech, language, and communication assessment
- A seating and positioning assessment
- A mobility assessment
- A switch use and input/output device assessment
- A writing evaluation, including hand and grip strength and fine-motor skills
- A visual and hearing assessment
- An assessment of home, school (classroom and campus), and community environmental factors

These assessments should be conducted in the child's naturally occurring environments, including her school building or home.

Zabala (1995) developed an outline of questions to help IEP teams make decisions about student assistive technology needs. Called the SETT framework, the process considers the Student's needs, interests, and abilities; the Environment in which the technology will be used; the Tasks for which the technology will be needed; and then the Tools that might be needed to meet the student's needs. Figure 10–2 illustrates the SETT framework.

Although experts must be involved in the assistive technology evaluation process, the student's family members and the student should participate to the maximum extent possible.

DESIGNING AN APPROPRIATE INDIVIDUALIZED EDUCATION PROGRAM

Partnering for Special Education and Related Services

It is increasingly common for teachers to design IEPs for students with severe and multiple disabilities by using person-centered planning. That term emphasizes the active participation of everyone involved with the student (family, teachers, administrators, and, of course, the student), focuses on the student's and family's dreams and visions, and seeks school and community inclusion (Holburn & Vietze, 2002).

Figure 10-2 SETT (student, environment, tasks, tools) framework for making evaluation decisions

Student
   What does the student need to do?
   What are the student's special needs?
   What are the student's current abilities?

Environment
   What materials and equipment are currently available in the environment?
   What is the physical arrangement? Are there special needs?
   What is the instructional arrangement? Are there likely to be changes?
   What supports are available to the student?
   What resources are available to the people supporting the student?

Tasks
   What activities take place in the environment?
   What activities support the student's curriculum?
   What are the critical elements of the activities?
   How might the activities be modified to accommodate the student's special needs?
   How might technology support the student's active participation in those activities?

Tools
   What no-tech, low-tech, and high-tech options should be considered when developing
      a system for a student with these needs and abilities doing these tasks in these
      environments?
   What strategies might be used to invite increased student performance?
   How might these tools be tried out with the student in the customary environments in
      which they will be used?

Source: Adapted from Zabala, J. (1995) *The SETT framework: Critical areas to consider when making informed assistive technology decisions.* Newton, MA: National Center to Improve Practice. (ERIC Document Reproduction Service No. ED381962).

Values: Person-centered planning emphasizes a student's *strengths,* interests, preferences, and dreams, thereby promoting self-determination.

   One of the most popular person-centered planning approaches is called making action plans (MAPs). The **MAPs** process customizes students' educational programs to their specific visions, strengths, and needs (Downing, 2002; Falvey, Forest, Pearpoint, & Rosenberg, 2002). It is especially effective in planning transitions from school to postschool activities (Mount & O'Brien, 2002).

   The MAPs process should involve the required members of multidisciplinary teams, including the student and his or her parents, as well as other family members such as brothers and sisters, the student's peers, and the family's friends. If the student cannot participate, one or more people need to represent the student's interest. The facilitator may be any one of these persons and should lead the participants in brainstorming centered on eight key questions (Turnbull, Turnbull, Erwin, & Soodak, 2006):

1. *What is MAPs?*   At the beginning of the meeting, the facilitator explains the purpose of the process, the type of questions that will be asked, and the general ground rules for open-ended and creative problem solving. The facilitator especially tries to create an upbeat, energized, and relational ambience.

2. *What is your history or story?*   Typically, the student and the student's family share background information, highlighting the triumphs and challenges that have been associated with living his life consistent with his visions, great expectations, strengths, and preferences.

3. *What are your dreams?*   The student shares his great expectations for the future. Family members also share their great expectations. The key aspect of the MAPs process is to identify these great expectations as the basis for planning the customized school schedule and extracurricular activities.

4. *What are your nightmares?*   Because students with exceptionalities and their families often have major fears that block their work toward great expectations, identifying their

nightmares lets everyone know what these fears are so the team can put adequate supports into place. Some fears cannot be prevented, such as those about the progressive course of AIDS in a young child, but sharing them can help everyone know where the student will need support.

5. *Who are you?* The group will use as many adjectives as it takes to avoid the student's exceptionality label and instead describe the student's noncategorical traits.

6. *What are your strengths, gifts, and talents?* Often teachers, friends, family members, and others can lose sight of the fact that the student has strengths on which to build. So the MAPs meeting takes time to identify them.

7. *What do you need?* What will it take to make the student's and family's great expectations come true? What barriers stand in the way? Identifying these needs and barriers lays the foundation for planning for the student to participate in academic, extracurricular, and other school activities.

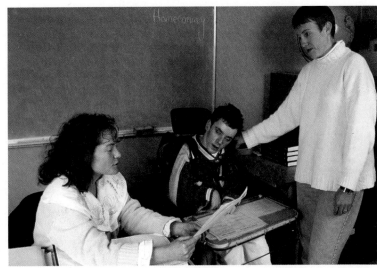

During the MAPS planning process, parents, family, friends, and teachers are involved in discussing the individual's strengths and challenges. What is unique to this process is that the student, himself, is also involved and offers a vital perspective.

8. *What is the plan of action?* A plan of action includes the specific steps that need to happen to accomplish the great expectations. The plan of action should identify the people, tasks, timelines, and resources that will help the student and family realize their expectations.

Naturally, a family's cultural values affect its great expectations and even its willingness to participate in the MAPs process. Box 10–2 points out how some Asian American families might regard the MAPs process.

Determining Supplementary Aids and Services

Supplementary aids and services can consist of support from teachers, paraprofessionals, and peers. **Peer tutoring** involves pairing students one on one so students who have already developed certain skills can help teach those and other skills to less advanced students and also help those students practice the skills they have already mastered. Can peer tutoring, which has worked so effectively for students without disabilities and for students with mild disabilities, also be successful for students with severe and multiple disabilities? Yes.

■ Peer tutors have successfully worked with middle school students in general education classrooms to teach them to record their own performance of skills (Gilberts, Agran, Hughes, & Wehmeyer, 2001).

■ A classwide peer-tutoring program involving middle school students with severe disabilities in inclusive classrooms increased the rates of academic responding and reduced the rates of problem behavior among students with disabilities (McDonnell, Mathot-Buckner, Thorson, & Fister, 2001).

■ Peer tutoring for students with moderate and severe disabilities in inclusive classrooms helped them to understand the tasks their teachers asked them to perform (Collins, Hendricks, Fetko, & Land, 2002).

■ Peer tutoring through cooperative-learning groups helped middle school students with severe disabilities acquire functional academic skills (Wilson, 1999).

Box 10–3 identifies the steps you should follow to implement peer tutoring with students with severe disabilities.

Diversity Tips ~ MAPs—When East Meets West   Box 10–2

You may face an unexpected challenge when you ask families from Vietnam, Korea, or China to engage in the MAPs process. That is because MAPs processes reflect European and American values, which may conflict with the Asian cultural values in several respects (Abery & McBride, 1998):

- Asian families operate on a hierarchical system. Elders, especially fathers, have a great deal of authority to make decisions, and children are expected to be dutiful toward their families. By contrast, MAPs focuses on what the person (in this case, the child) with a disability wants.
- Asian families tend to value the group (family) over the individual. By contrast, MAPs values the individual's preferences and desires. The group is the means for supporting the individual to accomplish his or her preferences.
- Asian families often defer to professionals and their knowledge. In contrast, MAPs asserts that everyone has worthwhile knowledge and expertise.
- Asian families often have a sense of pride in family (and shame related to disability) that may make it difficult for an outside MAPs facilitator to have any role.
- Asian families may tend to have a fatalistic view about disability ("it happened and we can't do anything about it") that may conflict with the MAPs expectation that the person with a disability will be self-determined and fully participate in his or her community.

Given these cultural disagreements, what should you do? These are the best rules of thumb:

- Explain MAPs and self-determination to Asian families and offer them the choice of doing MAPs or not.
- Do not be alarmed if some (perhaps those who have been in the United States for a longer period of time and have a relatively high socioeconomic status) say yes and others (perhaps more recent immigrants who are still not economically established) say no.
- Respect a family's elders and other authority figures (father and mother), and do not be disappointed if the student does not participate much.
- Consider asking for permission to use a translator (if needed), preferably one whom the family chooses. Language barriers can be great.

Self-determination is culturally grounded, and so is MAPs as a means for working toward it. Yet our country includes many cultures, some of which do not share your values and priorities. Because diversity is one of our country's strengths, educators should reinforce that diversity even if doing so means that MAPs is not appropriate for every student and family.

Source: Adapted from Bui, Y., & Turnbull, A. P. (2003). East meets west: Analysis of person-centered planning in the context of Asian American values. *Education and Training in Mental Retardation and Development Disabilities,* 28(1), 18–31.

Relying too much on students without disabilities to support their classmates who do have disabilities might lead to relationships that tend to be one-way rather than reciprocal. Clearly, there is nothing wrong with help; friends often help each other. But help is not and should never be the only basis for friendship. You should be careful not to overemphasize the helper-helpee aspect of a relationship. Unless help is reciprocal, the inherent inequity between tutor and tutee can distort the authenticity of a relationship (Van der Klift & Kunc, 1994). So you will want to find ways for your students to do something for each other, such as giving a compliment or nominating them for a class honor.

Planning for Universal Design for Learning

Many new advances in technology make it possible to include students with severe and multiple disabilities in the general curriculum. One of the exciting new technologies is the handheld personal computer.

Assume you are teaching three high school students with severe disabilities to get jobs in their communities. One student needs to learn how to set the tables in a restaurant or a senior citizens' home; another to wash, dry, and fold laundry in a school or university athletic center; the third to deliver the mail from a central mailroom to the offices of the judges and clerks of court in a county courthouse. Assume you have only one paraprofessional to assist you. How do you teach all three students, especially if they go off campus daily, to learn how to perform their duties?

One way to respond to that challenge is to use a software program called the Visual Assistant. The program operates on handheld computers running the Windows CE operating system. This innovative software, developed by Ablelink, Inc., of Colorado Springs, Colorado, is a "see-it, hear-it, do-it" example of universal design for learning. As you can see in Box 10–4, the Visual Assistant uses the capacity of handheld PCs to import and display digital pictures and to record and play audio messages to present information about tasks a student might be learning. In Chapter 2 we pointed out that universal design for learning modifies how teachers present and represent the curriculum that a student must learn. Using handheld PC technology and

Into Practice ~ Peer Buddies

Box 10-3

Suppose you could accomplish several goals with a single effort? For example, you could effectively integrate the educational programs of students with severe and multiple disabilities into the general curriculum, remove them from their separate and self-contained classrooms for at least one class period a day, help them learn functional academic and employment skills, and increase the number of genuine friendships they have with students who do not have disabilities. Would you be interested in adopting that program in your school? Probably.

What if that same strategy could simultaneously benefit students without disabilities in three or four different ways? Give them academic credit? Teach them how to be good citizens? Still interested? Definitely. After all, this is a win-win proposition for everyone.

The strategy we are talking about is called peer buddies, and it was designed by researchers at Vanderbilt University to promote social relationships among students with severe disabilities and their same-age peers without disabilities. In Nashville, Tennessee's, large urban school district, 9 of 11 comprehensive high schools paired 200 students with severe disabilities with 115 students who had no disabilities. The program was a great success (Hughes et al., 2001).

How does the peer buddies strategy work? Pretty simply, really, as these steps show:

Step 1: Introduce a 1-credit course. Many high schools already require their students to engage in some sort of service learning. The peer buddies model fulfills the requirements for service learning.

Step 2: Recruit peer buddies. Recruit students who hold high-status roles to serve as peer buddies—student government leaders, sport and cheerleading standouts, and high academic performers. These high-status students add credibility to the program process.

Step 3: Establish a screening process. Peer buddies must be responsible and reliable students, such as those who have a good attendance record and have shown they can juggle

extracurricular activities and academic demands. Once an initial screening has been completed, allow a potential peer buddy to observe existing peer buddy activities and allow him or her to ask questions to get a better idea about the purpose of the activities.

Step 4: Train the students. Topics include people-first language and disability awareness, effective communication strategies, sample activities in which to engage with students with severe disabilities, and how to deal with inappropriate behavior in an effective but respectful way.

Step 5: Establish expectations and evaluate progress. Observe peer buddies, provide feedback and reinforcement on their interactions, and answer questions. Establish regularly scheduled times for the peer buddies to meet and to discuss what worked for them and what did not. This is also a good venue to teach peer buddies skills related to time management and organizational and scheduling strategies.

Putting These Ideas to Work for Progress in the General Curriculum

1. What do you see as the benefits of participating in a peer buddies program for students with and without disabilities?

2. Peer buddies was set up at the high school level. Do you think the program could be adapted to the elementary level? If so, what changes would you recommend for using this program with younger children?

3. What might be some comfort and knowledge concerns of students without disabilities when interacting with the student and teachers you met in the vignette?

To answer these questions online, go to the Into Practice module in Chapter 10 of the Companion Website, www.prenhall.com/turnbull.

To learn more about Vanderbilt University's peer buddies model, go to our Companion Website, www.prenhall.com/turnbull, and link to the peer buddies website, http://www.transitionlink.com/index.htm.

---

software programs like Visual Assistant, teachers can import and display digital pictures that are individualized, like pictures of the student performing each step in a learning task, and can also play digital video clips.

Handheld PCs are ideal for introducing universally designed learning features into instruction. They are unobtrusive; fit into a pursue, a backpack, a waist pack, or the pockets of cargo pants; and unlike desktop computers, are very portable. Instead of using less accessible input modes, such as a keyboard, handheld computers operate by a touch screen. Moreover, other devices, including digital cameras and global positioning satellite devices, can be inserted into the handheld computer. Some researchers are even developing handheld PC programs that use global positioning systems data to help people with cognitive disabilities use public buses equipped with transmitters.

Research with the Visual Assistant has shown that students with severe disabilities can learn to do their jobs faster and with fewer errors and prompts from teachers or coaches than if they were doing the same work under the same conditions without a teacher or coach (Davies, Stock, & Wehmeyer, 2002a, 2002b; Riffel et al., in press). Now consider the possibilities for promoting a student's access to the general curriculum by using the Visual Assistant. In essence, the Visual Assistant is a multimedia version of a well-researched curriculum modification strategy—picture

To learn more about the Visual Assistant and other technologies that enable people with disabilities to experience greater independence, go to our Companion Website, *www.prenhall.com/turnbull*, and link to the AbleLink Technologies website, *http://www.ablelink-tech.com*.

Technology Tips ~ Visual Assistant: The See-It, Hear-It, Do-It Handheld Portable Prompter

Box 10–4

Pocket Compass—an instructional media task prompting system from AbleLink Technologies.

The Visual Assistant provides powerful task-prompting support by including digital pictures along with custom-recorded audio messages to provide step-by-step instructional support for students with intellectual and other disabilities. This allows educators to set up instructional tasks by recording instructions and incorporating pictures of each step—preferably of the student performing the step in the real-world environment—to provide multimodal cues for task completion. The Visual Assistant is ideal for more complex or detailed tasks where the addition of a picture can increase student accuracy. Its setup and use are simple and take into account principles of universal design and cognitive accessibility.

When the student initiates the Visual Assistant program by double-clicking (e.g., tapping twice using a stylus pen) on the Visual Assistant icon on the screen, the software opens to a screen showing all the tasks set up for the person. Those tasks are depicted using an icon or a picture that represents the task.

So, for example, if Dan, a student with severe disabilities, wants to use the Visual Assistant to make coffee, he taps on the icon with the picture of the coffee maker. That action, in turn, opens a screen with a larger picture of the coffee maker and initiates an audio message saying, "Dan, if you want to make a pot of coffee, tap on the *Next* button."

When Dan taps on the *Next* button, it opens another screen, which has a picture of the first step in the coffee-making process and two buttons, one that reads *Play* and one that reads *Done*. Dan's teacher has already taught Dan to press the *Play* button when he sees it, and when Dan does so, an audio message in the teacher's own voice says, "First, fill the glass coffee pitcher with water up to the 10-cup line."

Dan can play that message as often as he needs. If Dan needs more assistance, the picture of the pitcher can be closer or there can be more steps depicted, such as a picture of Dan himself filling the coffee pitcher at the sink.

When Dan completes the task depicted in the picture and described in the audio message, he presses the *Done* button. Tapping on that button takes him to the next screen, with a picture of the next step in the process and the *Play* and *Done* button.

So as you can see, the Visual Assistant is a "see it" (the visual image), "hear it" (the spoken voice), "do it" (the job being done and then finished) universally designed device!

Note: Images reproduced with permission of AbleLink Technologies © 2005. All Rights Reserved.

Visual Assistant—an instructional media task prompting system from AbleLink Technologies.

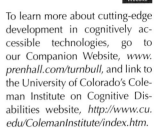

prompts—that uses pictures, graphics, or symbols prompting students to complete a multistep task. Those strategies help teach students to direct their own learning and are as appropriate for teaching math or reading as for teaching functional content.

Planning for Other Educational Needs

You have already learned that students with severe and multiple disabilities have limitations in communication. Everyone relies on communication for many important things, from learning to making friends. Fortunately, one form of assistive technology, **augmentative and alternative communication (AAC),** enables students who cannot communicate verbally or through other formats, such as sign language, to do so through technology. You learned a little about AAC in Chapter 6, but because those devices are so important for students with severe disabilities, it's worth learning more about them here.

AAC refers to the devices, techniques, and strategies used by students who are unable to communicate fully through natural speech and/or writing (Schlosser, 2003). AAC frequently involves the use of technology in the form of voice-output communication aids and synthesized speech, but it may also include a wide array of options for communication, from low-tech message boards, symbols, pictures, and visual prompts to very complex technology (Wehmeyer et al., 2004). The goal of AAC is to enable students to experience all the social, emotional, academic, recreational, and employment benefits that accrue from communication.

Like other forms of assistive and educational technology, AAC devices are supplementary aids and services. When making decisions about appropriate AAC devices, IEP teams need to identify those features that best meet the student's needs. AAC devices have four key features: symbols, displays, selection options, and output modes (Burstein, Wright-Drechsel, & Wood, 1998).

Symbols. Symbols represent meanings. Three forms of assistive technology use symbolic communication (Bigge, Best, & Heller, 2001; Heller, 2000):

- Non-electronic devices, such as communication boards and communication notebooks (see Figure 10–3)

- Dedicated communication devices specifically designed for communication

- Computer systems (not special devices)

Each form enables students to communicate through symbols such as drawings, photographs, letters, words, or a combination of them.

Displays. AAC devices have either fixed or dynamic displays. A fixed display offers an unchanging symbol arrangement. The pictures on the communication board in Figure 10–3 show a fixed display; all of these pictures remain the same. By contrast, dynamic displays enable students to make choices by changing the display on the computer screen. Figure 10–4 features DynaVox DV4, one of the most powerful and flexible AAC devices available.

DynaVox DV4 uses a touch-screen display that progresses (thus, is dynamic) through a natural process of forming and sending messages. The display has an extensive vocabulary. Students can have access to it by touching the screen or using a mouse. The display also includes preprogrammed communication pages suitable for individuals of all ages and a word-prediction dictionary of more than 100,000 word forms that enables individuals to create long messages quickly by offering a sequence of logical words.

Selection options. AAC devices typically offer two major types of selection options: scanning or direct selection. Scanning is suitable for the student who has extensive motor loss. Scanning involves pointing or

To learn more about cutting-edge development in cognitively accessible technologies, go to our Companion Website, *www. prenhall.com/turnbull,* and link to the University of Colorado's Coleman Institute on Cognitive Disabilities website, *http://www.cu. edu/ColemanInstitute/index.htm.*

Thanks, in part, to her inclusion in an integrated program, Sierra is on her way to becoming the self-governed and independent person that her future offers.

Figure 10–3   A communication board: Example of a fixed display

Figure 10–4   The DynaVox DV4: Example of a dynamic AAC System

Source: Photo reprinted with permission of DynaVox Technologies, Pittsburgh, PA (800-344-1778).

PRAXIS

Standard: Developing your competence related to AAC is a way to address PRAXIS™ Standard 3, Delivery of Services to Students with Disabilities.

using a cursor to scan an item at a time, a row of items, or a block of items. Many different options are available for scanning, and each can be tailored to the needs and preferences of a student (Glennen & DeCoste, 1997; Quist & Lloyd, 1997). The options allow the student to point to a symbol or word without having any physical contact, such as by looking at the symbol, using light pointers, or using head- or mouth-controlled pointers, touching or pressing the symbol or word, or using speech recognition, which is a computer program that understands user vocalizations and converts them into keyboard input (Quist & Lloyd, 1997, p. 112).

Output. The fourth AAC feature is output. Output options are either intrinsic (low tech) or extrinsic (high tech) (Burstein et al., 1998). Intrinsic output occurs when, for example, a student points to the letters on a non-electronic alphabet board and the student's communication partner observes each letter and then puts the letters together to understand the message. Alternatively, extrinsic output uses voice (such as DynaVox DV4) or print as extrinsic output modes.

The IEP team needs to include and work closely with speech and language pathologists in the design of AAC and instructional areas pertaining to AAC. As you have learned, instruction related to AAC is complex. Students will need to learn how to use the device in different communicative situations and with different partners and also how to care for the equipment. In addition, students must learn some of the basics of communication, whether you are using a device or communicating verbally. Those include how to maintain and sustain conversations (turn taking or showing interest in others) or when to use different kinds of messages (keeping secrets or telling jokes). Designing AAC to promote progress in the general curriculum is more than just buying a device; it involves thoughtful planning and effective instruction.

USING EFFECTIVE INSTRUCTIONAL STRATEGIES

Early Childhood Students: The Circle of Inclusion Model

Some people have long believed that students with severe and multiple disabilities should be in separate special programs, those in which they have no typically developing peers. But research suggests a different conclusion.

Researchers at the University of Kansas have developed and demonstrated a model for including infants, toddlers, and preschoolers with severe and multiple disabilities in typical programs (Thompson, Wegner, Wickham, & Ault, 1993; Thompson et al., 1991; Thompson, Wickham, Wegner, & Ault, 1996). Called the Circle of Inclusion, the model has been implemented in more than 20 preschool classrooms within 12 different early childhood programs (including two Head Start programs) and 10 K–3 programs. More than 600 typically developing children and 35 children with severe and multiple disabilities have participated in the program, including Sierra, whom you met in the vignette. What makes the Circle of Inclusion effective? Not surprisingly, there are many factors:

- A values-based commitment to including children with severe disabilities in programs available to typically developing children, not a "fix-up-the-child" approach that requires the child to meet certain developmental milestones before being "rewarded" with an inclusive placement
- Friendships between young children with and without disabilities
- Collaboration among all parents and professionals
- Development of children's choice-making skills
- Use of the MAPs process
- Ongoing evaluation of how to make inclusion work
- Commitment to child-initiated, child-centered education grounded in developmentally appropriate practice

The Circle of Inclusion model is more than a set of values, however; it incorporates a number of best practices:

- *Using facilitative and natural child-positioning procedures.* Position the child in as natural a position as possible, using a number of approaches, including support from an adult's body, modified furniture, or pillows and wedges.

- *Providing opportunities to use real materials within the context of meaningful applications.* Have the children use real materials, such as Sierra's picture book, and let them experience the natural consequences of their behaviors.

- *Encouraging cooperation and helpful interactions among peers and employing the principle of partial participation.* Apply the principle of **partial participation,** supporting children to take those actions they can do even when they cannot do everything that their nondisabled peers can do.

- *Using multiple instructional grouping strategies.* Vary the instructional arrangements according to the demands of the task, using small groups, cooperative learning groups, and one-to-one instruction as appropriate.

- *Embedding learning objectives for young children with disabilities within typical learning tasks.* Because most objectives important to young children with disabilities can be embedded into typical learning tasks, encourage a child with a disability to work on gross- or fine-motor objectives during a typical social play period, or work on a communication-related objective during a language arts/reading activity.

Ten years of research reveals that the implementation of the strategies within the model "offers a more desirable social and communicative environment for children with significant disabilities [than does a special education–only preschool] . . . and can match a high-quality special education program on environmental adaptations" (Thompson et al., 1996, p. 38). Students with severe and multiple disabilities learn to be part of the natural environment, just as IDEA's Part C requires, or of general education, as IDEA's Part B requires and as Sierra's teachers have made possible, with her parents' support.

To learn more about the Circle of Inclusion model, go to our Companion Website, *www. prenhall.com/ turnbull,* and link to the Circle of Inclusion website, *http://circleofinclusion.org.*

Elementary and Middle School Students: The Partial Participation Principle

Several principles govern the education of students with severe disabilities. The first is the principle of maximum participation (Baumgart et al., 1982), which asserts the right of students with severe disabilities to participate to the maximum degree possible in activities that contribute to their quality of life. The goal of the principle of maximum participation is to maximize participation in one's life.

A related principle is that of partial participation (Baumgart et al., 1982; Ferguson & Baumgart, 1991), which holds that students with severe and multiple disabilities should not be denied all access to general education and other inclusive activities solely because of their intellectual, adaptive skill, motor, sensory, and/or communication impairments (Snell & Brown, 2006). The principle rejects an all-or-none approach under which students either function independently in a given environment or not at all. Instead, it asserts that students with severe and multiple disabilities can participate, even if only partially, and indeed can often learn and complete a task if it is adapted to their strengths. Under the partial participation principle, "students are never denied access to preferred or meaningful activities because they lack the skills for complete independent participation" (Bambara, Browder, & Koger, 2006), so teachers should ask themselves three questions to implement partial participation:

- What noninstructional supports does the student need for meaningful participation?

- How much does the student wish to participate?

- How can teachers enhance the student's independence, especially partial independence?

Once you have answered these questions, you need to determine what parts of a task a student can do, observing the student performing a task and using observational methods like those discussed in the next section to determine what the student can do or can learn to do.

A frequently used and highly effective means for determining what tasks a student can perform is to conduct a task analysis. A task analysis identifies the individual steps that, when chained together, are required to perform a skill or activity. According to Snell and Brown (2006), a task analysis follows these steps:

1. Define the target skill or task.

2. Perform the task yourself and observe the student's peers performing the task, while noting the steps involved.

3. Identify the component or constituent parts or steps in the activity.

4. Write these parts or steps on a data collection form so that each is
   - Stated in terms of observable behavior
   - Ordered in a logical sequence
   - Written in second-person singular so it can serve as a verbal prompt (if used)

5. Observe the student performing the task and identify steps that he or she can or will be able to
   - Perform independently
   - Learn to perform
   - Use technology or other supports to perform if needed

Secondary and Transition Students: Student-Directed Learning Strategies

Consider this question and answer it: "If students were floated in life jackets for 12 years, would they be expected to swim if the jackets were suddenly jerked away?" (Martin, Marshall, Maxon, & Jerman, 1993, p. 4). The obvious answer is "of course not." Students would sink without specific instruction on how to swim. Being dependent on a life jacket does not ensure success once the life jacket is removed. Unfortunately, "the situation is similar for students receiving special education services. All too often these students are not taught how to self-manage their own lives before they are thrust into the cold water of post-school reality" (Martin et al., 1993, p. 4).

To reverse this situation, you can begin by using **student-directed learning strategies.** These strategies teach students with and without disabilities to modify and regulate their own learning (Agran, King-Sears, Wehmeyer, & Copeland, 2003). The educational supports that teachers use to implement the self-determined learning model of instruction (Chapter 9) include many student-directed learning strategies, but three are particularly important for students with severe disabilities: picture prompts or antecedent cue regulation, self-instruction, and self-monitoring.

Picture prompts or antecedent cue regulation strategies. You learned a little about these strategies when you learned about the Visual Assistant software program earlier in the chapter. This software provides visual and audio prompts for students to successfully complete multistep tasks. The antecedent cue regulation strategy involves a similar approach: providing visual and/or audio cues to support students to regulate their own behavior and to complete assigned tasks. The visual cues include photographs, drawings and illustrations, video clips, and even actual items involved in the task. Audio cues involve recorded instructions or directions on a tape, CD-ROM, or MP3 player. Technology platforms such as desktop or handheld computers provide both video and audio cues, just as the Visual Assistant software does.

Given the potential for multimedia devices to present cues in multiple formats, the term *antecedent cue regulation* is preferable to picture prompts; many cues are not visually oriented. *Antecedent* simply means "occuring before," so *antecedent cue regulation* simply means giving visual or auditory cues before a task to help the student regulate his or her own behavior.

Antecedent cue regulation has many benefits. First, it reduces your students' reliance on others to complete a task. Second, it supports those who cannot remember the steps or sequence in a multistep task. Antecedent cue regulation can also be a temporary support, not a permanent one. As a temporary strategy, it promotes learning.

The strategy is effective for students with severe and multiple disabilities. For example, Hughes and colleagues (2000) combined a peer-tutoring strategy with an antecedent cue regulation strategy and an augmentative communication strategy to improve social interactions among high school students with severe disabilities and their nondisabled peers. Peer tutors were taught how to support students with severe disabilities to use a picture communication book (an augmentative strategy) to initiate conversations with peers without disabilities. The strategy improved the number and quality of social interactions for students with severe disabilities.

Self-instruction strategies. **Self-instruction strategies** involve teaching students to use their own verbal or other communication skills to direct their own learning. Like the antecedent cue regulation strategies, students use self-instructions as cues to what they need to do next to perform the task. Self-instruction strategies are often even more flexible than antecedent cue regulation strategies because students use something they have with them at all times—their means of communicating (Agran et al., 2003). Several research-based templates for self-instruction exist, including the following (Agran et al., 2003):

- The traditional problem-solving self-instruction, in which students learn to verbally instruct themselves to identify the "problem" (What do I do next in this task?), identify a solution to the problem (I place the silverware in the napkin), evaluate the effectiveness of the solution (Does this look right?), and reinforce themselves (Yes, that looks good!)

- The task sequencing or "did-next-now" strategy, in which students learn self-instruction statements related to the step they just completed (I placed the silverware in the napkin), the next step (I need to roll the silverware in the napkin), and when they will perform the next step (I'll do the next step now)

- The "what-where" strategy, in which students learn statements about what they need to do (I need to roll the silverware in the napkin) and where they will do it (I roll the silverware in the napkin at my workstation in the restaurant), which helps them remember the context in which they engage in certain activities

- The interactive or "did-next-ask" strategy, in which students learn self-instruction statements similar to the task-sequencing strategy but complete the statement by instructing themselves to ask someone about the next step or about some aspect of the task (it is helpful to teach this in conjunction with the task-sequencing strategy in case students forget the next step)

Self-monitoring strategies. One of the most widely evaluated and effective student-directed learning strategies involves teaching students to monitor their own behavior or actions. Essentially, when using **self-monitoring strategies,** students learn to collect data on their progress toward educational goals. They can do this through traditional formats, such as charting their progress on a sheet of graph paper or completing a checklist. For students with severe and multiple disabilities, however, there are simpler ways to monitor themselves. They can place a marble in a jar each time they complete a task successfully or move a poker chip from one container to another. Once they fill the jar or move all of the chips from the original box, they learn that they have completed their specific goals. Agran and colleagues (2003) have provided these suggestions for implementing self-monitoring strategies:

- Implement self-monitoring strategies after the student has already learned to do the task that is being monitored.

- Teach the self-monitoring strategy to the student before implementing the strategy.

- Build in checks to determine the accuracy of the student's self-monitoring. Even when students are not entirely accurate, however, there are benefits to the use of self-monitoring.

Figure 10-5 Educational placement of students with multiple disabilities (2003–2004)

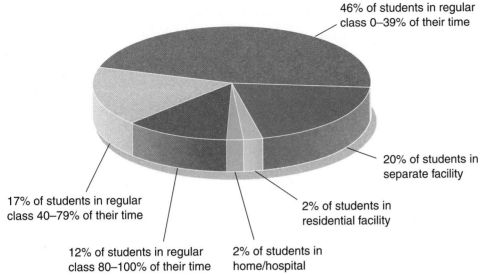

46% of students in regular
class 0–39% of their time

20% of students in
separate facility

17% of students in regular
class 40–79% of their time

2% of students in
residential facility

12% of students in regular
class 80–100% of their time

2% of students in
home/hospital

Source: U.S. Department of Education, Office of Special Education Programs. (2005). *IDEA data website* (http://www.ideadata.org/aboutThisSite.asp).

INCLUDING STUDENTS WITH SEVERE AND MULTIPLE DISABILITIES

Leaders in the field of severe and multiple disabilities have almost always advocated for inclusive education (Doyle, 2002; Kennedy & Fisher, 2001; Snell & Brown, 2006; Thousand, Villa, & Nevin, 2002). Indeed, the major professional organization in the field of severe and multiple disabilities, TASH (formerly, The Association for Persons with Severe Handicaps), has had a long-term commitment to inclusive education. Nevertheless, Figure 10–5 shows that most students with multiple disabilities still spend most of their time outside the regular classroom.

Advocacy alone does not ensure inclusion. Research into evidence-based practices is also necessary. There is now convincing evidence that students with severe disabilities can be successfully included in the general education classroom as well as extracurricular and other school activities (Ryndak & Fisher, 2003). As Sailor (2002) noted with regard to the "impressive amounts of published research" that has demonstrated that inclusion is feasible and beneficial, "after nearly two decades of special education efforts at policy reform in the direction of inclusive education, the corner has finally been turned and the question has shifted from 'should we do it?' to 'how do we do it?'" (p. 8).

A comprehensive synthesis of research studies on the inclusion of students with severe disabilities identified five strategies for inclusion (Hunt & Goetz, 1997):

- Collaborating among teachers and parents at classroom, building, and systems levels, as Sierra's teachers and parents do
- Teaching new skills in general education classrooms, as Kreg and Maureen do to Sierra
- Promoting friendships in inclusive settings, as Sierra is finding them in her classroom
- Facilitating positive outcomes for classmates without disabilities
- Adapting the students' curriculum (Wolfe & Hall, 2003), as Kreg and Maureen adapt Sierra's to her needs for sleep, her difficulty in holding a pencil, and her behavioral challenges (through the picture book)

Box 10–5 offers tips for promoting inclusion.

Given that educators know how to include students with severe disabilities, why do more than half of all students with severe and multiple disabilities spend most or all of their time outside the

Visit our Companion Website, *www.prenhall.com/turnbull*, to find a link to the TASH website, where you can read TASH's position statements on topics such as inclusive education and integrated employment (*www.tash.org*).

PRAXIS

Standard: Including students with severe and multiple disabilities is a way to enhance societal acceptance of these students in inclusive community settings after they graduate. Addressing societal attitudes ties to PRAXIS™ Standard 2, Legal and Societal Issues.

Inclusion Tips   Box 10–5

	What You Might See	**What You Might Be Tempted to Do**	**Alternate Responses**	**Ways to Include Peers in the Process**
Behavior	She may have temper tantrums and hit herself or others.	Discipline and isolate her from the rest of the class.	Learn to identify cues that trigger positive behavior. Reward appropriate behavior.	Support the peers closest to her and teach them to recognize and give cues that encourage positive behavior in a way that is respectful of her.
Social interactions	She is unable to communicate needs or wants using words.	Allow her to remain a class observer rather than a participant.	Use assistive technology to enable her to communicate her needs and wants.	Teach peers to communicate with her using her assistive technology.
Educational performance	He is not able to read or write, and his functional skills are extremely limited.	Give up and let him color or do something quiet.	Create opportunities for him to benefit from peer tutoring.	Arrange for peers to assist him with follow-through on task completion. Support them to be friends as well as peer tutors.
Classroom attitudes	He may appear bored or unresponsive and may sleep during class instruction.	Ignore him and focus on other, more attentive students.	Use times of alertness to teach self-instruction strategies to enable him to engage in more proactive learning.	Encourage peers to prompt him to use his preferred self-instruction strategies.

Values: Highly competent teachers, such as you can be, can provide their students with opportunities to be included in the general curriculum and to be *full citizens* in their schools and communities.

general education classroom? There are many reasons. Particularly at the high school level, many teachers still believe that students with severe disabilities cannot be appropriately served in general education classes or even in their neighborhood schools (Smith, 2000). Other teachers believe they are not prepared to teach students with severe and multiple disabilities (Smith, 2000). As you learned in Chapter 2, the better trained a teacher is, the more likely it is that teacher will support inclusion (Soodak et al., 2002). By contrast, the less well prepared teachers are, the less likely they are to support inclusion. Unfortunately, many parents also believe that general educators are not well prepared for inclusion (Palmer, Fuller, Arora, & Nelson, 2001). A survey of approximately 500 parents revealed that most of them believe that the nature of their child's disability is too severe and would overwhelm general education teachers; they are concerned about the mismatch between their child's needs in the general education curriculum, the lack of appropriate services, and peers' acceptance of their child (Palmer et al., 2001)

Yet there are effective practices that support students with severe disabilities in the general education classroom. (We highlight several of them in this chapter.) Furthermore, the emphasis that IDEA and NCLB place on all students and their progress in the general curriculum may encourage schools to change (Browder et al., 2006). And parents have reported that the primary benefit of inclusion is that their child has a greater chance to learn more academic and functional skills in general education classes because there are higher expectations in those classes than in special education classrooms (Palmer et al., 2001).

The key to successful inclusion for all students, especially students with severe and multiple disabilities, is partnerships among educators, families, and students. Box 10–6 describes how partnerships created inclusive supports and services at Whittier High School in Los Angeles County.

Partnership Tips ~ Facilitating Inclusion for Students with Severe and Multiple Disabilities
Box 10—6

A good example of how inclusion for students with severe disabilities can work exists at Whittier High School in southeastern Los Angeles County. This high school serves more than 2,000 students in grades 9 through 12, 84 percent of whom are Latino, 36 percent of whom participate in the free or reduced lunch program, and 19 percent of whom have limited ability to speak English.

In the mid-1990s, conscious that approximately 30 percent of its students were dropping out before graduating and that only 10 to 15 percent of its graduates went to 4-year colleges, and intent on implementing state-of-the-art inclusive practices, faculty members, staff, administration, parents, and community leaders adopted a mission statement that promotes academic excellence, respect for self and others, acceptance of the diversity of students' abilities and culture, involvement of all students in all aspects of the school, and a commitment that all students will reach their full potential. "All means all" at Whittier, including students with severe and multiple disabilities.

To improve the performance of students with disabilities as well as those not performing at grade level but not classified as having disabilities, students and faculty were divided into three teams at each grade level. Students remain in their team during their 9th- and 10th-grade years. Each team consists of the following:

- Eight to 10 core curriculum/general education teachers certified in math, science, social studies, and English
- Two support teachers certified in special education
- An administrator
- A school counselor

The teams share a common preparation period, their classes are located near each other, all teachers are responsible for teaching all students, and the teams provide seven different levels of support for the students in each team. These levels of support enable the teams to individualize their instruction without having to pull out students from the classroom. The levels begin with total staff support (nearly a one-to-one approach), range through daily in-class staff support and team teaching, and end in consultation (the least amount of support).

This tiered approach relies on the talents of each teacher and on the talents of the team as a whole. It also benefits students who receive special education services (including students with severe and multiple disabilities), students who have not qualified for special education services but are at risk of school failure, and students who have succeeded in traditional school systems. Whittier students do not carry special education labels; the support teachers are not called special education teachers; and the staff, by adopting this noncategorical approach, has discarded the idea that only specialists can work with students with disabilities. The result of these many changes is that Whittier High School has developed a community of learners that supports all students. Does it actually work? Yes. José, a student with severe and multiple disabilities, uses a wheelchair; his friends make sure he is wheeled from class to class each day. José works on recognizing numbers while most of his classmates study algebra. When it comes time for his math team to present its answer to an algebra problem, he writes the numbers (with help from his peers) on a poster using the lap tray attached to the front of his wheelchair as a desk (Eshilian et al., 2000; Falvey, Eshilian, & Hibbard, 2000; Thousand, Rosenberg, Bishop, & Villa, 1997). So including students with severe disabilities is possible; the data and the Whittier example show that to be the case.

Putting These Ideas to Work for Progress in the General Curriculum

1. From this description of partnerships at Whittier High School, extract a list of tips that you can follow in your own work to foster partnerships.

2. What impresses you most about the Whittier High School partnership practices?

3. What do you believe are two or three of the most important skills that you need to learn in order to be an effective partner at inclusive schools?

To answer these questions online, go to the Partnership Tips module in Chapter 10 of the Companion Website, www.prenhall.com/turnbull.

ASSESSING STUDENTS' PROGRESS

Measuring Students' Progress

Progress in the general curriculum. Many students with severe or multiple disabilities are unable to take typical paper-pencil assessments that measure their progress in core curriculum areas. Others cannot perform the tests even with accommodations. Furthermore, the curriculum-based measurement techniques that we discussed in Chapter 5 have not been validated with students with severe or multiple disabilities. So how can educators track those students' progress in the general curriculum? They can do so by using two strategies that resemble curriculum-based measurement techniques and that have been well developed for students with severe and multiple disabilities. We discussed one of them, data-based decision making, in Chapter 9. The second strategy is portfolio-based assessment (Kleinert & Kearns, 2001). Portfolio-based assessment also can be used for a student's alternate assessment, as we will point out later in this chapter.

Portfolio-based assessment requires teachers to accumulate permanent products that exemplify the student's work. These products are direct indicators of student performance, do not require continuous observation, as do the observational methodologies we discuss later, and allow for ongoing analysis (**formative analysis**) and comparisons between less and more mature products (**summative evaluation**) (Brown & Snell, 2006).

Portfolios should include a range of products that reflect a student's progress, including the data-based and performance data that we discussed in Chapter 9, graphs of student progress, student, peer, and parent reflections, student products, and video or audiotapes of a student's work (Kearns, Burdge, & Kleinert, 2006). Three portfolios foster greater independence and self-evaluation skills for students with disabilities (Duffy, Jones, & Thomas, 1999): the "everything portfolio," which is a broad compilation of the student's work across multiple subjects; the "product portfolio," in which products are specific to a topic or class/teacher; and the "showcase portfolio," which contains examples of the best of the student's work.

Values: By involving students with disabilities in identifying products for a portfolio and evaluating the portfolio, teachers can promote skills that lead to greater *choice* and *self-determination*.

Progress in addressing other educational needs. While evaluating student work in academic content areas often results in products and thus lends itself to portfolio assessment procedures, many areas of instruction, particularly those that fall outside the realm of core content areas, do not yield permanent products. For example, many students with severe disabilities engage in repetitive, stereotyped motor behaviors, and the reduction or elimination of those behaviors is an important part of the students' individualized educational programs. The only way to measure progress in reducing or eliminating these behaviors is to observe a student's behavior and record data about it. In this way, teachers can compile evidence of the student's involvement and progress in the general curriculum and in other school settings as well.

Observational methodologies are just what their names imply: ways of collecting data by watching or observing student behavior. Teachers can carry out these observations by watching the student (live observation) or by coding videotapes made of the student. Live observational methods include field observations, time sampling, and event recording. **Field observations** involve simply observing and recording, in a longhand, anecdotal format, what the student is doing. Those anecdotal records are often the first step in collecting observational data because they identify the specific behaviors or events that warrant more systematic observation.

Time sampling and event recording enable teachers to collect samples of a student's behavior. It is almost impossible to observe across the entire school day, so these two strategies are especially useful to you.

When **time sampling,** an observer records the occurrence or nonoccurrence of specific behaviors during short, predetermined intervals. For example, if a teacher wants to know whether a particular intervention reduces a student's stereotyped behavior, she may set up three 10-minute observation times daily. She selects those times randomly or chooses the times when the student's behavior is most likely to occur. During the observation, the teacher has a list of behaviors in which the student might be engaged, including the stereotyped behavior. During each 10-minute observation period, she observes for 20 seconds and then spends 10 seconds checking which of the behaviors occurred any time during the 20-second period. The entire 10-minute session yields data for 20 unique 20-second observation intervals, and the teacher will count the number of intervals in which the stereotyped behavior occurred and then tally those frequencies across time as more 10-minute observations occur. By contrast, when an observer is using **event recording,** he records every occurrence of a behavior during an observation period instead of using the yes/no recording per interval that is characteristic of time sampling.

Both methods are useful, and the one you use depends upon the behavior that you are counting. For example, some students with severe disabilities have small, hardly noticeable seizures, called **absence seizures,** which may occur every 2 to 5 seconds. Obviously, it would be difficult to observe for 10 minutes and reliably count every such seizure. Similarly, some behavior episodes, such as a temper tantrum, may last 5 to 10 minutes. Recording the frequency of one tantrum during a 10-minute observation is not very helpful: one tantrum is just that—a single tantrum.

Now consider the types of data collected through observational methods. Frequency counts involve literal counts of the number of times a behavior occurred or the number of intervals in which a behavior occurred. Frequency counts of intervals can be converted to percentage data by dividing the frequency of intervals in which a behavior occurred by the total number of intervals during which observations occurred. With event recording, frequency counts cannot be converted to percentage data, but they can be converted to rate data—namely, an average of the frequency over a specific period of time.

Another measure involves collecting duration data. This method requires a teacher to use a stopwatch or timer to record the length of a behavioral event. Still another measure involves collecting latency data, the time that lapses from one point to another—typically, the lapsed time between a direction or instruction and the student's response.

Most teachers who rely on observational methods collect data by using all or most of these methods and collecting all or most of these types of data. They do so because collecting observational data is inexpensive and provides detailed information about students' performance.

Making Accommodations for Assessment

Many students with disabilities receive accommodations in assessments and testing through the means we have already discussed. Many students with severe and multiple disabilities, however, will not be able to take state accountability assessments, even with accommodations. In Chapter 2, you learned that IDEA allows states to create alternate assessments for use with students with the most significant cognitive disabilities or other students who are identified by IEP teams as unable to take the regular assessment even with accommodations.

Alternate assessments must be aligned with the state's academic content standards. They serve the same purpose as the typical accountability assessment—namely, to determine how well a student has mastered content that is aligned with standards. As we noted in Chapter 2, the No Child Left Behind Act allows states to develop alternate student achievement standards, and increasingly alternate assessments are being aligned with those alternate achievement standards. Researchers at the National Center on Educational Outcomes (Quenemoen, Thompson, & Thurlow, 2003) have identified several other formats for alternative assessments:

- *IEP-linked body of evidence.* Teachers collect student products, similar to portfolio assessment, but link them to IEP goals and objectives.

- *Performance assessment.* Teachers use the data-based measurement techniques described in Chapter 9.

- *Checklist.* Teachers identify a student's skills and abilities on a checklist.

- *Portfolio-based alternate assessment.* Teachers rely on samples of student products that are related to a state's standards. Educators score these portfolios by relying on rubrics that "identify the quality and quantify a student's performance and their level of independence in demonstrating the academic skills linked to the state's standards" (Snell & Brown, 2006, p. 83).

Alternate assessment also relies on scoring criteria. Scoring criteria "are specific definitions of what a score means and how specific student responses are to be evaluated" (Quenemoen et al., 2003). Educators who are scoring a portfolio must have examples of high-quality work so that they will be able to distinguish high-quality from poor-quality portfolios. Many states are still struggling with developing alternate assessments that are genuinely comparable with other state accountability procedures, but it is clear that this is the goal under federal law.

Looking to Sierra's Future

By what name shall we call Sierra? Sierra the rarity? Yes. Sierra the paradox? Yes. Sierra the included? Yes. Sierra the sponge, soaking up pictures, books, computer games and toys, and adults' attention and affection? Yes. Sierra the well behaved and self-governed? Not Yet. Sierra the independent? Not yet.

All children are partially finished; education is one way of adding more finish to them. But Sierra will be an especially unfinished product for a long time to come. That's just the way it is with children with severe and multiple disabilities. Parts of them will develop more rapidly than others; parts will not develop much at all. Sierra is developing some of her parts—behavior, mainly. But then there's self-care and communication in a broader sense than changing her behaviors in order to communicate.

But however important these aspects of any child are, and they are very important aspects of Sierra's future, there are aspects of Sierra's life that transcend these immediate ones. Kreg captures one of them when he tells why he, Maureen, and Bea so strongly objected to Sierra's placement in the self-contained, separate, intensive-supports program and why they advocated so fiercely to keep her at Corrales School in an integrated program.

Despite, Kreg said, the daily grind of facing her behaviors, of going beyond a shared philosophy in favor of inclusion to its practice with Maureen, and of advocacy against segregation, Kreg sees Sierra as an always-included student. Why? Because, as he puts it, "Peer modeling is so crucial for teaching."

That's right: simply being in a place with nondisabled peers and learning from them advances Sierra's life prospects. It's not always about Sierra and Sierra alone. Her life depends on how others respond to her.

And what are those life prospects? David wants her to "keep up with her peers," and recognizes that, if she does, that in itself will be a "great accomplishment." Acknowledging that "keeping up" is just a buzz phrase for what he really sees in Sierra's future, David fixes on the word "independence."

"Independence. A skill, giving her some type of a skill that she can perform for the rest of her life and hopefully be independent. Maybe. Maybe not."

And why not? Sierra and her parents and teachers have already proved that her rarity and all the paradoxes involved in her life are just aspects of her life. They do not necessarily limit her. They do not necessarily liberate her. They just "are"—facets and facts that, under effective teachers, can assure Sierra's independence.

A job? Living on her own? Yes. With help, of course. But yes. It is possible. Indeed, it is likely. Not just because of her parents' support and her teacher' skills, but also because, like other people with SMS, her long-term memory, computer skills, and perceptual skills are inherent traits on which she and her teachers and parents can build for the future.

SUMMARY

Identifying students with severe and multiple disabilities

- The term "severe and multiple disabilities" defines a diverse group of people, and no single definition satisfies all occurrences. IDEA has two separate definitions, one for multiple disabilities and one for severe disabilities.
- Students with severe and multiple disabilities have impairments in intellectual functioning, adaptive skills, motor development, sensory functioning, health care needs, and communication.
- The causes include biological (particularly prenatal) ones and genetic ones.

Evaluating students with severe and multiple disabilities

- Physicians use screening tests such as the Apgar to determine the extent to which an infant is in distress immediately after birth.
- The evaluation process usually begins right after birth and may continue throughout a student's entire school career.

- Assistive technology evaluations are multidisciplinary efforts to determine the best fit between the student and the technology and to identify the instructional objectives that relate to language and communication skills associated with augmentative or alternative communication (AAC) systems.

Designing an appropriate individualized education program

- Person-centered planning procedures, such as the MAPs process, are effective tools for planning services and supports for students with severe and multiple disabilities.
- Peer tutoring has been used successfully one to one and classwide to improve students' achievement.
- Technological devices such as the Visual Assistant, which apply new and emerging technologies, offer greater access to universally designed learning materials and practices.
- Many students require AAC systems. The IEP team must identify the device and establish instructional goals related to language use and communication skills.

Using effective instructional strategies

- The Circle of Inclusion model combines many best practices in early childhood education to teach students in typical preschool settings, benefiting both the child with the disability and children without a disability.
- Partial participation enables students with severe and multiple disabilities to participate to the maximum extent possible for each of them in school, home, and community environments.
- Student-directed learning strategies such as antecedent cue regulation, self-instruction, and self-monitoring strategies are empirically validated ways to teach students to self-regulate learning and contribute to enhanced inclusion, generalization, and student empowerment.

Including students with severe and multiple disabilities

- Almost half of all students with severe and multiple disabilities are educated in separate classes; 30 percent are educated in separate schools, residential facilities, and homes/hospitals; and another 25 percent are educated in general education classroom/resource rooms.
- Students with severe and multiple disabilities can learn new skills, be involved and make progress in general education classrooms, and experience successful friendships.
- Preparing general educators to work with all students is a critical step in promoting inclusive practices.

Assessing students' progress

- Using portfolios to assess the progress of students with severe disabilities involves collecting examples of permanent products for students.
- Observational methodologies like field observations, time sampling, and event recording enable teachers to collect data such as behavioral frequency, percentage, rate, duration, and latency.
- Students who cannot take the state's general assessment even with modifications can still be involved in accountability decisions using alternate assessment procedures such as portfolios, performance assessments, IEP-linked content data, and checklist data.

Use your *Real Lives and Exceptionality* DVD to revisit Star, who has multiple disabilities. How has she enriched the lives of the educators and service professionals she has encountered?

WHAT WOULD YOU RECOMMEND?

Refer to chapter content and the PRAXIS™ and CEC standards in Appendix A to answer the following questions:

1. Find the statistics in your state for the number of students with severe and multiple disabilities. See if you can determine where these students are educated. Which PRAXIS™/CEC standards are you implementing?

2. Contact your local school district and find out how students with severe and multiple disabilities are accommodated on state tests. Which PRAXIS™/CEC standards are you implementing?

3. Develop a plan for how you could use peer tutoring to teach a student the correct change he should receive from one dollar when he buys a pencil for 25 cents at the school store. Which PRAXIS™/CEC standards are you implementing?

4. Visit the Companion Website module for this chapter and locate links to some of the websites noted in the chapter. Using information from these websites, compile a list of assessment tools that you would use if you had a student with severe and multiple disabilities in your class. Which PRAXIS™ or CEC standards are you implementing when you answer this question?

The Kansas City metropolitan area consists of two cities—Kansas City, Kansas, and Kansas City, Missouri—that are divided by the wide Missouri River. Within this area live nearly a million people; most do not live in the two cities but in some 20 or so suburbs. A ring of interstate and state highways encircles greater Kansas City, and those highways as well as lesser boulevards, avenues, roads, streets, alleys, and lanes also transect the area. The interstates lead north to Des Moines; east to St. Louis and Washington, DC; south to Little Rock and Oklahoma City; west to Denver and Los Angeles; southwest to Houston; and southeast to Atlanta.

Jeremy Jones, age 13, knows his way around the entire Kansas City area and how to get from "KC" to any of those cities, or nearly anywhere else for that matter. With fierce determination and increasing energy, he spends some of his class time drawing accurate maps of the interstate and local highways and other thoroughfares. With confidence born of certain knowledge, he asks, in a voice pitching lower with each month of adolescence, "Where were you born?" A teacher answers, "Topeka, Kansas." A speech therapist offers, "New Orleans." In a matter of seconds and with excitement that makes his hands shake (until he puts pencil to paper), he draws the map that will lead you there, city to city, interstates all the way. Between his cartographic excursions, he asks for simple school supplies: "Wal-Mart . . . Black Bic pens . . . Crayola supertips . . . markers . . . Papermate's Suspension pen . . . number-2 pencils . . . yellow pads . . . lined paper . . . three-ring notebooks . . . atlas of the USA."

Seemingly out of nowhere, he raises his right arm (his left hand holds fast to his pencil) and, upon being recognized by his teacher, exclaims: "Hands to self . . . don't touch others . . . not cool . . . no suspension, no discipline." Then, as if to make sure that he and his teachers are certain of his code of conduct, he writes: "Uncool: talk in class, touching, tardy in class, bad words."

What is surprising about Jeremy? Is it his skills in mapping? Yes, they are rather high for a boy who has autism and lives in the inner city of KC-Kansas. Are they at a level that makes him truly gifted? No, but they are considerable. Is it also remarkable that he rehearses his social skills: do not interrupt; raise your hand; wait to be called on; speak in a calm voice; keep your hands to yourself? No, because Jeremy and his teachers at Central Middle School, Kansas City, Kansas, together

Understanding Students with Autism

with a team of researchers at the University of Kansas, have been working on those skills, not just for Jeremy but also for all students at Central as part of an effort to ensure that schools are safe for everyone's learning. For Jeremy and other Central students, teachers applied a technique called positive behavior supports on universal, group, and individual bases. By creating schoolwide commitment to positive behavior supports and demonstrating that it helps all students, they have ensured that Jeremy—the only student with autism at Central—is included in and progressing through the general curriculum.

At Mt. Calvary Baptist Church, where his mother, Joyce, sings in the choir and his father, Richard, teaches Sunday School, Jeremy sometimes joins the choir. His favorite music (gospel has replaced jazz) starts him grinning. Richard believes Jeremy is having one of his epiphany moments—a time when Jeremy obtains a religious knowledge that belies his limited intelligence. Both at home and at school, when Jeremy's brain knows the word he wants to say but his mouth won't form it, he spells it out or simply claims victory over the intellectual challenge by declaring, "My brain is tired."

Is Jeremy over the hump of that mountain called autism? Hardly. He still chews his pencils and pens; rocks powerfully on his family's furniture, testing its resiliency to the breaking point; is obsessive about where his clothes and toiletries are laid out in his bedroom and bathroom; jumps incessantly on the trampoline or refuses to dismount after hours on the swings in a local park; fixates on oscillating fans; surfs the TV in search of weather reports; and remains aloof from his peers at school.

His repertoire of behaviors is mixed—some problematic, others not. He still exhibits some aggression (breaking the fan or putting pencils through window screens) and self-injurious behavior (biting his hands and biting his fingernails until they seem to disappear entirely). He still insists on routines and predictability, a prisoner of the school calendar and of his immediate personal history. But he has a powerful long-term memory for people, their names and faces, and their places of birth; and he is a superb cartographer-to-be.

IDENTIFYING STUDENTS WITH AUTISM

Defining Autism

Autism is a developmental disability that significantly affects a student's verbal and nonverbal communication, social interaction, and educational performance. It is generally evident before a child reaches age 3 and is manifest when the child engages in repetitive activities and stereotyped movements, resists environmental change or changes in daily routines, and displays unusual responses to sensory experiences. Under the current regulations implementing IDEA, a student may not be classified as having autism if his or her educational performance is adversely affected primarily by a serious emotional disturbance (34 C.F.R., Part 300, § 300.7[b][1]).

Autism is a severe form of a broader group of disorders referred to as **pervasive developmental disorders** (Lord & Risi, 2000; Nickel, 2000; Tanguay, 2000). The current *Diagnostic and Statistical Manual of Mental Disorders* of the American Psychiatric Association includes under that term five discrete disorders that have their onset in childhood (American Psychiatric Association, 2000): *autistic disorder, Rett's disorder, childhood disintegrative disorder, Asperger's disorder,* and *pervasive developmental disorder not otherwise specified.* Educators often use the term **autism spectrum disorder** when referring to some or all of these five disorders.

In this chapter we will concentrate on the condition known as autistic disorder, or simply autism, because it has the highest prevalence of the five disorders. We will also discuss issues related to Asperger's disorder, also known as Asperger syndrome. The characteristics of Rett syndrome are quite consistent with those characteristics associated with severe or multiple disabilities, which we discussed in Chapter 10.

The term **Asperger syndrome** describes individuals with significant challenges in social and emotional functioning but without significant delays in language development or intellectual functioning (Corothers & Taylor, 2004; Myles et al., 2003). During the 2003–2004 school year, the U.S. Department of Education (2005) reported that 132,333 students with autism were enrolled in school. The prevalence rate for Asperger syndrome is far less than for autism, which is 2.5 children in every 10,000 (Fombonne, 2003).

Fombonne (2003), a respected epidemiologist, reviewed 32 prevalence surveys published between 1966 and 2001 and reported that the prevalence of autism is 10 per 10,000. The prevalence of autism has increased over the past decade. Professionals and families have advanced different reasons for the increase in prevalence; these reasons include greater public awareness concerning the condition and its manifestation in young children, more refined diagnostic procedures, and the alleged negative effect of vaccines (especially mercury) on young children's brain development. Rates tend to be higher among students during elementary and secondary school years than in preschool years, probably because of more precise identification. Males outnumber females by approximately four to one, and research data suggest that there are no variations in the prevalence of autism according to race or ethnicity (Fombonne, 2003).

Describing the Characteristics

Autism has seven distinct characteristics: (1) atypical language development, (2) atypical social development, (3) repetitive behavior, (4) problem behavior, (5) the need for environmental predictability, (6) sensory and movement disorders, and (7) differences in intellectual functioning.

Atypical language development. Students with autism have a broad range of language abilities, ranging from no verbal communication to quite complex communication (Myles et al., 2003; National Research Council, 2001). They usually have a number of language impairments. Two common ones are delayed language and echolalia.

Delayed language. More than two decades ago, experts expected that only about 50 percent of individuals with autism would eventually develop useful speech (Prizant, 1983). Researchers now predict that as many as 85 to 90 percent of children with autism can learn to speak effectively if they receive state-of-the-art teaching and motivational approaches and begin their education before age 5 (Koegel, 2000). Nevertheless, children with autism often have limited communication skills.

To learn more about Asperger syndrome, go to the Web Links module in Chapter 11 of the Companion Website, *www. prenhall.com/turnbull,* to link to Tony Attwood's support web page on Asperger syndrome, *www.tonyattwood.com.*

Their communication may have the following characteristics (Carpenter & Tomasello, 2000; National Research Council, 2001; Prizant, Schuler, Wetherby, & Rydell, 1997):

■ Focus attention on one topic only

■ Limit a communication topic to fewer than a couple of interactions

■ Use limited gestures to supplement verbal skills

■ Reverse pronouns (For example, the student may look at his teacher and say, "You want have a snack now," meaning that he, not the teacher, wants a snack.)

■ Look away from the speaker rather than maintain eye contact

Echolalia. Echolalia is a form of communication in which a student echoes other people's language by constantly repeating a portion of what he or she hears (Prizant, Wetherby, & Rydell, 2000). This type of communication tends to happen with almost all young children who are beginning to talk, whether they have autism or not, but usually it begins to disappear around the age of 3. Some people with autism, however, may have echolalia throughout their lives.

Echolalia is either immediate or delayed (Prizant & Rydell, 1984). Students who engage in immediate echolalia may repeat what they have just heard because they are unaware of an appropriate response. Delayed echolalia includes verbal repetitions that a student has previously heard during periods of time ranging from a few minutes to many years ago.

Some specialists have described echolalia as speech that is repeated in an automatic manner without having communicative intent (Howlin, 1982). Those teachers who accept that view command their students, "Don't echo," to eliminate their echolalia (Lovass, 1977). Other specialists, however, reject the view that echolalia does not have communicative intent (Howlin, 1982). They believe that children and youth with autism may use echolalia to communicate a desire for a listener's attention, to fill the silence in a communication exchange, to make a request, to indicate affirmation, to protest the actions of others, and/or to provide information (Prizant & Rydell, 1984; Rydell & Prizant, 1995).

Atypical social development. Another hallmark of autism is atypical social development, characterized by delays in social interaction and social skills (McConnell, 2002; National Research Council, 2001). The American Psychiatric Association (2000) has adopted four criteria for diagnosing atypical social development in individuals with autism:

■ Impaired use of nonverbal behavior

■ Lack of peer relationships

■ Failure to spontaneously share enjoyment, interests, and achievements with others

■ Lack of reciprocity

One explanation for delayed social development is called the theory of mind: individuals with autism do not understand that their own beliefs, desires, and intentions may differ from those of others (Baron-Cohen, 2001; Baron-Cohen et al., 2002). They have difficulty comprehending others' feelings, preferences, and emotions even when other people directly say what their feelings are, and they often do not infer and intuit others' social cues and nonverbal signals.

Understandably, impairments in students' theory of mind often make it difficult for them to develop relationships with others. For example, Jeremy has distressed many people by running up to them, touching them, or even hugging them. What he seeks is their friendship; what he provokes is their alarm, fear, or hostility. Only when the hugged person knows him well does he receive affection and friendship. What Jeremy knows is that he likes to be hugged; what he does not know is that others generally don't want to hug or be hugged, especially if they do not know him. Because of the challenges he experiences related to theory of mind, his social networks are smaller than he, his teachers, and his family want them to be. Happily, researchers have developed strategies to teach students how to improve their social interactions (McConnell, 2002; National Research Council, 2001; Rogers, 2000).

Inappropriate social interactions in students with Asperger syndrome often are associated with hyperactivity, atypical behavior, verbal aggression, withdrawal, and depression (Myles et al., 2001; Safran, Safran, & Ellis, 2003). Depression is a frequent problem for these students and tends to cause them to blame themselves for various negative events in their lives and for their own social failures (Barnhill, 2001; Barnhill & Myles, 2001).

Values: By teaching your students how to be socially appropriate, you expand their opportunities to develop *relationships* that can bloom into genuine *friendships*.

PRAXIS

Standard: Understanding the impact of autism on social development is an application of PRAXIS™ Standard 1, Understanding Exceptionalities.

Repetitive behavior. **Repetitive behavior** involves obsessions, tics, and perseveration. **Obsessions** are persistent thoughts, impulses, or images of a repetitive nature that create anxiety. **Tics** are involuntary, rapid movements that occur without warning. **Perseveration** includes verbalizations or behaviors that are repeated to an inappropriate extent. For instance, Jeremy is adamant about how his clothes and toilet articles are to be stored, and he perseverates about maps and Wal-Mart stores: "Do you know how to get to . . . ? Have you been to the Wal-Mart at Bannister Mall? To the Wal-Mart at Oakridge? To the Wal-Mart at . . . ?" as he adds the names of the many shopping centers in the greater Kansas City area.

Repetitive acts involve repeated movements as well as repeated verbalization. Repeated movements include rocking back and forth, twirling objects, and/or waving fingers in front of the

face. Jeremy's bouncing on a trampoline or dismounting from a swing after hours of being on it are not so destructive as his constant jumping up and down on his bed, requiring his parents to replace the bed nearly every 6 months. You will find that your students use their repetitive behaviors as ways for communicating boredom and agitation or regulating their levels of awareness (Carr et al., 1994).

Obviously, these behaviors can interfere with your students' ability to learn and be included in typical work, school, and community settings. Simply decreasing their repetitive behaviors, however, is not sufficient; increasing their appropriate communication, social skills, and leisure activities is the state-of-the-art approach in today's schools (Kluth, 2003; McConnell, 2002; Myles & Simpson, 2003).

Regardless of Jeremy's autism, he still enjoys many leisure activities along with most students his age.

Problem behavior. IDEA requires educators to consider using positive behavior supports (which we discuss later in this chapter) when students perform behavior that impedes their or other students' learning. Four categories of problem behavior in students with autism are self-injurious behavior, aggression, tantrums, and property destruction. We will focus on the first two.

Self-injurious behavior. Some individuals have self-injurious behavior, such as head banging, biting (for example, Jeremy bites his hand and his fingernails), or scratching (Didden, Duker, & Korzilius, 1997; Mace & Mauk, 1999). These behaviors often persist into adulthood. Individuals with severe self-injurious behaviors may permanently injure themselves; sometimes and usually for only a few people, self-injurious behaviors are life-threatening. One of those life-threatening behaviors is called pica—eating nonedible items. Jeremy manifests pica when he chews on pencils and swallows some of the wood splinters.

Aggression. Aggressive behaviors are similar to self-injurious behaviors, but the behavior is directed toward others. Aggressive behaviors can be problematic in all settings. By using positive behavior supports, teachers enable their students to learn a wider repertoire of appropriate behaviors. Once students learn appropriate alternative behaviors, they often stop using aggressive behaviors.

Problem behavior can serve a communicative function, enabling the student to obtain something positive, avoid or escape something unpleasant, increase or decrease sensory stimulation, or achieve two or more of these results (Carr et al., 2002; Horner et al., 2002). Some researchers have predicted that as many as 75 to 80 percent of problem behavior may have a communicative function (Derby et al., 1992; Iwata et al., 1994). Given the functions that problem behavior serves, your role includes teaching the student other ways to communicate these same intentions (Chandler & Dahlquist, 2002; Horner, Albin, Todd, & Sprague, 2006).

Need for environmental predictability. Predictability and structure are important sources of security for many individuals with autism (Iovannone, Dunlap, Huber, & Kincaid, 2003;

Lewis & Bodfish, 1998). When their predictability and structure are interrupted by events such as school vacations, overnight stays with friends or extended family, the celebration of holidays, a change in television schedules, or a move from one classroom to another, students often experience a high degree of anxiety. In addition, "things in their place" mean a great deal to some students. Most of us do not think much about whether the telephone is straight on a desk, whether the cosmetics are always in the same place on the bathroom counter, or whether a door is open or closed. Disruptions in these seemingly insignificant environmental patterns, however, disturb many students with autism and impede their ability to learn.

You can enhance your students' ability to predict what happens to them by adhering to schedules, not varying routines, and supporting your students to develop strategies to accept changes (Iovannone et al., 2003; Markes et al., 2003). For example, you might offer picture schedules to students who do not read, outlining the schedule of the different activities or classroom periods they will have each day. Students who have higher cognitive abilities may find that both daily and weekly work schedules are helpful.

Routines also enable students to understand when things will occur. For example, some students need to have activities that are almost always associated with the same time of day or the same day of the week. Because that kind of highly regular routine can create a problem when those times need to change, many students require instruction and support in learning to accept schedule changes. You might find it helpful to let students know in advance when there will be a change and when schedules and routines will return to the typical schedule. ("We will not have music this afternoon because there is a special school program. You will get to go to music again next Tuesday afternoon. You can look forward to having music and fun then.")

Sensory and movement disorders. Between 42 percent and 88 percent of children and youth with autism and Asperger syndrome have sensory and movement disorders (Anzalone & Williamson, 2000; National Research Council, 2001). Some have under- or overresponsiveness to sensory stimuli, although more have overresponsiveness (National Research Council, 2001; Talay-Ongan & Wood, 2000). Temple Grandin (1997), who was identified as having autism as a child and then Asperger syndrome as an adult, is now one of the most successful designers of livestock equipment in the world. In Figure 11–1, she describes some typical problems with overresponsiveness to sensory stimuli as well as some practical solutions.

Movement disorders also are associated with autism (Dawson & Watling, 2000; Donnellan, 1999; National Research Council, 2001). Examples include abnormal posture; abnormal movements of the face, head, trunk, and limbs; abnormal eye movements; repeated gestures and mannerisms; and awkward gait (Leary & Hill, 1996). Motor clumsiness and disorders are also present in the majority of individuals who have Asperger syndrome (Barnhill, 2001).

Differences in intellectual functioning. Autism occurs in children with all levels of intelligence, ranging from students who are gifted to those who have mental retardation. Recent research has indicated that approximately 64 to 70 percent of children and youth with autism also have mental retardation (Fombonne, 2003; Yeargin-Allsopp et al., 2003).

Individuals with Asperger syndrome tend to have higher intellectual functioning than do individuals with autism (Volkmar, Klin, & Cohen, 1997; Myles & Simpson, 2003). Their IQ scores tend to fall in the average range and to reveal a frequency distribution similar to that of the general population.

Some people with autism also display **savant syndrome**. Savant syndrome is an unusual condition in which individuals display extraordinary abilities in areas such as calendar calculating, musical ability, mathematical skills, memorization, and mechanical abilities (Kelly, Macaruso, & Sokol, 1997; Miller, 1999; O'Connor, Cowan, & Samella, 2000; Saloviita, Ruusila, & Ruusila, 2000). For example, a student with savant syndrome may be able to recite the baseball game scores and the batting averages of all players who ever participated in the major leagues. A familiar example of savant ability is the betting calculations of Raymond in the movie *Rain Man*. But a student's unusual ability in these areas also occurs in conjunction with low ability in most other areas (Cheatham et al., 1995; Nettelbeck & Young, 1996). It is not likely that Jeremy would be classified as having the savant syndrome, despite his cartography skills, because his skills are not terribly refined.

Values: It is important to build on the strengths of students with autism who have extraordinary abilities to increase the likelihood that they will make *positive contributions* to others.

Figure 11-1 Temple Grandin: Insights on how she experiences autism

- As an adult I find it difficult to determine exactly when I should break into a conversation. I cannot follow the rhythmic give and take of conversation. People have told me that I often interrupt, and I still have difficulty determining where the pauses are.
- Noise was a major problem for me. When I was confronted with loud or confusing noise, I could not modulate it. I either had to shut it all out and withdraw or let it all in like a freight train.
- I think a classroom should be quiet and free from distracting noises, such as a high pitched vent fan. Some teachers have found that disturbing noises can be blocked out with headphones and music. When a child has to make a trip to a busy shopping center, a headset with a favorite tape can help make the trip more peaceful.
- I often misbehaved in church and screamed because my Sunday clothes felt different—scratchy petticoats drove me crazy; a feeling that would be insignificant to most people may feel like sand paper rubbing the skin raw to an autistic child . . . . Most people habituate to different types of clothes, but I keep feeling them for hours.
- Calming sensory activities immediately prior to school lessons or speech therapy may help to improve learning. These activities should be conducted as fun games.
- Abstract concepts such as getting along with people have to have a visual image. For example, my visual image for relationships with people was a sliding glass door. If you push it too hard it will break. To make the abstract concept more real, I would some times act it out—for example, by walking through a real sliding door.
- At puberty I was desperate for relief from the "nerves." . . . At my aunt's ranch, I observed that the cattle sometimes appeared to relax when they were held in the squeeze chute, a device for holding cattle for veterinary procedures. The animal is held tightly between two sides, which squeeze the body. After a horrible bout of the "nerves" I got in the squeeze chute. For about 45 minutes I was much calmer. I then built a squeeze-chute-like device which I could use to apply pressure (which I controlled). . . . I have made a successful career based on my fixation with cattle squeeze chutes. I have designed livestock handling systems for major ranches and meat companies all over the world. When I was in high school, many of my teachers and psychologists wanted to get rid of my fixation on cattle chutes. I am indebted to Mr. Carlock, my high school science teacher. He suggested that I read psychology journals and study so I could learn why the cattle chute had a relaxing effect. If my fixation had been taken away, I could have ended up in an institution. Do not confuse fixations with stereotyped behavior, such as hand flapping or rocking. A fixation is in interest in something external that should be diverted and used to motivate.

Source: From "Teaching Tips from a Recovered Autistic" by T. Grandin, 1988. *Focus on Autistic Behavior, 3*(1). Copyright 1998 by PRO-ED, Inc. Reprinted by permission.

Determining the Causes

Historical perspective on causes. When autism was diagnosed in the early 1940s, parents of children with autism were often regarded as intelligent people of high socioeconomic status who were also "cold." At that time, incredibly, some professionals referred to mothers of children with autism as "refrigerator mothers."

By the 1970s, research established that autism is caused by brain or biochemical dysfunction that occurs before, during, or after birth and that it is totally unwarranted to blame parents. In 1977 the National Society for Autistic Children (now known as the Autism Society of America) asserted, "No known factors in the psychological environment of a child have been shown to cause autism." Today parents are not seen as the cause of problems; they are seen as partners with educators, contributing to solving their children's problems.

Biomedical causes. An international network of 10 collaborative research programs sponsored by the National Institutes of Health has been organized to identify subgroups within autism; to find causes for each; and to develop effective biological, behavioral, and/or alternative treatments (Bristol, McIlvane, & Alexander, 1998). There is broad agreement that autism is caused by abnormalities in brain development, neurochemistry, and genetic factors (Courchesne, 2004; Prater & Zylstra, 2002; Towbin, Mauk, & Batshaw, 2002). Biomedical research now focuses on the normal and atypical development of the central nervous system and the genetic and biological influences that lead to autism, particularly on deviations in brain size during the early years of the child's life that then lead to disruptions in the brain's circuit formation (Courchesne, 2004). One theory is that the deviations in brain size are caused by an early brain overgrowth followed by a period of atypical slow growth.

Evaluating Students with Autism

Determining the Presence of Autism

Many children receive the initial diagnosis of autism from an interdisciplinary evaluation team, typically during their early childhood years (Prelock et al., 2003). Evaluators usually administer some of the same tests given to students with mental retardation and students with severe and multiple disabilities (Mayes & Calhoun, 2003). Figure 11–2 highlights the standard techniques used for observations, screening, and nondiscriminatory evaluation.

Various diagnostic tools can detect the presence of autism (Lord, 1997; Lord et al., 1997). One is the Autism Diagnostic Interview—Revised (Lord, Rutter, & Le Couteur, 1994). This semistructured interview is administered by a professional to caregivers of children and adults who are thought to have autism. Special training is required to administer and score the interview, especially since scoring is based on clinical judgment regarding the caregiver's description of the child's development and behavior. The interview takes about $1\frac{1}{2}$ hours and focuses on three main areas—social interaction, communication and language, and repetitive and stereotyped behaviors. These three areas represent six factors—spoken language, social intent, compulsions, developmental milestones, savant skills, and sensory aversion (Tadevosyan-Leyfer et al., 2003). The six factors cover the broad range of characteristics that you have already learned about in this chapter. Children must meet the criteria for autism in all three content areas, and a child's atypical development in at least one content area must be manifest by 36 months of age. This tool helps differentiate between children and youth who have autism and those who have mental retardation.

Standard: Using a variety of diagnostic tools to identify the exceptional learning needs of students is an application of CEC Standard 8, Assessment.

Determining the Nature of Specially Designed Instruction and Services

You have already learned that positive behavior supports are an important part of Jeremy Jones's educational program. Like any other instructional area, assessment is an important step in determining the need for and nature of positive behavioral supports. (You will learn more about positive behavior support later in this chapter.) The assessment process used to determine necessary positive behavior support is called a functional behavioral assessment. A **functional behavioral assessment** identifies specific relationships between a student's behaviors and the circumstances that trigger those behaviors, especially those that impede a student's ability to learn (Chandler & Dahlquist, 2002; Crone & Horner, 2003; Ryan, Halsey, & Matthews, 2003). Although a functional behavioral assessment is helpful for many students, regardless of their specific category of exceptionality, it is particularly apt for students with autism (Horner et al., 2002).

You will use these basic steps when you conduct a functional behavioral assessment:

1. Describe as precisely as possible the nature of the behaviors that are impeding the student's learning or the learning of others.

Careful observation is especially important in conducting a functional behavioral assessment.

Figure 11–2 Nondiscriminatory evaluation process for determining the presence of autism

Observation ↓	***Medical or psychological professionals and parents observe:*** The child is challenged by social conversations, does not play with others, is frequently unresponsive to voices, may exhibit echolalia or other unusual speech patterns, has language development delays, has problem behavior, is disrupted by changes in daily routine, engages in stereotypical behaviors, and has sensory and movement disorders.
Screening ↓	***Assessment measures:*** **Physical examinations:** A physician notes that the child is not reaching developmental milestones, especially in areas of social and language development. The child's physical health is usually normal. The physician may refer the child to a psychiatrist or psychologist for further evaluation.

Psychological evaluations: The child meets the *Diagnostic Standards Manual—IV* criteria for autism, including (1) qualitative impairment in social interaction, (2) qualitative impairment in communication, and (3) restricted repetitive and stereotyped patterns of behavior. |
| Prereferral ↓ | The student is usually identified before starting school. In rare circumstances in which the student is not identified before starting school, the severity of the disability may preclude the use of prereferral. |
| Referral ↓ | Children with autism should be referred by medical personnel or parents for early intervention during infancy or the preschool years. The child is referred upon reaching school age. |
| Nondiscriminatory evaluation procedures and standards | ***Findings that suggest autism:*** **Individualized intelligence test:** About 70 percent of students with autism perform two or more standard deviations below the mean, indicating mental retardation. Others have average or even gifted intelligence. Evaluating intelligence is generally difficult because of challenging social and language behaviors.

Individualized achievement tests: Students with autism who have average or above-average intelligence may perform at an average or above-average level in one or more areas of achievment. Some individuals with autism have unusual giftedness in one or more areas. Students with autism typically have below-average achievement.

Adaptive behavior scales: The student usually scores significantly below average in areas of adaptive behavior, indicating severe deficits in skills such as communication, daily living, socialization, gross- and fine-motor coordination, and socially appropriate behavior.

Autism-specific scales: The student's scores meet the criteria for identifying him or her as having autism.

Direct observation: The student's self-initiated interactions with teacher and peers are limited. The student exhibits language delays and may use unusual speech patterns such as echolalia. The observer may notice that the student has difficulty with changes in routines and manifests stereotypical behaviors.

Anecdotal records: Records suggest that performance varies according to moods, energy level, extent and pile-up of environmental changes, and whether or not individual preferences are incorporated. |

2. Gather information from teachers, family members, the student, related service providers, and any other individuals who have extensive firsthand knowledge about the circumstances that are regularly associated with the occurrence and nonoccurrence of the problem behavior. Determine as specifically as possible the events that occur before, during, and after the student's appropriate and inappropriate behavior.

3. Determine why the student engages in the problem behavior. What is the student trying to accomplish through the behavior? What is the student communicating? For example, does the student want to obtain something positive, avoid or escape something unpleasant, or increase or decrease sensory stimulation (Reese, Richman, Zarcone, & Zarcone, 2003)?

4. Hypothesize the relationship between the problem behavior and the events occurring before, during, and after the behavior.

5. Incorporate the functional assessment information into the student's IEP. Focus on changing the environmental events and circumstances so that the student does not need to engage in problem behavior to accomplish his or her purpose.

6. Help the student develop alternative behaviors and new skills so that he or she can accomplish the same purpose in more socially acceptable ways.

Jeremy's support team gained valuable information when they administered a functional behavioral assessment to him. Highlights of what they learned are included in Box 11–1. The box also provides information about Jeremy's positive behavior support plan as it is implemented at each of the three levels of universal, group, and individual.

When Jeremy's team knows about his problem behavior and when it occurs and does not, it can develop an IEP for him that can include a behavioral intervention plan. Thus, functional behavioral assessment leads to a behavioral intervention plan, one that incorporates positive behavior support.

DESIGNING AN APPROPRIATE INDIVIDUALIZED EDUCATION PROGRAM

Partnering for Special Education and Related Services

Partnerships are essential if you, other educators, and family members of students with autism want to be successful in responding to students' needs (Ruble & Dalrymple, 2002). That is so because all of you will need to develop coherent instructional strategies and use them in school, home, and community settings. Creating coherent instruction means having the key people in each of those environments collaborate to plan and implement the curriculum and use the same methods of instruction. For example, you will find that positive behavior support is far more effective when teachers, parents, and community service providers are all responding to a student's problem behavior in similar ways. It is especially important to have a person on the evaluation and IEP team who has expertise in positive behavior support. This person might be a teacher, a school psychologist, a counselor, or a behavior specialist.

Standard: Being a part of collaborations and partnerships reflects CEC Standard 10, Collaboration.

The Individual Support Program is a model program for children with autism (Dunlap & Fox, 1999; Dunlap et al., 2001; Fox, Benito, & Dunlap, 2002). Under the program, a behavior specialist, the child's family, and the child's teacher carry out planning based on the outcomes of a functional assessment of the child's problem behavior in which all stakeholders are involved. They ask questions such as

- What is the nature of the behavior?
- In what contexts does it occur or not occur?
- What are its antecedents and consequences?
- What are its communicative functions?

Their collaborative assessment always assumes that problem behavior is purposeful: the child uses it to communicate certain needs or desires and to get certain results.

Into Practice ~ Highlights of Jeremy's Positive Behavior Support Plan for Inappropriate Verbal Disruptions (Talk-Outs) — Box 11–1

1. Description of target problem behavior
   - Asks the teacher repetitive questions (e.g., "Have I been bad?")
   - Uses loud voice and/or repeats person's name in a loud voice (e.g., "You mean, Ms. B.")
   - Makes out-of-context comments while other students are working quietly (e.g., "I don't like spiders. Spiders are unsanitary.")

2. Functional behavior assessment findings
   - Has difficulty when other peers whisper near him in class
   - Tends to begin to talk more loudly when he hears other students whisper
   - Appears to calm down when adults whisper and even tries to model or imitate the "whisper voice"
   - Imitates peers' appropriate verbal behaviors or peers' imitation of his loud and excited talk
   - Talks out when teachers demonstrate anxious behaviors (e.g., shaking, cringing) or provide high levels of corrective feedback to students

3. Hypothesis statement
   - Uses excessive and repetitive talk-out behaviors to get what he wants and to escape from frustrating or less preferred tasks, especially when he is told to wait for something he wants or is told that he cannot interact with a particular preferred person or object
   - Uses talk-outs to get or obtain adult and/or peer attention
   - Uses talk-outs to reduce/alleviate stress, anxiety, or tension and/or to express his emotions, especially when his energy level is high and he needs to interact with peers and adults

4. Desired replacement behavior
   - To work quietly in class and refrain from making out-of-context comments that disrupt the lesson
   - To raise his hand and wait to be acknowledged before calling out answers to questions and before talking out in class
   - To ignore peers' comments that taunt or mimic him
   - To engage in quiet self-talk to remind himself of the class rules about not talking out in class
   - To read and recopy social stories as a way of reinforcing positive behaviors in writing

5. IEP goals and objectives
   - Goal: Jeremy will improve his skills in language and communication.

     Objective 1: Jeremy will work quietly in class and refrain from making out-of-context comments that disrupt the class.

     Objective 2: Jeremy will raise his hand and wait to be acknowledged before calling out answers to questions and/or talking out about things in class.

     Objective 3: Jeremy will ignore and/or redirect himself by practicing quiet self-talk or reading social stories to himself in response to comments made by peers that taunt or mimic him.

6. Interventions based on functional behavior assessment
   - *Strategies to change setting events.* Schedule functional activities and build routines that offer opportunities for Jeremy to move around and burn energy, especially before times/activities that are predictable triggers for disruptive talk-outs, such as a class period that lasts longer than 50 minutes.
   - *Strategies to change immediate antecedent events.* Offer more assistance—with minimal verbal interaction—when presenting new or difficult tasks or when working on assigned tasks at nonpreferred times of the day—e.g., fifth hour or late in the day when disruptive talk-outs are much more likely.
   - *Strategies to teach new, desired replacement behaviors.* Teach Jeremy to self-monitor and self-manage talk-outs by using his social stories.
   - Teach him how to appropriately terminate a nonpreferred task without talking out disruptively. This communication form could be to raise or wiggle his hand, wait to be acknowledged, then say "Stop, please," or "Need to cool down now."

7. Crisis management/emergency procedures
   - Intervene physically between Jeremy and others to prevent injury or damage to property.
   - Remove Jeremy from the situation/setting that is triggering the problem behavior by escorting him down the hallway and prompting him to review social stories and work on self-management skills.

8. Monitoring procedures for IEP team
   - Use a frequency count of problem behavior occurrences on a daily basis using Jeremy's self-monitoring data and teacher-maintained data.
   - Assess the percentage of times and situations where problem behavior is not used and alternative skills are practiced.
   - Review data at a monthly meeting with the team (including his family).

Putting These Strategies to Work for Progress in the General Curriculum

1. To what extent do the positive behavior support strategies address the functional behavior assessment? Give specific examples.

2. If you were Jeremy's classroom teacher, what challenges would you foresee in implementing these strategies? How would you overcome these challenges?

3. How will a trusting partnership between Jeremy's teachers and his parents and other family members assist in the implementation of his positive behavior support plan?

To answer these questions online, go to the Into Practice module in Chapter 11 of the Companion Website, www.prenhall.com/turnbull.

Next, the specialist, the family, and the teacher decide how to change the environments in which the child uses these behaviors, the interactions that the family and others have with the child, and the child's own skills. They develop a plan, to be used in all settings where the child will be (home, school and community), that addresses the following issues:

■ Long-term supports for the child and family

■ Strategies that the child and his or her family and teachers can use to extinguish the child's problem behavior

■ Strategies to replace the problem behaviors with more appropriate behaviors

■ Consequences that teach the child that more functional skills work better

In Box 11–2, you will read about Rosie Mack, a young child with autism, and how educators at the University of New Hampshire and Rosie's family adapted the Individual Support Program to implement positive behavior support. Rosie experienced dramatic improvement in a very short time.

Determining Supplementary Aids and Services

In implementing positive behavior support (which we discuss later in this chapter), a student's IEP team should consider supplementary aids and services that address the domains of access, classroom ecology, and task modifications. Supplementary aids and services that address access involve modifications to the community, campus, building, or classroom to ensure physical and cognitive access. These supplementary aids and services also provide "behavioral access"—that is, modifications that promote positive behavior and minimize disruptive behavior. In a research synthesis of behavior interventions for young children with autism, Horner and colleagues (2002) determined that "strategies for changing the physical characteristics of a setting, altering schedules, modifying curricula, and redesigning social groupings have all been demonstrated to alter the future likelihood of problem behaviors" (p. 425). It is important, then, to look beyond simply student-focused interventions for creating positive support and to include supplementary aids and services that modify the environment or the classroom ecology as well.

There are other campus or building modifications that IEP teams should address. The lunchroom is a frequent environment in which problem behaviors occur. It's noisy, there is not as much direct supervision, and there is constant movement. By simply modifying the lunchroom environment, educators can reduce the opportunity for problem behavior to occur. For example, they might replace long rows of tables, at which lots of students sit, with round tables around which fewer students congregate or create rotating lunch periods to reduce the number of students in the cafeteria at any one time. Educators can make similar modifications during other times in which problem behavior might occur, including before and after school and in the hall between classes. Schools might provide activities in which students can participate before entering the school building, minimizing the potential for other, less positive behaviors.

Some behavioral problems emerge because students are having difficulties that their teachers do not recognize. At the simplest level, a student may be acting out because he can't see or hear well, so a teacher might reseat him or modify the classroom arrangement to ensure better visual or acoustic access. Seating arrangements can also precipitate problem behavior, so teachers can change where they seat a student or how many students interact with each other at any given time. They also can create visual schedules for students to follow, thereby reducing off-task time and curtailing the times during which problems may occur. Finally, problem behavior may arise as students become frustrated because they are unable to complete required tasks. IEP teams should consider modifications, such as extended time, as a means to limit problem behavior.

Planning for Universal Design for Learning

Up to this point we have discussed the characteristics of autism that cause students' problems in learning and developing. Paradoxically, some characteristics associated with autism spectrum disorders, particularly with Asperger syndrome, are potential areas of learning strengths and

Partnership Tips ~ Implementing Positive Behavior Supports — Box 11–2

It took only 6 months, an amazingly short period, for Rosie Mack, age 3, to change dramatically—so dramatically that progress in the general curriculum was not just a phrase but a reality. The challenge was to help Rosie behave in such a way that she could be included in a preschool with students who do not have disabilities. What stood in the way was Rosie's erratic behavior: she was alternatively hyperactive or withdrawn and sobbing. Rosie's behaviors were rather typical for a preschooler with autism. She needed to learn appropriate behavior (such as how to calm down), how to comply with safety instructions ("Don't touch the hot stove") and other directions, and how to express her needs and choices other than by acting out ("Tell me what you want, Rosie").

The partners consisted of Rosie's mother, Kathy; Kathy's parents, Lorraine and John Mack; Ann Dillon of the University of New Hampshire's "Jump Start" program (where positive behavior support is linked to family support and person-centered planning); Ann's graduate students; and the teachers and therapists in Rosie's early intervention program and elementary school.

Under Ann's direction but with Kathy's diligent participation, they began by conducting a functional assessment of Rosie's behavior; then they developed and carried out a plan for positive behavior support for Rosie. The plan included social stories (with graphic design by Kathy and photographs by Rosie's grandmother, Lorraine). At Ann's suggestion, Kathy or Ann's students read the stories to Rosie before she went to different places (for example, the preschool or the elementary school, a swimming pool, and a theater) or engaged in various activities (for example, being a patient at a dentist's or physician's office). The stories prepped her for what lay ahead, gave her a sense of predictability, and helped her be calm when places changed and people entered her life.

Again under Ann's guidance, the team engaged in family support. Following the guidance of Kathy, Lorraine, and John, they developed a shared vision for Rosie, which was for her to be included in general education and have friends—those who do and do not have disabilities. They also helped Kathy find child care, learn how to advocate for Rosie's inclusion in school and the community, and meet some of Rosie's needs for strenuous physical activity. Grandfather John himself built Rosie's swing-gym set. Finally, the team worked with Rosie's teachers in the preschool and the elementary school to help them learn how to deliver positive behavior support to Rosie. And even though Ann herself pointed her team members in the

right direction, seeming to lead, everyone participated equally in leading and following. As in the best partnerships, a teacher can jump-start the process, but everyone has to be a leader.

The results were remarkable. Rosie's problem behavior is a thing of the past. She progressed through the preschool and is now fully included, with support, in a typical first-grade classroom. She uses words and phrases to express her choices. If she doesn't know a word, she tells herself, "I will be okay," and uses hand signals, not acting-out behaviors, to communicate. She is fully included in her elementary school (with an aide), has friends who have and don't have disabilities, and has progressed from no literacy skills to knowing how to read and being a regular visitor to the community library. Rosie's favorite book is her well-worn copy of *The Tale of Peter Rabbit*.

As Kathy said, "We wouldn't be so much in control of our lives without Jump Start"; and as Ann said, "It's about the family and in turn about Rosie."

The key in partnerships, as Rosie's story illustrates, is to

- Involve family members other than "just" the student's parents (remember how we defined "family" in Chapter 4?)
- Involve all school-based personnel and other professionals who work for the student
- Seek and apply what researchers and their students know about interventions
- Carry out a functional behavioral assessment, make it the basis for a positive behavioral intervention plan, and implement the plan diligently and across all settings and times
- Support each other, not just the student but also the student's family and teachers

Putting These Tips to Work for Progress in the General Curriculum

1. Provide a rationale of why it is important to conduct a functional assessment and implement positive behavior support in multiple settings.

2. Identify related service providers who might be available to assist you as a teacher in providing family support. What types of assistance would you expect from each related service provider that you identify?

3. How can you involve family members to address problem behavior and enhance student outcomes?

To answer these questions online, go to the Partnership Tips module in Chapter 11 of the Companion Website, www.prenhall.com/turnbull.

provide a basis for curriculum adaptation and augmentation strategies that enable students to progress in the general curriculum. For example, some students with autism spectrum disorders may have the capacity to focus attention on detailed information for a long period of time, while others excel in areas of the curriculum that are not as language-based, such as math or science. As we noted in Chapter 2, curriculum adaptations modify either the way in which teachers present or represent curriculum content or the way in which students respond to the curriculum, and curriculum augmentations expand the general curriculum to teach students "learning-to-learn" strategies that will enable them to succeed in the general curriculum.

Mnemonic strategies. Some students with Asperger syndrome are skilled in memory tasks (Ozonoff, Dawson, & McPartland, 2002) that can form the basis for curriculum adaptations and augmentations; you should take their memory strengths into account when planning for universally designed instruction. One such curriculum modification involves mnemonic strategies (Lee et al., 2004; Marks et al., 2003). Mnemonic, or memory, strategies help students learn and retain information. There are generally three types of mnemonic strategies employed: keyword, pegword, and letter strategies.

Keyword. **Keyword strategies** teach students to link a keyword to a new word or concept to help them remember the new material. The keyword is a word that sounds like the word or concept in question and can be easily pictured (Uberti, Scruggs, & Mastropieri, 2003). For example, to remember the three bones in the inner ear, you might use the following keyword strategies:

- *Malleus* sounds like mallets, and you can picture an image of hitting a bell with a mallet and causing it to ring (e.g., make sound).

- *Incus* sounds like ink, and you can picture an image of a large ear holding an ink pen and writing the word "incus."

- *Stapes* sounds like staple, and you can picture an image of a stapler with ears.

Pegword. The **pegword strategy** helps students remember numbered or ordered information by linking words that rhyme with numbers. The visual images help students remember a number or number sequence. There are standard pegwords that have come to represent numbers, such as the pegword "bun" representing the number one, the pegword "shoe" representing the number two, and so forth.

Letter. **Letter strategies** employ acronyms or a string of letters to help students remember a list of words or concepts. Recalling the acronym helps them recall the list or sequence. The fact that "IDEA" stands for Individuals with Disabilities Education Act helps people remember the act's name. Another common letter strategy is using the acronym "HOMES" to help people remember the list of the great lakes (Huron, Ontario, Michigan, Erie, Superior). Another version of the letter strategy involves acronyms that do not form recognizable words. The letter mnemonic for the notes that fall on the lines of the musical staff of the treble clef is EGBDF, which is not a useful mnemonic in and of itself. However, forming an acrostic (that is, using each letter to identify a word in a sentence) helps: the acrostic letter strategy for remembering the notes on the treble clef is "Every Good Boy Deserves a Favor."

Planning for Other Educational Needs

The most common characteristics of autism are impairments in language development and social development. We discussed language development in Chapter 6, so we will focus here on social development for children with autism. Impairments in social skills and social interactions can result in problems in many areas, but for students with autism, none may be more of a problem than the impact of poor social skills on developing friendships. It is important for educators to be systematic in making sure that they provide students with instructional supports that enable them to develop and maintain friendships.

Promoting friendships. We all know what friends are—people we like to be around and who like to be with us! Having friends is important at all points in life, perhaps especially during the school years. But difficulties with communication, poor social skills, and problem behavior too often can cause students with autism to be isolated from their peers with and without disabilities. Orsmond, Krauss, and Seltzer (2004) studied peer relationships of more than 200 adolescents and adults with autism and found that only 8 percent of them had at least one "friend," where "friend" was defined as a person of the same age with whom the person engaged in varied activities outside the home. Twenty-one percent of them had a peer relationship that fell short of the standard of a friend but involved some activities out of the home, while 24 percent were involved in peer relationships only in prearranged settings, such as school. Finally, almost half of them (46 percent) had no peer relationships whatsoever that met the criteria of same-age peer within or outside prearranged settings. It is clear, then, that the IEPs of many students with autism must address how to promote friendships.

While you probably knew immediately what we were talking about when we mentioned the word *friend,* you may not know quite as intuitively how one goes about planning for and teaching friendship skills. These are skills that most children just learn through typical play activities and, of course, with the guidance of their parents or brothers and sisters.

Values: All students with disabilities have *strengths* as well as limitations. Too often, teachers emphasize only the limitations. To promote your students' access to the general curriculum, however, you will want to build on their *strengths*.

Values: *Friendships* don't just happen for many students with autism, and that is why educators should create opportunities for their students to interact with peers with and without disabilities.

Council for Exceptional Children

Standard: Promoting friendships is one way to apply CEC Standard 5, Learning Environments and Social Interactions. Positive social interactions help prepare learners with realistic expectations for social behaviors.

The first step toward promoting friendships involves including students with autism in general education classrooms as well as in extracurricular and nonacademic activities such as school clubs, plays, sporting events, dances, and field trips. The peer buddy program you learned about in Chapter 10 involves linking same-age peers with and without mental retardation in a wide array of activities, including those outside the classroom, and could be equally useful for students with autism. As we discussed in that section, however, you have to support students without disabilities to interact with and respond appropriately to students with disabilities. A common mistake in teaching friendship skills for students with disabilities is to assume that simply placing students in proximity of their peers without disabilities will be sufficient. But research tells us that is not the case (Snell & Janney, 2000); teachers need to do more than ensure that their students with autism interact with their classmates in general education settings.

Using person-centered planning models (described in Chapter 10) that involve peers is a good first step. A second step is considering the environment itself: the lack of friends may reflect a general lack of peer acceptance in the environment, so you should make sure that a student's peers learn about the goals of inclusion. Some teams have developed an environmental support plan that addresses activities such as the support peers will need to interact more appropriately, the role of supplementary aids and services in supporting interactions, and the types of extracurricular activities that are important to make available (Snell & Janney, 2000). This plan can contribute to planning for positive behavior support as well. Another step in the planning process is to identify the interests and abilities of your students with autism and then to connect your students with others who share those interests and abilities.

Obviously, planning for promoting friendship involves setting goals for instructional activities. So students' IEPs should address the following instructional areas (Kluth, 2003; McConnell, 2002; Snell & Janney, 2000):

Use your *Real Lives and Exceptionalities* DVD to view Jonathan, another young man with autism, participating with disabled and nondisabled peers in Project Success, a community service organization. Click on "Beyond School," and then select, "Jonathan" (Clip 6).

- *Trustworthiness and loyalty:* teaching students how important it is to be a loyal friend by keeping secrets and promises, standing up for one's friends, and supporting the rights of friends.

- *Conflict resolution:* teaching students how to resolve conflicts between and among friends and acquaintances, and helping peers to do so.

- *General friendship skills:* teaching students how to act around a friend, such as taking turns speaking, asking about the well-being or feelings of a friend, asking questions about hobbies and areas of shared interest, and so forth.

- *Positive interaction style:* teaching students to be active listeners, give positive feedback, ask questions, and respond to the needs of others.

- *Taking the perspective of others:* teaching students to consider the needs, feelings, and interests of others; compromise on activity choices; and listen to others' ideas.

Finally, as the IEP team members consider the types of interventions to implement, they should keep in mind the role of strategies such as peer tutoring, social skills groups, student-directed learning strategies, Circles of Friends, and social stories (which we will discuss later in this chapter) for promoting social skills, social competence, social interactions, and friendships for students with autism (Rogers, 2000).

USING EFFECTIVE INSTRUCTIONAL STRATEGIES

Early Childhood Students: Social Stories

Early intervention and education, with special attention to communication and social competence, are essential services for children with autism and their families (Handleman & Harris, 2001; Koegel, 2000; Rogers, 2000; Simpson & Myles, in press). Early intervention and preschool programs use different approaches, including the following:

- Applied behavior analytic techniques, such as discrete trial training (which we discuss later in this chapter) that emphasize assessment, programming, systematic reinforcement of appropriate behavior, and generalization of skills and behavior across settings (places) and people (Smith, 2001; Smith, Green, & Wynn, 2000)

- Incidental teaching in natural environments, similar to that discussed in Chapter 9, such as the child's home, a child-care center, and the community (McGee, Morrier, & Daley, 1999)
- Communication, sensory processing, motor planning, and shared affect with caregivers and peers (Koegel, 2000; Rogers, 2000)

A strategy that is useful across ages, including for preschool children with autism, is the use of social stories. As you have read, students with autism and Asperger syndrome often need additional instruction to learn how to interact appropriately with others in social situations: knowing what is cool and uncool behavior, understanding the perspectives of other people, and knowing the unwritten codes of conduct—what educators call the "hidden curriculum" (Myles & Simpson, 2001). **Social stories** are written by educators, parents, or students and describe social situations, social cues, and appropriate responses to those cues. These stories usually consist of four different types of sentences (Gray, 1998, pp. 178–179):

- Descriptive sentences objectively define where a situation occurs, who is involved, what they are doing, and why.
- Perspective sentences describe a person's internal physical state or desire. Perspective sentences also frequently describe another person's thoughts, feelings, beliefs, and motivations.
- Directive sentences directly define what is expected as a response, to a given cue or in a particular situation.
- Control sentences are statements written by a student to identify strategies the student may use to recall the information in a social story, reassure him- or herself, or define his or her own responses.

Social stories can incorporate a wide range of creative approaches. For example, a teacher in a resource room embedded social stories within a comic strip to enable a teenager with Asperger syndrome to tune into the nuances of conversations with peers (Rogers & Myles, 2001). A music therapist composed original music using the text of a social story as the lyrics (Brownell, 2000). He compared the effectiveness of reading the social stories to students with teaching the students to sing the story. The singing condition was significantly more effective for one of the four students involved in the research; the inappropriate behavior of the three other students decreased during the singing condition but not significantly. These results are promising in terms of adding a musical dimension to social stories. Box 11–3 shows how to use multimedia to present social stories.

The positive effects of social stories occur with preschool-age children across multiple settings (Gray & White, 2002). For example, social stories enabled a 5-year-old boy with autism to decrease the number of tantrums he had at home (Lorimer, Simpson, Myles, & Ganz, 2002). Indeed, a recent synthesis of research on the efficacy of social stories concluded that they yielded positive effects for students with autism, although the authors also called for more research on the strategy (Sansosti, Powell-Smith, & Kincaid, 2004).

Elementary and Middle School Students: Positive Behavior Support

Positive behavior support is a proactive, problem-solving, and data-based approach to improving appropriate behavior and achieving important academic, social, and communication outcomes (Sugai et al., 2000). Teachers instruct students to replace their problem behavior with appropriate behavior, enabling them to benefit much more effectively from the general curriculum.

In addition, positive behavior support also seeks to rearrange school environments and change school systems to prevent students from engaging in problem behaviors in the first place. Because a student's problem behavior often results from someone else's failure to provide individualized and comprehensive support (Turnbull & Ruef, 1996, 1997), positive behavior support seeks to tailor students' environments to their preferences, strengths, and needs.

Technology Tips ~ Multimedia Social Stories

Box 11–3

You certainly remember your parents' or teachers' admonition, given to you as a child: wash your hands before and after meals, after going to the bathroom, and at other important times. And you probably did what they asked—so often that it is now your habit, one you practice without even thinking about it.

But what if you are a young boy with autism who doesn't want to wash his hands? What if you resist "wash" instructions because you don't like the feel of soap (a sensory reason), want to escape from instructions, or want to get attention by not complying? The challenge is clear—to learn rudimentary, life-long cleanliness habits. Would it help to have a social story that you can "see" and practice, using one of your favorite toys—a computer? The answer is yes.

What Is the Technology?

Researchers at the University of Kansas developed a social story about hand washing using HyperCard software (Apple Computer, 1994). First, they developed the story; then they programmed it into the student's computer. The program consisted of a movie showing the student washing his hands, a synthesized computer voice telling the student what to do, and a navigational button that the student could use to key the computer to "tell" his story.

What Do You Do with It?

Together, the student's teachers and parents and the researcher repeatedly exposed the student to the programmed story; the student enjoyed using the computer and also learned every time he turned on his program what he should do about hand washing. The story helped the student learn that there are three settings in which he should wash his hands: before morning snack, before lunch, and after recess. The result: the student made impressive gains in each setting, and the teacher succeeded in combining the student's interest in computers with his need to learn a lifelong skill.

Source: Adapted from Hagiwara, T., & Myles, B. S. (1999). A multimedia social story intervention: Teaching skills to children with autism. *Focus on Autism and Other Developmental Disabilities, 14*(4), 82–95.

A review of more than 100 research articles published between 1985 and 1996 to investigate the behavioral outcomes for individuals with problem behavior (primarily individuals with mental retardation, autism, or both) who were part of this data base concluded the following (Carr et al., 1999):

- Positive behavior support was successful in achieving at least an 80 percent reduction in problem behavior for approximately two-thirds of the behavioral outcomes that were studied in this research.

- A functional assessment substantially increases the success of positive behavior support.

- Positive behavior support is more effective when the focus is not just on the individual with problem behavior but also on other significant people, helping teachers and families change their behavior to support the individual more effectively.

- Positive behavior support is more effective when teachers and families reorganize environments to support the student's success.

- Positive behavior support is just as effective with individuals who have pervasive needs for support as it is with individuals who have only intermittent needs.

Schoolwide positive behavior support includes three components: (1) universal support, (2) group support, and (3) individual support.

How do teachers use these three components? The answer comes from research data. Approximately 76 percent of students receive no more than one office discipline referral during a school year; these students do not have serious problem behavior and can benefit from universal support. Another 15 percent of students receive two to five office referrals; these students are at risk for having problem behavior and can benefit from group support. Finally, about 9 percent receive six or more office referrals; these students have intense problem behavior (Lewis & Sugai, 1999; Sugai et al., 2000). Figure 11–3 illustrates the proportions of students whose behaviors vary from not problematic at all to intensely problematic. Typically, students with autism require individual support to learn appropriate behavior.

The primary goal of universal support is to create a positive learning context for all students. Educators carry out this goal by setting clear expectations for student behavior in all places and activities in a school (cafeteria, hallways, bathrooms, library, and playgrounds), making sure the students agree to those expectations, giving the students many opportunities to meet these expectations, and rewarding them when they do. And educators succeed in implementing universal support when they do the following:

PRAXIS

Standard: Using positive behavior support to manage behavior is an application of PRAXIS™ Standard 3, Delivery of Services to Students with Disabilities. As you manage behavior, organize the classroom, and provide an appropriate physical-social environment, you are acting on behalf of your students.

Figure 11-3 Percentages of students with, at risk for, and without serious problem behavior

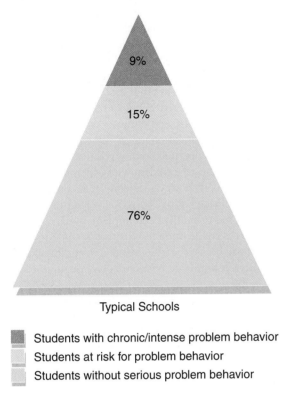

Typical Schools

■ Students with chronic/intense problem behavior
■ Students at risk for problem behavior
■ Students without serious problem behavior

- Clearly define behavioral expectations. These expectations should be defined as simply, positively, and succinctly as possible.

- Teach behavioral expectations. Each expectation should be explicitly taught so that students know exactly what is expected of them.

- Frequently acknowledge appropriate behaviors. A rule of thumb is to have at least four times as many positive affirmations as negative sanctions.

- Evaluate problems and make adaptations on an ongoing basis through a team approach. The team should involve all stakeholders and should review data on behavioral incidences, attendance rates, detentions, and suspension rates and implement proactive strategies to ensure the decline of negative behavior and the increase of positive behavior.

- Target support to address students who need more intense skill development and practice than is offered through universal support. The targeted support might relate to particular behavior in the hallways or cafeteria, social skills, conflict resolution, and/or communication training.

Group support is the second component of positive behavior support (Hawken & Horner, 2001; Turnbull et al., 2002). Group support addresses problem behavior that is occurring with at least 10 to 15 students, each of whom has received universal support but has not yet learned appropriate behavior. Group support typically involves

- Observing the students individually and as a group

- Interviewing the ones who are having problem behaviors

- Developing hypotheses that deal with the behaviors of all of the members of the group

- Teaching the specific skills that all of the students need to eliminate their problem behaviors

Group support is often provided in those places where students have higher rates of problem behaviors, such as hallways, lunchrooms, and playgrounds.

The most intense level of positive behavior support is individual support—the type of support that Jeremy receives. Individual support is for students who are not able to sufficiently eliminate their problem behavior through universal and group support.

Individual support begins with a functional behavioral assessment of the student; the functional behavioral assessment becomes part of the student's nondiscriminatory evaluation and is the basis on which educators then develop the student's IEP. If a student has a behavior that impedes his or other students' learning, IDEA requires the student's IEP team to consider the use of positive behavior interventions and supports as well as other strategies to address the behavior. That is why, for example, Jeremy's IEP team adopts positive behavior support to address his behaviors—namely, his touching, interrupting, talking in class, and tardiness to class. Note, then, that the functional behavioral assessment becomes the foundation for an IEP whose goals include reducing problem behavior, teaching appropriate behavior, maximizing positive outcomes such as communication and social skills, and thereby providing the student with access to the school's general curriculum. In adopting positive behavior support, however, Jeremy's team, and indeed his entire school, also decided to put into place a schoolwide positive behavior support program (Turnbull et al., 2002).

Positive behavior support has primarily been implemented to address the needs of students with externalizing behavior. As you learned in Chapter 5, students with externalizing behavior typically disrupt the class, break the rules, and act out in substantial ways. Box 11–4 addresses the extent to which schoolwide positive behavior support also addresses behaviors that are not disruptive.

We caution you that not all parents adhere to the basic premise of positive behavior support, which is that students learn more effectively when they have positive consequences for their behavior and that punishment might lead them to suppress a behavior temporarily but does not teach them alternative appropriate behavior. Their perspective is represented in Box 11–5.

To read an article about the comprehensive positive behavior support plan at Jeremy's school, go to the Companion Website, *www. prenhall.com/turnbull*, for a link, *http://www.beachcenter.org/PBS-Blueprint.asp.*

Secondary and Transition Students: Discrete Trial Training

You have learned that positive behavior support is important for many students with autism. The behavioral change techniques underlying positive behavior support emerged from a set of strategies and techniques referred to as applied behavior analysis. **Applied behavior analysis** uses the principles of operant psychology to develop techniques that reduce problem behavior or increase positive behavior. In a classic article introducing applied behavior analysis, Baer, Wolf, and Risley (1968) noted that the "process of applying sometimes tentative principles of behavior to the improvement of specific behaviors and simultaneously evaluating whether or not any changes noted are indeed attributable to the process of application" (p. 91).

The principles of applied behavior analysis have been used to design a number of instructional techniques and strategies that are critical to the success of students with disabilities, particularly students with autism. One such strategy is discrete trial training. **Discrete trial training** is based on the three-term contingency outlined by applied behavior analysis: the discriminative stimulus, the response, and the reinforcer or consequence.

Like all other students at Central Middle School, Jeremy is expected to do homework, as he is about to do at his desk at home.

- **Discriminative stimulus.** The discriminative stimulus is a specific event or environmental condition that elicits the desired response. This stimulus acquires control over the desired response when the response is paired with a reinforcer. A common discriminative stimulus is a teacher instruction or command to perform a task.

Your Own Voice ~ Exasperation, Pride, and Hope — Box 11–4

Imagine that you are the 16-year-old sister of a 20-year-old student with autism. You and he attend the same high school. (He can stay there until he's 21 and ages out of IDEA eligibility.) It's hard enough for you to be 16 and a bright girl, mature beyond your age. The raging hormones of your puberty are not a distant memory, but they don't control you like they used to.

What controls you now is equally internal but far less biological. You are searching for your own identity, for a reliable sense of yourself, in a family not so long ago beset by a divorce (you live with your mother during the school year and with your out-of-state father during holidays and summers). And you are also struggling to cope with your brother's autism.

The many different cliques in your school offer you all kinds of choices for "finding yourself." You know you shouldn't accept every offer that comes your way. Illegal and dangerous behavior attends some of the choices you might make. Yet there is the lure of escaping from your brother's autism simply by joining a group whose members and their boyfriends retreat into alcohol and drugs.

Why do you want to escape your brother's autism? That's easy to answer. One answer takes you back to your childhood. You recall his uncontrollable outbursts when you were much younger; you felt defenseless and ran from your parents' home to a neighbor's house, and you still haven't wholly forgiven your parents and him for letting you think you were in jeopardy.

Another answer is entirely contemporary. You are embarrassed by your brother's insistence on hugging your girlfriends and giving excessively enthusiastic high-fives to your boyfriends. You are ashamed by how he is always staring at girls. You feel pity for the ones he has a crush on; each seems helpless to say that she just wants to be his friend, not his girlfriend. You are abashed by how often he interrupts conversations among his teachers and your peers. You almost go through the floor when he picks his nose or farts. Sometimes you just want not to be his sister, but to live with your father a long distance away. You are convinced that his behavior stigmatizes you.

Yet you are proud that he has learned to read, albeit at an elementary-school level. You are delighted that he has held part-time jobs in school. You revel in the fact that he has a wide circle of youthful and middle-aged musicians who are drawn to him by his obvious appreciation of their music and let him listen in on their jam sessions; that he is welcome and understood by your mother's colleagues at her work; and that the school-bus drivers enjoy his presence, often more than they enjoy other students'.

And sometimes you are just so proud, as when he earned his varsity letter as the manager of the football team. You remember the co-captains offering him their varsity-letter jackets, noting that he would not get his for a few months but that he had earned the right to wear one now. What a symbolic gesture, you thought to yourself: my brother brings them towels when they are sweaty and bleeding, and now they bring him symbols of their success. Inclusion works, you know.

So exasperation and pride mingle with each other. And now there is hope.

Your teachers and school administrators have just launched a new program, "Got You Being Good." It's the brand name for something called schoolwide positive behavioral support (PBS).

The program, at least as it is operating now, seems to be tailored for some bad-acting students who don't have disabilities and for a few students with disabilities who disrupt class. Your brother is neither a bad actor nor a disruptive student. He's just a good guy who has some behaviors that really embarrass you. You wish there was more concern about awkward, annoying behavior and not just disruptive behavior. It is almost as if your brother does not disrupt the class enough to get attention from the PBS specialist.

Do you research PBS, hoping it will help your brother? Do you push your brother into it? Do you get your friends to learn about it so they—and you—will be more able to handle your brother's embarrassing behavior? If you take any of these actions, is it because of your concern for him and him alone? Or because you want to shed the stigma that his disability casts onto you?

Whatever action you take will tend to define you in these years of searching for your own authentic identity. So you cannot escape asking, "Who really is supposed to benefit from positive behavior support?"

How do you want to answer the questions in these last two paragraphs? What does Chapter 4 suggest the answers might be?

Diversity Tips ~ When Cultures Clash over Positive Behavior Support — Box 11–5

Positive behavior support reflects certain cultural values. That is obvious if you consider just one word—the key word. *Positive* means that the ways of shaping a child's behavior should not be punishing. *Positive* means that teachers and families will redesign children's physical environments, change the curriculum (what they teach children) and instruction (how they teach children), and deny the child any rewards for problem behavior (for example, not give attention to the student in response to yelling and screaming).

Not punishing means that teachers and families will not use aversive techniques to change a child's behavior. For example, they will not inflict pain or tissue damage; they will not humiliate the child; and they will not deny the child the necessities of life (food, clothing, shelter, and health and educational care).

But what if a child's family has strong cultural beliefs about punishment? What if the family believes that to spare the rod is to spoil the child? Some families come from cultures in which punishment is not only acceptable but mandatory. These families may think of "using the rod" as loving and responsible discipline rather than punishment.

Positive behavior support clashes directly with the rod approach. It also conflicts with what some families and educators believe about discipline in light of their cultural values. We encourage you to work with your school principal and other school colleagues to inform parents about different approaches to problem behavior and then invite their input on how you and they can discipline children in a way that is consistent with research-based practices but does not violate family values.

- **Response.** The response is the behavior the student performs when presented with the discriminative stimulus. The response is the behavior you are trying to teach the child.
- **Reinforcing stimulus.** The reinforcer, or reinforcing stimulus, is an event or action that follows the response and increases the possibility that the response will be exhibited again.

Let's use a simple example to illustrate these principles. You want to teach an adolescent with autism the steps in a vocational task, such as sorting silverware into bins. To do so, the student needs to be able to distinguish each type of utensil (spoon, fork, knife). So you lay a spoon, a fork, and a knife in front of the student and provide a discriminative stimulus by saying, "Show me the spoon." The most likely response from the student would be to point to or touch one of the utensils or, if she is not certain, not to respond at all. If the student points to the spoon, you immediately praise her, saying, "Great job. That's right, that's the spoon." Your praise constitutes the reinforcing stimulus. If the student points to a different utensil or to none of them, she does not get the reinforcer (verbal praise) and instead may be prompted to try again to identify the spoon.

Eventually, if the correct response (pointing to the spoon) to the discriminative stimulus ("Show me the spoon") is reinforced ("Great job!") while other responses to the stimulus are ignored or not reinforced, the student will more consistently respond to the stimulus with the appropriate response.

Discrete trial training is, then, a single instructional trial consisting of the following elements:

- Presentation of the discriminative stimulus, sometimes called a cue
- Presentation of a prompting stimulus, if needed
- The response
- The reinforcing stimulus

In discrete trial training, this trial is followed by a brief interval, called the intertrial interval, before the sequence is repeated. You will notice that we have added a step to the three-term contingency—a prompting stimulus. If a student is learning a brand-new concept, he may need a variety of levels of prompts to be able to exhibit the correct response. A prompting stimulus is any stimulus that, when paired with the discriminative stimulus, increases the probability that the student will exhibit the correct response.

Let's go back to our example of sorting utensils. If a student does not know what a spoon is, the probability is one in four that she will choose the right utensil. That means there is a three in four probability that she will not select the right utensil and will instead point to the fork or knife or simply not respond. If, however, when you present the discriminative stimulus ("Show me the spoon") you also provide a prompt (pointing to the spoon yourself, taking the student's hand and placing it on the spoon, looking at the spoon), you increase the probability that the appropriate response will occur.

Discrete trial training is particularly useful for teaching students with autism new forms of behavior (e.g., behaviors not previously in the child's repertoire) and how to discriminate among events and activities (Smith, 2001). It improves communication outcomes for students with autism (Goldstein, 2003), teaches them how to use augmentative communication, and is effective for instructing them in transition-related skills (Smith, 2001).

INCLUDING STUDENTS WITH AUTISM

Though research demonstrates the success of teaching behavior change techniques to students with autism, these students have one of the lowest rates of inclusion in general education classes. As illustrated in Figure 11–4, fewer than one-third of students with autism spend the majority of their time in general education classes (U.S. Department of Education, 2005). Yet effective educators can assure their progress in the general curriculum. Researchers examined the relationship that general education teachers have with second and third graders with autism who were in an inclusive classroom (Robertson, Chamberlain, & Kasari, 2003). Their findings were encouraging:

1. General education teachers reported that they have positive relationships with students with autism included in their classes. Students with higher rates of problem behavior had less favorable relationships with their teachers.

Values: Student-directed strategies, such as those suggested in Chapter 9, should also be included to promote student *choices* and self-direction.

Figure 11-4 Educational placement of students with autism (2001–2002)

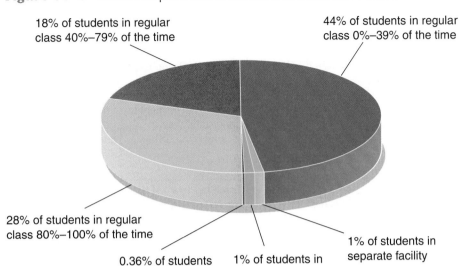

18% of students in regular class 40%–79% of the time

44% of students in regular class 0%–39% of the time

28% of students in regular class 80%–100% of the time

0.36% of students in home/hospital

1% of students in residential facility

1% of students in separate facility

Source: U.S. Department of Education, Office of Special Education Programs. (2005). *IDEA data website* (http://www.ideadata.org/aboutThisSite.asp).

2. A relationship was found between the quality of the teacher-student relationship and the peer status of the child with autism. Children with autism who had more positive relationships with their teachers also were included more by their peers.

3. Half of the children with autism have paraprofessionals, and the presence of a paraprofessional did not interfere with the child's relationship with the teacher.

Box 11–6 offers suggestions for promoting successful inclusion for students with autism.

ASSESSING STUDENTS' PROGRESS

Measuring Students' Progress

Progress in the general curriculum. Most of the procedures for measuring a student's progress in the general curriculum are assessment strategies. Educators often combine them with other strategies to get a more robust understanding of a student's progress. When they bundle assessment strategies with other strategies, they create a holistic assessment or evaluation system. There are several such systems in use in the field of autism.

The Autism Screening Instrument for Educational Planning (ASIEP-2) (Krug, Arick, & Almond, 1993) exemplifies the potential benefits of a more comprehensive assessment system. The ASIEP-2 has five components or subtests that enable educators to evaluate a student's capacity across multiple domains, including communication, social interactions, behavior, and academic content. The most frequently used subtest of the ASIEP-2 is the Autism Behavior Checklist, which is a screening tool to identify the need for further assessment with regard to the presence of autism (Volkmar et al., 1988; Wadden, Bryson, & Rodger, 1991). The Sample of Vocal Behavior subscale and the Social Interaction Assessment both help teachers track their students' progress in areas of other educational needs.

Positive relationships for teachers, peers, and students with autism are often the happy result of including students in regular education classrooms.

279

Inclusion Tips

Box 11–6

	What You Might See	What You Might Be Tempted to Do	Alternate Responses	Ways to Include Peers in the Process
Behavior	She often rocks back and forth over and over during class activities she's not interested in.	Ignore her behavior or tell her to stop.	Conduct a functional behavior assessment to understand why rocking is occurring.	Help peers to understand her behavior. Encourage and support their acceptance of her.
Social interactions	On the playground she is almost always left out of group interactions.	Assume that being alone is how she prefers to spend her time.	Teach her to ask if she can be included and to develop the skills to participate in play with one or two peers.	Pair her with students who understand her preferred communication method.
Educational performance	He learns very slowly and needs a great deal of extra help to learn simple concepts.	Expect less and make the requirements less structured.	Use visual images and music to teach abstract concepts.	Provide opportunities for peer tutoring with visual images and music.
Classroom attitudes	He becomes antagonistic during activities in which there is much noise or confusion.	Remove him from class activities to work alone in the library.	Use social stories to learn ways to concentrate in noisy environments.	Teach peers to write social stories that include all students. Have small groups, including the student, revise and work out different scenarios.

To learn more about the ASIEP-2 and its use to track progress, go to the Companion Website, *www.prenhall.com/turnbull*, and follow the link to the Autism Spectrum Disorders Outcome Study web page, *http://www.autism-study.pdx.edu/Participants.htm*.

To learn more about the SWIS, go to the Companion Website, *www.prenhall.com/turnbull*, and follow the link to the Positive Behavior Intervention and Supports website and tool page, *http://www.swis.org/*.

Of particular relevance to tracking students' progress in the general curriculum, however, is the Educational Assessment subscale of the ASIEP-2. Although designed for screening and planning activities, the Educational Assessment subscale also has been administered to determine students' progress in school and at home (Arick et al., 2003).

Progress in addressing other educational needs. As with any intervention, it is important for educators to measure outcomes related to schoolwide positive behavior interventions and supports. Measurement strategies such as the data-based measurement techniques discussed in Chapter 9 are effective for measuring students' behavioral changes. Since positive behavior support involves multiple levels, however, it is necessary for educators to measure students' behavioral change at the school and district level or else they will not have a full understanding of how well their interventions are reducing problem behavior.

What types of data do educators need to collect to determine the effectiveness of schoolwide positive behavior interventions? Some data are direct counts of problem behavior, including the number of office referrals for the school or district on a weekly or monthly visit or the types of problem behavior reflected in those office referrals. Other types of data involve problem behavior reported by environment or time of day. Some data are indirect indicators of success, including student absences or attendance rates, both as a function of student enrollment. This type of data can be collected by hand or can be collected and analyzed using an online data collection system called the School Wide Information System (May et al., 2003).

Another data-collection tool is the School-Wide Evaluation Tool (SET) (Sugai, Lewis-Palmer, Todd, & Horner, 2001). It assists educators in assessing and evaluating the features of schoolwide behavior support across the academic year and from year to year. Finally, the Self-Assessment of Contextual Fit in Schools (Horner, Salentine, & Albin, 2003) enables teams to assess the need for and impact of the types of supplementary aids and services we have already discussed, such as access and classroom ecological modifications.

Making Accommodations for Assessment

A number of accommodations have been shown to improve students' outcomes on standardized assessments. One such accommodation differs from typical test modifications because it considers not the test itself but the examiner giving the test and his or her interactions with the student. Koegel, Koegel, and Smith (1997) found that students with autism performed better on standardized assessments when provided with more frequent positive reinforcement. Szarko (2000) found that students with autism performed better on standardized assessments when they were administered by a familiar person. These findings are not specific to students with autism. In a meta-analysis of the impact of examiner familiarity, Fuchs and Fuchs (1986) found that students with a wide array of disabilities performed better with a familiar examiner.

Part of the benefit of a familiar examiner for students with autism comes from the fact that the presence of the examiner minimizes the students' anxiety and stress associated with testing. Students with autism frequently have difficulty during times of transition or stress. Typically, on days during which students complete standardized testing, the normal schedule is not followed. Between the disruption to the schedule and the stress associated with testing, particularly high-stakes testing, teachers and school administrators must do whatever they can to reduce the anxiety that students normally will experience, including providing a familiar examiner.

To learn more about these and other tools for assessing positive behavior support, go to the Companion Website, *www.prenhall. com/ turnbull*, and follow the link to the Positive Behavior Intervention and Supports website and tool page, *http://www.pbis.org/ tools.htm*.

Looking to Jeremy's Future ■ ■ ■ ■ ■ ■ ■ ■

At age 13, soon to be 14, Jeremy has another 7 years of schooling ahead of him. Looking ahead and assuming that the positive behavior supports that he has received at Central Middle School continue when he enters Wyandotte High School, and further assuming that his mother, Joyce, father, Richard, and brothers and sisters follow the regimen that they have already begun, it is a safe bet that Jeremy will achieve the goals that IDEA sets for him and other students with disabilities.

He can fully participate in the life of Kansas City. At home, he's a "weather-news hound," accurate about which TV channels show what weather news when. Because good news about Central Middle School has been broadcast within the African American community (news that the need for discipline is down and good behavior and learning are up), a celebrity weatherman, Bryan Busby, himself an African American, has taken an interest in the school. So it is not out of the question for Jeremy to be a production assistant for Busby.

How would Jeremy get to work, crossing the Missouri River from Kansas City, Kansas, to Kansas City, Missouri? Using the city's bus transportation system (remember, Jeremy knows Kansas City as few other people do) seems entirely feasible. Volunteering at Mt. Calvary Baptist Church can enrich him, just as it enriches his mother and father. Continuing education at Donnelly College, just a mile or so from where he lives, or at Kansas City Community College may be just the ticket to increasing his mapping skills. And hanging out with the young men and women who are part of the Central Avenue Betterment Association (the neighborhood Chamber of Commerce) seems quite likely. Indeed, as the word gets out that Central Middle School offers a good learning environment, especially for students whose behaviors otherwise would impede their and others' learning, it is certain that not only Jeremy but all other students will have community opportunities that otherwise would be out of their reach.

You see, it's not only Jeremy who benefits from positive behavior support and other state-of-the-art techniques; all students and their entire community do. What's good for one seems to be good for all. Special education's contributions—and the lessons of Jeremy Jones and his school and family—have a way of radiating across Kansas City, just as those interstate highways that he so loves to draw radiate throughout the entire metropolitan area. Are Jeremy's maps a metaphor for special education's impact? No doubt, they are.

SUMMARY

Identifying students with autism

- Autism is a developmental disability significantly affecting verbal and nonverbal communication and social interaction. It is generally evident before age 3 and adversely affects educational performance. Other characteristics include repetitive activities, stereotyped movements, behavioral challenges, need for environmental predictability, unusual responsiveness to sensory stimulation, and below-average intellectual functioning.

- Autism is part of a broader group of disorders called pervasive developmental disorders. Among the group is the disorder known as Asperger syndrome.

- The majority of people with autism function intellectually as though they have mental retardation. Some, however, have the savant syndrome.

- Autism is caused by abnormalities in brain development, neurochemistry, and genetic factors, but the specific biological trigger is unknown at this time.

- The prevalence of autism is approximately 10 per 10,000 children.

Evaluating students with autism

- The Autism Diagnostic Interview—Revised is an assessment tool that frequently is used to determine whether children have autism.

- A functional behavioral assessment (which is one type of ecological assessment) identifies specific relationships between environmental events and a student's problem behavior. It is used to tailor an intervention plan aimed at helping students to function as successfully as possible.

Designing an appropriate individualized education program

- Planning to implement positive behavior support requires a team effort, with particular emphasis on creating an effective partnership among special educators, family members, and behavior specialists.

- Implementing positive behavior support involves ensuring that issues pertaining to behavioral accessibility are addressed, including building and classroom ecological supplementary aids and supports that promote positive behavior.

- Mnemonic strategies are effective curriculum adaptations and augmentations that enable students with autism to succeed in the general curriculum.

Using effective instructional strategies

- Social stories are effective ways to teach young children with autism a number of skills, particularly social interaction skills.

- Positive behavior support, including schoolwide, group, and individual strategies, have been shown to decrease problem behavior and improve the opportunities for learning.

- Discrete trial training is one strategy derived from applied behavior analysis and applies learning principles from operant psychology to provide an effective way of teaching skills to students with autism.

Including students with autism

- Relative to other students with disabilities, students with autism have one of the lowest rates of inclusion in general education classes.

Assessing students' progress

- Sometimes systems or assessment packages, such as the Autism Screening Instrument for Educational Planning, provide teachers with organized ways to collect data on student progress, including progress in the general curriculum, across multiple domains.

- There are multiple means for collecting data on progress as a function of the implementation of positive behavior supports, most of which focus on collecting data from school referrals, types of problem behavior, or changes in absenteeism or tardiness.

- For students with autism, having a familiar person administer standardized tests may reduce test and schedule anxiety and improve the performance of students with autism.

WHAT WOULD YOU RECOMMEND?

Refer to chapter content and the PRAXIS™ and CEC standards in Appendix A to answer the following questions:

1. Describe the steps of a functional behavior assessment and state the purpose for using this type of evaluation. As you do this, what CEC standards are you addressing?

2. How could you use social stories to help prepare a secondary student with autism for job training in a local pet store? What PRAXIS™ standard are you addressing?

3. Identify five tips that you might specifically remember to enable you as a teacher to facilitate the friendships of students with autism. To which CEC standards does facilitating friendships relate?

4. Visit the Companion Website module for this chapter and locate the link for *www.pbis.org/tools*. Make a list of assessment tools that would be useful in the classroom. What CEC or PRAXIS™ standards are you applying as you do this research and evaluate assessment tools?

Companion Website

Chapter
12

Who is Ryan Frisella?

Let's describe an all-American middle school student, shall we? Let's do it by referring to Ryan Frisella, an eighth grader at Pershing Middle School in San Diego, California, enrolled in the gifted and talented education (GATE) program. With the help of sponsors whom he solicits for funds on behalf of his wheelchair sports team, he participates in a half-marathon annually by riding his hand-cycle, a three-wheeled bike that he propels with his hands instead of his feet. He also is on the junior varsity soccer team sponsored by the San Diego parks and recreation program for individuals with disabilities and travels to interstate competitions. He has endeared himself to his classmates and teachers. According to his mother, Mary, he's bright, witty, concerned about other students, and caring. According to his drama teacher, Terry Miller, he's got the courage of his convictions and a not-to-be-daunted work ethic. He has no fear of standing up for what he believes in: he has advocated for drama education by addressing the San Diego Unified City School District Board of Education. He acts, sings, and dances on stage. Terry says he is "an inspirational person because he is so commanding, in a soft way. His strong will gives him the power of presence."

Have you got a good picture of Ryan? Now add this dimension: he has cerebral palsy; uses crutches, a walker, and a wheelchair; and has had two major surgeries on his legs and feet. When he was advocating before the school board, he hoisted himself out of his wheelchair, grasped a podium designed for standing-up adults, pulled himself to a standing position, and spoke his mind. His most recent surgery, in March 2005, did not prevent him from taking center stage in June as the sultan in his school's production of *Aladdin.* Nor does his disability keep him from dancing if that is what his role calls for, as it did in *The King and I.* He simply balances on his walker, fixes himself into place, and dances with his hands, his feet (holding fast to his walker), and, in Terry's words, "his whole being."

Dancing and taking a leading role, says Terry, is the extra dimension that theater—indeed, all of education—allows: the opportunity to innovate, to make the drama or any form of education believable even though the actor or student has an obvious disability.

So Ryan follows his muse, the muse of the theater. Asked why, he says simply, "I like being on stage and pretending that I'm someone else." Not that he needs to pretend: in spite of the added dimension of his cerebral palsy, Ryan already is the all-American kid.

Why is that so? Terry does not hesitate to answer: Mary, John, and his sister Nicole (a fifth grader) have always expected something unusual from Ryan, so Ryan expects that from himself and teaches his teachers to do likewise. The circle of great expectations began at home, but it is not confined to that one site.

Use your *Real Lives and Exceptionalities* DVD to "Meet Ryan."

Understanding Students with Physical Disabilities and Other Health Impairments

Since the completion of the mapping of the human genome, it has become fashionable to believe that genes are destiny. In one sense, that is true of Kwashon Drayton, a nine-year-old fourth-grader at Meadowfield Elementary School in Columbia, South Carolina. Like his great-grandmother, grandmother, and mother, Kwashon has asthma.

But the genes-as-destiny statement does not acknowledge the beneficial effects of medication for asthma. If it did, perhaps the saying would go something like "Genes are destiny, but medication mitigates them and changes a person's destiny." That's not quite as catchy a phrase, but it is far more accurate for Kwashon. The four medicines he takes daily to treat his asthma make it possible for him to participate fully in all of his school's activities except one, track, which takes a greater lung capacity than the basketball he now enjoys and the football that he plans to start in the fall of his fifth-grade year. And the one medicine he takes to counteract the effects of asthma attacks makes it possible for him to recover quickly, after lying down for a while, and to return to his normal activities in the general academic curriculum, extracurricular activities, and other school activities.

There is very little his mother, Michelle, and father, Vic, or his teachers have to do for him, but that "very little" makes a huge difference:

- Keep him away from peanuts and pets.
- Be sure he dusts his desk and around his home daily.
- Buy an expensive vacuum cleaner, one that has a filter on it, and use it every day.
- Keep the windows shut and, in the summer, the air conditioning on to filter out as much dust, pollen, and grass as possible.

- Encase his mattress and pillows so that their contents do not irritate his lungs.
- Above all, make sure that he takes his medicines daily and that he and his allergy specialist, school nurse, and parents communicate regularly about his health, usually by cell phone.

It's not asthma itself that requires Kwashon to have an IEP. Instead, it's the fact that he has some speech delays that result from his being born prematurely and from having contracted viral meningitis when he was only 3 months old. Two early surgeries partially corrected his hearing and speech: the insertion of tubes into his ears and the removal of his adenoids. But he has needed therapy ever since then, though it is likely that he'll phase out of that next year, in fifth grade.

So Kwashon has a health-care plan for his asthma (under Section 504 of the Rehabilitation Act), an IEP for his speech challenges, nothing except kudos for being an honor-roll student, and an insatiable case of "super-fanitis" for the Miami Heat professional basketball team and the Atlanta Falcons professional football team. As his mother, Michelle, puts it, "He's all boy." So, too, are his younger brothers, Isiah, now 8 years old, and Joshua, now 1 year old. Yet they have defied the genes-as-destiny maxim: neither has asthma or any other challenges.

When asked to compare her years in elementary, middle, and secondary school (before she graduated with her bachelor's degree from the University of South Carolina in 1995) with Kwashon's first 4 years in school, Michelle gave a simple answer: "There's much more awareness and education now than before. And there are prescription medicines, not just the over-the-counter ones I used to use." Yes, genes are destiny, but they are not, by any means, a person's entire destiny.

Who is Kwashon Drayton?

IDENTIFYING STUDENTS WITH PHYSICAL DISABILITIES AND OTHER HEALTH IMPAIRMENTS

Unlike previous and subsequent ones, this chapter discusses two categories of exceptionality: physical disabilities and other health impairments. We begin, as in the other chapters, by providing an overview of these categories. Since there are common educational issues involving students with physical disabilities and other health impairments, we address these common issues throughout the chapter.

PHYSICAL DISABILITIES

Defining Physical Disabilities

IDEA and its current regulations refer to physical disabilities, such as Ryan's cerebral palsy, as orthopedic impairments:

> "Orthopedic impairment" means a severe orthopedic impairment that adversely affects a child's educational performance. The term includes impairments caused by congenital anomaly (e.g., clubfoot, absence of some member, etc.), impairments caused by disease (e.g., poliomyelitis, bone tuberculosis, etc.), and impairments from other causes (e.g., cerebral palsy, amputations, and fractures or burns that cause contractures). (34 C.F.R., sec. 300.7[b][7])

Although IDEA uses the term *orthopedic impairments,* educators typically use the term *physical disabilities* when referring to these same conditions. So there are two terms in use: the IDEA term and the educators' term. But special educators also sometimes refer to students with severe and multiple disabilities (see Chapter 10) or traumatic brain injury (see Chapter 13) as having physical disabilities. All of this different usage means that there is also an aggregate usage: the term *physical disabilities* typically refers to a large group of students who are subcategorized into groups that are quite different from each other, even though they may have the same condition. You may recall that Thomas Ellenson, from Chapter 1, also has cerebral palsy. Like Ryan, he has mobility challenges; unlike Ryan, however, he also has communication challenges.

Because physical disabilities often occur in combination with other disabilities, it is hard to determine their prevalence. Nevertheless, the U.S. Department of Education (2005) reported that schools served 68,188 students, ages 6 to 21, who have physical disabilities during the 2003–2004 school year. This number represents 0.1 percent of all students receiving special education services. We focus here on cerebral palsy and spina bifida.

Cerebral Palsy: Describing the Characteristics and Determining the Causes

What is cerebral palsy? *Cerebral* refers to the brain. *Palsy* describes the lack of muscle control that affects a student's ability to move and to maintain balance and posture. That is why Ryan uses crutches, a walker, and (like Thomas Ellenson), a wheelchair, choosing the assistance he needs according to the particular challenges of his environment or his activities. **Cerebral palsy,** then, is a disorder of movement or posture. It occurs because a person's brain cannot control his or her muscles. The impairment occurs in the brain's development (usually by 6 years of age), and the brain damage is nonprogressive (Pellegrino, 2002). Cerebral palsy is a lifetime condition; but it is not a disease, so it is inappropriate to consider children and youth with cerebral palsy to be sick (Taft, 1999). The prevalence of cerebral palsy is 1.5 to 2.5 individuals with cerebral palsy per 1,000 individuals in the population (Hagberg et al., 1996; Nickel, 2000).

There are four types of cerebral palsy; each refers to the person's movement patterns:

- **Spastic** involves tightness in one or more muscle groups and affects 70 to 80 percent of individuals with cerebral palsy. Ryan has this type.

Visit the Companion Website, *www.prenhall.com/turnbull*, for a link to United Cerebral Palsy, the largest professional and consumer organization focusing on cerebral palsy, *www.ucp.org*.

PRAXIS

Standard: Understanding the characteristics and needs of students with physical disabilities or other health impairments is an application of PRAXIS™ Standard 1, Understanding Exceptionalities.

- **Athetoid** involves abrupt, involuntary movements of the head, neck, face, and extremities, particularly the upper ones.

- **Ataxic** involves unsteadiness, lack of coordination and balance, and varying degrees of difficulty with standing and walking.

- **Mixed** combines spastic muscle tone and the involuntary movements of athethoid cerebral palsy.

In addition to characterizing cerebral palsy by the nature of a person's movement, professionals also refer to the part of the person's body that is affected. In this **topographical classification system,** the specific body location of the movement impairment correlates with the location of the brain damage. Figure 12–1 describes the topographical classification system.

What other conditions are associated with cerebral palsy? Many health and developmental problems may accompany cerebral palsy (Croen, Grether, Curry, & Nelson, 2001; Nickel, 2000). Because cerebral palsy results from brain damage, there is a significant relationship between cerebral palsy and mental retardation. Fifty to about 70 percent of people with cerebral palsy also have mental retardation (Pellegrino, 2002). It is important to remember, however, that some individuals with cerebral palsy, such as Ryan Frisella and Thomas Ellenson, are intellectually quite capable.

Children and youth with cerebral palsy also are more likely to have other limitations:

- Forty to 50 percent develop seizures (Aksu, 1990).

- Thirty percent have hearing, speech, and/or language impairments (Pellegrino, 2002).

- More children with cerebral palsy than children without it experience visual impairments, feeding and growth difficulties, and emotional and behavioral disorders (Azcue et al., 1996; Reilly, Skuse, & Poblete, 1996). For example, Ryan has some vision challenges, so he uses enlarged graph paper to do his math problems.

What are the causes of cerebral palsy? Cerebral palsy is caused by **prenatal** (e.g., infection or brain malformation before birth), **perinatal** (e.g., lack of oxygen or infection during birth), or **postnatal** (e.g., brain injury or meningitis after birth) factors (Griffin, Fitch, & Griffin, 2002). The vast majority of children and youth with cerebral palsy have causes related to prenatal development and prematurity (Croen et al., 2001). That's the cause of Ryan's disability. He was born at 33½ weeks, weighed 4 pounds, 5 ounces, and was on a respirator for his first 24 hours of life. Not until his mother, Mary, mentioned to his physicians, when Ryan was 9 months old, that his legs seemed stiff was he diagnosed as having cerebral palsy.

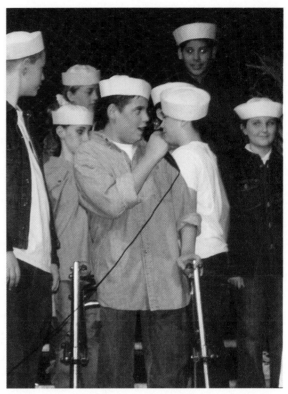

Despite his cerebral palsy, Ryan Frisella is a song-and-dance man. Disabilities limit but they do not always prevent a student from participating in general extracurricular activities.

Values: Cerebral palsy may impair a student in some ways, but it should not disguise a student's *strengths,* such as Ryan's literary and dramatic skills.

Use your *Real Lives and Exceptionality* DVD to see what it is like living with cerebral palsy. Click on Beyond Schools and view "Maxine" (Clip 3).

Figure 12-1   Topographical classification system

Monoplegia: one limb.
Paraplegia: legs only.
Hemiplegia: one half of body.
Triplegia: three limbs (usually two legs and one arm).
Quadriplegia: all four limbs.
Diplegia: more affected in the legs than the arms.
Double hemiplegia: arms more involved than the legs.

The severity of a person's cerebral palsy generally depends on the type and timing of the injury. For example, bleeding in the brain of very premature babies can cause extensive damage.

Spina Bifida: Describing the Characteristics and Determining the Causes

What is spina bifida? **Spina bifida** refers to a malformation of the spinal cord (Liptak, 2002). The spine is made up of separate bones called vertebrae, which normally cover and protect the spinal cord. In a person with spina bifida, the spinal column does not close completely and cover the spinal cord, usually resulting in a protrusion of the spinal cord, its coverings, or both. A saclike bulge may occur in any part of the person's spine, from neck to buttocks. The higher on the spinal column the impairment appears, the more severe the person's loss of function. Typically, the impairment occurs in the lower region and causes complete or partial paralysis of only the person's lower extremities and loss of skin sensation. The prevalence of spina bifida is 0.32 per 1,000 births and is declining (Lary & Edmonds, 1996; Stevenson et al., 2000). Spina bifida occurs more frequently in people who have a lower socioeconomic status or who live in neighborhoods characterized by lower socioeconomic status (Wasserman et al., 1998). Spina bifida is not a progressive condition and has three common forms (see Figure 12–2):

- **Spina bifida occulta.** The spinal cord or its covering do not protrude and only a small portion of the vertebrae, usually in the low spine, is missing. This is the mildest and most common form.

- **Meningocele.** The covering of the spinal cord, but not the cord itself, actually protrudes through the opening created by the defect in the spine. This more serious form usually does not cause a person to experience mobility impairments.

- **Myelomeningocele.** The protrusion or sac contains not only the spinal cord's covering but also a portion of the spinal cord or nerve roots. This is the most serious form and results in varying degrees of leg weakness, inability to control bowels or bladder, and a variety of physical problems such as dislocated hips or club feet.

The location of the insult to the spine determines the degree to which mobility is affected. If the insult occurs at the thoracic vertebra T-12 or above, total paralysis of the legs results. The **lumbar nerves** move the leg muscles, and the **sacral nerves** control the foot muscles. As we have already noted, the lower the impairment in the lumbar or sacral regions, the greater the person's ability to walk without braces and crutches.

What are other conditions associated with spina bifida? Approximately 75 percent of children and youth with spina bifida have typical intelligence (Friedrich et al., 1991; Liptak, 2002), but some students with spina bifida do have learning difficulties (Bigge, Best, & Heller, 2001; Russell, 2004).

Myelomeningocele almost always occurs above the part of the spinal cord that controls the bladder and bowels (Liptak, 2002; Nickel, 2000). Constipation, bladder paralysis, urinary tract infections, and resulting incontinence are common. Kidney failure can also result. Many students can be taught the technique of **clean intermittent catheterization** and effective bowel management (Lutkenhoff, 1999). Working with a school nurse trained in these techniques, teachers can monitor students' self-management abilities (Heller et al., 2000).

What causes spina bifida? The exact causes of spina bifida are unknown, but the condition occurs during the very early days of pregnancy (Nickel, 2000). Parents do not carry any particular gene that specifically causes spina bifida, although their genes may interact with environmental factors (e.g., nutrition, medication, and exposure to high temperatures) to trigger the malformation in the developing embryo (Hall & Solehdin, 1998; Nickel, 2000).

A woman who uses daily vitamin supplements containing folic acid reduces the risk that her baby will have neural tube defects such as spina bifida (Berry et al., 1999; Liptak, 2002). Folic acid is a B-vitamin that enables bodies to build healthy cells. Beginning in 1998, the federal Food and Drug Administration has required breads and enriched cereal grain products to be fortified with synthetic folic acid. Since then, there has been a 19 percent reduction in the number of cases of spina bifida and related conditions (Honein et al., 2001).

Figure 12–2 Types of spina bifida

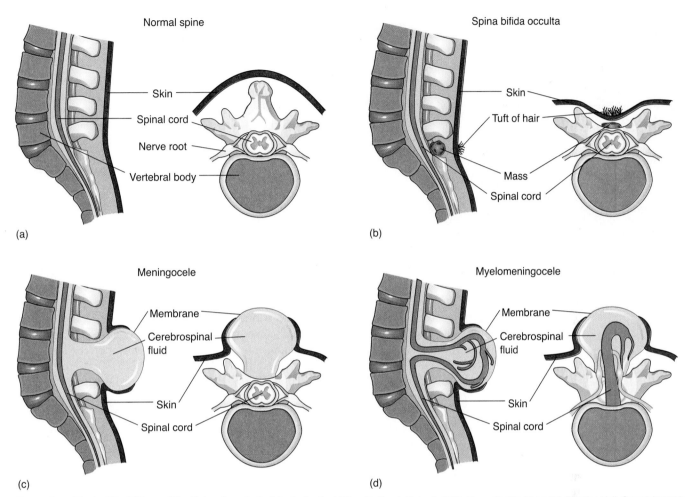

Normal spine

- Skin
- Spinal cord
- Nerve root
- Vertebral body

(a)

Spina bifida occulta

- Skin
- Tuft of hair
- Mass
- Spinal cord

(b)

Meningocele

- Membrane
- Cerebrospinal fluid
- Skin
- Spinal cord

(c)

Myelomeningocele

- Membrane
- Cerebrospinal fluid
- Skin
- Spinal cord

(d)

Source: From *Physical Disabilities and Health Impairments: An Introduction* (p. 118), edited by J. Umbreit, 1983, Upper Saddle River, NJ: Prentice Hall. Copyright 1983 by Prentice Hall. Reprinted with permission.

OTHER HEALTH IMPAIRMENTS

Defining Other Health Impairments

The current regulations implementing IDEA define students with other health impairments as those "having limited strength, vitality or alertness, including a heightened alertness to environmental stimuli, that results in limited alertness with respect to the educational environment, that

1. is due to chronic or acute health problems such as asthma, attention deficit disorder or attention deficit hyperactivity disorder, diabetes, epilepsy, a heart condition, hemophilia, lead poisoning, leukemia, nephritis, rheumatic fever, and sickle cell anemia; and

2. adversely affects a child's educational performance." (34 C.F.R., sec. 300.7[c] [9])

The word *other* in the categorical name *other health impairments* distinguishes these conditions from severe and multiple disabilities (Chapter 10), physical disabilities (this chapter), and traumatic brain injury (Chapter 13). To be served under the "other health impairments" category, the student's health condition, such as Kwashon Drayton's, must limit his strength, vitality, or alertness to such a degree that the student's educational progress is adversely affected. Kwashon does not qualify under IDEA; his educational progress is just fine, as evidenced by his receiving academic honors. But because his asthma requires accommodations in school (such as

Kwashon Drayton is fully included in his school's academic program, as this photograph portrays.

On the Companion Website, *www.prenhall.com/turnbull*, you will find a link to the Epilepsy Foundation, which has the mission of promoting research, education, advocacy, and service for individuals with epilepsy, *www.ef.org*.

screening his food so he will not eat any peanuts or derivatives of them and so that his school nurse will be authorized to administer medication in an emergency and his teachers will be trained to perform CPR), he does qualify under Section 504 of the Rehabilitation Act (which you learned about in Chapter 8).

As you also learned in Chapter 8, AD/HD falls into the category of other health impairments. In terms of the three criteria of limitations in strength, vitality, or alertness, students with AD/HD, including Kelsey, whom you met in Chapter 8, generally experience difficulty only with alertness.

Under the current IDEA definition, a student may have a chronic or an acute condition. A chronic condition develops slowly and has long-lasting symptoms. Students with diabetes, a chronic condition, experience lifelong medical needs. A student with asthma, such as Kwashon, has a chronic condition; when he has an asthma episode involving severe shortness of breath and violent coughing, he has an acute condition and must take medication (an inhaled spray) and then rest briefly to recover his strength. An acute condition typically develops quickly and has symptoms that last for a relatively short period of time. A student with pneumonia may need temporary homebound services; however, once she recovers from this acute condition, she no longer is eligible for special education services.

In the 2003–2004 school year, schools served 452,045 students (0.7 percent of the school-age population) ages 6 to 21 under IDEA as other health impaired (U.S. Department of Education, 2005). Ten to 30 percent of all students will experience a childhood chronic illness lasting 3 months or longer (Kliebenstein & Broome, 2000). More than 200 specific health impairments exist, and most are rare (Thies, 1999). For that reason, we focus on two relatively prevalent conditions: epilepsy and asthma.

Epilepsy: Describing the Characteristics and Determining the Causes

What is epilepsy? Epilepsy is a condition characterized by **seizures,** which are temporary neurological abnormalities that result from unregulated electrical discharges in the brain, much like an electrical storm. If a person has seizures only once or temporarily, perhaps from a high fever or brain injury, he or she does not have epilepsy. To be classified as having epilepsy, an individual must have two or more seizures more than 24 hours apart (Shinnar, 2000). Most people associate epilepsy with convulsive seizures, but students can also have seizures that manifest as a brief period of unconsciousness or altered behavior that is sometimes misinterpreted as daydreaming.

The majority of seizures can be classified into two types: seizures with primarily altered consciousness and partial seizures (Weinstein, 2002). Seizures with **primarily altered consciousness** affect large areas of the brain and may manifest in limited activity (absence seizures) or extreme motor behaviors (tonic-clonic seizures). During **absence seizures** (pronounced ab-SAHNZ) (formerly known as *petit mal*), the student also loses consciousness but only for a brief period lasting from a few seconds to a half-minute or so. The student, teachers, and peers might not realize a seizure has taken place. Absence seizures can occur up to hundreds of times a day and can severely affect learning.

Tonic-clonic seizures (once known as *grand mal*) cause the student to lose consciousness and often to fall to the ground and have sudden, involuntary contractions of groups of muscles. "Clonic (repetitive jerking occurring at a regular rate) and tonic (sustained stiffening) seizures often occur within the same event" (Weinstein, 2002, p. 499). Students may make unusual noises during tonic-clonic seizures, have a bluish hue, lose bladder control, require sleep or rest after the seizure, and typically have no memory of the seizure (Weinstein, 2002).

A second major type of seizure is **partial seizures.** During partial seizures, a student may be affected in the motor control center of the brain as well as in sensory, behavioral, and cognitive areas. Partial seizures can occur in only one region of the brain or spread to other brain hemispheres. Approximately 60 percent of all children with epilepsy have partial seizures (Eriksson & Koivikko, 1997). Following are some trends related to the occurrence of seizures (Shinnar, 2000):

- After a first seizure, approximately 40 to 50 percent of children have another seizure.

- Approximately three-fourths of children with epilepsy enter a state of remission, which means having no seizures whether they take or don't take medication.

- Approximately two-thirds to three-fourths of children with epilepsy who are seizure-free for more than 2 to 4 years on medication are able to stop taking medication and remain seizure-free.

- The majority of children who experience seizures after they stop medication become seizure-free after they start medication again.

Figure 12–3 lists appropriate first-aid measures for different seizure types.

Figure 12–3   First aid for seizures

Seizure Type	Characteristics	First Aid	Possibility of Injury
General seizures			
Tonic-clonic	Uncontrolled jerking Loss of consciousness Disorientation Violent reactions Cessation of breathing Vomiting Loss of continence	Lay the person on side. Move potentially dangerous or fragile objects. Place pillow under her head. Never attempt to restrain her or place anything in her mouth.	Fairly high; person often bumps into objects during seizure
Tonic	Sudden stiffening of muscles Rigidity Falling to ground	Reassure the individual. Provide a place to lie down afterward. Stay calm.	Quite high; person may strike an object while falling
Atonic	Sudden loss of muscle tone resulting in a collapse on ground	Reassure the individual. Provide a place to rest.	High; person may fall into an object
Absence	Very brief interruption in consciousness Appearance of momentary déjà-vu	Reassure the individual following the event.	Fairly low
Partial seizures			
Simple partial	Twitching movements Sensation of déjà-vu	Reassure the student.	Fairly low
Complex partial	Altered state of consciousness Psychomotor movements	Provide verbal reassurance during occurrence.	Fairly low unless there is increased physical activity

Seek medical attention immediately if . . .

- There is no previous history of seizures, especially if the student is experiencing a tonic-clonic seizure.
- Several tonic-clonic seizures follow one another in rapid succession.
- A tonic-clonic seizure lasts for more than 2 to 3 minutes.

Source: From "What Every Teacher Should Know about Epilepsy," by G. L. Spiegel, S. K. Cutler, and C. E. Yetter, 1996, *Intervention in School and Clinic, 32*(1), pp. 35–37. Copyright 1996 by PRO-ED, Inc. Adapted and reprinted with permission.

Values: Because epilepsy and other disabilities can impair a person physically and emotionally, it is important for educators to instill *great expectations* in their students with disabilities, sometimes by asking students to write a short biography about the success stories of relatively well known people with a particular disability.

What are other conditions associated with epilepsy? Most children with epilepsy have average IQs; however, children with epilepsy are more likely to experience learning disabilities as compared to those without epilepsy (Black & Hynd, 1995; Mitchell & Flourie, 1999). Their academic challenges often include math, reading, and any other tasks requiring memory. A study that followed students with epilepsy over 4 years revealed that their academic achievements still remain low after their epilepsy had improved (Austin, Huberty, Huster, & Dunn, 1999). Students with absence seizures are at risk for being misidentified as having AD/HD (Agnew, Nystul, & Conner, 1998). A higher-than-average prevalence of depression has been reported in adolescents with epilepsy. Youths who have negative attitudes about their epilepsy and who experience dissatisfaction with family relationships are more likely to experience depression (Dunn, Austin, & Huster, 1999).

What are the causes of epilepsy? Insults to the brain create a level of brain vulnerability that can result in the onset of seizures. Brain insults can have prenatal (infections), perinatal (birth trauma), or postnatal (poisoning, stress, fatigue, sleep deprivation) causes (Frucht, Quigg, Schwaner, & Fountain, 2000; Roberts, 2000). In approximately three-fourths of individuals with epilepsy, the precise cause of the brain insult that triggers epilepsy is unknown (DePaepe, Garrison-Kane, & Doelling, 2002).

The prevalence of epilepsy changes over the lifespan. Up to 10 percent of all children experience a seizure at some point in their childhood or youth, but only 1 percent of the population has epilepsy by the age of 20 (Hauser, 1994).

Asthma: Describing the Characteristics and Determining the Causes

What is asthma? Asthma is a chronic lung condition characterized by airway obstruction, inflammation, and increased sensitivity (Aronson, 1995; Eisenberg, 2000). The symptoms and severity of asthma vary widely from person to person and are generally classified in the following ways (National Heart, Lung, and Blood Institute, 1997):

- Mild intermittent (two or fewer episodes per week)

- Mild persistent (more than two per week)

- Moderate persistent (daily)

- Severe persistent (continual and interferes with physical activity, such as Kwashon's running track)

Although most students with asthma have mild to moderate symptoms, asthma episodes (the attacks that Kwashon's parents or the school nurse treat with medication) account on an annual basis for approximately 500,000 hospitalizations, 2 million emergency department visits, 14 million absences from school, and 5,000 deaths (Mannino et al., 2002). Common symptoms requiring prompt attention include wheezing or chronic cough, shortness of breath, rapid breathing, and blue-hued lips or nails (DePaepe et al., 2002). Figure 12–4 includes a list of symptoms requiring emergency treatment.

Asthma is the most common chronic disease among children in the United States. Approximately 7 to 10 percent of the general childhood population has a diagnosis of asthma (Aronson, 1995; National Heart, Lung, and Blood Institute, 1999). The risk of asthma increases among students from diverse backgrounds. A study of the prevalence of asthma in children attending Head Start reported that the prevalence rate was two to five times higher than the rate that occurs in the general population of children (Ladebauche et al., 2001; Slezak et al., 1998; Walders, McQuaid, & Dickstein, 2004). Researchers attribute this high level of asthma to the high-risk factors in low-income communities and, as in Kwashon's case, to genetic factors. In addition, asthma is the most common chronic illness among Latino children; their condition is associated with their quality of life, the reduced likelihood that they will use

Michelle and Kwashon Drayton are the poster-family for asthma prevention and treatment efforts in South Carolina.

Diversity Tips ~ Teaching Parents and Changing Bedrooms   Box 12–1

Throughout this book, we have emphasized how important it is for educators and parents to be partners with each other in the child's education. The partnership can extend beyond a narrowly defined understanding of "education" (namely, one that is classroom- or school-based) to those aspects of a child's health that impair his or her ability to benefit from an education.

A parent education program in San Diego, California, exemplifies how educators can teach parents of students with asthma and improve the students' health. Health educators worked with approximately 200 low-income, underserved Latino families to teach them about the causes of asthma (triggers) and what they might do to reduce them in their children's bedrooms (controllers).

The triggers typically are household items associated with dust, dust mites, and mold spores, such as carpeted flooring, window drapes, stuffed animals, plants, and household pets (dogs and cats). The controllers are the household items that typically help control exposure to dust mites and mold, such as nonfeather pillows, zippered mattress encasements, and covered or sealed air vents in the child's sleeping area.

First, the educators tested family members (98 percent were mothers of children with asthma) to learn what they knew about the causes/triggers and preventions/controllers. The testing was done in the families' homes and in the language (English, Spanish, or both) that the family preferred to use.

Then the educators spent an average of an hour and 45 minutes teaching the families, in their homes, about triggers and controllers. Finally, they tested the families to determine what they had learned and whether they took any action to reduce the triggers and increase the controllers. The results were encouraging. There was a 30 percent increase on average in the families' knowledge about how to manage asthma, a 25 percent reduction in the number of triggers in a child's bedroom, and a 29 percent increase in the number of controllers in the child's bedroom.

Teachers can supplement these types of activities by doing the following:

- Providing information to their students' families, in the families' native language, about how teachers are controlling the triggers at school and how families can follow through at home
- Teaching their students to understand their own asthma and how to regulate themselves to minimize its effects
- Reinforcing, through regular communication with their students' families, how trigger control is benefiting their child in school

Source: Adapted from Jones, J. A., Wahlgren, D., Meltzer, S. B., Meltzer, E. O., Clark, N. M., & Hovell, M. F. (2001). Increasing asthma knowledge and changing home environments for Latino families with asthmatic children. *Parent Education and Counseling, 42,* 76–79.

preventive medications and receive nebulizers to treat their condition after they have been hospitalized, and the increased probability that they will use an emergency room for the treatment of acute asthma episodes (Jones, Wahlgren, Meltzer, Meltzer, Clark, & Hovell, 2001). In Box 12–1, you will learn how an intervention to educate Latino families increased their knowledge about asthma and their capacity to take action to reduce the prevalence of allergies in a child's sleeping area. Kwashon's mother Michelle operates a similar program in Columbia, South Carolina, serving 77 families by educating them about the triggers that bring on asthma and the countermeasures that families should take to control dust, pollen, mold, and mites.

What are other conditions associated with asthma? Children and youth who have asthma often experience fatigue from waking during the night because of breathing difficulties, and they are absent from school due to symptoms. Both fatigue and school absenteeism are associated with lower academic performance (Celano & Geller, 1993; Diette et al., 2000), although some students, such as Kwashon, earn academic honors.

Figure 12–4   When to seek emergency care for asthma

- Symptoms worsen, even after the medication has had time to work (generally 5 to 10 minutes).
- The student cannot speak a sentence without pausing for breath, has difficulty walking, and/or stops playing and cannot start again.
- Chest and neck are pulled or sucked in with each breath.
- Peak flow rate lessens or does not improve after bronchodilator treatment or drops below 50 percent of the student's personal best.
- Lips and fingernails turn blue: emergency care is needed immediately!
- A second wave occurs after an episode subsides; the student is uncomfortable and having trouble breathing but does not wheeze.

What are the causes of asthma? Individuals with asthma have airways that are especially sensitive. Asthma symptoms are triggered by food, exercise, cold air, respiratory infections, and environmental allergens, including cigarette smoke, dust, mold, gases, and chemicals (DePaepe et al., 2002; Sotir, Yetts, & Shy, 2003). Sometimes, as we have noted, asthma is an inherited condition, as it is for Michelle Drayton and her son Kwashon.

A research study investigating triggers for asthma early in life reported that an asthma diagnosis before the age of 5 was associated with many environmental allergens, including smoke, exhaust, cockroaches, and pesticides (Salam, Li, Langholz, & Gilliland, 2004). Additionally, children who attended daycare centers had a 1.6 times higher risk of developing childhood asthma than did children who did not attend them.

EVALUATING STUDENTS WITH PHYSICAL DISABILITIES AND OTHER HEALTH IMPAIRMENTS

Determining the Presence of Physical Disabilities and Other Health Impairments

Figures 12–5 and 12–6 highlight the nondiscriminatory evaluation processes for determining the presence of physical disabilities and other health impairments, respectively. In both cases, a physical examination from a physician is often the first step in determining whether or not the student has a disability. Although medical exams are individualized according to the particular symptoms of each student, a neurological exam is frequently administered when there is any concern about the brain's involvement in a particular condition. In Chapter 13, you will learn about the use of neuroimaging with students who have brain injuries. **Neuroimaging** provides detailed pictures of various parts of the brain that are helpful in determining the presence of a disability. Neuroimaging is exceedingly helpful in determining the presence of cerebral palsy, spina bifida, and epilepsy (Pellegrino, 2002; Weinstein, 2002). Neuroimaging is not needed, however, for students who have symptoms associated only with asthma.

Prenatal screening is now used to detect spina bifida, and in the future it is likely to be used to detect many other conditions. The most frequently used prenatal test to detect spina bifida is **maternal serum alpha-fetoprotein.** Alpha-fetoprotein is made by babies during their prenatal development. When a baby has spina bifida, its alpha-fetoprotein is higher than normal. If a blood test of the mother, at 16 weeks' gestation, reveals a higher-than-normal level of alpha-fetoprotein, further testing can confirm or disconfirm the presence of spina bifida.

One way to prevent serious loss of neurological functioning due to spina bifida is to perform fetal surgery. Only a few medical centers have the capability to perform such surgery. Currently, the surgery does not restore neurological functioning that has already been lost but is designed to prevent further malformation before delivery. During the surgery, the neurosurgeon exposes the fetus, closes the lesions on the baby's back, and then closes the incision in the mother.

Although fetal surgery has many benefits, it also has risks. The risk for the fetus includes the greater likelihood of a premature delivery. The risk for the mother can include infection, gestational diabetes, and blood loss. Box 12–2 challenges you to weigh the pros and cons of fetal surgery.

Determining the Nature of Specially Designed Instruction and Services

Many students with physical disabilities or other health impairments need assistance with functional tasks such as changing positions, recreational movement, hygiene, and safety. Ryan, for example, receives help from Hank Jurczak, a special education technician for the past 28 years, in putting books and his laptop computer into and taking them out of his backpack, which he carries on the back of his wheelchair; Hank also is with Ryan whenever Ryan has to use the bathroom, making sure that Ryan does not fall when transferring from or to his crutches, walker, or chair. In Hank's words, "I help Ryan do whatever he needs to do and can't do, but I push him to

Figure 12–5 Nondiscriminatory evaluation process for determining the presence of physical disabilities

Observation	***Parents or teacher observe:*** The student has difficulty moving in an organized and efficient way; with fine-motor activities; with gross-motor activities; with activities of daily living, such as dressing; with postural control; and with speaking.
	Physician observes: The child is not passing developmental milestones. Movement is better on one side of the body than the other. Muscle tone is too floppy or stiff. The child has problems with balance or coordination or has neurological signs that suggest a physical disability.
Screening	***Assessment measures:***
	Developmental assessment: The child is not meeting developmental milestones or shows poor quality of movement on measures administered by a physician, physical therapist, occupational therapist, and psychologist.
	Functional assessment: Activities of daily living are affected.
Prereferral	Prereferral is typically not used with these students because of the need to quickly identify physical disabilities. Also, most children with physical disabilities will be identified by a physician before starting school.
Referral	Students with physical disabilities who are identified before starting school should receive early intervention services and a nondiscriminatory evaluation upon entering school. Because some physical disabilities may develop after a student enters school, teachers should refer any student who seems to have significant difficulty with motor-related activities.
Nondiscriminatory evaluation procedures and standards	***Assessment measures:***
	Individualized intelligence test: Standard administration guidelines may need to be adapted because the student's physical disability interferes with the ability to perform some tasks. Results may not be an accurate reflection of ability. The student may be average, above average, or below average in intelligence.
	Individualized achievement test: The student may be average, above average, or below average in specific areas of achievement. Standard administration guidelines may need to be adapted to accommodate student's response style. Results may not accurately reflect achievement.
	Motor functioning tests: The student's differences in range of motion, motor patterns, gaits, and postures may present learning problems. Also, length and circumference of limbs and degrees of muscle tone or muscle strength may affect his or her ability to learn specific skills.
	Tests of perceptual functioning: The student is unable or has difficulty in integrating visual/auditory input and motor output in skills such as cutting and carrying out verbal instructions in an organized manner.
	Adaptive behavior scales: The student may have difficulty in self-care, household, community, and communication skills because of the physical disability.
	Anecdotal records: Reports suggest that the student has functional deficits and requires extra time or assistance in mobility, self-care, household, community, and communication skills because of the physical disability.
	Curriculum-based assessment: The student's physical disability may limit accuracy of curriculum-based assessments.
	Direct observation: The student is unable to organize and complete work or has difficulty doing so.
Determination	The nondiscriminatory evaluation team determines that the student has a physical disability and needs special education and related services.

Figure 12–6 Nondiscriminatory evaluation process for determining the presence of other health impairments

Observation	***Parents or teacher observe:*** The student may seem sluggish or have other symptoms that suggest illness. The parent takes the student for a medical examination. ***Physician observes:*** During a routine physical or a physical resulting from symptoms, the physician determines why the student needs further medical assessment. Some health impairments are detemined before or shortly after birth.
Screening	***Assessment measures:*** **Battery of medical tests prescribed by physician and/or specialists:** Results reveal that the student has a health impairment. A physician makes the diagnosis.
Prereferral	Prereferral may or may not be indicated, depending on the severity of the health impairment. Some students function well in the general classroom. A decision may be made to serve the student with a 504 plan if accommodations are needed solely to monitor medications and/or to make sure the faculty knows what to do if the student has a medical emergency.
Referral	Students with health impairments that adversely affect their learning or behavior need to be referred for educational assessment.
Nondiscriminatory evaluation procedures and standards	***Assessment measures:*** **Medical history:** Completed jointly by parents, medical, and school personnel, the history yields information needed to develop a health care plan. **Individualized intelligence test:** The student's condition or treatment may contribute to a decrease in IQ. **Individualized achievement test:** The student's medical condition and/or treatment regimen may affect achievement. **Behavior rating scales:** The student is not mastering the curriculum in one or more areas as a result of the condition, treatment, and/or resulting absences. **Curriculum-based assessment:** The student is not mastering the curriculum in one or more areas as a result of the condition, treatment, and/or resulting absences. **Direct observation:** The student may experience fatigue or other symptoms resulting from the condition or treatment, detrimentally affecting classroom progress.
Determination	The nondiscriminatory evaluation team determines that the student has an other health impairment and needs special education and related services.

do it himself. I have to restrain myself from doing things for Ryan. My job, ironically, is trying to put myself out of work."

Often physical therapists and occupational therapists test a student's functional competence, but many of their assessments do not focus on the functional tasks that are required in school settings. (Ryan's physical therapist, Dan Ciccheli, works with Ryan on building his muscles to improve his mobility and stamina.) One such test has been developed especially for elementary students with disabilities—the School Function Assessment (Coster, Mancini, & Ludlow, 1999). It has three parts:

Your Own Voice ~ Surgery or Not?   Box 12-2

As part of your training to be an early intervention specialist, you sit in on a meeting that involves the mother and father of a baby not yet born, two surgeons, and two members of the ethics committee of a major research hospital. The only purpose of the meeting is to decide whether to perform surgery on the fetus to try to correct an obvious condition of spina bifida.

The parents speak for themselves and the baby the mother is carrying. Or so it seems to you. But you have some reservations about whether they really do.

The parents are clear about their position: they oppose abortion, are eager for the surgery, understand the risks, and want to do everything they can for their baby right now. They are willing to shoulder the responsibility for anything that goes wrong in the surgery and for any long-term consequences for the mother, the baby, and the entire family (mother, father, and child).

The surgeons are clear about the risks and benefits of this experimental surgery. The mother undergoes a general anesthesia, which risks brain damage; she might become infected; she will need complete bed rest for the rest of her pregnancy; she will have to go to her doctor twice a month and have a weekly sonogram of her womb; she will have a Caesarean delivery; and she will have a long recuperative period after that procedure. The fetus risks becoming infected during the surgery; there also is a risk of premature birth, which itself creates the likelihood of physical or cognitive delays, or both. Without the surgery, however, the baby, if born alive, may be unable to walk; may have little or no control over her bladder; and may need an operation to drain spinal fluid from her skull so that her brain can develop normally, free of the fluid's pressure that can damage her

brain and cause intellectual or physical disabilities or both. The father risks losing his wife and baby.

The benefits are attractive: a child who will come into this world with only minimal, if any, intellectual or physical disabilities.

The ethicists ask the parents about their emotional state: are they calm and cool enough to make a decision? About the costs of the surgery: can they meet the emotional, physical, and financial costs of having a child with a disability? Have they really thought about the responsibilities of caring for a child with a disability? There are, they say, no guarantees in this surgery.

You sit and listen, and you ask yourself: what do the parents know about disability? This is their first child; their families have been untouched by disability, so they have no history to consult when making a decision. How can they make an informed decision about anything except the surgery?

And then you begin to ask yourself about disability itself. Is it really so burdensome to have a child with a disability? Why don't the doctors talk about what can be done for the baby even if the baby has a disability? About special education and other services? And why don't the ethicists say that children with disabilities make many positive contributions to their families and communities? That having great expectations about any baby, especially this one, is a "right" posture, not just expecting the "worst" in the sense of having a child with a disability? Why does everyone freak out about disability?

Somewhere you read a phrase that sticks in your mind like your own last name: "Less able is not less worthy" (Turnbull, 1976, p. 769).

For more information, read Renkle, M. (2001). A miracle for Isaac. *Parenting, 15*(1), 106–111.

- ■ "Participation" evaluates the student's level of participation in school activities and environments.

- ■ "Task Supports" evaluates the extent to which students need supplementary aids and services to participate in school activities and environments.

- ■ "Activity Performance" evaluates the student's ability to complete functional activities requiring cognitive and physical skills.

The School Function Assessment is criterion-based. The items in each of its three parts represent increasing difficulty, from simpler to more complex tasks. Educators who are very familiar with the student in school settings are the respondents. They usually can complete the entire instrument in 5 to 10 minutes.

The reliability, validity, and psychometric characteristics of the School Function Assessment have been

Lori Kauffman-Faison is more than Ryan's special education itinerant teacher; she's his friend, too.

established at a respectable level (Coster et al., 1999; Coster et al., 1998). Validity studies have demonstrated that it differentiates among the profiles of students with and without disabilities and also distinguishes between groups of students with different disabilities such as the performance profiles of students with cerebral palsy and learning disabilities (Coster & Haltiwanger, 2004; Hwang et al., 2002).

Council for Exceptional Children

Standard: Understanding the impact that asthma has on Kwashon's life is an application of CEC Standard 3, Individual Learning Differences.

DESIGNING AN APPROPRIATE INDIVIDUALIZED EDUCATION PROGRAM

Partnering for Special Education and Related Services

Students are entitled to the benefits of IDEA and to an IEP if their health condition limits their strength, vitality, or alertness and adversely affects their educational performance. But not all students who have health impairments get an IEP; that's how it is for Kwashon. He and other students do not get an IEP because their impairments do not affect their educational performance. Instead, they usually need and have a Section 504 plan (which we explained in Chapter 8) that covers their health services and other accommodations as well as a health care plan (DePaepe et al., 2002). Figure 12–7 describes the content of a health plan.

The health care plan for a student with asthma should identify the triggers and prevention protocol and should include a treatment plan developed by the student's asthma specialist, allergist, or pediatrician, describing the student's daily preventive medicines (Kwashon takes his regular meds at home), treatment for mild asthma attacks, and treatment regimens and procedures for more serious attacks (Kwashon receives emergency medication and post-attack rest at school) (Meadows, 2003). Similarly, health care plans for students with epilepsy should identify procedures to follow when seizure activity occurs, medicine for prevention and treatment, and emergency procedures. Box 12–3 illustrates how to integrate therapy services into the classroom.

A student, such as Kwashon, who has a health care plan will be involved with many different professionals. A partnership among the professionals, family members, and student is essential to assure agreement and consistent treatment. Box 12–4 describes how Kwashon's health care plan can be regarded as an agreement among partners.

Asthma does not prevent Kwashon Drayton from playing basketball with his brother.

Figure 12–7 Health Care Plans

A health care plan should include the following:
- Statements about who will know about the student's condition, how they will get this information, and how they will be trained in CPR, emergency, and standard first-aid procedures (Kleiberstein & Broome, 2000)
- Specified procedures and standards for taking naps, receiving medications, and making up work missed during absences
- Emergency-response plans, listing emergency-contact telephone numbers (DePaepe et al., 2002)
- Instructions on how to inventory and regularly check emergency medical kits (DePaepe et al., 2002)
- Written consents from the student's physicians and the student's parents or guardians
- Instructions on storage and administration of medication
- Descriptions of health goals and adaptations to school regimens
- Plans for transition from hospital to school (if the student has been hospitalized), especially to the general curriculum
- Descriptions of occupational, physical, respiratory, or other therapy the student will receive at school, or, if not at school, how the therapies will affect the student's education

Into Practice ~ Physical and Occupational Therapy in General Education Classrooms

Box 12–3

Imagine for a moment that you are a general education teacher of third graders and that Maddie is enrolled in your classroom. Maddie has several challenges. For one thing, she has spastic quadriplegic cerebral palsy. She can't use her right arm for any purpose except to stabilize objects: it serves as a sort of wall because it is fixed into a half-cocked position. She can, however, use her left arm and hand. In addition, she uses a wheelchair throughout the school day because she cannot walk; and she also has a very weak back and poor posture. Finally, she has a learning disability. Ask yourself, "How can I include Maddie?"

The answer is that you ask for assistance from an occupational therapist and a physical therapist. Although these therapists often work together, they bring different talents to the general classroom. The physical therapist is concerned with the student's sensory and gross-motor functions and particularly with the student's nervous and musculoskeletal systems. That means the physical therapist will assist the student to coordinate her body positions in order to complete certain tasks, learn how to move about in certain environments and overcome barriers in those environments (such as classrooms and playgrounds), and acquire and learn how to use mobility-facilitating equipment.

By contrast, the occupational therapist is concerned with the student's fine-motor skills: manipulating small objects, handwriting, organizing to do certain tasks, orienting her body to certain spaces, and completing activities of daily living (such as dressing, bathing, and toileting). To carry out their duties, these therapists either work directly with the student, providing hands-on training, or they advise, consult, and monitor, providing indirect services.

The following list describes some of the ways in which these therapists can make it possible for you to teach Maddie in general education classrooms:

Learning outcomes. Maddie will use a computer at her desk to complete 25 percent of her work independently.
Physical therapy. Maddie will work on postural control and stabilization of her upper body to improve use of her hands and head control for desktop work.
Occupational therapy. The therapist will introduce a computer at her desk with adaptations. Maddie will work on fine-motor coordination and equipment use.

Putting These Strategies to Work for Progress in the General Curriculum

1. How could a physical therapist assist you as a classroom teacher in ensuring that your student is safe on the playground?

2. Identify three ways that an occupational therapist might assist you in providing literacy instruction.

3. What contributions do you believe physical and occupational therapists can make to IEP development?

To answer these questions online, go to the Into Practice module in Chapter 12 of the Companion Website, www.prenhall.com/turnbull.

Source: Adapted from Szabo, J. L. (2000). Maddie's story: Inclusion through physical and occupational therapy. *Teaching Exceptional Children, 33*(2), 26–32.

Determining Supplementary Aids and Services

You have already read how important technology can be and about word processors that promote a student's written performance. PDAs that help the student with sequencing tasks, digital talking books and e-text formats, and adapted and augmentative communication devices. Students with physical disabilities, particularly those with cerebral palsy, will often benefit from the use of a variety of technologies, including AAC devices to help them overcome communication limitations.

Sometimes simple is better when it comes to technology; not every student needs high-end equipment. The only device that some students with physical disabilities may need as a supplementary aid is a simple switch to operate an educational tool such as a computer, mobility equipment such as an electric wheelchair, or a tape recorder that the student uses to record teachers' lessons (Cole & Swinth, 2004; Lancioni et al., 2002). Figure 12–8 describes various switches. Box 12–5 provides more information about another technology that benefits students with physical disabilities and other health impairments: power wheelchairs.

Planning for Universal Design for Learning

In Chapter 2, you learned that the 2004 amendments to IDEA included provisions for a national standard for electronic text materials, called the National Instructional Materials Accessibility Standard (NIMAS). NIMAS establishes technical standards about how electronic texts should be set up to ensure that they are accessible to students

When Kwashon Drayton has an asthma attack, the school nurse assists him in taking his medication and recovering his strength, consistent with his health-care plan.

Partnership Tips ~ Agreement Among Professionals and Family   Box 12–4

There are, of course, general rules about partnerships. Some derive from IDEA, as we described in Chapter 2. Others derive from the best practices we described in Chapter 4. When students with other health impairments are the focus of a partnership, however, the general rules warrant some modifications. Here, for example, are modifications—described as partnership roles for various professionals—that could apply to Kwashon or other students with asthma.

None of these roles will produce any benefit for Kwashon unless all of the partners adhere to the seven principles of partnership: communicate, be professionally competent, respect each other, advocate for Kwashon and each other, treat each other as equally qualified to contribute to Kwashon, stay committed to him and each other, and build trust.

For Kwashon himself: know what asthma is, be aware of his symptoms, especially acute attacks, and know where to get help in school.

For Michelle, his mother: stay up to date on medications and other interventions, control the asthma triggers at home, monitor Kwashon's health.

For Kwashon's regular physician (family or internal medicine): conduct regular physical examinations and alert Kwashon's asthma specialist whenever there are any alarming signs of change in his health.

For Kwashon's asthma specialist (pulmonologist): conduct regular lung evaluations, monitor and change as necessary any medications, respond to and contact Kwashon's regular physician as needed.

For Kwashon's school nurse: secure authority from Kwashon's two physicians and his mother to administer emergency medication or other treatment, know what the medications and treatments are and when and why to use them, assist school administrators and especially the maintenance crews to eliminate as many asthma triggers as possible, and stay in regular contact with Kwashon and Michelle.

For Kwashon's teachers: be able to recognize symptoms of an asthma attack, know where the school nurse is at all times, know how to intervene if the nurse is not available, know what other emergency measures to take, and monitor Kwashon for any signs of asthma reactions or acute episodes.

Clearly, a health plan for a student such as Kwashon requires a partnership. But it also requires a "senior partner"; so these professionals, Michelle, and Kwashon must designate one person to coordinate all of the information.

Putting These Tips to Work for Progress in the General Curriculum

1. Provide a rationale for including the student with a disability on the partnership team.

2. If you had a child with asthma in your classroom, how could partnering with the child's parents benefit you as a teacher?

3. Review websites that focus on asthma. What information and resources can you identify that could be helpful to you as a teacher?

To answer these question online, go to the Partnership Tips module in Chapter 12 of the Companion Website, www.prenhall.com/turnbull.

Figure 12–8   Adaptive switches

Switches vary according to how they are activated, how many functions they can operate, or what happens when you start them:

- Most single switches operate by pressure, which performs the switch-on, switch-off function (Johnston, 2003).
- Some pressure switches activate a timed sequence, instead of a simple on-off switch, thus allowing the device to begin operating and then to shut off at predetermined times.
- Other pressure switches perform only as long as they are depressed—for example, a motorized wheelchair activated by a joystick or similar switch.
- **Pneumatic, or puffing, switches** operate when the student, such as one who has no arm control, puffs air into a strawlike tube. If a student's lung capacity limits her ability to expel air, she can operate switches by sipping or inhaling air through the tube.
- Still other switches operate by detecting the user's movements, such as head movement, eyebrow twitching, or eye movement.
- Some switches can be activated by sounds.

Values: Even the use of simple technologies, like switches or a walker, can build on students' *strengths* and enable them to be more independent and *self-determined.* Relatively simple ideas can have a big impact!

For more information about the National Instructional Materials Standard and about technical assistance regarding NIMAS, go to *http://nimas.cast.org/*.

with sensory or learning disabilities. Technology standards assure the widest possible access to written text. Just as DVDs are standardized, NIMAS sets a standard so that all e-text materials are identical in their accessibility.

E-text is created from a digital source file; the term *digital source files* refers to computer files or programs written in some digital format. Digital text can range from formats used for word

Technology Tips ~ Powered Mobility Equals Freedom! Electric Wheelchairs ~ Box 12–5

Students with physical disabilities and other health impairments benefit considerably from technology such as the switches you learned about in Figure 12–8. Electronic wheelchairs are an advanced technology that create access to home, school, and community environments and the fellow students and adults in each of those places. Electric wheelchairs, often called power wheelchairs, can indeed mean freedom.

Electric wheelchairs involve a combination of technology applications. There's the motorized chair itself. Then there's the switch that operates the chair. Often people incorporate other technologies, like AAC devices, into the structure of the chair itself.

There are a number of issues that must be considered in supporting a student to purchase or use a power chair:

- *Transporting the chair.* Power chairs are heavy; transporting them requires the use of a modified van (modified to include a lift and internal equipment to stabilize the rider). If customized transportation is not available, perhaps a non-powered chair is a better option or, alternatively, a smaller motorized vehicle, like a scooter. There are smaller, collapsible power chairs available that have two small motors

and are for indoor use only, so perhaps having one of these at school would be better than a heavy power wheelchair.

- *Adjusting the size.* A power wheelchair's size limits the student's opportunity to navigate in school environments. Particularly for children, smaller is better.
- *Recharging the batteries.* Power chairs are battery-operated, and their batteries need to be recharged. Teachers should place the student's chair near a power outlet.
- *Selecting navigation tools.* Many types of switches are available, and virtually any one can be used to operate a power chair, though joysticks are the most common type of navigation tool. These should be configured with regard to the student's physical capacities and personal preferences.
- *Assuring safety.* Power wheelchairs can be hazardous for the student and others. They are often hard to stop and navigate. Training is the first step in ensuring safe use, and teaching classmates about safety around the chair is also important. Power chairs can come with various configurations of braking mechanisms based on the student's needs, although most brake systems are not intended to stop a wheelchair but to keep it from rolling.

---

processors, to markup languages such as HTML or XML, to computer codes such as JAVA. Currently, XML (extensible markup language) and XSL (extensible stylesheet language) are the most widely used digital formats to create electronic texts. The NIMAS standard is based on these digital formats. The electronic text is an output of the digital file.

The digital file can be read by commercially available media players that allow the information in the source file to be presented in multiple ways. Media players can convert digital source files into audio and video media, flexible text, or electronic braille and can even create avatars (digitally created figures) that virtually present content in sign language. Think of these media players as similar to a web browser, which takes HTML (hypertext markup language) and converts it to output that includes text, pictures, graphics, audio, and so forth. Within a few years, most school textbooks will be available in a digital file format.

The NIMAS standard and media players are, however, mainly directions for the future. There are ways of accessing e-text and digital documents today. For example, Tom Snyder Productions publishes a series of digital texts under its Thinking Reader series. Thinking Readers were designed by researchers at CAST and are digital talking book (DTB) formats of popular books, like *Tuck Everlasting*; *Bud, Not Buddy*; and *A Wrinkle in Time*, often taught in middle or junior high school. The DTB versions of these classics allow learners who are not reading at grade level to access the book through audio and video outputs and through supports programmed into the software and, as a result, improve reading skills. This approach can benefit students who have severe physical impairments that limit their ability to use print materials easily or see print-based books. It also benefits students with more severe cognitive disabilities who otherwise could not read the book.

You can create many of your own electronic texts through simple programs like Microsoft Word or PowerPoint. Many of the materials that teachers use are not subject to copyright or have been developed by the teacher or the school district. Those can be converted to electronic versions.

Also, there are copyright-free digital audio and video materials that can be incorporated into other materials to make them more accessible. Internet browsers such as Netscape and Microsoft Explorer can present HTML content in multiple ways, including through video streams. Sometimes even using simple e-text options can allow students with physical and other disabilities to have access to general education content and provide evidence of their knowledge and skills.

For more information about CAST and e-text formats, go to *http://www.cast.org/*.

Values: Ensuring that students with disabilities have access to core content information through electronic and digital text materials ensures that they have *rights and opportunities* for learning.

Planning for Other Educational Needs

For more information on the RRTC on Health and Wellness, go to *http://www.healthwellness. org/index.htm.*

One area in which both students with physical disabilities and students with other health impairments may need IEP goals to address other educational needs is in the area of physical education. Like Ryan and Kwashon, students with these disabilities usually are limited with respect to the types, intensity, and duration of physical activities in which they can engage.

Accordingly, their IEP teams—Ryan's is one of them—need to consider adapted physical education (PE) goals and supports for the educational programs of these students. Adapted physical education is, quite simply, "physical education which has been adapted or modified so that it is appropriate for the person with a disability" (Cantu & Buswell, 2003, p. 58).

For people with disabilities, physical activities are undoubtedly important. The U.S. Department of Education's Rehabilitation Research and Training Center (RRTC) on Health and Wellness has documented the barriers that often limit access to physical activities for people with physical and other disabilities as well as the importance of physical activities for this population (Krahn, 2003; Powers, 2003; Putnam et al., 2003).

Adapted physical education allows a student with a disability to participate in a typical sport or physical activity. Adapted PE specialists may suggest modifying the environment in which the sport or physical activity will occur or providing some equipment or modifing existing equipment to ensure the inclusion of students. For example, a student who is blind can participate in typical softball activities if the players use a beeping softball—an ordinary softball with an auditory sound (typically, beeps) that enable the person with the visual impairment to hear, and thus sense, the approaching ball.

In addition to developing these types of modifications and accommodations, however, adapted PE responds to students' unique or specific educational needs in areas such as sensory awareness systems, reflexes, fine- and gross-motor skills, body image, locomotor skills, manipulation skills, muscular endurance, and agility or speed (Mears, 2004). Enabling students with physical disabilities or other health impairments to participate in sports and recreation activities may link that student to an area of life-long enjoyment. Ryan's adapted physical education teacher concentrates on building Ryan's strength and then on how he can participate in warmups and some sports.

USING EFFECTIVE INSTRUCTIONAL STRATEGIES

Early Childhood Students: Token Economy Systems

A number of instructional strategies you read about in this text are not specific to any disability category but are useful for students across disability categories and ages. Indeed, some are useful across age ranges for all students, with or without disabilities! One such strategy, the use of token economy systems, is useful in all classrooms.

As you learned in Chapter 10 when reading about discrete trial training, the basic laws governing the use of techniques from the field of applied behavior analysis involve the delivery of a discriminative stimulus intended to elicit a response, which is then followed by a reinforcing stimulus. In Chapter 8 you learned about errorless learning and how using prompts is one way for modifying the three-term contingency sequence (discriminative stimulus, response, and reinforcing stimulus) to ensure learning.

Another way to modify the three-term contingency is by changing aspects of the reinforcing stimulus, such as by altering the schedule on which a reinforcer is delivered (e.g., every time the student performs a behavior, every other time, infrequently) or modifying the type of reinforcer provided. In token economy systems, students are provided with tokens such as points, poker chips, or tickets to reinforce their behavior. You should remember from Chapter 10 that a reinforcer (or reinforcing stimulus) is anything that increases the probability that the desired response will be performed. How, then, can points, poker chips, or tickets serve that function? Well, think about the most common token economy system, one that you use every day. What is that? Money! The reason most people are willing to work hard to receive money is not that they eat or collect the money itself but because they can use that money to buy items or activities—commodities—that they value.

Buying a valued commodity is the crux of token economy systems. Tokens take on a reinforcing value because the student can trade them for a desired commodity. In some ways, token economy systems make it simpler to implement applied behavior analysis procedures. It is difficult and of questionable ethics to use primary reinforcers like food all of the time, and there are only so many other primary reinforcers available to teachers.

Smith (2004) and colleagues at the University of Minnesota's Early Childhood Behavior Project have identified the important elements of a token economy system for young children with disabilities. First, you need to make sure that the token keeps its value to the student by providing frequent-enough opportunities to exchange the token and by setting the rate at which tokens can be earned on a frequent-enough schedule. Requiring the accumulation of 1,000 points to get a candy bar but making it possible to acquire those points only over a period of, say, 6 months, creates a situation in which the tokens have no real value to the student. Early in the year it is probably important to set up the token system so the student can trade in his or her tokens once a day to get a desired reinforcer.

Second, determine, along with the student, what the tokens can be used to buy. Again, students will only work for tokens if the tokens can be exchanged for something they want! Students can buy a wide array of commodities, such as Pokemon cards, inexpensive bracelets, time on the computer, a homework pass, extra recess, or extra free time.

Third, you want to fade out the token reinforcement system. You can do this by pairing the token reinforcers with other forms of reinforcement, such as verbal praise, and then slowly increasing the number of tokens needed to obtain reinforcers.

Smith (2004) and colleagues noted that token economy systems are particularly useful in early childhood settings because they can easily be used at both school and home. Parents frequently find these systems manageable at home, and that using them provides helpful consistency between the two environments.

Standard: Assisting students with self-awareness and emotional health is an example of CEC Standard 5, Learning Environments and Social Interaction.

Elementary and Middle School Students: Self-Awareness

The middle school years are difficult for most students, whether the student has or does not have a disability. Disabilities can adversely affect emerging adolescent milestones, one of which is the development of a student's self-awareness as distinct from the disability, health condition, or disorder. The term *self-awareness* refers to one's understanding of oneself as a unique individual and is often used in conjunction with the notions of self-understanding and self-knowledge. This includes the process referred to as *disability awareness*, which involves the capacity of an individual to appraise his or her own abilities as a function of a specific disabling condition.

Too frequently the only time the issue of student self-awareness comes to the forefront in education is when people other than the student question the degree to which he or she has accepted his or her disability or, in less positive terms, accepts what he or she cannot do because of the disabling condition. Figure 12–9 describes some strategies to promote healthy disability- and self-awareness.

Too frequently, students with disabilities and other health impairments begin to think of themselves only in the context of their disability. Yet self-awareness is mediated by and tied to executive functioning capabilities, like decision making, problem solving, and self-regulation (you will learn more about executive functions in Chapter 13) (Turner & Levine, 2004). In addition, positive self-awareness is an important component in the development of effective coping behavior.

What strategies promote positive self-awareness for students with disabilities?

Terry Miller, Ryan's drama teacher, shows her pride in his success in the play Aladdin.

Figure 12-9 Promoting self-awareness

- Do not regard a student's self-awareness as consisting only of acceptance of a limitation.
- Do not force the student to accept the disability and to do nothing more about the student's self-awareness.
- Recognize that although disability awareness is an important part of self-awareness, understanding one's disability and its effects in typical situations should not be the goal of educational efforts to promote self-awareness.
- Instead, promote a student's self-acceptance through self-understanding and self-knowledge.
- Enable the student to use her unique skills and abilities to her greatest advantage (Wehmeyer, Sands, Knowlton, & Kozleski, 2002).

■ Avoid overprotecting students with health impairments at any age but especially during early adolescence, when students want to fit in instead of standing out (Sullivan, Fulmer, & Zigmond, 2001).

■ Begin instruction in self-awareness by identifying a student's basic physical and psychological needs, interests, and abilities.

■ Help students distinguish between their physical and psychological needs and then learn how to meet these needs.

■ Encourage role-playing and brainstorming activities that explore students' interests and abilities.

■ Ask students to discuss common emotions, such as self-worth; their own positive physical and psychological attributes and how these attributes make them feel; how other people's actions affect their feelings of self-worth, fear, love, hate, and sadness; how these feelings affect their and others' behavior; and how to cope with these emotions.

■ Transition from emotional to basic physical awareness, teaching students about their physical selves and how their physical health and capacities affect their actions.

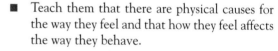

■ Teach them that there are physical causes for the way they feel and that how they feel affects the way they behave.

■ Import additional materials involving health, sexuality, and body systems.

■ Help students explore others' perceptions of them, listing others' potential reactions and constructing a view of how others see them; discuss differences among people, including interests and abilities.

■ Teach students how to give and accept praise and criticism appropriately and inappropriately, list the effects and purposes of praise and criticism, and offer strategies to give and receive both.

■ Ask students to identify their own positive characteristics, how to express confidence in themselves, how to react to others' expressions of confidence, and how to appropriately make positive statements about themselves (Wehmeyer et al., 2002).

Ryan's parents, Mary and John, and his sister, Nicole, have been important partners on Ryan's team. Their support and attitude have contributed to Ryan's confidence and independence.

The most important theme is that, in all such efforts, the student must be the catalyst for change. Students need to be actively involved in identifying their interests, abilities, strengths, and unique learning needs as well as applying this knowledge to identify strategies and supports that can enable them to overcome limitations.

Secondary and Transition Students: Driver's Education

You can probably remember the day you passed your driver's test and received your license. It's a big day in any young person's life. Having a driver's license is sort of like having a license to freedom! You can go places without your parents, and you can do more things you want to do. Many people assume that students with disabilities cannot drive, but many people with physical disabilities are quite capable drivers. In fact, given the lack of accessible public transportation in many communities, a driver's license becomes the key to getting to a job and earning the money needed to live more independently.

Vogtle, Kern, and McCauley (2000) surveyed adolescents with and without disabilities on several issues pertaining to social inclusion and found that, although 88 percent of adolescents without disabilities had a driver's license, only 46 percent of students with disabilities (across all categories) did. McGill and Vogtle (2001) interviewed adolescents with physical disabilities, particularly those with cerebral palsy and spina bifida, about their feelings about learning to drive. These students indicated that driving would give them the chance to be like everyone else, would provide the usual benefits of being an adult, and would minimize their isolation. They thought that their involvement in high school drivers' education classes would contribute to their social inclusion as well.

What strategies exist to teach driving to young people with physical disabilities? Mainly, this involves direct instruction on using vehicle adaptations that enable a person with a physical disability to drive. For example, steering wheels can be outfitted with handles that allow students with limited motor control to grip and turn the wheel more easily. Vehicles can be reconfigured with a left-foot accelerator, additional mirrors, additional room for wheelchair stowage and access, hand controls for accelerating and braking, and even a joystick modification to allow steering with one's foot instead of hands.

Not all students with physical disabilities may be able to obtain a driver's license, but if schools provide direct instruction with modified vehicles, perhaps more students will be able to do so. Just as important, students with physical disabilities will have the opportunity to undergo a right of passage for adolescence—driver's education!

INCLUDING STUDENTS WITH PHYSICAL DISABILITIES AND OTHER HEALTH IMPAIRMENTS

Figures 12–10 and 12–11 display the percentage of students with physical disabilities and other health impairments, respectively, in inclusive placements.

As compared to students with other types of disabilities, students with other health impairments are more likely to receive services in home/hospital settings. Receiving an appropriate education while in the hospital and at home is important if students are to avoid grade retention, inappropriate special education placement, learned helplessness, or early dropout (Bessell, 2001b). In addition, students often feel isolated by homebound services (Bessell, 2001a). The Committee on School Health (2000) emphasizes that "homebound instruction is meant for acute or catastrophic health problems that confine a child or adolescent to home or hospital for a prolonged but defined period of time and is not intended to relieve the school or parent of the responsibility for providing education for the child in the least restrictive environment" (p. 1154).

Parents, school administrators, teachers, and the student's primary care physician need to partner with each other to consider how to address the curriculum standards and IEP goals/objectives that the student would achieve if still in school, the specific duration of the

Values: *Relationships* among students with physical disabilities, such as Ryan, or other health impairments, such as Kwashon, can prosper when the students and their teachers are candid about the causes and treatment of a condition and about the prospects for students with the condition. Knowledge is power; it trumps ignorance every time.

Figure 12–10 Educational placement of students with physical disabilities (2003–2004)

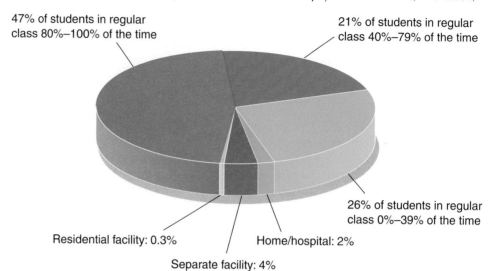

47% of students in regular class 80%–100% of the time

21% of students in regular class 40%–79% of the time

26% of students in regular class 0%–39% of the time

Residential facility: 0.3%

Home/hospital: 2%

Separate facility: 4%

Source: U.S. Department of Education, Office of Special Education Programs. (2005). *IDEA data website* (http://www.ideadata.org/aboutThisSite.asp).

Figure 12–11 Educational placement of students with other health impairments (2003–2004)

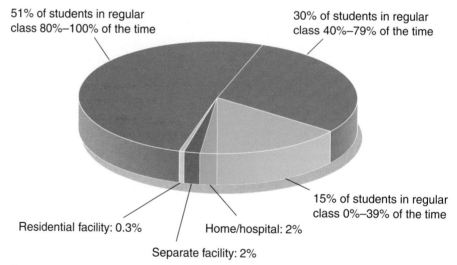

51% of students in regular class 80%–100% of the time

30% of students in regular class 40%–79% of the time

15% of students in regular class 0%–39% of the time

Residential facility: 0.3%

Home/hospital: 2%

Separate facility: 2%

Source: U.S. Department of Education, Office of Special Education Programs. (2005). *IDEA data website* (http://www.ideadata.org/aboutThisSite.asp).

homebound services, and how to return the student to school as quickly and smoothly as possible. Receiving dual enrollment in homebound and school-based instruction enables students to continue functioning as a classroom member (Bessell, 2001b). Box 12–6 offers suggestions for including students with other health impairments and physical disabilities in general education classrooms.

ASSESSING STUDENTS' PROGRESS

Measuring Students' Progress

Progress in the general curriculum. Many means of assessing progress in the general curriculum involve paper/pencil examinations or other tests. But students with physical disabilities often

Inclusion Tips

Box 12–6

	What You Might See	What You Might Be Tempted to Do	Alternate Responses	Ways to Include Peers in the Process
Behavior	The student becomes very anxious when she is not able to complete assignments at the same speed as her classmates.	Tell her to be realistic and face her own limitations.	Develop a 504 plan that incorporates the use of technology to enable the student to complete assignments more quickly.	Explore ways that all class members can benefit from assistive technology.
Social interactions	He may be self-conscious or embarrassed, so he withdraws from others.	Allow him to work alone, assuming he is merely low on energy or needs to be by himself.	Work with the school counselor to provide the student with self-awareness instruction.	Recognize that all students deal with self-esteem issues and involve the class in self-awareness instruction.
Educational performance	Lack of strength and use of a wheelchair hinder her capacity for full participation in physical education.	Excuse her from physical education and have her attend a study hall instead.	Use curriculum-based assessment to evaluate the student's strengths and needs related to adapted physical education.	Explore opportunities for her to participate in a wheelchair basketball league.
Classroom attitudes	He appears to be overwhelmed by class activities when feeling fatigued.	Tell the student that his only choice is to deal with it.	In a 504 plan, specify the appropriate length of work and rest periods for him.	Have classmates serve as scribes for him or offer other support as needed.

have fine- and gross-motor limitations that reduce their capacity to demonstrate their abilities on these assessments; similarly, students with other health impairments may lack the stamina required to complete them on time.

An increasing number of alternatives to handwritten performance examinations involve computer technology. In Chapter 5 you learned how curriculum-based measurement tracks student progress in the general curriculum. Computer-based assessment augments curriculum-based measurement (Fuchs & Fuchs, 2001). As you learned in Chapter 5, curriculum-based measurement (CBM) involves frequent measurements of indicators that are tied to the curriculum, can be measured repeatedly, and provide indicators of student improvement. Using a computer for CBM purposes is an obvious accommodation for students with physical disabilities or other health impairments, but it also assists educators in assessing the progress of all of their students.

Progress in addressing other educational needs. As you have learned, physical activities have various important benefits for students with physical disabilities or other health impairments, and adapted physical education services can give these students the exercise they need. There are a variety of ways to track student progress in the area of physical education, including teacher observations, tracking students' correct performances of a physical task, or measuring the frequency in which a student can engage in an activity. Haynes (2002) suggests that measurement in adapted physical education include the following:

- Cardiovascular function, including resting and target heart rate (important for Kwashon, given his asthma)
- Body composition, mass, and weight

Council for Exceptional Children

Standard: Using technology to assist students with physical disabilities during assessments is an application of CEC Standard 8, Assessment.

- Muscle strength and endurance (what Ryan works on when he does adaptive physical education)
- Muscle and joint flexibility
- Posture evaluation
- Mobility

Making Accommodations for Assessments

You have already learned that computer-based assessment can be an important strategy for measuring progress in the general curriculum for students with physical disabilities and other health impairments, and computer-based assessment is also an important accommodation to enable students to participate in standardized testing. Students with other health impairments may require more frequent breaks in order to complete a test or sit for multiple test sessions. If a computer-based assessment is not available, students with physical disabilities may need a scribe to record answers or extended time to complete the test. Because his disability also affects his fine-motor coordination and his prematurity affected his eyesight, Ryan has accommodations in taking his mathematics examinations and assessments.

You have also learned that there are many universal accommodations—those that benefit students with different disabilities. One particular accommodation that may be specific to students with physical disabilities, however, involves physical access to the testing environment. In many cases, concerns about ensuring security and minimizing the potential for cheating or disruption of the testing environment take priority over ensuring physical access. Test situations should consider mobility access, including the availability of an elevator, access to needed test materials to make sure students with physical disabilities can participate in the test, and environmental controls, such as the air conditioning that Kwashon needs to minimize pollen.

Looking to Ryan's Future

Let's assume that Ryan, while in high school, continues to play sports, hand-cycle in half-marathons, act, advocate, and remain in the gifted-talented program; that he applies to attend one of California's many excellent colleges or universities; and that neither he nor any of his faculty say a single word about his cerebral palsy.

Now envision him at, say, University of California at San Diego. He learns that the university theater is putting on the classic rock musical *Hair*. Ryan comes to the auditions, having used his chair to traverse the hilly campus. The stage director, musical director, and other actors look his way. Some turn away; some stare, puzzled, silently wondering, "How can that freshman kid, in his chair, possibly be in this play?"

Obliquely, the director asks that question: "Are you looking for something or someone? Can I help you find your way?"

"No," answers Ryan. "I'm where I want to be, for now. Auditioning. For the role of the hippie who befriends the cowboy. Soon I'll be where I want to be. Rehearsing and then performing that role."

There it is again—Ryan's persistence, his and his family's great expectations, his middle school teachers' lessons about strengths and capacity motivating him.

Another actor—a girl who knew Ryan when he was at Pershing Middle School and acting in Terry Miller's program—speaks out: "This guy's good. Change your stereotype, folks. Imagine the hippie as having a disability. Imagine Ryan as the hippie. That's the extra dimension we can add to our performance." Adding the extra dimension is what special education is all about, in Terry's words. And adding an extra dimension to the theater, to Pershing Middle School, and then to the University of California at San Diego is what Ryan's all about.

We don't have to guess the ending of this vision. Let's simply say that it takes Ryan from California to graduate school at New York University (Terry's alma mater), and then back to San Diego as a cast member at the Old Globe Theatre.

Looking to Kwashon's Future

Children sometimes track their parents' careers, and so it is with Kwashon. Genes may be part of one's destiny, and surely Kwashon's asthma tracks his ancestors', but parents' examples shape a child's destiny, too.

That is why, after Kwashon graduates from school in Columbia, South Carolina, he matriculates at the University of South Carolina, his mother's alma mater. There he majors in health, sports administration, and education, following his father's example as a member of the staff of the Columbia Parks and Recreation Department.

While studying the health aspect of that major, Kwashon discovers that he has a nearly insatiable curiosity about physiology and particularly about how family traits—genetics, if you will—affect a person's health. His interest coincides with his "all boy" enthusiasm for sports; so having completed his major, he faces a choice.

It's a good one: whether to take an internship with the Miami Heat as a sports medicine trainer or to accept the offer of the university's medical school to study to be a physician. The job with the Heat would lead eventually to a well-paid position with that team or any other basketball program; a degree in medicine would open the door to specialty-based practices that are only dimly perceived and that can be exceptionally remunerative.

Would you be surprised if Kwashon were to earn his M.D. and become a pulmonologist, specializing in diseases of the lungs? And that he would then earn his Ph.D. in public health. And then establish himself in Columbia, enlarging the work that his mother has undertaken by treating, training, and advocating for families and individuals affected by asthma and by being an environmentalist who regards public health as a product of a good environment? There is nothing about Kwashon's asthma that limits him in any activity he wants to do, except one: you won't find him running track. He's too busy as a physician, a public health specialist, and a superfan of the Heat and the Falcons.

SUMMARY

Identifying students with physical disabilities

■ The term *physical disability* refers to a large group of students who, though quite different from each other, share the common challenge of mobility limitations.

■ Cerebral palsy refers to a disorder of movement or posture occurring when the brain is in its early stages of development. The damage is not progressive or hereditary.

■ Spina bifida is a malformation of the spinal cord. Its severity depends on both the extent of the malformation and its position on the spinal cord.

Identifying students with other health impairments

■ Other health impairments are chronic or acute health problems that result in limitations of strength, vitality, or alertness and adversely affect a student's educational performance.

■ Epilepsy is a condition characterized by seizures that can manifest as a brief period of unconsciousness or altered behavior that is sometimes misinterpreted as daydreaming.

■ Asthma can be defined as a chronic lung condition characterized by airway obstruction, inflammation, and increased sensitivity. It is the most common chronic disease among children in the United States.

■ A physical examination from a physician is often the first step in determining whether or not the student has a physical disability or other health impairment.

■ The School Function Assessment is a criterion-based measure of functional skills required of elementary students in school settings.

Evaluating students with physical disabilities and other health impairments

- A physical examination, performed by a physician, is a standard method of evaluating a student with a physical disability or other health impairment.

- Sometimes a neurological examination is appropriate, and neuroimaging is a technique for that kind of examination.

- Prenatal screening assists in identifying some physical disabilities.

- Occasionally, prenatal surgery will be used to correct a physical disability.

Designing an appropriate individualized education program

- Students with physical disabilities and other health impairments will benefit from a thoughtful health plan that prepares for a student's transition to and support in the general education classroom.

- IEP teams should consider the use of switches to provide greater access to the general curriculum for students with physical disabilities and other health impairments.

- Electronic or digital text formats enable educators to deliver core academic content in multiple ways.

- Physical exercise is important for *all* children. Adapted physical education provides students with opportunities for inclusion, exercise, and recreation.

Using effective instructional strategies

- Token economy systems involve the use of tokens to reinforce positive behavior and academic outcomes. They can be incorporated into the educational programs of young children with disabilities to promote positive outcomes.

- Students with physical disabilities and other health impairments may have self-images that are derived more from their physical impairment or health status than their many capacities and abilities. Teachers should include instruction on student self-awareness as part of the educational program.

- Driver's education is a part of the transition to adulthood for most adolescents and should be for students with physical disabilities and other health impairments. Some students may learn to drive if they have instruction and are provided with vehicle modifications.

Assessing students' progress

- Students with physical disabilities and other health impairments may perform more effectively on curriculum-based measurement and mastery learning assessments if such measures are computer-based.

- There are multiple means to measure progress in physical education, but teachers should focus on a wide array of health outcomes, including cardiovascular and other outcomes.

- Students with physical disabilities and other health impairments may need multiple accommodations for testing, such as extended time, a scribe, or computer administration. Physical access to the testing site is also important.

WHAT DO YOU RECOMMEND?

Refer to chapter content and the PRAXIS™ and CEC standards in Appendix A to answer the following questions:

1. Specify four tips related to first aid for people with seizures that are especially important for teachers to know. Then identify what PRAXIS™ or CEC standards you are applying.

2. View the DVD section that features Ryan Frisella. How does his involvement in sports affect your understanding of adapted physical education. What PRAXIS™ or CEC standards apply to being able to implement instruction in these key areas?

3. Compare and contrast physical education and adapted physical education and state the CEC or PRAXIS™ standards that apply in being able to implement instruction in these key areas.

4. Visit the Companion Website for this chapter and locate a link to one of the websites mentioned in the chapter, investigate an area of physical disabilities or other health impairments, and make a list of five important tips for teachers to remember regarding this disability. What CEC or PRAXIS™ standards apply to your answers?

Use your *Real Lives and Exceptionalities* DVD to critically think about working with Ryan under "Questions," located below "Meet Ryan."

Chapter 13

Who is Jarris Garner?

There are at least two challenges in growing up with a brain injury: first, having limitations in your ability to think and imagine; and second, coping with difficult and frustrating aspects of your physical development. Yet Jarris Garner has grown up with a brain injury and still has a vivid imagination and great expectations for a lifetime of success.

Jarris and her father and mother, Brent and Shawn, were involved in a very serious automobile accident when she was all of 7 months old. So growing up with a brain injury is part of Jarris's life, all 10 years of it.

Both Jarris and Shawn were hospitalized after the accident. For 6 days following it, Jarris experienced many seizures. When her physicians finally were able to control her seizures and after all of her external wounds were treated and healed, they discharged her, making only two recommendations to her parents. First, go to a quiet place. Second, be prepared for long periods of rehabilitation and uncertain outcomes because no one can precisely foresee the trajectory of Jarris's life.

The "quiet place" certainly could not be Jarris's home; she has two older brothers and an older sister. Grandmother's home, however, would work. So while Shawn recovered at her mother's, so did Jarris, with this difference: Shawn's mother devoted a great deal of attention to Jarris, playing and talking with her—all of which helped Jarris recover some of her lost physical and communication skills.

Grandmother's help was invaluable, but Jarris needed more. Shawn took a proactive approach, searching the Internet and local libraries for information about the effects of traumatic brain injury on infants and toddlers. What she learned was both alarming and hopeful: alarming because so little research had been conducted on the effects of moderate to severe head injury on infants; more research had focused on toddlers and young children, but Jarris was just an infant when she was injured. Yet Shawn found hope when she learned that the Language Acquisition Program (LAP) at the University of Kansas would accept Jarris and work with her and her family on retrieving her language, boosting her communication skills, even teaching her how to use sign language, and preparing her for school.

LAP serves 36 children, ages 3 to 5: 18 in the morning and the same number in the afternoon. A third of the children are like Jarris in that they have significant language delays, a third speak English as a second language, and a third have no language challenges at all.

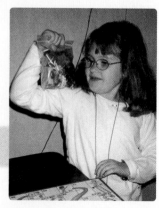

Understanding Students with Traumatic Brain Injury

Instead of "feeling our way through the dark," as Jarris's physicians warned they would, Jarris, Shawn, Brent, and her brothers and sister have nearly "talked" their way out of the injury. That is because the staff focused first and foremost on Jarris's language. They taught her how to use American Sign Language. In time and out of necessity, Shawn, Brent, and Jarris's brothers and sister also have learned to sign, and her siblings expanded their knowledge by taking American Sign Language as a second language while in high school.

Teaching Jarris a different way to communicate was not, however, the only focus of the LAP intervention. By assuring that Jarris would be with children who do not have disabilities (but may not yet speak English), the LAP staff subtly taught her how to be part of a social community. She learned the social skills and appropriate behavior that she would have acquired naturally had she not been injured but that, in her and other children with traumatic brain injuries, are usually impaired as a result of the injury.

Now, at the age of 10, Jarris attends general education classes in her local school in Lawrence, Kansas. She is an avid football fan, although she will not play that sport and may have to be careful about participating in other contact sports so as not to reinjure herself. She is also a Walt Disney groupie: not a single Disney movie escapes her rapt attention. Indeed, Disney movies not only entertain her but also spark her interest in acting. She reenacts the roles that Disney's heroines play, using her—yes, you guessed it—imagination.

So let's return to the challenge of imagining growing up with a brain injury. Imagine your parents being told that you and they are starting a journey that few physicians can chart reliably. Imagine learning to speak by using signs and acquiring special ways to remember and behave in a world in which most of your peers do not understand you or your behavior because they have never experienced brain injury.

And then imagine, as in a Disney movie, that there is a way out—but it is a lap that you have to run once, and then once again, and then once again, and so on, interminably. Could you run those laps? Jarris may not now be able to imagine what we ask you to imagine, but she has to run the laps. Who will run alongside her?

IDENTIFYING STUDENTS WITH TRAUMATIC BRAIN INJURY

Defining Traumatic Brain Injury

IDEA defines **traumatic brain injury** (TBI) as

> an acquired injury to the brain caused by an external physical force, resulting in total or partial functional disability or psychosocial impairment, or both, that adversely affects a child's educational performance. The term applies to open or closed head injuries resulting in impairments in one or more areas, such as cognition; language; memory; attention; reasoning; abstract thinking; judgment; problem-solving; sensory, perceptual, and motor abilities; psychosocial behavior; physical functions; information processing; and speech. The term does not apply to brain injuries that are congenital or degenerative, or to brain injuries induced by birth trauma (34 Code of Federal Regulations, § 300.7 [C] [12]).

We call your attention to three aspects of this definition: First, TBI must be an **acquired injury** (occurring after a child is born). It is inappropriate to classify a student as having TBI if his brain injury was **congenital** (present at birth) or if it occurred at the time of delivery. Second, TBI must be caused by an external physical force. Thus, if a student had **encephalitis** (inflammation of the brain) and her brain was injured as a result of the inflammation, it would not be classified as TBI. Finally, the term *TBI* applies to both open and closed head injuries. An **open head injury** penetrates the bones of the skull, allowing bacteria to have contact with the brain and potentially impairing specific functions, usually only those controlled by the injured part of the brain. Figure 13–1 illustrates the six areas of the brain (including the brain stem) and their related functions. A **closed head injury** does not involve penetration or a fracture of the bones of the skull. It results from an external blow or from the brain being whipped back and forth rapidly, causing it to rub against and bounce off the rough, jagged interior of the skull. Figure 13–2 illustrates how a closed head injury can occur in an automobile accident.

Figure 13–1   Areas of the brain and related general functions

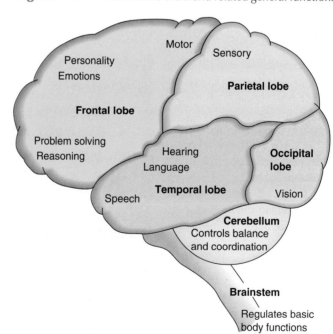

Source: From *Missouri Head Injury Guide for Survivors, Families, and Caregivers,* by Missouri Head Injury Foundation, 1991, Jefferson City, State of Missouri. Copyright 1991 by State of Missouri. Reprinted with permission.

Figure 13-2 Closed head injury accident

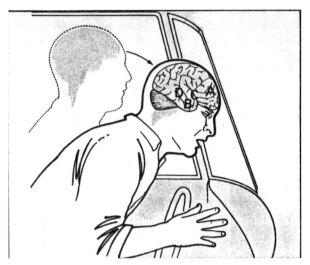

Source: From the U.S. Department of Health and Human Services. (1984). *Head injury: Hope through research.* Bethesda, MD: Author.

In the 2003–2004 school year, 22,509 students received services under the IDEA category of TBI (U.S. Department of Education, 2005). This represents 0.03 percent of the total school population. Other prevalence data indicate the effects of TBI:

- For children ages birth to 14, TBI results in approximately 400,000 emergency department visits, 29,000 hospitalizations, and 3,000 deaths (Langlois & Gotsch, 2001).

- Eighty thousand to ninety thousand people have a TBI of lifelong duration (Thurman et al., 1999).

- Approximately 75 percent of individuals who have TBI have a mild version (CDC, 2003).

- Males are approximately twice as likely to sustain a TBI as contrasted to females (CDC, 1997).

Describing the Characteristics

Students with TBI differ in onset, complexity, and recovery from students with other disabilities (Bigler, Clark, & Farmer, 1997). Their injuries may affect them in many areas of their functioning; however, they often have the same or similar characteristics as students who have learning disabilities (Chapter 5), communication disorders (Chapter 6), emotional or behavioral disorders (Chapter 7), mental retardation (Chapter 9), health impairments (Chapter 11), and/or physical disabilities (Chapter 12). Jarris, for instance, has a communication impairment.

The number and magnitude of each student's functional changes, post-TBI, will vary according to the site and extent of injury, the length of time the student was in a **coma** (an unconscious state), and the student's maturational stage at the time of the injury (Tyler & Mira, 1999). The extent of functional changes and the course of recovery after the injury depend largely on whether it was mild, moderate, or severe. Twenty-nine percent of individuals with moderate to severe TBI die within 30 days of their accident, whereas only 0.2 percent of individuals with mild TBI die within the same period (Brown et al., 2004).

A person's cognitive functioning often improves as a result of rehabilitation. For example, the initial limitations in cognitive functioning of children with mild closed head injuries were partially resolved, with rehabilitation, within 3 months after the injury (Yeates et al., 1999). Although many people believe that recovery of cognitive functioning happens only soon after the injury occurs, a 5-year longitudinal study found that 18 percent of the injured adults continued to improve from year 1 to year 5, approximately 75 percent stayed the same, and 7 percent increased their cognitive functioning (Hammond et al., 2004).

On our Companion Website, *www.prenhall.com/turnbull*, you will find a link to fact sheets on the characteristics of TBI published by the Centers for Disease Control and Prevention (CDC), *www.cdc.gov/cts.do/sort/date/id/0900s3ec8000dbdc/content1.1/134.* You also may go to *www.tbiguide.com/howbrainhurt.html.*

Individuals with traumatic brain injury may benefit from physical rehabilitation, which can help address fatigue, poor coordination, and other temporary or permanent physical injuries as a result of an accident.

Values: After a student experiences a head injury, it is especially important to maintain *great expectations* for the future.

Values: Because of the changes in their cognitive functioning, you should offer *self-determination* training so your students can make and carry out good *choices* and decisions.

Council for Exceptional Children

Standard: Learning about the characteristics of learners with TBI is an application of CEC Standard 2, Understanding the Development and Characteristics of Learners.

Physical changes. The extent of students' physical changes can range from nonexistent to mild, moderate, or severe. "The site(s) of brain injury determines the type of motor dysfunction that follows. Spasticity, rigidity, and **ataxia**/tremor are the most common motor abnormalities" (Michaud, Semel-Concepción, Duhaime, & Lazar, 2002, p. 534).

Coordination problems, physical weakness, and fatigue are also common effects. Students who were previously athletic find these changes to be especially frustrating. Fortunately, however, their coordination and physical strength usually improve as their brains heal and they undergo rehabilitation, especially occupational therapy, to reacquire the fine-motor skills that help them function independently. Their fatigue often lingers, though, and if occupational therapy and other rehabilitation interventions are not brought to bear, their muscles may **atrophy,** resulting in lost or reduced muscle strength.

For example, before her accident, Megan Kohnke had been awarded a full scholarship to Pepperdine University because she was an exceptionally talented soccer player. After her accident, Megan had to be retaught everything, even how to walk and run, much less how to kick a soccer ball. Although she recovered to the point that she could practice with the Pepperdine University team and indeed started for Albertson College after transferring from Pepperdine between her sophomore and junior years, Megan will never be the player she was. She certainly will not "head" a soccer ball again.

Typically, students also experience headaches (Buyer, 1999). Almost one-third of students with TBI report headaches during the first year after the injury (Chapman, 1998). If your students have frequent headaches, you will need to make accommodations in their academic or other school schedules and assignments, give them opportunities to rest, and provide times and places for them to take medications.

Children and youth with TBI frequently have visual impairments, and about one-fifth of children and youth experience hearing loss immediately following the onset of TBI (Cockrell & Nickel, 2000). Other students may have perceptual impairments; often their vision and hearing are within normal limits with correction, but they have difficulty interpreting the information they receive through their senses. They also may experience adverse changes in their senses of taste, touch, and smell (Ponsford et al., 1999).

Cognitive changes. We encourage you to look back at Figure 13–1 and note the frontal lobe region of the brain. Closed head injuries often tend to be targeted in the frontal lobes, resulting in impairments in cognitive functioning (Yeates et al., 1999). Characteristics of cognitive changes in TBI include the following:

- Problems with attention and memory (Anderson et al., 2000; Yeates et al., 1999)

- Disruptions in higher-order social cognition tasks such as understanding ambiguous emotions and instructions (Dennis et al., 1999)

- Disruptions in executive functioning associated with reasoning, abstract thinking, and organizational skills (Cockrell & Nickel, 2000; Ylvisaker & DeBonis, 2000)

Obviously, impairments in cognitive functioning affect your students' educational performances and typically cause them to need special education services. The more severe the injury, the greater the chance the student will need those services (Arroyos-Jurado et al., 2000).

A child's age at the time of injury significantly affects his or her cognitive functioning and rehabilitation prospects. Infants or preschoolers tend to have a greater impairment of cognitive abilities than do children whose injury occurs at a later age (Gil, 2003). Moreover, very young children have greater brain vulnerability, and the manifestation of impairment often occurs at a later time. Again, as with all aspects of TBI, specific changes are highly influenced by the area of the brain that is damaged. Children and youth with more severe TBI have a much higher likelihood of developing AD/HD within the first couple of years after their injury (Max et al., 1997, 1998).

Communication changes. Communication impairments are likely when the damage is to the left hemisphere of the brain. With respect to your students' receptive language, you can expect that approximately 10 to 20 percent will have difficulty with **central auditory processing,** which involves the ability to track individual and group conversations that occur in both quiet and noisy backgrounds (Cockrell & Gregory, 1992; Cockrell & Nickel, 2000). With respect to their expressive language, you can expect that your students will often be unable to coordinate the movement of their lips, tongue, and palate, making it difficult for them to pronounce words (Cockrell & Nickel, 2000; Michaud et al., 2002), find the particular word they want to say, and speak at a normal pace.

Despite her difficulties with communication, Jarris has a full life and is able to enjoy her interactions with her siblings and other friends.

Behavioral, emotional, and social changes. Behavioral, emotional, and social changes can be especially problematic for children and youth with TBI. These students are three times more likely to develop serious problem behavior than are their nondisabled peers (Clark, 1997); these challenges are the most problematic aspect of TBI for many students (Cattelani, Lombardi, Brianti, & Mazzucchi, 1998; Koskinen, 1998). Depending upon the extent of injury and the particular location in the brain, their problems often include aggressive behavior, agitation, and anxiety (Andrews, Rose, & Johnson, 1998). They will have a significantly higher rate of emotional and behavioral disorders, especially depression, than will other students (Bloom et al., 2001); indeed, approximately 25 percent of them who have severe TBI have major depression (Max et al., 1998). In addition, the very fact of the trauma of the head injury and the hospitalization associated with it places them at risk for post-traumatic stress disorder (Daviss et al., 2000; Kassam-Adams & Winston, 2004).

Most of your students with TBI face the major challenge of dealing with their sense of loss—their reduced ability to be as competent as they were before they were injured. Their sense of loss can affect their self-concept and their confidence in interacting with peers, teachers, and families. Many of your students also will have problems in social relationships, such as accepting no for an answer, dealing with teasing, feeling socially isolated, and controlling emotions (Bohnert, Parker, & Warschausky, 1997; Clark, Russman, & Orme, 1999; Dykeman, 2003).

Determining the Causes

As we have already noted, the term *brain injury* under IDEA applies to *acquired* brain injuries. But the term also includes, although not under IDEA's definition, cogenital or degenerative injuries or injuries that are induced by a birth trauma (Lea, 2001). Figure 13–3 illustrates the causes of brain injury.

The four major causes of acquired TBI are accidents, falls, violence-related incidents, and sports and recreational injuries. Accidents typically involve motor vehicle, bicycle, or pedestrian-vehicle incidents (National Institutes of Health, 1998). Indeed, motor vehicle accidents are the leading cause of TBI that requires the victim to be hospitalized (CDC, 2001). Jarris was involved in a serious automobile accident and was life-flighted to receive emergency assistance. In your role as an educator, we encourage you to teach students to wear seatbelts every time they ride in a motor vehicle.

Falls are a second cause of TBI. The cause of children's falls vary but includes falls from beds, chairs, tables, shopping carts, and playground equipment (CDC, 2001).

Violence-related incidents are a third cause of TBI. These incidents are almost equally divided into firearm and non-firearm assaults. Approximately two-thirds of firearm-inflicted brain injuries are associated with suicidal attempts (CDC, 1999). Box 13–1 addresses the subculture of violence and suggests checks for you to consider in thinking about how to decrease violence-related incidents.

Non-firearm assaults often include child abuse that results in infant head injuries (National Institutes of Health, 1998). Child abuse involving TBI accounts for approximately one-fifth of hospital admissions in children younger than $6\frac{1}{2}$ years old and approximately one-third of admissions of children younger than 3 years old (Reece & Sege, 2000). **Shaken baby syndrome** refers to TBI resulting from a caregiver who has shaken a child violently, often in situations when

Diversity Tips ~ TBI and the Subculture of Violence

Box 13–1

The statistics about TBI and violence are alarming (CDC, 2001):

- Firearms are the leading cause of death from TBI.
- Teenagers, especially males, are more likely to die from TBI than are any other people.
- Brain injury that kills boys and young men often results from shootings or motor vehicle crashes.
- African American citizens are at a much greater risk of dying from TBI that is related to firearms than are people of any other race.
- Teenagers and people over age 75 are more likely than any other people to sustain TBI because of a motor vehicle crash or violence.
- Shootings cause less than 10 percent of all TBI yet are the leading cause of death-related TBI.
- People who are involved in assaults without firearms have a much greater chance of surviving TBI than do those involved in assaults with firearms.

These data tell us that multiculturalism and diversity are not matters of ethnicity, language, and place of origin alone. Instead, they tell us that there is a culture of violence in America. Fortunately, the culture is a "sub" one, relatively small but nonetheless exceedingly potent: the power of a weapon or a motor vehicle to destroy a life or damage a brain cannot be denied.

What can teachers do about one part of this subculture—the part that engenders a subculture of violence? Here, the challenge to a teacher is not how to assure that a student with TBI makes progress in the general curriculum. The challenge is to help prevent that student's placement into special education as a result of TBI; prevention means never having to face the challenge of reentering the general curriculum in the first place.

- Talk about the danger of firearms. Ask students who have TBI as a result of deadly-weapon assaults to explain how the TBI affects them: what were their lives like before and after their injuries?
- Develop conflict-resolution programs that involve peers, adults, members of law enforcement agencies, staff from local emergency centers and rehabilitation facilities, and family members.
- Show films about TBI and its effects. Display the data about firearms, violence, and violent environments on classroom walls and bulletin boards.
- Do not single out any one race of students for special attention; violence is everywhere.
- Tell students about the zero tolerance policy of your school (see Chapter 1 and the special provisions about IDEA and discipline) and why zero tolerance of weapons makes good sense.

Figure 13-3 Causes of brain injury

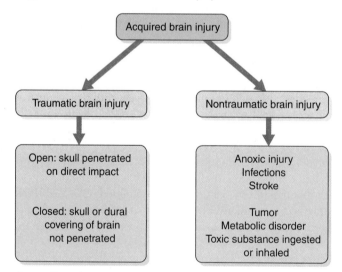

Source: From *Pediatric Traumatic Brain Injury: Proactive Interventions,* by J. L. Blosser and R. DePompei, 1994, San Diego, CA: Singular Press. Copyright 1994 by Singular Press. Reprinted with permission by Singular Publishing Group, Inc.

the caregiver is frustrated because of the child's crying (Michaud et al., 2002). In these situations, the brain can be injured by contact with the skull as well as when the child's head hits surfaces such as furniture and walls (David, 1999).

Sports and recreational injuries (sledding, skiing, snowboarding, diving, skateboarding, playing contact sports, or being hit by a ball) are the fourth major cause of TBI.

EVALUATING STUDENTS WITH TRAUMATIC BRAIN INJURY

The evaluation of students with TBI needs to be comprehensive (across the student's physical, cognitive, emotional-behavioral, and developmental faculties) and ongoing because children change, just as Jarris changed after her injuries (D'Amato & Rothlisberg, 1997). Figure 13–4 illustrates the necessary steps that an evaluation team must take.

Determining the Presence of Traumatic Brain Injury

The comprehensive educational evaluation usually occurs simultaneously with extensive evaluations by medical and rehabilitation personnel, including physical and occupational therapists (Ylvisaker, Hanks, & Johnson-Green, 2002). Physicians often run a variety of tests to determine the location and severity of the student's injury. **Computerized tomography** (CT) or **computerized axial tomography** (CAT) uses X rays to show a cross-section of the brain and skull. These pictures can be useful in identifying large areas of bleeding or large contusions. Unlike X rays, **magnetic resonance imaging** (MRI) uses a strong magnetic field and radio waves to provide detailed pictures of smaller and subtler brain anomalies or differences that a CT scan cannot provide. A newer procedure is **functional magnetic resonance imaging** (fMRI), which provides a map of brain activity by producing images of tiny metabolic changes that occur as the brain functions. Another test for determining the location and severity of an injury to the brain is the **positron emission tomography** (PET) scan, which produces three-dimensional pictures based on recording a radioactive chemical that is injected into the body and absorbed by organs. The PET scan detects early changes at the cellular level that the CT and MRI are not able to detect.

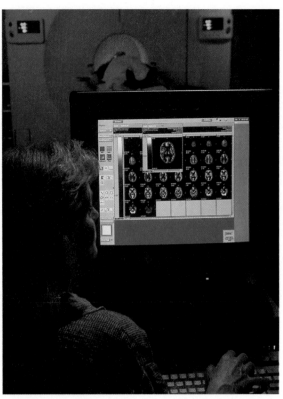

A technician uses a computer scan to secure an image of a person's brain in order to diagnose the precise location and type of disease (if any).

Typically, school psychologists administer IQ tests to students with TBI, but IQ scores often underestimate their students' specific cognitive deficits and overestimate their overall cognitive functioning (Gutentag, Naglieri, & Yeates, 1998). Moreover, IQ score patterns often tend to show less impairment in verbal skills than in performance areas (Dalby & Obrzut, 1991; Donders, 1997).

For these reasons, educators supplement IQ testing with a neurological assessment that measures cognitive processing skills more precisely (Ylvisaker et al., 2001). One such assessment is the Test of Problem Solving—Elementary, Revised, which focuses on critical thinking and problem-solving skills and analyzes a student's strengths and weaknesses:

- Solving problems
- Determining solutions
- Drawing emphasis
- Empathizing
- Predicting outcomes
- Using context clues
- Comprehending vocabulary

The Test of Problem Solving is designed for children between the ages of 6 and 11 and takes approximately 35 minutes to administer.

Teachers and rehabilitation specialists use the results of neuropsychological testing for **cognitive retraining** (Keyser-Marcus et al., 2002). Cognitive retraining involves instruction to recapture lost skills such as processing information, communication, and socialization.

Go to our Companion Website, *www.prenhall.com/turnbull*, to find a link to a website that provides information and images on CTs and MRIs, *www.nlm.nih. gov/medline-plus/headandbrain-injuries.html.*

Figure 13-4 Nondiscriminatory assessment process for determing the presence of traumatic brain injury

Observation	***Parents observe:*** The student receives a head injury from an accident, fall, sports injury, act of violence, or other cause.
	Physicians observe: The student has an open or closed head injury caused by an external physical force.
	Teacher observes: In the case of a mild head injury that might not have been treated by a physician, the teacher observes changes—physical, cognitive, communication, and/or social, behavioral, and personality.
Screening	***Assessment measures:***
	Scanning instruments: EEGs, CAT scans, MRIs, PETs, and other technology determine the extent of injury.
	Neurological exam: A neurologist examines the student for indications of brain injury.
	Coma scale: In instances of moderate to severe head injuries that induce comas, these scales provide some information about probable outcome.
Prereferral	Prereferral typically is not used with these students because the sudden onset and severity of the disability indicates a need for special education or related services.
Referral	Students with moderate to severe TBI should be referred to special education evaluation while still in rehabilitation. Teachers should refer students with mild head injuries if they notice any changes—physical; cognitive, communication, and/or social, behavioral, and personality.
Nondiscriminatory evaluation procedures and standards	***Assessment measures:***
	Individualized intelligence test: The student tends to score higher on the verbal section of the test as contrasted to performance.
	Individualized achievement tests: The student usually has peaks and valleys in scores. The student often retains skills in some areas while other skills are affected adversely by the injury.
	Adaptive behavior scales: The student may have difficulty in social, self-care, household, and community skills as a result of the injury.
	Cognitive processing tests: The student may have difficulty in areas of attention, memory, concentration, motivation, and perceptual integration.
	Social, emotional, and behavioral changes: The student may demonstrate difficulty relating to others and behaving in socially appropriate ways. The student may have problem behavior and/or emotional disorders.
	Anecdotal records: The student's cognitive, communication, motor, and behavior skills appear to have changed from what was indicated in records before the accident.
	Curriculum-based assessment: The student may have difficulty in areas of curriculum that were not problematic before the injury.
	Direct observation: The student appears frustrated, has a limited attention span, fatigues easily, or lacks motivation to perform academic tasks. The student may have difficulty relating appropriately to others. Skills can improve rapidly, especially during the early postinjury stage.
Determination	The nondiscriminatory evaluation team determines that special education and related services are needed.

Figure 13–5 Classroom observation checklist for students with TBI

Functional Domain	Examples of Problems
Memory	____ Cannot remember the previous day's lecture ____ Difficulty finding the location of classrooms, bathroom ____ Cannot remember class schedule, locker combination ____ Constantly losing books, assignments ____ Struggles to learn new information
Attention and Concentration	____ Loses track of conversations with peers ____ Constantly repeats him/herself when talking to teacher/peers ____ Difficulty listening to lectures, instructions ____ Does not know homework assignments ____ Does not complete tasks
Executive Functioning	____ Gets easily confused with changes in daily routine ____ Disorganized and cannot accomplish simple tasks ____ Cannot give directions to others (e.g., how to get to his or her house) ____ Difficulty starting and completing assignments
Self-Awareness	____ Believes he or she already knows material to be presented ____ Falsely assumes he or she has gotten an A on a failed test ____ Does not give himself or herself ample time to complete work
Language	____ Knows what he or she wants to say, but cannot find the right words to express him/herself ____ Gets teased by classmates because speech sounds slurred ____ No longer understands written language ____ Cannot name familiar objects in the classroom (e.g., desk, pencil) ____ May use inappropriate word or substitute a nonsense word for a real one

Source: From Enhancing the schooling of students with traumatic brain injury by Keyser-Marcus, L., Briel, L., Sherron-Targett, P., Yasuda, S., Johnson, S., & Wehmen, P., *Teaching Exceptional Children, 38*(4), (2002), pp. 62–67. Copyright 2002 by The Council for Exceptional Children. Reprinted with permission.

Determining the Nature of Specially Designed Instruction and Services

Students with TBI need frequent evaluation and reevaluation because of the nature and trend of their recovery, especially in the first couple of years after the onset of injury (Arroyos-Jurado et al., 2000). To evaluate frequently, teachers make classroom observations of the key neurological skills affected by TBI. Figure 13–5 is a classroom observation checklist that includes the cognitive and academic domains frequently associated with TBI. Teachers can complete this checklist monthly during the first year after a head injury, and less frequently thereafter.

DESIGNING AN APPROPRIATE INDIVIDUALIZED EDUCATION PROGRAM

Partnering for Special Education and Related Services

One of the challenges related to designing an appropriate education program for these students involves their reentry into the school setting. Special and general education teachers and related school personnel, physicians, other health care providers, and rehabilitation professionals will all be able to contribute when teachers develop IEPs for their students. Physicians and rehabilitation professionals can describe a student's brain functioning and prognosis and can assist in designing and carrying out an IEP. Many rehabilitation centers realize the particular importance of the student's reentry to school and employ a hospital-school liaison (sometimes referred to as

Partnership Tips ~ Starting with and Keeping a Team

Box 13–2

Because students with TBI must have a traumatic, external injury to their brains to qualify under the IDEA category for TBI, they almost always have been patients before they become special education students.

Jarris and Megan were in automobile accidents. Each was immediately taken to a hospital for patients in her first treatment. Only after being a patient in a hospital were they in rehabilitation. They became students again only after they returned to their schools, but they were not the same students they were before their accidents, and their programs were not the same either.

Partnerships among the various professionals and between them and their families can make all this movement back and forth—from one kind of person to another, from one kind of program to another—less traumatic for student and family. But collaboration is not always easy to achieve.

For one thing, physicians and other health care providers have a focus different from that of the other professionals. In some instances, they are intent on saving the student's life; that certainly was the case when Megan was life-flighted to a hospital and underwent several hours of brain surgery. If they are successful, they then focus on rehabilitation, itself a specialized field of medicine that involves not only physicians but also other professionals:

- Pulmonary therapists (to develop the student's lung and heart capacity)
- Physical therapists (to develop the student's muscle strength and stamina)
- Occupational therapists (to develop the student's ability to do the chores of daily living, such as brushing her teeth and tying her shoes)
- Psychologists or cognitive retrainers (to help the student learn how to think again)
- Speech-language therapists (to help the student regain the ability to communicate)

Whether these professionals work in a hospital or a rehabilitation center, they are trying to restore the student's ability to learn.

The educator, on the other hand, is trying to teach the student what he once knew and to move him to the next lesson, always increasing his cognitive abilities. The educator is also trying to help the student cope with behavioral and social challenges that invariably arise in school.

Finally, the student's family members are experiencing their own grief; essentially, they have lost one child and now have a different one. Their goals may include all of the rehabilitation and educational goals of the professionals, but they also have to learn to integrate their child into their lives and family.

Partnerships, then, require everyone to do the following:

- Acknowledge that each has different specific goals, techniques, and talents.
- Identify the short-term goals and techniques needed to achieve those goals.
- Focus on the ultimate goal of assuring that the student recovers as much preinjury capacity as possible and learns to accommodate as effectively as possible to the challenges of postinjury limitations.

So partnerships consist of

- Keeping the same long-term goal in mind
- Identifying the short-term goals and how they will help achieve the long-term goals
- Showing how one professional's techniques complement another's
- Acknowledging that the different professionals bring different but equally valuable strategies to the collaborative effort, albeit at different times

Putting Partnerships to Work for Progress in the General Curriculum

1. If you find out at the beginning of a school year that you are going to have a student with TBI, what steps would you take to find out who the partnership team has been who has worked with the student and his or her family in the past?

2. As an educator, what are the unique contributions that you could make to a partnership team for a student with TBI as contrasted to the other professional disciplines that are likely to be represented?

3. Compare and contrast the members of a partnership team for a student with TBI as contrasted with the team for a student with autism.

To answer these questions online, go to the Partnership Tips module in Chapter 13 of our Companion Website, www.prenhall.com/turnbull.

---

a school reentry specialist). In Box 13–2, you will read about a partnership model that can help students with TBI and students with other disabilities as well.

Ensuring successful reentry depends on timing; when is it best for students to move from medical and rehabilitation settings back into the school? Semrud-Clikeman (2001, p. 112) summarized the key abilities that predict a student's successful reentry:

- To attend to the instructor and instruction
- To understand and retain information
- To reason and express ideas
- To solve problems
- To plan and monitor his own performance

An expert panel on TBI recommended the following with regard to hospital-to-school transitions (Ylvisaker et al., 2001, p. 83):

- Involve educators during the hospital stay
- Keep school personnel updated on student medical progress
- Make the time for homebound instruction as short as possible
- Frequently monitor the student's progress after reentry
- Assign someone to be the point person for coordinating the transition

In many cases, teams formed for reentry remain intact to support the student in school. Jarris's school has developed a core team to foster partnerships. It consists of her general and special education teachers, her parents, a speech pathologist, a physical therapist, an occupational therapist, and the school district's director of curriculum. The team meets monthly to discuss how she is developing and to consider how to respond to her learning needs. Rather than supporting her needs in isolation, the team has been able to propose solutions that members can implement and evaluate as a team and with the cooperation of her parents. For example, realizing that sign language is an effective augmentative communication for Jarris, Linda (her third-grade general education teacher) sought assistance in learning how to sign by inviting the district's deaf education teacher into the classroom to teach her and her students basic sign language.

Values: Partnering to ensure effective school reentry is necessary for the student's inclusion and *peer relationships*.

Determining Supplementary Aids and Services

Many of the classroom modifications that we discussed in the chapter on students with autism (Chapter 11) also benefit students with TBI. There are also technology devices to support students with TBI, particularly to compensate for their impaired memory skills. O'Neil-Pirozzi, Kendrick, Goldstein, and Glenn (2004, p. 183) conducted a study that identified the potential uses of memory aids:

- Following a routine schedule
- Keeping appointments that are not routine
- Taking medications
- Remembering to perform a new task
- Marking when to start or end a task

The Visual Assistant software you learned about in Chapter 9 (mental retardation) exemplifies how handheld computers can help people with cognitive impairments overcome limitations in memory and organization skills, as shown in Box 13–3.

For more information about the Brain Injury Association of America's work with PDAs as memory and organization support devices, go to our Companion Website, *www.prenhall.com/turnbull*, and look for the link to the Assistive Technologies and Cognitive Disabilities Project information, *http://www.biausa.org/pda*.

Technology Tips ~ **Personal Digital Assistants for Memory and Organization Support**

Box 13–3

The proliferation of personal data assistants (PDAs) in today's society is astounding. While some people may prefer the traditional appointment book, many individuals with disabilities are enhancing their academic and work proficiency through the use of PDAs. Individuals with TBI who have challenges in organizing information or recalling specific appointments or important dates find the PDA to be essential for them to successfully participate in school or the workplace. The PDA can store information, offer automatic reminders, and present opportunities to share information that goes beyond the capabilities of the individual.

What Is the Technology?

PDAs (e.g., Palm Pilots) offer users the capacity to store, organize, and access information. Initially seen as an electronic calendar, today's versions allow the user to access the Internet, use most computing software, download entire novels, and access more than 100 wireless functions.

What Do We Do with It?

For the individual with TBI, the answer to this question seems to be endless. Today, a student might use a PDA to take class notes; beam assignments from his or her PDA to a teacher's PDA, or vice versa; organize scheduled activities; or use it as a mobility tool to map out where she is now and where she is going. For individuals with more significant needs, software such as the Schedule Assistant (developed by AbleLink, Inc.) offers options that provide timed prompts during morning routines and keep track of bus schedules, appointments, work schedules, and so on. It also enables caregivers to record audio messages or reminders that will automatically activate at the prescribed time and day for the user to hear and then follow.

Simple assistive technology devices can be invaluable tools for helping students with TBI complete their day-to-day tasks.

For more information about available memory-prompting technology for people with TBI, go to our Companion Website, *www. prenhall.com/turnbull*, and find the link to the Brain Injury Association Assistive Technology catalog, *http://www.biausa.org/Pages/ AT/*.

Values: Providing technology to enable students to compensate for memory and other limitations enables them to be more independent and increases their *self-determination.*

In some cases, the student does not need anything as complex as a PDA but may need only prompts to help him remember an appointment, when to change classes, or when to take medication. In fact, when IEP teams are considering technology, the motto "simple is better" is worth keeping in mind. There is a tendency to want to get the latest and coolest technology support, but in most cases, a device's reliability, not its newness, is its most important feature. Quite simply, less complex devices usually require less maintenance and are more reliable than more complex devices.

Available low-tech memory aids include pagers or electronic watches. A pager (also called a beeper) is a small radio receiver that produces sounds (beeps, tones, buzz) or visual stimuli (flashing lights, text messages) or vibrates when it receives a signal. The most common way to activate a pager is through a phone call, but any device that can send a radio signal can activate pagers.

Pagers and digital beepers require a subscription service like a cellular phone or an Internet account. Simple and inexpensive ($10 to $15) electronic watches can also be used to provide audio (beeps) prompts. Most of those watches have different functions, including a timer, a stopwatch, and an alarm function. At least one watch also comes with a built-in pager. All of these can be used as memory aids. The downside with regard to the use of off-the-shelf electronic watches is that they can often be very confusing to set up and use.

Other devices contain the same functions as electronic watches but are use-specific and may be simpler to operate. For example, "medication reminder" devices provide prompts to remind people to take their medicine. Most are built into a pill tray or holder, into which the appropriate dosage can be inserted, and can be set to emit auditory sounds (beeps, chimes, rings) or to vibrate between 4 and 12 times per day. In too many cases, the lack of training on how to use a device renders the device ineffective. O'Neil-Pirozzi and colleagues (2004) studied the use of memory aids and found that training the user and offering technical assistance enhanced the device's usability.

Some teachers and students will want to combine technology with other strategies to help students remember what they need to know. Box 13–4 describes a mnemonic approach for solving problems.

Planning for Universal Design for Learning

With a traumatic brain injury, students may have difficulty paying attention as teachers present a course's content; they also may have difficulty processing the information presented to them, particularly when it is presented in lecture format. Universal design for learning modifies how teachers present information; almost every IEP team should consider the "how" challenge.

Teachers can use the evidence-based practice of instructional pacing. This strategy involves delivering course content in smaller increments or packets of information, modifying the time between their delivery of new information, and allowing students to respond to smaller chunks of information (Ylvisaker et al., 2001). Hall (2002) identified instructional pacing as one evidence-based instructional strategy. There are others (Hall, 2002, pp. 4–5):

- *Appropriate instructional pacing:* Varying how fast you present information and how often you ask your students to respond, bearing in mind their differences in attention, information processing, and cognitive ability.

- *Frequent student responses:* Asking for frequent responses and requiring your students to respond through different formats so as to actively engage them in learning.

- *Adequate processing time:* Allowing your students varying times to respond, taking into account their processing capacity, giving some students more "think" time than others.

Into Practice ~ Mnemonics for Solving Problems   Box 13–4

A good mnemonic must

- Solve a problem (i.e., make sense to people and their challenges); without this connection, a student will not integrate the strategy into his learning
- Relate to the actual activity it is designed to address
- Have a sing-song quality, like a rhyme, that helps the student connect the word to the sound
- Imply activity and elicit a good mental image
- Be simple and easy to rehearse and recall

Often students with TBI have a great deal of difficulty solving a problem in a logical way. They benefit from a step-by-step method that can be applied in various situations. Using rhyming verse and word mnemonics, Parente and his colleagues (2001) developed a mnemonic called SOLVE. Each letter of the word SOLVE reminds the person of some important aspect of a problem-solving process. Here is how SOLVE works:

- Specify the problem—define the problem
- Organize your solution—keep several options in mind
- Listen to advice—take others' advice
- Vary your thinking—ask, "what makes the problem worse?"
- Evaluate if your solution worked—read this verse again (p. 18)

The next step is for students to decide which of the several possible options would be the best solution. The DECIDE acronym teaches a rhyme that a student can follow to start thinking about a decision and to consider the decision from several possible viewpoints. DECIDE seeks to get the opinions of different people so that the student will make more correct than incorrect decisions (Parente et al., 2001, p. 18).

- Do not procrastinate—decide to begin
- Evaluate each option—choose those that are WIN-WIN
- Create new options when the others won't do
- Investigate existing policies—limit what you choose
- Discuss the decision with others and listen to them
- Evaluate your feelings—before acting, think twice

Putting These Strategies to Work for Progress in the General Curriculum

1. How might one of Jarris's teachers integrate the SOLVE and DECIDE strategies into Jarris's education?

2. Propose a plan for how Jarris might serve as a peer tutor, using the SOLVE and DECIDE strategies in teaching problem solving to a younger student.

3. How can a partnership among the special and general education teacher and Jarris's family assist in implementing the use of mnemonics for solving problems? How could Brent or Shawn incorporate mnemonics at home?

To answer these questions online, go to the Into Practice module in Chapter 13 of our Companion Website, www.prenhall.com/turnbull.

- *Monitoring responses:* Monitoring the quality and nature of your student's responses to determine if they are mastering the content of your course. If this monitoring suggests they are not, adjust your instruction soon; do not wait until the lesson is over.

- *Frequent feedback:* Providing supportive and specific feedback to your students on correct and incorrect responses and correcting the latter in "real time" instead of waiting until after the lesson.

Chapter 7 (emotional and behavioral disorders) discusses mastery assessment and mastery learning as a way to ensure ongoing progress. So you should be able to recognize that the strategies in appropriate pacing and explicit instruction incorporate a mastery learning approach, frequently assessing your students' knowledge and pacing your instruction accordingly.

IEP teams should simultaneously consider instructional pacing strategies and technology to deliver content information. For example, watching a film may have the benefit of visual input, but in many cases information presented in video format is paced briskly. Students may have a difficult time paying attention throughout the entire film and processing the information it presents. Teachers can pause the videos to pace the video presentation, using that time to solicit student responses and determine student mastery. Alternatively, digital presentation of information in computer formats allows students to regulate the presentation of information and gives their teachers the opportunity to probe their students' understanding.

Planning for Other Educational Needs

The long-term effects of frontal lobe injuries in children and adolescents require interventions to address their present and anticipated future needs. Often at the middle and high school levels, they need to develop or refine their self-management, learning, thinking, and problem-solving abilities, especially when planning their transition from school to adulthood, including the transition to college.

For more information about explicit instruction, go to our Companion Website, *www.prenhall. com/turnbull*, and find the link to CAST, *http://www.cast.org/ncac/ ExplicitInstruction2875.cfm*.

Council for Exceptional Children

Standard: Selecting and adapting strategies to meet the needs of exceptional learners directly relates to CEC Standard 4, Instructional Strategies.

It can be challenging and even frightening for a student with TBI to transition from school to a college or university. Take Megan, for example. Megan's near-fatal car accident happened just four days after she graduated from high school. A gifted student and soccer player, she had plans to attend Pepperdine University on a full athletic scholarship. After her intensive rehabilitation, Megan entered Pepperdine University a semester late. To prepare for her entry, Megan and her mother met with her rehabilitation team. Her neuropsychologist mapped out strategies and modifications that Megan would need to be successful.

Immediately after arriving at Pepperdine, Megan met with each professor and introduced herself and explained her disability. To illustrate her injury, she brought pictures of herself immediately after the accident, showing significant damage to her skull and featuring a bald Megan with a scar reaching from ear to ear. She wasn't seeking sympathy; rather, she used the pictures to show the professors what had happened to her. Her hair had grown back and now covered the scar, but she wanted them to know that, even though she looked fine, she had significant challenges because of this injury. She also brought information about her high school grades and information about the rehabilitation she had recently completed. Megan explains,

> I wasn't looking for a handout but, instead, I wanted my professors to know what I had been through. I let them know that I was going to try extra hard, but without accommodations I wouldn't succeed. This wasn't easy for me. I used to be a very social person; but like most people who suffer from a TBI, I had lost confidence in myself and was uncomfortable talking with people, especially about me. However, I met with every professor and told them what my neurologist suggested and how I would need additional time to complete tests, I would need to tape every lecture, I would benefit from any type of handout that would further illustrate the lecture, and I would need the assistance of the writing center.

Megan's first semester at Pepperdine consisted of a number of other hurdles. One of the first involved being independent and attending to her basic needs. Unfortunately, simple activities such as selecting food at the cafeteria proved to be a challenge. Her mother explains,

> I went to Pepperdine with Megan and spent the first week with her. The first morning, we went over to the cafeteria, and I told Megan to get something to eat. I left to allow her the opportunity to make the appropriate selection. After a long time, she returned to the room not having eaten a thing. With all the choices, Megan didn't know how to make a selection. I quickly learned she needed direct instruction in how to select food items from the cafeteria if she was going to eat in this environment. So we went through the various lines and reviewed what a balanced meal would include and selected various items. This involved further demonstration and practice before Megan was comfortable and able to eat on her own.

When her classes began, Megan, armed with a tape recorder, recorded every lecture. At the end of the day, she returned home and transcribed these lectures by hand. Next, she reviewed her handwritten transcription and created another outline that would help her study. This was exceedingly time-consuming but necessary for Megan's learning needs. On test days, Megan was allowed to arrive early and begin the test 30 to 60 minutes ahead of the rest of her peers. As Megan explains, "I was the first person there and the last to leave for every one of my tests." Megan's hard work and postsecondary accommodations have paid off. She successfully completed her undergraduate degree.

In Chapter 5 (on learning disabilities), we discussed the importance of teaching students with learning disabilities the self-advocacy skills they need to transition from high school to college. These skills are equally important for students with TBI, as Megan so clearly demonstrates. Students with TBI need to be equipped with the knowledge and skills required to succeed in postsecondary education, and that begins with the IEP planning team's efforts to identify the assistance that students will need and the instructional and support strategies that will help the student achieve a positive transition to college.

USING EFFECTIVE INSTRUCTIONAL STRATEGIES

Early Childhood Students: Collaborative Teaming

When you think of instructional strategies, you probably think of methods a teacher uses when teaching students. But you have already learned about strategies that involve students teaching other students and students teaching themselves, so it is obvious that not all instructional strategies focus on the teacher-student interaction. Collaborative teaming is an important strategy to promote inclusive practices for all students with disabilities, from early childhood to high school, that focuses on the role of teachers and not specifically on teacher-student interactions. Quite simply, collaborative teaming involves two or more people working together to educate students with disabilities. Thousand and Villa (2000) have identified a collaborative team as a group of people who

- Partner to achieve a shared goal
- Believe that all team members have unique and needed expertise and skills, and value each person's contribution
- Distribute leadership throughout the team

Janney and Snell (2000) have identified five principle components of collaborative teaming.

Building team structure. This involves making sure that school policies support team teaching, defining the core team (those team members who are most directly responsible for the student's education) and the whole team (core team plus members who might occasionally teach the student), and creating time to plan for instruction.

Learning teamwork skills. To succeed, team members need to learn and practice teamwork skills such as active listening, negotiation and compromise skills, and role-release skills (turning over some of one's own responsibilities to other team members). Teams should discuss and agree on shared values and a shared goal related to a student's progress.

Taking team action. Teams begin by problem solving, creating an action plan, determining a schedule for program delivery, and identifying assessment and program evaluation components.

Teaching collaboratively. After the groundwork has been layed, teaching collaboratively feels natural and is effective. Co-teachers learn one another's areas of instructional strength and how to best use those strengths to all students' benefit.

Improving communication and handling conflict. Along with experience comes more open communication, stronger (and more effective) partnerships, and trust (as we pointed out in Chapter 4). In some circumstances, however, conflicts can arise, and it is important that team members treat one another with respect and practice effective conflict-resolution skills, especially when the student with a traumatic brain injury participates in team meetings.

Collaborative teaming is important across all age levels, including early childhood. Hunt and colleagues (2004) implemented collaborative teaming to support preschoolers with severe disabilities, including TBI. The core team consisted of the early childhood teacher, the special education teacher, an instructional assistant, the speech-language therapist, and a parent. The collaborative teaming strategies resulted in positive outcomes for the children, including reduced student nonengaged time, higher levels of social interactions with peers, and higher levels of child-initiated interactions with an adult in the classroom.

Elementary and Middle School Students: Cooperative Learning

One of the most important strategies to ensure progress in the general curriculum for students with disabilities, including students with TBI, involves the use of cooperative learning strategies. These strategies involve small groups of students who together focus on a common learning task or activity. Successfully implementing cooperative learning, however, involves much more than

Use your *Real Lives and Exceptionalities* DVD to view Jamie, involved in cooperative activity. Click on, "Beyond School," and then select "Jamie" (Clip 5). What characteristics of successful cooperative learning groups can you identify in this clip?

Standard: Participating in collaborative teaming is an example of how you can address CEC Standard 10, Collaboration.

Cooperative learning can be a successful strategy when teachers allow the students to be both independent and accountable for their own and others' work.

simply putting students together in small groups and giving them an assignment. A haphazard approach to group learning can result in the outcome that a few students do most of the work and, consequently, most of the learning.

Early seminal work in cooperative learning by Johnson and Johnson (1991) identified the primary characteristics of cooperative learning groups, two of which are very important: positive interdependence and individual accountability.

Positive interdependence. Positive interdependence refers to "linking students together so one cannot succeed unless all group members succeed" (Johnson, Johnson, & Holubec, 1998, p. 4). In essence, students are compelled to support and enable their fellow group members to succeed. Positive interdependence is created by assigning group members tasks that are critical to the overall goal and are individualized to the student's ability level. Students engage in different levels of learning and their tasks vary, as is the case in universally designed learning, but each task is essential to the overall success of the group.

Individual accountability. A second drawback of haphazardly created learning groups is that all students benefit or are punished equally by the group outcome, not necessarily by their individual contribution. One student may do all the work and that work may earn the group an A, but other students may not have individually deserved that grade. Similarly, one student may perform his or her portion of the task at a high-quality level, but the overall quality of her product may be dragged down by other students' performances; that one student is unfairly punished with a grade lower than she deserved.

By assigning students in cooperative learning groups with discrete, identifiable tasks that contribute to the whole, teachers can individually assess their students on the quality of that one component task. However, more important to the implementation of cooperative learning is that students understand that each group member has a role and that the group as a whole will be accountable for the quality of the product.

Johnson and colleagues (1998) identified several ways to structure cooperative learning groups to ensure both individual and group success. One factor is group size; the smaller the group, the easier it is to fairly distribute tasks and to individualize those tasks to the unique needs of students. A second factor is detailing each student's individual task, providing examples of quality outcomes pertaining to that task, and making sure the student understands the contribution of his or her task to the group's task or goal. Instead of waiting until the group is finished, teachers should use frequent probes to determine what each group member is doing and learning. Additionally, peers can hold one another accountable. Researchers suggested that teachers assign one group member to be a "checker" and to question other group members to ensure that everyone understands (Johnson et al., 1998).

Secondary and Transition Students: Problem-Solving and Decision-Making Instruction

Even after a student has recuperated from a traumatic brain injury, he or she may still have difficulties in executive function areas. These are higher-level brain or intellectual functions that govern complex activities like making plans and decisions, solving problems, and setting goals. Impairments of executive function systems are not easily detected, at least not until the student is called upon to perform one of these tasks. So it is important to provide students with systematic instruction that will enable them to improve their executive functioning skills, including problem-solving or decision-making skills.

A problem is "a task, activity, or situation for which a solution is not immediately identified, known, or obtainable" (Agran & Wehmeyer, in press). Teaching problem-solving skills involves teaching students skills to identify a solution that solves the problem. Solving a problem, therefore, is the process of identifying a solution that resolves the initial perplexity or difficulty. The skills typically involved in teaching problem solving are (1) problem identification, (2) problem explication or definition, and (3) solution generation.

Problem identification. The first step in solving a problem is to recognize that a problem exists. Agran and Wehmeyer (in press) suggested that, as a part of this step, students should address the following questions: (1) is the problem caused by myself or someone else? and (2) How important is the problem? Students should also learn to estimate the time needed to solve a problem during this step.

Problem explication or definition. In many cases, students are too global in their definition of the problem. That is, they attribute the problem to broad factors ("That teacher is mean") rather than the real problem at hand (failing a class, not meeting class deadlines, or arriving late). It is important to teach students to narrow the problem down to one that is solvable. This is accomplished by teaching the student to specify or define the problem.

Solution generation. Once a student has defined the problem she must solve, she will need to learn how to generate potential solutions to problems. Initially, it is important to allow students to generate as many solutions as feasible, even if they do not adequately address the problem. Discuss with students why a given solution does or does not solve the problem and whether the solution's implementation is feasible.

At this point students are ready to make a decision about the best option available, learning how to select from a pool of potential solutions the one that best fits their needs, circumstances, and capacity. This is, in essence, a decision-making action, the process for which is discussed next.

When teaching problem solving, teachers should use real-world situations. Adolescents face a myriad of problems, from relationship troubles to tobacco and alcohol use; using these problems as examples can enable students to learn problem-solving strategies and also can provide a means to address issues in adolescence.

As we have noted, the problem-solving process ends with making a decision about the best solution to the problem from among several possible solutions. Many people view problem solving and decision making as one and the same. This is not accurate, however. As you have learned, a problem-solving process requires students to identify potential solutions. The decision-making process involves coming to a judgment or conclusion, selecting the best potential solution.

Just as the typical problem-solving process ends with making a decision, the typical decision-making strategy begins with a problem-solving step. Teaching students to make decisions involves a number of steps:

Identify relevant alternatives or options. If students already know the alternatives from which to make a decision, then this step is straightforward: have the students write down the solution. More often than not, the students do not know all of the options or alternatives available to them, so the decision-making process begins by implementing a problem-solving process to identify relevant options.

Identify consequences of alternatives. One characteristic of many students with disabilities (indeed, many adolescents in general) is their tendency to act impulsively or without adequate thought about the consequences of their actions. When this involves some circumstances, like taking drugs, their impulsivity can be more than just exasperating; it can be life-threatening. Students need to be taught systematically to think through all the possible consequences of each alternative.

Identify the probability of each consequence. Teachers need to be clear about the consequences of a student's behavior. Consequences range from positive to neutral to negative. They also range from highly likely to occur to unlikely to occur. Students with TBI should learn to weigh the relative risk of the alternative with the relative likelihood that it will occur and with its potential benefits. The potential risks of some activities (cancer from smoking or AIDS from unprotected sex) are so negative that even the slightest possibility that they could occur should warrant discarding that option.

Determine the value placed on each option or alternative. Students should be supported to consider relevant issues as they consider risks, benefits, and consequences. Their values, preferences,

Standard: Teaching students problem solving and other cognitive strategies addresses CEC Standard 4, Instructional Strategies.

Values: By promoting students' problem-solving and decision-making skills, teachers ensure that students become more *self-determined* and have more opportunity to obtain full *citizenship*.

and interests should come into play and often become the dominant factors in reaching a decision. Also, cultural, ethical, and religious factors can play a role in their decisions.

Integrate values and consequences to select a preferred option. The final step is to choose one option based on all the factors considered. As Ylvisaker and DeBonis (2000) noted, students with TBI (and AD/HD) are at increased risk for impairments in executive function skills. Moreover, research has shown that students with TBI benefit from instruction in these areas. For example, researchers showed that students with TBI who were involved in an intervention that included problem-solving instruction and instruction on student-directed learning strategies made significant improvements in their problem-solving abilities (Suzman, Morris, Morris, & Milan, 1997). (See Chapters 5 and 11 for information on student-directed learning strategies and Chapter 7 for discussion of the importance of multicomponent interventions to address complex problems.)

INCLUDING STUDENTS WITH TRAUMATIC BRAIN INJURY

Figure 13–6 indicates the educational placement of students with TBI, and Box 13–5 provides tips for increasing their success in general education classrooms.

ASSESSING STUDENTS' PROGRESS

Measuring Students' Progress

Progress in the general curriculum. One strategy for determining progress in the general curriculum involves the use of analytic rubrics (Nolet & McLaughlin, 2000). A rubric is a scale developed by a teacher (or others) as a guide to scoring a student's performance. To create an analytic rubric, teachers identify specific outcomes linked to a standard, ranking them from less to more positive and assigning a score (typically from 0 or 1 to 4 or 5) to each outcome. For example, an analytic rubric for a first-grade writing standard might set the following outcomes:

1 = handwriting not legible; cannot be read by adult

2 = some words legible, but most are not

Figure 13–6 Educational placement of students with TBI (2003–2004)

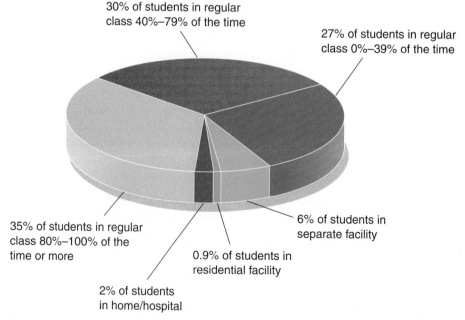

30% of students in regular class 40%–79% of the time

27% of students in regular class 0%–39% of the time

35% of students in regular class 80%–100% of the time or more

0.9% of students in residential facility

6% of students in separate facility

2% of students in home/hospital

Source: U.S. Department of Education, Office of Special Education Programs. (2005). *IDEA data website* (http://www.ideadata.org/aboutThisSite.asp).

Inclusion Tips

Box 13–5

	What You Might See	What You Might Be Tempted to Do	Alternate Responses	Ways to Include Peers in the Process
Behavior	The student may show behavior and personality changes, such as temper outbursts, anxiety, fatigue, or depression.	Respond with strong disapproval of her new behavior.	Teach problem solving, using the SOLVE mnemonic to reduce frustration that is associated with problem behavior.	Give her time to work in natural settings with peers who will encourage appropriate behavior yet show acceptance during the relearning stage.
Social interactions	She may have forgotten social skills and experience social misunderstandings because of her new identity struggles.	Ignore her social difficulties and hope they go away.	Partner with both the speech and language pathologist and the school counselor to plan the best ways to use language and social skills in successful situations.	Allow friends with whom she feels secure to role-play social activities. Structure many opportunities for successful interactions. Use videotapes for self-evaluation.
Educational performance	Learning new information may be difficult for her, or it may take her much longer to process information.	Require extra work in areas of difficulty.	Use cooperative learning groups to aid her in organization, memory, and cognitive processes.	Have her brainstorm and work with her peers/friends to practice skills as well as to plan future projects and educational aspirations.
Classroom attitudes	She may be confused about exactly what is expected on assignments.	Excuse her from assignments.	Use rubrics as a way to delineate four months' worth of expectations for assignments.	Pair her with a partner and friend who can help her focus and participate meaningfully during instruction.

3 = most words legible; some cannot be read

4 = all words legible

When considering the development of rubrics to determine progress in the general curriculum, Nolet and McLaughlin (2000) suggest:

- The rubrics should link directly to specific content and student achievement standards.
- A rubric should focus on only one dimension of student performance (i.e., legibility versus content knowledge).
- There should be enough points in the scale to adequately judge performance but not so many as to confuse the issue. Nolet and McLaughlin recommend 3 to 7 points.
- The rubric should focus on specific outcomes rather than a process.
- Teachers should provide students with information about the rubrics and examples of high-quality performance that would meet the standard and be scored high.

Progress in addressing other educational needs. Traumatic brain injuries can often result in perceptual and motor impairments that include difficulty with handwriting due to poor eye-hand coordination. Perceptual-motor skills are those skills that coordinate visual and sensory input with motor activities. There are a number of widely used tests of perceptual-motor skills. For example, the Bender-Gestalt Visual Motor test provides a relatively quick way to

PRAXIS

Standard: Identifying and using appropriate assessments reflects PRAXIS™ Standard 3, Delivery of Services to Students with Disabilities.

For more information about the Bender Test, go to our Companion Website, *www.prenhall.com/turnbull*, and search for the link to the American Orthopsychiatric Association, *http://www.amerortho.org/*.

measure children's visual-motor functioning, visual-perception skills, and the impact of brain injury on these functions. The test involves the administration of nine geometric designs, presented one at a time to the student, who is asked to reproduce them. Like many such standardized tests, the administration of the Bender-Gestalt test should be performed by a school psychologist.

On a more applied level, teachers can assess student progress in specific perceptual-motor areas through collaborations among special and general educators and occupational or physical therapists. For example, evaluating students' handwriting is a common activity performed by occupational therapists. Working with special educators, occupational therapists can determine whether a student's handwriting difficulties are a function of visual impairments, perceptual difficulties, eye-hand coordination problems, motor tone problems, hand grasping or pinching difficulties, or general hand functioning. In turn, the teacher and occupational therapists can establish an instructional program to improve the student's handwriting or, if necessary, identify assistive writing devices, including adaptive word processors (such as those discussed in Chapter 7).

Making Accommodations for Assessment

Students with TBI may experience difficulties concentrating and attending for long periods of time; like students with AD/HD, they will benefit from the accommodations we discussed in Chapter 8.

In addition, as you have learned in this chapter, problems with memory and retention are often barriers for students with TBI, and testing situations are no different. One accommodation involves the way in which test items are constructed. Students with TBI may perform better on exams that present multiple-choice or true-false options than on tests that rely on memory and recall, such as short answer or essay formats. While it is not usually a reasonable accommodation to reword items from one format to another, the use of a scribe (someone who writes the answer for the student) may benefit students with TBI. Having someone write the answer allows the student to focus or concentrate on recalling information, and students can most likely provide more information verbally than in writing, particularly if they have handwriting difficulties.

Looking to Jarris's Future

Nearly 9 years have elapsed since Jarris's injury, and 6 since her entry into the LAP program, where she took her first steps on the journey to rejoining the world that she would have occupied except for her injury. Where is she now?

She has mastered ASL; her family has, too. Her teachers use some signs with her, and when they cannot communicate satisfactorily through signs to and from each other, Jarris's classmates lend a hand—literally! Her teachers have adopted universal design in their curriculum and instruction, giving Jarris access to the same opportunities to learn that her classmates without disabilities have. She still struggles to communicate and to master her academic subjects. But she has traveled a very long route and done it successfully, albeit with a great deal of support.

Brent and Shawn concur when asked about Jarris's future: "We want and expect Jarris to be able to choose what it is she wants to do and be able to pursue her dream just like anyone else. It's quite simple, actually. We believe Jarris has the potential, and we want to ensure that we do whatever is necessary for her to reach her potential."

So let's return to the initial challenge, the one we confronted when we first met Jarris. Can you imagine growing up with a brain injury? Ask that of Jarris, her family, and her teachers, and the answer will be, "Of course." The reason the answer comes so quickly and unanimously? History is prologue. The LAP was where Jarris's history began, and its end is not yet in sight.

SUMMARY

Identifying students with traumatic brain injuries

- The IDEA definition of TBI includes acquired injuries to the brain caused by an external force but does not include brain injuries that are congenital, degenerative, or induced at birth.
- Closed head injuries and open head injuries are the two types of brain injuries included under the IDEA definition.
- Students with TBI often experience physical, cognitive, communication, and social, behavioral, and personality changes.
- No generalizations can be made about prognosis based on the injury's mildness or severity.
- The four major causes of TBI are accidents, falls, violence, and sports and recreational injuries.

Evaluating students with TBI

- Medical evaluations include CAT scans, MRIs, and PET scans to determine the location and severity of the student's injury.
- The Test of Problem Solving—Elementary, Revised, is a neuropsychological assessment particularly aimed at evaluating the critical-thinking and problem-solving skills of elementary-age students.
- On an ongoing basis, teachers can use a classroom observation guide to pinpoint a student's precise cognitive functioning.

Designing an appropriate individualized education program

- It is critical that educators partner with medical and other professionals to ensure an effective reentry into the public school system.
- Simple technologies, like pagers, alarms, and watches, can provide the support students need to be more independent and to minimize memory impairments.
- The rate at which teachers present content information affects student success when they have attention and processing difficulties related to TBI. Instructional pacing is important to consider.
- Many students with TBI can succeed in college if the appropriate planning occurs and the student is prepared to provide ideas for accommodations.

Using effective instructional strategies

- Collaborative teaming involves two or more educators working collaboratively to meet shared goals pertaining to student achievement.
- Cooperative learning groups are critical to the success of inclusive classrooms. Teachers need to be sure, however, that all students have a meaningful role in the process and contribute to the outcome.
- Problem-solving and decision-making skills are important for students with TBI, whose injuries often result in lifelong difficulties in these areas of executive function.

Including students with traumatic brain injury

- Approximately one-third of students with TBI spend 80 percent or more of their time in general education classrooms.

Assessing students' progress

■ Rubrics provide a means for teachers to quantify student progress in the general curriculum.

■ A variety of neuropsychiatric assessments may help teachers who are working with students with TBI. Teachers should definitely focus on determining perceptual-motor skills since they directly impact handwriting.

■ The use of a scribe and test item formats that minimize the use of essay exams are accommodations for students with TBI who have memory impairments.

WHAT WOULD YOU RECOMMEND?

Refer to chapter content and the PRAXIS™ and CEC standards in Appendix A to answer the following questions:

1. If you were Jarris's teacher, what kind of collaborative teaming would provide you with the support and resources that you would need to be successful? What PRAXIS™ or CEC standards apply to cooperative teaming?

2. Design a rubric for an assignment that you have in one of your current courses. Identify the PRAXIS™ or CEC standards that apply to developing competency in the use of rubrics.

3. Develop a list of each of the characteristics of TBI, and state one potential educational challenge associated with each characteristic. Visit the Companion Website and find links to the websites mentioned in the chapter. Use the information you find there to help you with your response. What PRAXIS™ or CEC standards apply to this area of knowledge?

Who are Mariah, Ricquel, and Shylah Thomas?

by *Sally L. Roberts, University of Kansas*

Who, indeed, are these three sisters? There are several ways we can describe them. Let's try a comparative approach, choosing the words *unusual* and *usual* as our criteria.

Mariah, Ricquel, and Shylah (ages 9, 7, and 3, respectively) are unusual in that they are the profoundly deaf daughters of Sharon and Sheddrick Thomas and the younger sisters of Bradley (age 11), who has no hearing loss at all. Three sisters with the same degree of hearing loss is an unusual constellation of disability.

Unusual, yes, in one sense, but not in another. Like so many other students with disabilities and their families, the Thomas family is determined to move forward with their lives, undisturbed by the fact that Sharon is pregnant with their next child.

The sisters are unusual in that, unlike many students with disabilities, they do not attend school in their home school district in Poway, California. Instead, they ride the school bus to schools operated by the San Diego Unified School District. Mariah and Ricquel attend the Lindbergh Schweitzer Elementary School, and Shylah attends the Lafayette Elementary School, schools on separate campuses but near each other. Sharon insisted on out-of-district busing so that all three would receive the most appropriate education available in the greater-metropolitan San Diego area.

They are usual in that, like many students with disabilities, they are included in their school's general education curriculum, receive some of their education in a pullout program operated by a teacher of the deaf, and have friends with and without disabilities. They are unusual in that they have the same disability, but they are usual in that two of them, Mariah and Ricquel, are auditory learners for whom the oral method comes easily, whereas Shylah is a visual learner who picks up sign language more readily than her sisters.

Enough of the comparisons! What is especially notable about Mariah, Ricquel, and Shylah is that the way they receive their education is deeply controversial. They receive it—and thus communicate with their parents, teachers, and peers, with and without disabilities—through a cochlear implant. This implant is an electronic device that compensates for the damaged or absent hair cells in a person's cochlea by stimulating the person's auditory nerve fibers. Unlike a hearing aid, the implant does not make sounds louder. Instead, it provides sound information by directly stimulating the functional auditory nerve fibers in the cochlea. The implant has two parts. The internal part is surgically implanted under the skin with electrodes inserted into the cochlea. The external part, worn like a hearing aid, consists of a microphone, a speech processor, and a transmitting coil.

Understanding Students with Hearing Loss

Why is a cochlear implant controversial? Isn't it like eyeglasses for a person with a visual impairment or a prosthesis for a person who has lost an arm or a leg? In part, the implant is comparable to eyeglasses or a prosthesis. It restores lost function. If we return to Mariah, Ricquel, and Shylah and their unusual and usual attributes, the implant seems quite usual. But it is also quite unusual because not all people with hearing loss can benefit from one.

Most of all, however, the cochlear implant is quite unusual because some individuals who are deaf or hard of hearing strongly object to it. They are opposed to any alteration of a deaf person's inherent deafness. They believe that deafness is only part of a person's being, so any mechanical alteration denies that person's essence and may diminish his or her worth. Further, they believe that deafness creates a subpopulation among Americans of people who have their own language, history, and culture. To alter a person mechanically, then, is tantamount to subverting a proud population.

Other people who are deaf or hard of hearing disagree. Along with Sharon and Sheddrick, they hold that any intervention that helps a deaf person communicate with hearing people is worthwhile. Their position is not grounded on cultural identity but on pragmatics and efficacy: if an intervention benefits a person, use it.

That's the same position Sharon and Sheddrick took when they decided to transfer their children from the Poway School District to the one in San Diego. Individualized benefit governs their decision to follow two unusual courses of action, braving a transfer and a loss of opportunity to be with neighborhood peers. But being brave does not mean acting alone.

Three professionals play special roles in supporting Sharon, Sheddrick, and their daughters. One is Vicki Maley, herself a woman who is deaf and who taught Mariah and Ricquel until she retired a few years ago. Sharon describes Vicki as her "deaf mentor," a person who introduced the concept of Deaf culture, recounted what it means to be a member of that culture and how a deaf person can get along in the deaf and in the hearing worlds alike. Mary gave Sharon hope for her daughters and entire family at a time when, in Sharon's words, "I felt that my life was over." Predictably, Sharon herself looks forward to the time when she, too, will be a mentor for another parent, in a parent-to-parent relationship (see Chapter 4).

The second professional is Mary Maussang, the girls' deaf educator. She is, as Sharon puts it, "my lifeline." Mary is a member of a team of educators committed to Sharon's daughters. She team-teaches with a general educator in the kindergarten and third-grade classrooms. They teach in voice and sign language simultaneously, relying on an interpreter and on Mary's assistant teacher, both of whom sign the instruction. As these team members work collaboratively, they make it possible for the class of two deaf students and 17 hearing students to organize itself into smaller groups. Each group learns through both sign and oral communication, with the result that the deaf students have a support and communication network that consists of their hearing peers.

The other significant benefit of team teaching is that each teacher works with small groups for guided reading, vocabulary, and other skill building; and each teacher works with each small group once a day, so that every group receives two daily sessions of instruction. And a third professional source of help consists of the girls' team of physicians, audiologists, and speech-language therapists at San Diego's Children's Hospital.

Let's return to the first question: who are Mariah, Ricquel, and Shylah? They are unusual and yet usual. They themselves are noncontroversial, yet they are in the middle of controversy. It's hard to pigeon-hole them or any other students who are deaf or hard of hearing. The range of human variety is great. The Thomas family not only illustrates that fact but also is cause to celebrate it.

IDENTIFYING STUDENTS WITH HEARING LOSS

Defining Hearing Loss

Two terms, *deaf* and *hard of hearing,* describe hearing loss. Two other terms, **unilateral** and **bilateral,** relate to whether the loss occurs in one or both ears. The term *deaf* is often overused to describe all individuals with hearing loss. The current regulations implementing IDEA define *deafness* as a hearing impairment that is so severe that the student is impaired in processing linguistic information through hearing, with or without amplification, and that it adversely affects the student's educational performance.

The severity, or level, of a student's hearing determines whether the student will be classified as deaf. A person is considered to be **deaf** who has a hearing loss of 70 to 90 decibels (dB) or greater and cannot use hearing, even with amplification, as the primary means for developing language. Figure 14–1 illustrates the degrees of hearing loss. By contrast, a person is considered to be **hard of hearing** who has a hearing loss in the 20 to 70 dB range, benefits from amplification, and communicates primarily through speaking. **Congenital deafness** is a low-incidence disability, affecting a small number of people. The majority of the people with whom they interact are hearing—including most of their family members.

Although some people use the term *hearing impaired* to describe a student with a hearing loss, special educators prefer to use person-first language ("student who is deaf") when referring to students with hearing loss. The **Deaf community,** however, believes that the term *impaired* has negative connotations and prefers *deaf child* (Batshaw, 2002). Its members particularly resist the term *hearing impaired* because it implies a condition in need of correction or repair. Members of the Deaf community do not view themselves as needing to be fixed or cured but as a distinct cultural and linguistic group (Lane, Hoffmeister, & Bahan, 1996).

Prevalence. Compared to other groups of students with disabilities, students with hearing loss are a relatively small group. The U.S. Department of Education (2003) reported that 70,349 students with hearing loss between the ages of 6 and 21 received some type of special education services in 2002–2003. Preschool programs (ages 3 to 5) served another 7,474 children, equivalent to about 1 percent of the total numbers of young children in preschools.

Figure 14–1 Degrees of hearing loss

	125	250	500	1,000	2,000	4,000	8,000
0 10	(0–15 dB) *Normal*—There is no impact on communication.						
20	(16–25 dB) *Slight*—In noisy environments, faint speech is difficult to understand.						
30	(26–40 dB) *Mild*—Faint or distant speech is difficult to hear, even in quiet environments. Classroom discussions are challenging to follow.						
40 50	(41–55 dB) *Moderate*—Conversational speech is heard only at a close distance. Group activities in a classroom present a challenge.						
60	(56–70 dB) *Moderate-severe*—Only loud, clear conversational speech can be heard, and group situations present great difficulty. Speech is intelligible, though noticeably impaired.						
70 80	(71–90 dB) *Severe*—Conversational speech cannot be heard unless it is loud; even then, many words cannot be recognized. Environmental sounds can be detected, though not always identified. Speech is not always intelligible.						
90 100 110 120	(91+ dB) *Profound*—Conversational speech cannot be heard. Some loud environmental sounds may be heard. Speech is difficult to understand or may not be developed at all.						

The Hearing Process

Before you can understand hearing loss, you must first understand what is involved in hearing sound. The hearing process is called **audition.** When we hear sounds, we are really interpreting patterns in the movement (vibration) of air molecules. Sounds are described in terms of their pitch or frequency (very low to very high) and intensity or loudness (very soft to very loud). Frequency is measured in **hertz (Hz),** named in honor of Heinrich Hertz, and loudness is measured in **decibels (dB),** named in honor of Alexander Graham Bell. Speech has a mix of high and low frequencies and soft and loud sounds.

Most of the sounds we hear every day occur in the 250 to 6,000 Hz range. Conversational speech is usually at about 45 dB to 50 dB of loudness. You have normal hearing if you can hear frequencies between 20 and 20,000 Hz and 0 and 120 dB. A whisper is about 20 dB, and a shout can be as loud as 70 dB. Vowel sounds like "o" have low frequencies; consonants like "f" and "sh" have higher frequencies. An individual who cannot hear high-frequency sounds will have a very hard time understanding speech. To help you approximate what these ranges sound like, refer to Figure 14–2 to compare familiar sounds to these speech ranges.

The hearing mechanism. To understand what can go wrong with the hearing process, it is important to begin with the anatomy of the hearing mechanism, which consists of three parts: the outer, middle, and inner ear. Figure 14–3 illustrates the structure and anatomy of the ear. Look at it as you read the next few paragraphs.

The outer ear consists of the **auricle,** or **pinna,** and the **ear canal.** Its purpose is to collect the sound waves and funnel them to the tympanic membrane (or eardrum). The vibrating air molecules hit the eardrum and cause it to vibrate.

The middle ear is behind the eardrum and consists of three little bones, the **malleus, incus,** and **stapes.** Because of their shape, you may know them as the hammer, anvil, and stirrup. We also call these bones the **ossicular chain.** The vibration of the eardrum transfers energy to the ossicular chain, causing the bones to vibrate and transmit the sound through the middle ear cavity.

Council for Exceptional Children

Standard: Understanding the hearing process conforms to CEC Standard 2, Development and Characteristics of Learners.

Figure 14–2 Frequency spectrum of familiar sounds plotted on a standard audiogram

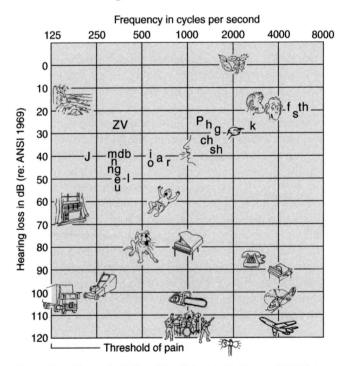

Source: From *Hearing in Children* (5th ed.), by J. L. Northern and M. P. Downs, 2002, Philadelphia, Lippincott. Copyright 2002 by Lippincott Williams & Wilkins. Reprinted with permission.

Figure 14–3 Anatomical structure of the ear and a cross-section of the cochlea

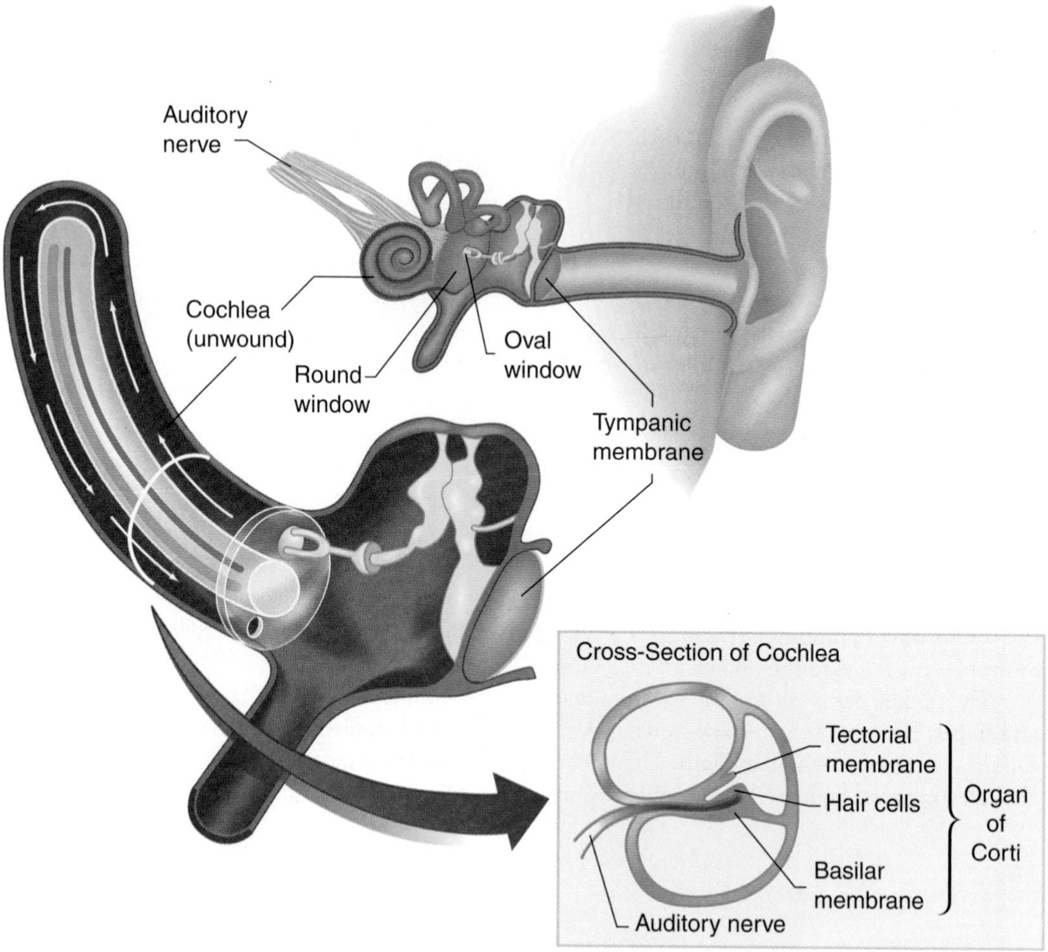

Also found in the middle ear is the **eustachian tube.** It extends from the throat into the middle-ear cavity, and its primary purpose is to equalize the air pressure on the eardrum when we swallow or yawn. This is why our ears feel plugged in the mountains and when an airplane is landing.

The inner ear contains the cochlea and the vestibular mechanism. The cochlea is just beyond the **oval window,** the membrane that separates the middle and the inner ear. The **cochlea** is a snail-shaped bony structure that houses the actual organ of hearing (**organ of Corti**) and the vestibular mechanism, the sensory organ of balance. The cochlea has multiple rows of delicate hair cells that are connected to the auditory nerve. These hair cells are actually sensory receptors for the auditory nerve. The cochlea is arranged **tonotopically,** meaning that the hair cells closest to the oval window respond to high-frequency sounds and those at the center (if the cochlea were unrolled) are more sensitive to low-frequency sounds. The vibration of the middle-ear bones transfers the sound waves to the oval window, moving the fluid in the cochlea across the hair cells. This movement generates impulses to the auditory nerve.

The other structure in the inner ear, the **vestibular mechanism,** a group of semicircular canals, controls balance. These canals are also filled with the same fluid found in the cochlea, and this fluid is sensitive to our head movement. The vestibular mechanism helps our body maintain its equilibrium. It is sensitive to both motion and gravity.

Sound is transported from the inner ear by way of the auditory nerve to the temporal lobe of the brain. The route from the ear to the cochlea passes through at least four neural relay stations on its way to the brain. Think of this transfer of sound to the brain as a train trip that has stops at several stations along the route. Once sound reaches the auditory cortex, it can then be associated with other sensory information and memory, allowing us to perceive and integrate what we have heard (Batshaw, 2002).

Describing the Characteristics

Hearing loss impairs the development of spoken language. The IQ range of students who are deaf or hard of hearing is much the same as it is in the general population (Moores, 2001). Most often, their academic problems are related to difficulties in speaking, reading, and writing, not to cognitive challenges.

Speech and English-language development. Children are born with an innate ability and desire to communicate. Normal language acquisition for hearing children follows a predetermined sequence that is similar across most languages and cultures. Children will usually become a native speaker of at least one language just by being exposed to it. They usually do not need direct instruction.

The language development of children who are born deaf or hard of hearing will also follow this sequence; however, their language delays will range from mild to severe. These delays are a direct result of their inability to process auditory information or their lack of exposure to a visually encoded language. Their delays will vary, depending on the level of hearing loss and the amount of visual and auditory input they receive (Spencer & Meadow-Orlans, 1996).

This teacher uses sign language to supplement the student's assistive technology hearing aid.

Even the speech of a student with a moderate loss may be affected. Although the student may be able to hear speech sounds, crucial information will elude her. By contrast, a child born deaf will be unable to hear most speech sounds, even with amplification. Her receptive speech will be significantly impaired unless she is an exceptional **speech reader** (able to interpret words by watching the speaker's lips and facial movements without hearing the speaker's voice), and her expressive speech will most likely show problems with articulation, voice quality, and tone, making her difficult to understand.

Communication options. Professionals commonly use three approaches to teach communication skills to students with hearing loss, and there is a long history of controversy over which approach is the most appropriate. There is, however, probably no one single method that meets the needs of *all* students. That is why IDEA now provides that a student's IEP team must consider the variety of languages and communication modes that the student who is deaf or hard of hearing might use in the educational setting.

Oral/aural communication. This approach includes two primary teaching formats. The **auditory-verbal format** encourages early identification and subsequent amplification or cochlear implant. It emphasizes the amplification of sound and helping the child use what hearing remains (residual hearing). Auditory training enhances the student's listening skills and stresses using speech to communicate.

The **oral/aural format** also emphasizes the use of amplified sound to develop oral language. In contrast to a strict auditory-verbal approach, however, this method allows for the use of visual input—speech reading—to augment auditory information. Unfortunately, this skill is extremely difficult to master since such a small amount of what is being said is actually visible on the lips.

Manual communication. The **manual approach** to teaching communication stresses the use of some form of sign language. This approach makes use of the student's intact visual modality to get information. Manual communication includes several different sign systems, each with its own proponents. **Sign language** uses combinations of hand, body, and facial movements to convey both words and concepts rather than individual letters. **Fingerspelling** uses a hand representation for all 26 letters of the alphabet. Figure 14–4 shows you the accepted forms of manual communication for the letters of the alphabet.

Figure 14–4   Chart of the manual alphabet

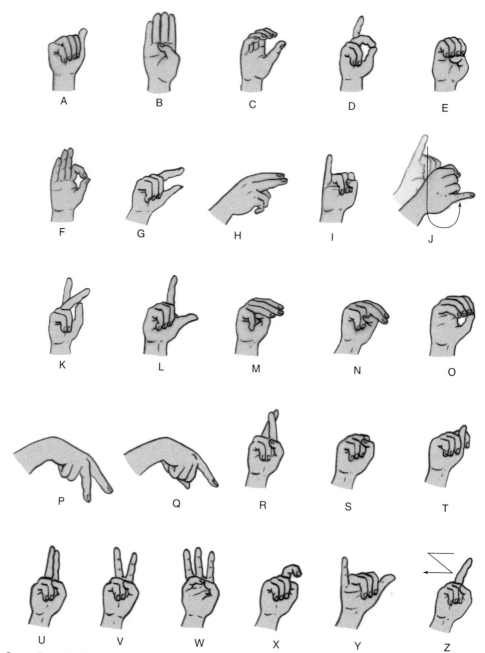

Source: From *The Signed English Starter,* by H. Bornstein and K. Saulnier, 1984, Washington, DC: Gallaudet University Press. Copyright 1984 by Gallaudet University Press. Reprinted with permission.

Visit the Companion Website, *www.prenhall.com/turnbull,* to acquire more information on American Sign Language and other sign systems used in the United States.

Use your *Real Lives and Exceptionality* DVD to see Star doing American Sign Language. Click on "Who is Star" (Clip 1) under "Meet Star."

American Sign Language (ASL) is the most widely used sign language among deaf adults in North America. Although some individual ASL signs may have comparable English words, its signs are meant to represent concepts rather than single words. For example, the sign for "look" is made by pointing the index and middle fingers in the shape of a V at the eyes and then turning to point forward. If the V moves from the eyes and then points upward, that small change indicates that the person is looking up.

Manually coded English sign language systems differ from ASL in that they are designed to be a visual representation of the English language. The primary sign systems used in the United States are **Pidgin Sign English (PSE); Seeing Essential English, Signing Exact English (SEE2); and Conceptually Accurate Signed English (CASE).**

An alternative to natural sign language and English sign systems is **cued speech.** Cued speech supplements spoken English and is intended to make its features fully visible (LaSasso & Metzger, 1998). Since many sounds look the same on the lips when they are pronounced, cued speech uses 36 different cues to clarify the 44 different sounds in English. The placement of the cues on the face also indicates vowels and consonants. Unlike sign languages that provide information about meaning rather than about sound, cued speech communicates about sounds.

Total or simultaneous communication. This approach combines as many sources of information as possible, including simultaneous communication of both sign and spoken language and support for residual hearing. Thus, amplification, speech reading, speech training, reading, and writing are all used in combination with signs.

The three Thomas girls are good examples of individuals who use a variety of communication options. All three learned sign language as their first language (before receiving their cochlear implants). Mariah and Ricquel now use a combination of oral and manual communication (total communication). They receive information auditorally and through sign, and they are able to express themselves by speaking and signing. Even with her cochlear implant, Shylah is more comfortable using sign language both receptively and expressively and has been slower to adapt to a strictly oral input.

Academic achievement. The academic achievement of students with hearing loss depends on their individual characteristics as well as the characteristics of their parents, teachers, and school programs. Most of these children have specific educational challenges in the areas of reading and writing (Easterbrooks & Baker, 2002). Because educational curricula are so language-based, communication and learning are strongly linked.

Two issues have confounded researchers who have attempted to identify the causes of the relatively low academic achievement of students who are deaf and hard of hearing. The first concerns the effects of inclusive education settings versus segregated ones. Much research has shown that students in general education classrooms demonstrate higher academic achievement than do students in self-contained classrooms or segregated settings (Kluwin, 1993).

Sheddrick and Sharon Thomas have chosen a regular education (mainstream) setting for their three daughters, although they opted for an out-of-district program that would provide other peers with hearing loss, a deaf educator who could work closely with the regular educators, trained educational interpreters, and specialized individual support in reading, phonics, and speech. The choice seems to be a good one since all three are working at grade level and have friends who are both deaf and hearing.

The second issue involves the rising numbers of students with hearing loss who are from diverse racial, ethnic, and linguistic backgrounds. In 2002, more than 40 percent of school-age deaf and hard-of-hearing children were from culturally-diverse groups (Wolbers, 2002). The increase in the Latino population in school is mirrored in deaf education. In 1995, Latinos were the fastest-growing ethnic group among deaf and hard-of-hearing students (Gerner de Garcia, 1995).

Families and teachers struggle to find appropriate methods for improving language and literacy for students with hearing loss. For students with a hearing loss whose families do not use English as their primary language, educational opportunities and outcomes look even bleaker. Those students who are both Latino and deaf or hard of hearing are less successful than those with either single characteristic (Walker-Vann, 1998). Box 14–1 gives you tips for teaching students who are deaf or hard of hearing and who use ASL as their first language.

Academically, students who are hard of hearing are still among the least appropriately served groups. The issues and challenges of students with mild and moderate hearing losses are complex and have severe implications for their academic and social success. Their needs are often overlooked and misunderstood. Because these students can hear some sounds, they may not be immediately referred for services. Accumulated years of misunderstanding what they are hearing can result in grade retention and a gap between ability and academic achievement. They are also at risk socially because they may miss the small social nuances in schools' hallways, cafeterias, and gyms (Easterbrooks & Baker, 2002).

Use your *Real Lives and Exceptionalities* DVD to review George who has hearing loss. Click on "Meet George" and while watching the clips, look for specific communication barriers he faces. How does George, his family, his teachers, and his peers foster his development?

Diversity Tips ~ Bilingual/Bicultural Educational Programs

Box 14-1

Bilingual/bicultural ("bi-bi") programs seek to develop a student's competence in two languages, ASL and English, and two cultures, Deaf culture and the culture of the student's hearing parents. They also recognize why the English-As-a-Second-Language (ESL) models that have been developed for children who are learning spoken languages have not been easily adapted to children learning one visual-gestural language and one spoken language. First, ASL has no written form, yet a written form of both languages appears to facilitate acquisition of both languages. Second, except for children with parents who are deaf, children who are deaf are not likely to learn ASL as a first language from their parents, the individuals from whom almost all children learn their first language. Indeed, their parents are often struggling to learn ASL themselves.

Effective bilingual-bicultural programs should result in students who are both capable and enlightened about diversity. Following are the underlying principles of bi-bi programs:

- Acknowledge the continuum of language skills that allow each child to reach his or her potential.
- Recognize the value of linguistic and cultural pluralism within society and understand that Deaf individuals constitute a linguistic and cultural group.
- Promote equality of opportunity regardless of language, disability, ethnicity, or gender.
- Advance competence in American Sign Language.

To learn more about the bi-bi model, go to http://clerccenter. gallaudet.edu/Literacy/programs/starschools.html.

Deaf and hearing students sign to each other and contribute to each others' social development.

Values: *Relationships* and attitudes interact with each other. So when teachers include students who are deaf or hard of hearing in the general curriculum, they create opportunities for hearing students to learn how their hearing-challenged peers contribute to everyone's education and how peer relationships can blunt discriminatory attitudes.

Social and emotional development. The communication barriers that result from the difficulty of acquiring oral language, compounded by preconceived ideas of deafness held by the hearing world, significantly affect a student's psychosocial development. The average hearing person will have difficulty communicating with a person with hearing loss, and deaf students soon become aware of these communication problems as they try to make their wants and needs known. This situation is unsettling for both parties.

Four factors affect deaf students' social and emotional development. First, parent-child interaction plays a fundamental role in every child's development. Hearing parents may very early find it difficult to communicate with their child who is deaf or hard of hearing. This difficulty will affect their interactions as well as parent-child bonding.

Second, peers and teachers play a significant role in the student's social development. When communication is easy, students learn social norms, rules of conversation, appropriate ways of responding in various situations, and how to develop relationships. If, however, there is a communication barrier among the student, teachers, and peers, the resulting lack of interaction is likely to hamper the student's development of a positive self-concept as well as close friendships.

A third influence on a developing social presence involves the awareness of social cues. These cues are most often spoken, and while the student may pick up on some visual cues to appropriate social behaviors, he may miss the auditory ones.

Finally, deaf children may feel an increasing sense of isolation and loneliness as they realize that others may not be comfortable interacting with them (Scheetz, 2004). They may even begin to see themselves through the eyes of society and develop a feeling of being outsiders in a hearing world. According to Stuart, Harrison, and Simpson (1991), "deafness *per se* does not determine the emotional and social development of the individual. Rather, it is the attitudes of hearing people that cause irreparable harm to the personality of the deaf person" (p. 124).

Determining the Causes

Determining the cause of hearing loss is often complicated by a delay in diagnosis, and many causes remain unknown. When a hearing loss is present at birth, we use the term **congenital** loss, regardless of the cause. We describe losses that occur after birth as **acquired.** A number of factors can result in hearing loss. They include hereditary or genetic reasons, an event or injury during pregnancy (prenatal), or injury at or just following birth. Factors that can cause an acquired hearing loss include trauma, disease, and exposure to excessive noise.

Genetic causes. Hereditary loss occurs in approximately 1 in 2,000 children. Most hereditary hearing loss is a result of an inherited autosomal recessive gene (80 percent) and is not associated with any type of **syndrome.** There are more than 70 documented inherited syndromes associated with deafness; they can result in either a conductive, a sensorineural, or a mixed loss (Batshaw, 2002).

Prenatal causes. Exposure to viruses, bacteria, and other toxins before or after birth can result in a hearing loss. During delivery or in the newborn period, a number of complications such as lack of oxygen (**hypoxia**) can damage the hearing mechanism, particularly the cochlea.

The major cause of congenital deafness is infection that occurs during pregnancy or soon after the baby is born. Before the development of a vaccine, **rubella** was one of the leading causes of deafness. The rubella epidemic in the United States in 1964–1965 resulted in a huge increase in the incidence of deafness. Beginning with the use of an anti-rubella vaccine, the incidence has decreased considerably.

Toxoplasmosis, herpes virus, syphilis, and **cytomegalovirus (CMV)** are other prenatal infections that can cause hearing loss. The most prevalent of these infections is CMV, which has an incidence of 5 to 25 cases per 1,000 births (Batshaw, 2002). This viral infection is spread by close contact with an individual who is shedding the virus through body fluids. No vaccine is available for protection against CMV, but care should be taken to wash hands and avoid contact with individuals who have the disease. Toxoplasmosis is characterized by **jaundice** and **anemia** and results in hearing loss in about 15 percent of infants born to mothers who have this disease. Pregnant women should avoid contact with cat feces or raw or undercooked meat, which may be contaminated with this virus. The herpes virus is transferred to the infant during the birth process as the infant passes through the birth canal. Mothers with genital herpes disease most often deliver babies by Caesarean section to avoid transferring the infection to their infant (National Center on Birth Defects and Developmental Disabilities, 2004).

Premature infants, particularly those weighing less than 1,500 grams ($3\frac{1}{3}$ pounds), have an increased susceptibility to hypoxia, **hyperbilirubinemia,** and **intracranial hemorrhage,** all of which have been associated with sensorineural hearing loss. Other factors associated with congenital sensorineural hearing loss are Rh incompatibility and the use of ototoxic drugs (Batshaw, 2002). **Maternal Rh incompatibility** used to be a much more common cause of hearing loss before the development of anti-Rh gamma globulin (**RhoGAM**) in 1968. The injection of RhoGAM in the first 72 hours following delivery of her first child will keep the mother from producing antibodies that could harm her later babies. Certain antibiotics are considered **ototoxic** and can destroy the outer row of hair cells in the cochlea. Physicians can monitor drug levels in the blood to prevent them from reaching toxic levels.

Postnatal causes. Infections in infancy and childhood also can lead to a sensorineural hearing loss. For example, **bacterial meningitis** has a 10 percent risk of hearing loss from damage to the cochlea. The most common cause of hearing loss in young children is middle-ear disease or **acute otitis media** (ear infection). Fluid collects in the middle ear behind the eardrum. This disease can go undiagnosed, and although it does not result in a permanent conductive hearing loss, it can cause hearing to fluctuate in young children during the time that they are acquiring speech and language in the first two years of life. In fact, 75 to 90 percent of all young children have at least one ear infection before they are 2 years old. As a teacher, you will want to be aware of the fluctuating conductive hearing loss that can occur in your students who have middle-ear infections; those students might be missing important information while they have an ear infection. You should be aware of any signs (such as inattention or cocking the head) that might indicate that the child is not hearing what you are saying.

Postlingual causes. A blow to the skull can cause trauma to the cochlea and may lead to a sensorineural hearing loss. It can also damage the middle-ear bones, resulting in a conductive loss. Mild to moderate sensorineural hearing loss can occur as a result of being around excessive noise such as firecrackers and air guns. Transient or permanent sensorineural loss may also occur with exposure to very loud sound over time. Using headphones at high-intensity levels or attending rock concerts where noise levels can reach 100 to 110 dB may be damaging. In fact, any sustained exposure to sound levels of 90 dB or greater is potentially harmful to the cochlea and should be avoided (Batshaw, 2002).

EVALUATING STUDENTS WITH HEARING LOSS

Determining the Presence of Hearing Loss

Diagnostic assessment. The earlier hearing loss is identified, the more quickly intervention can begin. Figure 14–5 illustrates a recommended infant hearing screening process. Most states now have an early hearing detection and intervention (EHDI) system that

1. Screens all newborns for hearing loss before 1 month of age, preferably before leaving the hospital

2. Refers all infants who screen positive for a diagnostic audiologic evaluation before 3 months of age

3. Provides all infants identified as having a hearing loss with appropriate early intervention services before 6 months of age

Figure 14–5 Infant hearing screening process

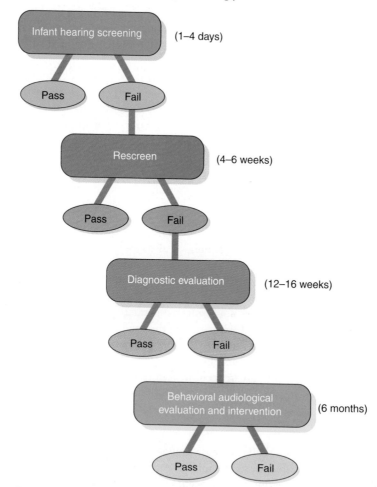

Source: From "Universal Newborn Hearing Screening Using Transient Evoked Otoacoustic Emissions: Results of the Rhode Island Hearing Assessment Project," by K. R. White, B. R. Vohr, and T. R. Behrens, 1993. *Seminars in Hearing, 14*(1), pp. 18–29. Copyright 1993 by Thieme Medical Publishers. Reprinted with permission.

The diagnosis of a hearing loss is made by a combination of professionals, including the child's own doctor, an **otologist** (a physician who specializes in diseases of the ear), and an **audiologist.** Audiologists have special training in testing and measuring hearing and are able to evaluate the hearing of any child at any age. Audiologists also have the skills to participate in the child's rehabilitation and treatment and to prescribe and evaluate the effectiveness of hearing aids and cochlear implants.

Hearing aids. Audiologists provide assistance in the selection and use of hearing aids. Hearing aids amplify sound but do not correct hearing. In other words, they can make sound louder but not necessarily clearer.

The behind-the-ear aid is probably the most common type of hearing aid used both by children and adults. The case holding all of the components of the hearing aid is worn behind the ear, and the signal is delivered through a tube into the ear using an earmold. For children, this type of aid has the advantage of durability and flexibility. Behind-the-ear hearing aids are larger than the hearing aids worn inside the ear, making them easier to keep track of and better able to withstand the daily wear and tear of young children.

In addition, behind-the-ear aids provide flexibility. As the child grows, the size of the ear also increases. When this happens, the earmold may no longer fit. With a behind-the-ear aid, accommodating growth means simply replacing the earmold rather than the entire hearing aid. Children can wear this type of aid behind one or both ears.

Cochlear implants. A **cochlear implant,** which Mariah, Ricquel, and Shyla have, is an electronic device that is surgically implanted under the skin behind the ear and contains a magnet that couples to a magnet in a sound transmitter that is worn externally.

A surgeon inserts an electrode array into the cochlea to provide direct stimulation to the nerve fibers. A speech processor that can be worn on the body or behind the ear is connected to a headpiece by a cable. Sound is picked up by a microphone and sent to the speech processor, which then filters, analyzes, and digitizes the sound into coded electrical signals. These coded signals are sent through a coil across the skin to the internal implanted receiver/stimulator via an FM radio signal. The receiver delivers electrical stimulation to the appropriate implanted electrodes in the cochlea, and then this signal is carried to the brain through the auditory nerve.

The cochlear implant does not restore normal hearing or amplify sound. Rather, it provides a sense of sound to individuals who are profoundly deaf and cannot otherwise receive auditory signals. It "gets around" the blockage of damaged hair cells in the cochlea by bypassing them and directly stimulating the auditory nerve (National Institute on Deafness and Other Communication Disorders, 2000).

Assistive listening devices. Hearing aids provide maximum benefit when the environment is relatively quiet, the acoustics are good, and the student is close to the speaker. Noisy environments, such as many classrooms, blunt the effects of hearing aids.

Assistive listening devices can solve problems created by noise and distance. Assistive listening devices that use FM radio frequencies are often referred to as FM systems. The teacher wears a wireless microphone, enabling both the teacher and the student to move about freely. However, the individual hearing aid will pick up sound only from the microphone, so activities such as group discussions can be cumbersome to carry out because the microphone must be passed from teacher to student or student to student.

Determining the Nature of Specially Designed Instruction and Services

Educational evaluation. As we pointed out in Chapter 2, nondiscriminatory evaluation has two purposes: to determine whether the student has a disability and, if so, to determine an appropriate program and placement for the student. The test for eligibility for special education services for students with hearing loss is usually their initial assessment, the hearing test. Figure 14–6 illustrates the evaluation process.

Visit the Companion Website, *www.prenhall.com/turnbull,* for more information on cochlear implants.

Figure 14–6 Nondiscriminatory evaluation process for determining the presence of a hearing loss

Observation	***Medical personnel observe:*** The baby does not show a startle reflex to loud noises. As the child matures, speech and language are delayed.
	Teachers and parents observe: The child (1) does not respond to sound; (2) does not babble or engage in vocal play; and (3) experiences communication misunderstandings, speech difficulties, and inattention.
Screening	***Assessment measures:***
	Newborn screening: Most states require newborn screening for hearing loss.
	Auditory brain stem response: Results may show inadequate or slow response to sound.
	Transient evoked otoacoustic immittance: Results may show that measurement of sound in the ear is lower than normal.
	Behavioral audiological evaluation: Hearing thresholds are higher than 15 dB.
Prereferral	Prereferral is typically not used with these students because of the need to identify hearing loss quickly.
Referral	Children receive nondiscriminatory evaluation procedures as soon as they enter school. Intervention should occur as soon as the child is diagnosed. Students with mild hearing loss may be referred.
Nondiscriminatory evaluation procedures and standards	***Assessment measures:***
	Audiological reassessment: Recent audiograms may indicate that the student's hearing loss has stabilized or is worsening. Testing for hearing aid function is a regular need.
	Speech and language evaluation: The student may have significant problems with receptive and expressive language. The student's speech is usually affected.
	Individualized intelligence test: The student's scores show a discrepancy between verbal and nonverbal measures. Nonverbal tests are considered the only reliable and valid measures of intelligence for this population.
	Individualized achievement test: The student may score significantly lower than peers.
	Adaptive behavior: The student may score below average in communication and possibly in other areas of adaptive behavior.
	Anecdotal records: The student's performance may indicate difficulty with reading, writing, or language arts.
	Curriculum-based assessment: The student may be performing below peers in one or more areas of the curriculum because of reading and/or language difficulties.
	Direct observation: The student may be difficult to understand and may misunderstand others.
Determination	The nondiscriminatory evaluation team determines that the student has a hearing loss and needs special education and related services. The team proceeds to develop appropriate education options for the child.

How hearing is tested. Audiologists measure the type and severity of a hearing loss. The simplest test of hearing ability is called *pure tone audiometry*. Audiologists use a machine called an **audiometer** to test hearing. It measures hearing threshold, the softest level at which sound can first be detected, at various sound frequencies.

Infants up to 6 months of age can be screened for hearing loss in two ways: evoked otoacoustic emissions (EOAE) and screening auditory brain stem response (SABR). EOAE is a fast and noninvasive test for a newborn that assesses how well the baby's cochlea is functioning and transmitting sound to the brain. The ear canal is sealed with a plastic probe, and clicks or tones of various frequencies are introduced into the ear canal. A computer records responses that are evoked from the cochlea.

The other newborn screening method, SABR, assesses more than the child's cochlea. It tests the child's auditory neural pathway as well. EEG sensors are placed in various places on the baby's scalp. Using an external or inserted earphone, tones or clicks are presented separately to each ear, stimulating neural activity along the path. The electrodes detect sound, and the computer averages the responses.

Finally, diagnostic ABR audiometry is a highly sensitive test for both hearing loss and problems in the neural pathway. The ABR generates waveforms composed of three distinct waves (I, II, and III); the absence of waveform at a given intensity suggests a hearing loss, whereas the complete absence of a particular wave suggests an abnormality at a particular location along the brain pathway (Batshaw, 2002).

According to Sharon, the diagnosis of hearing loss was very different for her three daughters. She began to suspect a problem when Mariah was 2 years old and was not yet speaking. An ABR exam showed that Mariah had a severe to profound loss. When Ricquel and Shylah were born, early hearing screening was provided in the hospital, resulting in a much earlier identification.

Behavioral audiological evaluations are appropriate for testing the hearing of older children. This test requires the child to respond in order to indicate that she hears a sound. The child listens to a series of beeps called pure tones and indicates when she hears the sound.

The child's responses are recorded on an **audiogram,** a picture of what is heard. Figure 14–7 is Ricquel's audiogram, showing a severe to profound hearing loss, the type of loss all three Thomas sisters had at birth. It shows how much the hearing varies from normal if there is a loss (severity) and where the problem might be located in the auditory pathway (type). The vertical lines on an audiogram represent pitch or frequency (Hz), and the horizontal lines represent loudness or intensity (dB). The top of the audiogram on the left side shows 125 Hertz, a very low-pitched sound. As you look across, each line represents a higher and higher pitch. The critical pitches for speech are 500 to 3,000 Hz.

When you read down the left side of the audiogram, you can see the increasing loudness of sound represented by decibels. The first number listed is minus 10 dB because there is never a complete absence of sound in our world. Moving downward, each number represents a louder and louder sound as if the volume were being turned up on your stereo. Responses to sound are plotted on the graph in terms of how loud a sound must be at each frequency before you can hear it. Every point on an audiogram represents a different sound.

The audiologist tests the student's hearing by using air conduction (through earphones) and marks the hearing threshold on a graph with an O (for the right ear) and an X (for the left ear). The sound leaves the earphones, traveling through the air in the ear canal, through the middle ear, and to the cochlea in the inner ear.

The audiologist tests the sensitivity of the student's cochlea by using bone conduction through a small vibrator placed on the bone behind the ear. Sounds presented this way travel through the bones of the skull directly to the cochlea and auditory nerve, bypassing the outer and middle ear. When a bone-conduction vibrator is used to test for thresholds, a "<" symbol or a "[" symbol is used for the right ear and a ">" symbol or a "]" symbol is used for the left ear.

Audiologists retest the hearing of children with suspected or known hearing loss four times a year until age 3, twice a year until age 6, and annually after 6 years of age.

Visit the Companion Website, *www.prenhall.com/turnbull*, to see babies having their hearing tested and to learn more about early hearing detection and intervention.

Figure 14–7 Ricquel's audiogram, showing profound hearing loss in both ears

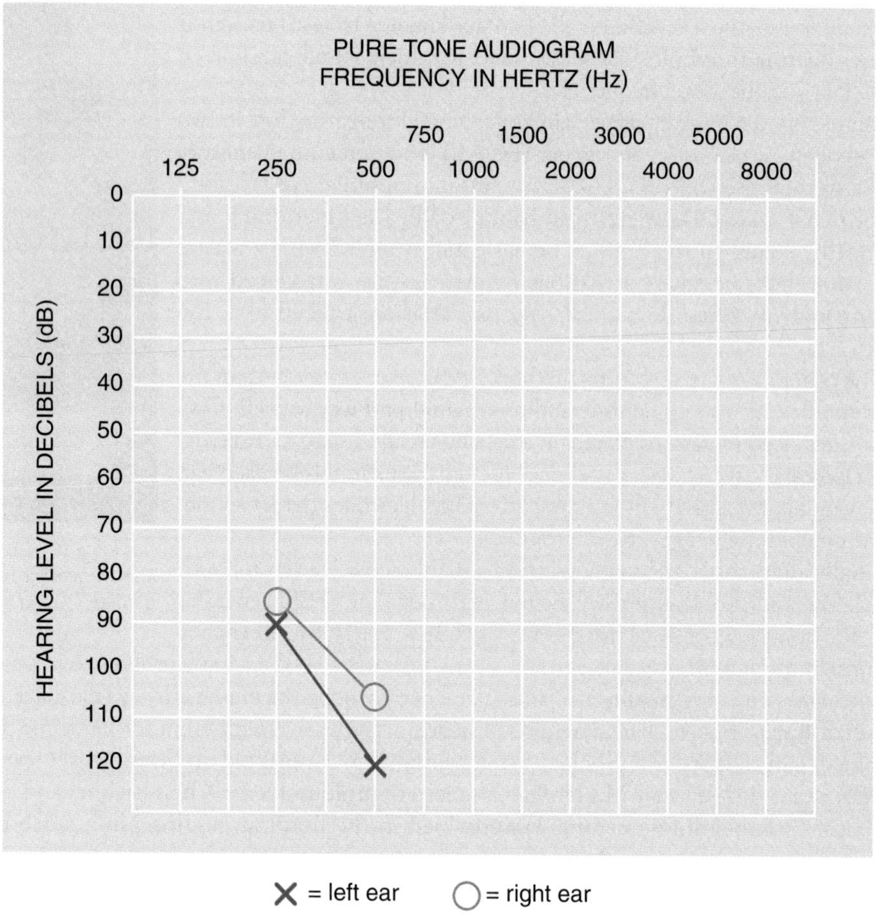

PURE TONE AUDIOGRAM
FREQUENCY IN HERTZ (Hz)

X = left ear   ◯ = right ear

By comparing the headphone thresholds with the bone conduction thresholds at each pitch, the audiologist can determine whether a hearing loss is conductive, sensorineural, or mixed. If the air-conduction thresholds show a hearing loss but the bone-conduction thresholds are normal, then the individual has a conductive loss. If the hearing thresholds obtained by bone conduction are the same as by air conduction, there is no blockage of sound in the outer or middle ear and the hearing loss is caused by a loss of sensitivity in the cochlea or auditory nerve.

The audiologist usually will perform two additional tests, **tympanography** and speech **audiometry.** Tympanography is not a hearing test but a test of how well the middle ear is functioning and how well the eardrum can move. To conduct this test, the audiologist places a small rubber tip in the ear and pumps a little air into the outer ear canal. If the middle ear is functioning properly, the air causes the eardrum to move. If there is a problem in the middle ear, it may show up as no eardrum movement. Very little movement of the eardrum may indicate fluid behind the eardrum as a result of a middle-ear infection (otitis media).

The ability to use speech for communication is a function of two things—the ability to detect the sounds of speech and the ability to understand speech. The pure tone audiogram shows how much sound someone can detect, but it does not tell us how clearly speech can be heard. We can make predictions based on the degree and type of hearing loss, but to measure a person's speech discrimination—how well he or she can understand speech—special tests are used.

For speech audiometry, words are presented at different levels of loudness and the student is asked to repeat them. A student with a sensorineural hearing loss may have a problem understanding the words, even when they are loud enough. Generally, the greater the student's sensorineural hearing loss, the poorer the student's speech discrimination.

Students who are deaf or hard of hearing may also require specific tests to determine the nature and extent of their disability. This is particularly true if a student has other problems in addition to hearing loss. Testing to provide feedback is important because teachers need to know whether their instruction is successful and parents want to know about their child's progress. The assessment of communication involves testing speech and/or sign language skills depending on the communication modality the student is using. Finally, assessment is used to guide instruction. It can be as complex as state-mandated testing programs for all students and as simple as a 10-item spelling test.

The norm-referenced test most frequently used to test the school achievement of students with hearing loss is the Stanford Achievement Test. Educators usually administer this test to students who are 8 years of age or older. The current version (ninth edition) is referred to as "the Stanford 9." It is designed to measure a student's achievement in the areas of reading, language, spelling, mathematics, science, and social studies. Educators select a test level for a student who takes the Stanford 9 by screening the student first (Stewart & Kluwin, 2001).

The Stanford 9 used for deaf students is identical to the Stanford Achievement Test used for hearing students. In fact, the test items and questions are exactly the same. What makes the deaf-only version unique is that it was normed on a sample of deaf students by the Gallaudet Research Institute. This allows the performance of students with hearing loss to be compared to the performance of other deaf students.

There are, however, some limitations to the Stanford 9. The test was designed to measure curriculum appropriate for hearing students at specific academic grade levels. If the student with hearing loss is performing below grade level, she may not have covered the content material. Also, the use of some types of question forms developed for students who can hear may be biased against deaf students, resulting in lowered scores. Material and reports with age-based percentiles for deaf and hard-of-hearing students for the Stanford Achievement Test, 10th edition, are currently available from the Gallaudet Research Institute (2002).

Values: IDEA and NCLB provide that students with disabilities, including those who are deaf or hard of hearing, will participate in state and district assessments. These laws express the sense of *great expectations,* and the Stanford 9, as modified at Gallaudet Research Institute, accommodates deafness to that expectation and the law's commands.

DESIGNING AN APPROPRIATE INDIVIDUALIZED EDUCATION PROGRAM

Partnering for Special Education and Related Services

Special and general educators, speech-language pathologists, audiologists, interpreters, paraprofessionals, family members, friends, and community members often become partners to contribute to the student's language, academic, and social development. With the increased use of cochlear implants, participation by members of the medical implant team is needed. Also, an itinerant deaf educator sees many students who are served in the general classroom only intermittently. Thus, the child's educational interpreter may be the most constant member and best advocate for the student. Box 14–2 gives you tips on how partners educate Ben, who has a profound hearing loss.

Using interpreters in educational settings. According to IDEA, related services under Part B (ages 3–21) include interpreting services. Educational interpreters provide an essential service to both students and teachers. They translate the spoken word into signs for the student with a hearing loss. Some perform additional duties within the school or classroom such as tutoring, general classroom assistance, educational planning, and sign language instruction (Stuckless, Avery, & Hurwitz, 1989). The educational interpreter is often a student's communication bridge to the hearing world around him.

Interpreter services, illustrated here and consisting of the translation of the spoken word into signs and signs into the spoken word, are now a related service under IDEA.

Partnership Tips ~ A Three-Pronged Visual Approach   Box 14–2

Partnerships among general and special educators, deaf educators, related service providers, interpreters, and students who are deaf or hard of hearing are indispensable if the students are to make progress in the general curriculum. That much is obvious. But how to apply this proposition—that's another matter.

As you have already learned, regardless of how effectively the child with hearing loss can comprehend complex concepts presented from teacher to student, reading about these concepts requires that he be able to manipulate English sentence structure, which is a daunting task for the child who is not proficient in English.

Because the vocabulary is difficult and the sentence structures complex, the social studies and science texts that Ben, age 10, must master for statewide assessment purposes are eluding him. The challenge is to provide Ben, who has a profound hearing loss, with the support he needs to continue being included in general instruction for these subject areas. The partners in this endeavor include Ben; Linda, his classroom teacher; Katie, his deaf educator; Todd, Ben's friend, who is hearing; John, his interpreter; and Ben's parents.

Linda has taught several reading strategies to her class of 28 children, knowing that Ben is not the only child in the class who can benefit from improved ability to read content-area material. Katie uses these same strategies with Ben and several other students during small-group time in the resource room.

Strategies

1. Semantic mapping for vocabulary development
   - Provide visual cues to assist in comprehension.
   - Before reading, choose a few words that represent new or complex concepts.
   - Put each word inside a circle and draw lines from the word. Then from each line, draw a new circle. In each circle, write questions such as "What is it? What is it like? What are examples?"
   - Pause for interpretation. John, Ben's interpreter, makes sure that Ben has opportunities to contribute to the discussion by reminding Linda to pause between calling on children because the lag time between Linda's question and John's interpreting means that Ben is a few seconds behind the other children in "hearing" the question.
2. The K-W-L approach: *Know, what, learn*
   - Before reading, ask the children to brainstorm what they know about the topic.

   - Write all their ideas on the computer, project through an LCD projector, and then ask students to put their ideas into categories.
   - After this group activity, ask them to create individual questions regarding what they want to learn about the topic.
   - Assign the text material for homework.

   Ben's parents make sure to dedicate a few minutes in the evening so that Ben can show them his questions and the answers he finds. The next day, Linda asks her students to discuss what they have learned. She focuses their responses specifically on answering the questions they have written the previous day. She also draws their attention to similarities and differences between what they had previously known about the topic and what they have learned by reading the assignment.
3. Thematic organizers
   - Create an outline or flow chart of major concepts and vocabulary the students will encounter in the material.
   - When students are comfortable using thematic organizers, leave blanks for information that the children can fill in. Todd works as Ben's study buddy, and they share ideas about what to fill in for each blank. Todd often helps explain a concept in a way that is understandable to Ben.

Ben has been able to keep up with his fourth-grade peers in comprehending the content material assigned as homework. His teachers and parents realize, however, that as text material becomes more difficult, Ben will be increasingly challenged to be independent in reading material written at grade level. In the future, Ben's teachers may wish to find supplementary material written at his reading level.

Putting These Tips to Work for Progress in the General Curriculum

1. Who are the partners?
2. What are the challenges?
3. What can the team do?
4. What are the results?

To answer these questions online and learn more about these strategies, go to the Partnership Tips module in Chapter 14 of the Companion Website, www.prenhall.com/turnbull.

Determining Supplementary Aids and Services

Managing the listening environment/acoustics. When a classroom is equipped with a **sound-field amplification system,** the teacher transmits her voice by using a lavaliere microphone and ceiling- or wall-mounted speakers. These in turn amplify her voice to 8 to 10 dB above the ambient room noise.

A student's hearing aid also allows access to **loop systems.** These involve closed-circuit wiring that sends FM signals from an audio system directly to an electronic coil in the student's hearing aid. The receiver picks up the signals, much as a remote control sends infrared signals to a television. These systems allow students with residual hearing to participate in a variety of educational settings.

PRAXIS

Standard: Learning about and using technology for students with hearing loss is an application of PRAXIS™ Standard 3, Delivery of Services to Students with Disabilities.

Technology Tips ~ Real-Time Captioning in Classrooms   Box 14-3

Undoubtedly, you have seen movies in which a court stenographer is recording what the judges, lawyers, and witnesses say. The stenographer is making a record that the participants in the trial can consult later. Now technology takes that service to a new level, making the words instantly available to students who are deaf or hard of hearing.

Communication Access Realtime Translation (CART) is a technology that instantly converts the spoken word into English text, using a stenotype machine, a notebook computer, and real-time software. An individual types the spoken word into the stenotype machine, and a software program converts the shorthand into text that then appears on a computer monitor. The real-time captionist is a related service provider, just like the student's educational interpreter. The regulations implementing the Americans with Disabilities Act recognize

CART as an assistive technology that affords "effective communication access." Thus, communication access is what truly distinguishes CART from real-time reporting in a traditional courtroom sense. Real-time captioning in a classroom can give deaf and hard-of-hearing students instant access to a teacher's and peers' communications. Its power to advance students' inclusion is staggering.

Deaf students have had access to captioned movies and videos for many years, and captioning increases students' comprehension and their reading skills (Caldwell, 1973). In fact, captions help both deaf and hearing students, particularly in classroom environments with poor acoustics (e.g., a large room or noisy conditions), where hearing students also have difficulties in hearing everything that is said.

Assistive technology. Just as a caption in a book is the text under a picture, **closed-captioned technology** translates dialogue from a spoken language to a printed form (captions) that is then inserted at the bottom of the television, movie, or videotape. Captioning increases the deaf or hard-of-hearing student's ability to comprehend the speaker and understand the information presented (Block & Okrand, 1983). Box 14-3 provides you with tips on how real-time captioning in a classroom benefits students who are deaf or hard of hearing.

Computers and the Internet. Personal computers provide students with hearing loss access to information in remarkably innovative ways. They can provide instructional support and can even assist students in learning sign language. A computer system (C-print) developed by the National Technical Institute for the Deaf (NTID) provides students who use software-equipped laptop computers with real-time translations of the spoken word. Students with hearing loss can attend a lecture, watch an interpreter without having to look down to take notes, and view the simultaneous written text of what is being said.

Planning for Universal Design for Learning

As discussed, children who are deaf or hard of hearing typically communicate in one of three ways: oral/aural, manual (ASL or English system), or simultaneous communication.

Communication methods. Oral/aural methods include instruction in spoken English, a curriculum in speech and aural habilitation, and the expectation that students will use speech, speech reading, and auditory skills for communication. Not all students benefit from speech instruction; indeed, as many students become older, their motivation for speech intervention often declines.

Speech-language pathologists are responsible for carrying out instruction in speech and aural habilitation (teaching the child to use his remaining hearing). Because many students with significant hearing loss do not hear speech or do not hear it without distortion, it is difficult for them to produce speech and to monitor their own speech without assistance. Their problems can also include trouble with volume, pitch, and nasality. The speech-language pathologist helps them develop breath control, vocalization, voice patterns, and sound production.

Here, both the student and the teacher wear an assistive technology device (a transmitter and receiver), but neither relies on it alone to communicate.

Council for
Exceptional
Children

Standard: Supporting and enhancing communication skills of individuals with hearing loss is an implementation of CEC Standard 6, Communication.

Values: Communication—in all of its many forms for students who are deaf or hard of hearing—is the instrument by which students express their *self-determination*.

The speech-language pathologist also usually encourages students with hearing loss to use even their minimal residual hearing effectively. The pathologist teaches the student about awareness of sound, localization of sound, discrimination of sound differences, recognition of the sound, and, ultimately, comprehension of others' speech.

Total communication methods include instruction in simultaneous communication. Students are expected to use simultaneous communication for their academic and social discourse. Total communication methods also incorporate curriculum in speech and aural habilitation, and they sometimes include curriculum in ASL.

Total communication is somewhat out of favor. One reason is that it is unrealistic to expect a student to use every available communication technique and mode. Teachers typically emphasize speech and audition at the expense of sign language, or vice versa. And students often attend more to one mode than to the other.

A second reason for its decreasing use is that total communication uses speech and sign language simultaneously. It is nearly impossible to speak and use ASL at the same time, so teachers use either manually coded English or Pidgin Sign English.

Many educators and members of the Deaf community are vociferous opponents of manually coded English sign systems because they believe that these systems are not languages at all but distortions of features of ASL. But researchers have found that most teachers using total communication methods actually use Pidgin Sign English, which is essentially an incomplete version of both ASL and English, providing none of the grammatical complexity of either language (Coryell & Holcomb, 1997; Hype, Power, & Cliffe, 1992; Mayer & Lowenbraun, 1990; Woodward & Allen, 1993).

A bilingual/bicultural model. One method of communication that interests both deaf and hearing parents of students with hearing loss is the bilingual/bicultural (bi-bi) program. This model is a bilingual/English-As-a-Second-Language model for deaf students acquiring and learning two languages—American Sign Language and English.

Visit the Companion Website, *www.prenhall.com/turnbull*, for more information about the Star School Project and some schools where it is being used.

The Star Schools Project (Nover & Andrews, 1999) is a multi-state distance-learning project to implement and test this model. The project is looking at methods for teaching language and literacy to students who are deaf and hard of hearing. The model takes the theories and knowledge from ESL research and applies it to deaf education (Easterbrooks & Baker, 2002). The student learns ASL as a first language and English as a second language.

Planning for Other Educational Needs

When the majority of students with hearing loss attended residential schools for the deaf, they were exposed to the culture of deafness as a normal part of their lives. The school played an integral part in the Deaf community. Deaf adults spent large amounts of time at the schools, attending sports events and social affairs, serving as role models for the students, and providing them with direct access to the critical elements of Deaf culture. This included information about Deaf history, the arts, and stories about their lives. The schools contained a treasure trove of photos, trophies, and artwork from the past.

Values: Deaf and hard-of-hearing students can be *full citizens* in two different worlds—the one that their hearing peers occupy and the one that their non-hearing peers occupy.

Today most students with hearing loss attend public school programs, so "deaf immersion" is not an option (Stewart et al., 2001). As a result, schools and communities must purposefully provide students with a study of their native language (ASL), Deaf culture, and opportunities to socialize with deaf adults. Making Deaf studies an indispensable part of a student's educational program is an essential part of the growth and development of the student's identity, awareness of diversity, and self-esteem. The successful deaf adult is likely to function in both the hearing and the deaf world, so deaf children need to be taught about both communities.

USING EFFECTIVE INSTRUCTIONAL STRATEGIES

Early Childhood Students: Language-Rich Environments

Early intervention. Early intervention for children with hearing loss and their families is critical for developing the child's language, social, and academic skills. Programs should provide young children with similar peers, role models, appropriate developmental skills training, and support for acquiring communication and language. Early intervention programs should also help parents understand their child's needs so they can make informed decisions about issues that will affect their child's and family's future (Marschark, Lang, & Albertini, 2002).

Early access to a language-rich environment is critical. This means better education for parents concerning strategies to enhance communication with their deaf or hard-of-hearing children, whether they use spoken or sign language. Getting and maintaining attention, labeling and commenting on objects, and explaining events are important components of a child's early language, social, and cognitive development. Hearing parents need to learn the effective visual communication techniques that are typically used by deaf parents (Marschark et al., 2002).

Early childhood programs include children from birth through kindergarten who are deaf, hard of hearing, and hearing. The curriculum should provide a developmentally appropriate learning environment that fosters the growth of the whole child.

One well-recognized system is the Reggio Emilia approach to early childhood education. This approach cultivates and guides each child's intellectual, emotional, social, and moral potentials (Edwards, Gandini, & Foreman, 1998). The child is regarded as an active learner in the development of knowledge, skills, and attitudes. One of the key aspects of the Reggio Emilia system is the collaboration among the school, parents, and community. Other principles include the environment as the "third teacher," learning through child-driven projects, a curriculum that comes from collaboration between child and teacher, symbolic representation through visual arts, and documentation of learning. The topics and projects are child-driven and emerge from the child's interests. The program is particularly appropriate for young children with hearing loss because it stresses ASL and English vocabulary and language development; book awareness; visual discrimination; matching signs and words in print for meaning; and matching fingerspelling, signs, and printed words. Children who are hard of hearing learn auditory skills and sound/letter correspondence (phonics), and families learn visual phonics.

Shared reading. Another appropriate program for young children with hearing loss was developed by teachers and researchers at the Clerc National Deaf Education Center at Gallaudet University: the Shared Reading Project (Schleper, 1997). It depends heavily on the use of ASL, fluency in signing, and a knack for reading signs and is based on how deaf adults read to deaf children. Dramatization, connecting English sentences with the way they are signed in ASL, and engaging the children in the reading process are emphasized. This project was found to be of particular benefit to families who were not sharing books before their training and those who spoke a language other than English. The Shared Reading Project is effective in helping parents learn to share books with traditionally underserved deaf and hard-of-hearing children (Delk & Weidekamp, 2001).

Elementary and Middle School Students: Reading and Writing Intervention

Since students with hearing loss suffer in the academic areas of reading and writing, teachers give high priority to instruction in these content areas. Students should be given hands-on experiences and be taught the relationships among concepts and the multiple meanings of words. Visual aids can show links between words and their categories (e.g., animal-dog-golden retriever).

Use authentic experiences. Students acquire language and knowledge only when they are presented in ways that are meaningful to the students. Clarke (1983) noted that many of the traditional language programs for students who are deaf or hard of hearing are limited because the programs have no connection to the students' real-world or authentic experiences.

A list of sentences in a book is relevant only if the student has had experiences that are related to what is described. Authentic experiences are particularly important for students with hearing loss because they may not have had the same experiences as their hearing peers nor had them in the same way. For example, we explain to the hearing child why he or she must put on mittens to go outside ("It's below freezing today, and your hands will turn blue!"). For the child with hearing loss who lacks the language for this explanation, the parent may just put the mittens on without explanation. When the child later encounters a written sentence about freezing temperatures, he or she will have had no authentic experience with this situation.

Standard: Learning about appropriate methods and strategies to use with students with hearing loss is an application of CEC Standard 4, Instructional Strategies.

Integrate vocabulary development. The process of integrating vocabulary occurs by showing that words are parts of related concepts, are presented in context, and are everywhere. Words occur in bunches and context. The contexts help define the word and its meanings. "Spring" is a season of the year, a coiled piece of metal, a jump, a small body of water, and many other things. Words are everywhere. There is writing on toys, on clothing labels, and even on cereal boxes. In an integrated approach to vocabulary development, words appear on charts, bulletin boards, and objects in the room. As a teacher, you may find yourself using one of the standard models for increasing your students' language proficiency, the Cummins model, which Box 14–4 describes.

Create opportunities for self-expression. Self-expression is a large part of a student's learning process. Teachers provide their students with an opportunity to practice their verbal skills and to define and refine ideas. They allow the student to convert the information into another form and then express it. Self-expression shows how deeply and for what purposes a student has processed certain information.

Provide deaf role models. Students with hearing loss should have the opportunity to meet and interact with deaf adults. A role model can be a positive example of adult behavior and show the student what he can become. If the only adults in their world have hearing, it may be difficult for students with hearing loss to visualize their capabilities and to create future goals (Stewart & Kluwin, 2001).

Teach about Deaf studies. Learning about deafness, the Deaf community, Deaf history, and famous Deaf adults should be a part of the curriculum for students with hearing loss. Teachers can incorporate this information into social studies, health, and science content for all students, but for their deaf and hard-of-hearing students in particular. Just as teachers provide students with information about diverse ethnic and racial cultures, they should provide them with information about deafness. The subject matter should include the basics for interacting with people with hearing loss, sensitivity activities, ASL as a language, Deaf social interaction norms, Deaf history and organizations, Deaf literature and arts, and Deaf values.

The Kendall Demonstration Elementary School at Gallaudet University in Washington, DC, has developed a Deaf studies curriculum guide that provides an approach to teaching Deaf studies (Miller-Nomeland & Gillespie, 1993). The guide is for teaching students at elementary through middle school levels, using strands that repeatedly cover six topic areas in each of the 9 years of school from first through ninth grade. The topics are Deaf identity, American Deaf culture, American Sign Language, communication, history, and social change. The guide provides activities appropriate to each grade level; the activities can be modified to meet a variety of educational goals.

Visit the Companion Website, *www.prenhall.com/turnbull*, to find out more information about the Kendall Demonstration Elementary School at Gallaudet University.

Secondary and Transition Students: Community-Based Instruction

In the early years of deaf education, schools for the deaf typically prepared their students to get a job. A few students went on to college, but the majority graduated expecting to join the workforce. For example, an 1893 survey of graduates from the Ohio School for the Deaf reported that 62 of its graduates were typesetters, 152 were farmers, 31 were shoemakers, 29 were laborers, 27 worked in shoe factories, 25 were teachers, 3 were principals, and 17 were bookbinders. The number of graduates working in the printing trade was not surprising or unusual because most schools for the deaf had a print shop as part of their vocational training. This was true until the early 1970s (Stewart & Kluwin, 2001).

Today the advances in technology in America have changed the nature of jobs and employment. It is almost impossible to prepare students with the kinds of skills they will need to immediately obtain employment. Obviously, a high school diploma is no longer a guarantee for a well-paying job.

The result is that all schools must prepare their students with hearing loss for postsecondary education and training rather than for a specific job. This is particularly critical because deaf people experience higher unemployment and underemployment than do their hearing counterparts

Into Practice ~ Using the Cummins Model of Language Proficiency   Box 14–4

James Cummins (1980, 1992), a Canadian linguist, investigated how people acquire language, doing most of his work in Quebec and studying French and English. He observed that language has two dimensions—*conversational* and *academic*. He used two terms to describe these dimensions: (1) BICS (basic interpersonal communicative skills) and (2) CALP (cognitive academic linguistic proficiency).

When a child begins to learn language and eventually enters school, he arrives with BICS in his first language. This is the language he uses at home and on the playground. When we talk to our friends about the ballgame on Friday night, we are using BICS. Most children enter kindergarten with a fully developed BICS, basically a receptive and expressive vocabulary of about 2,500 words. Their teachers then expand and build on that knowledge to develop CALP, the academic dimension of language that is necessary for school success. Teachers and students use CALP to explain the structure of a cell, summarize a book passage, write a research paper on medieval castles, and take an academic test. So if a student has BICS in one language, learns to read in that language, and uses that language in thinking and analyzing, he develops a relatively clear relationship between speech and print and between language and thought. For a student to be successful both socially and academically, both dimensions must be developed: BICS + CALP = academic success. The Cummins model is used in both deaf education and in ESL programs to support students in those programs. Here's how it works.

The Cummins Model consists of a continuum along which the student's progress in challenging material is increased while the amount of concrete material the student is asked to learn decreases, as the illustration/model shows. The model has four quadrants. The easiest way to understand each quadrant is to place some tasks inside each quadrant. Quadrant A might include tasks related to art, music, and physical education, all being activities that are very much hands-on and visual. Quadrant B offers math computation, science experiments, and social studies projects—activities that are visual yet tied to content. Quadrant C includes a telephone conversation, a note on the refrigerator, written instructions without examples, which demand a much higher cognitive level for comprehension to occur. Finally, language competence at the Quadrant D level allows the student to take a test, present a paper, listen to a lecture, and understand abstract concepts. There is a progression from more visual, less content-based tasks to much more language-dependent tasks. How can you use this model for students who are deaf and hard of hearing?

■ *Improve listening skills.* Add context to listening skills by improving the room's acoustics, repeating directions two or three times, adding gestures, using a graphic support such as a picture or a drawing, or providing a word clue ("It rhymes with moon"). Use the model to remind the team to be aware of one student's need to reduce some cognitive demands while recognizing that others may be ready for higher-level thinking skills.

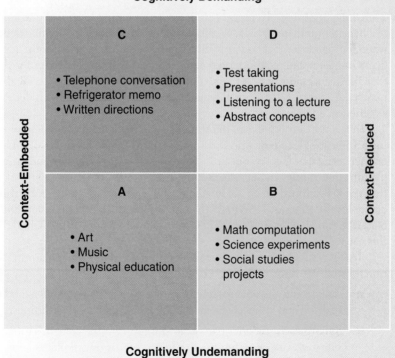

Cognitively Demanding

Context-Embedded

C
- Telephone conversation
- Refrigerator memo
- Written directions

D
- Test taking
- Presentations
- Listening to a lecture
- Abstract concepts

A
- Art
- Music
- Physical education

B
- Math computation
- Science experiments
- Social studies projects

Context-Reduced

Cognitively Undemanding

(continued)

■ *Add language-comprehension skills.* Add language-comprehension material to each quadrant. Quadrant A could include cognitively undemanding, context-embedded questions: "What color is this table?" "Who is sitting by you?" "Which one is red?" Quadrant B may include cognitively undemanding, context-reduced questions: "Where is your sister's classroom?" "What color is your house?" "What is your teacher's name?" Quadrant C may have more cognitively demanding questions but the context is still embedded: "What do you think this story is about?" "Why are shoes made of leather?" "How does electricity make a lamp go on?" Quadrant D represents the most cognitively demanding language level with the context reduced: "How is a state different from a country?" "What is similar about a horse and a cow?" "Is a mile longer than a kilometer?"

■ *Identify levels of student support.* When planning activities, take into consideration the needed CALP for success (i.e., what is the degree of linguistic ability necessary to comprehend and express a particular concept?). For example, in Quadrant D is listed a skill that is difficult for the student: Joe will understand the written directions in his textbook. Quadrant A includes directly teaching the necessary subskills with mediation (define key words using terms Joe knows, provide a picture or diagram). Quadrant B involves directly teaching the substeps to the objective

(have Joe paraphrase the main ideas of the instructions or construct a graphic organizer of the steps). Quadrant C activities are teacher-led rather than teacher-directed (assist Joe in verbalizing his thought process by using open-ended questions—"What does 'identify the subject' mean?").

The Cummins Model can assist team members to analyze tasks, write objectives, and plan appropriate mediated activities for students with hearing loss.

Putting These Strategies to Work for Progress in the General Curriculum

1. What word clues would you use for a hearing-impaired student to whom you are teaching American history (e.g., "1776" clues the student to the Declaration of Independence)?

2. What question would you ask about the Declaration of Independence if you were teaching a student who is competent in language-comprehension skills at the level of Quadrant C?

3. How would you use Quadrants A through D to explain the concept of equality (as expressed in the Declaration of Independence)?

To answer these questions online and learn more about these strategies, go to the Into Practice module in Chapter 14 of the Companion Website, www.prenhall.com/turnbull.

(Garay, 2003; Hanks & Luckner, 2003). Thus, transition planning is a critical component of a student's education.

Transition planning. To prepare students with hearing loss for the world beyond school, their teachers inform them about what employment, education, and living opportunities are available when they graduate. Beyond providing this information, teachers must actively engage their students in meaningful goal-oriented activities that will prepare them for the future. This means that IEP teams must plan for an extensive evaluation of each individual student, coordinate a number of educational and employment experiences, and help the student match her knowledge, experience, and preferences.

In the transition process, the student's reading level has implications for the future. Imagine a 16-year-old student who is reading at a fifth-grade level. His IEP has continually focused on increasing that level by one year. But this goal is inappropriate and probably unrealistic when planning for transition. Let's say that the student wants to enter a particular vocational program that requires a ninth-grade reading level. The questions to ask are, "Is this student a good candidate for this program?" "With sufficient support, such as help in learning the course's written materials and an interpreter to help with in-class communication, could this student succeed in this career?"

Teachers should consider several important activities when planning for a successful transition for students who are deaf and hard of hearing:

■ Talk to the students to determine their interests and understanding of work. Are they realistic and knowledgeable about possible career opportunities?

■ Talk to each student's parents for insight into the student's interests or even the possibility of work opportunities at the parents' own workplaces.

■ Assess the student's communication and social skills to determine whether he is comfortable interacting with hearing people and can request help if he encounters difficulty. Assess all aspects of his communication, including reading, writing, interpersonal communication, signing, and speaking.

- Examine the accommodations the student will need in order to meet the demands of the job, including the use of an interpreter or job coach.

- Determine if the student is willing and able to take an entry-level examination if he is going on to postsecondary education. Often there are entrance exams required for both entry into colleges and technical schools.

- Explore any financial needs for postsecondary education. Encourage the student to seek support from vocational rehabilitation agencies. Make sure the student is aware of how to contact these agencies.

- Investigate the availability of workplaces in the area that are sensitive to the communication needs of individuals with hearing loss.

The Americans with Disabilities Act requires employers to offer reasonable accommodations for deaf employees, such as installing a telecommunications device for the deaf (TDD). This device consists of a keyboard, a display screen, and a modem. The user types into the machine, and the letters are converted into electrical signals that can travel over regular phone lines. When the signals reach another TDD, they are converted back into letters that appear on a display screen so that the individual with hearing loss can read them. Employees are also using pagers and interpreters for meetings and training.

Postsecondary education. During the past few years, many colleges and universities have experienced a growth in the numbers of students who are deaf or hard of hearing. This increase has made the transition from high school to postsecondary education easier because students with hearing loss now may have a small community of supportive peers in attendance.

In addition, most colleges and universities provide direct support through on-campus offices for students with disabilities. These offices often provide counselors, interpreters, tutoring, and training for professors who will have the students in their classes. They also make arrangements for note takers and even real-time captioning of lectures.

For example, Kent State University, in Ohio, uses a remote captioning service designed specifically for educational settings. The professor wears a lapel microphone that connects to a phone line, while the captioner, who is at another location, hears the lecture from the phone and word-processes it. The captioner's computer has a phone line that sends the information directly to the student's laptop computer. The student sees the professor's lecture across his or her laptop screen at almost the same time as the professor is talking, which is why the process is called real-time captioning.

New technology and electronics are making education accessible in many new ways for students with hearing loss. While it may be too soon to judge the effectiveness of each new method or device on student achievement and success, it is clear that the environment, both educational and vocational, is changing.

INCLUDING STUDENTS WITH HEARING LOSS

Educational Quality

When the Commission on the Education of the Deaf (1988) assessed the quality of all educational services provided to students with hearing loss, it concluded that the present status of education for persons who are deaf in the United States is unsatisfactory. The commission recommended promoting English language development and recognizing the unique needs of students who are deaf. It requested that service providers take these needs into account when developing IEPs and urged the Department of Education to reconsider how the fourth principle of IDEA, placement in the least restrictive environment, should apply to deaf and hard-of-hearing students. It also requested that educators focus on the appropriateness of placement, taking into consideration the student's need to be taught by, and be able to interact with, others who use the same mode of communication (Commission on Education of the Deaf, 1988).

Values: The debates about methods for teaching students who are deaf or hard of hearing should not obscure this simple fact: any effective means builds on the students' *strengths* and therefore is appropriate for the student.

In direct response to the commission's report, the federal government issued new policy guidelines relative to the education of students who are deaf. The guidelines pointed out that "any setting, including a regular classroom, that prevents a child who is deaf from receiving an appropriate education that meets his or her needs, including communication needs, is not the LRE (least restrictive environment) for that child" (U.S. Department of Education, 1992, p. 49275). Educators have understood these guidelines to mean that the least restrictive environment for students who are deaf or hard of hearing may not be the regular education classroom. Accordingly, educators balance appropriateness (i.e., the student's opportunity to benefit) against placement (i.e., inclusion) and place the priority on appropriateness when there is a conflict between it and an inclusive placement.

This approach seems defensible. When Congress reauthorized IDEA in 2004, it directed the IEP team for a student who is deaf or hard of hearing to consider the student's language and communication needs, opportunities for direct communications with peers in the student's language and mode of communication, and full range of needs, including opportunities for direct instruction in the student's language and mode of communication. In Box 14–5, you will learn about a national movement to create a bill of rights to communication for deaf and hard-of-hearing students. It should prompt you to ask, in your own voice, where you place your priorities.

Educational Placement

Access to communication should drive decisions about educational placement for students with hearing loss, but access and placement can be in the general curriculum for many students. As Figure 14–8 shows, more and more students with hearing loss are educated in regular education

---

Your Own Voice ~ What Is a Deaf Child's Bill of Rights?   Box 14–5

Do you have a right to communicate? Arguably, no: the right does not appear in any constitutions or laws, and according to current conservative theories about government, judges should not confer a right that the people and their representatives do not make explicit in their laws. There's the opposite answer, of course: arguably, there *is* a right to communicate. Here liberal theories hold; otherwise, rights to free speech would mean little, if anything. Neither would IDEA-valued outcomes such as full participation in American society.

A unique collaboration of parents, professionals, and consumers, working as equal partners to achieve a common vision (the right to communicate) and representing different philosophies and beliefs (e.g., manual programs, oral programs, residential programs, mainstream programs, the Deaf community, etc.), is now trying to create an explicit right to communicate. It has developed a "white paper," a sort of manifesto, entitled the *National Agenda for Moving Forward on Achieving Educational Equality for Deaf and Hard of Hearing Students* (April 2005). The *National Agenda* sets out priorities for improving the quality and nature of educational services and programs for these students.

Key to the agenda is the belief that there is a fundamental right to have access to communication and language. Members of the agenda team are asking each state department of education to sponsor a law or adopt a regulation entitled the Deaf Child's Bill of Rights to make sure that children with hearing loss have access to communication in their own mode.

Imagine that you are a teacher in a small town in a rural area. You have a deaf child in your classroom who communicates using American Sign Language. No other children in your school are deaf, but a deaf couple who use ASL live in a nearby town. You ask your district board of education to hire them to be related service professionals in your classroom, even though they are not certified to teach or be interpreters. You refer to the importance of a Deaf culture and deaf adult mentors. Most of all, you talk about IDEA and the student's communication mode. Finally, you mention the proposed bill of rights.

A member of the board reminds you about NCLB and IDEA and their provisions for highly-qualified teachers and other professionals. Another board member says that if you start hiring nonprofessionals for one group of students, especially for just one student, you will start a precedent that has no limits: "Who's next to be hired?" A third member says, "The problem with the schools is that there already are too many rights. When are you going to stop advocating for rights?"

To help you answer these questions, see the following:

- *The national agenda: Moving forward on achieving educational equality for deaf and hard of hearing students.* (2005, April). (*http://www.deafed.net/*).

- The Colorado Department of Education for information about implementing a deaf child's bill of rights (*http://www.cde.state.co.us/cdesped/*).

- Siegel, L. (2000). The educational and communication needs of deaf and hard of hearing children: A statement of principle regarding fundamental systematic educational changes. *American Annals of the Deaf, 145*(2), 64–77.

- Hands and Voices, an organization for parents of children who are deaf and hard of hearing (*http://www.handsandvoices.org/*).

Figure 14–8   Educational placement of students with hearing loss (2003–2004)

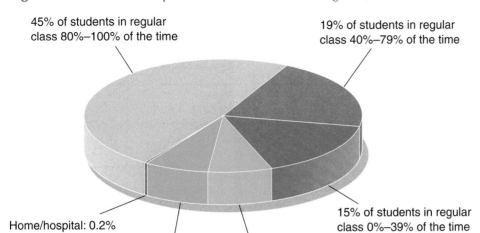

45% of students in regular class 80%–100% of the time

19% of students in regular class 40%–79% of the time

15% of students in regular class 0%–39% of the time

Home/hospital: 0.2%

Residential facility: 7%

Separate facility: 7%

Source: U.S. Department of Education, Office of Special Education Programs. (2005). *IDEA data website* (http://www.ideadata.org/aboutThisSite.asp).

classrooms. They may be receiving special services, including classroom amplification, audiological evaluation, speech-language therapy, resource support from a trained deaf educator, instructional accommodations, and an educational **interpreter,** now an IDEA related service. Interpreting services include, but are not limited to, oral transliteration services, cued language services, and sign language interpreting.

Another placement option is a special classroom in the public school with other students who are deaf or hard of hearing. The teacher is usually a trained deaf educator, and the students may be included with their hearing peers for some academic subjects or for art, music, or physical education.

Yet another placement option is a segregated setting. Before the 1980s, most students with hearing loss (particularly those who were deaf) were educated in large residential schools for the deaf or in separate public or private day schools. They often entered those schools at age 5, learned to communicate from their peers and deaf adults who worked at the schools, made lifetime friendships, met their spouse, and settled in the area to live and work. In fact, this educational setting was the basis for the development and perpetuation of the Deaf community and Deaf culture.

IDEA has changed the nature and prevalence of these residential and day programs. Given the wider range of placement options in public schools, enrollment in residential schools has declined and many have closed, although members of the Deaf community and some professionals in the field of deafness continue to advocate for the right to choose this placement option (Moores, 2001).

Mariah and Ricquel are being educated using a unique educational model for students with hearing loss, an approach that is used in only a few school systems. Their school employs a team-teaching model that pairs a deaf educator with a regular educator. The girls are taught

The general education classroom, with supports, offers many opportunities for academic and social success for students who are deaf or hard of hearing.

in voice and sign language simultaneously, using an educational interpreter and an assistant teacher who also signs. The teachers work collaboratively, allowing for small-group instruction within the larger classroom setting. As they work with small groups for subjects like guided reading and vocabulary, both the students with hearing loss and any other students in the class who might also need special support benefit. In this classroom, all of the children (both deaf and hearing) are exposed to sign language throughout the day, and the other

Inclusion Tips   Box 14–6

	What You Might See	What You Might Be Tempted to Do	Alternate Responses	Ways to Include Peers in the Process
Behavior	The student might not participate in cooperative learning activities.	Tell her in front of the rest of the class to participate appropriately.	Be sure she understands the activity and what is expected of her beforehand.	Use a buddy system to foster her greater participation.
Social interactions	Her speech may be difficult to understand, the other students may not know how to sign, and this may limit her ability to interact during small-group discussions.	Randomly assign her to a group; assume the group will work out roles and participations.	Discuss the situation with the deaf educator and the educational-interpreter. The deaf educator can work on making sure she is prepared for small-group discussions. The interpreter can encourage the other students to follow the teacher's rules for turn taking.	Arrange instruction for peers to learn more sign language. Use a student to facilitate with a more structured approach that allows comments and input from everyone. Practice taking turns with everyone.
Educational performance	She may miss some things other students say and appear not to understand.	Tell her to ask her interpreter.	Ensure that the other students face her when they are talking. Make sure the other students raise their hand before speaking so she can visually orient to the speaker. Have the interpreter move to the student who is talking so she can see both the interpreter and the student who is talking. If the vocabulary in the cooperative learning activity is unfamiliar, provide a study guide.	Check the notes taken by the student note taker to be sure they are adequate. Arrange for peer tutoring of unfamiliar vocabulary.
Classroom attitudes	She may appear bored or inattentive because of not hearing all that is said or not watching the interpreter.	Discipline her for inattentiveness.	Be sure her hearing aid or cochlear implant is working and that her interpreting needs are being met during cooperative learning activities.	Group her with peers who are helpful and caring but do not "mother" her.

students are learning to sign along with their deaf peers. This provides a great support for socialization for the girls because all of the students are learning to communicate directly with each other. Mariah and Ricquel are benefiting from inclusion, as are other students who are deaf and hard of hearing. Box 14–6 provides you with tips on how to include them in the general curriculum.

ASSESSING STUDENTS' PROGRESS

Measuring Students' Progress

Many of the problems that educators face in assessing the progress of students with hearing loss relate to the following (Stewart & Kluwin, 2001):

1.   Many students are users of nonstandard English. (English is their second language if they use American Sign Language to communicate.)
2.   A student's speech intelligibility may be impaired.
3.   Many tests will be difficult for the deaf child who has reading delays.
4.   Standardized achievement tests are rarely norm-referenced for deaf or hard-of-hearing students.

Among some of the issues affecting deaf education under NCLB and state-mandated assessments of student progress are the goals of the state testing system and how deaf students can be accommodated within that system.

Progress in the General Curriculum

Educators of students with hearing loss typically test their hearing, communication, and school achievement. The assessment of communication depends on the particular mode used by the child. Students who are oral will be assessed for speech and hearing skills; students who are manual will be assessed on sign language skills.

The assessment of academic achievement (or lack thereof) often focuses specifically on the child's reading and writing skills. There are three classic ways to assess reading: questions on comprehension following the reading of a short passage, cloze procedures, and reading performance measures (Stewart & Kluwin, 2001).

A **cloze procedure** involves the modification of a text of at least 250 words by eliminating every fifth word and replacing it with a blank. The student then supplies the missing word without prompting. Cloze procedures emphasize prediction of content rather than comprehension and offer the teacher a quick and simple assessment of the match between reading materials and a student's abilities.

Reading performance measures can include oral reading tests in which the student is given a passage to read aloud and is scored on how well she reads the text. This type of test can cause problems for deaf or hard-of-hearing students for whom English is a second language. They tend to substitute a dialect phrase for the exact wording of the text. The teacher must decide whether to score the dialect phrase as wrong or allow it to substitute for the printed word. Often this type of reading assessment becomes a test of speech intelligibility.

Story retelling is a form of performance measure in which the student reads a passage to herself and then tells the teacher what was in the passage (French, 1999). Although there are no scoring norms for this approach, the approach allows the student to show that she understands what has been read even though she may not be able to sound out each individual word.

Teachers can assess a student's writing skills in three ways: surrogate skills, editing skills/ grammar correction, and holistic or impressionistic scoring (Stewart & Kluwin, 2001). Surrogate skills measure the components of writing with spelling or vocabulary tests. If a student can do well on tests of spelling or vocabulary, then she will probably be a good writer. Editing skill involves assessing the student's ability to correct her own grammar. For example, she might be asked to select the right grammatical form from among several options.

Researchers at the National Technical Institute for the Deaf and Gallaudet University developed the holistic or impressionistic measure of writing skills. This procedure provides the student with a writing prompt, such as a scenario or issue to be addressed, a likely audience for the writing, and some parameters for the writer to consider in his paper. For example, a student might be asked to write a letter to a child in a foreign country, asking to be a pen pal. Scoring protocols are rubrics for scoring the written document.

Progress in Addressing Other Educational Needs

Often a student with hearing loss is educated in a general education classroom with support from an itinerant deaf educator who provides direct services in a resource room. The student's general educator and deaf educator create a team-teaching situation in which there may be different criteria for grading. Who will assign the grade, and what will the child be expected to do to achieve a specific grade? Will a normative criterion be applied, based on what is expected of her hearing peers?

These two educators might agree to use contract grading, IEP grading, level grading, and narrative grading. In contract grading, they grade the student on a negotiated contract based on a predetermined amount of work. IEP grading addresses the student's specific needs relative to the IEP goals and objectives. Level grading makes the student responsible for the same work and achievement as his hearing peers, and narrative grading allows the itinerant deaf educator to report in narrative form on the student's work in the resource room.

Portfolio assessment is particularly effective as a performance assessment for students who are deaf and hard of hearing. A student's signing ability can be videotaped; the assessment and monitoring of speech production lends itself well to audiotapes. Examples of the student's written work can be included in the portfolio.

A good portfolio contains more than random collections of various assessments. It should be a thoughtful assembly of materials that address a clear purpose for inclusion (e.g., progressive drafts of an essay), evidences appropriate performance criteria (e.g., sign or speech production is scored as absent, emerging, or proficient), and shows not only the student's best work but examples of her typical work. A videotape of the student giving a speech to his class about a famous Deaf adult for a unit on Deaf studies exemplifies appropriate content in a portfolio.

Making Accommodations for Assessment

Elliot, Kratochwill, and Schulte (1998) identified eight possible accommodations to state formats for students with disabilities. Using these categories, Stewart and Kluwin (2001) adapted the list and made the accommodations specific for deaf students. Their suggestions include providing assistance before testing to teach any new forms of test taking, providing a longer time period for the assessment, interpreting the directions, and even changing the format and content (rephrasing an item) if this can be done without altering the intent of the question. Accommodations allow for the greatest level of success for the students—the accurate measure of knowledge and performance on a level playing field.

Looking to Mariah's, Ricquel's, and Shylah's Future

When you ask Sharon to look ahead to the years that will follow her daughters' graduation from high school, she says that she wants them to be mainstreamed and to be as normal as possible. She talks vaguely about their attending college.

It is interesting that she uses a word, *mainstreaming*, that is somewhat dated, yet her expectations for her daughters are thoroughly up-to-date. To participate fully in American life; to hold jobs and be economically self-sufficient; to live on their own, independently; and to have equal opportunities to be all they can and want to be: these are, of course, the national policy goals that IDEA and the Americans with Disabilities Act set out. And they are goals that Sharon adopts as her and her daughters' own.

To be as normal as possible is a noble policy goal. Yet it can conflict with a Deaf culture that asserts that being "normal" means being—indeed, staying—as deaf as possible. How will the girls resolve the dilemma of adhering to the policy goals, honoring their mother's and teachers' great expectations for them, building on their strengths, yet being loyal to their peers in the Deaf community?

One—let's say, Mariah—demonstrates extraordinary athletic ability. She excels in sports, such as gymnastics and soccer, where communication is either not needed or, if needed, is less auditory than seen and anticipated. Nothing prevents her from graduating with a degree in physical education, earning her teaching certificate, and becoming a physical education teacher and coach.

Another—let's say, Ricquel—is gifted in mathematics and physics. She turns these high school talents into a career in computers and information technology. Again, nothing prevents her from using assistive technologies. For her, the cochlear implant is "just another technology."

And the third, Shylah, is so inspired by her teachers that she earns her doctorate in special education, with a concentration in deaf education, and takes a position as a professor at a leading research university, preparing new teachers to work with students who are deaf.

All three continue to model their parents' and their teachers' pragmatic approach to deafness. Use those places, programs, and interventions that work. Celebrate the variety of human difference. And make sure that your own talents benefit others.

SUMMARY

Identifying students with hearing loss

- Children are typically classified as deaf or hard of hearing. Degree of hearing loss is categorized as mild, moderate, moderate-severe, severe, and profound.
- Conductive loss is caused by a problem in the outer and middle ear; sensorineural loss is caused by a problem in the inner ear or along the nerve pathway to the brain.
- Achievement levels, specifically in the areas of reading and writing, are primary concerns for students with hearing loss. They can be particularly problematic among children from diverse racial, ethnic, and linguistic backgrounds.
- Hearing loss in children is considered a low-incidence disability and is estimated at about 1.3 percent of the school-age population.

Evaluating students with hearing loss

- An audiologist diagnoses hearing loss using an auditory brain stem response or otoacoustic immittance test with infants and young children and behavioral audiological evaluation with older children.
- Hearing aids make sound louder but do not restore normal hearing; there is always some distortion of sound.
- Cochlear implants provide sound information by directly stimulating the functioning auditory nerve fibers in the cochlea. Cochlear implants do not make sound louder.
- Assessment of language, speech, speech reading, signing, academic achievement, and socialization are essential for providing an appropriate education for students who are deaf and hard of hearing.

Designing an appropriate individualized education program

- The increase in cochlear implants has resulted in increased input from the medical implant team.
- The educational interpreter is often the student's bridge to the hearing world around him.
- The various communication modes used by individuals with hearing loss include oral/aural, manual, and total communication.

- A bilingual/bicultural educational model combines the use of American Sign Language as the student's first language, English as his or her second language, and Deaf studies to teach the culture of deafness.

Using effective instructional strategies

- Intervention for young children with hearing loss includes access to a language-rich environment.
- Shared reading emphasizes the importance of reading to young children as they connect the English sentences in the book to the way the sentences are signed in ASL.
- Real-world or authentic experiences are particularly important for students with hearing loss if they are to make a connection with what they know and what they read.
- Learning about deafness, the Deaf community, Deaf history, and famous Deaf adults can be incorporated into social studies, health, and science curricula for all students.

Including students with hearing loss

- Access to communication is critical when deciding on placement for students with hearing loss.
- IDEA now includes interpreting services as related services; oral transliteration, cued speech, and sign language interpreting are part of interpreting.

Assessing students' progress

- There may be problems in the assessment of students with hearing loss if the student uses English as a second language (ASL being the first language), has unintelligible speech, or has difficulty with reading.
- Story retelling allows the student to show that he understands what he has read, even though he may not have been able to sound out each individual word.

WHAT WOULD YOU RECOMMEND?

Refer to chapter content and the PRAXIS™ and CEC standards in Appendix A to answer the following questions:

1. Go to the Companion Website, *www.prenhall.com/turnbull*, and locate the link to ASL. Using this link, practice signing 10 words that you will teach to your class. Which PRAXIS™ or CEC standards are you using as you complete this activity?

2. Develop a room arrangement that maximizes opportunities for visual and/or auditory learning. Which PRAXIS™ or CEC standards are you using as you complete this activity?

3. Go to the Companion Website, *www.prenhall.com/turnbull*, and locate the link to hearing loss. Listen to the replications of hearing loss. As a teacher, how might you use this exposure to assist a student in your classroom? Which PRAXIS™ or CEC standards are you using as you complete this activity?

Who is Haley Sumner?

by Sandra Lewis, Florida State University

As Mrs. Benson's second-grade class walks down the hallway of Robey Elementary School in Indianapolis, Indiana, one can't help but notice the petite, brown-haired girl with a big grin on her face who is leading the girls' line. She walks with a bounce in her step, moving her white cane in rhythm with her strides.

Haley Sumner's class is headed to the gymnasium for P.E. This week the class is working on bounce-passing balls and catching the ball after one bounce. Haley is prepared; she has practiced this activity for a few weeks with some of her friends during recess. Many of her friends have had to learn how to pass the ball correctly to Haley so that she can catch it more easily. She stands with her arms out in front of her, prepared to move her hands and arms quickly to embrace the ball after she hears it bounce.

Haley also enjoys attending music class, where they are practicing for the upcoming second-grade concert. Art is another favorite subject. She proudly displays an art project she made in first grade that won honorable mention in a national art competition. Pumping the swings is her chosen activity during recess, but when it is too cold to be outside, she plays Connect Four or Uno inside with her peers.

Every evening, Haley practices her spelling words, works on addition and subtraction facts, and reads to her parents from her reading book. On Thursdays, Haley attends Brownies with several of her classmates.

Haley seems to be a typical second grader, but she does have to do some things differently than her peers because she is visually impaired. Haley was born with some ability to perceive light but is considered blind. At age 3, Haley and her family began to work in their home and a pre-school classroom with Miss Katie Culbertson, a teacher of students with visual impairments (TVI). Haley showed spunk and determination even then, telling adults, "I do it myself!" Since then, she has learned many new techniques and developed key blindness skills so that she can, indeed, do it herself.

Haley continues to work with Miss Katie during and sometimes after school, in her general education classroom and a resource room, at home, and in the community. Haley and Miss Katie focus on a wide variety of skills that are enabling her to be much more independent. Over summer break, they particularly emphasize independent living skills and other community-based activities.

Understanding Students with Visual Impairments

Haley is reading fluently in braille at a third-grade level. She has learned how to write in braille using a Perkins braille writer and an electronic braille writer called the Mountbatten. She has also started to master the computer keyboard and loves typing letters to family members that can be read in print. Haley is anxiously awaiting the arrival of a new note taker, a mini braille computer device she will be able to use to complete assignments in braille and then print out one copy for herself in braille, another for her teacher in print.

In addition to using braille for reading, Haley has learned to read the Nemeth code, a special braille code for math and science. She uses this code daily in math. She is also continuing to develop skills in reading tactile graphs, tables, and charts for math and tactile maps and diagrams for science and social studies. Haley is also becoming quite proficient in using an abacus for solving addition and subtraction problems, although she and her classmates prefer to hear the talking calculator read the answer after she has entered a problem.

Miss Katie is also a certified orientation and mobility specialist (COMS). Haley has received orientation and mobility (O&M) services at home and school since she was in preschool. She now displays confidence when traveling throughout school independently. She is even quite willing to give a tour to anyone unfamiliar with the building. "How did you know how to find the computer lab?" someone asked her one day. "I've known that since I was 4!" Haley answered. "I learned that from Miss Katie on a mobility lesson." Now that she is 7, Haley's O&M lessons have extended far beyond the walls of her school building.

Use your *Real Lives and Exceptionalities* DVD to view Kristen, a woman with a visual impairment. Click on, "Beyond School," and then Select, "Kristen" (Clip 7). Kristen's mother says she believes Kristen will always need, "someone to trust" to help her with certain tasks. What kind of assistant might Haley continue to require into adulthood?

She has learned how to detect driveways and curbs with her cane, how to travel safely and independently around an unfamiliar block, and how to get clues from traffic noises around her. She has made numerous trips in the community to work on her cane technique and learn how to navigate using a sighted guide in busy stores and restaurants.

One of Haley's biggest struggles in the public school and community has been convincing others that she can do things on her own. "I don't like it when everyone asks me if they can do things for me all the time," Haley told her TVI one day. "But I try to be polite, and I just tell them, 'No, thank you; I can do it myself.'" But after working with her parents, her TVI, and her COMS in the community, Haley has begun to recognize that there are times when she might need someone's help, just as there are times when she can offer her assistance to others.

IDENTIFYING STUDENTS WITH VISUAL IMPAIRMENTS

Defining visual impairments

When you think about visual impairments and blindness, you might imagine someone such as Haley, who sees nothing at all and must use adaptive techniques for tasks that typically require vision, such as braille for reading or a cane to detect objects when traveling. It may surprise you to learn that most individuals with **legal blindness** have usable vision and that most students who have visual impairments are print readers.

Two different definitions describe visual impairment. The legal definition of blindness is based on a clinical measurement of visual acuity. **Acuity** is determined by having the individual read the letters on a chart, each line of which is composed of letters written with a certain size of print. The ability to read the 20 line from a distance of 20 feet is typical, and a person who can read at that line is said to have 20/20 acuity. Individuals who can read only the top line from 20 feet, where the print size is 200 (the big E), when using both eyes and wearing their glasses, have 20/200 acuity; these people are legally blind. People are also legally blind if their **field of vision** (the area around them that they can visually detect when looking straight ahead) is less than 20 degrees (normal is 160 degrees), even if their visual acuity is normal. These individuals have **tunnel vision.** Figure 15–1 shows what people with various types of visual impairment might see.

The legal definition of blindness, as established by federal law in 1935 (Koestler, 1976), is an arbitrary clinical measure that is used to determine eligibility for special government allowances, such as an extra income tax deduction, specialized job training, and eligibility for certain support services such as the Talking Book Program. Many state, local, and private agencies also use legal blindness as their eligibility requirement. A person who is legally blind may have a great deal of useful vision. The legal definition of blindness is simply an eligibility standard; it does not provide any meaningful information about the way in which a person experiences and learns about the world (Huebner, 2000).

How a person experiences and learns about the world is, however, at the core of the IDEA definition of visual impairments. The current regulations implementing IDEA define **visual disability (including blindness)** as "an impairment in vision that, even with correction, adversely affects a child's educational performance. The term includes both partial sight and blindness" (34 C.F.R., sec. 300.7[13]). Key to this definition is that the student has some kind of disorder of the visual system that interferes with learning.

Students with visual impairments represent a wide range of visual abilities. Educators classify these students by their ability to use their vision or their tendency or need to use tactile means for learning (Lewis & Allman, 2000):

- **Low vision** describes individuals who read print, although they may depend on optical aids, such as magnifying lenses, to see better. A few read both braille and print; all rely primarily on vision for learning. Individuals with low vision may or may not be legally blind.

- **Functionally blind** describes individuals who typically use braille for efficient reading and writing. They may rely on their ability to use functional vision for other tasks, such as moving through the environment or sorting items by color. Thus, they use their limited vision to supplement the combination of tactile and auditory learning methods.

- **Totally blind** describes those individuals who do not receive meaningful input through the visual sense. These individuals use tactile and auditory means to learn about their environment, and they generally read braille.

These broad categories are only minimally useful. Every individual with visual impairment uses vision differently and in a way that is difficult to predict. When you teach these students, it is important to avoid the common errors of assuming that students who are functionally blind cannot see anything and that students with low vision are efficiently using that sense. Teachers should observe carefully how a student functions and then present instructional activities to maximize that student's learning.

To learn more about how impaired vision might look, go to the Web Links module in Chapter 15 of the Companion Website, *www. prenhall. com/turnbull.*

Figure 15-1 Estimate of how a view appears for (a) individuals with 20/20 vision, (b) reduced visual acuity, (c) and (d) restricted fields of vision.

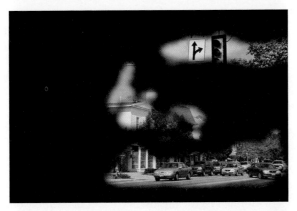

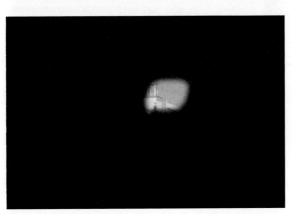

Because state and local educational agencies vary so widely in how they measure and report visual impairments, it is extremely difficult to accurately count the number of students with visual impairments who are served in schools (Kirchner & Diament, 1999). The best estimates are that approximately one to two students in 1,000 have a visual disorder that interferes with learning; those children are eligible to receive special education services (Nelson & Dimitrova, 1993). Visual impairment accounts for about 0.04 percent of the total special education population (U.S. Department of Education, 2002).

Describing the Characteristics

The population of students with visual impairments is surprisingly heterogeneous. The students differ from each other in how they learn and in their visual functioning, socioeconomic status, cultural background, age of onset of visual impairment, the presence of other disabilities, and cognitive abilities. Some are gifted or have special talents. A large number also have multiple disabilities (Huebner, 2000; Pogrund, 2002; Silberman, 2000). Yet each possesses a characteristic in common: the limited ability to learn incidentally from the environment (Hatlen & Curry, 1987).

Almost from the moment they are born, children with good vision learn seemingly effortlessly through their visual sense. Their vision helps them organize, synthesize, and give meaning to their perceptions of the environment (Ferrell, 2000; Liefert, 2003; Lowenfeld, 1973). For example, a sighted baby spends hours looking at his or her hand before that hand becomes an efficient tool. A young child will drop a toy repeatedly, watching its path to the floor until he or she learns to understand "down." Through these repeated observations, the child is learning about how to move his hands, the effects of his hands' movement (on himself, the toy, and his caretakers), and, as similar and diverse experiences occur with various objects, about the properties of nature (sound, gravity, weight, etc.). This learning occurs without direct instruction from others but almost exclusively through the power of observation.

Think about the way in which a young child learns the concept of *table*. Even before she has a name for that object, she has observed a variety of tables in her environment: in the kitchen, living room, and family room, at the homes of relatives and friends, and at preschool. Tables are everywhere, and the sighted child begins to recognize that the things people call tables ("Put your cup on the table," or "Leave the magazine on the table," or "Go get Daddy's glasses off the table") have certain features in common. Soon she perceives a relationship between the object and the word. Later, after more visual experiences, she will distinguish among desks, tables, counters, and other flat surfaces. Children learn this kind of conceptual information incidentally with little or no direct instruction.

Young children develop a "scheme" about tables through their experience with them. This incidental learning differs for a child who has always been visually impaired.

Incidental learning is problematic for all visually impaired children (Ferrell, 1996; Hatlen & Curry, 1987; Liefert, 2003). The child with limited visual access to her environment may find it necessary for her family and teachers to provide her with opportunities to explore carefully and completely, either visually at a close distance or through tactile means, every part of a variety of tables before she can acquire, organize, and then synthesize information about "tableness."

Incidental learning also affects how children come to perform skills. For example, most children need little training when they make toast for the first time. They have few problems with any of the steps involved in this rather complex task because they have observed adults make toast hundreds of times. Without hands-on instruction, children with visual impairments may not even be aware that a special machine is used in this task. Even youngsters with low vision, who may not see clearly beyond a distance of 2 or 3 feet, usually need special instruction and practice time to perform this and other tasks.

Because of the important role played by incidental learning for most individuals, the presence of a visual impairment has the potential to influence motor, language, cognitive, and social skills development. Generally, however, these influences are not long-lasting if the student receives appropriate interventions (Ferrell, 2000). Interventions must be designed to reduce the limitations imposed on an individual by a significant visual impairment, including limitations in the range and variety of experiences, limitations in the ability to get around, and limitations in interactions with the environment.

Standard: By learning about the characteristics of students with visual impairments, you put into practice CEC Standard 2, Development and Characteristics of Learners.

Limitations in range and variety of experiences. Vision allows a person to experience the world meaningfully and safely from a distance. Touch is an ineffective substitute for vision: some objects are too big (skyscrapers, mountains), too small (ants, molecules), too fragile (snowflakes, moths), too dangerous (fire, boiling water), or too distant (the sun, the horizon) for their characteristics to be learned tactilely (Lowenfeld, 1973). The other senses do not fully compensate for what can be learned visually: the song of a bird or the smell of baking bread may provide evidence that those objects are nearby but do not provide useful information about many of their properties. Individuals with visual impairment often have not shared the experiences of their peers with typical vision, so their knowledge of the world may be different.

Students with visual impairments also experience different social interactions because they cannot share common experiences with sighted friends. The student who has not seen the latest movie, played the newest video game, or taken driver's training may be at a disadvantage within the school culture. The potential for inadequate development of social skills and the related negative impact on self-esteem are serious concerns that may have a lifelong impact (Sacks & Silberman, 2000).

Similarly, career development can be limited. While individuals with visual impairments are employed in a variety of occupations, many young adults struggle with determining an appropriate vocation because they are unaware of the jobs that people (with or without vision) perform (Wolffe, 2000).

Limitations in the ability to get around. Individuals who are visually impaired are limited in their spontaneous ability to move safely in and through their environment. This restriction influences a child's early motor development and exploration of the world; in turn, the same restriction affects the child's knowledge base and social development. The ability to move through the environment spontaneously is probably one area over which only moderate control can be exercised and is a continuing source of frustration for many adults (Corn & Sacks, 1994).

Individuals who have significant visual impairment are limited in their movement through space. This limitation directly affects their opportunities for experiences (Barraga & Erin, 2001). The child with impaired vision may not know what is interesting in the environment. Even if that child is aware of something to explore, he or she may not know how to get to the desired object. These children can become passive and in turn have fewer opportunities for intellectual and social stimulation (Anthony et al., 2003; Pogrund, 2002).

Limitations in interactions with the environment. Knowledge about and control over the environment often are areas of concern for individuals with visual impairments. In some cases, their limited vision reduces their level of readily acquired information about their environment and their ability to act on that information. For instance, they cannot determine at a glance the source of a loud crash or a burning smell, so they cannot quickly determine an appropriate reaction. Similarly, they cannot adequately inform themselves about the effects of their actions on the people and things around them.

In young children, reduced vision correlates with poor motivation to move through the environment, manipulate toys, and initiate interactions (Ferrell, 2000). Their tendency toward physical and social detachment (Wolffe, Sacks, & Thomas, 2000) and low motivation can have the long-lasting consequence of limiting their sense of competence and mastery. Individuals who have a poor sense of their ability to effect change in their lives are at risk for the development of poor self-esteem, poor academic achievement, and reduced language and social skills (Harrell, 1992).

The limitations in the range and variety of experiences, in the ability to get around, and in interactions with the environment influence how a student with a visual impairment experiences the world. Visual impairment can result in experiential and environmental deprivation. Students with visual impairments, even children who have other concomitant disabilities, can learn, but because

Young children with impaired vision need opportunities to explore a variety of environments to develop a healthy sense of competency.

To learn about the structures of the eye, go to the Web Links module in Chapter 15 of the Companion Website, *www.prenhall.com/turnbull.*

they receive unclear, incomplete, or no visual input, they require directed interventions to develop an understanding of the relationships between people and objects in their environment (Freeman, Goetz, Richards, & Groenveld, 1991). Visual impairment primarily affects how students learn skills but does not prevent the acquisition of skills when appropriate interventions are provided.

Determining the Causes

As you can tell from Figure 15–2, seeing involves both the eye and brain. Damage to or malfunction of any part of the visual system can impair how the student functions.

Damage to the structures involved in the visual process can be the result of an event that happens during the development of the embryo, can occur at or immediately after an infant's birth, or can result from an injury or disease that occurs at any time during a person's development. **Congenital** visual impairment occurs at birth or, in the case of blindness, before visual memories have been established. Haley has a congenital visual impairment. That type of impairment can affect any child's earliest access to information and experiences. Students who acquire a vision loss after having normal vision have an **adventitious** visual impairment. That is, their impairment results from an advent (e.g., loss of sight caused by a hereditary condition that has just manifested itself) or an event (e.g., loss of sight caused by trauma). Although the educational needs of students with adventitious and congenital visual impairments may be similar, even a short period of good vision can enrich the student's understanding of self, others, and the relationships among people, objects, and events in the environment (Scott, Jan, & Freeman, 1995).

EVALUATING STUDENTS WITH VISUAL IMPAIRMENTS

Determining the Presence of Visual Impairments

Like students with other disabilities, a student with visual impairment receives a nondiscriminatory evaluation (see Figure 15–3). Of course, evaluations of students with visual impairments do have several highly specialized aspects.

Figure 15-2   Anatomy of the eye

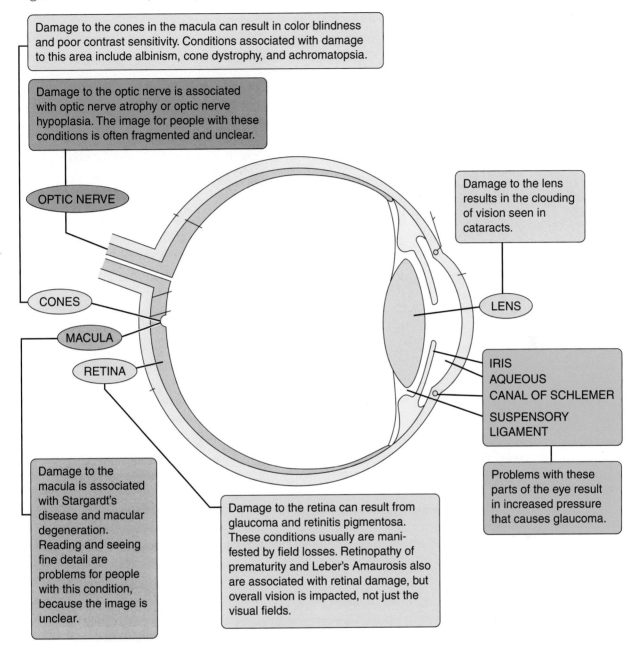

Damage to the cones in the macula can result in color blindness and poor contrast sensitivity. Conditions associated with damage to this area include albinism, cone dystrophy, and achromatopsia.

Damage to the optic nerve is associated with optic nerve atrophy or optic nerve hypoplasia. The image for people with these conditions is often fragmented and unclear.

Damage to the lens results in the clouding of vision seen in cataracts.

OPTIC NERVE

CONES

MACULA

RETINA

LENS

IRIS
AQUEOUS
CANAL OF SCHLEMER
SUSPENSORY LIGAMENT

Problems with these parts of the eye result in increased pressure that causes glaucoma.

Damage to the macula is associated with Stargardt's disease and macular degeneration. Reading and seeing fine detail are problems for people with this condition, because the image is unclear.

Damage to the retina can result from glaucoma and retinitis pigmentosa. These conditions usually are manifested by field losses. Retinopathy of prematurity and Leber's Amaurosis also are associated with retinal damage, but overall vision is impacted, not just the visual fields.

Medical specialists usually determine the presence of a disorder of the child's visual system. Physicians often detect a serious visual disorder when the child is very young or has just experienced a trauma. Their diagnosis generally is followed by a search for medical solutions to correct vision. When no such correction is possible, referrals to the schools occur.

It is important for educators to know the cause of a student's visual impairment. Although a diagnosis of the cause, or **etiology,** may not provide accurate information about how much a student sees, this information is invaluable as educators plan the student's program. An accurate diagnosis suggests typical characteristics associated with a particular eye condition, including probable lighting needs, a potential prognosis, and possible related medical disorders or learning problems.

When a referral for services is received by a school district, the teacher of students with visual impairments first evaluates the referred student to determine how he or she uses any vision that is available and then whether the student learns b5est using the visual or tactile sense.

Figure 15-3 Nondiscriminatory evaluation process for determining the presence of visual impairments

Observation	**Parents observe:** The child may not have any eye turn or may not respond to visual stimuli as expected.
	Physicians observe: The newborn or infant may have an identifiable visual disorder.
	Teacher observes: The student squints or seems to be bothered by light, the student's eyes water or are red, the student holds books too close, or the student bumps into objects.
Screening	**Assessment measures:**
	Ophthalmological: Medical procedures indicate the presence of a visual disorder or reduced visual functioning that cannot be improved to typical levels through surgery or medical intervention.
	Functional vision evaluation: A visual disorder interferes with the student's ability to incidentally learn from the environment and the student's use of vision for performance of tasks.
	Low vision specialist: A specialist evaluation indicates that visual functioning cannot be improved to typical levels through the use of lenses.
	Vision screening in schools: For students with low vision who have not been identified before entering school, screening indicates the need for further evaluation.
Prereferral	Prereferral typically is not used with these students because the severity of the disability indicates a need for special education or related services.
Referral	Students with visual impairments should be referred by medical personnel or parents for early intervention during the infancy/preschool years. Many states have child-find organizations to make sure these students receive services. Children are referred for protection in evaluation procedures upon entering school. Teachers should refer any students with possible vision impairments for immediate evaluation.
Nondiscriminatory evaluation procedures and standards	**Assessment measures:**
	Individualized intelligence test: Standardization may need to be violated because the student's visual impairment interferes with the ability to perform some tasks. Therefore, results may not be an accurate reflection of ability. Students may be average, above average, or below average in intelligence.
	Individualized achievement tests: The student may not achieve in concept development and academic areas at levels of peers. Also, standardization of these tests, unless developed for students with visual impairments, may have to be violated because of the visual impairment. Results may not accurately reflect achievement.
	Adaptive behavior scales: The student may have difficulty in self-care, household, and community skills because of vision and mobility problems.
	Orientation and mobility evaluation: The student's ability to orient to the environment and to travel to desired locations may be limited.
	Anecdotal records: The student may not participate in age-appropriate self-help, social, and recreational activities in home, community, or school.

376

	Curriculum-based assessment: The student may not possess age-appropriate knowledge or skills in areas of communication, daily living, career awareness, sensory and fine motor, social, and self-advocacy. **Direct observation–learning media assessment:** The student is unable to respond or has difficulty responding to print media without the use of magnification or alternative strategies, or the student cannot sustain reading in these texts for long periods of time.
Determination	The nondiscriminatory evaluation team determines that student has a vision impairment or blindness and needs special education and related services.

Determining how a student uses vision. Even given an accurate diagnosis and standard visual acuity measurements, it is impossible to predict exactly how a student with usable vision puts that vision to work to learn incidentally from the environment and to perform age-appropriate tasks. Educators, especially those who teach students with visual impairments, work with a student and her family to determine the effects of the disorder on the student's visual functioning when they conduct a **functional vision assessment (FVA)** (Anthony, 2000; Lueck, 2004). While the results of an examination by an eye specialist are reported in clinical terms (such as 20/120), the results of an FVA are reported in language that informs educators and others in more concrete ways. For example, an FVA report might read, "The student can see 3-inch-high printed letters at a distance of no more than 5 feet," or "The student can pick up a raisin on a white table when seen from 6 inches." Figure 15–4 shows part of an FVA designed for preschoolers.

Functional vision assessments describe how a student uses his vision in a variety of natural environments, such as under the fluorescent lights in a grocery store, on the playground in the glare of the midday sun, or in a dimly lit corridor leading to the school library. Appropriate functional vision assessments also consider the different activities that occur in these environments. For example, a student at a grocery store may be able to see the products on the shelves but not be able to read the aisle labels that hang directly below the bright lights or the value of paper money at the checkout counter. Obviously, this kind of information is extremely valuable to educators who work with the student because it helps them design relevant instructional strategies (Anthony, 2000).

Most youngsters with usable vision benefit from periodic evaluations by a low vision specialist, an optometrist, or an ophthalmologist with special training in the evaluation of people with severe visual impairment who can prescribe optical and nonoptical devices, as appropriate (Lueck, 2004; Simons & Lapolice, 2000). Ideally, an FVA should occur before an examination by a **low vision specialist** so the TVI can share information about the student's functioning. If optical aids are recommended, a follow-up FVA may be necessary to describe the student's improved functioning while using these devices.

Values: When teachers carefully evaluate a student's functional vision and then use teaching strategies that emphasize those capabilities, they build on student *strengths,* an important value of special educators.

Determining the appropriate reading medium. For students such as Haley, it is easy for teachers to determine how educational materials should be presented. Since she cannot see, braille clearly is the appropriate reading medium for her. Remember, however, that most students who are visually impaired have some usable vision; determining the appropriate learning medium for them is more complex.

Learning medium is the term used to describe the options for the format of reading and literacy materials and may include braille, print, audiotapes, and access technology. Many children who can read print do so at such slow speeds or with such inefficiency that they also benefit from using braille. Teachers determine the appropriate reading media for students by conducting a **learning media assessment (LMA)** (Koenig & Holbrook, 1993). The LMA begins with a functional vision assessment but also includes additional considerations, such as the student's approaches (tactual or visual) to new situations or environments, the nature and stability of the eye condition, visual stamina, and motivation.

Figure 15–4   Example of a functional vision assessment at the pre-kindergarten level

Distant Vision

- Mimics teacher's facial expressions at _____ feet.
- Locates the drinking fountain at _____ feet.
- Recognizes own name, shapes, numbers at _____ feet.
- Identifies classmates at _____ feet.
- Locates personal possessions (lunchbox, jacket, backpack) in closet at _____ feet.
- Locates own cubby at _____ feet.
- Locates _____ of four dropped coins on a _____ (color) floor: quarter at _____ feet; nickel at _____ feet; dime at _____ feet; penny at _____ feet.
- Tracks and locates a _____ (size) moving ball at _____ feet.
- Avoids obstacles when moving round P.E. apparatus. Yes _____ No _____.
- Visually detects and smoothly navigates contour changes in surfaces such as ramps and steps. Yes _____ No _____ .

Near Vision

- Completes _____ (number of pieces) puzzle with head _____ inches from the board (describe how student performs task: e.g., trial and error, quickly, visually, tactually, etc.).
- Places pegs in pegboard at _____ inches from head _____ inches from pegs (describe how student performs task).

Source: From *Functional Visual Evaluation,* by the Los Angeles Unified School District, 1990. Copyright 1990 by the Los Angeles Unified School District. Adapted with permission.

Do you remember the special factors IDEA requires members of IEP teams to consider, which you learned about in Chapters 1 and 2? IDEA requires that members of the team consider the use of braille or other appropriate reading and writing media for a student who is blind or visually impaired. Like an FVA, the LMA needs to be repeated at regular intervals to determine whether circumstances or the student's skills have changed and whether additional instruction in a different reading medium is necessary. Students who use both braille and print have the advantage of being able to choose the reading medium that works best for them under different conditions, such as when they are in a dimly lit restaurant or when reading assignments are long and eye fatigue is a problem.

Determining the Nature of Specially Designed Instruction and Services

The provision of special education and related services must be based on a student's specific needs as identified through a comprehensive assessment of the student's current level of functioning and knowledge in both the general education curriculum and what has been identified as the **expanded core curriculum** (Hatlen, 1996). The expanded core curriculum includes the following areas: compensatory and communication skills, social and interaction skills, **orientation and mobility (O&M)** skills, independent living skills, recreation and leisure skills, use of assistive technology, visual efficiency skills, and career/vocational skills (Hatlen, 1996). Figure 15–5 describes the skills educators will evaluate in a complete assessment.

Assessment is best accomplished by a team of individuals with experience working with students with visual disabilities. In addition to those people who, under IDEA, must be members of the team, the team also should consist of an O&M specialist and a certified teacher of the visually impaired (TVI). The outcome of a comprehensive assessment should be a description of the

Figure 15–5 Expanded core curriculum

Concept Development and Academic Skills

- Development of concepts
- Determination of learning mode
- Academic support
- Listening skills
- Organization and study skills
- Reading charts, maps, graphs
- Use of reference materials

Social/Emotional Skills

- Knowledge of self
- Knowledge of human sexuality
- Knowledge of visual impairment
- Knowledge of others
- Development of interaction skills
- Development of social skills
- Lifelong recreation and leisure skills
- Self-advocacy skills

Orientation and Mobility Skills

- Development of body image
- Development of concrete environmental concepts
- Development of spatial concepts
- Development of directional concepts
- Understanding traffic and traffic control
- Trailing techniques
- Sighted guide techniques
- Use of vision for travel and orientation
- Development of orientation skills
- Use of long cane
- Independent travel in a variety of environments
- Public interaction skills

Communication Skills

- Handwriting
- Development of legal signature
- Use of braille writer
- Use of slate and stylus
- Use of word processors
- Use of adaptive equipment
- Note-taking skills

Sensory/Motor Skills

- Development of maximum use of vision
- Development of gross-motor skills
- Development of fine-motor skills
- Development of auditory skills
- Development of strength, stamina, and endurance in legs, arms, and hands
- Identification of textures tactually and under foot

Daily Living Skills

- Personal hygiene
- Eating
- Dressing
- Clothing care
- Food preparation
- Housekeeping
- Basic home repair
- Money identification and management
- Use of telephone and information
- Use of desk tools
- Time and calendar
- Shopping skills
- Restaurant skills
- Community skills
- Knowledge and use of community services

Career and Vocational Skills

- Knowledge of relationship between work and play
- Understanding of value of work
- Knowledge of characteristics of valued workers
- Awareness of the variety of jobs people hold
- Awareness of jobs people with visual impairments often hold
- Awareness of jobs teenagers hold
- Job acquisition skills (want ads, résumés, applications, interviews)
- Typical job adaptations made by workers with visual impairments
- In-depth knowledge of a variety of jobs of interest
- Work experience
- Laws related to employment
- Management of readers, drivers

student's current level of functioning in all areas of the general and expanded core curriculum and the identification of skills to be addressed for that child to function optimally in current and future home, school, and community environments (Barclay, 2003; Lewis & Russo, 1997; Pugh & Erin, 1999).

Few teachers would consider it important to evaluate a straight-A high school student's ability to order a meal at a fast-food restaurant or to launder clothes, yet a student with a visual impairment who achieves at grade level may not function appropriately outside of the classroom. Many students with visual impairments lack these outside-school skills. Informal assessment techniques, including family and student interviews, the use of checklists, observation in natural environments, and authentic and performance assessments, are the most valuable methods for determining the level of functioning of students with visual impairments in the expanded core curriculum.

When assessing a student's needs, educators should evaluate the age-appropriateness of a task from two perspectives. First, what are the student's peers doing? If Haley's friends are at the stage of social development where participating in groups, such as Brownies, is common, an assessment of Haley's social skills should investigate this aspect of her functioning. Second, because sighted students are incidentally learning to perform some skills long before it is age-appropriate to expect mastery of these tasks, educators should evaluate a student's involvement in these tasks earlier than they might for sighted students. For example, while many students are not expected to launder their clothes independently until their late teens, an educator assessing Haley would want to assess her participation in this task's component parts, such as scooping soap, sorting clothes by color, or folding freshly laundered towels and socks, since these skills are within the range of her capability now and are being learned visually by her peers.

Teachers also should avoid making assumptions about a student's previously learned information. For example, an 18-year-old woman with low vision, when tested to determine her knowledge of contraceptive devices, might reveal that she is unaware that men's sexual organs differ from her own. It would be unfortunate if she did not learn this fact until after the class had been discussing contraception for several days. Unaware of the role of incidental learning in understanding gender differences, the teacher had assumed that all of her students, including her blind student, had acquired this knowledge.

DESIGNING AN APPROPRIATE INDIVIDUALIZED EDUCATION PROGRAM

Partnering for Special Education and Related Services

Nearly 69 percent of students with visual impairments spend most of their school day in the general education classroom, and students who are blind or who have low vision often learn differently from most students. In order to include these students successfully in the general curriculum, close partnerships must be nurtured among the general educator, the TVI, the O&M specialist, the student's parents or guardians, and other professionals involved in the student's education.

In particular, these individuals must collaborate when designing the IEP to make some important decisions about the following:

- Provision of instruction to support the child's success in the general education curriculum
- Nonacademic priorities on which the special educators will focus
- Location of special education and related services
- Ways in which partners will communicate to meet the student's needs

Providing specialized instruction. Because of the complex or highly visual nature of some academic areas, such as mathematics, students with visual impairments may need specialized instruction to master the curriculum. In addition, many students need specialized instruction to master skills related to writing braille with a **slate and stylus;** use of the **abacus** for calculating; and development of listening, study, and organizational skills. For these purposes, special and general educators must collaborate to provide appropriate learning experiences. As you read about how students who are blind learn braille, think about the level of interaction that must occur between the general and special educator.

Reading instruction. Students who do not learn efficiently through their visual sense may access the academic curriculum through **braille,** a tactile method of reading. Like the print alphabet,

Figure 15–6 English braille symbols, including contractions

| | 1 | 2 | 3 | 4 | 5 | 6 | 7 | 8 | 9 | 0 |
| | a | b | c | d | e | f | g | h | i | j |

| | k | l | m | n | o | p | q | r | s | t |

| | u | v | w | x | y | z |

about	ab	bb		can		day	
above	abv	be		cannot		dd	
according	ac	because	bec	cc		deceive	dcv
across	acr	before	bef			deceiving	dcvg
after	af	behind	beh	ch		declare	dcl
afternoon	afn	below	bel	character		declaring	dclg
afterward	afw	beneath	ben	child		dis	
again	ag	beside	bes	children	chn	do	
against	agst	between	bet				
ally		beyond	bey	com		ea	
almost	alm	ble		con		ed	
already	alr	blind	bl	conceive	concv	either	ei
		braille	brl	conceiving	concvg		

Source: Courtesy of Victor H. Hemphill.

braille is a code, a way of presenting spoken language in written form. As Figure 15–6 shows, there is one braille symbol for each of the 26 letters of the English alphabet. The early publishers of braille developed numerous shortcuts for writing common words or letter combinations. These shortcuts are called **braille contractions.** Because of the contractions, there is not a one-to-one correspondence between print and braille. In Figure 15–7, you can compare a print passage with its braille translation.

The number of braille contractions in this passage requires the braille reader to learn more difficult material much earlier than sighted students do, sometimes even before all the print letters of the alphabet have been introduced to sighted students. Many new readers who are blind learn to read using *Patterns* (Caton, Pester, & Bradley, 1980), a special reading series that introduces the braille symbols in a logical manner. The TVIs of other students who are blind collaborate closely with the general educator to introduce the braille contractions, regardless of difficulty, in a way that allows the student to participate fully in the reading instruction offered in the classroom. The introduction of braille contractions to blind children who are included in general education reading classes is a subject of controversy today. You can learn more about this issue in Box 15–1.

To learn more about braille, go to the Web Links module in Chapter 15 of the Companion Website, *www.prenhall.com/turnbull.*

Figure 15-7 Comparison of "Old Mother Hubbard" in braille and print

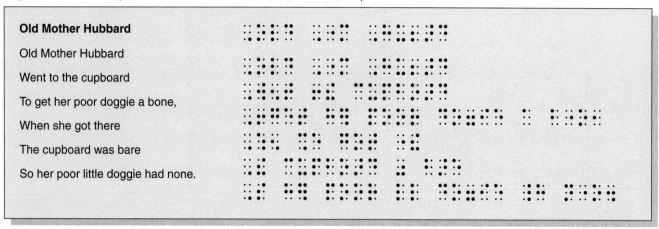

Old Mother Hubbard

Old Mother Hubbard

Went to the cupboard

To get her poor doggie a bone,

When she got there

The cupboard was bare

So her poor little doggie had none.

Your Own Voice ~ Teaching Children Who Are Blind to Read   Box 15-1

By the time that Haley finished kindergarten, she recognized most of the letters of the braille alphabet and knew their sounds. She and her parents had worked with Miss Katie so that she would be ready to learn to read in first grade.

The IEP team was faced with a difficult decision with regard to Haley's reading instruction. They could remove Haley from the general education program during reading to work on learning to read braille using *Patterns,* a familiar curriculum designed specifically for students with blindness. *Patterns* offers many advantages: it introduces the braille contractions in a carefully sequenced manner, it includes stories about children who are blind or events that are familiar to them, and it has a carefully designed teacher's manual—something that is unusual for TVIs and makes using this curriculum easy. The primary disadvantage of using *Patterns,* however, was significant: Haley wouldn't be learning to read with her peers. In addition, it would be difficult to include her in those moments during the day when her general education teacher referred to a new word or story that had been the focus of the reading lesson.

Another factor influencing this decision was how Miss Katie should introduce the braille contractions to Haley if she were taught to read with the general education class. Although Haley recognized the 26 alphabet letters, she did not know the other 143 symbols used in literary braille. These symbols very likely would show up in the reading series used by Haley's teacher. And they wouldn't show up in any organized or systematic way. Easy contractions wouldn't necessarily come first, and a contraction might be used in one word and then not be seen again for several weeks.

TVIs such as Miss Katie are trying to discover new approaches for supporting the reading instruction that occurs in general education classes. In the past, they usually pulled a student like Haley out of the class for specialized instruction in reading in grades 1 through 3 and always introduced reading words using their contracted form. Today, TVIs are experimenting with introducing early reading words in braille in their uncontracted form. Using this approach, when the general education teacher tells students to find the "a" in the word "sand," the braille reader can actually find an "a," not the "and" contraction. Teaching uncontracted braille facilitates inclusion, as there is a one-to-one correspondence between the print and the braille. Little research, however, exists to support this approach as best for teaching blind children to read.

One problem with adopting this approach is that most textbooks and materials in braille are written in the contracted form. Children who are blind must learn contracted braille in order to access their math, social studies, and science books. In addition, statewide accountability measures are usually available in contracted braille. At some point, the child who reads uncontracted braille must begin to learn the contractions and the 450 rules for using them.

Use the resources listed below to help Miss Katie determine how she should begin to introduce the contractions to Haley. Or do you think it would be best to have Haley learn to read using *Patterns?*

- Herzberg, T. S., Stough, L. M., & Clark, C. M. (2004). Teaching and assessing the appropriateness of uncontracted braille. *Journal of Visual Impairment and Blindness, 98*(12), 773–777.

- Swenson, A. M. (1991). A process approach to teaching braille writing at the primary level. *Journal of Visual Impairment and Blindness, 85*(5), 217–221.

- Caton, H. (1979). A primary reading program for beginning braille readers. *Journal of Visual Impairment and Blindness, 73*(8), 309–313.

You can imagine that the situation becomes even more complex for students who are second language learners. No curriculum exists for teaching literacy skills to students whose first language is not English (Milian, 2000). Teachers of students with visual impairments, teachers of English as a second language, and general education teachers must collaborate to create appropriate materials that enhance acquisition of language, reading, and braille skills. Box 15–2 shows some strategies for teaching braille to these students.

Diversity Tips ~ Strategies for Teaching Braille to ESL Students

Box 15–2

General Strategies

- Collaborate with the ESL teacher, the O&M specialist, and others involved with the student's education to coordinate teachers' activities and address the student's language and visual needs.
- Sequence language activities and structure lessons based on the school district's ESL curriculum.
- Use real objects instead of visual examples.
- Use thematic instruction whenever possible.

Strategies for the Early-Production Stage of Developing English

- Bring real objects that belong to the same category, such as fruits, to school. Make braille cards with words matching the objects. Assist the student in creating first verbal and then written sentences using adjectives describing the objects (e.g., "The orange is bumpy.").
- Create braille cards on which are written the names of classroom objects, such as *door, desk, book*. Read each noun, give the card to the student, and ask the student to place the card on the correct classroom item.
- Read aloud simple stories, poems, or rhymes that contain repeated phrases. Provide the student with a braille copy of material presented orally and ask her to move her fingers, held in the correct reading position, over phrases.

Strategies for the Emergence-of-Speech Stage of Developing English

- Ask the student to participate in an activity and then assist him in writing about the activity on the brailler.
- Give the student an audiotape and a braille version of an age-appropriate story. Encourage the student to read the braille while listening to the story. Also, have the student write sentences or phrases about the story on the brailler.
- Have the student participate in an activity of daily living or an O&M activity, audiotape the sequence of activities, and then write keywords related to it on the brailler.

Strategies for the Intermediate Fluency Level

- Have the student create a book about an experience and share it with classmates.
- Have the student keep a braille list of vocabulary words and a journal related to each of the content areas.
- Create meaningful activities that require the student to speak, listen, read, write, and interact with others.

For more information about teaching braille to second language learners, refer to Milian, M. (1997). Teaching braille reading and writing to students who speak English as a second language. In D. P. Wormsley & F. M. D'Andrea (Eds.), *Instructional strategies for braille literacy* (pp. 189–230). New York: AFB Press.

Even before reading instruction begins, many students with visual impairments may not have had the same kind of exposure to literacy events as their sighted peers have. Think of all of the opportunities that Haley's 3-year-old peers with typical vision had to see letters, long before they were expected to read. Letters are everywhere: they appear on cereal boxes, on toys, on the newspaper and envelopes delivered daily to the house, on billboards, on street signs, on television, and in books. Even if these children were not learning the letter names, they saw them and incidentally compared their outlines and shapes, setting the stage for future learning.

Collaborating teachers need to make certain that young students who have low vision have opportunities to be exposed to letters and words that can be seen clearly. For preschoolers who are blind, two essential components of an early literacy program include systematically introducing braille and flooding the environment with incidental opportunities to find braille, such as on labels, notes, books, schedules, and lunch menus.

Determining nonacademic priorities. As you reviewed Figure 15–5, you may have felt a bit overwhelmed at the list of areas in which a student with visual impairment may need specialized instruction. Once a child's performance in these areas is assessed and any needs for instruction identified, it becomes the task of the IEP team to prioritize those needs for instruction. Often, not all of the skills of the expanded core curriculum can be addressed every year. Nonetheless, it is critical that needed skills in these areas not be ignored in favor of the academic skills that are the focus of statewide achievement and accountability testing since all are skills needed for success in adult life. Ideally, the IEP team will identify some skills in each expanded core curriculum area for intensive instruction each year. The TVI must carefully monitor a student's acquisition and use of these skills so that by the time the student is ready to transition from school to adult life, the student has the skills necessary for success.

Into Practice ~ Strategies for Supporting Mathematics Instruction for Students with Visual Impairments

Box 15–3

Students preparing to be teachers of children with visual impairments are often reminded that they are not supposed to be academic tutors. The example that is usually shared is that it is the job of the math teacher to teach math; the TVI only supports the math teacher's efforts. These roles, however, easily become clouded in practice since so much of mathematics is visual in nature. It is difficult to know if one is teaching a math concept or trying to overcome a basic lack of information related to the visual impairment.

The responsibilities of the TVI in math instruction include the following:

- Teaching students specialized computation methods
- Teaching students who are blind the Nemeth code of braille mathematics
- Teaching students to use tactile charts, diagrams, and graphs
- Consulting with general education teachers on appropriate modifications for teaching mathematics to students with visual impairments
- Modifying materials used in mathematics instruction

Practices that support the general educator who is teaching mathematics to a class in which a student with visual impairments is enrolled include the following:

- Have the TVI preteach concepts or techniques before they are introduced in the general education class.
- Have the TVI present during math instruction to assist with the student's understanding of the concepts.

- Encourage the mathematics teacher to speak about mathematics consistently and unambiguously so that all students can understand.
- Have the math teacher verbalize whatever is written on the blackboard or overhead projector transparencies.
- Have the math teacher provide advance copies of transparencies and notes from the chalkboard to the TVI so that the student has access to them at the same time as peers.
- Teach the student to be a self-advocate and to speak up when concepts or strategies are not understood.
- Use manipulatives, real objects, and appropriate three-dimensional models as much as possible for activities.
- Provide opportunities to apply basic concepts and operations in real-life situations.
- Illustrate problems for students in a way that allows them to experience the principles that are being taught.

Putting These Strategies to Work for Progress in the General Curriculum

1. As a classroom teacher, what are the advantages of your attendance at the IEP conference for a student with visual impairments who will need accommodations in math?

2. Use information from this box to design a math lesson for a student who is blind.

3. How could you incorporate peer tutoring in the instruction of students with visual impairments in academic subjects?

To answer these questions online, go to the Into Practice module in Chapter 15 of the Companion Website, www.prenhall.com/turnbull.

Determining the location of special education and related services. Once decisions have been made about what is going to be taught, the IEP team must collaborate to determine where that instruction should take place. Sometimes it is more appropriate to provide initial instruction privately and then practice emerging skills within the general education classroom. To meet other needs, such as the acquisition of skills related to human sexuality, cooking, or shopping, instruction in specialized environments will be essential.

Communicating to meet students' needs. For students who rely on adapted materials, especially in braille, and who need increased opportunities for meaningful, hands-on activities, the level of communication necessary among all collaborators is extensive. General educators need to feel confident that the lessons that they prepare will be accessible to their students with visual impairments. Since these adaptations, especially of math, science, and social studies materials, require significant time to create, the TVI must receive the materials well in advance of the date of their intended use.

Close communication to meet students' needs is also necessary when determining modifications to assigned work, if any. Haley requires at least twice as much time as her peers do to complete a typical math assignment, in part because the braille math code is unfamiliar to her. Her teachers discussed the possibility of reducing the length of her assignments, but it was also obvious that, because of her lack of experience with numbers, she needs additional opportunities in order to achieve at the level of her classmates. The IEP team had to deal with her competing needs for more time to complete the assigned work and more experiences to understand it thoroughly. They ultimately decided that her need for practice of these basic mathematical skills was critical to her long-term academic success, and her IEP team did not recommend this modification. Box 15–3 presents other strategies TVIs use to support the mathematics instruction of students with visual impairments.

Determining Supplementary Aids and Services

To participate in general education, many students who are blind or have low vision require curriculum modifications for accessing print and access to appropriate assistive technology.

Providing adapted materials. A variety of adapted materials are available for use by students with visual impairments, including braille and large-print maps, measuring devices, graph paper, writing paper, calendars, flash cards, and geometric forms. A good source of adapted materials is the American Printing House for the Blind (*http://www.aph.org/catalogs/*).

Often, it is the teacher of students with visual impairments who must adapt specific materials for assignments designed by general educators. Making these adaptations requires careful judgment by the special educator, who must determine what the essential and secondary purposes of the lesson are and what information can reasonably and meaningfully be represented in a tactile form. Adaptations can be simple, such as when a child is given real coins instead of pictures of coins to complete a math assignment. Occasionally, meaningful adaptations are impossible to create and alternative assignments that focus on the same skill must be prepared.

Students with low vision access print primarily through the use of optical devices such as glasses, telescopes, and magnifying lenses. In some instances, they may read large-print books, though some researchers suggest that this practice does not lead to faster reading rates or more comfortable reading distances (Lussenhop & Corn, 2002). One of the advantages of magnification devices is that they allow the student access not only to materials at school but also to the printed materials that are available at home, at work, and in the community.

Accessing appropriate assistive technology. As you have learned, students with visual impairments often require alternative methods to assure progress in the general education curriculum. Today, several types of devices make access to the curriculum much easier for people with visual impairment. Box 15–4 describes some of these technologies.

Technology Tips ~ Assistive Technology for Students with Visual Impairments   Box 15–4

Students with visual impairments often need to use a variety of technologies to access print materials and to create the products expected of all students engaged in the general curriculum. It helps to know the types of devices that your students might use to solve their access challenges.

- *When you have a student with low vision who needs to view a small object closely,* the student can use a handheld magnifier or a closed circuit television (CCTV), a device that comes in either a handheld or desktop model that enlarges the image to the desired size and projects it on a television screen or computer monitor. The camera on some CCTVs can be adjusted to focus on a distant object, such as a demonstration or a whiteboard, thereby bringing the information to the computer screen directly in front of the student.
- *When you have a student who needs to scan a print document that is not available electronically,* the student can use an optical character reader (OCR) or scanner. Special software can be used with an off-the-shelf scanner to increase the accuracy with which material is scanned. Some OCRs are specifically designed for people who are visually impaired and can even scan information in columns accurately.
- *When you have a student with low vision who needs to read information displayed electronically on a computer screen,* the student can use a screen enlargement and navigation system. These systems increase the size of the characters on

the screen, the cursors, and the menu and dialogue boxes. Because it is easy to get lost within the document when the characters have been enlarged too much, many screen enlargement programs also offer screen navigation systems.
- *When you have a student for whom electronic text on a computer screen is difficult to see,* the student can use a screen reader. Using synthesized speech, screen readers read the text that is displayed as the user moves the cursor (usually using keyboard strokes, not the mouse) or inputs from the keyboard. Some screen readers can read Internet websites fairly well these days.
- *When you have a student who needs to take notes in class,* the student can use a note-taking device. Several lightweight electronic note-taking devices (with either braille or qwerty keyboards) are available to efficiently take notes. The student can then download these notes to a computer for study or to be printed or embossed as braille. Most of these devices have audio output; some also create braille on an electronic display.
- *When you have a blind student who needs to create a personal braille copy of an assignment that has been created electronically,* the student can use a braille embosser, which, when connected to a computer and used in conjunction with braille translation software, will "print" a braille version of the text. Some braille embossers also print the ink-print translation on the same page.

Standard: CEC Standard 5 relates to learning environments and social interactions. When you encourage students with visual impairments to use technology to complete assignments, you are applying this standard.

Many students use these technologies in combination. For example, when she is older and is required to write a paper, Haley will probably access the library's online catalog with JAWS, which speaks the text on the monitor aloud to her. She may take notes about which books and articles to check out at the library on her braille note taker. Then, when she has the copies of the articles, she will scan them with her optical character reader, which will convert the print to an electronic form that she can either emboss in braille or read aloud using the computer's voice synthesizer. With braille translation software, Haley will be able to print her paper in braille to proofread before making the final print copy to turn in to her teacher.

These technologies create the opportunity for students with significant visual impairments to access and participate in the general education curriculum—as long as it remains print-based. There is a dark side to the technological revolution, however, particularly for students who are blind. As teachers supplement more and more of the general education curriculum with graphics-based sources, such as dramatic interactive software programs, they make it less likely that the curriculum is accessible to students who cannot see the images on the screen. Already, vast areas of the Internet, because they are graphics-based, are not accessible to students with visual impairments. Even if these materials are presented with audio descriptions, they may be meaningless to the student who is blind simply because the student has limited or no experience with the object being described.

The challenge for classroom educators is to remain flexible in their use of curricular materials that are interesting and that can be meaningfully accessed by all students, including students with visual impairments. Through universally designed instruction, teachers can make a dark future bright.

Planning for Universal Design for Learning

The principles of universal design can be particularly beneficial for students with visual impairments. As described in Chapter 2, the NIMAS project will make available electronic versions of print materials that can be easily accessed in a variety of ways by students who are blind or who have low vision. Similarly, when general and special educators partner to create learning experiences and assessments that are universally designed and use visual, auditory, and experiential activities, students with visual impairments benefit.

As valuable as the principles of universal design are, educators should be cautious about how they apply the principles to curriculum and instruction for students with visual impairments. Educators tend to underestimate these students' abilities and to provide too much support, leading to learned helplessness. In general, educators should expect these students to master the same content and meet the same performance standards as students with vision, even though the students with vision impairments may use adapted methods to access the curriculum and demonstrate these standards. In addition, because of the impact of visual impairment on students' basic knowledge of the world around them, teachers should augment the curriculum with additional areas of instruction.

Often, students with visual impairments have difficulty understanding some of the ideas that their teachers are presenting because they have not directly experienced these concepts. They may need many additional experiences to make up for their lack of incidental learning. Universally designed instruction provides for these meaningful experiences and can benefit all students.

For example, early reading books designed for sighted children rely heavily on pictures to convey the meaning of the story. In addition, the pictures reveal to young readers information about the world that they may not have directly experienced. Not all new readers have been for a walk in a forest or have gone for a ride in a rowboat, but from pictures they can discern what the words in the story convey (Koenig & Farrenkopf, 1997). General educators of students with visual impairments must provide more experiential activities in their classrooms to assure that all students understand the text.

Older students with visual impairments also benefit from instruction that incorporates real experiences. Effective teachers use a tactile/kinesthetic approach to adapt instruction in some academic subject areas. Many of the concepts related to science, social studies, mathematics, art, and other subjects are especially appropriate for a tactile/kinesthetic approach. For example, next year when Haley's science class studies germination, her teachers can arrange for students to use larger seeds so that Haley can feel them easily. Instead of having Haley plant her seed in the dirt

Inclusion Tips   Box 15–5

	What You Might See	**What You Might Be Tempted to Do**	**Alternate Response**	**Ways to Include Peers in the Process**
Behavior	She is a loner on the playground, choosing to play or walk alone.	Allow her to stay in class and read or do homework.	Teach her board or card games.	Once she has mastered the games, set up a game table during recess where anyone who wants to play can.
Social interactions	She doesn't say hello to peers in hallways or acknowledge peers' presence when entering room.	Assume she is stuck up and unfriendly.	Have the entire class prepare autobiographies, including life history, special interests, and photos or objects for her and others to study.	Teach peers to say both her name and their own in greeting, as she may not be able to recognize them from their voices alone.
Educational performance	She is completing her arithmetic assignments more slowly than her peers are.	Immediately shorten the assignment for her.	Assess to determine if she understands the arithmetical concepts. Provide concrete objects and manipulatives, if necessary, for mastery. Shorten assignment if concepts are mastered.	Have her act as a cross-age tutor to younger students who benefit from use of concrete materials in learning.
Classroom attitudes	She might seem bored or uninterested during class demonstrations or teacher-directed activities.	Assume it is too difficult or simply ignore the inattention.	Make sure that she can "see" the teacher's materials by having copies of printed/ brailled materials at her desk during the lesson.	Have her and peers help the teacher prepare a lesson by getting out materials and preparing overheads and hands-on materials for class use.

in a yogurt container, as her classmates will, Haley will plant her seed in water. Then she and her classmates will check daily for changes in how the seed feels and smells. By using this method, she can learn about root growth (which will be accessible to her classmates through pictures in her science book) and also about seed germination and the growth of the leafy part of the plant.

You can read about how teachers promote success in general education through high expectations and meaningful interaction with peers in Box 15–5.

Planning for Other Educational Needs

As you have already read, students with visual impairments may have difficulty acquiring many of the functional life and social skills that students with adequate vision learn simply by watching parents, siblings, other adults, and peers. Effective teachers recognize how a visual impairment impedes development in the skills of the expanded core curriculum.

You might ask yourself how instruction in these areas affects the student's progress in the general education curriculum. When children with visual impairments have had the same experiences as their sighted peers and when they are encouraged to be autonomous and allowed to make

Council for Exceptional Children

Standard: Instruction in the skills of the expanded core curriculum reflects an application of CEC Standard 7, Instructional Planning.

All students with visual impairments benefit from an education that focuses on such daily living skills as taking care of their own living space.

Values: Envisioning *great expectations* is the first of the values that you learned about in Chapter 1.

Go to Chapter 15 of the Companion Website, *www.prenhall.com/turnbull*, for more information on orientation and mobility. Look for the information on promoting travel in schools.

decisions for themselves, they are more interested and engaged in the content of the general curriculum and understand and appreciate it better. Mastery of these kinds of skills is critical to students' long-range educational and life outcomes. Students will need social, living, travel, and career skills to manage as competent adults and to apply the content and performance standards acquired in their general education programs. Typically, teachers need to focus on three of the areas in the curriculum of students with visual impairments: daily living skills, orientation and mobility, and self-advocacy.

Daily living skills. Students with visual impairments require ongoing instruction in important skills of daily living, such as clothing management and kitchen skills. Generally, effective teaching strategies involve repeated visual or hand-over-hand kinesthetic demonstrations (or both), systematic instruction, gradual fading of assistance and prompts, and significant periods of practice (Koenig & Holbrook, 2000).

Often, people do not think to include a child with visual impairment in simple activities of daily living. Involving the student in an activity and having high expectations that the skill can be acquired are critical factors in the acquisition of daily living skills. Because many adults think of people who are blind as helpless, they have low expectations for students with visual impairments to acquire typical skills. In addition, because adults may assume that students with low vision see more clearly than they do, the adults do not show these youngsters how to perform some of the activities that sighted children learn incidentally, such as buttoning a shirt, holding a spoon correctly, or making a bed. When these students do not spontaneously develop these skills, teachers may mistakenly think that the students also have additional cognitive disabilities and may reduce their expectations even more.

Low and inaccurate expectations of their abilities are students' worst enemies. Skilled teachers know to be constantly alert to what students are not doing for themselves. These teachers are prepared to challenge these students to promote independence and self-motivation.

Orientation and mobility. O&M skills, an IDEA-related service, are those that people with visual impairment use to know where they are in their environment and how to move around that environment safely. Unlike sighted students, students with visual impairments must learn to listen to the flow of traffic; react to changes of street and road surfaces; and use their vision, other senses, and perhaps a cane or other mobility device to detect objects in the environment and to help them know where they are.

The development of O&M skills begins in infancy and continues until the student can reach a destination safely by using a variety of techniques. Young children concentrate on developing body image, mastering spatial and positional concepts, learning the layout of their homes and schools, and developing environmental awareness. Older students focus on crossing streets safely and negotiating travel in increasingly complex situations, such as a town's business district or a shopping mall.

Some blind adults learn how to travel with a guide dog. Primarily because of the responsibility associated with the care of these service animals, individuals under the age of 18 who still attend local schools rarely learn to use a guide dog, but children can be prepared to use guide dogs by learning to care for animals as pets (Young, 1997) and by becoming proficient at orientation skills, which are necessary for efficient traveling.

Self-advocacy. In Chapter 5, you learned that self-advocacy skills were important for students with disabilities. As adults, most people with visual impairments are required to explain their abilities and special needs to other people they meet: bus drivers, prospective employers, landlords, restaurant and hotel workers, and flight attendants. Sometimes these explanations are simple, such as asking a bus driver to call out the name of every bus stop, but sometimes they require more detailed descriptions. For example, as a college student, Haley may need to ask permission of each of her teachers to tape-record lectures, request personal copies of overhead transparencies, explain that it will be necessary to say aloud what they write on the board, and describe special accommodations that she needs (e.g., a reader or additional time during testing). Very likely, she will need to convince each of her professors that she can do the work for the class. In brief, she will have to be an effective self-advocate.

Haley has already begun developing self-advocacy skills. At first, she simply listened as Miss Katie explained her needs to her teachers, but she is increasingly participating in this task, taking on the responsibility of explaining about the special tools that she uses to her general education teacher.

As an adult, Haley will very likely need to advocate for her rights with landlords and, if she gets a guide

These students work with an orientation and mobility specialist to learn how to move safely within their school neighborhood before tackling the challenge of a busy city street.

dog, for access to public buildings. Her teachers will need to help her learn the laws (especially the Americans with Disabilities Act) and the communication techniques she can use to avoid confrontations (if possible) and to assert herself (as necessary). As part of Haley's lessons in self-advocacy, Miss Katie is introducing her to successful adults who are blind.

Partnering is key. Meeting the academic, social, and functional life-skills needs of students with visual impairments frequently becomes a balancing act that demands considerable finesse and dexterity (Hatlen, 1996; Koenig & Holbrook, 2000; Pugh & Erin, 1999), prioritizing goals, and creative problem solving.

Creativity is the answer to many questions: creativity in scheduling, in instruction, in use of free time, and in collaboration among the many adults involved in each pupil's program. Critical to the success of this endeavor is that team members assume responsibility for the instruction and practice of newly learned skills whenever the natural opportunity to do so occurs. Each IEP team member also must believe that ultimate successful adult functioning depends on the student's attainment of skills in all of the curriculum areas—that no one area is more or less important than the others. It's a delicate balance.

In Box 15–6, you can read about the collaboration of general and special educators to meet the needs of a student who wanted to participate in his school's band.

Values: Teaching students to be their own advocates supports the value of enhancing *self-determination*.

Go to Chapter 15 of the Companion Website, *www.prenhall.com/turnbull*, to read a statement about the placement of students with visual impairments that was signed by all the major organizations involved in the education of these students.

USING EFFECTIVE INSTRUCTIONAL STRATEGIES

Early Childhood Students: Programming That Focuses on Real Experiences

Early intervention programs for young children with visual impairments generally are home-based, although many successful interventions, such as the BEGIN program at the Center for the Visually Impaired in Atlanta, also offer a center-based component where parents of infants go to observe preschool children with visual impairments and to meet the families of other youngsters who are blind or have low vision. The focus of early intervention is to help parents understand the effects of visual impairment on learning and to present effective methods that reduce the impact of these effects on development. These programs emphasize strategies that enhance the child's acquisition of body image, language, early self-help skills, sensorimotor skills, concepts, orientation, and early social interactions in home, school, and community environments where young children spend their time.

Partnership Tips ~ Making Beautiful Music Together   Box 15–6

Adults who are not familiar with the techniques used by individuals with visual impairments to accomplish tasks often have difficulty imagining that the students can participate at all. Often, effective problem solving to change attitudes and create practical answers requires both local and distant collaborators.

One such partnership occurred when Ja'dine, a saxophone player in his school's orchestra, mentioned to his mother that he wanted to participate in the school's marching band. His mother's first thought was that Ja'dine was asking for too much—that, because of his blindness, he was going to be disappointed. She called Eloisa Ramirez, Ja'dine's special education teacher, and asked for her advice.

Eloisa was pleased that Ja'dine was interested in becoming involved in this extracurricular activity and wanted to support him. She recognized, though, that others at the school, like Ja'dine's mother, would have doubts about the wisdom of the idea. She talked with the school principal, who, though not entirely supportive of the idea, was willing to meet with the individuals most likely to be involved in implementing the plan.

In preparation for this meeting, Eloisa and Ja'dine made two lists. The first set out the benefits he would experience as a member of the marching band. The second identified the adaptations that he might need. Before the meeting, Ja'dine practiced with Eloisa how he would present this information.

Attending the meeting were the orientation and mobility specialist, the marching band director, the principal, Eloisa, and, of course, Ja'dine and his mother. Ja'dine persuasively presented his case for being involved in the marching band. Having decided that he was committed to the work that would be required to make his idea a reality, the group then began examining how it might be accomplished.

They identified two issues that had to be resolved. First, the principal was concerned that the district would use insurance liability as an excuse to prevent Ja'dine from marching. Eloisa offered to contact a state advocacy group of blind adults to get information that he could use to counter any arguments that the school district's insurance expert presented. This group even sent a representative to meet with district representatives.

The marching band director, who was uncertain how Ja'dine would be able stay in step, voiced the second concern. The O&M instructor suggested that there might be several ways in which Ja'dine could stay in formation with the rest of the band members. One strategy might be to use rigid poles to connect Ja'dine to the band members in front of and behind him. The band director wasn't too keen on this idea but agreed to allow the O&M specialist to attend band practice to work with him to identify other solutions.

During the summer, as the O&M specialist and the band director worked with Ja'dine and the other band members who were learning formations, other partners became involved. Eloisa had to contract with a faraway braillist who knew the braille music code and could emboss the needed braille sheet music. Ja'dine's peers in the band also became involved when his mother's work shift changed to early evenings and she was unable to get him to and from practice. Other band members had learned a lot about Ja'dine and his sense of humor as they practiced; they wanted to be with him and were willing to offer him rides.

At the first game of the season, Ja'dine proudly marched with his fellow band members. Watching from the stands were the team members who had helped to make this night possible. Farther away, but also smiling, were the advocate and the braillist. Indeed, success for students with visual impairments involves both distant and local collaboration.

Several steps led to this successful collaboration:

- Adults responded to a desired goal expressed by the student.
- The student's TVI arranged a meeting with the partners who might be involved in making the student's desired goal possible.
- The TVI and the student brainstormed potential benefits and obstacles to achieving the goal, which the student presented to the potential partners.
- Possible strategies for overcoming identified obstacles were discussed and assigned to specific partners for further investigation.
- The group worked as a team to resolve new issues that arose; new partners were added as necessary to achieve the goal.

Putting These Tips to Work for Progress in the General Curriculum

1. Take what you learned from this example and apply it to the extracurricular activity of track and field. List four accommodations that might be made so that a blind student could participate in track and field.

2. Identify four accommodations needed so that a blind student could perform in a musical.

3. Identify four accommodations needed so that a blind student could participate in a field trip to a natural history museum.

To answer these questions online, go to the Partnership Tips module in Chapter 15 of the Companion Website, www.prenhall.com/turnbull.

Preschool programs for children with visual impairments continue early intervention goals and provide many experiences that are the foundation for learning. Most of the activities are hands-on, meaningful, and related to real-life activities. Students make their own snacks, wash their dishes, and find opportunities to change their clothes often, thereby practicing needed daily living skills. They collect tangible memories of their day and include them in braille or print experience stories that they dictate to their teachers. TVIs facilitate students' movement, meaningful language, exploration, and control of the environment to reduce the impact of visual impairment on development.

Many students with visual impairments are in heterogeneously grouped preschools and in preschools for children without disabilities. With the proper supports, these programs can be valuable learning environments for some children. It is easy to forget, however, that sighted children are acquiring many of the benefits of these programs through incidental learning, which is often unavailable to those with visual impairments. Although students with visual impairments participate, there is a potential that they will fall behind others in the class unless they get supplemental help.

Elementary and Middle School Students: Accommodations to Develop Basic Skills

Elementary school is a key time for sighted children to develop a positive self-image, lay a solid foundation in academic skills, and safely explore the world. For pupils with visual impairments, the focus of the educational program is the same as that for students with vision; however, the techniques for accomplishing these goals may be different, requiring TVIs to teach or reinforce concepts presented in class. In addition, and depending on the student's needs, the TVI emphasizes the development of career-awareness skills, social skills, knowledge of human sexuality, additional self-help skills, knowledge of one's visual impairment, and early advocacy skills. At the same time, the O&M specialist may be increasing the environments in which the youngster can travel safely.

TVIs spend much of their time adapting materials for students in elementary programs. As one TVI, Mary Gordon, from Lawrence, Kansas, explained, "When you can't see the chalkboard, and you can't see exactly where the rooms are, and you can't see this, and you can't see that, it takes twice as much energy to get through the day as it does for someone with sight. I provide instruction, materials, and support for students who may require many hours to master what a sighted child can learn through casual observation." TVIs who support inclusion of

A trip to the sculpture garden at the zoo provides a natural opportunity to encourage peer interactions.

their students create braille sheet music for music class, provide maps with raised continents and tactilely different countries for social studies, and encourage peer-supported learning as students handle formaldehyde-soaked specimens in science. For students to fully participate, TVIs must assure that every handout, graph, and instructional device used by the general educator is accessible to their students.

TVIs also promote inclusion. As Mary Gordon noted, "Each blind and visually impaired student should also become a real and integral part of the classroom. Since so much of our social interaction is visual, blind children must learn behaviors of sighted persons in order to obtain acceptance from their peers. To accomplish this, my students and I spend many hours practicing social skills that other students learn by observing. Learning to face the person to whom they are speaking, standing or sitting with appropriate postures, and eliminating mannerisms that might detract from their appearance are all imperative."

Secondary and Transition Students: Preparing for Adult Life

For many students with visual impairments, the middle and high school years are a time to catch up, to learn skills that students with good vision have been learning incidentally but that are not used until the teen years. TVIs generally have to spend more time with them to meet needs related to the expanded core curriculum, while at the same time students are enrolled in general education classes to meet the state's graduation requirements. Sometimes they choose to delay

Using your *Real Lives and Exceptionalities* DVD to view Kristen, located under "Beyond School" (Clip 7), how would you work with Haley so that she is able to participate in the kinds of community-based activities accessed by Kristen?

Education includes training for job skills. Economic self-sufficiency is an obtainable goal for most people with visual impairments.

their graduation in order to master all the skills they will need for a successful transition to independent adult living.

Sandy Serventi, an itinerant TVI from Tallahassee, Florida, works with her students on the transition skills they need. For example, her student Martin Vasquez could not make a sandwich or clean a sink when he entered high school. Because of his family's cultural attitude about the abilities of students labeled as blind, he had not been expected to help with general household tasks, and because of his visual impairment, he had not learned how to perform these tasks incidentally. Sandy met several times at Martin's house with his mother and gradually persuaded her that Martin needed to learn to do more for himself at home—and that his educational program needed to focus on both his academic and nonacademic needs.

Today Martin and Sandy are making a list of the utility services that he will need to contact when he moves into an apartment. Martin practices his note-taking skills as he contacts directory assistance to request the telephone numbers of the different utility companies and keys them into his electronic note taker. Later, he will retrieve the number and call to request information about having the utilities started.

On some days, Martin also works with his O&M specialist. Recently, they have been exploring apartment complexes close to the vocational school where Martin will enroll next year. He knows he must spend many long hours learning to negotiate safely the routes to use around the school's campus and to the grocery store, the mall, and other community areas he will be using.

INCLUDING STUDENTS WITH VISUAL IMPAIRMENTS

As you have already read, blindness and low vision do not affect what a student can learn as much as they affect *how* a student learns. In the 2003–2004 school year, 55 percent of students spent 80 to 100 percent of their time in the general education classroom, like Haley, with another 17 percent receiving services from 40 to 79 percent of the school day in this setting (U.S. Department of Education, 2005). Residential schools across the nation educated about 6 percent of the total number of students with visual impairments. Since 1990, the percentage of students with visual impairments receiving most of their education in the general education class has risen by 7 percent. This change may reflect the increased access to the general education curriculum that has been made possible through new technologies. Figure 15–8 illustrates patterns of educational placement.

You've met Haley, who is included in Ms. Benson's second-grade class and is expected to complete the same work that the other students are. Although she spends most of her school day with Ms. Benson, Haley occasionally is pulled from class to work with Miss Katie in the resource room or the community. Depending on the subject of instruction, however, there are times when Miss Katie will provide support to Haley in Ms. Benson's class. This flexible approach to placement benefits many students with visual impairments. There are, however, some students who are best served in the general education classroom all day and who are never pulled from that environment for special services. Still other students receive educational benefit through placement at a school for the blind or in a special class.

The nature of visual impairment and how youngsters with visual impairments learn about the world mitigate against successful inclusion in all cases. Inclusion is thought to be most successful when both the academic needs and the needs identified in the expanded core curriculum are adequately addressed. For students with visual impairments, inclusion in society is best thought of as the goal of special education; it is not always the means to that goal.

Values: Meeting students' needs through individualized programming and placement decisions is one way to ensure that students with visual impairments are given the opportunities to develop the skills that lead to *full citizenship*.

Figure 15-8 Educational placement of students with visual impairments (2003–2004)

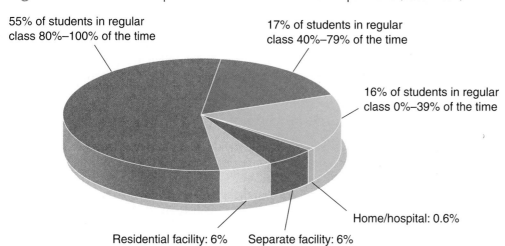

55% of students in regular class 80%–100% of the time

17% of students in regular class 40%–79% of the time

16% of students in regular class 0%–39% of the time

Home/hospital: 0.6%

Residential facility: 6%   Separate facility: 6%

Source: U.S. Department of Education, Office of Special Education Programs. (2005). *IDEA data website* (http://www.ideadata.org/aboutThisSite.asp).

ASSESSING STUDENTS' PROGRESS

Measuring Students' Progress

As is true for all other children, it is important to measure students' progress in school in order to make well-informed decisions about programming. The progress of students with visual impairments is measured in both the general and the expanded core curriculum.

Progress in the general curriculum. Since most students with visual impairments are provided with educational services in the general education classroom, their progress is measured at the same time as their peers. They take the same math, social studies, language arts, and science tests as the other students in their class. Sometimes, of course, it is necessary to transcribe print materials into braille or for the student to use a magnifier when reading the test, but these accommodations are not designed to modify the purpose or difficulty of the test in any way. When students prepare their answers in braille, their specialist teacher interlines their work for the general educator—that is, she writes in print exactly what is written in braille above the braille. After the general educator has graded the interlined work, the TVI prepares the general educator's comments in braille for the student.

You may remember that there are some braille symbols that represent more than one print letter. Because of this situation, when students who are blind take spelling tests in braille, they must spell the words both with and without the braille contractions because knowing both formats is important for their success in school and future environments.

It is not uncommon for students with visual impairments to take their tests in a separate classroom. Sometimes they must leave the general education classroom to use the specialized technology equipment that is stored in another area; sometimes additional space is necessary to spread out their materials. Usually, though, these students require extra time to complete tests because of the slow reading rates often associated with having a visual impairment.

Progress in addressing other educational needs. Teachers of students with visual impairments are responsible for measuring students' progress in the expanded core curriculum. Generally, students' skill levels are determined through the use of informal measures, such as teacher observation, evaluation of needed prompt levels, and curriculum-based tests prepared by the TVI. For example, after Haley completes a unit of study on her eye condition, Miss Katie may prepare a test to determine Haley's level of retention and understanding of the information taught. To measure Haley's progress in learning to make a grilled cheese sandwich, however, Miss Katie may use a checklist of the steps needed to complete this task and note on the list the level of prompting (indirect verbal, specific verbal, physical, or guided) that Haley required. In keyboarding, a computer-based test may be available to measure Haley's speed and accuracy.

As with initial assessments to determine a child's level of functioning for the IEP, teachers of students with visual impairments must have knowledge of the kinds of skill development that is influenced by the presence of a visual impairment and the limitations in incidental learning that are related to it. They must devise progress measurements that measure changes in a variety of skill areas.

Making Accommodations for Assessment

Comprehensive assessments frequently include standardized and norm-referenced tests, which are often timed. An issue to consider about some tests is the additional time needed by students that is directly related to their visual impairment. Taking tests often requires complex use of vision, such as frequent eye movements between the test booklet and the answer sheet or scanning of multiple-choice answers and stimulus paragraphs. Similarly, readers who use braille, who tend to have reading rates significantly below their peers with sight and whose system of reading is not conducive to efficient scanning, have difficulty with tests (Bradley-Johnson, 1994). The amount of time needed should be determined individually (Allman, 2004).

Other accommodations used frequently by students with visual impairments when participating in formal assessments include a reader (for the nonreading sections of the test), a scribe, or a computer; placement in a quiet testing area; and frequent breaks. Of course, these accommodations must be listed on the IEP and be the types of accommodations typically used by the student to complete assignments.

Looking to Haley's Future

It is the year 2025. Miss Katie enters the church where Sissa, a former peer tutor to her students at the high school, is to be wed in an hour. Miss Katie looks around the unfamiliar church when her eyes focus on the bridesmaids, chattering excitedly near their chairs in the front. She immediately recognizes several of the young women; she stops as she sees Haley, beautiful in the dress that Sissa has chosen, giggling with the others. Miss Katie approaches Haley, whom she hasn't seen since Haley left for college, and they embrace with great fondness. They sit to catch up when Miss Katie spies a braille book under Haley's chair, next to her folded cane. They laugh together as Miss Katie recalls aloud that Haley couldn't go anywhere without a book to read, "just in case" it got too quiet. Some things never change.

The vision for Haley's future is bright today because her parents and teachers have focused on that bright vision since she was an infant. They have looked far enough into the future to see what skills she would need as an adult and have designed flexible educational programs to develop those skills. Recognizing that her blindness could prevent Haley from easily discovering much about the world, they have provided her with the tools to be successful and encouraged her to take the risks necessary to know herself, others, and the world around her.

SUMMARY

Identifying students with visual impairments

- Legal blindness is a measurement that is used primarily to entitle people for government- or private-assistance programs.

- Within education, visual impairment, including blindness, is defined as an impairment in vision that adversely affects a student's educational performance.

- Students with visual impairments have a limited ability to learn incidentally from the environment and must be directly exposed to or taught much of what they need to know.

Evaluating students with visual impairments

- Ophthalmologists determine the presence of a visual disorder, and optometrists and low vision specialists determine if a visual disorder can be corrected through lenses or optical devices.

- A functional low vision evaluation determines how the student uses his or her vision in a variety of situations and places.

- A learning media assessment assists TVIs to determine the most efficient mode of reading and learning such as braille, magnification, or large print.

- Educators determine the effects of the visual impairment on the student's development of skills in the expanded core curriculum, including compensatory skills, orientation and mobility, career education, independent living, technology, self-determination, recreation and leisure, visual efficiency, and social skills. They use observations, parent and student interviews, and other informal testing procedures.

Including students with visual disabilities

- Most students with visual impairments who do not have other disabilities are educated for most of the school day in general education classrooms.

- Special education services are provided by a TVI who is assigned to that school either on a part-time or full-time basis.

Designing an appropriate individualized education program

- Students learn through meaningful involvement in activities from beginning to end. Often they take a hands-on approach that maximizes the use of all senses. Through practice, they have increased opportunities to develop new skills.

- Educators meet the academic needs of students through the principles of universally designed instruction.

- TVIs meet the functional and life-skill needs of students to facilitate their eventual integration and full participation in adult society.

- Instruction must focus on the skills acquired incidentally by sighted students and those skills that are specific to students who have visual impairments.

Using effective instructional strategies

- In the early childhood years, TVIs emphasize teaching parents of young children with visual impairments to think like someone who can't see and teaching children to learn hands-on, real-life skills, such as changing clothes and making snacks.

- In the elementary years, the emphasis is on teaching through tactile methods (braille, raised maps, handling specimens), practicing social skills that facilitate inclusion, and developing orientation and mobility and self-advocacy skills.

- In the secondary and transition years, the focus is on transition from school to adulthood; from living at home with parents to living on one's own; on orientation and mobility training in the community; on choosing lifestyles, places of residence, and leisure-time activities; and on refining skills so that these choices can become realities.

Assessing students' progress

- Progress in the general curriculum is measured through materials selected by the general education teacher that are adapted appropriately by the TVI.

- Progress in the expanded core curriculum is measured by the TVI and O&M specialist using informal assessment techniques, including interviews, teacher-made tests, and rubrics.

■ Options for the use of accommodations on statewide tests are determined by the IEP team and often include different presentation (braille or print), additional time, a quiet setting, and use of a reader or scribe.

What Would You Recommend?

Refer to chapter content and the PRAXIS™ and CEC standards in Appendix A to answer the following questions:

1. Visit the Companion Website, *www.prenhall.com/turnbull*, to locate links to help you learn more about how impaired vision might look. After viewing this information, discuss what kind of support you would expect the TVI to provide you and your student in reading. Identify the CEC standards that would apply in this situation.

2. How might partnering with the O&M specialist facilitate the development of skills in this area by a student who is blind who is enrolled in your class? Identify the CEC standards that would apply in this situation.

3. How might you assist other students in your class to understand the learning style of their blind peer? Identify the CEC standards that would apply in this situation.

4. Locate the braille alphabet at the back of the book. Find the letters that spell your name. How does your awareness of this assistive device impact how you would plan curriculum for a student with low vision who uses braille? Which PRAXIS™ or CEC standards would apply to your response?

Who is Briana Hoskins?

"Where are you taking me?" That is the question Forrester (played by Sean Connery) asked his gifted teenage neighbor Jamal (played by Rob Brown) in the 1996 movie *Finding Forrester* (Sony Pictures, 2000). The movie depicts an unlikely friendship between a gifted 16-year-old African American student living in the Bronx (a borough of New York City) and a reclusive Pulitzer Prize–winning author, William Forrester. As the movie develops, Forrester teaches Jamal to make the most of one of his gifts: his writing.

There is a single simple reason why Tyrone Hoskins encouraged his daughter Briana to watch this movie. It is because Jamal and Briana share several traits. Both excel in their academic and athletic pursuits, and both usually hide their gifts from their peers.

Briana's mother, Deborah, first noticed there was something unusual about her daughter when Briana was 3 years old. At that time, Briana's older sister Candice often baby-sat Briana. One day, Candice was reciting "And Still I Rise," a poem by Maya Angelou, while Briana sat quietly listening. Later that day, Briana surprised her family by reciting the entire poem from memory.

Deborah soon realized that Briana was able to read by herself many of the books that they read together at bedtime. By age 4, Briana was pronouncing challenging words.

Briana's kindergarten teacher was the first professional to talk with Deborah about Briana's development and how advanced she was for her age. By first grade, Briana was being pulled out of her general education class 1 to 2 days a week to receive enrichment opportunities. Evaluations authenticated what Briana's family and teachers had been witnessing: Briana had an IQ of 154.

The results required Deborah to make some difficult choices. The pullout support was helping Briana, but the other 3 days a week were boring and frustrated her. Briana had exceptional abilities, but unfortunately the staff at her school were not fully prepared to meet her academic needs at such an early age.

They certainly would have allowed Briana to remain in her current setting. They recommended, however, that she and Deborah consider a more challenging environment. The closest and probably most appropriate school program for Briana meant an hour, round trip, in the car each day. Nevertheless, Deborah chose to enroll her daughter in this school because it offered an enrichment model that would challenge Briana academically and expand her educational opportunities.

Although the move to the new school offered academic benefits, it also created social challenges. At first, Briana's friends from her neighborhood asked her why she wasn't going to their school anymore. Like Jamal in *Finding Forrester,* Briana doesn't like to be regarded as smart. "Actually, she is often quite modest, which sets her apart from the norm," Deborah explains.

Understanding Students Who Are Gifted and Talented

Not wanting to be seen as brainy, Briana began to remain inside the house more, preferring books to her old neighborhood friends. "It was a lot for a third grader to handle, being asked where she was and why she didn't go to school anymore," Deborah says.

Although Briana sometimes continues to prefer books to a social life, her social life is busy. Part of it consists of practicing and performing with her church dance and choir group. Recently, the group was invited to perform at the University of Missouri at Kansas City and to attend training under the instruction of the Alvin Ailey dance troupe from New York City. These days, dance practice and performances across the Kansas City metropolitan area keep Briana and her mother quite busy.

Briana also runs track. On most weekday afternoons, you'll find her running either for her middle school cross-country team or for her local Amateur Athletic Union track team. Briana started running during the summer after her fifth-grade year and is a "natural talent in the 400 and 200 meter," according to Deborah. "Every weekend we seem to be traveling to some city or another. She just missed qualifying for nationals last year but did qualify for regionals in the 400 meter."

For Briana, running is serious business, as is the classroom. She is competitive and takes losing seriously. When she thinks she should have won, she often cries after a race. At the same time, she really cares for her other team members. According to her mother, "In cross-country events this year Briana was known to run beside a team member offering words of encouragement."

From all accounts, Briana is a well-rounded middle school student, but her teachers often find it demanding to create learning situations that challenge her and encourage her talents. Briana often exceeds her teachers' expectations and demands; she challenges them to think beyond the borders of typical curricula and related assignments. Currently, the school district's Program for Exceptional Gifted Students is addressing many of her intellectual needs as a seventh grader. However, Deborah wonders whether transitioning to high school and the ninth grade (skipping the eighth grade) might be an appropriate plan for next year. Although Deborah and Briana's teachers are considering the social consequences, Deborah says, "Briana is tall for her age and is often mistaken for being older than she actually is. She has always been able to interact well with older children and adults." So the questions facing Briana, her family, and her teachers are the same ones that Forrester put to Jamal: "Where are you taking me? Where are you headed?"

Use your *Real Lives and Exceptionalities* DVD to "Meet Briana."

IDENTIFYING STUDENTS WHO ARE GIFTED

Defining Gifted and Talented

Currently, 29 states (57 percent) have state laws or policies requiring schools provide gifted and talented education; 19 states (37 percent) do not. In those states, the choice of whether to provide services belongs to state or local education agencies. This right of local choice distinguishes gifted education from special education for students with disabilities, for whom IDEA controls state definitions and actions (as we pointed out in Chapter 1). Surprisingly, given the emphasis on school reform and educational outcomes that we discussed in that chapter, the availability of education for gifted and talented students has not increased over the last 10 years (Purcell, 1992; Shaunessy, 2003).

Unlike the disability categories you have read about in this book, giftedness is not well or easily defined. Most states adopt the definition the federal government promulgated in 1978 (Stephens & Karnes, 2000):

> [T]he term "gifted and talented children" means children and, whenever applicable, youth, who are identified at the preschool, elementary, or secondary level as possessing demonstrated or potential abilities that give evidence of high performance capability in areas such as intellectual, creative, specific academic or leadership ability or in the performing and visual arts and who by reason thereof require services or activities not ordinarily provided by the school (P.L. 95-561, Title XIV, sec. 902)

This definition differs from earlier ones in two respects. First, it excludes psychomotor ability, making the definition more narrow; second, it adds "preschool" and "youth" in place of "children," enlarging the age range (Stephens & Karnes, 2000).

Based on 2003 data, 40 states (91 percent) define *gifted and talented* (Council of State Directors of Programs for the Gifted and National Association for Gifted Children, 2003). The percentage of states who recognize particular attributes of giftedness are as follows:

- 35 percent address intellectually gifted.
- 30 percent address academically gifted.
- 23 percent address performing visual arts.
- 22 percent address creatively gifted.
- 15 percent address leadership.

Not only do the states' definitions and categories vary, but so do the terms that state agencies use to describe these exceptional children. Most use "gifted and talented"; 13 use only "gifted"; still others use "highly capable student" and "learner of high ability" (Stephens & Karnes, 2000).

Definitions of gifted and talented are multidimensional (spanning several domains). What, for example, are Briana's areas of giftedness and talent? Is she like those students who exhibit more than one area of giftedness, or is she like those who excel in one area only?

To account for the fact that giftedness spans more than one area of human development and achievement, Gardner (1983, 1993a, 1993b, 1999) has proposed a **multidimensional model of intelligence** that is both broader yet more specific than the federal definition. He described eight specific intelligences found across cultures and societies: musical, bodily-kinesthetic, linguistic, logical-mathematical, spatial, interpersonal, intrapersonal, and naturalistic. Figure 16–1 lists the typical characteristics and distinctive features common in gifted individuals in each of these eight areas. Later in the chapter, you'll learn about how this theory can be applied to education.

It is difficult to identify how many students are gifted and talented. That is because state and local educational agencies use so many different definitions and criteria for classifying a student as gifted and talented. Most agencies apply an IQ score of 125 to 130 as baseline for identifying these students. On that measure alone, the top 2 or 3 percent of the general population is gifted (Piirto, 1998). A contrasting perspective does not rely on IQ alone but holds that the top 15 to 20 percent of students in general ability or specific performance areas are gifted so long as they also have an IQ of at least 115 (Renzulli & Reis, 2003).

Visit the Companion Website, *www.prenhall.com/turnbull,* for a link to interviews with Gardner on a variety of topics, *www.ed.psu. edu/insys/ESD/gardner/menu.html.*

Figure 16–1 Potential areas of giftedness: An adaptation of Howard Gardner's eight areas of intelligence

Area	Gifted Person	Possible Characteristics of Giftedness	Early Indicators of Giftedness
Musical	Ella Fitzgerald Itzhak Perlman Ray Charles Carlos Santana Yo Yo Ma	Unusual awareness and sensitivity to pitch, rhythm, and timbre Ability may be apparent without musical training Uses music as a way of capturing feelings	Ability to sing or play instrument at an early age Ability to match and mimic segments of song Fascination with sounds
Bodily-kinesthetic	Michael Jordan Nadia Comanici Marla Runyon Jim Abbot	Ability can be seen before formal training Remarkable control of bodily movement Unusual poise	Skilled use of body Good sense of timing
Logical-mathematical	Albert Einsten Stephen Hawking John Nash	Loves dealing with abstraction Problem solving is remarkably rapid Solutions can be formulated before articulated: Aha! Ability to skillfully handle long chains of reasoning	Doesn't need hands-on methods to understand concepts Fascinated by and capable of making patterns Ability to figure things out without paper Loves to order and reorder objects
Linguistic	Virginia Woolf Maya Angelou Helen Keller Ralph Ellison Sandra Cisneros	Remarkable ability to use words Prolific in linguistic output, even at a young age	Unusual ability in mimicking adult speech style and register Rapidity and skill of language mastery Unusual kinds of words first uttered
Spatial	Pablo Picasso Frank Lloyd Wright I.M. Pei Frida Kahlo	Ability to conjure up mental imagery and then transform it Ability to recognize instances of the same element Ability to make transformations of one element into another	Intuitive knowledge of layout Able to see many perspectives Notices fine details, makes mental maps
Interpersonal	Martin Luther King, Jr. Madeleine Albright Rosa Parks Nelson Mandela	Great capacity to notice and make distinctions among people, contrasts in moods, temperaments, motivations, and intentions Ability to read intention and desire of others in social interactions; not dependent on language	Able to pretend or play-act different roles of adults Easily senses the moods of others; often able to motivate, encourage, and help others
Intrapersonal	Sigmund Freud Plato	Extensive knowledge of the internal aspects of a person Increased access to one's own feelings and emotions Mature sense of self	Sensitivity to feeling (sometimes overly sensitive) Unusual maturity in understanding of self
Naturalist	Rachel Carson John James Audubon Cesar Chavez Jacques Cousteau	Relates to the world around him or her In tune with the environment	Recognizes and differentiates among many types of an environmental item, such as different makes of cars Recognizes many different rocks, minerals, trees

A third approach is to examine how many students receive gifted services. If a school chooses a 4.5 percent figure, then, of 350 students, about 16 students would receive services. Under the IQ approach, 7 to 9 or 10 students would be served. According to Renzulli and Reis's approach, about 70 students would be served.

There is a substantial and long-standing underrepresentation of students from racially diverse backgrounds. This disparity occurs on all traditional achievement indicators (standardized test scores, grade-point averages, and class rank) and at all grades from kindergarten through high school (Miller, 2000). The National Research Council (2002) reported that European American first and third graders were approximately three times more likely to score at the 75th percentile in reading and math as compared to African American and Latino students. Poverty undoubtedly affects the prevalence data.

> In many ways, children of poverty are behind the eight ball from the moment of conception onward. . . . Fewer of the marginalized children will develop to the full measure of their potential or acquire advanced intellectual competencies and academic skills that are clearly ahead of the norm for their age. In the ordinary course of events, they will be under-represented among academically gifted children. (Robinson, 2003, p. 257)

In part because many gifted students from ethnically-, linguistically-, and culturally-diverse backgrounds live in families that experience poverty or attend neglected inner-city schools, they may not have the opportunity to benefit from special education designed particularly for them. Box 16–1 describes how some African American students regarded their opportunities when

Partnership Tips ~ Hearing Students' Voices

Box 16–1

Here are several disturbing aspects about gifted African American students in schools that are predominantly white (as reported in recent research). First, fewer gifted black students (at all grades) were in gifted programs in the 1990s than were in them in the 1970s. Second, the academic achievement and self-esteem of African American students (at all grades) have not increased as a result of desegregation or, if they did increase, did not increase at the level of white students during the same time period. Third, it seems that gifted black students in elementary schools prefer to be in segregated schools, not integrated schools. Fourth, they want to sacrifice their opportunities for allegedly higher-quality educational opportunities (in magnet schools) because they will continue to be minority students and because they also expect to be socially segregated and educationally underchallenged.

Given these research results, imagine yourself on the board of education in the state where you went to elementary school. The state education commissioner confronts the board with the four facts just set out. The state board conducts a hearing about the research and the four facts. Experts testify. Parents protest. Students sit silently. Then you decide, "It's all about them. Let's bring them into the decision-making process." So you point to a half-dozen young black students and ask them, "Do any of you have anything you want to say? You've got to be partners with us in finding a better way to educate you."

One of them stands up and says, "They won't teach us," and he makes it clear that the "they" include some but not all of the teachers in his elementary school.

"What do you want us to do about that?" asks the commissioner. To which the student answers, "Ask us what a good teacher is and what a poor teacher is, and we'll let you know. You have no idea."

Shocked, the commissioner and your colleagues on the board sit silent. You, however, speak up.

"It's a good idea. We need to know what the students think about teachers' attitudes. We need to know whether they think their teachers are trained to be culturally competent and whether they act sensitively to their students from racially-diverse

backgrounds. We need to know how the students want their teachers to interact with them and their families. Most of all, we need to invest in gifted students, all of them, and especially those from racially-diverse backgrounds. We can't be good policymakers unless we are also good partners with the students. What do they tell us? Why should we be afraid to find out?"

"Good point," adds a person who has identified herself as a researcher. "Everyone else has a voice; everyone else is a full partner. But not the students. So in our research, we asked them. We wanted them to be our partners. So why don't you let them be your partners as you make policy that affects them?"

To learn what students from racially-diverse backgrounds (African American students) have said about effective and ineffective teachers and about how you can do your own research about effective teaching, in partnership with gifted minority students, read about these four facts and the students' voices in Harmon, D. (2001). They won't teach me: The voices of gifted African American inner-city students. *Roeper Review*, 24(2), 68–75.

Putting Partnership Tips to Work for Progress in the General Curriculum

1. What is your opinion about the appropriateness of students having input into solving significant educational problems?

2. How might you incorporate into your curriculum more instruction on leadership development to enable students to have more opportunities for partnership?

3. How would you address the situation if you wanted a student to be involved in key educational decisions but the student's parents thought that it was inappropriate for their son or daughter to have input, preferring that their child withhold opinions from educators who should be the "boss"?

To answer these question online, go to the Partnership Tips module in Chapter 16 of the Companion Website, www.prenhall.com/turnbull.

Standard: When you learn about the characteristics of students who are gifted, you are applying CEC Standard 2, Having Knowledge and Skill Related to Similarities and Differences of Individuals with and without Exceptional Learning Needs.

bused from their own neighborhoods to schools whose students were, on the whole, white; what they expected from their teachers; and how they and their teachers responded to the challenges of educating them in a school they did not want to attend.

Describing the Characteristics

It is difficult to identify the characteristics of all people who are gifted and talented. Indeed, "no one profile exists of a gifted child or a gifted education program. Gifted children are a diverse group, and we need to move beyond a 'one-size-fits-all' conception both for identification and programming" (Rizza & Gentry, 2001, p. 175). Nevertheless, those who are gifted share these traits: high general intellect; specific academic aptitude; creative, productive thinking; leadership ability; and visual and performing artistry. Paradoxically, high-ability students may have language, hearing, visual, physical, or learning disabilities, but they also may have a specific aptitude in another area, such as the visual and performing arts (Baldwin & Vialle, 1999). Thus, giftedness may co-occur with disability.

High general intellect. From its earliest conceptions, giftedness has been associated primarily with students' high general intellectual ability (Nevo, 1994). That is still the case, as you have learned, with 26 states making intellectual ability the defining trait. These students are able to grasp concepts, generalize, analyze, or synthesize new ideas or products far more easily than can other students their age (Bloom, 1956; Noble, 2004). Even as young children, they may be concerned about issues or events relating to values, ethics, or justice. Some of the differentiating characteristics of students with high general intellect include having flexible thought processes, having an extraordinary amount of information, being able to synthesize large bodies of information, and being able to use and create conceptual frameworks (Clark, 2002). Students' general intellect is expressed through their application of these characteristics to various academic subjects and life problems.

As you have learned, typically an IQ score of 125 to 130 is the baseline for identifying giftedness. Students who have an IQ range from about 130 to 144 are considered to be moderately gifted; those with an IQ range of 145 to 159 are considered to be highly gifted; and those with an IQ range over 160 are considered to be exceptionally gifted (Clark, 2002). Although IQ tests typically can record scores as high as 160, scores of 180 to 200 have been estimated by other methods. This means that the IQ of people in the gifted population ranges from 125 to 200 and that those at one end of the gifted spectrum may be very different from those at the other.

According to Gardner, "*giftedness* is a sign of precocious biopsychological potential in whichever domains exist in a culture," whereas "*prodigiousness* is an extreme form of giftedness in a domain" (1993b, p. 51). In other words, a gifted individual shows unusual promise in a specific task or domain, but a **prodigy** surpasses unusual promise to being unmistakably extraordinary (Morelock & Feldman, 1997).

Students with exceptional ability may have an unusual aptitude in specific scholastic areas such as verbal or mathematical reasoning. Some, like Briana, read at a much earlier age than an average student, and many read independently and avidly.

Many people believe that males far outnumber females in programs for gifted students. But in fact, they appear to be equally represented in those programs (Council of State Directors of Programs for the Gifted and National Association for Gifted Children, 2003). Differences, however, occur in the academic interests of gifted males and females.

- Girls tend to have more positive attitudes toward English, writing and reading, while boys have more positive attitudes toward science and computers (Swiatek & Lupkowski-Shoplik, 2000).

- Boys are twice as likely to score higher than girls on mathematics tests (Olszewski-Kubilius & Turner, 2002).

- Girls tend to have a much higher interest in language arts and foreign language, two subjects that boys identify as least interesting (Olszewski-Kubilius & Turner, 2002).

Creative, productive thinking. Educators have long regarded creativity as a defining trait of gifted and talented students (Torrance, 1964). Creativity is often associated with the visual and

Figure 16–2 Four aspects of creativity

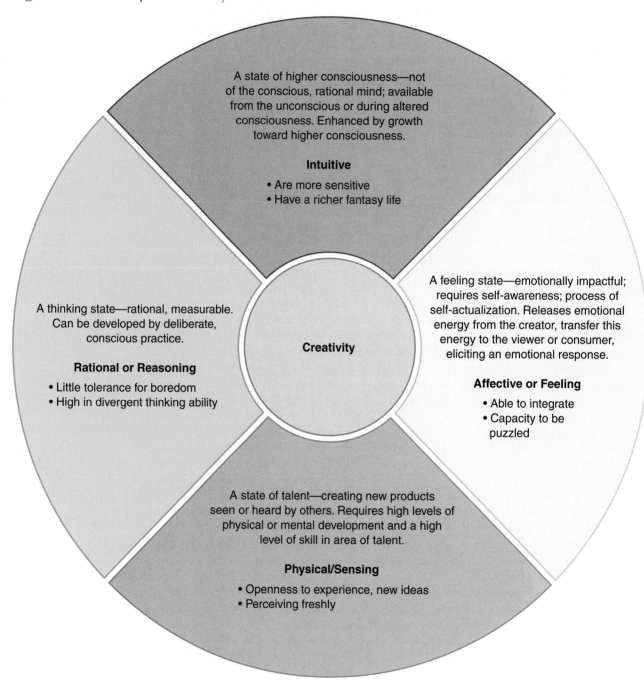

Source: Clark, B. (2000). *Growing up gifted* (6th ed.). Upper Saddle River, NJ: Merrill/Prentice Hall, p. 76.

performing arts, but students can express it in other ways, as illustrated in Figure 16–2. Researchers agree that creativity correlates with higher-order cognitive thinking, intrinsic motivation, and a sheer love of creating (Amabile, 1990; Mumford, 1998; Piirto, 1998). It is impossible to think of Einstein's creation of the theory of relativity without seeing the characteristics of his creativity: independence, risk taking, originality, and intuition surely were all part of the process (Karolyi, Ramos-Ford, & Gardner, 2003).

Leadership ability. As we have reported, 15 states include leadership in their definitions, even though "leadership" is not well conceptualized or researched (Bean & Karnes, 2001). One recent model describes leaders as those who emerge in situations in which there is not a designated leader (Guastello, 2002). Four indices of emergent leadership are being a role model for others, inspiring or motivating others when they are unsure about what action to take, affirming others' perspectives and ideas, and assigning tasks to people with corresponding strengths. One of the most important characteristics of leadership is "*wisdom in spontaneity*—the ability to assess situations quickly and step forward or backward in taking direction for the benefit of the group" (Roach et al., 1999, p. 17).

Authentic assessment procedures, in which students are asked to apply acquired knowledge to real-world tasks to assess progress, can pinpoint leadership skills (Jolly & Kettler, 2004). The behaviors most attributed to emerging leaders are (1) keeping the group focused, (2) offering compromises that are accepted by the group, (3) being listened to and respected by group members, and (4) eliciting agreement from others (Jolly & Kettler, 2004).

Another type of leadership involves taking action related to values, ethics, and/or justice. Renzulli (2002) described characteristics of people who "mobilize their interpersonal, political, ethical, and moral lives in such ways that they place human concerns in the common good above materialism, ego enhancement, and self-indulgence" (p. 35). Their characteristics are optimism, courage, avid interest in a topic or discipline, sensitivity to human concerns, physical/mental energy, and vision/sense of destiny.

Leaders and prodigies can occur in sports as well as in other areas.

Visual and performing arts. The visual and performing arts are media in which students show many of the traits associated with creativity, general intellect, and specific academic aptitude, including rapid mastery of a subject matter. In addition, they may have highly developed nonverbal communication skills; physical coordination; exceptional awareness of where they are in relation to other things and people; or specific skills in music, dance, theater/acting and mime, storytelling, drawing, or painting. For example, although Stravinsky was immersed in music as a child, he was not a musical prodigy (Gardner, 1993). He had, however, a keen sense of sound and with his violin was able to imitate the unison singing of village women on their way home from work.

Values: Promoting *self-determination* is one aspect of leadership development.

Behavioral characteristics. Some students who are gifted behave well, and some behave poorly (Seeley, 2003). Some have a strong sense of humor or unquenchable curiosity that can be a distraction in class. Indeed, these students are not any less well adjusted than their so-called typical or not-gifted peers (Neihart, Reis, Robinson, & Moon, 2002). Some may have fewer friends or try to hide their talents so that they will be more accepted by their typical peers (Neihart et al., 2002). Some may experience perfectionism or its opposite, the tendency to underachieve (Reis & McCoach, 2002; Schuler, 2002). Females who are gifted and talented may believe that it is socially unacceptable for them to achieve at high levels (Reis, 1998).

Although students with these characteristics can be perfectionists, easily distracted by external stimuli, unable to maintain attention, or have difficulty controlling their impulses, they also have a positive view of others, are sensitive, have a forgiving nature, and are able to produce work of significant quality when motivated and valued (Wallace, 1999/2000).

There is growing concern about the number of students who are being misdiagnosed as having a specific learning disability (Chapter 5) or an attention-deficit/hyperactivity disorder (Chapter 8) when in fact they are gifted (Silverman, 1998). Because many of the characteristics of giftedness are also associated with these other conditions, it is not always easy to recognize students' giftedness.

Social and emotional characteristics. Traditionally, educators have valued students' social intelligence (Guilford, 1967; Salovey & Mayer, 1990; Sternberg, 1985). Salovey and Mayer (1990)

Students who are gifted often excel in other areas such as creativity and dramatic arts.

Go to the Companion Website, *www.prenhall.com/turnbull,* for a link to websites that provide illustrations and information about early brain development, *http://faculty.washington.edu/chudler/dev.html* and *www.zerotothree.org/brain-wonders/caregivers.html.*

Values: A nondiscriminatory evaluation will identify a student's *strengths* in the several domains of giftedness.

first described emotional intelligence (a different trait from social intelligence), but Goleman (1995) has more recently popularized that concept and described emotional intelligence as including the capacity to know one's emotions, manage one's emotions, motivate oneself, recognize others' emotions, and effectively develop relationships with others. He describes emotionally intelligent individuals as having specific characteristics associated with self-awareness, impulse control, persistence, self-motivation, empathy, hope, and optimism.

According to Goleman, these factors contribute to a different way of being smart—one he terms *emotional intelligence*. Having high cognitive intelligence does not imply exemplary skills in any other area of life, and indeed Goleman claims that emotional intelligence shapes everything from personal success to physical well-being. His theory of intelligence, similar to Gardner's interpersonal and intrapersonal domains of giftedness, provides a broader explanation for how giftedness can be demonstrated. Although Goleman's conceptualization of emotional intelligence is generally well known, the originators of this concept point out that his conceptualization is too broad. They characterize emotional intelligence as having "the ability to perceive, understand, and manage emotions on the one hand and to allow emotions to facilitate their thought on the other" (Mayer, Perkins, Caruso, & Salovey, 2001, p. 132).

Determining the Origins

Does giftedness originate from nature or nurture? The answer has long been debated (Doman & Doman, 1994; Elkind, 1981; Henderson & Ebner, 1997) and may well be determined as the Human Genome Project (you read about it in Chapter 11) reveals more about the biological aspects of brain development.

Clark (2002) asserts that it is unwise to conclude that either inherited abilities or environmental opportunities are more important than the other. That is so because any "restriction on either would inhibit high levels of actualized intellectual ability." Indeed, the brain's plasticity is the key to this conclusion. A person's actions, sensations, and memories shape the brain's function and anatomy. "High levels of brain development do not occur without a high level of interaction between the inherited abilities and appropriately enriching experiences" (p. 43).

EVALUATING STUDENTS WHO ARE GIFTED AND TALENTED

To identify and serve students who are gifted and talented, educators often conduct a two-step diagnostic evaluation similar to the nondiscriminatory evaluation they use to identify and evaluate students with disabilities.

Determining the Presence of Giftedness and Talents

There are at least two challenges in evaluating a student for giftedness and talent. One is that the validity and reliability of standardized tests is questionable (Pfeiffer, 2003). The other is that some of the standardized tests may discriminate against some students: "typically used measures do not work as well with culturally diverse populations, students from low socioeconomic status (SES) or rural areas, and students in which language is not the primary language spoken in the home" (Pfeiffer, 2003, p. 163). You may recall that students from culturally- and linguistically-diverse backgrounds are underrepresented in gifted programs (Ford & Grantham, 2003; Grantham, 2004; National Research Council, 2002).

To protect against discrimination, researchers advocate using more than one means of evaluation (Dickson, 2003; Gallagher, 2002). They advise balancing IQ test results against other documentation criteria such as creativity tests, behavior rating scales, samples of artwork or creative writing, photographs of a previously completed project, a videotape of an oral presentation, a leadership profile, or other material from parents or teachers.

One of the challenges in using more than one measure is deciding how to combine the scores and results to determine whether to classify a student as being gifted and talented. Gallagher (2002) recommends against "merely simple aggregation of the findings"; instead, he favors "creatively combining the results" (p. 104). Unhappily, guidelines for ensuring creative combinations are inexplicit. Figure 16–3 shows the standard process for evaluating students for the presence of giftedness.

You learned about intelligence testing in Chapter 5; in this chapter we will focus on alternative assessments for identifying giftedness among students from diverse backgrounds. These assessments acknowledge the multiple domains of intelligence, the nearly exclusive reliance on IQ tests (Nevo, 1994), and the increasing concern about test bias (Baker, 1996; Sarouphim, 2001).

DISCOVER (Discovering Intellectual Strengths and Capabilities through Observation while allowing for Varied Ethnic Responses) is a performance-based, research-reliable, and research-validated assessment for identifying giftedness in students from diverse backgrounds (Maker, 2001; Sarouphim, 1999, 2001). It requires the student to undertake problem-solving tasks in six of Gardner's domains of intelligence: spatial, logical-mathematical, linguistic, bodily-kinesthetic, interpersonal, and intrapersonal. The tasks increase in complexity and openness as the assessment progresses. Assessments are available at four grade levels: K–2, 3–5, 6–8, and 9–12.

The instrument draws on Maker's (1993) definition of giftedness as "the ability to solve the most complex problems in the most efficient, effective, or economical ways" (p. 71). During the evaluation process, students work in small groups, while highly trained observers use standard observation sheets, pictures, and a video camera to note the students' problem-solving processes and products. Over a 2½-hour period, observers accept all products, give helpful clues when asked, adopt a nonjudgmental attitude, and rotate regularly to minimize bias.

Afterward, the observers work as partners to rate the students' strengths on a scale of 1 to 5, from "no strength observed" to "definite strength observed." Students with a superior problem-solver rating are those with definite ratings in two or more activities.

By using DISCOVER instead of other approaches, educators identify as gifted and talented a higher proportion of students from diverse ethnic, socioeconomic, and linguistic backgrounds (Castellano, 2003; Maker, 2001; Sarouphim, 1999).

Standard: Finding appropriate assessment instruments for children who are gifted is an application of CEC Standard 8, Assessment.

Determining the Nature of Specially Designed Instruction and Services

In addition to measuring intellectual functioning, educators evaluate students' creativity. Because creativity is not a discrete personal trait but occurs through interaction with the sociocultural context (Nakamura & Csikszentmihalyi, 2001), it is difficult to find assessments that bring these interactions together.

Many tests assess creativity (Fishkin, Cramond, & Olszewski-Kubilius, 2001), but divergent-thinking tests are among the most popular techniques (Davis, 2003). For example, the two Torrance Tests of Creative Thinking (Torrance, 1966a, 1966b, 1990) assess different aspects of creativity. They are untimed tests, may be administered individually or in groups, and predict adult achievement as accurately as frequently used intelligence or achievement tests (Torrance & Wu, 1981; Torrance, 1984).

Thinking Creatively with Words focuses on the verbal, linguistic side of creativity from fourth grade through graduate school and asks students to complete seven verbal activities, such as writing all the questions you can conceive about a simple picture, listing possible causes for the action shown in the picture, and listing all the possible consequences of the action in the picture.

Figure 16–3   Evaluating whether or not a student is gifted, using an IDEA-like process

Observation	**_Teacher and parents observe:_** The student may be bored with school or intensely interested in academic pursuits, has high vocabulary or specialized talents and interests, shows curiosity and frequently asks questions (especially _how_ and _why_), is insightful, and has novel ideas and approaches to tasks.
Screening	**_Assessment measures:_** **Classroom work products:** Her work is consistently superior in one or more academic areas; or in the case of the underachieving gifted, products are inconsistent, with only work of special interest being superior. **Group intelligence tests:** Tests often indicate exceptional intelligence. **Group achievement tests:** The student usually performs above average in one or more areas of achievement. (Cutoff for screening purposes is an IQ of 115.)
Prereferral	Generally, prereferral is not used for students who may be evaluated as gifted.
Referral	Schools will vary on their procedures for referral; in some cases, referral will be handled very similarly to the process of referring students who have disabilities.
Nondiscriminatory evaluation procedures and standards	**_Assessment measures:_** **Individualized intelligence test:** The student scores in the upper 2 to 3 percent of the population. Because of cultural biases of standardized IQ tests, students from minority backgrounds are considered if their IQs do not meet the cutoff but other indicators suggest giftedness. **Individualized achievement test:** The student scores in the upper 2 to 3 percent in one or more areas of achievement. **Creativity assessment:** The student demonstrates unusual creativity in work products as judged by experts or performs exceptionally well on tests designed to assess creativity. The student does not have to be academically gifted to qualify. **Checklists of gifted characteristics:** These checklists are often completed by teachers, parents, peers, or others who know the student well. The student scores in the range that suggests giftedness as established by checklist developers. **Anecdotal records:** The student's records suggest high ability in one or more areas. **Curriculum-based assessment:** The student is performing at a level beyond peers in one or more areas of the curriculum used by the local school district. **Direct observation:** The student may be a model student or could have behavior problems as a result of being bored with classwork. If the student is a perfectionist, anxiety might be observed. Observations should occur in other settings besides the school.

> **Visual and performing arts assessment:** The student's performance in visual or performing arts is judged by individuals with expertise in the specific area. The student does not have to be academically gifted to qualify.
>
> **Leadership assessment:** Peer nomination, parent nomination, and teacher nomination are generally used. However, self-nomination can also be a good predictor of leadership. Leadership in extracurricular activities is often an effective indicator. The student does not have to be academically gifted to qualify.
>
> **Case-study approach:** Determination of a student's giftedness is based on looking at all areas of assessment just described without adding special weight to one factor.

| Determination | The nondiscriminatory evaluation team determines that the student is gifted and needs special education. |

Thinking Creatively with Pictures evaluates a student's figural and spatial creativity from kindergarten through graduate school and determines a student's spatial abilities by using pictures and asking her to make as many objects or pictures as she can from identical shapes, such as squares or triangles, all within 10 minutes.

Educators apply several criteria to the test results. For example, they score the verbal creativity tests for fluency, originality, and flexibility according to a scoring guide that accompanies the test and that gives examples for evaluating student answers. They then summarize, interpret, and report their scores.

DESIGNING AN APPROPRIATE INDIVIDUALIZED EDUCATION PROGRAM

Partnering for Special Education and Related Services

Differentiated instruction is an effective strategy for teaching students who are gifted and talented, as well as many students with disabilities, in the general classroom. (See Chapter 9 for more information about differentiated instruction.) Differentiated instruction requires general education teachers and gifted-education specialists to partner with each other. The gifted specialists partner with grade and content-level teachers to plan and implement differentiated instruction, co-teach, help to compact or expand the curriculum, and provide direct instruction to gifted and talented students.

Differentiated instruction involves differentiation strategies such as flexible student instructional grouping, learning stations and learning centers, compacted or expanded curriculum (discussed later in this chapter), and co-teaching. Teachers and administrators need regularly scheduled time to plan and collaborate around differentiation (Pettig, 2000).

Co-teaching (which we also discuss in Chapter 13 under "collaborative teaming") involves two educators teaching in the same classroom. Hughes and Murawski (2001) described co-teaching in gifted education as requiring "dialogue, planning, shared and creative decision making, and follow-up between at least two co-equal professionals with diverse expertise, in which the goal of the interaction is to provide appropriate services for students, including high achieving and gifted students" (p. 196).

Co-teaching typically involves a general education or content teacher and a specialist in an area such as special education, English as a second language, or, in this case, gifted and talented education. There are different types of co-teaching. Sometimes one teacher delivers content while the other supports students in learning the skills they need to succeed in the lesson; at

Values: Differentiated instruction builds on students' *strengths* by identifying how students learn best and then matching them with appropriate instructional settings and activities.

For a discussion about how differentiated instruction contributes to universal design for learning, go to our Companion Website, *www. prenhall.com/turnbull,* and then link to the National Center on Accessing the Curriculum website, *http://www.cast.org/ncac/index. cfm?i=2876.*

Co-teaching typically involves a general and special education teacher working together for the benefit of students with special needs.

other times the second teacher works with smaller groups while the content teacher provides instruction on core content.

Partnerships between general educators and specialists in giftedness remain important as students get older, but the nature of the partnership may change. As students enter high school, the role of content experts, such as science or math teachers, becomes more critical. Students taking high school advanced placement or honors math or science courses, in which most gifted and talented students will be enrolled, will have the knowledge and capacity to succeed in such courses. The students' IEP teams need to plan how the specialist in gifted education will partner with the content expert on specific instructional strategies, not about content issues.

Gifted education also requires partnerships between educators and members of the students' communities (Melber, 2003). For example, Melber described a program in which gifted students went to a museum to learn the standards-related science content. By interacting with the museum staff, the students learned about both the content and science as a career.

Determining Supplementary Aids and Services

One of the most important decisions facing an IEP team is how best to challenge a student in one or more content areas. IEP teams can achieve this goal through supplementary aids and services that modify the scope and sequence of the curriculum.

The first option is **acceleration,** which involves moving students "more rapidly through the standard sequence" of the curriculum (Gallagher, 2003, p. 17) by having the student move up a grade or skip a course in the normal sequence. That is what Geoff does; he is an eighth-grade gifted student who goes to the high school each morning to take honors geometry at the ninth-grade level and then returns to his middle school for the remainder of his educational program. His IEP team carefully considers the social effects of acceleration. Geoff is mature and fits in fine at the high school, but if a student is physically, emotionally, or socially immature, it may not be in his or her best interest to be placed in classes with older students. Then the IEP team needs to consider other options.

One way to accelerate a student without moving her up a grade or class sequence is to **compact the curriculum.** Compacting involves tests that reveal the aspects of the content that a student has already mastered; the teacher then provides instruction only on that content that the student has not yet mastered (Clark, 2002). Compacting often makes it possible for students to complete a couple of sequenced courses in a single semester (Stamps, 2004).

A variation on acceleration is the "most difficult first" strategy. Instead of doing all problems or activities on a task, the students complete the most difficult tasks (as identified in advance by the teacher). If they get all of the tasks correct, they move on to the next activity or task in the sequence. If they do not, they do the complete assignment. This variation allows for curriculum compacting on a day-to-day and lesson-to-lesson basis. Teachers often combine these modifications to the scope and sequence of the curriculum with universal design. The students' IEPs should identify both the modifications and the universal design features.

Planning for Universal Design for Learning

Two strategies that provide curriculum adaptations or augmentations involve (1) the use of curriculum extension techniques and (2) the application of cognitive taxonomies to the design of activity, lesson, and unit plans.

Standard: Using differentiation strategies is one way to address CEC Standard 4, Instructional Strategies. By selecting and adapting strategies and materials, you are adapting for the individual.

For more information on co-teaching as a strategy, go to our Companion Website, *www.prenhall.com/turnbull,* for a link to LDOnline's discussion of co-teaching, *http://www.ldonline.org/ld_indepth/teaching_techniques/tec_coteaching.html.*

Standard: Addressing the similarities, differences, and varying needs of students who are gifted and talented is an application of CEC Standard 2, Development and Characteristics of Learners.

Curriculum extension refers to efforts to expand the breadth and depth of the coverage of a given topic. Students who are gifted learn content quicker than their peers do; they do not need as much repetition, so their curriculum extension activities should not simply repeat the same task but should challenge them at a higher level.

Teachers take their students to a higher level by using cognitive taxonomies. A taxonomy is an ordered list or classification of something. **Cognitive taxonomies** are ordered lists of cognitive skills or activities that can be used to differentiate expectations for students. The most familiar taxonomy is the one developed by Bloom and associates (1956). Bloom's taxonomy categorizes the cognitive skills that students use when achieving their learning goals. As a student ascends Bloom's taxonomy, he or she faces increasingly complex cognitive demands.

Teachers can differentiate what they expect from students by designing lesson and activity objectives that range from less to more complex levels of interaction with materials. They also can extend the curriculum for gifted students by having their students engage in activities that move up the taxonomy, from applying information and knowledge to solve novel problems to synthesizing information to create new patterns or structures. These activities will teach students the skills they need to be more creative and to develop effective thinking skills.

Go to our Companion Website, *www.prenhall.com/turnbull*, where you can link to more information about curriculum compacting, acceleration, and other strategies at the Center for Gifted Education and Talent Development's website, *http://www.gifted.uconn.edu/*.

Planning for Other Educational Needs

It is not always easy being gifted. If schools do not plan for and implement practices like differentiated instruction, acceleration, compaction, curriculum extension, and cognitive taxonomies, schools can bore their gifted students.

But there is more, as Reis and Renzulli (2004) have noted: "current press and popular television portray a rather skewed view of gifted and talented youth as the 'dorky' misfit" (p. 119). In fact, though, a study commissioned by the National Association for Gifted Children and the National Research Center on the Gifted and Talented concluded that "high ability students are generally at least as well adjusted as any other group" (Reis & Renzulli, 2004, p. 119).

Even if gifted students do not conform to media stereotypes, there are some aspects of the experience of being gifted that IEP teams should address to ward off potential socioemotional problems. As we have noted, students who are gifted tend to be perfectionists and highly competitive. Their advanced cognitive abilities may make their age-appropriate socioemotional skills seem immature. They are more likely to be highly active, independent, nonconforming, persistent, curious, and self-critical (Clark, 2002).

One response to their needs is the **autonomous learning model** (Betts & Kercher, 1999). It assists the students in dealing with the socioemotional issues that might accompany their giftedness. This model is effective for helping elementary through secondary school students explore the socioemotional aspects of being gifted and to enable them to become lifelong learners. Students involved with the autonomous learning model do the following (Clark, 2002):

- Explore what it means to be gifted
- Explore what intelligence and creativity mean
- Explore aspects of their personal/social development
- Consider their strengths and limitations
- Learn organizational skills
- Engage in self-directed study about topics in which they are interested
- Learn the importance of autonomous lifelong learning

The activities in the autonomous learning model can benefit all students. Uresti, Goertz, and Bernal (2002) found that implementing the model with first-grade Latino children increased their independence and higher-order thinking skills and improved their scores on achievement tests. Box 16–2 provides a step-by-step guide for implementing the model.

Values: Because gifted students often know what modifications work best for them, teachers should consider giving them a *choice* about all of the modifications we have just discussed. When students choose how to learn, they often are more successful in their schoolwork.

You can learn about the six levels of Bloom's taxonomy by going to the Companion Website, *www.prenhall.com/turnbull*, and following the link to *www.coum.uvic.ca/learn/program/hndouts/bloom.html*.

Council for Exceptional Children

Standard: Using the autonomous learning model reflects CEC Standard 4, Instructional Strategies, in regard to teaching self-assessment and problem-solving strategies.

Into Practice ~ Autonomous Learning Model

Box 16–2

Like problem-based learning, the autonomous learning model develops independent, self-directed learners—not just those who are exceptionally smart but those who are developed in social, emotional, and cognitive domains. The model features five areas in which students receive support and enrichment experiences:

1. *Orientation:* understanding giftedness, talent, intelligence, and creativity.
2. *Individual development:* inter/intrapersonal skills, learning skills, technology, college and career involvement, organizational skills, productivity.
3. *Enrichment:* explorations, investigations, cultural activities, service, adventure trips.
4. *Seminars:* futuristic, problem-based, controversial, general interest, advanced knowledge.
5. *In-depth study:* individual projects, group projects, mentorships, presentations, assessments.

The strengths of this program lie in its flexibility. As students and teachers work together, roles change and adapt to the experience. The teacher may become the student and the learner may become a facilitator of others' learning. By changing roles, all students develop and appreciate their own strengths and become independent learners.

Putting These Strategies to Work for Progress in the General Curriculum

1. Assign students (individually or in groups) to develop a PowerPoint presentation in which the student(s) relate one of their academic or emotional strengths to a contemporary issue (easily identified in news magazines over the past 12 months).

2. Require your students to write an essay that describes how their academic talents affect their emotional or social lives in a positive or a negative way, or in both ways.

3. Require your students to write an essay in which they predict how their academic, emotional/social, or other talents will contribute to society.

To answer these questions online, go to the Into Practice module in Chapter 16 of the Companion Website, www.prenhall.com/turnbull.

USING EFFECTIVE INSTRUCTIONAL STRATEGIES

Early Childhood Students: Multiple Intelligences

There are few gifted programs for very young children whose giftedness is in its most formative stage. Briana did not receive specialized support until the first grade. Unlike her, some gifted students may lose their capacity for reflection and creative thinking if the schools fail to meet their educational needs (Hodge & Kemp, 2000).

One theoretical model of intelligence that has been translated into instructional practice is Howard Gardner's multiple intelligences theory. Gardner defined intelligence as "the capacity to solve problems or to fashion products that are valued in one or more cultural settings" (Gardner & Hatch, 1989). Look back at Figure 16–1, which describes Gardner's eight areas of potential giftedness and lists the typical characteristics and distinctive features common in gifted individuals.

The theory of multiple intelligences has the potential to fundamentally reshape schools. Learning activities reflect student strengths across the eight areas of potential giftedness. Instead of just presenting information in words through texts or lectures, teachers use physical and social experiences, music, and engagement with the natural world. Sounds a lot like universal design, doesn't it? In fact, in schools incorporating multiple-intelligences theory, there is a "school-community broker," a person who searches for educational opportunities for students within the wider community. In one school in which the school day has been designed within this framework, students spend half of their day at school studying traditional subject areas through project-oriented learning activities and the other half in the community exploring the contexts in which they can apply what they have learned in school (Gardner, 1993).

The multiple intelligence theory encourages learning in real environments.

Educator Thomas Armstrong, who has pioneered the application of the theory to education, explained it like this: "For whatever you wish to teach, link your instructional objective to words, numbers or logic, pictures, music, the body, social interaction and/or personal experience" (Armstrong, 1994, p. 26).

In Project Spectrum, Gardner and his colleagues applied the model to early childhood and early elementary education settings. Montgomery Knolls Elementary School in Silver Spring, Maryland, has based its early childhood gifted program on the Project Spectrum principles. There, teachers identify and serve different types of giftedness, ensuring that instruction and content correlate with their students' aptitudes, interests, and abilities. The teachers look for different types of giftedness, plan activities specific to these areas, and then provide options for each child. Twice a year, they fill out a strengths checklist for each child.

For instance, during a study of dinosaurs, children with a strong spatial orientation wanted to know how big the dinosaurs were. To find out, they projected enlarged pictures onto the school wall to grasp the concept of size. By contrast, children with a linguistic orientation developed seven questions and then e-mailed them to a paleontologist, who answered their questions. Children with artistic talents used papier-mâché to make life-sized features of the dinosaurs, and those with a musical ability wrote and sang songs about dinosaurs.

Values: Restructuring schools to reflect the multiple intelligence model is a concrete way to challenge students to meet and exceed their own, their teachers', and their parents' *great expectations* for them.

Elementary and Middle School Students: Schoolwide Enrichment

Because their gifted students have unique cognitive and other characteristics and in order to address their students' challenges in motivation, attention, and behavior, good teachers match the content of their courses to their students' aptitudes, sophistication, and interests. Often they use enrichment strategies to engage their students.

The term *enrichment* refers to "curriculum as well as program delivery services" (Schiever & Maker, 2003, p. 164). Enrichment activities include the following (Clark, 2002, p. 264):

- Adding instruction on disciplines or learning domains not found within the typical curriculum
- Using more challenging or complex material to present content
- Using an expanded range of instructional strategies
- Teaching critical thinking and problem solving skills

Renzulli and colleagues developed and implemented an enrichment model known as the **schoolwide enrichment model** (Renzulli & Reis, 2003). Its major goal is to promote challenging, high-end learning across a range of school types, levels, and demographic differences by creating services that can be integrated across the general education curriculum to assist all students, not just those who are gifted. There are three types of enrichment approaches under the model.

Type I enrichment exposes the students to a wide variety of topics, disciplines, occupations, hobbies, persons, places, and events that ordinarily would not be included in the general education curriculum. For example, Type I experiences may involve community speakers, demonstrations, performances, multimedia presentations, or other illustrative formats.

Type II enrichment focuses on resources that promote creative thinking, problem solving, and critical-thinking skills. This kind of enrichment consists of how-to-learn skills, including written, oral, and visual communication skills. Other Type II skills are specific to a particular student's talents and interests.

When a student becomes interested in pursuing a self-selected area of interest and commits the time necessary for this endeavor, Type III enrichment occurs. It consists of

1. Providing opportunities for applying interests
2. Acquiring advanced-level understanding of the content and process that are used within particular disciplines
3. Developing authentic products

4. Developing self-directed learning skills

5. Empowering the student to control learning through organization and feelings of accomplishment

Blue Valley School District, a suburban district located in Johnson County, Kansas, integrates features of the schoolwide enrichment model and the autonomous learning model (discussed previously) for students in grades 1 through 6. For example, Lucie Medbery and her colleagues at Heartland Elementary School use this combined approach to address the specific needs of gifted students. Her instruction aims to expand the problem-based experiences that a student can complete individually or share with a group of learners. The results are promising, even with the youngest of her students, Graham.

A recent example of Lucie's efforts to facilitate group as well as problem-based learning involved simple household refrigerator magnets. "I brought in some refrigerator magnets one day and shared them with the group," she explains. "I asked them to investigate and problem-solve how these magnets are being used or what possible uses there are for magnets." Soon Graham and his peers were discussing magnetic resonance imaging. Next they researched the technology and its various applications. "It was fascinating to watch and listen to the students move from magnets to magnetic resonance imaging. One student quoted Einstein's statement about the power of observation and related this quote or idea to what they were doing as a group," Lucie notes. To learn more, the group sought her help in identifying experts.

Lucie's group is also tracking the progress of a number of turtles that regularly visit the class with a local marine biologist. The biologist initially visited Lucie's class because he knew that one of her students was fascinated by turtles. That first visit led to others. Instead of simply marveling at the variety of turtles brought in for display, the students decided they wanted to track the turtles' growth and progress. During each visit, students collect data on the growth of each turtle, changes in it characteristics, and other information; they store that information in a Microsoft Excel document.

Lucie clearly sees herself as a facilitator, creating the appropriate environment for individual or group problem-based learning. She helps her students find research information and introduces technology applications that can help them learn. Lucie explains, "My role is to facilitate the learning experience, presenting problems for them to solve. I also feel it is my responsibility to help these students realize what it is to be gifted. That is why we like the autonomous learning model. It features problem-based learning but also stresses an understanding of what it is to be gifted, the characteristics one has as a gifted child, the issues that tend to come along with this exceptionality, as well as some of the skills one needs to fully develop, for example, time management."

Lucie also uses technology to benefit students, like Graham, who receive enrichment services. One innovative use of technology involves using the Internet to conduct WebQuests. Box 16–3 provides an overview of how to conduct WebQuests.

Secondary and Transition Students: Promoting Creativity and Critical-Thinking Skills

You have already learned that students who are gifted are highly original, independent, risk takers, curious, motivated, and attracted to complexity. They are creative and effective critical thinkers. It would be wrong, however, for a teacher to assume that students who are gifted are already highly skilled in creativity and critical thinking and do not need instruction in that area. Instead, the teacher should focus on enhancing the students' innate strengths by honing their creative talents and thinking abilities. According to Davis (2003, p. 319), a teacher can promote creativity by

- Fostering creative attitudes
- Improving student understanding of creativity
- Practicing and exercising creativity
- Teaching critical thinking and creative thinking skills
- Engaging students in creative activities

Technology Tips ~ WebQuests

Box 16–3

Today, most schools and many homes have Internet connections. In classrooms all across the United States, teachers and students are integrating the content of web pages into their daily instruction. To do just that is increasingly easy, for web applications and resources seem to proliferate overnight. At the same time, educators are often challenged by the amount of information available and how to apply specific resources as they teach.

What Is the Technology?

A WebQuest is an inquiry-oriented activity in which most or all of the information that students use comes from the web. Web-Quests are designed to use students' time well; to focus on using information rather than looking for it; and to support students' thinking at the levels of analysis, synthesis, and evaluation. Web-Quests are appealing because they provide structure and guidance for both students and teachers. The ideal of engaging higher-level thinking skills by making good use of limited computer access seems to resonate with many educators.

What Do We Do with It?

A WebQuest allows teachers and students to create activities around web-based resources. Instead of simply using a website,

the teacher or student is directed through a quest in how to interact with the site(s), what activity to undertake, and how to evaluate success with the site(s). For example, a WebQuest begins with an introduction about the purpose of the quest. Next the teacher assigns a task that focuses students on what they are going to do: specifically, the culminating performance or product that drives all the learning activities. Subsequently, an outline tells the student how he will accomplish the task. Using scaffolding (the process of building one skill on top of another, and so on, up through the skill levels), the student uses clear steps, resources, and tools for organizing information. Each WebQuest also includes an evaluation component that enumerates the specific criteria students must meet to satisfy performance and content standards. Finally, the WebQuest conclusion brings closure and encourages the student to reflect on his learning experience.

You can find more about WebQuests at *http://webquest.org/*. The website *http://webquest.sdsu.edu/adapting/* provides helpful suggestions for adapting existing WebQuests for your use. Like other materials, it's important to seek permission to use existing resources, like WebQuests.

Developing critical thinking skills involves teaching students to develop more effective problem-solving skills, such as those assessed by the DISCOVER process you have already learned about; to think more productively; and to apply those skills to broader, meaningful problems.

Productive thinking refers to focusing on fluency, flexibility, originality, and elaboration in the thinking process (Feldhusen, 2003). Promoting fluency involves teaching students to consider a lot of ideas in addressing a problem. Flexible thinking refers to considering lots of types of ideas. Promoting originality involves teaching students to come up with ideas that are their own. Teaching elaboration skills involves teaching students to expand their ideas.

How does one teach these skills? Sometimes it's a matter of teaching students how to optimize their time and talents to achieve better results. Most people think more clearly and perform more effectively at certain times of the day, and teachers can help gifted students identify what tasks to undertake during the more productive times. Teaching strategies focused on developing creativity are less memory-based and have students do more thinking activities, focus their evaluation on big ideas and issues instead of on the microlevel of evaluation (such as handwriting or neatness), develop learning communities that support spontaneity and risk taking, pose provocative questions, and provide explicit models of the steps involved in solving problems and thinking through issues (Clark, 2002).

In many cases, the best way to teach these types of creative thinking is to involve students in some of the many competitions—those in math, science, or history. Examples of these competitions include MathCounts, Odyssey of the Mind, or Science Olympiad. These programs are appealing because students can compete with other students who are talented.

For more information about competitions in which gifted students might participate, go to our Companion Website, *www.prenhall.com/turnbull*, and link to the Duke Talent Identification Program, *http://www.tip. duke.edu/*.

INCLUDING STUDENTS WHO ARE GIFTED AND TALENTED

Within the field of gifted education, there is an ongoing debate regarding student placement. On the one hand, IDEA's principle of the least restrictive environment (access to the general curriculum and inclusion) has prompted state and local educational agencies to promote the inclusion of students who are gifted and talented, even though these students are not covered as part

Exploring the range of options available to students who are gifted can include accelerating learning for some.

of IDEA (Robinson, 2003; Shaunessy, 2003). On the other hand, some leaders within the field of gifted education have expressed grave concern about the lack of curricula breadth, depth, and specificity in general education classrooms (Pfeiffer, 2003). They have underscored the need to consider a broad range of options:

- **Cluster grouping:** assigning three to six students who are gifted and talented to the same general education classroom so that they can work together.

- **All-school enrichment programs:** addressing the top 20 percent of students in a school through special-interest groups, specialized instruction in small groups, and mentoring on individual projects (Renzulli & Reis, 2003).

- **Accelerative method:** starting to kindergarten or college early, skipping one or more grades in order to experience higher levels of instruction, and/or attending a higher grade level program for part of the school day (Schiever & Maker, 2003).

- **Magnet schools, charter schools, self-contained classes, special day schools, and residential schools:** drawing students together who are gifted and talented (Gallagher, 2002; Robinson, 2003).

Box 16–4 provides tips that can be integrated with these practices to enhance success in the general education setting. As you read the tips, bear in mind that you must understand each student's needs in order to achieve the best match between those needs and the curriculum. And remember that inclusion means one thing for students who have disabilities and another for students who are gifted. Read Box 16–5 and answer its challenge to justify either a great deal of inclusion or a great deal of exclusion of gifted students.

Throughout this book, we have driven home the point that special education overenrolls a disproportionate number of students from racially-diverse backgrounds. The one great exception to this general rule relates to gifted education, where there is disproportionate underenrollment of students from racially-diverse backgrounds. In Box 16–6, you will find tips on how teachers can assure that they do not contribute to that shameful condition.

ASSESSING STUDENTS' PROGRESS

Measuring Students' Progress

Progress in the general curriculum. After identifying a student as gifted, educators evaluate her progress by measuring performance on the student's goals. In addition, they can place some of the evaluation responsibility on the student herself.

Product evaluation. Teachers commonly base academic assessment of students on written products of the student's learning, often one or more tests. The test results help teachers track grades and learning, but they do not provide teachers or students with tools for understanding the students' learning processes.

Moreover, some students have both gifts and talents as well as obvious disabilities; product measures/evaluation and process measures/evaluation do not fully address the students' progress. These product and process approaches are appropriate for a student's gifted aspects, but the other measures should be based on a student's IDEA-type disability.

Good teachers use product measures not just for grading but also for helping students who are gifted record their own progress and compete with themselves rather than with classmates. In addition, good teachers use product measures to assess the thoroughness of their teaching, looking for areas that need further or different instruction.

Inclusion Tips   Box 16–4

	What You Might See	What You Might Be Tempted to Do	Alternate Responses	Ways to Include Peers in the Process
Behavior	The student asks so many questions that there is time for nothing else.	Tell her to be quiet and pay attention to her work.	Begin a dialogue journal. Ask her to write down her questions. Then research and discuss some of the answers together.	Have an all-class "Challenge Box," where students can write questions they think are difficult. Then enable the students who are gifted to work on these in small groups with their peers.
Social interactions	He is unable to see another person's perspectives.	Avoid calling on him in class in order to avoid potential conflict.	Build on his leadership by giving him responsibility for leading a class discussion of major concepts.	Have him work with small groups, teaching the other students to be discussion facilitators.
Educational performance	She is very bored in class and is refusing to do homework.	Discipline her for inattentiveness or give additional work to reinforce the lesson.	Modify the scope and sequence of the student's curriculum through acceleration to create more challenge.	Explore the possibility of this student attending one or more classes in the next grade.
Classroom attitudes	He is achieving slightly below grade level, but he has unusual talents related to leadership and emotional intelligence.	Assume that he is being academically lazy and give him extra work to try to get him up to grade level.	Recognize his gifts and strengths and work with the school principal to find a school citizenship project for which he can provide leadership.	Identify other students with similar talents and get them involved in a cooperative citizenship project.

Process evaluation. Educators should also evaluate a student's learning process (Andrade, 2000). Process evaluation happens when a teacher attempts to observe and learn from a student's comments or work. Teachers formalize "kid watching" when they take notes on their students' strengths and weaknesses in solving problems and carrying out various learning activities. These notes are good resources during parent-teacher conferences. Likewise, reflective assessment or evaluation (White & Frederiksen, 1998) involves teaching students to become aware of the process of their own learning. Reflective assessment helps students monitor their own learning. Figure 16–4 shows how four areas of assessment work together on the student's behalf.

Progress in addressing other educational needs. One of the objectives of the autonomous learning model that you learned about earlier is to teach students who are gifted to become more independent thinkers and autonomous learners. Using learning contracts can be a good way to support this and to help students evaluate their own progress toward their educational goals.

Learning contracts are agreements between a student and his or her teacher. They describe in detail the outcome of the student's learning, the product(s) that will provide evidence of that outcome, and, if necessary, the criteria for determining whether the products are of acceptable quality. The contracts also specify timelines, resources, and, importantly, reinforcement.

Your Own Voice ~ I'm For/Against Inclusion   Box 16–5

Assume that you are the Latino parent of two school-age children, born just a year apart from each other. Your son, Alejandro, clearly has an intellectual or emotional limitation. Your daughter, Anita, clearly is gifted. Both have been classified into special education.

Ever since you enrolled Alejandro in school, you have advocated for him to have the maximum feasible access to the general education curriculum; you want him to learn how to read and calculate because both skills will make him more independent as an adult. You also have insisted that he be included in the school's extracurricular and other activities. You know that the social security safety net for him is the network of friendships that he will develop among his classmates who do not have disabilities. So you have relied on IDEA's least restrictive environment principle—on its assurances of access to the general curriculum.

Now that his younger sister, Anita, is enrolled in school, however, you are of a different mind about her education. You want her to be given every possible opportunity to make maximum use of her innate talents. No one in your family has ever attended college; she has bright prospects for not just going to college but being admitted to the honors programs in your state's flagship university or in any number of tier-one colleges or universities. So you have asked her teachers and their principals to accelerate her, compress her curriculum, pull her out of the general education classes, and put her into separate, self-contained classes that are for gifted students only.

Alejandro and Anita are in the same school. When you meet with their teachers and the school's principal and curriculum specialists, you advocate for inclusion for Alejandro and separate education for Anita.

"How can you be so inconsistent?" asks the principal.

"We can make some modifications to the curriculum for both of your children, but without pulling Anita out and pushing Alejandro in," says the curriculum specialist.

"Mrs. Huerta," says the teachers, "you can't have it both ways. It's either in or out. Which will it be?"

Justify your position.

Diversity Tips ~ Effective Teaching in Gifted Education   Box 16–6

In today's multicultural schools, there is no place for teachers who

- Expect little of their students from racially-diverse backgrounds
- Do not understand how to teach them
- Treat them unfairly and unequally
- Condone racial prejudice among any of their students

There is always a place, however, for teachers who

- Expect high academic and behavioral accomplishments from all students, especially those from racially-diverse backgrounds (teachers' "deficit perspectives" are the first barrier that gifted students from diverse backgrounds meet)
- Are specially motivated to teach students from diverse backgrounds (teachers' motivations shape their practices)
- Admit that they themselves may harbor prejudices (teachers' self-knowledge leads to self-reform)
- Refuse to judge the students' families as being not interested in their children's education (teachers who don't walk in others' shoes should refrain from evaluating another's worthiness as a parent)
- Guard against misinterpreting their students' behavior (for example, the oral tradition encourages frank, direct, and honest communication and the use of puns, jokes, and innuendoes, but some teachers may misinterpret it as rudeness, lack of social skills, and lack of intelligence; likewise, verve and movement, also known as tactile and kinesthetic preferences, may be misinterpreted as hyperactivity; and an affective orientation, with easy expression of feelings, may be misinterpreted as immaturity, irrationality, or low cognitive ability, meaning that teachers' own ignorance compounds teacher prejudice and thwarts their students' gifts and talents)
- Work with other committed teachers and administrators to identify gifted students from diverse backgrounds and educate them effectively (a loner tires soon, but a team can endure)
- Immediately squelch any forms of prejudice in their classrooms and throughout their schools (intolerance of intolerance can breed tolerance)
- Incorporate multicultural and diversity issues into their classes whenever possible, throughout the entire year, not just during special weeks or months that acknowledge different races, cultures, and ethnic heritages (giftedness and diversity are not occasional traits with their own birthdays and anniversaries)
- Invite members of racially-diverse communities to lead classes, be mentors, and serve as role models (teaching by example is powerful)
- Adopt multicultural gifted curriculum materials, such as that offered by Ford, D.Y., & Harris, J. J., III. (1999). *Multicultural gifted education.* New York: Teachers College Press.

Source: Adapted from Grantham, T. C. (2002). Underrepresentation in gifted education: How did we get here and what needs to change? *Roeper Review, 24*(2), 50–88; Morris, J. E. (2002). African-American students and gifted education: The politics of race and culture, *Roeper Review, 24*(2), 59–62; Harmon, D. (2002). They won't teach me: The voices of gifted African American inner-city students, *Roeper Review 24*(2), 68–80.

Learning contracts are effective with a wide range of students with disabilities and across many content areas. Their effectiveness derives, in part, from the fact that learning contracts are individualized and child-centered and promote independence and autonomy (Greenwood, 2003). These contracts are important components in high-quality gifted education programs, just as

Figure 16–4 Four areas of assessment

	Product	**Process**
Teacher uses	*Written Tests/Projects* • Teacher's grade book • Report card • How student compares to other students	*Kid Watching: Teacher Portfolios* • Teacher's understanding of student • Teacher's instructional planning • Parent conferences
Student uses	*Written Tests/Projects* • Student understanding of what still needs to be learned • Review of material • How student compares to peers in the class	*Reflective Evaluation: Student Portfolios* • Active participation and responsibility in the assessment process • Development of self-monitoring strategies that use higher-order thinking skills

important as differentiated instruction, multiple intelligences, acceleration, and flexible grouping (Kapusnick & Hauslein, 2001).

Making Accommodations for Assessments

Given that students who are gifted and talented have achieved at high levels and have unusual cognitive abilities, they usually do not need assessment accommodations. That is not true, however, if they also have a disability, like a learning disability, attention disorder, or a physical or sensory disability. Those students may need some of the same accommodations we discussed in the chapters about those disabilities.

Although many students who are gifted do not need specific accommodations, they still warrant teachers' special attention. As you have learned, they tend to be very competitive and expect to perform very well. They may feel additional pressure to do well on standardized tests and, as a result, may not perform as well as they could otherwise do. Teachers can help them keep the testing in perspective and reinforce that they should simply do as well as they can but not push too hard.

Among the standardized tests that gifted students will take are those used for college admission, typically the Scholastic Aptitude Test (SAT) or the American College Test (ACT). Students may feel extreme pressure to succeed on these examinations, particularly if they feel they need to qualify for exclusive colleges and/or scholarships. Whether a test is a state assessment or a college examination, students can learn skills like deep breathing that help them to relax and perform well. Basic preparation skills, like pacing out study sessions (instead of cramming all at once) and being well rested before taking a test, are also important. Gifted students will not need as much of the rote practice that often accompanies test preparation in the schools, so teachers adjust test preparation schedules accordingly (Moon, Brighton, & Callahan, 2003).

Looking to Briana's Future ■ ■ ■ ■ ■ ■

"Where are you taking me?" asked the author Forrester of his young protégé, Jamal. Forrester put the question to Jamal in the context of the boy's writing; he wanted Jamal to be crystal-clear about his message.

Turn the question around and let Briana ask it to herself: "Where are you, my many gifts, taking me?" Assume that Briana has skipped a grade as she left elementary and entered middle school. That's a fair assumption, given that she moved from one school to another during her elementary school years. Assume further that she also continued to develop her academic, athletic, and artistic skills. Picture her, like Jamal, in her last year of high school. "Where," she asks herself, "am I taking myself?"

For Briana and others who have multiple gifts, life after high school offers an abundance of opportunity. Already she has been besieged by college and university solicitations promising admission to the state university's honors programs, offering the benefits of the most select private colleges and universities, and asking her to come to summer sports camps. Dance and music conservatories have reminded her of the summer she spent in Kansas City with the Alvin Ailey dance troupe and of her ability not only to dance but also to imagine a dance ensemble performing to, say, Duke Ellington's jazz symphony "Black and Tan Fantasy." Like the colleges and universities, these conservatories plead, "Come spend the next 4 years of your life with me."

Like Jamal in the movie, Briana cannot keep her gifts under wraps, and again like him, she is finding ways to be socially accepted and remain emotionally and behaviorally balanced. Indeed, "Balanced Briana" has found a way to reach the golden mean, which the ancient Greeks advocated and which you may know in its Latin version: "mens sana in corpore sano," or "a healthy mind in a sound body."

Where, then, are her gifts taking her? A good question, but one that cannot be answered without also acknowledging that Briana's history in special education—with its flexibility, acceleration, and variety—are the keys to answering it. Wherever she goes after high school, she will seek and need flexibility in her academic and extracurricular activities, acceleration in all that she undertakes, and variety in the way in which she learns and indeed in what she does.

"Where are you taking me?"

"Anywhere your gifts lead, Briana; anywhere they lead."

SUMMARY

Identifying students who are gifted and talented

- Students who are gifted and talented demonstrate unusual capabilities in an intellectual, creative, academic, leadership, or performing and visual arts area. These students require special services not ordinarily provided by the public schools or covered under IDEA.

- Forty states have a definition of *gifted and talented*, and 19 states have a mandate to provide educational services and supports to students who are gifted and talented.

- The characteristic of gifted and talented students most recognized in schools is high intellectual ability.

- Students from ethnically-diverse and poverty backgrounds are vastly underrepresented in current gifted programs.

- The origins of giftedness are from an interaction of environmental and biological factors.

- When IQ test scores are equated with giftedness, the top 2 or 3 percent of the general population is considered gifted.

Evaluating students who are gifted and talented

- Recent innovative evaluation procedures based on multiple domains of giftedness, such as the DISCOVER assessment, offer an alternative form of assessment for identifying and serving students who are gifted.

- The Torrance Test of Creative Thinking is a valid and reliable way to assess the strengths and needs of students in the area of creativity.

Designing an appropriate individualized education program

- Differentiating instruction requires thoughtful planning and partnerships between regular education teachers and specialists in gifted education. Co-teaching is a model of partnerships, and IEP teams should consider what factors would support co-teaching and other needed partnerships.

- Modifications to the scope and sequence of a student's educational program through practices such as acceleration and compacting can ensure that students who are gifted have access to a challenging curriculum.

- Extending the curriculum through the use of cognitive taxonomies can ensure that unit, lesson, and activity objectives are appropriate for the needs of students who are gifted or talented.

- Addressing the socioemotional needs of students who are gifted through activities like the autonomous learning model is a critical feature of a student's IEP to which planning teams must attend.

Using effective instructional strategies

- Gardner's multiple intelligences theory has direct and significant impact on education. As with universal design, schools that focus on the multiple intelligences can ensure that a wider array of students will succeed, beginning with preschool children.

- The schoolwide enrichment model provides an effective way to implement important instructional strategies across a campus, thus ensuring that students who are gifted can be educated in the general education classroom.

- Even though students who are gifted are already ahead of their peers in many ways, they can still learn important skills related to creativity and critical thinking.

Including students who are gifted and talented

- The majority of students who are gifted and talented spend most of their school day in general education classrooms.

- Leaders in gifted education disagree about the appropriateness of the general education classroom curriculum for students who are gifted and talented.

Assessing students' progress

- Product and process evaluations and learning contracts are ways in which students who are gifted can be involved in evaluating progress in their educational programs.

WHAT WOULD YOU RECOMMEND?

Refer to chapter content and the CEC standards in Appendix A to answer the following questions:

1. For each of Gardner's multiple areas of intelligence, plan one instructional activity. Select whether to do this at the early childhood, elementary, middle, or secondary level and identify which CEC standard you would be applying.

2. Reflect on the definition of emotional intelligence. How might you incorporate emotional intelligence into your classroom instruction? Visit the Companion Website, *www.prenhall.com/turnbull*, and locate links to the websites mentioned in the chapter. Use these to help with your answer. Identify which PRAXIS™ or CEC standard you would be applying.

3. Using the eight areas of intelligence illustrated in Figure 16–1, create at least one learning objective (for elementary, middle, or secondary-school students who are gifted and talented) related to at least three of the areas of intelligence.

4. View the section on your DVD that features Briana. Write a profile of Briana, discussing her strengths and gifts. Identify 4 or 5 additional ways you might help her develop these outstanding talents. What PRAXIS™ or CEC standards are you applying?

Use your *Real Lives and Exceptionalities* DVD to critically think about working with Briana under "Questions," located below "Meet Briana." Do you believe students that are gifted and talented should be required to have IEPs? How about federal funding allocated for special education? Why or why not?

Appendix A

PROFESSIONAL STANDARDS FOR SPECIAL EDUCATION

There are two important strands of professional standards referenced in this text. One derives from a separate professional organization in special education, the Council for Exceptional Children; another from standards that appear on professional assessment necessary for teacher creditation. Content in the margin notes of the text refers you to the Standards listed below. The margin notes assist you in connecting the Standards to chapter content. In doing so, the margin notes will help you better apply the Standards in your teaching practice.

One strand includes those standards of the Council for Exceptional Children (CEC), one of the leading advocacy and awareness agencies for individuals with disabilities (*www.cec.sped.org*). A second strand includes the Standards of PRAXIS™, the professional assessments for beginning teachers developed by Educational Testing Service (*www.ets.org*).

THE COUNCIL FOR EXCEPTIONAL CHILDREN— PROFESSIONAL STANDARDS *

Established by the Council for Exceptional Children (CEC), these professional standards address ten critical areas of professionalism:

1. Foundations
2. Development and characteristics of learners
3. Individual learning differences
4. Instructional strategies
5. Learning environments and social interactions
6. Communication
7. Instructional planning
8. Assessment
9. Professional and ethical practice
10. Collaboration

---

*Used with permission of the Council for Exceptional Children.

Each of these broad Standards includes an overview statement and more detailed measurable knowledge and skill statements. The knowledge and skills are limited to the CEC Common Core and do not include any standards from the CEC Area of Specialization Standards. The descriptions provided by CEC have been used verbatim and also appear in the Student Study Guide and on the companion website (*http://www.prenhall.com/turnbull*).

Foundations

Special educators understand the field as an evolving and changing discipline based on philosophies, evidence-based principles and theories, relevant laws and policies, diverse and historical points of view, and human issues that have historically influenced and continue to influence the field of special education and the education and treatment of individuals with exceptional needs both in school and society. Special educators understand how these influence professional practice, including assessment, instructional planning, implementation, and program evaluation. Special educators understand how issues of human diversity can impact families, cultures, and schools, and how these complex human issues can interact with issues in the delivery of special education services. They understand the relationships of organizations of special education to the organizations and functions of schools, school systems, and other agencies. Special educators use this knowledge as a ground upon which to construct their own personal understandings and philosophies of special education. Knowledge and skills addressed in this standard include:

1. Models, theories, and philosophies that form the basis for special education practice.
2. Laws, policies, and ethical principles regarding behavior management planning and implementation.
3. Relationship of special education to the organization and function of educational agencies.
4. Rights and responsibilities of students, parents, teachers, and other professionals, and schools related to exceptional learning needs.
5. Issues in definition and identification of individuals with exceptional learning needs, including those from culturally and linguistically diverse backgrounds.
6. Issues, assurances, and due process rights related to assessment, eligibility, and placement within a continuum of services.

7. Family systems and the role of families in the educational process.

8. Historical points of view and contribution of culturally diverse groups.

9. Impact of the dominant culture on shaping schools and the individuals who study and work in them.

10. Potential impact of differences in values, languages, and customs that can exist between the home and school.

11. Articulate personal philosophy of special education.

Development and Characteristics of Learners

Special educators know and demonstrate respect for their students first as unique human beings. Special educators understand the similarities and differences in human development and the characteristics between and among individuals with and without exceptional learning needs. Moreover, special educators understand how exceptional conditions can interact with the domains of human development and they use this knowledge to respond to the varying abilities and behaviors of individuals with ELN. Special educators understand how the experiences of individuals with ELN can impact families, as well as the individuals ability to learn, interact socially, and live as fulfilled contributing members of the community. Knowledge and skills addressed in this standard include:

1. Typical and atypical human growth and development.

2. Educational implications of characteristics of various exceptionalities.

3. Characteristics and effects of the cultural and environmental milieu of the individual with exceptional learning needs and the family.

4. Family systems and the role of families in supporting development.

5. Similarities and differences of individuals with and without exceptional learning needs.

6. Similarities and differences among individuals with exceptional learning needs.

7. Effects of various medications on individuals with exceptional learning needs.

Individual Learning Differences

Special educators understand the effects that an exceptional condition can have on an individual's learning in school and throughout life. Special educators understand that the beliefs, traditions, and values across and within cultures can affect relationships among and between students, their families, and the school community. Moreover, special educators are active and resourceful in seeking to understand how primary language, culture, and familial backgrounds interact with the individual's exceptional condition to impact the individual's academic and social abilities, attitudes, values, interests, and career options.

The understanding of these learning differences and their possible interactions provide the foundation upon which special educators individualize instruction to provide meaningful and challenging learning for individuals with ELN. Knowledge and skills addressed in this standard include:

1. Effects an exceptional condition(s) can have on an individual's life.

2. Impact of learners' academic and social abilities, attitudes, interests, and values on instruction and career development.

3. Variations in beliefs, traditions, and values across and within cultures and their effects on relationships among individuals with exceptional learning needs. Family, and schooling.

4. Cultural perspectives influencing the relationships among families, schools and communities as related to instruction.

5. Differing ways of learning of individuals with exceptional learning needs, including those from culturally diverse backgrounds, and strategies for addressing these differences.

Instructional Strategies

Special educators possess a repertoire of evidence-based instructional strategies to individualize instruction for individuals with ELN. Special educators select, adapt, and use these instructional strategies to promote challenging learning results in general and special curriculum and to appropriately modify learning environments for individuals with ELN. They enhance the learning of critical thinking, problem solving, and performance skills of individuals with ELN, and increase their self-awareness, self-management, self-control, self-reliance, and self-esteem. Moreover, special educators emphasize the development, maintenance, and generalization of knowledge and skills across environments, settings, and the lifespan. Knowledge and skills addressed in this standard include:

1. Use strategies to facilitate integration into various settings.

2. Teach individuals to use self-assessment, problem solving, and other cognitive strategies to meet their needs.

3. Select, adapt, and use instructional strategies and materials according to characteristics of the individual with exceptional learning needs.

4. Use strategies to facilitate maintenance and generalization of skills across learning environments.

5. Use procedures to increase the individual's self-awareness, self-management, self-control, self-reliance, and self-esteem.

6. Use strategies that promote successful transitions for individuals with exceptional learning needs.

Learning Environments and Social Interactions

Special educators actively create learning environments for individuals with ELN that foster cultural understanding, safety and emotional well being, positive social interactions, and active engagement of individuals with ELN. In addition, special educators foster environments in which diversity is valued and individuals are taught to live harmoniously and productively in a culturally diverse world. Special educators shape environments to encourage the independence, self-motivation, self-direction, personal empowerment, and self-advocacy of individuals with ELN. Special educators help their general education colleagues integrate individuals with ELN in regular environments and engage them in meaningful learning activities and interactions. Special educators use direct motivational and instructional interventions with individuals with ELN to teach them to respond effectively to current expectations. When necessary, special educators can safely intervene with individuals with ELN in crisis. Special educators coordinate all these efforts and provide guidance and direction to paraeducators and others, such as classroom volunteers and tutors. Knowledge and skills addressed in this standard include:

1. Demands of learning environments.
2. Basic classroom management theories and strategies for individuals with exceptional learning needs.
3. Effective management of teaching and learning.
4. Teacher attitudes and behaviors that influence behavior of individuals with exceptional learning needs.
5. Social skills needed for educational and other environments.
6. Strategies for crisis prevention and intervention.
7. Strategies for preparing individuals to live harmoniously and productively in a culturally diverse world.
8. Ways to create learning environments that allow individuals to retain and appreciate their own and each others' respective language and cultural heritage.
9. Ways specific cultures are negatively stereotyped.
10. Strategies used by diverse populations to cope with a legacy of former and continuing racism.
11. Create a safe, equitable, positive, and supportive learning environment in which diversities are valued.
12. Identify realistic expectations for personal and social behavior in various settings.
13. Identify supports needed for integration into various program placements.
14. Design learning environments that encourage active participation in individual and group activities.
15. Modify the learning environment to manage behaviors.
16. Use performance data and information from all stakeholders to make or suggest modifications in learning environments.
17. Establish and maintain rapport with individuals with and without exceptional learning needs.
18. Teach self-advocacy.
19. Create an environment that encourages self-advocacy and increased independence.
20. Use effective and varied behavior management strategies.
21. Use the least intensive behavior management strategy consistent with the needs of the individual with exceptional learning needs.
22. Design and manage daily routines.
23. Organize, develop, and sustain learning environments that support positive intracultural and intercultural experiences.
24. Mediate controversial intercultural issues among students within the learning environment in ways that enhance any culture, group, or person.
25. Structure, direct, and support the activities of paraeducators, volunteers, and tutors.
26. Use universal precautions.

Communication

Special educators understand typical and atypical language development and the ways in which exceptional conditions can interact with an individual's experience with and use of language. Special educators use individualized strategies to enhance language development and teach communication skills to individuals with ELN. Special educators are familiar with augmentative, alternative, and assistive technologies to support and enhance communication of individuals with exceptional needs. Special educators match their communication methods to an individual's language proficiency and cultural and linguistic differences. Special educators provide effective language models, and they use communication strategies and resources to facilitate understanding of subject matter for individuals with ELN whose primary language is not English. Knowledge and skills addressed in this standard include:

1. Effects of cultural and linguistic differences on growth and development.
2. Characteristics of one's own culture and use of language and the ways in which these can differ from other cultures and uses of languages.
3. Ways of behaving and communicating among cultures that can lead to misinterpretation and misunderstanding.
4. Augmentative and assistive communication strategies.
5. Use strategies to support and enhance communication skills of individuals with exceptional learning needs.

6. Use communication strategies and resources to facilitate understanding of subject matter for students whose primary language is not the dominant language.

Instructional Planning

Individualized decision-making and instruction is at the center of special education practice. Special educators develop long-range individualized instructional plans anchored in both general and special curricula. In addition, special educators systematically translate these individualized plans into carefully selected shorter-range goals and objectives, taking into consideration an individual's abilities and needs, the learning environment, and a myriad of cultural and linguistic factors. Individualized instructional plans emphasize explicit modeling and efficient guided practice to assure acquisition and fluency through maintenance and generalization. Understanding of these factors, as well as the implications of an individual's exceptional condition, guides the special educator's selection, adaptation, and creation of materials, and the use of powerful instructional variables. Instructional plans are modified based on ongoing analysis of the individual's learning progress. Moreover, special educators facilitate this instructional planning in a collaborative context including the individuals with exceptionalities, families, professional colleagues, and personnel from other agencies as appropriate. Special educators also develop a variety of individualized transition plans, such as transitions from preschool to elementary school and from secondary settings to a variety of postsecondary work and learning contexts. Special educators are comfortable using appropriate technologies to support instructional planning and individualized instruction. Knowledge and skills addressed in this standard include:

1. Theories and research that form the basis of curriculum development and instructional practice.

2. Scope and sequences of general and special curricula.

3. National, state or provincial, and local curricula standards.

4. Technology for planning and managing the teaching and learning environment.

5. Roles and responsibilities of the paraeducator related to instruction, intervention, and direct service.

6. Identify and prioritize areas of the general curriculum and accommodations for individuals with exceptional learning needs.

7. Develop and implement comprehensive, longitudinal individualized programs in collaboration with team members.

8. Involve the individual and family in setting instructional goals and monitoring progress.

9. Use functional assessments to develop intervention plans.

10. Use task analysis.

11. Sequence, implement, and evaluate individualized learning objectives.

12. Integrate affective, social, and life skills with academic curricula.

13. Develop and select instructional content, resources, and strategies that respond to cultural, linguistic, and gender differences.

14. Incorporate and implement instructional and assistive technology into the educational program.

15. Prepare lesson plans.

16. Prepare and organize materials to implement daily lesson plans.

17. Use instructional time effectively.

18. Make responsive adjustments to instruction based on continual observations.

19. Prepare individuals to exhibit self-enhancing behavior in response to societal attitudes and actions.

Assessment

Assessment is integral to the decision-making and teaching of special educators, and special educators use multiple types of assessment information for a variety of educational decisions. Special educators use the results of assessments to help identify exceptional learning needs and to develop and implement individualized instructional programs, as well as to adjust instruction in response to ongoing learning progress. Special educators understand the legal policies and ethical principles of measurement and assessment related to referral, eligibility, program planning, instruction, and placement for individuals with ELN, including those from culturally and linguistically diverse backgrounds. Special educators understand measurement theory and practices for addressing issues of validity, reliability, norms, bias, and interpretation of assessment results. In addition, special educators understand the appropriate use and limitations of various types of assessments. Special educators collaborate with families and other colleagues to assure non-biased, meaningful assessments and decision-making. Special educators conduct formal and informal assessments of behavior, learning, achievement, and environments to design learning experiences that support the growth and development of individuals with ELN. Special educators use assessment information to identify supports and adaptations required for individuals with ELN to access the general curriculum and to participate in school, system, and statewide assessment programs. Special educators regularly monitor the progress of individuals with ELN in general and special curricula. Special educators use appropriate technologies to support their assessments. Knowledge and skills addressed in this standard include:

1. Basic terminology used in assessment.

2. Legal provisions and ethical principles regarding assessment of individuals.

3. Screening, pre-referral, referral, and classification procedures.

4. Use and limitations of assessment instruments.

5. National, state or provincial, and local accommodations and modifications.

6. Gather relevant background information.

7. Administer nonbiased formal and informal assessments.

8. Use technology to conduct assessments.

9. Develop or modify individualized assessment strategies.

10. Interpret information from formal and informal assessments.

11. Use assessment information in making eligibility, program, and placement decisions for individuals with exceptional learning needs, including those from culturally and/or linguistically diverse backgrounds.

12. Report assessment results to all stakeholders using effective communication skills.

13. Evaluate instruction and monitor progress of individuals with exceptional learning needs.

14. Create and maintain records.

Professional and Ethical Practice

Special educators are guided by the profession's ethical and professional practice standards. Special educators practice in multiple roles and complex situations across wide age and developmental ranges. Their practice requires ongoing attention to legal matters along with serious professional and ethical considerations. Special educators engage in professional activities and participate in learning communities that benefit individuals with ELN, their families, colleagues, and their own professional growth. Special educators view themselves as lifelong learners and regularly reflect on and adjust their practice. Special educators are aware of how their own and others' attitudes, behaviors, and ways of communicating can influence their practice. Special educators understand that culture and language can interact with exceptionalities, and are sensitive to the many aspects of diversity of individuals with ELN and their families. Special educators actively plan and engage in activities that foster their professional growth and keep them current with evidence-based best practices. Special educators know their own limits of practice and practice within them. Knowledge and skills addressed in this standard include:

1. Personal cultural biases and differences that affect one's teaching.

2. Importance of the teacher serving as a model for individuals with exceptional learning needs.

3. Continuum of lifelong professional development.

4. Methods to remain current regarding research-validated practice.

5. Practice within the CEC Code of Ethics and other standards of the profession.

6. Uphold high standards of competence and integrity and exercise sound judgment in the practice of the profession.

7. Act ethically in advocating for appropriate services.

8. Conduct professional activities in compliance with applicable laws and policies.

9. Demonstrate commitment to developing the highest education and quality-of-life potential of individuals with exceptional learning needs.

10. Demonstrate sensitivity for the culture, language, religion, gender, disability, socio-economic status, and sexual orientation of individuals.

11. Practice within one's skill limit and obtain assistance as needed.

12. Use verbal, nonverbal, and written language effectively.

13. Conduct self-evaluation of instruction.

14. Access information on exceptionalities.

15. Reflect on one's practice to improve instruction and guide professional growth.

16. Engage in professional activities that benefit individuals with exceptional learning needs, their families, and one's colleagues.

Collaboration

Special educators routinely and effectively collaborate with families, other educators, related service providers, and personnel from community agencies in culturally responsive ways. This collaboration assures that the needs of individuals with ELN are addressed throughout schooling. Moreover, special educators embrace their special role as advocate for individuals with ELN. Special educators promote and advocate the learning and well being of individuals with ELN across a wide range of settings and a range of different learning experiences. Special educators are viewed as specialists by a myriad of people who actively seek their collaboration to effectively include and teach individuals with ELN. Special educators are a resource to their colleagues in understanding the laws and policies relevant to individuals with ELN. Special educators use collaboration to facilitate the successful transitions of individuals with ELN across settings and services. Knowledge and skills addressed in this standard include:

1. Models and strategies of consultation and collaboration.

2. Roles of individuals with exceptional learning needs, families, and school and community personnel in planning of an individualized program.

3. Concerns of families of individuals with exceptional learning needs and strategies to help address these concerns.

4. Culturally responsive factors that promote effective communication and collaboration with individuals with exceptional learning needs, families, school personnel, and community members.

5. Maintain confidential communication about individuals with exceptional learning needs.

6. Collaborate with families and others in assessment of individuals with exceptional learning needs.

7. Foster respectful and beneficial relationships between families and professionals.

8. Assist individuals with exceptional learning needs and their families in becoming active participants in the educational team.

9. Plan and conduct collaborative conferences with individuals with exceptional learning needs and their families.

10. Collaborate with school personnel and community members in integrating individuals with exceptional learning needs into various settings.

11. Use group problem solving skills to develop, implement, and evaluate collaborative activities.

12. Model techniques and coach others in the use of instructional methods and accommodations.

13. Communicate with school personnel about the characteristics and needs of individuals with exceptional learning needs.

14. Communicate effectively with families of individuals with exceptional learning needs from diverse backgrounds.

15. Observe, evaluate, and provide feedback to paraeducators.

THE PRAXIS™ STANDARDS FOR SPECIAL EDUCATION †

Established by Educational Testing Services (ETS), these professional standards address three components of special education, including understanding, delivery, and legal issues. Each standard is comprehensive, as shown below.

As discussed by ETS (ETS, 2003), the Special Education: Knowledge-Based Core Principles are attentive to understanding exceptionalities, legal and social issues, and delivery of

---

† PRAXIS™ materials selected from The PRAXIS™ Series: Professional Assessments for Beginning Teachers. Reprinted by Permission of Educational Testing Service, the copyright owner.

Disclaimer Permission to reprint PRAXIS™ materials does not constitute review of Endorsement by Educational Testing Service of this publication as a whole or of any other testing information it may contain.

services to students with disabilities. Each of these areas, as described by ETS, is detailed below.

Understanding Exceptionalities

1. Theories and principles of human development and learning, including research and theories related to human development; theories of learning; social and emotional development; language development; cognitive development; and physical development, including motor and sensory

2. Characteristics of students with disabilities, including medical/physical; educational; social; and psychological

3. Basic concepts in special education, including definitions of all major categories and specific disabilities; causation and prevention of disability; the nature of behaviors, including frequency, duration, intensity, and degrees of severity; and classification of students with disabilities, including classifications as represented in IDEA and labeling of students

Legal and Societal Issues

1. Federal laws and landmark legal cases related to special education

2. Issues related to school, family, and/or community, such as teacher advocacy for students and families, including advocating for educational change and developing student self-advocacy; family participation and support systems; public attitudes toward individuals with disabilities; and cultural and community influences.

Delivery of Services to Students with Disabilities

1. Conceptual approaches underlying the delivery of services to students with disabilities (for example, medical, psychodynamic, behavioral, cognitive, sociological, eclectic)

2. Professional roles and responsibilities of teachers of students with disabilities (for example, teacher as a collaborator with other teachers, parents, community groups, and outside agencies); teacher as a multidisciplinary team member; teacher's role in selecting appropriate environments and providing appropriate services to students; knowledge and use of professional literature, research (including classroom research), and professional organizations and associations; and reflecting on one's own teaching

3. Assessment, including how to modify, construct, or select and conduct nondiscriminatory and appropriate informal and formal assessment procedures; how to interpret standardized and specialized assessment results; how to use evaluation results for various purposes, including monitoring instruction and IEP/ITP

development; and how to prepare written reports and communicate findings to others

4. Placement and program issues (including continuum of services; mainstreaming; integration; inclusion; least restrictive environment; non-categorical, categorical, and cross-categorical programs; related services; early intervention; community-based training; transition of students into and within special education placements; postschool transitions; and access to assistive technology)

5. Curriculum and instruction, including the IEP/ITP process; instructional development and implementation (for example, instructional activities, curricular materials, resources and equipment, working with classroom personnel, tutoring and the use of technology); teaching strategies and methods (for example, direct instruction, cooperative learning, diagnostic-prescriptive method); instructional format and components (for example, individualized instruction, small- and large-group instruction, modeling, drill and practice); and areas of instruction (such as academics, study and learning skills, social, self-care, and vocational skills)

6. Management of the learning environment, including behavior management (for example, behavior analysis—identification and definition of antecedents, target behavior, and consequent events, data-gathering procedures, selecting and using behavioral interventions); classroom organization/management (for example, providing the appropriate physical-social environment for learning—expectations, rules, consequences, consistency, attitudes, lighting, seating, access, and strategies for positive interactions, transitions between lessons and activities); grouping of students; and effective and efficient documentation (such as parent/ teacher contacts and legal records)

Glossary

Abacus is a tool composed of beads on vertical rods that is used by students with visual impairments to help them with mathematical calculations. The abacus is not a calculator but is similar to solving a math problem with paper and pencil.

Absence seizures are a type of generalized seizure that cause the person to lose consciousness only briefly.

Academic content standards define the knowledge, skills, and understanding that students should attain in academic subjects.

Acceleration involves students' skipping one or more grades in order to experience higher levels of instruction and/or attending a higher-grade-level program for part of the school day.

Acquired refers to hearing losses that occur after birth.

Acquired disorder is a disorder that occurs well after birth.

Acquired injury means that the injury occurred after a child was born.

Activity task analysis identifies each step the student needs to master within ecological activities that are embedded in community-based instruction.

Acuity is a measure of the sharpness and clarity of vision. It is determined by having an individual stand at a specified distance to read a standard eye chart, each line of which is composed of symbols printed at a certain size.

Acute otitis media is an infection in the middle ear that can result in conductive hearing loss.

Adaptive behavior refers to the typical performance of individuals without disabilities in meeting the expectations of their various environments.

Additions occur when students place a vowel between two consonants.

Adventitious visual impairment means that the impairment results from an advent (e.g., loss of sight caused by a hereditary condition that has just manifested itself) or an event (e.g., loss of sight caused by trauma).

All-school enrichment programs address the top 20 percent of students in a school through special-interest groups, specialized instruction, small groups, and mentoring on individual projects.

Alternate achievement standards must align with the same academic content standards for all students so that these students will be able to make progress in the general curriculum.

Alternate assessment means evaluating performance for students for whom test accommodations are not sufficient to enable them to participate in the typical state- or district-wide assessment.

Alternative teacher certification refers to teachers who do not go through traditional routes to obtain teacher certification. Often they hold emergency certification that allows them to start teaching before they complete the full certification program.

American Sign Language (ASL) is the most widely used sign language among deaf adults in North America.

Anemia is a disorder in which the blood has too few red blood cells or too little hemoglobin.

Anxiety disorder is characterized by overwhelming fear, worry, and/or uneasiness. The condition includes phobia, generalized anxiety disorder, panic disorder, obsessive-compulsive disorder, and post-traumatic stress disorder.

Apgar test is a method for determining the health of a newborn immediately in transition to life outside the womb. The screening occurs in the first minute after birth and again at the fifth minute after birth.

Applied behavior analysis uses the principles of operant psychology to develop techniques that reduce problem behavior and/or increase positive behavior.

Appropriate education is an IDEA principle that requires schools to provide an Individualized Educational Program for students with disabilities that is appropriate to their educational strengths and needs.

Apraxia is a motor speech disorder that affects the way in which a student plans to produce speech.

Aptitude-achievement discrepancy refers to a discrepancy between different abilities and areas of achievement.

Articulation is a speaker's production of individual or sequenced sounds.

Asperger syndrome describes the traits of individuals on the autism spectrum who have significant challenges in social and emotional functioning but without significant delays in language development or intellectual functioning.

Asthma is a chronic lung condition characterized by airway obstruction, inflammation, and increased sensitivity.

Ataxia refers to the inability to coordinate voluntary muscular movements.

Ataxic cerebral palsy involves unsteadiness, lack of coordination and balance, and varying degrees of difficulty with standing and walking.

Athetoid cerebral palsy involves abrupt, involuntary movements of the head, neck, face, and extremities, particularly the upper ones.

Atrophy refers to lost or reduced muscle strength.

Audiogram is a graphic representation of an individual's response to sound in terms of frequency (Hz) and loudness (dB).

Audiologist has special training in testing and measuring hearing.

Audiometer is a machine that measures hearing threshold, the softest level at which sound can first be detected at various sound frequencies.

Audiometry refers to a hearing test, using a device called an audiometer, which provides a graph showing hearing thresholds at various levels of pitch and loudness.

Audition is the hearing process.

Auditory-verbal format encourages early identification and subsequent amplification or cochlear implant. It emphasizes the amplification of sound and helping the child use what hearing remains (residual hearing).

Augmentative and alternative communication (AAC) refers to the devices, techniques, and strategies used by students who are unable to communicate fully through natural speech and/or writing.

Auricle or pinna is the top of the external ear; it channels sound into the ear canal.

Autism spectrum disorder refers to five types of pervasive developmental disorders, including autistic disorder, Rhett's disorder, childhood disintegrative disorder, Asperger syndrome, and pervasive developmental disorder not otherwise specified.

Autonomous learning model assists students in dealing with the socioemotional issues that might accompany their giftedness.

Bacterial meningitis is an infection of the meninges, the three membranes enveloping the brain and the spinal cord.

Behavioral audiological evaluations are hearing tests that require the child to respond to a series of beeps called pure tones to indicate that she hears a sound.

Bidialectal refers to someone who uses two variations of a language.

Bilateral is a hearing loss that occurs in both ears.

Bilingual refers to someone who uses two languages equally well.

Bipolar disorder refers to a condition in which a person experiences exaggerated mood swings—for example, sometimes feeling depressed and other times experiencing heightened activity, energy, and a sense of strength. (These latter experiences are sometimes referred to as *mania*.)

Braille is a method of writing that uses raised dots in specific configurations that can be read and interpreted by people who are blind (and who have received appropriate instruction) by running their fingers across the dots.

Braille contractions are shortcuts for writing letter combinations in braille. Intended to save space and reading time, these contractions may represent a whole word or part of a word. As a result, the braille version of printed material is usually composed of fewer symbols than the print version, even though both include the same words.

Central auditory processing involves the ability to track individual and group conversations that occur in both quiet and noisy backgrounds.

Cerebral palsy refers to a lack of muscle control that affects a student's ability to move and to maintain balance and posture; it has a neurological basis.

Child maltreatment involves neglect, physical abuse, sexual abuse, and emotional abuse.

Chromosomes direct each cell's activity and contain DNA and genes that determine a person's physical and mental condition.

Circle of friends refers to the individuals who surround a person with a disability with support that is consistent with the person's choices and that advances the person's self-determination, full citizenship, relationships, positive contributions, strengths, and choices.

Classroom-centered intervention refers to classroom-based strategies to intervene against poor academic achievement and aggressive or shy behavior.

Clean intermittent catheterization refers to the procedure whereby a person or an attendant (a trained health aide) inserts a tube into the person's urethra to induce urination. It is "clean" because the procedure is done under sterile conditions, and it is "intermittent" because it is done as needed or on a regular schedule; the tube is not permanently placed in the person's urethra.

Cleft palate or lip describes a condition in which a person has a split in the upper part of the oral cavity or the upper lip.

Closed-captioned technology translates dialogue from a spoken language to a printed form (captions) that is then inserted at the bottom of a television or movie screen.

Closed head injury results when the brain whips back and forth during an accident, causing it to bounce off the inside of the skull. It does not involve penetration or a fracture of the bone of the skull.

Cloze procedure involves the modification of a text of at least 250 words by eliminating every fifth word and replacing it with a blank.

Cluster grouping involves grouping three to six students who are gifted and talented in the same general education classroom so that they can work together.

Cochlea is a snail-shaped bony structure that houses the actual organ of hearing.

Cochlear implant is an electronic device that provides sound information by directly stimulating the functional auditory nerve fibers in the cochlea. The internal part is surgically implanted under the skin with electrodes inserted into the cochlea; the external part consists of a microphone, a speech processor, and a transmitting coil.

Cognitive behavioral therapy involves teaching the use of inner speech ("self-talk") to modify underlying cognitions that affect overt behavior.

Cognitive retraining helps students regain perceptual processing, communication, behavioral, and social skills that were lost as a result of traumatic brain injury.

Cognitive taxonomies are ordered lists of cognitive skills or activities that can be used to differentiate expectations for students.

Cognitive tetonomies classify the cognitive demands related to learning targets.

Coma is a state of deep or prolonged unconsciousness usually caused by injury or illness.

Compacting the curriculum involves first testing students to identify the content they have already mastered and then teaching them only the concepts that they have not yet mastered.

Computerized axial tomography (CAT) is another term for computerized tomography, which refers to a method of producing a cross-section image of the body from a thin X-ray beam that rotates around a patient.

Computerized tomography is a method of producing a cross-section image of the body from a thin X-ray beam that rotates around a patient.

Conceptually Accurate Signed English (CASE) is a sign system used in the United States that involves signing concepts rather than the literal English translation.

Conduct disorder consists of a persistent pattern of antisocial behavior that significantly interferes with others' rights or with schools and communities' behavioral expectations.

Congenital refers to an impairment that is present from birth or from the time very near birth; visual impairment occurs at birth or, in the case of blindness, before visual memories have been established.

Congenital deafness is a hearing loss that is present at birth.

Congenital disorder is a disorder that occurs at or before birth.

Cued speech is an alternative to natural sign language and English sign systems. Cued speech supplements spoken English and is intended to make its features fully visible.

Cultural deficit theory blames the failure of students from culturally- and linguistically-diverse backgrounds on the disadvantages that they experienced within their own cultures.

Cultural difference theories also called cultural mismatch theories; contend that failure of students from culturally- and linguistically-diverse backgrounds in school cannot be attributed solely to their lack of assimilation into European culture.

Curriculum-based measurement involves direct assessment of a student's skills in the content of the curriculum that is being taught.

Curriculum extension refers to efforts to expand the breadth and depth of the coverage of a given topic.

Cytomegalovirus (CMV) is a virus that may have very few symptoms in adults or might resemble mononucleosis. In a fetus, however, it can lead to severe malformations.

Deaf is a term used to describe a hearing loss greater than 70 to 90 dB that results in severe oral speech and language delay or that prevents a person from understanding spoken language through hearing.

Deaf community is a group of individuals who are deaf; share a culture, attitudes, and a set of beliefs; and use American Sign Language to communicate.

Decibel (dB) is the unit used to express how loud sound is.

Dialect is a regional variation of a language, as when someone speaks English using terms or pronunciations common only in that region.

Differentiated instruction involves using different strategies such as flexible student instructional grouping, learning stations and learning centers, and two educators in the same classroom.

Discrepancy analysis examines where and how the two ecological inventories differ and whether the points of difference can be the basis for instruction or can be addressed through other means, such as assistive technology.

Discrete trial training is based on the three-term contingency outlined by applied behavior analysis: the discriminative stimulus, the response, and the reinforcer or consequence.

Discriminative stimulus is a specific event or environmental condition that elicits a desired response. This stimulus "acquires control" over the desired response when the response is paired with a reinforcer.

Distortions are modifications of the production of a phoneme in a word.

Domains of family life include emotional well-being, parenting, family interaction, physical/material well-being, and disability-related support.

Dopamine is one of the brain's neurotransmitters, carrying signals between neurons.

Duration is the length of time any speech sound requires.

Dyscalculia refers to a lack of ability to perform mathematical functions.

Dysgraphia refers to the partial inability to remember how to make certain alphabet or arithmetic symbols in handwriting.

Dyslexia refers to the condition of having severe difficulty in learning to read.

Ear canal is the channel through which sounds flow to the middle ear.

Echolalia is a form of communication in which a student echoes other people's language by constantly repeating a portion of what he or she hears. It is either immediate or delayed.

Ecological inventories identify the subenvironments in which students function, the activities involved in them, and the skills needed in them.

Encephalitis refers to inflammation of the brain.

Errorless learning refers to a procedure that presents the discriminative stimuli and arranges the delivery of prompts in a learning situation in such a way as to ensure that the student gives only correct responses.

Etiology describes the cause or origin of a medical condition.

Eustachian tube is the structure that extends from the throat into the middle ear cavity; its primary purpose is to equalize the air pressure on the eardrum when a person swallows or yawns.

Event recording involves an observer recording every occurrence of a behavior during an observation period instead of using the yes/no recording per interval that is characteristic of time sampling.

Exclusionary standard refers to embedding particular exemptions within a definition. For example, in the IDEA definition of learning disabilities, learning disabilities do not include learning problems that primarily result from visual impairment; hearing loss; mental retardation; emotional disturbance; or environmental, cultural, or economic disadvantages.

Executive functioning includes being able to process information to make decisions, take actions, and solve problems.

Expanded core curriculum describes the areas of instruction in which students with visual impairments need additional instruction because of the impact of their visual impairment on incidental learning. It includes compensatory skills, orientation and mobility, social interaction skills, independent living skills, recreation and leisure skills, career education, use of assistive technology, visual efficiency skills, and self-determination.

Expressive language disorder is characterized by difficulty in formulating ideas and information.

Externalizing behaviors are behavior disorders comprising aggressive, acting-out, and noncompliant behaviors.

Family means two or more people who regard themselves to be a family and who carry out the functions that families typically perform.

Family-professional partnerships are relationships in which families and professionals collaborate, capitalizing on each other's judgments and expertise in order to increase the benefits of education for students, families, and professionals.

Family quality of life refers to the extent to which the family's needs are met, family members enjoy their life together, and family members have the chance to do the things that are important to them.

Field observation involves observing and recording, in a longhand, anecdotal format, what a student is doing.

Field of vision (visual field) is the entire area of which an individual is visually aware when the person is directing his or her gaze straight ahead, typically 160 degrees.

Fingerspelling uses a hand representation for all 26 letters of the alphabet.

Fluency is the rate and rhythm of speaking.

Formative analysis means that analysis is conducted on an ongoing basis.

Functional behavioral assessment is a process used to determine a specific relationship between a student's behaviors and the circumstances that triggered those behaviors, especially those that impede a student's ability to learn.

Functional disorders are those with no identifiable organic or neurological cause.

Functionally blind describes individuals who can use their available vision to some limited degree but acquire information about the environment primarily through their auditory and tactile senses.

Functional magnetic resonance imaging provides a map of brain activity by producing images of tiny metabolic changes that occur as the brain functions.

Functional visual assessment (FVA) is an evaluation of how an individual uses his or her vision to perform tasks. It results in a description of what an individual with a visual impairment does with his or her available vision, not an acuity measurement.

General education curriculum refers to the curriculum used by nondisabled students.

Generalization refers to the ability to transfer knowledge or behavior learned for doing one task to another task and to make that transfer across different settings or environments.

Generalized anxiety disorder consists of excessive, overwhelming worry not caused by any recent experience.

Genetic deficit theories typically support the notion that nonwhites are genetically deficient when compared to whites.

Goal attainment scaling is a process that enables teachers to compare goals and to quantify student goal attainment.

Hard of hearing is a term used for individuals who have hearing loss of 25 to 70 dB in the better ear, who benefit from amplification, and who communicate primarily through spoken language.

Herpes virus is a virus leading to symptoms that range from cold sores, to genital lesions, to encephalitis; it causes disabilities in early infancy.

Hertz (Hz) is the unit used to express the frequency of sound and is measured in terms of the number of cycles that vibrating sound molecules complete per second.

Hyperactivity refers to behaviors associated with frequent movement, difficulty concentrating, and talking excessively.

Hyperbilirubinemia results from an excess accumulation of bilirubin in the blood, which can result in jaundice a yellowing of the complexion and the whites of the eyes.

Hyperfocus refers to demonstrating intense levels of concentration and attention in completing tasks.

Hypernasality is when air is allowed to pass through the nasal cavity on sounds other than /m/, /n/, and /ng/.

Hyponasality occurs because air cannot pass through the nose and comes through the mouth instead.

Hypoxia is the lack of oxygen.

Impulsivity refers to behaviors such as difficulty awaiting one's turn, interrupting or intruding on others and blurting out answers before questions have been completed.

Incidental learning occurs when an individual learns about a process or concept primarily through observation and without others knowingly providing instruction.

Inclusionary standard refers to embedding certain criteria within a definition so as to clearly state the conditions that the definition covers. For example, in the IDEA definition of learning disabilities, perceptual disabilities, brain injury, minimal brain dysfunction, dyslexia, and developmental aphasia are included conditions.

Individualized Education Program (IEP) is a written plan for serving students with disabilities ages 3 to 21.

Individualized Family Services Plan (IFSP) is a written plan for providing services to infants and toddlers, ages zero to 3, and their families.

Intensity (loudness or softness) is based on the perception of the listener and is determined by the air pressure coming from the lungs through the vocal folds.

Internalization of speech is an executive function that includes talking to oneself in order to plan what to do and say and recognizing when it is appropriate to speak these thoughts.

Internalizing behaviors are behavior disorders comprising social withdrawal, depression, anxiety, obsessions, and compulsions.

Interpreter is an individual who translates a spoken message into sign. Oral interpreters silently repeat with clear lip movements the message of the speaker. A transliterator provides word-for-word translation using signs in English word order.

Intra-achievement discrepancy refers to a discrepancy between different areas of academic achievement.

Intracognitive discrepancy refers to discrepancies between different abilities such as performance and verbal scores.

Intracranial hemorrhage is a neurological complication of extremely premature infants in which the immature blood vessels bleed into the brain.

IQ-achievement discrepancy refers to a discrepancy between the student's intellectual ability, as measured by an IQ test, and the student's achievement, as measured by a standardized achievement test.

Jaundice is a yellowing of the complexion and the whites of the eyes resulting from hyperbilirubinemia.

Karyotyping involves arranging the chromosomes under a microscope so that they can be counted and grouped according to size, shape, and pattern.

Keyword strategies teach students to link a keyword to a new word or concept to help them remember the new material.

Kinship care refers to the situation where children receive their basic care from some member of their family other than their parents.

Language is a structured, shared, rule-governed symbolic system for communicating.

Language disorder is difficulty in receiving, understanding, and formulating ideas and information.

Learning media assessment (LMA) is an evaluation of students who have visual impairments to determine the learning medium in which they function most efficiently as well as to identify those media in which additional instruction may be necessary.

Learning medium is the term used to describe the format(s) of reading and literacy materials available to individuals who have visual impairments and may include braille, print, large print, audiotapes, and access technology.

Learning strategies help students with learning disabilities to learn independently and to generalize, or transfer, their skills and behaviors to new situations.

Least restrictive environment (LRE) is an IDEA principle that requires that students with disabilities be educated to the maximum extent appropriate with students who do not have a disability and that they be removed from regular education settings only when the nature or severity of their disability cannot be addressed with the use of supplementary aids and services.

Legal blindness is a term that refers to individuals whose central visual acuity, when measured in both eyes and when they are wearing corrective lenses, is 20/200 or whose visual field is no more than 20 degrees.

Letter strategies employ acronyms or a string of letters to remember a list of words or concepts.

Life space analysis is a process in which teachers collect two kinds of data: first, baseline data about how well a student functions in certain community settings; next, information about the student's current environments and prospective environments for community-based instruction.

Loop systems involve closed-circuit wiring that sends FM signals from an audio system directly to an electronic coil in a student's hearing aid. The receiver picks up the signals, much as a remote-control device sends infrared signals to a television.

Low vision is experienced by individuals with a visual impairment who can use their vision as a primary channel for learning.

Low vision specialist is an individual, usually an optometrist, who has specialized in the measurement of the basic visual skills of individuals with low vision and who is knowledgeable about and prescribes glasses and other assistive devices that facilitate visual functioning in people whose vision is impaired.

Lumbar nerves move the leg muscles.

Magnetic resonance imaging (MRI) uses a strong magnetic field and radio waves to provide detailed pictures of smaller and more subtle brain anomalies or differences that cannot be detected by computerized tomography.

Manifestation determination is used when disciplining students who receive special education. The school must determine whether the student's behavior is a manifestation "caused by" his or her disability. This process must occur when the school proposes to change the student's placement for more than 10 days.

Manual approach involves teaching the use of sign language for communication.

MAPs is a process that customizes students' educational programs to their specific visions, strengths, and needs. It is especially effective in planning transitions from school to postschool activities.

Maternal Rh incompatibility is a condition that occurs when a baby with Rh+ blood is born to a mother with Rh− blood. This leads to a breakdown of red blood cells in the baby.

Maternal serum alpha-fetoprotein is a prenatal test to detect spina bifida.

Mean refers to an average.

Meningocele refers to the condition in which the covering of the spinal cord, but not the cord itself, protrudes through the opening created by the defect in the spine. This condition usually does not cause a person to experience mobility impairments.

Mixed cerebral palsy combines spastic muscle tone and the involuntary movements of athetoid cerebral palsy.

Mnemonic is a device such as a rhyme, formula, or acronym that is used to aid memory.

Mood disorder involves an extreme deviation in either a depressed or an elevated direction or sometimes in both directions at different times.

Morpheme is the smallest meaningful unit of speech.

Morphology is the system that governs the structure of words.

Multidimensional model of intelligence considers multiple domains of intelligence as contrasted to concentrating only on intellectual ability or academic achievement.

Multimodal treatments involves multiple interventions or treatments across modes or types of therapies.

Myelomeningocele refers to a condition in which the protrusion or sac contains not only the spinal cord's covering but also a portion of the spinal cord or nerve roots. This condition results in varying degrees of leg weakness, inability to control bowels or bladder, and a variety of physical problems such as dislocated hips or club feet.

Neuroimaging provides non-invasive detailed pictures of various parts of the brain that are helpful in determining the presence of a disability.

Neurotransmitters are substances that transmit nerve impulses across synapses in the brain.

No cessation is a term that refers to the discipline of students under IDEA and means that the school may not expel or suspend a student with a disability for more than 10 school days in any one school year, regardless of what the student does to violate a school code.

Nondiscriminatory evaluation is an IDEA principle that requires schools to determine what each student's disability is and how it relates to the student's education. The evaluation must be carried out in a culturally responsive way.

Nonverbal working memory is an executive function that involves the ability to retrieve auditory, visual, and other sensory images of the past.

Norm group is a comparison group usually representing an average standard of achievement or development for a specific age group or grade level.

Norm-referenced achievement test compares a student with his or her age- or grade-level peers in terms of performance.

Obsessions are persistent thoughts, impulses, or images of a repetitive nature that create anxiety.

Obsessive-compulsive disorder are obsessions manifesting as repetitive, persistent, and intrusive impulses, images, or thoughts (i.e., repetitive thoughts about death or illness) and/or compulsions manifesting as repetitive, stereotypical behaviors (i.e., handwashing or counting).

Omissions occur when a child leaves a phoneme out of a word.

Open head injury penetrates the bones of the skull, allowing bacteria to have contact with the brain and potentially impairing specific functions, usually only those controlled by the injured part of the brain.

Oppositional defiant disorder causes a pattern of negativistic, hostile, disobedient, and defiant behaviors.

Oral/aural format emphasizes the use of amplified sound to develop oral language.

Oral motor exam is examination of the appearance, strength, and range of motion of the lips, tongue, palate, teeth, and jaw.

Organic disorders are those caused by an identifiable problem in the neuromuscular mechanism of the person.

Organ of Corti refers to the organ of hearing.

Orientation and mobility (O&M) is a term used to describe the two components of travel: orientation (knowing where you are and where you want to go) and mobility (the safe, efficient, graceful movement between two locations). For students with visual impairments, instruction in O&M often is necessary.

Ossicular chain consists of the three small bones in the middle ear (**malleus, incus,** and **stapes**—hammer, anvil, and stirrup) that transmit the sound vibrations through the middle-ear cavity to the inner ear.

Otologist is a physician who specializes in diseases of the ear.

Ototoxic drugs affect the organs or nerves involved in hearing or balance.

Outer-directedness is a condition in which individuals distrust their own solutions and seek cues from others.

Oval window is the membrane that separates the middle from the inner ear.

Panic disorder involves overwhelming panic attacks resulting in rapid heartbeat, dizziness, and/or other physical symptoms.

Part B refers to the section of IDEA that addresses the social education of students who range from 3 to 21 years of age.

Part C represents the section of IDEA that addresses the needs of infants and toddlers ranging in age from birth through age 2.

Partial participation rejects an all-or-none approach under which students either function independently in a given environment or not at all. Instead, it asserts that students with severe and multiple disabilities can participate, even if only partially, and indeed can often learn and complete a task if it is adapted to their strengths.

Partial seizures cause the student to lose consciousness and often to fall to the ground and have sudden, involuntary contractions of groups of muscles.

Peer tutoring involves pairing students one on one so that students who have already developed certain skills can help teach those and other skills to less advanced students and also help those students practice the skills they have already mastered.

Pegword strategy helps students remember numbered or ordered information by linking words that rhyme with numbers.

Perinatal means at birth.

Perseveration includes verbalizations or behaviors that are repeated to an inappropriate extent.

Pervasive developmental disorders include five discrete disorders that are part of the autism spectrum, including autistic disorder, Rhett's disorder, childhood disintegrative disorder, and Asperger syndrome.

Phobia consists of the unrealistic, overwhelming fear of an object or situation.

Phonemes are individual speech sounds and how they are produced, depending on their placement in a syllable or word.

Phonological processing refers to the ability to process written and oral information by using the sound system of language.

Phonology is the use of sounds to make meaningful syllables and words.

Pidgin Sign English (PSE) is a sign system used in the United States and employs a basic ASL sign vocabulary in English word order.

Pitch is affected by the tension and size of the vocal folds, the health of the larynx, and the location of the larynx.

Pneumatic, or Puffing, Switches operate when the student, such as one who has no arm control, puffs air into a strawlike tube.

Portfolio-based assessment is a technique for assembling exemplars of a student's work, such as homework, in-class tests, artwork, journal writing, and other evidence of the student's strengths and needs.

Positive behavior support is a proactive, data-based approach to ensuring that students acquire needed skills and environmental supports.

Positron emission tomography (PET) produces three-dimensional pictures by recording a radioactive chemical that is injected into the body and absorbed by organs.

Postnatal means after birth.

Post-traumatic stress disorder refers to flashbacks and other recurrent symptoms following exposure to an extremely distressing and dangerous event such as witnessing violence or a hurricane.

Pragmatics refers to the use of communication in context.

Prelinguistic milieu teaching is an effective language-acquisition instructional strategy based on the principle that children will learn if their instruction matches their interests and abilities.

Prenatal means before birth.

Prereferral occurs when a student's general education teacher asks others (educators and families) to help problem-solve in order to identify instructional strategies to adequately address learning and behavioral challenges.

Procedural due process is the principle of IDEA that seeks to make the schools and parents accountable to each other through a system of checks and balances.

Procedural problems in math refer to difficulty in sequencing the steps of complex problems.

Prodigy is a person who is gifted to the point of being unmistakably extraordinary.

Receptive language disorder is characterized by difficulty in receiving or understanding information.

Reconstitution is an executive function that includes the skill of analyzing and synthesizing behaviors.

Referral occurs when an educator or a parent submits a formal request for the student to be considered for a full and formal nondiscriminatory evaluation.

Reinforcing stimulus is an event or action that follows the response and increases the possibility that the response will be exhibited again.

Repetitive behavior involves obsessions, tics, and perseveration.

Resonance is determined by the way in which the tone coming from the vocal folds is modified by the spaces of the throat, mouth, and nose.

Response is the behavior a student performs when presented with a discriminative stimulus. The response is the behavior you are trying to teach the child.

Response-to-intervention model refers to procedures for providing generally effective instruction to students, monitoring their progress, and assessing the extent to which students make sufficient progress in response to their instruction.

Reverse-role tutoring refers to using students with disabilities as tutors for their peers without disabilities.

RhoGAM is a drug used for mothers who have Rh− blood to keep them from producing antibodies that could harm their future babies.

Rubella is a viral infection, also called German measles, that causes a mild fever and skin rash. If a woman in the first 3 months of her pregnancy gets this disease, it can lead to severe birth defects in her child.

Sacral nerves control the foot muscles.

Savant syndrome is a condition in which individuals typically display extraordinary abilities in areas such as calendar calculating, musical ability, mathematical skills, memorization, and mechanical abilities.

Schizophrenia is characterized by psychotic periods resulting in hallucinations, delusions, inability to experience pleasure, and loss of contact with reality.

Schoolwide enrichment model promotes challenging, high-end learning across a range of school types, levels, and demographic differences by creating services that can be integrated across the general curriculum to assist all students, not just students who are gifted.

Screening is a routine test that helps school staff identify which students might need further testing to determine whether they qualify for special education.

Seeing Essential English, Signing Exact English (SEE2) is a sign system used in the United States that borrows sign from ASL and then adds signs that correspond to English morphemes.

Seizures are temporary neurological abnormalities that result from unregulated electrical discharges in the brain, much like an electrical storm.

Seizures with primarily altered consciousness affect large areas of the brain and may manifest in limited activity (absence seizures) or extreme motor behaviors (tonic-clonic seizures).

Self-determination refers to the ability of individuals to live their lives as they choose, consistent with their own values, preferences, and abilities.

Self-instruction strategies involve teaching students to use their own verbal or other communication skills to direct their own learning.

Self-monitoring strategies enable students to learn to collect data on their progress toward educational goals. They can do this through various formats, such as by charting their progress on a sheet of graph paper or completing a checklist.

Self-regulation of affect, motivation, and arousal is an executive function that refers to being less objective and more emotional in responding to events, understanding the effect of one's behavior on others, and generating energy and enthusiasm to carry out behavior.

Semantic memory problems in math refer to difficulty in remembering math facts.

Semantics refers to the meaning of what is expressed.

Separation anxiety disorder is excessive and intense fear associated with separating from home, family, and others with whom a child has a close attachment.

Service learning is a method for students to develop newly acquired skills by active participation and structured reflection in organized opportunities to meet community needs.

Shaken baby syndrome refers to a brain injury resulting from a situation in which a caregiver has shaken a child violently, often because the caregiver is frustrated by the child's crying.

Short-term memory is the mental ability to recall information that has been stored for a few seconds to a few hours.

Sign language uses combinations of hand movements to convey words and concepts rather than individual letters.

Skilled dialogue is a strategy that involves **anchored understanding** (having a compassionate understanding of differences that comes from truly getting to know someone) and **third space** (a situation in which people creatively restate each other's diverse perspectives in order to reach a new perspective without abandoning individual points of view).

Slate and stylus is a tool used by people who are blind to write short notes to themselves. It consists of a slate, a hinged metal template, and a stylus (a small awl) that is used to punch the dots of a message in braille on a piece of paper inserted in the slate.

Social interaction theories emphasize that communication skills are learned through social interactions.

Social stories are written by educators, parents, or students and describe social situations, social cues, and appropriate responses to those cues.

Sound-field amplification system enables the teacher to transmit her voice by using a lavaliere microphone and ceiling- or wall-mounted speakers.

Spastic cerebral palsy involves tightness in one or more muscle groups.

Specially designed instruction refers to adaptations of the content, methodology, or delivery of instruction to address a student's unique needs and ensure that the student can participate and make progress in the general curriculum.

Specific language impairment   describes a language disorder with no identifiable cause in a person with apparently normal development in all other areas.

Specific learning disability   means a disorder in one or more of the basic psychological processes involved in understanding or using spoken or written language.

Speech   is the oral expression of language.

Speech disorder   refers to difficulty in producing sounds as well as disorders of voice quality (for example, a hoarse voice) or fluency of speech, often referred to as stuttering.

Speech reader   is someone who is able to interpret words by watching the speaker's lips and facial movements without hearing the speaker's voice.

Spina bifida   is a condition in which the person's vertebral arches (the connective tissue between one vertebra and another) are not completely closed; the person's spine is split—thus, spina (spine) bifida (split). Spina bifida is the most common form of neural tube defect.

Spina bifida occulta   refers to a condition in which the spinal cord or its covering do not protrude and only a small portion of the vertebra, usually in the lower spine, is missing. This is the mildest and most common form of spina bifida.

Standard deviation   is a way to determine how much a particular score differs from the mean.

Standards-based reform   is a process that identifies the academic content (reading, mathematics) that students must master, the standards for the students' achievement of content proficiency, a general curriculum aligned with these standards, assessment of student progress in meeting the general curriculum and standards, and information from the assessments to improve teaching and learning and to demonstrate that the schools are indeed accountable to the students, their families, and the public.

Student achievement standards   define the levels of achievement that students must meet to demonstrate their proficiency in the subjects.

Student-directed learning strategies   teach students with and without disabilities to modify and regulate their own learning.

Substitutions   occur when a person substitutes one sound for another, as when a child substitutes /d/ for the voiced /th/ ("doze" for "those"), /t/ for /k/ ("tat" for "cat"), or /w/ for /r/ ("wabbit" for "rabbit").

Summative evaluation   is an evaluation that occurs after a product or project is completed.

Supplementary aids and services   are aids, services, and other supports provided in general education classes or other education-related settings to enable children with disabilities to be educated with nondisabled children to the maximum extent appropriate.

Syndrome   is a collection of two or more features that result from a single cause.

Syntax   provides rules for putting together a series of words to form sentences.

Syphilis   is a sexually transmitted disease that can cause an intrauterine infection in pregnant woman and result in severe birth defects in her child.

System for Augmenting Language (SAL)   focuses on augmented input of language.

T-Charts   are charts that are laid out in the form of a capital letter *T*, which allow teachers to track two aspects of a behavior together.

Teratogens   refer to aspects of the environment that cause developmental malformations in humans.

Tics   are involuntary, rapid movements that occur without warning.

Time sampling   involves an observer who is recording the occurrence or nonoccurrence of specific behaviors during short, predetermined intervals.

Tonic-clonic seizures   affect a student's motor control area of the brain, as well as sensory, behavioral, and cognitive areas. Tonic-clonic seizures can occur in only one region of the brain or spread to other brain hemispheres.

Tonotopically   means that the hair cells closest to the oval window respond to high-frequency sounds and those at the center (if the cochlea were unrolled) are more sensitive to low-frequency sounds.

Topographical classification system   correlates the specific body location of the movement impairment with the location of the brain damage.

Totally blind   describes those individuals who do not receive meaningful input through the visual sense.

Toxoplasmosis   is an infectious disease caused by a microorganism that can cause severe fetal malformations.

Transition services   focus on planning educational services and supports for students who are moving from one level of education to another, such as from high school to postsecondary services.

Traumatic brain injury   is caused by an external physical force, resulting in impaired functioning in one or more areas. Educational performance is adversely affected. The injury may be open or closed.

Tunnel vision   occurs when an individual's visual field is reduced significantly so that only a small area of central visual acuity remains. The affected individual has the impression of looking through a tunnel or tube and is unaware of objects to the left, right, top, or bottom.

Tympanography   is not a hearing test but a test of how well the middle ear is functioning and how well the eardrum can move.

Unilateral   is hearing loss in one ear only.

Universal design for learning (UDL) is the application of principles to the design of curricular and instructional materials to provide students across a wide range of abilities and from a variety of backgrounds with access to academic content.

Vestibular mechanism (semicircular canals) controls balance, helps a body maintain its equilibrium, and is sensitive to both motion and gravity.

Visual disability (including blindness) is an impairment in vision that, even with correction, adversely affects a child's educational performance. The term includes both partial sight and blindness.

Visual-special problems in math refer to difficulties in reproducing numerals.

Wraparound refers to a philosophy of care that includes a definable planning process involving the child and family that results in a unique set of community services and natural supports individualized for that child and family to achieve a positive set of outcomes.

Zero reject is an IDEA principle that requires schools to enroll all students who have disabilities.

References

Chapter 1

Bahr, M. W., Fuchs, D., & Fuchs, L. S. (1999). Mainstream assistance teams: A consultation-based approach to prereferral intervention. In S. Graham & K. Harris (Eds.), *Teachers working together: Enhancing the performance of students with special needs* (pp. 87–116). Cambridge, MA: Brookline.

Bahr, M. W., Whitten, E., Dieker, L., Kocarek, C. E., & Manson, D. (1999). A comparison of school-based teams: Implications for educational and legal reform. *Teaching Exceptional Children 66*(1), 67–83.

Belkin, L. (2004, September 12). The lessons of classroom 506. *New York Times Magazine*, pp. 40–49.

Brown v. Board of Education. 347 U.S. 483. (1954).

Bush, G. W. (2001a). *Foreword: No Child Left Behind* (http://www.whitehouse.gov/news/reports/no-child-left-behind.html).

Bush, G. W. (2001b). *Overview: No Child Left Behind* (http://www.ed.gov/nclb/overview/intro/presidentplan/page_pg3.html).

Carlson, E., Brauen, M., Klein, S., Schroll, K., & Willig, S. (2002). *Key findings for SPeNSE* (http://ferdig.coe.ufl.edu/spense).

Chambers, J. G., Shkolink, J., & Pérez, M. (2003). *Total expenditures for students with disabilities, 1999–2000: Spending variation by disability.* Palo Alto, CA: Center for Special Education Finance/American Institutes for Research.

Council of State Directors of Programs for the Gifted and National Association for Gifted Children. (2003). *State of states: Gifted and talented education report, 2001–2002.* Washington, DC: National Association for Gifted Children.

Coutinho, M. J., & Oswald, D. P. (2005). State variation in gender disproportionality in special education: Findings and recommendations. *Remedial and Special Education, 26*(1), 7–15.

deBettencourt, L. U. (2002). Understanding the differences between IDEA and Section 504. *Teaching Exceptional Children 34*(3), 16–23.

Denbo, S. M. (2003). Disability lessons in higher education: Accommodating learning-disabled students and student-athletes under the Rehabilitation Act and the Americans with Disabilities Act. *American Business Law Journal, 41*(1), 145–203.

Donne, J. (1986 [1624]). *Devotions upon emergent occasions.* In M. H. Abrams (Ed.), *The Norton Anthology of English Literature* (Meditation 17, pp. 1107–1108). New York: Norton.

Goffman, E. (1963). *Behavior in public places: Notes on the social orgnization of gatherings.* Glencoe, IL: Free Press.

Huber, J., & Jones, G. (2003). Renovating to meet ADA standards. *School Planning and Management, 42*(2), 62–63.

Katsiyannis, A., Zhang, D., & Conroy, M. A. (2003). Availability of special education teachers: Trends and issues. *Remedial and Special Education, 24*(4), 246–253.

Kemp, C. E., Hourcade, J. J., & Parette, H. P. (2000). Building an initial information base: Assistive technology funding resources for school-aged students with disabilities. *Journal of Special Education Technology, 15*(4), 15–24.

Kliewer, C., & Biklin, D. (1996). *Labeling: Who wants to be called retarded?* (2nd ed.). Boston: Allyn & Bacon.

Lahm, E. A., Bausch, M. E., Hasselbring, T. S., & Blackhurst, A. E. (2001). National Assistive Technology Research Institute. *Journal of Special Education Technology, 16*(3), 19–26.

Lapadat, J. C. (1998). Implicit theories and stigmatizing labels. *Journal of College Reading and Learning, 29*(1), 73.

Mesibov, G. B., Adams, L. W., & Klinger, L. G. (1997). *Autism: Understanding the disorder.* New York: Plenum.

Mills v. Washington, DC, Board of Education. 348 F. Supp 866 (D.DC 1972); contempt proceedings, EHLR 551: 643 (D.DC 1980).

National Center for Education Statistics. (2000). *Dropout rates in the United States.* Washington, DC: U.S. Department of Education.

National Council on Disability. (2000). *Federal policy barriers to assistive technology.* Washington: Author.

National Organization on Disability. (2004). *N.O.D./Harris survey of Americans with disabilities.* (Study No. 20839). New York: Harris Interactive.

No Child Left Behind Act. (2002). P.L. 107–110.

Norwich, B. (1999). The connotation of special education labels for professionals in the field. *British Journal of Special Education, 26*(4), 179–183.

Obiakor, F. E. (1999). Teacher expectations of minority exceptional learners: Impact on "accuracy" of self-concepts. *Exceptional Children, 66*(1), 39–53.

Parrish, T., Harr, J., Wolman, J., Anthony, J., Merickel, A., & Esra, P. (2004). *State special education finance systems, 1999–2000: Part 2: Special education revenues and expenditures.* Palo Alto, CA: Center for Special Education Finance/American Institutes for Research.

Patton, J. M. (1998). The disproportionate representation of African Americans in special education: Looking behind the curtain for understanding and solutions. *Journal of Special Education, 32*(1), 25–31.

Pennsylvania Association for Retarded Children (PARC) v. Commonwealth of Pennsylvania. 334 F. Supp. 1257, 343 F. Supp. 279 (1971, 1972).

Rea, P. J., & Davis-Dorsey, J. (2004). ADA in the public school setting: Practitioners' reflections. *Journal of Disability Policy Studies, 15*(2), 66–69.

Reschly, D. J. (1996). Identification and assessment of students with disabilities. *Future in Children, 6*(1), 40–53.

Stoddart, T., & Floden, R. (1995). *Traditional and alternate routes to teacher certification: Issues, assumptions, and misconceptions.* East Lansing, MI: National Center for Research on Teacher Learning.

Turnbull, A. P., Turnbull, H. R., Erwin, E., & Soodak, L. (2006). *Families, professionals, and exceptionality: Positive outcomes through partnerships and trust* (5th ed.). Upper Saddle River, NJ: Merrill/Prentice Hall.

Turnbull, H. R., Turnbull, A. P., Stowe, M., & Wilcox, B. L. (2000). *Free appropriate education: The law and children with disabilities* (6th ed.). Denver: Love.

U.S. Department of Education. (1998). *To assure the free appropriate public education of all children with disabilities: Twentieth annual report to Congress on the implementation of the Individuals with Disabilities Education Act.* Washington, DC: Author.

U.S. Department of Education. (2001). *To assure the free appropriate public education of all children with disabilities: Twenty-third annual report to Congress on the implementation of the Individuals with Disabilities Education Act.* Washington, DC: Author.

U.S. Department of Education Office of Special Education Programs. (2005). *IDEA data* (http://www.ideadata.org).

Wall, P. S., & Sarver, L. (2003). Disabled student access in an era of technology. *Internet and Higher Education, 6*(3), 277–284.

Yell, M. (1998). *The law and special education.* Upper Saddle River, NJ: Merrill/Prentice Hall.

Chapter 2

American Federation of Teachers. (1999). *Making standards matter 1996: An annual fifty-state report on efforts to raise academic standards*. Washington, DC: Author.

Andrews, J. E., Carnine, D. W., Continho, M. J., Edgar, E. B., Forness, S. R., Fuchs, L. S., Jordan, D., Kauffman, J. M., Patton, J. M., Paul, J., Rosell, J., Rueda, E. S., Schiller, E., Skrtic, T. M., & Wong, J. (2000). Bridging the special education divide. *Remedial and Special Education, 21*(5), 258–260, 267.

Barnett, C., & Monda-Amaya, L. E. (1998). Principals' knowledge of and attitudes toward inclusion. *Remedial and Special Education, 19*(3), 181–192.

Bennett, T., DeLuca, D., & Bruns, D. (1997). Putting inclusion into practice: Perspectives of teachers and parents. *Exceptional Children, 64*(1), 115–131.

Bolt, S. E., & Thurlow, M. (2004). Five of the most frequently allowed testing accommodations in state policy. *Remedial and Special Education, 25*, 141–152.

Boyer, W. A. R., & Bandy, H. (1997). Rural teachers' perceptions of the current state of inclusion: Knowledge, training, teaching practices, and adequacy of support systems. *Exceptionality, 7*(1), 1–18.

Browder, D. M., Spooner, F., Algrim-Delzell, L., Flowers, C., Algozzine, R., & Karvonen, M. (2004). A content analysis of the curricular philosophies reflected in states' alternate assessments. *Research and Practice for Persons with Severe Disabilities, 28*, 105–131.

Brown, L., Udvari-Solner, A., Frattura-Kampschroer, E., Davis, L., Ahlgren, C., Van Daventer, P., & Jorgensen, J. (1991). Integrated work: A rejection of segregated enclaves and mobile work crews. In L. H. Meyer, C. A. Peck, & L. Brown (Eds.), *Critial issues in the lives of people with severe disabilites* (pp. 219–228). Baltimore: Brookes.

Duhaney, L. M. G., & Salend, S. J. (2000). Parental perceptions of inclusive educational placements. *Remedial and Special Education, 21*(2), 121–128.

Erickson, R. (1998). *Accountability, standards, and assessment*. Washington, DC: Academy for Educational Development, Federal Resource Center.

Erwin, E., Soodak, L., Winton, P., & Turnbull, A. (2001). "I wish it wouldn't all depend upon me": Research on families and early childhood inclusion. In M. J. Guralnick (Ed.), *Early childhood inclusion: Focus on change* (pp. 127–158). Baltimore: Brookes.

Etscheidt, S. K., & Bartlett, L. (1999). The IDEA amendments: A four-step approach for determining supplementary aids and services. *Exceptional Children, 65*(2), 163–174.

Finn, J. D., & Achilles, C. M. (1999). Tennessee's class size study: Findings, implications, misconceptions. *Educational Evaluation and Policy Analysis, 21*, 97–109.

Fisher, D. (1999). According to their peers: Inclusion as high school students see it. *Mental Retardation, 37*(6), 458–467.

Fisher, D., Pumpian, I., & Sax, C. (1998). High school students' attitudes about and recommendations for their peers with significant disabilities. *Journal of the Association for Persons with Severe Handicaps, 23*(3), 272–280.

Ford, A., Davern, L., & Schnorr, R. (2001). Learners with significant disabilities: Curricular relevance in an era of standards-based reform. *Remedial and Special Education, 22*(4), 214–222.

Fox, N. E., & Ysseldyke, J. E. (1997). Implementing inclusion at the middle school level: Lessons for a negative example. *Exceptional Children, 64*(1), 81–98.

Fryxell, D., & Kennedy, C. H. (1995). Placement along the continuum of services and its impact on students' social relationships. *Journal of the Association for Persons with Severe Handicaps, 20*, 259–269.

Gartner, A., & Lipsky, D. K. (1987). Beyond special education: Toward a quality system for all students. *Harvard Educational Review, 57*(4), 367–395.

Grosenick, J. K., & Reynolds, M. C. (1978). *Teacher education: Renegotiating roles for mainstreaming*. Minneapolis: National Support Systems Project.

Grove, K. A., & Fisher, D. (1999). Entrepreneurs of meaning: Parents and the process of inclusive education. *Remedial and Special Education, 20*(4), 208–215, 256.

Halvorsen, A., Neary, T., Hunt, P., & Piuma, C. (1996). *A model for evaluating the cost-effectiveness of inclusive and special classes*. Hayward: California State University, PEERS Project.

Hollowood, T. M., Salisbury, C. L., Rainforth, B., & Palombaro, M. M. (1994). Use of instructional time in classrooms serving students with and without severe disabilities. *Exceptional Children, 61*(3), 242–253.

Hunt, P., & Hirose-Hatae, A., Doering, K., Karasoff, P., and Goetz, L. (2000). "Community" is what I think everyone is talking about. *Remedial and Special Education, 21*(5), 305–317.

Hunt, P., Staub, D., Alwell, M., & Goetz, L. (1994). Achievement by all students within the context of cooperative learning groups. *Journal of the Association for Persons with Severe Handicaps, 19*(4), 290–301.

Kauffman, J. M. (1995). How we might achieve the radical reform of special education. In J. M. Kauffman & D. P. Hallahan (Eds.), *The illusion of full inclusion* (pp. 193–211). Austin, TX: Pro-Ed.

Kavale, K. A., & Forness, S. R. (1999). *Efficacy of special education and related services*. Washington, DC: American Association on Mental Retardation.

Kavale, K. A., & Forness, S. R. (2000). History, rhetoric, and reality: Analysis of the inclusion debate. *Remedial and Special Education, 21*(5), 279–296.

Kennedy, C. H., Shukla, S., & Fryxell, D. (1997). Comparing the effects of educational placements on the social relationships of intermediate school students with severe disabilities. *Journal of the Association for Persons with Severe Handicaps, 19*(4), 277–289.

King-Sears, M. E. (2001). Three steps for gaining access to the general education curriculum for learners with disabilities. *Intervention in School and Clinic, 37*(2), 67–76.

Klingner, J. K., Vaughn, S., Schumm, J. S., Cohen, P., & Forgan, J. W. (1998). Inclusion or pull-out: Which do students prefer? *Journal of Learning Disabilities, 31*(2), 148–158.

MacMillan, D. L., Gresham, F. M., & Forness, S. R. (1996). Full inclusion: An empirical perspective. *Behavioral Disorders, 21*(2), 145–159.

Massachusetts Department of Education. (2001). *Resource guide to the Massachusetts Curriculum Framework for students with significant disabilities*. Malden, MA: Author.

McDonnell, J., Hardman, M., Hightower, J., & Kiefer-O'Donnell, R. (1991). Variables associated with in-school and after-school integration of secondary students with severe disabilities. *Education and Training in Mental Retardation, 26*, 243–257.

McDonnell, J., Thorson, N., McQuivey, C., & Kiefer-O'Donnell, R. (1997). Academic engaged time of students with low-incidence disabilities in general education classes. *Mental Retardation, 35*(1), 18–26.

McDougall, D., & Brady, M. P. (1998). Initiating and fading self-management interventions to increase math fluency in general education classes. *Exceptional Children, 64*(2), 151–166.

McGregor, G., & Vogelsberg, R. T. (1998). *Inclusive schooling practices: Pedagogical and research foundations: A synthesis of the literature that informs best practices about inclusive schooling*. Pittsburgh: Allegheny University of the Health Sciences.

McLaughlin, M. W., & Warren, S. H. (1994). The costs of inclusion: Reallocating financial and human resources to include students with disabilities. *School Administrator, 51*, 8–18.

McLeskey, J., Waldron, N. L., So, T. H., Swanson, K., & Loveland, T. (2001). Perspectives of teachers toward inclusive school programs. *Teacher Education and Special Education, 24*(2), 108–115.

Minke, K. M., Bear, G. G., Deemer, S. A., & Griffin, S. M. (1996). Teachers' experiences with inclusive classrooms: Implications for special education reform. *Journal of Special Education, 30*, 152–186.

Molnar, A., Smith, P., Zahorik, J., Palmer, A., & Ehrle, K. (1999). Evaluating the SAGE program: A pilot program in targeted pupil-teacher reduction in Wisconsin. *Educational Evaluation and Policy Analysis, 21*(2), 165–177.

National Assessment of Educational Progress. (2005a). *The nation's report card: Reading highlights 2003* (http://nces.ed.gov/nations reportcard/pdf/main2003/2004452.pdf).

National Assessment of Educational Progress (2005b). *Racial/ethnic gaps in average mathematics scores, grades 4, 8, and 12: 1990–2000* (http://nces.ed.gov/nationsreportcard/mathematics/resultsscale-ethnic-compared.asp).

National Center on Educational Statistics (2000). *Digest of educational statistics.* Washington, DC: U.S. Department of Education, Office of Educational Research and Improvement.

National Research Council. (1993). *National science education standards.* Washington, DC: National Committee on Science Education Standards and Assessment.

Nolet, V., & McLaughlin, M. (2000). *Accessing the general curriculum: Including students with disabilities in standards-based reform.* Thousand Oaks, CA: Corwin.

O'Connor, R. E., & Jenkins, J. R. (1996). Cooperative learning as an inclusion strategy: A closer look. *Exceptionality, 6*(1), 29–51.

O'Neill, P. T. (2001). Special education and high stakes testing for high school graduation: An analysis of current law and policy. *Journal of Law and Education, 30*(2), 185–222.

Orkwis, R., & McLane, K. (1998, Fall). *A curriculum every student can use: Design principles for student access.* ERIC/OSEP Topical Brief, pp. 3–19.

Praisner, C. L. (2003). Attitudes of elementary school principals toward the inclusion of students with disabilities, *Exceptional Children, 69,* 135–145.

Pugach, M. C., & Johnson, L. J. (2002). *Collaborative practitioners, collaborative schools* (2nd ed.). Denver: Love.

Pugach, M. C., & Warger, C. L. (2001). Curriculum matters: Raising expectations for students with disabilities. *Remedial and Special Education, 22*(4), 194–196, 213.

Reynolds, M. C., Wang, M. C., & Walberg, H. J. (1987). The necessary restructuring of special and general education. *Exceptional Children, 53,* 391–398.

Sailor, W. (Ed.). (2002). *Building partnerships for learning, achievement, and accountability.* New York: Teachers College Press.

Salisbury, C., & Chambers, A. (1994). Instructional costs of inclusive schooling. *Journal of the Association for Persons with Severe Handicaps, 19*(3), 215–222.

Schnorr, R. F. (1997). From enrollment to membership: "Belonging" in middle and high school classes. *Journal of the Association for Persons with Severe Handicaps, 22*(1), 1–15.

Schumm, J. S., & Vaughn, S. (1995). Getting ready for inclusion: Is the stage set? *Learning Disabilities Research and Practice, 10,* 169–179.

Scruggs, T. E., & Mastropieri, M. A. (1996). Teacher perceptions of mainstreaming/inclusion, 1958–1995: A research synthesis. *Exceptional Children, 63,* 59–74.

Soodak, L. C., Erwin, E. J., Winton, P., Brotherson, M. J., Turnbull, A. P., Hanson, M. J., & Brault, L. M. (2002). Implementing inclusive early

childhood education: A call for professional empowerment. *Topics in Early Childhood Special Education, 22*(2), 91–102.

Soodak, L. C., Podell, D. M., & Lehman, L. R. (1998). Teacher, student, and school attributes as predictors of teachers' responses to inclusion. *Journal of Special Education, 31,* 480–497.

Study of Personnel Needs in Special Education (2002). Key findings. Washington, DC. U.S. Department of Education.

Taylor, S. (1988). Caught in the continuum: A critical analysis of the principle of least restrictive environment. *Journal of the Association for Persons with Severe Handicaps, 13*(1), 41–53.

Thompson, S., & Thurlow, M. (2003). *2003 state special education outcomes: Marching on.* Minneapolis: University of Minnesota, National Center on Educational Outcomes (http://education.umn.edu/NCEO/OnlinePubs/2003StateReport.htm./).

Thousand, J. S., Villa, R. A., & Nevin, A. I. (Eds.). (2002). *Creativity and collaborative learning* (2nd ed.). Baltimore: Brookes.

Thurlow, M. L. (2000). Standards-based reform and students with disabilities: Reflections on a decade of change. *Focus on Exceptional Children, 33*(3), 1–16.

Thurlow, M. L., House, A., Boys, C., Scott, D., & Ysseldyke, J. (2000). *State assessment policies on participation and accommodation for students with disabilities: 1999 update* (Synthesis Report 33). Minneapolis: University of Minnesota, National Center on Educational Outcomes.

Thurlow, M., Ysseldyke, J., Gutman, S., & Geenen, K. (1998). *An analysis of inclusion of students with disabilities in state standards documents* (Technical Report 19). Minneapolis: University of Minnesota, National Center on Educational Outcomes.

Turnbull, A. P., & Schultz, J. B. (1979). *Mainstreaming handicapped students: A guide for the classroom teacher.* Boston: Allyn & Bacon.

Turnbull, H. R., Turnbull, A. P., Wehmeyer, M. L., & Park, J. (2003). A quality of life framework for special education outcomes. *Remedial and Special Education, 24,* 67–74.

U.S. Department of Education. (2000). *To assure the free appropriate public education of all children with disabilities: Twentieth annual report to Congress on the implementation of the Individuals with Disabilities Education Act.* Washington, DC: Author.

U.S. Department of Education. (2001). *To assure the free appropriate public education of all children with disabilities: Twenty-third annual report to Congress on the implementation of the Individuals with Disabilities Education Act.* Washington, DC: Author.

Van Reusen, A. K., Shoho, A. R., Barker, K. S. (2000). High school teacher attitudes toward inclusion. *High School Journal, 84*(2), 7–20.

Vaughn, S., & Klingner, J. (1998). Students' perceptions of inclusion and resource room settings. *Journal of Special Education, 32*(2), 79–88.

Voltz, D. L., Brazil, N., & Ford, A. (2001). What matters most in inclusive education: A practical guide for moving forward. *Intervention in School and Clinic, 37*(1), 23–30.

Walther-Thomas, C., Korinek, L., & McLaughlin, V. L. (1999). Collaboration to support students' success. *Focus on Exceptional Children, 32*(3), 1–18.

Wehmeyer, M. L., Lance, G. D., Bashinski, S. (2002). Promoting access to the general curriculum for students with mental retardation: A multi-level model. *Education and Training in Mental Retardation and Developmental Disabilities, 37*(3), 223–234.

Wehmeyer, M. L., Lattin, D., Lapp-Rincker, G., & Agran, M. (2003). Access to the general curriculum of middle-school students with mental retardation: An observational study. *Remedial and Special Education, 24,* 262–272.

Wehmeyer, M. L., Sands, D. J., Knowlton, H. E., & Kosleski, E. B. (2002). *Teaching students with mental retardation: Providing access to the general curriculum.* Baltimore: Brookes.

Will, M. C. (1986). Educating children with learning problems: A shared responsibility. *Exceptional Children, 52,* 411–416.

Zigmond, N., Jenkins, J., Fuchs, L. S., Deno, S., Fuchs, D., Baker, J. N., Jenkins, L., & Couthino, M. (1995, March). Special education in restructured schools: Findings from three multi-year studies. *Phi Delta Kappan,* pp. 531–540.

Chapter 3

Arreaga-Mayer, C., & Perdomo-Rivera, C. (1996). Ecobehavioral analysis of instruction for at-risk language-minority students. *Elementary School Journal, 96,* 245–258.

Artiles, A. J. (2003). Paradoxes and dilemmas in special education's changing identity: Culture and space in inclusion and racial representation discourses. *Harvard Educational Review, 73*(2), 164–202.

Artiles, A. J., & Ortiz, A. (Eds.) . (2002). *English language learners with special needs: Identification, placement and instruction.* Washington, DC: Center for Applied Linguistics.

Artiles, A. J., Rueda, R., Salazar, J., & Higareda, I. (2005). Within-group diversity in minority disproportionate representation: English language learners in urban school districts. *Exceptional Children, 71,* 283–300.

Artiles, A. J., Trent, S. C., & Palmer, J. (2004). Culturally diverse students in special education: Legacies and prospects. In J. A. Banks & C. M. Banks (Eds.), *Handbook of research on multicultural education* (2nd ed., pp. 716–735). San Francisco: Jossey-Bass.

August, D., & Hakuta, K. (Eds.). (1997). *Improving schooling for language-minority children: A research agenda.* Washington, DC: National Academy Press.

Baca, M., & Cervantes, H. (2004). *The bilingual special education interface.* Upper Saddle River, NJ: Merrill/Prentice Hall.

Banks, J. A. (1993). The canon debate, knowledge construction, and multicultural education. *Educational Researcher, 22*(5), 4–14.

Banks, J. A. (1995). The historical reconstruction of knowledge about race: Implications for transformative teaching. *Educational Researcher, 24*(2), 15–25.

Banks, J. A., & Banks, C. A. M. (2001). *Multicultural education: Issues and perspectives.* New York: Wiley.

Bos, C. S., & Reyes, E. I. (1996). Conversations with a Latina teacher about education for language-minority students with special needs. *Elementary School Journal, 96,* 343–351.

Brown v. Board of Education, 348 U.S. 483 (1954).

Children's Defense Fund. (2004). *The state of America's children 2004.* Washington, DC: Author.

Chinn, P. C., & Hughes, S. (1987). Representation of minority students in special education classes. *Remedial and Special Education, 8,* 41–46.

Cochran-Smith, M., Davis, D., & Fries, K. (2004). Multicultural teacher education: Research, practice, and policy, In J. Banks & C. A. M. Banks (Eds.), *Handbook of research on multicultural education* (2nd ed., pp. 931–975). San Francisco: Jossey-Bass.

Cole, M. (1996). *Cultural psychology.* Cambridge, MA: Harvard University Press.

Correa, V. I., & Heward, W. L. (1996). Special education in a culturally and linguistically diverse society. In W. L. Heward (Ed.), *Exceptional children: An introduction to special education* (5th ed., pp. 91–129). Upper Saddle River, NJ: Merrill/Prentice Hall.

Cummins, J. (1989). A theoretical framework for bilingual special education. *Exceptional Children, 56,* 111–119.

DeCuir, J. T., & Dixson, A. D. (2004). "So when it comes out, they aren't that surprised that it is there": Using critical race theory as a tool of analysis of race and racism in education. *Educational Researcher, 33*(5), 26–31.

Delpit, L. D. (1988). The silenced dialogue: Power and pedagogy in educating other people's children. *Harvard Educational Review, 58,* 280–298.

Delpit, L. D. (1995). *Other people's children.* New York: New Press.

Deschenes, S., Cuban, L., & Tyack, D. (2001). Mismatch: Historical perspectives on schools and students who don't fit them. *Teachers College Record, 103,* 525–547.

Diana v. State Board of Education, No. C-70-37 RFP (N. Cal. 1973).

Dunn, L. M. (1968). Special education for the mildly retarded: Is much of it justifiable? *Exceptional Children, 35*(1), 5–22.

Fierros, E. G., & Conroy, J. W. (2002). Double jeopardy: An exploration of restrictiveness and race in special education. In J. Losen & G. Orfield (Eds.), *Racial inequality in special education* (pp. 39–70). Cambridge, MA: Harvard Education Press.

Fletcher, T. V., Bos, C. S., & Johnson, L. M. (1999). Accommodating English language learners with language and learning disabilities in bilingual education classrooms. *Learning Disabilities Research and Practice, 14,* 80–91.

Gallego, M A., Cole, M., & the Laboratory of Comparative Human Cognition (LCHC). (2001). Classroom cultures and cultures in the classroom. In V. Richardson (Ed.), *Handbook of research on teaching* (4th ed., pp. 951–997). Washington, DC: American Educational Research Association.

Garcia, E. E. (1993). Language, culture and education. *Review of Research in Education, 19,* 51–97.

Garcia, E. E. (2004, November). *A profile of the ELL population and subpopulations.* Paper presented at the research conference "English Language Learners Struggling to Learn: Emergent Research on Linguistic Differences and Learning Disabilities," Scottsdale, AZ.

Gay, G. (2000). Preparing for culturally responsive teaching. *Journal of Teacher Education, 53*(2), 106–116.

Gay, G., & Kirkland, K. (2003). Developing cultural critical consciousness and self-reflection in preservice teacher education. *Theory into Practice, 42,* 181–187.

Gersten, R., & Baker, S. (2000). What we know about effective instructional practices for English-language learners. *Exceptional Children, 66,* 454–470.

Gersten, R., & Jiménez, R. T. (1996). The language-minority student in transition [Special Issue]. *Elementary School Journal, 96*(3).

Gersten, R., & Woodward, J. (1994). The language-minority student and special education: Issues, trends, and paradoxes. *Exceptional Children, 60,* 310–332.

Gollnick, D. M., & Chinn, P. C. (1994). *Multicultural education in a pluralistic society* (4th ed.). New York: Macmillan.

Herrstein, R. J., & Murray, C. (1994). *The bell curve: Intelligence and class structure in American life.* New York: Free Press.

Hoffman-Kipp, P., Artiles, A. J., & López-Torres, L. (2003). Beyond reflection: Teacher learning as praxis. *Theory into Practice, 42*(3), 248–254.

Jacob, E. (1999). Cultural inquiry process (http://classweb.gmu.edu/cip/cip-ind.htm).

Jiménez, R. T., Gersten, R., & Rivera, A. (1996). Conversations with a Chicana teacher: Supporting students' transition from native to English language instruction. *Elementary School Journal, 96,* 333–341.

Kauffman, J. M., Mostert, M., Trent, S. C., Pullen, P., & Hallahan, D. P. (in press). *Managing classroom behavior: A reflective case-based approach.* (4th ed.). Boston: Allyn & Bacon.

Klingner, J., Artiles, A. J., & Méndez Barletta, L. (2004, November). *English language learners and learning disabilities: A critical review of research.* Paper presented at the research conference "English Language Learners Struggling to Learn: Emergent Research on

Linguistic Differences and Learning Disabilities," Scottsdale, AZ.

Ladson-Billings, G. (1992). Culturally relevant teaching: The key to making multicultural education work. In C. A. Grant (Ed.), *Research and multicultural education: From the margins to the mainstream* (pp. 107–121). London: Falmer.

Ladson-Billings, G. (1994). *The dreamkeepers: Successful teachers of African American children.* San Francisco: Jossey-Bass.

Ladson-Billings, G. (1995). Toward a theory of culturally relevant pedagogy. *American Educational Research Journal, 32,* 465–491.

Larry, P. v. Riles, 343 F. Supp. 1306 (N.D. Cal. 1972), 502 F. 2d 963 (9th Cir. 1974), No. C-71-2270 RFP (N.D. Cal., October 16, 1979), 793 F. 2d 969 (9th Cir. 1984).

Losen, D. J., & Orfield, G. (2002). *Racial inequity in special education.* Cambridge, MA: Harvard Education Press.

Marston, D. B. (1989). A curriculum-based measurement approach to assessing academic performance: What it is and why do it. In M. R. Shinn (Ed.), *Curriculum-based measurement: Assessing special children* (pp. 18–78). New York: Guilford.

McCray, A. D., Webb-Johnson, & Neal, L. I. (2003). The disproportionality of African Americans in special education: An enduring threat to equality and opportunity. In C. C. Yeakey & R. D. Henderson (Eds.), *Surmounting all odds: Education, opportunity, and society in the new millenium* (pp. 455–485). Greenwich, CT: Information Age Publishing.

McLaughlin, M. J., Artiles, A. J., & Pullin, D. (2003). Challenges for the transformation of special education in the 21st century: Rethinking culture in school reform. *Journal of Special Education Leadership, 14*(2), 51–62.

Mehan, H., Okamoto, D., Lintz, A., & Wills, J. S. (2004). Ethnographic studies of multicultural education in classrooms and schools. In J. A. Banks & C. M. Banks (Eds.), *Handbook of research on multicultural education* (2nd ed., pp. 129–144). San Francisco: Jossey-Bass.

Mercer, J. R. (1973). *Labeling the mentally retarded.* Los Angeles: University of California Press.

Mercer, J. R., & Richardson, J. G. (1975). Mental retardation as a social problem. In N. Hobbs (Ed.), *Issues in the classification of children* (Vol. 2, pp. 463–496). San Francisco: Jossey-Bass.

Merriam-Webster's Collegiate Dictionary (11th ed.). (2003). Springfield, MA: Merriam-Webster.

Mickelson, R. A. (2003). When are racial disparities in education the result of racial discrimination? A social science perspective. *Teachers College Record, 105,* 1052–1086.

Miller, L. S. (2000). *Minority high academic achievement patterns and their implication for the gifted and talented education community.* Paper prepared for the National Academies' Committee on Minority Representation in Special Education and Gifted and Talented Programs, Washington, DC.

Moll, L. C., & Gonzales, N. (1997). Teachers as social scientists: Learning about culture from household research. In P. M. Hall (Ed.), *Race, ethnicity and multicuralism* (Vol. 1). New York: Garland.

National Research Council. (1982). *Placing children in special education: A strategy for equity.* Washington, DC: National Academy Press.

National Research Council. (2002). *Minority representation in special education.* Washington, DC: National Academy Press.

Nieto, S. (2004). *Affirming diveristy: The sociopolitical context of multicultural education* (4th ed.). Boston: Pearson.

Obiakor, F. E., & Ford, B. A. (2002). Educational reform and accountability: Implications for African Americans with exceptionalities. *Multiple Voices for Ethnically Diverse Exceptionalities, 5,* 83–93.

Parrish, T. (2002). Racial disparities in the identification, funding, and provision of special education. In D. J. Losen & G. Orfield (Eds.), *Racial inequity in special education* (pp. 15–37). Cambridge, MA: Harvard Education Press.

PASE v. Hannon, 506 F. Supp. 831 (N.D. III. 1980).

Putnam, R., & Borko, H. (2000). What do new views of knowledge and thinking have to say about research on teacher learning? *Educational Researcher, 29*(1), 4–15.

Reyes, M. (1992). Challenging venerable assumptions: Literacy instruction for linguistically different students. *Harvard Educational Review, 62,* 427–446.

Richardson, V. (Ed.). (2001). *Handbook of research on teaching* (4th ed.). Washington, DC: AERA.

Rogoff, B. (2003). *The cultural nature of human development.* New York: Oxford University Press.

Safford, P. L., & Safford, E. H. (1998). Visions of the special class. *Remedial and Special Education, 19,* 229–238.

Safran, S. P., & Safran, J. S. (1996). Intervention assistance programs and prereferral teams: Directions for the twenty-first century. *Remedial and Special Education, 17,* 363–369.

Scott, S. S., McGuire, J. M., & Shaw, S. F. (2003). Universal design for instruction: A new paradigm for adult instruction in postsecondary education. *Journal of Learning Disabilities, 24,* 369–379.

Skiba, R. J., Simons, A. B., Ritter, S., Kohler, K. R., & Wu, T. C. (2003). The psychology of disproportionality. *Multiple Voices for Ethnically Diverse Exceptional Learners, 6,* 27–40.

Span, C. M. (2003). "Knowledge is light, knowledge is power": African American education in antebellum America. In C. C. Yeakey & R. D. Henderson (Eds.), *Surmounting all odds: Education, opportunity, and society in the new millenium* (pp. 3–29). Greenwich, CT: Information Age Publishing.

Trent, S. C. (1997). Serving urban African-American students with learning disabilities in inclusive settings: Using study groups to facilitate change, *Learning Disabilities Research and Practice, 12*(2), 132–142.

Turnbull, A., Turnbull, R., Erwin, E., & Soodak, L. (2006). *Families, professionals, and exceptionality: Positive outcomes through partnership and trust.* Upper Saddle River, NJ: Merrill/Prentice Hall.

U.S. Department of Education, National Center for Education Statistics. (2003). *Condition of education.* Washington, DC: Author.

Valencia, R. R. (1997). *The evolutions of deficit thinking.* New York: Palmer.

Villegas, A. M., & Lucas, T. (2002). *Educating culturally responsive teachers.* Albany: State University of New York Press.

Chapter 4

Algozzine, B., Browder, D., Karvonen, M., Test, D. W., & Wood, W. M. (2001). Effects of interventions to promote self-determination for individuals with disabilities. *Review of Educational Research, 71*(2), 219–277.

Baier, A. C. (1986). Trust and antitrust. *Ethics, 96,* 231–260.

Bailey, D. B., & Winton, P. J. (1989). Friendship and acquaintance among families in a mainstreamed day care center. *Education and Training in Mental Retardation, 24,* 107–113.

Baker, B. L., McIntyre, L. L., Blacher, J., Crnic, K., Edelbrock, C., & Low, C. (2003). Pre-school children with and without developmental delay: Behaviour problems and parenting stress over time. *Journal of Intellectual and Developmental Disability, 47*(4/5), 217–230.

Balli, S. J., Demo, D. H., & Wedman, J. F. (1998). Family involvement with children's homework: An intervention in middle grades. *Family Relations, 47*(2), 149–157.

Barrera, I., & Corso, R. M. (2002). Cultural competency as skilled dialogue. *Topics in Early Childhood Special Education, 22*(2), 103–113.

Beach Center. (1999). *Unpublished transcripts.* Lawrence: University of Kansas, Beach Center.

Beach Center. (2000). *Unpublished research transcripts of focus groups.* Lawrence: University of Kansas, Beach Center.

Blue-Banning, M. J., Summers, J. A., Frankland, H. C., Nelson, L. L., & Beegle, G. (2004). Dimensions of family and professional partnerships: Constructive guidelines for collaboration. *Exceptional Children, 70*(2), 167–184.

Board of Education v. Rowley. (1982). 458 U.S. 176.

Burton, S. L., & Parks, A. L. (1994). College-aged siblings of individuals with disabilities. *Social Work Research, 18*(3), 178–185.

Callahan, K., Rademacher, J. A., & Hildreth, B. L. (1998). The effect of parent participation in strategies to improve the homework performance of students who are at risk. *Remedial and Special Education, 19*(3), 131–141.

Cedar Rapids Community School District v. Garrett F., 526 U.S. 6 (1999).

Chavkin, N. E., Gonzalez, J., & Rader, R. (2002). A home-school program in Texas-Mexico border school: Voices from parents, students,

and school staff. *School Community Journal, 10*(2), 127–137.

Comer, J. P., & Haynes, N. M. (1991). Parent involvement in schools: An ecological approach. *Elementary School Journal, 91*(3), 271–277.

Faires, J., Nichols, W. D., & Rickelman, R. J. (2000). Effects of parental involvement in developing competent readers in first grade. *Reading Psychology, 21*(3), 195–215.

Falvey, M. A., Forest, M. S., Pearpoint, J., & Rosenberg, R. L. (2002). Building connections. In J. S. Thousand, R. A. Villa, & A. I. Nevin (Eds.), *Creativity and collaborative learning.* Baltimore: Brookes.

Fiedler, C. R. (2000). *Making a difference: Advocacy competencies for special education professionals.* Boston: Allyn & Bacon.

Fisman, S., Wolf, L., Ellison, D., & Freeman, T. (2000). A longitudinal study of siblings of children with chronic disabilities. *Canadian Journal of Psychiatry, 45,* 369–375.

Frederickson, N., & Turner, J. (2003). Utilizing the classroom peer group to address children's social needs: An evaluation of the circle of friends intervention approach. *Journal of Special Education, 36*(4), 234–245.

Fuijiura, G. T., & Yamaki, K. (2000). Trends in demography of childhood poverty and disability. *Exceptional Children, 66*(2), 187–200.

Gallagher, P. A., Floyd, J. H., Stafford, A. M., Taber, T. A., Brozovic, S. A., & Alberto, P. A. (2000). Inclusion of students with moderate or severe disabilities in educational and community settings: Perspectives from parents and siblings. *Education and Training in Mental Retardation and Developmental Disabilities, 35*(2), 135–147.

Gerdel, P. (1986). *Who are the researchers and why are they saying these horrible things about me?* Lawrence: University of Kansas, Beach Center.

Goddard, R. D., Sweetland, S. R., & Hoy, W. K. (2000). Academic emphasis of urban elementary schools and student achievement in reading and mathematics: A multilevel analysis. *Educational Administration Quarterly, 36*(5), 683–702.

Guralnick, M. J., Conner, R. T., & Hammond, M. (1995). Parent perspectives of peer relationships and friendships in integrated and specialized settings. *American Journal on Mental Retardation, 99,* 457–476.

Hamre-Nietupski, S., Hendrickson, J., Nietupski, J., & Sasso, G. (1993). Perceptions of teachers of students with moderate, severe, or profound disabilities on facilitating friendships with nondisabled peers. *Education and Training in Mental Retardation, 28*(2), 111–127.

Hamre-Nietupski, S., Hendrickson, J., Nietupski, J., & Shokoohi-Yekta, M. (1994). Regular educators' perceptions of facilitating friendships of students with moderate, severe, or profound disabilities with nondisabled peers. *Education and Training in Mental Retardation, 29*(2), 102–117.

Hara, S. R., & Burke, D. J. (1998). Parent involvement: The key to improved student achievement. *School Community Journal, 8*(2), 385–413.

Hart, B., & Risley, T. R. (1995). *Meaningful differences in the everyday experience of young American children*. Baltimore: Brookes.

Hastings, R. P., Daley, D., Burns, C., & Beck, A. (in press). Maternal stress and expressed emotion: Cross-sectional and longitudinal relationships with behavior problems of children with intellectual disabilities. *American Journal on Mental Retardation*.

Henderson, A. T., & Berla, N. (Eds.). (1994). *A new generation of evidence: The family is critical to student achievement*. Washington, DC: Center for Law and Education.

Hoy, W. K. (2002). Faculty trust: A key to student achievement. *Journal of Public School Relations, 23*, 88–103.

Hoy, W. K., & Tarter, C. J. (1997). *The road to open and healthy schools: A handbook for change (Elementary and secondary school ed.)*. Thousand Oaks, CA: Corwin.

Iceland, J. (2000). *The "family/couple/household" unit of analysis in poverty measurement* (http://www.census.gov/hhes/poverty/povmeas/papers/famhh3.html#2).

Irving Independent School District v. Tatro, 703 F. 2d 823 (5th Cir., 1983), aff'd. in part, rev'd. in part, 468 U.S. 883 (1984).

Jackson, C. (2004). *Family outcomes of children who are deaf: Results of a national survey*. Lawrence: University of Kansas.

Johnson, J., Duffett, A., Farkas, S., & Wilson, L. (2002). *When it's your own child: A report on special education from the families who use it*. New York: Public Agenda.

Jordan, L., Reyes-Blanes, M. E., Peel, B. B., Peel, H. A., & Lane, H. B. (1998). Developing teacher-parent partnerships across cultures: Effective parent conferences. *Intervention in School and Clinic, 33*(3), 141–147.

Kaiser, A., & Delaney, E. (1996). The effects of poverty on parenting young children. *Peabody Journal of Education, 71*, 66–85.

Kaufman, P., Kwon, J. Y., Klein, S., & Chapman, C. D. (2000). *Dropout rates in the United States: 1999*. Washington, DC: National Center for Educational Statistics.

Korenman, S., Miller, J. E., & Sjaastad, J. E. (1995). Long-term poverty and child development in the United States: Results from the National Longitudinal Survey of Youth. *Children and Young Services Review, 17*, 127–151.

Lake, J. E., & Billingsley, B. S. (2000). An analysis of factors that contribute to parent-school conflict in special education. *Remedial and Special Education, 21*(4), 240–251.

Lord-Nelson, L. G., Summers, J. A., & Turnbull, A. P. (2004). Boundaries in family-professional relationships: Implications for special educators. *Remedial and Special Education, 25*(3), 153–165.

Madden, M. (2003). *The changing picture of who's on line and what they do*. Pew Internet &

American Life Project. (http://www.pewtrusts.com/pdf/pew_internet_yearend_2003.pdf).

Mannan, H. (2005). *Examining family outcomes in early childhood services for families of children with disabilities*. Unpublished doctoral dissertation, University of Kansas, Lawrence.

Martin, J. E., & Marshall, L. H. (1995). ChoiceMaker: Infusing self-determination instruction into the IEP and transition process. In D. J. Sands & M. L. Wehmeyer (Eds.), *Self-determination across the life span: Independence and choice for people with disabilities* (pp. 211–232). Baltimore: Brookes.

Merriam-Webster, Inc. (1996). *Merriam-Webster's Collegiate Dictionary* (10th ed.). Springfield, MA: Author.

Meyer, D. J., & Vadasy, P. F. (1994). *Sibshops: Workshops for siblings of children with special needs*. Baltimore: Brookes.

Mills v. District of Columbia Bd. of Ed., 348 F. Supp. 866 (D.D.C. 1972).

Orsillo, S. M., McCaffrey, R. J., & Fisher, J. M. (1993). Siblings of head-injured individuals: A population at risk. *Journal of Head Trauma Rehabilitation, 8*(1), 102–115.

PARC v. Commonwealth, 334 F. Supp. 1257 (E.D. Pa. 1971); 343 F. Supp. 279 (E.D. Pa. 1972).

Park, J., Hoffman, L., Marquis, J., Turnbull, A. P., Poston, D., Mannan, H., Wang, M., & Nelson, L. (2003). Toward assessing family outcomes of service delivery: Validation of a family quality of life survey. *Journal of Intellectual Disability Research, 47*(4/5), 367–384.

Park, J., Turnbull, A. P., & Park, H. S. (2001). Quality of partnerships in service provision for Korean-American parents of children with disabilities: A qualitative inquiry. *Journal of the Association for Persons with Severe Handicaps, 26*(3), 158–170.

Poston, D., Turnbull, A., Park, J., Mannan, H., Marquis, J., & Wang, M. (2003). Family quality of life: A qualitative inquiry. *Mental Retardation, 41*(5), 313–328.

Ruef, M., & Turnbull, A. P. (2001). Stakeholder opinions on accessible informational products helpful in building positive practical solutions to behavioral challenges of people with mental retardation and/or autism. *Education and Training in Mental Retardation and Developmental Disabilities, 36*(4), 441–456.

Salembier, G., & Furney, K. S. (1997). Facilitating participation: Parents' perceptions of their involvement in the IEP/transition planning process. *Career Development for Exceptional Individuals, 20*(1), 29–42.

Sanders, M. G., & Herting, J. R. (2000). Gender and the effects of school, family, and church support on the academic achievement of African-American urban adolescents. In M. G. Sanders (Ed.), *Schooling students placed at risk: Research, policy, and practice in the education of poor and minority adolescents* (pp. 141–161). Mahwah, NJ: Erlbaum.

Satir, V. (1972). *Peoplemaking*. Palo Alto, CA: Science and Behavior Books.

Shapiro, J., Blacher, J., & Lopez, S. R. (1998). Maternal reactions to children with mental retardation. In J. A. Burack, R. M. Hodapp, & E. Zigler (Eds.), *Handbook of mental retardation and development* (pp. 606–636). New York: Cambridge University Press.

Shapiro, J., Monzo, L. D., Rueda, R., Gomez, J. A., & Blacher, J. (2004). Alienated advocacy: Perspectives of Latina mothers of young adults with developmental disabilities on service systems. *Mental Retardation, 42*(1), 37–54.

Shaver, A. V., & Walls, R. T. (1998). Effect of Title I parent involvement on student reading and mathematics achievement. *Journal of Research and Development in Education, 31*(2), 90–97.

Shumow, L., & Miller, J. D. (2001). Parents' at-home and at-school academic involvement with young adolescents. *Journal of Early Adolescence, 21*(1), 68–91.

Singer, G. H. S. (in press). A meta-analysis of comparative studies of depression in mothers of children with and without developmental disabilities. *American Journal on Mental Retardation*.

Summers, J. A., Poston, D. J., Turnbull, A. P., Marquis, J., Hoffman, L., Mannan, H., & Wang, M. (in press). Conceptualizing and measuring family quality of life. *Journal of Intellectual Disability*.

Sweetland, S. R., & Hoy, W. K. (2000). School characteristics and educational outcomes: Toward an organizational model of student achievement in middle schools. *Educational Administration Quarterly, 36*(5), 703–729.

Tschannen-Moran, M., & Hoy, W. (2000). A multidisciplinary analysis of the nature, meaning, and measurement of trust. *Review of Educational Research, 70*(4), 547–593.

Turnbull, A. P., Brown, I., & Turnbull, H. R. (2004). *Family quality of life: An international perspective*. Washington DC: American Association on Mental Retardation.

Turnbull, A. P., & Ruef, M. (1996). Family perspectives on problem behavior. *Mental Retardation, 34* 280–293.

Turnbull, A. P., & Ruef, M. (1997). Family perspectives on inclusive lifestyle issues for individuals with problem behavior. *Exceptional Children, 63*(2), 211–227.

Turnbull, A. P., Turnbull, R., Erwin, E., & Soodak, L. (2006). *Families, professionals, and exceptionality: Positive outcomes through partnerships and trust*. Upper Saddle River, NJ: Merrill/Prentice Hall.

Turnbull, H. R., Turnbull, A. P., Stowe, M., & Wilcox, B. L. (2000). *Free appropriate education: The law and children with disabilities*. Denver: Love.

Turnbull, H. R., Turnbull, A. P., & Wheat, M. (1982). Assumptions about parental participation: A legislative history. *Exceptional Education Quarterly, 3*(2), 1–8.

Turnbull, K. (1997). Untitled essay. In D. Meyer (Ed.), *Views from our shoes: Growing up with a brother or sister with special needs* (pp. 90–93). Bethesda, MD: Woodbine House.

U.S. Department of Education. (2002). *To assure the free appropriate education of all children with disabilities: Twenty-fourth annual report to Congress on the implementation of the Individuals with Disabilities Education Act.* Washington, DC: Author.

Wang, M., Mannan, H., Poston, D., Turnbull, A. P., & Summers, J. A. (2004). Parents's perceptions of advocacy activities and their impact on family quality of life. *Research and Practice for Persons with Severe Disabilities, 29*(2), 144–155.

Wehmeyer, M. L. (1996). Self-determination as an educational outcome: Why is it important to children, youth and adults with disabilities? In D. J. Sands & M. L. Wehmeyer (Eds.), *Self-determination across the life span: Independence and choice for people with disabilities* (pp. 15–34). Baltimore: Brookes.

Chapter 5

Allor, J. H. (2002). The relationships of phonemic awareness and rapid naming to reading development. *Learning Disabilities Quarterly, 25,* 47–57.

Al Otaiba, S., & Fuchs, D. (2002). Characteristics of children who are unresponsive to early literacy intervention: A review of the literature. *Remedial and Special Education, 23*(4), 300–316.

Ausubel, D. (1963). *The psychology of meaningful verbal learning: An introduction to school learning.* New York: Grune & Stratton.

Bear, C. G., Minke, K. M. (1996). Positive bias in the maintenance of self-worth among children with LD. *Learning Disability Quarterly, 19,* 23–32.

Blair, C., & Scott, K. G. (2002). Proportion of LD placements associated with low socioeconomic status: Evidence for a gradient? *Journal of Special Education, 36*(1), 14–22.

Bricker, D., Pretti-Frontczak, K., & McComas, N. (1998). *An activity-based approach to early intervention* (2nd ed.). Baltimore: Brookes.

Calhoon, M. B., & Fuchs, L. (2003). The effects of peer assisted learning strategies and curriculum-based measurement on the mathematics performance of secondary students with disabilities. *Remedial and Special Education, 24*(4), 235–245.

Calhoon, M. B., Fuchs, L., & Hamlett, C. (2000). Effects of computer-based test accommodations on mathematics performance assessments for secondary students with learning disabilities. *Learning Disability Quarterly, 23,* 271–282.

Catts, H. W., Gillispie, M., Leonard L. B., Kail, R. B., & Miller, C. A. (2002). The role of speed of processing, rapid naming, and phonological awareness in reading achievement. *Journal of Learning Disabilities, 35*(6), 509–524.

Chard, D. J., & Kame' enui, E. J. (2000). Struggling first-grade readers: The frequency and progress of their reading. *Journal of Special Education, 34,* 28–38.

Compton, D. L., Appleton, A. C., & Hosp, M. K. (2004). Exploring the relationship between text-leveling systems and reading accuracy and fluency in second-grade students who are average and poor decoders. *Learning Disabilities Research and Practice, 19*(3), 176–184.

Coyne, M. D., Kame' enui, E. J., & Simmons, D. C. (2001). Prevention and intervention in beginning reading: Two complex systems. *Learning Disabilities, 16*(2), 62–73.

Davis, M. D., Kilgo, J. L., & Gamel-McCormick, M. (1998). *Young children with special needs.* Boston: Allyn & Bacon.

DeFries, J. C., & Alarcon, M. (1996). Genetics of specific reading disability. *Mental Retardation and Developmental Disabilities Research Reviews, 2,* 39–47.

Deshler, D. D., Schumaker, J. B., Lenz, B. K., Bulgren, J. A., Hock, M. F., Knight, J., & Ehren, B. J. (2001). Ensuring content-area learning by secondary students with learning disabilities. *Learning Disabilities Research and Practice, 16*(2), 96–108.

Espin, C. A., Busch, T. W., Shin, J., & Kruschwitz, R. (2001). Curriculum-based measurement in the content areas: Validity of vocabulary matching as an indicator of performance in social studies. *Learning Disabilities Research and Practice, 16*(3), 142–151.

Fletcher, J. M., Foorman, B. R., Boudousquie, A., Barnes, M. A., Schatschneider, C., & Francis, D. J. (2002). Assessment of reading and learning disabilities: A research-based intervention-oriented approach. *Journal of School Psychology, 40*(1), 27–63.

Frankenberger, W., & Fronzaglio, K. (1991). A review of states' criteria and procedures for identifying children with learning disabilities. *Journal of Learning Disabilities, 24,* 495–500.

Friend, M., & Bursuck, W. D. (2002). *Including students with special needs: A practical guide for classroom teachers.* Boston: Allyn & Bacon.

Fuchs, D. M., Fuchs, L. S., Mathes, P. G., Lipsey, M. W., & Roberts, P. H. (2001). Is "learning disabilities" just a fancy term for low achievement: A meta-analysis of reading differences between low achievers with and without the label (http://www.air.org/1dsummit/).

Fuchs, D. M., Mock, D., Morgan, P. L., & Young, C. L. (2003). Responsiveness-to-intervention: Definitions, evidence, and implications for the learning disabilities construct. *Learning Disabilities: Resource & Practice, 18*(3), 157–171.

Fuchs, L., & Fuchs, D. (2002). Linking assessment to instructional interventions: An overview. *School Psychology Review, 15,* 318–324.

Fuchs, L. S., Fuchs, D., Eaton, S. B., Hamlett, C. L., & Karns, K. M. (2000). Supplementing teacher judgments of mathematics test accommodations with objective data sources. *School Psychology Review, 29,* 65–85.

Gans, A. M., Kenny, M. C., & Ghany, D. L. (2003). Comparing the self-concept of students with and without learning disabilities. *Journal of Learning Disabilities, 36*(3), 287–295.

Georgiewa, P., Rzanny R., Hopf, J. M., Knab, R., Glauche, V., Kaiser, W. A., & Blanz, B. (1999). FMRI during word processing in dyslexic and normal reading children. *Neuroreport, 10*(16), 3459–3465.

Gersten, R. (1998). Recent advances in instructional research for students with learning disabilities: An overview. *Learning Disabilities, 13,* 162–170.

Glassberg, L. A., Hooper, S. R., & Mattison, R. E. (1999). Prevalence of learning disabilities at enrollment in special education students with behavioral disorders. *Behavioral Disorders, 25*(1), 9–21.

Graham, S., Harris, K. R., & Larsen, L. (2001). Prevention and intervention of writing difficulties for students with learning disabilities. *Learning Disabilities, 16*(2), 74–84.

Harter, S., Whitesell, N. R., & Junkin, L. J. (1998). Similarities and differences in domain-specific and global self-evaluations of learning-disabled, behaviorally disordered, and normally achieving adolescents. *American Education Research Journal, 35,* 653–680.

Hemmeter, M. L., & Grisham-Brown, J. (1997). Teaching language and communication skills in the context of ongoing activities and routines in inclusive preschool classrooms. *Dimensions in Early Childhood Education, 25,* 6–13.

Higgins, E. L., Raskind, M. H., Goldberg, R. J., & Herman, K. L. (2002). Stages of acceptance of a learning disability: The impact of labeling. *Learning Disability Quarterly, 25,* 3–18.

Hock, M. F., Deshler, D. D., & Schumaker, J. B. (1999). Tutoring programs for academically underprepared college students: A review of the literature. *Journal of College Reading and Learning, 29*(2), 101–121.

Horn, E., Leiber, J., & Li, S. (2000). Supporting young children's IEP goals in inclusive settings through embedded learning opportunities. *Topics in Early Childhood Special Education, 20,* 206–223.

Hosp, M. K., & Hosp, J. L. (2003). Curriuclum-based measurement for reading, spelling, and math: How to do it and why. *Preventing School Failure, 48,* 10–17.

International Dyslexia Assocation. (2002). *Frequently asked questions: What is dyslexia?* (www.interdys.org/servlet/compose?section_id=5&page_id-95).

Izzo, M. V., Hertzfeld, J. E., & Aaron, J. H. (2001). Raising the bar: Student self-determination + good teaching = success. *Journal of Vocational Special Needs Education, 24,* 26–36.

Jacob, H. H. (2004). *Getting results with curriculum mapping.* Alexandria, VA: Association for Supervision and Curriculum Development.

Janney, R., & Snell, M. E. (2004). *Teachers' guides to inclusive practices: Modifying schoolwork* (2nd ed.). Baltimore: Brookes.

Jorm, A., & Share, D. (1983). Phonological recoding and reading acquisition. *Applied Psycholinguistics, 4,* 103–147.

Kavale, K. A., & Forness, S. R. (2000). What definitions of learning disability say and don't say: A critical analysis. *Journal of Learning Disabilities, 33*, 239–256.

Kavale, K. A., & Reese, J. H. (1992). The character of learning disabilities: An Iowa profile. *Learning Disability Quarterly, 15*, 74–94.

Kibby, M. Y., & Hynd, G. W. (2001). Neurobiological basis of learning disabilities. In D. P. Hallahan & B. K. Keogh (Eds.), *Research and global perspectives in learning disabilities* (pp. 25–42). Mahwah, NJ: Erlbaum.

Kotkin, R. A., Forness, S. R., & Kavale, K. A. (2001). Comorbid ADHD and learning disabilities: Diagnosis, special education, and intervention. In D. P. Hallahan & B. K. Keogh (Eds.), *Research and global perspectives in learning disabilities* (pp. 43–64). Mahwah, NJ: Lawrence Erlbaum Associates.

Lancaster, P. E., Schumaker, J. B., & Deshler, D. D. (2002). The development and validation of an interactive hypermedia program teaching a self-advocacy strategy to students with disabilities. *Learning Disability Quarterly, 25*(4), 277–302.

Lenz, K., Deshler, D., & Kissam, B. (2003). *Teaching content to all: Evidence-based inclusive practices in middle and secondary schools.* Boston: Allyn & Bacon.

Lyon, G. R., Fletcher, J. M., Shaywitz, S. E., Shaywitz, B. A., Torgesen, J. K., Wood, F. B., Schulte, A., & Olson, R. (2001). Rethinking learning disabilities. In C. E. Finn, A. J. Rotherham, & C. R. Hokanson (Eds.), *Rethinking special education for a new century.* Washington, DC: Fordham Foundation.

MacMaster, K., Donovan, L. A., & MacIntyre, P. D. (2002). The effects of being diagnosed with a learning disability on children's self-esteem. *Child Study Journal, 32*(2), 101–108.

Martin, J. E., Marshall, L. H., Maxson, L., & Jerman, P. (1998). *ChoiceMaker.* Longmont, CO: Sopris West.

Martin, J. E., Marshall, L. H., & Sale, P. (2004). A 3-year study of middle, junior high, and high school IEP meetings. *Exceptional Children, 70*, 285–297.

McLeskey, J., Waldron, N. L., & Wornhoff, S. A. (1990). Factors influencing the identification of black and white students with learning disabilities. *Journal of Learning Disabilities, 23*, 362–366.

Meese, R. L. (2001). *Teaching learners with mild disabilities: Integrating research and practice* (2nd ed.). Belmont, CA: Wadsworth.

Meltzer, L., Roditi, B., Houser, R. F., Jr., & Perlman, M. (1998). Perceptions of academic strategies and competence in students with learning disabilities. *Journal of Learning Disabilities, 31*, 437–451.

Mercer, C. D., & Pullen, P. C. (2005). *Students with learning disabilities.* Upper Saddle River, NJ: Merrill/Prentice Hall.

Murphy-Brennan, M. G., & Oei, P. S. (1999). Is there evidence to show that fetal alcohol syndrome can be prevented? *Journal of Drug Education, 29*(1), 5–24.

National Reading Panel. (2000). *Research-based approaches to reading instruction.* Washington, DC: Author.

O'Shaughnessy, T. E., & Swanson, L. H. (1998). Do immediate memory deficits in students with learning disabilities in reading reflect a developmental lag or deficit? A selective meta-analysis of the literature. *Learning Disability Quarterly, 21*, 123–148.

Raskind, W. H. (2001). Current understanding of the genetic basis of reading and spelling disability. *Learning Disability Quarterly, 24*(3), 141–157.

Reis, S. M., McGuire, J. M., & Neu, T. W. (2000). Compensation strategies used by high-ability students with learning disabilities who succeed in college. *Gifted Child Quarterly, 44*, 123–134.

Sandall, S., Schwartz, I., & Joseph, G. (2001). A building blocks model for effective instruction in inclusive early childhood settings. *Young Exceptional Children, 4*(3), 3–9.

Schumaker, J., & Deshler, D. (2003). *The self-advocacy strategy.* Lawrence, KS: Edge Enterprises.

Settle, S. A., & Milich, R. (1999). Social persistence following failure in boys and girls with LD. *Journal of Learning Disabilities, 32*, 201–212.

Shapiro, B. K. (2001). Specific reading disability: A multiplanar view. *Mental Retardation and Developmental Disabilities Research Reviews, 7*, 13–20.

Shapiro, B. K., Church, R. P., & Lewis, M. E. B. (2002). Specific learning disabilities. In M. L. Batshaw (Ed.), *Children with disabilities* (5th ed., pp. 417–442). Baltimore: Brookes.

Shaywitz, B. A., Fletcher, J. M., & Shaywitz, S. E. (1995). Defining and classifying learning disabilities and attention-deficit/hyperactivity disorder. *Journal of Child Neurology, 10*, S50–S57.

Shaywitz, S. E., Escobar, M. D., Shaywitz, B. A., Fletcher, J. M., & Makuch, R. (1992). Evidence that dyslexia may represent the lower tail of a normal distribution of reading ability. *New England Journal of Medicine, 326*(3), 145–150.

Shaywitz, S. E., Shaywitz, B. A., Pugh, K. R., Fulbright, R. K., Constable, R. T., Mencel, W. E., Shankweiler, D. P., Liberman, A. M., Skudlarski, P., Fletcher, J. M., Katz, L., Marchione, K. E., Lacadie, C., Gatenby, C., & Gore, J. C. (1998). Functional disruption in the organization of the brain for reading dyslexia. *Proceedings of the National Academy of Sciences of the United States of America, 95*(5) 2636–2641.

Sofie, C. A., & Riccio, C. A. (2002). A comparison of multiple methods for the identification of children with reading disabilities. *Journal of Learning Disabilities, 35*(3), 234–244.

Stuebing, K. K., Fletcher, J. M., LeDoux, J. M., Lyon, G. R., Shaywitz, S. E., & Shaywitz, B. A. (2002). Validity of IQ-discrepancy classification of reading disabilities: A meta-analysis. *American Educational Research Journal, 39*(2), 469–518.

Swanson, H. L. (2000). Are working memory deficits in readers with learning disabilities hard to change? *Journal of Learning Disabilities, 33*, 551–566.

Swanson, H. L. (2001). Research on interventions for adolescents with learning disabilities: A meta-analysis of outcomes related to higher-order processing. *Elementary School Journal, 101*, 331–348.

Swanson, H. L., & Deshler, D. (2003). Instructing adolescents with learning disabilities: Converting a meta-analysis to practice. *Journal of Learning Disabilities, 36*(2), 124–135.

Test, D. W., Mason, C., Hughes, C., Konrad, M., Neale, M., & Wood, W. (2004). Student involvement in individualized education program meetings. *Exceptional Children, 70*, 391–412.

Thoma, C., & Wehmeyer, M. L. (in press). Self-determination and the transition to postsecondary education of students with disabilities. In E. E. Getzel & P. Wehman (Eds.), *Going to college: The next frontier for persons with disabilities.* Baltimore: Brookes.

Tomlinson, C. A. (2001). *How to differentiate instruction in mixed abilities classrooms* (2nd ed.). Alexandria, VA: Association for Supervision and Curriculum Development.

Tomlinson, C. A. (2003). *Fulfilling the promise of differentiated classrooms: Strategies and tools for responsive teaching.* Alexandria, VA: Association for Supervision and Curriculum Development.

Torgesen, J. K. (2002). The prevention of reading difficulties. *Journal of School Psychology, 40*(1), 7–26.

Torgesen, J. K., & Wagner, R. K. (1998). Alternative diagnostic approaches for specific developmental reading disabilities. *Learning Disabilities, 13*, 220–232.

Udelhofen, S. (2005). *Keys to curriculum mapping: Strategies and tools to make it work.* Thousand Oaks, CA: Corwin.

U.S. Department of Education, Office of Special Education Programs. (2005). *IDEA data website* (http://www.ideadata.org/aboutThisSite.asp).

Vaidya, S. R. (2004). Understanding dyscalculia for teaching. *Education, 124*(4), 717–720.

Valas, H. (1999). Students with learning disabilities and low-achieving students: Peer acceptance, loneliness, self-esteem, and depression. *Social Psychology of Education, 3*, 173–192.

Vaughn, S., Elbaum, B., & Boardman, A. G. (2001). The social functioning of students with learning disabilities: Implications for inclusion. *Exceptionality, 9*, 47–65.

Vaughn, S., & Fuchs, L. S. (2003). Redefining learning disabilities as inadequate response to instruction: The promise and potential problems. *Learning Disabilities Research and Practice, 18*(3), 137–146.

Wagner, R. K., & Torgesen, J. K. (1997). The nature of phonological processing and its causal role in the acquisition of reading skills. *Psychological Bulletin, 101*, 192–212.

Warner, T. D., Dede, D. E., Garban, C. W., & Conway, T. W. (2002). One size still does not fit all in specific learning disability assessment across ethnic groups. *Journal of Learning Disabilities, 35*(6), 500–508.

Weaver, S. M. (2000). The efficacy of extended time on tests for postsecondary students with learning disabilities. *Learning Disabilities: A Multidisciplinary Journal, 10*(2), 47–56.

Wehmeyer, M. L. (2002). Self-determined assessment: Critical components for transition planning. In C. Thoma & C. Sax (Eds.), *Transition assessment: Wise practices for quality lives* (pp. 25–38). Baltimore: Brookes.

Wehmeyer, M. L., Palmer, S., Agran, M., Mithaug, D., & Martin, J. (2000). Promoting causal agency: The self-determined learning model of instruction. *Exceptional Children, 66,* 439–453.

Wehmeyer, M. L., Sands, D. J., Knowlton, H. E., & Kozleski, E. B. (2002). *Teaching students with mental retardation: Providing access to the general curriculum.* Baltimore: Brookes.

Woodcock, R. W. (1990). Theoretical foundations of the WJ-R measures of cognitive ability. *Journal of Psychoeducational Assessment, (8)*3, 231–258.

Chapter 6

Allington, R. L., & Cunningham, P. M. (1996). *Schools that work: Where all children read and write.* New York: HarperCollins.

American Speech-Language-Hearing Association (ASHA). (1984). *Clinical management of communicatively handicapped minority language populations.* Rockville, MD: Author.

American Speech-Language-Hearing Association (ASHA). (1991). Report: Augmentative and alternative communication. *ASHA, 33* (Suppl.), 912.

American Speech-Language-Hearing Association (ASHA). (1999). *Guidelines for the roles and responsibilities of the school-based speech-language pathologist.* Rockville, MD: Author.

American Speech-Language-Hearing Association (ASHA). (2003). *A workload analysis approach for establishing speech-language caseload standards in the schools.* Rockville, MD: Author.

American Speech-Language-Hearing Association (ASHA). (2004a). *Accents and dialects* (http://www.asha.org/about/leadership-projects/multicultural/ad.htm).

American Speech-Language-Hearing Association (ASHA). (2004b). *Communication facts: Incidence and prevalence of communication disorders and hearing loss in children—2004 edition* (http://www.asha.org/members/reports/children.htm).

American Speech-Language-Hearing Association (ASHA). (2005). *How does your child hear and talk?* (http://www.asha.org/public/speech/development/child_hear_talk.htm).

Apel, K., & Swank, L. K. (1999). Second chances: Improving decoding skills in the older student. *Language, Speech, and Hearing Services in Schools, 30,* 231–242.

Battle, D. (1998). *Communication disorders in multicultural populations* (2nd ed.). Boston: Butterworth-Heinemann.

Barry, L., & Burley, S. (2004). Using social stories to teach choice and play skills to children with autism. *Focus on Autism and Other Developmental Disabilities, 19,* 45–51.

Beukelman, D. R., & Mirenda, P. A. (2005). *Augmentative and alternative communication: Supporting children and adults with complex communication needs* (3rd ed.) Baltimore: Brookes.

Bloom, L., & Lahey, M. (1978). *Language development and language disorders.* New York: Wiley.

Bunce, B. (2003). *Using a language-focused curriculum in a preschool classroom: Language and literacy facilitation and intervention.* Workshop presented at the University of Virginia.

Bunce, B., & Watkins, R. (1995). Language intervention in a preschool classroom: Implementing a language focused curriculum. In M. Rice & K. Wilcox (Eds.), *Building a language-focused curriculum for the preschool classroom. Vol. I: A foundation for lifelong communication.* Baltimore: Brookes.

Caruso A., & Strand, E. (1999). *Clinical management of motor speech disorders in children.* New York: Thieme.

Catts, H., & Kamhi, A. (1999). *Language and reading disabilities.* Needham, MA: Allyn & Bacon.

Chomsky, N. (1957). *Syntactic structures.* The Hague, the Netherlands: Mouton.

Cunningham, P. M., & Allington, R. L. (2003). *Classrooms that work: They can all read and write* (3rd ed.). New York: Addison-Wesley.

Downing, J. E. (2005). *Teaching communication skills to students with severe disabilities* (2nd ed.). Baltimore: Brookes.

Foley, B., & Staples, A. (2000). *Literature-based language intervention for students who use AAC.* Paper presented at the International Society for Augmentative and Alternative Communication Convention, Washington, DC.

Giangreco, M. (2000). Related services research for students with low-incidence disabilities: Implications for speech-language pathologists in inclusive classrooms. *Language, Speech, and Hearing Services in Schools, 31*(3), 230–239.

Gray, C. (2004). Social stories 10.0: The new defining criteria and guidelines. *Jenison Autism Journal, 14*(4), 2–21.

Howell, K. W., & Nolet, V. (2000). *Curriculum-based evaluation teaching and decision making* (3rd ed.). Belmont, CA: Wadsworth/Thompson Learning.

Hulit, H., & Howard, M. (2002). *Born to talk: An introduction to speech and language development* (3rd ed.). Boston: Allyn & Bacon.

Ivey, M., Heflin, J., & Alberto, P. (2004). The use of social stories to promote independent behaviors in novel events for children with PDD-NOS. *Focus on Autism and Other Developmental Disabilities, 19,* 164–176.

Kumin, L. (2001). *Classroom language skills for children with Down syndrome: A guide for parents and teachers.* Bethesda, MD: Woodbine House.

Kuoch, H., & Mirenda, P. (2003). Social story interventions for young children with autism spectrum disorders. *Focus on Autism and Other Developmental Disabilities, 18,* 219–227.

Loeb, D. (2003). Language theory and practice. In L. McCormick, D. Loeb, & D. Schiefelbusch (Eds.), *Supporting children with communication difficulties in inclusive settings: School-based language intervention* (2nd ed., pp. 43–70). Boston: Allyn & Bacon.

Lombardino, L. J., Riccio, C. A., Hynd, G. W., & Pinheiro, S. B. (1997). Linguistic deficits in children with reading disabilities. *American Journal of Speech-Language Pathology, 6,* 71–78.

Losardo, A., & Notari-Syverson, A. (2001). *Alternative approaches to assessing young children.* Baltimore: Brookes.

McCormick, L. (2003). Introduction to language acquisition. In L. McCormick, D. Loeb, & D. Schiefelbusch (Eds.), *Supporting children with communication difficulties in inclusive settings: School-based language intervention* (2nd ed., pp. 1–42) Boston: Allyn & Bacon.

McCormick, L., & Loeb, D. (2003). Characteristics of students with language and communication difficulties. In L. McCormick, D. Loeb, & D. Schiefelbusch (Eds.), *Supporting children with communication difficulties in inclusive settings: School-based language intervention* (2nd ed., pp. 71–112). Boston: Allyn & Bacon.

Myles, B., & Simpson, R. (2003). *Asperger syndrome: A guide for educators and parents* (2nd ed.). Austin, TX: Pro-Ed.

Nelson, N., & Van Meter, A. (2004). *The writing lab approach to language instruction and intervention.* Baltimore: Brookes.

Owens, R. (2001). *Language development: An introduction* (5th ed.). Boston: Allyn & Bacon.

Owens, R. (2005). *Language development: An introduction* (6th ed.). Boston: Allyn & Bacon.

Pannbacker, M. (1999). Treatment of vocal nodules: Options and outcomes. *American Journal of Speech-Language Pathology, 8*(3), 209–217.

Rice, M. L. (1993). "Don't talk to him, He's weird": A social consequences account of language and social interactions. In A. P. Kaiser & D. B. Gray (Eds.), *Enhancing children's communication: Research foundations for intervention* (pp. 139–158). Baltimore: Brookes.

Rice, M., & Wilcox, K. (1995). *Building a language-focused curriculum for the preschool classroom. Vol. I: A foundation for lifelong communication.* Baltimore: Brookes.

Romski, M. A., & Sevcik, R. A. (1988). Augmentative communication system acquisition and use: A model for teaching and assessing progress. *NSSLHA Journal, 16,* 61–74.

Romski, M. A., & Sevcik, R. A. (1992). Developing augmented language in children with severe mental retardation. In S. F. Warren & J. Reichle (Eds.), *Communication and language intervention series. Vol. 1: Causes and effects in communication and language intervention* (pp. 113–130). Baltimore: Brookes.

Romski, M. A., & Sevcik, R. A. (1996). *Breaking the speech barrier: Language development through augmented means*. Baltimore: Brookes.

Romski, M. A., & Sevcik, R. A. (2003). Augmented input. In J. Light, D. Beukelman, & J. Reichle (Eds.), *Communicative competence for individuals who use AAC: From research to effective practice*. Baltimore: Brookes.

Romski, M. A., Sevcik, R. A., & Forrest, S. (2001). Assistive technology and augmentative communication in inclusive early childhood programs. In M. J. Guralnick (Ed.), *Early childhood inclusion: Focus on change* (pp. 465–479). Baltimore: Brookes.

Sandall, S., & Schwartz, I. (2002). *Building blocks for teaching preschoolers with special needs*. Baltimore: Brookes.

Stuart, S. (2002). Communication: Speech and language. In M. Batshaw (Ed.), *Children with disabilities* (5th ed., pp. 229–241). Baltimore: Brookes.

Sturm, J., & Rankin-Erickson, J. (2002). Effects of hand-drawn and computer-generated concept mapping on the expository writing of middle school students with learning disabilities. *Learning Disabilities Research and Practices, 17*(2), 124–139.

Trelease, J. (1995). *The read-aloud handbook* (4th ed.). New York: Penguin.

U.S. Department of Education. (2001). *To assure a free appropriate public education: Twenty-third annual report to Congress on the implementation of the Individuals with Disabilities Education Act*. Washington, DC: Author.

U.S. Department of Education. (2002). *To assure a free appropriate public education: Twenty-fourth annual report to Congress on the implementation of the Individuals with Disabilities Education Act*. Washington, DC: Author.

Verdolini, K. (2000). Voice disorders. In J. Tomblin, H. Morris, & D. Spriestersbach (Eds.), *Diagnosis in speech-language pathology* (2nd ed., pp. 233–280). San Diego: Singular.

Vygotsky, L. S. (1978). *Thought and language*. Cambridge, MA: Harvard University Press.

Vygotsky, L. S. (1987). *The collected works of L. S. Vygotsky* (Vol. 1). New York: Plenum.

Wang, P. P., & Baron, M. A. (1997). Language and communication: Development and disorders. In M. L. Batshaw (Ed.), *Children with disabilities* (4th ed., pp. 275–292). Baltimore: Brookes.

Zebrowski, P. (2000). Stuttering. In J. Tomblin, H. Morris, & D. Spriestersbach (Eds.), *Diagnosis in speech-language pathology* (2nd ed., pp. 199–231). San Diego: Singular.

Chapter 7

Ackerman, B. P., Brown, E., & Izard, C. E. (2003). Continuity and change in levels of externalizing behavior in school of children from economically disadvantaged families. *Child Development, 74*(3), 694–709.

Adams, G. B. (2004). Identifying, assessing, and treating obsessive-compulsive disorder in school-aged children: The role of school personnel. *Teaching Exceptional Children, 37*(2), 46–53.

Addison, M. M., & Westmoreland, D. A. (2000). Over the net: Encouraging win-win solutions through conflict resolution. *Reaching Today's Youth, 5*(1), 51–54.

Administration for Children and Families. (2004). *What everyone can do to prevent child abuse* (2nd ed.). Washington, DC: Author.

Albano, A. M., Chorpita, B. F., & Barlow, D. H. (2003). Childhood anxiety disorders. In E. J. Mash & R. A. Barkley (Eds.), *Child psychopathology* (pp. 233–278). New York: Guilford.

Algozzine, R., Serna, L., & Patton, J. R. (2001). *Childhood behavior disorders: Applied research and educational practices* (2nd ed.). Austin, TX: PRO-ED.

American Psychiatric Association. (2000). *Diagnostic and statistical manual of mental disorders* (4th ed., revised). Washington, DC: Author.

Anderson, R. N., & Smith, B. L. (2003). Deaths: Leading causes for 2001. *National Vital Statistics Report, 52*(9), 1–52.

Asarnow, J. R., & Asarnow, R. F. (2003). Childhood-onset schizophrenia. In E. J. Mash & R. A. Barkley (Eds.), *Child psychopathology* (pp. 455–485). New York: Guilford.

Bassarath, L. (2001). Conduct disorder: A biopsychosocial review. *Candian Journal of Psychiatry, 46*(7), 609–617.

Benner, G. J., Nelson, J. R., & Epstein, M. H. (2002). Language skills of children with EBD. *Journal of Emotional and Behavioral Disorders, 10*(1), 43–57.

Billingsley, B. S. (2001). *Beginning special educators: Characteristics, qualifications, and experiences*. Rockville, MD: Weststat. (ERIC Document Reproduction Service No. ED 467269).

Bostic, J. Q., Rustuccia, C., & Schlozman, S. C. (2001). The suicidal student. *Educational Leadership, 59*(2), 92–93.

Brendtro, L. K., Brokenleg, M., & Van Bockern, S. (1991). The circle of courage. *Beyond Behavior, 2*(1), 5–12.

Breunlin, D. C., Cimmarusti, R. A., Bryant-Edwards, T. L., & Hetherington, J. S. (2002). Conflict resolution training as an alternative to suspension for violent behavior. *Journal of Educational Research, 95*, 349–357.

Brooks-Gunn, J. B., & Duncan, G. J. (1997). The effects of poverty on children. *Future of Children*, pp. 55–71.

Bruns, E. J., Burchard, J. D., Suter, J. C., Leverentz-Brady, K., & Force, M. M. (2004). Assessing fidelity to a community-based treatment for youth. *Journal of Emotional and Behavioral Disorders, 12*, 19–89.

Bullis, M., & Cheney, D. (1999). Vocational and transition interventions for adolescents and young adults with emotional or behavioral disorders. *Focus on Exceptional Children, 31*(7), 1–24.

Bullock, C., & Foegen, A. (2002). Constructive conflict resolution for students with behavioral disorders. *Behavioral Disorders, 27*(3), 289–295.

Burke, J. D., Loeber, R., & Birmaher, B. (2002). Oppositional defiant disorder and conduct disorder: A review of the past 10 years, part II. *Journal of the American Academy of Child and Adolescent Psychiatry, 41*(11), 1275–1293.

Burns, B. J., & Goldman, S. K. (Eds.). (1999). *Promising practices in wraparound for children with serious emotional disturbance and their families. Systems of care: Promising practices in children's mental health, 1998 series* (Vol. 4). Washington, DC: American Institutes for Research, Center for Effective Collaboration and Practice.

Christenson, S., Sinclair, M., Thurlow, M., & Evelo, D. (1995). *Tip the balance: Policies and practices that influence school engagement for youth at high risk for dropping out*. Minneapolis: University of Minnesota, Institute on Community Integration.

Clausen, J. M., Landsverk, J., Ganger, W., Chadwick, D., & Litrownik, A. (1998). Mental health problems of children in foster care. *Journal of Child and Family Studies, 7*, 283–296.

Cohen, N. J., Barwick, M. A., Horodezky, N. B., Vallance, D. D., & Im, N. (1998). Language, achievement, and cognitive processing in psychiatrically disturbed children with previously identified and unsuspected language impairments. *Journal of Child Psychology and Psychiatry, 39*, 865–877.

Coles, R. (1989). *The call of stories*. Boston: Houghton Mifflin.

Collett, B. R., Ohan, J. L., & Myers, K. M. (2003). Ten-year review of rating scales. IV: Scales assessing externalizing behaviors. *Journal of American Academy of Child and Adolescent Psychiatry, 42*(10), 1143–1170.

Corbett, W. P., Sanders, R. L., Clark, H. B., & Blank, W. (2002). Employment and social outcomes associated with vocational programming for youths with emotional or behavioral disorders. *Behavioral Disorders, 27*, 358–370.

Coutinho, M. J., Oswald, D. P., Best, A. M., & Forness, S. R. (2002). Gender and socio-demographic factors and the disproportionate identification of minority students as emotionally disturbed. *Behavioral Disorders, 27*, 109–125.

Cullinan, D., Evans, C., Epstein, M. H., & Ryser, G. (2003). Characteristics of emotional disturbance of elementary school students. *Behavioral Disorders, 28*(2), 94–110.

Cullinan, D., Osborne, S., & Epstein, M. H. (2004). Characteristics of emotional disturbance among female students. *Remedial and Special Education, 25*(5), 276–290.

Daunic, A. P., Smith, S. W., Robinson, T. W., Miller, M. D., & Landry, K. L. (2000). School-wide conflict resolution and peer mediation programs: Experiences in three middle schools. *Intervention in School and Clinic, 36*(2), 94–100.

References

Duncan, B. B., Forness, S. R., & Hartsough, C. (1995). Students identified as seriously emotionally disturbed in day treatment: Cognitive, psychiatric, and special education characteristics. *Behavioral Disorders, 29,* 238–252.

Emslie, G. J., Rush, A. J., Weinberg, W. A., Kowatch, R. A., Hughes, C. W., Carmody, T., & Rintelmann, J. (1997). A double-blind, randomized, placebo-controlled trial of fluoxetine in children and adolescents with depression. *Archives of General Psychology, 54,* 1031–1037.

Epstein, M. H. (1999). The development and validation of a scale to assess the emotional and behavioral strengths of children and adolescents. *Remedial and Special Education, 20*(5), 258–262.

Epstein, M. H., Cullinan, D., Ryser, G., & Pearson, N. (2002). Development of a scale to assess emotional disturbance. *Behavioral Disorders, 28*(1), 5–22.

Epstein, M. H., Hertzog, M. A., & Reid, R. (2001). The behavioral and emotional rating scale: Long-term test-retest reliability. *Behavioral Disorders, 26*(4), 314–320.

Epstein, M. H., Nordness, P. D., Cullinan, D., & Hertzog, M. (2002). Scale for assessing emotional disturbance: Long-term test-retest reliability validity with kindergarten and first-grade students. *Remedial and Special Education, 24*(3), 141–148.

Epstein, M H., Nordness, P. D., Nelson J. R., & Hertzog, M. (2002). Convergent validity of the behavioral and emotional rating scale with primary grade-level students. *Topics in Early Childhood Special Education, 22*(2), 114–121.

Epstein, M. H., & Sharma, J. (1998). *Behavioral and emotional rating scale: A strength-based approach to assessment.* Austin, TX: PRO-ED.

Faedda, G., Baldessarini, R., Suppes, T., Tondo, L., Becker, I., & Lipschitz, D. (1995). Pediatric onset bipolar disorder: A neglected clinical and public health problem. *Harvard Review of Psychiatry, 3*(4), 171–195.

Foley, R. M. (2001). Academic characteristics of incarcerated youth and correctional educational programs: A literature review. *Journal of Emotional and Behavioral Disorders, 9*(4), 248–259.

Forness, S. R., Walker, H. M., & Kavale, K. A. (2003). Psychiatric disorders and treatments: A primer for teachers. *Teaching Exceptional Children, 36*(2), 42–49.

Frey, L. M. (2003). Abundent beautification: An effective service learning project for students with emotional or behavioral disorders. *Teaching Exceptional Children, 35,* 66–75.

Fujiki, M., Brinton, B., Morgan, M., & Hart, C. H. (1999). Withdrawn and sociable behavior of children with language impairment. *Language, Speech, and Hearing Services in Schools, 30,* 183–195.

Fujiura, G. T., & Yamaki, K. (2000). Trends in demography of childhood poverty and disability. *Exceptional Children, 66*(2), 187–199.

Gagnon, J. C., & McLaughlin, M. J. (2004). Curriculum, assessment, and acountability in day treatment and residential schools. *Exceptional Children, 70,* 263–283.

Geller, B., Williams, M., Zimmerman, B., Frazier, J., Beringer, L., & Warner, K. (1998). Prepubertal and early adolescent bipolarity differentiate from ADHD by manic symptoms, grandiose delusions, ultra-rapid or ultradian cycling. *Journal of Affective Disorders, 51,* 81–91.

George, N. L., George, M. P., Gersten, R., & Grosenick, J. (1995). To leave or to stay: An exploratory study of teachers of students with emotional and behavioral disorders. *Remedial and Special Education, 16,* 227–236.

Glassberg, L. A., Hooper, S. R., & Mattison, R. E. (1999). Prevalence of learning disabilities at enrollment in special education: Students with behavioral disorders. *Behavioral Disorders, 25*(1), 9–21.

Gresham, F. M., & Elliott, S. N. (1990). *Social skills rating system.* Circle Pines, MN: AGS.

Gresham, F. M., Lane, K. L., MacMillan, D. L., & Bocian, K. M. (1999). Social and academic profiles of externalizing and internalizing groups: Risk factors for emotional and behavioral disorders. *Behavioral Disorders, 24*(3), 231–245.

Gunter, P. L., Callicott, K., & Denny, R. K. (2003). Evaluation and use of data in classrooms for students with emotional and behavioral disorders. *Preventing School Failure, 48,* 4–9.

Gunter, P. L., Coutinho, M. J., & Cade, T. (2002). Classroom factors linked with academic gains among students with emotional and behavioral problems. *Preventing School Failure, 46*(3), 126–132.

Gunter, P. L., Denny, R. K., & Venn, M. (2000). Modification of instructional materials and procedures for curricular success of students with emotional and behavioral disorders. *Preventing School Failure, 44,* 116–122.

Gunter, P. L., Hummell, J. H., & Venn, M. L. (1998). Are effective academic instructional practices used to teach students with behavioral disorders? *Beyond Behavior, 9*(3), 5–11.

Hallowell, E. M. (1996). *When you worry about the child you love: Emotional and learning problems in children.* New York: Fireside.

Hammen, C., & Rudolph, K. D. (2003). Childhood mood disorders. In E. J. Mash & R. A. Barkley (Eds.), *Child psychopathology* (2nd ed., pp. 233–278). New York: Guilford.

Hasselbring, T. S., & Glaser, C. H. W. (2000). Use of computer technology to help students with special needs. *Future of Children, 10*(2), 102–122.

Hewitt, M. B. (1999). The control game: Exploring oppositional behavior. *Reclaiming Children and Youth, 8*(1), 30–33.

Hinshaw, S. P., & Lee, S. S. (2003). Conduct and oppositional defiant disorders. In E. J. Mash & R. A. Barkley (Eds.), *Child psychopathology* (2nd ed., pp. 144–198). New York: Guilford.

Hunt, M. H., Meyers, J., Davies, G., Meyers, B., Grogg, K. R., & Neel, J. (2002). A comprehensive needs assessment to facilitate prevention of school dropout and violence. *Psychology in the Schools, 39,* 399–416.

Ialongo, N., Poduska, J., Werthamer, L., & Sheppard, K. (2001). The distal impact of two first-grade preventive interventions on conduct problem and disorder in early adolescence. *Journal of Emotional and Behavioral Disorders, 9*(3), 146–161.

Institute for Children and Poverty. (2001). *Déjà vu: Family homelessness in New York City.* New York: Author.

Jolivette, K. (2000). *Improving post-school outcomes for students with emotional and behavioral disorders.* ERIC/OSEP Digest, E597.

Kamps, D., Kravits, T., Rauch, J., Kamps, J. L., & Chung, N. (2000). A prevention program for students with or at risk for ED: Moderating effects of variation in treatment and classroom structure. *Journal of Emotional and Behavioral Disorders, 8,* 141–152.

Kauffman, J. M. (2001). *Characteristics of emotional and behavioral disorders of children and youth* (7th ed.). Upper Saddle River, NJ: Merrill/Prentice Hall.

Kavale, K. A., Forness, S. R., & Walker, H. M. (1999). Interventions for ODD and CD in the school. In H. Quay & A. Hogan (Eds.), *Handbook of disruptive behavior disorders* (pp. 441–454). New York: Plenum.

Kelly, J. E., Buehlman, K., & Caldwell, K. (2000). Training personnel to promote quality parent-child interaction in families who are homeless. *Topics in Early Childhood and Special Education, 20*(3), 174–185.

King-Sears, M., & Mooney, J. F. (2004). Teaching content in an academically diverse class. In B. K. Lenz, D. D. Deshler, & B. R. Kissam (Eds.), *Teaching content to all: Evidence-based inclusive practices in middle and secondary schools* (pp. 221–257). Boston: Allyn & Bacon.

Knowlton, D. (1995). Managing children with oppositional behavior. *Beyond Behavior, 6*(3), 5–10.

Kochanek, K. D., & Smith, B. L. (2004). Deaths: Preliminary data for 2002. *National Vital Statistics Report, 52*(13), 1–48.

Kovacs, M. (1996). Presentation and course of major depressive disorder during childhood and later years of the life span. *Journal of the American Academy of Child and Adolescent Psychiatry, 35,* 705–715.

Kumra, S., Shaw, M., Merka, P., Nakayama, E., & Augustin, R. (2001). Childhood-onset schizophrenia: Research update. *Canadian Journal of Psychiatry, 46,* 923–930.

Langley, A. K., Bergman, L., & Piacentini, J. C. (2002). Assessment of childhood anxiety. *International Review of Psychiatry, 14,* 102–113.

Laursen, E. K. (2000). Strength-based practice with children in trouble. *Reclaiming Children and Youth, 9*(2), 70–75.

Lee, D. L., Belfiore, P. J., & Toro-Zambrana, W. (2001). The effects of mastery training and explicit feedback on task design preference in a vocational setting. *Research in Developmental Disabilities, 22,* 333–351.

Leone, P. E., Meisel, S. M., & Drakeford, W. (2002). Special education programs for youth with disabilities in juvenile corrections. *Journal of Correctional Education, 53*, 46–50.

Leslie, L. K., Landsverk, J., Ezzet-Lofstrom, R., Tschann, J. M., Slymen, D. J., & Garland, A. F. (2000). Children in foster care: Factors influencing outpatient mental health service use. *Child Abuse and Neglect, 24*(4), 465–476.

Levy, S., & Vaughn, S. (2002). An observational study of teachers' reading instruction for students with emotional or behavioral disorders. *Behavioral Disorders, 27*, 215–235.

Loeber, R., Burke, J. D., Lahey, B. B., Winters, A., & Zera, M. (2000). Oppositional defiant and conduct disorder: A review of the past 10 years, part I. *Journal of American Academy of Child and Adolescent Psychiatry, 39*(12), 1468–1484.

Mahoney, J. L. (2000). School extracurricular activity participation as moderator in the development of antisocial patterns. *Child Development, 71*, 502–516.

Martin, E. J., Tobin, T. J., & Sugai, G. M. (2002). Current information on dropout prevention: Ideas from practitioners and the literature. *Preventing School Failure, 47*, 10–15.

Mash, E. J., & Dozois, D. J. A. (2003). Child psychopathology: A developmental systems perspective. In E. J. Mash & R. A. Barkley (Eds.), *Child psychopathology* (2nd ed., pp. 3–74). New York: Guilford.

Mattison, R. E., Spitznagel, E. L., & Felix, B. C. (1998). Enrollment predictors of the special education outcome for SED students. *Behavioral Disorders, 23*, 243–256.

McCulloch, A., Wiggins, R. D., Joshi, H. E., & Sachdev, D. (2000). Internalising and externalising children's behaviour problems in Britain and the US: Relationships to family resources. *Children and Society, 14*(5), 368–383.

McIntosh, P. I., & Guest, C. L. (2000). Suicidal behavior: Recognition and response for children and adolescents. *Beyond Behavior, 10*(2), 14–17.

Miklowitz, D. J., & Goldsteing, M. J. (1997). *Bipolar disorder. A family-focused treatment approach.* New York: Guilford.

Milne, J. M., Edwards, J. K., & Murchie, J. C. (2001). Family treatment of oppositional defiant disorder: Changing views and strength-based approaches. *Family Journal, 9*(1), 17–28.

Mishara, B. L. (1999). Conceptions of death and suicide in children ages 6–12 and their implications for suicide prevention. *Suicide and Life-Threatening Behavior, 29*(2), 105–118.

Mitchem, K. J. (2001). CWPASM: A classwide peer-assisted self-management program for general education classrooms. *Education and Treatment of Children, 24*(2), 111–141.

Mooney, P., Denny, R. K., & Gunter, P. L. (2004). The impact of NCLB and the reauthorization of IDEA on academic instruction of students with emotional or behavioral disorders. *Behavioral Disorders, 29*(3), 237–246.

Muscott, H. S. (2000). A review and analysis of service-learning programs involving students with emotional/behavioral disorders. *Education and Treatment of Children, 23*(3), 346–368.

Nelson, J. R., Benner, G. J., Lane, K., & Smith, B. W. (2004). Academic achievement of K–12 students with emotional and behavioral disorders. *Council for Exceptional Children, 71*(1), 59–73.

Nelson, J. R., Gonzalez, J. E., Epstein, M. H., & Benner, G. J. (2003). Administrative discipline contacts: A review of the literature. *Behavioral Disorders, 28*(3), 249–281.

Oseroff, A., Oseroff, C. E., Westling, D., & Gessner, L. J. (1999). Teachers' beliefs about maltreatment of students with emotional/behavioral disorders. *Behavioral Disorders, 24*(3), 197–209.

Osher, D. M., Quinn, M. M., & Hanley, T. V. (2002). Children and youth with serious emotional disturbances: A national agenda for success. *Journal of Child and Family Studies, 11*, 1–11.

Panico, A. (1998). Service learning as a community initiation. *Reaching Today's Youth, 3*(1), 37–41.

Park, J., Turnbull, A. P., & Turnbull, H. R. (2002). Impacts of poverty on quality of life in families of children with disabilities. *Exceptional Children, 68*(2), 151–170.

Pierce, C. D., Reid, R., & Epstein, M. H. (2004). Teacher-mediated interventions for children with EBD and their academic outcomes: A review. *Remedial and Special Education, 25*(3), 175–188.

Qi, C. H., & Kaiser, A. P. (2003). Behavior problems of preschool children from low-income families: Review of the literature. *Teaching Exceptional Children, 23*(4), 188–216.

Reid, R., Epstein, M. H., Pastor, D. A., & Ryser, G. R. (2000). Strengths-based assessment differences across students with LD and EBD. *Remedial and Special Education, 21*(6), 346–355.

Reid, R., Gonzalez, J. E., Nordness, P. D., Trout, A., & Epstein, M. H. (2004). A meta-analysis of the academic status of students with emotional/behavioral disturbance. *Journal of Special Education, 38*(3), 130–143.

Rubin, K., Chen, X., McDougall, P., Bowker, A., & McKinnon, J. (1995). The Waterloo Longitudinal Project: Predicting internalizing and externalizing problems in adolescence. *Development and Psychopathology, 7*, 751–764.

Rudolph, S. M., & Epstein, M. H. (2000). Empowering children and families through strength-based assessment. *Reclaiming Children and Youth, 8*(4), 207–209, 232.

Rutter, P. A., & Behrendt, A. E. (2004). Adolescent suicide risk: Four psychosocial factors. *Adolescence, 39*(154), 295–302.

Saavedra, L. M., & Silverman, W. K. (2002). Classification of anxiety disorders in children: What a difference two decades make. *International Review of Psychiatry, 14*, 87–101.

Scanlon, D., & Mellard, D. F. (2002). Academic and participation profiles of school-age dropouts with and without disabilities. *Exceptional Children, 68*, 239–259.

Sitlington, P. L., & Neubert, D. A. (2004). Preparing youths with emotional or behavioral disorders for transition to adult life: Can it be done within the standards-based reform movement? *Behavioral Disorders, 29*, 279–288.

Sternberg, R. J., & Grigorenko, E. L. (1999). Myths in education and psychology regarding the gene-environment debate. *Teachers College Record, 100*(3), 536.

Thurlow, M. L., Lazarus, S., Thompson, S., & Robey, J. (2002). *2001 state policies on assessment participation and accommodations* (Synthesis Report 46). Minneapolis: University of Minnesota, National Center on Educational Outcomes (http://education.umn.edu/NCEO/OnlinePubs/Synthesis46.html).

Tournaki, N., & Criscitiello, E. (2003). Using peer tutoring as a successful part of behavior management. *Teaching Exceptional Children, 36*(2), 22–29.

Trout, A. L., Nordness, P. D., Pierce, C. D., & Epstein, M. H. (2003). Research on the academic status of children with emotional and behavioral disorders: A review of the literature from 1961–2000. *Journal of Emotional and Behavioral Disorders, 11*(4), 198–210.

U.S. Department of Education. (1998). *To assure the free appropriate public education of all children with disabilities: Twentieth annual report to Congress on the implementation of the Individuals with Disabilities Education Act.* Washington, DC: Author.

U.S. Department of Education. (2002). *To assure the free appropriate public education of all children with disabilities: Twenty-third annual report to Congress on the implementation of the Individuals with Disabilities Education Act.* Washington, DC: Author.

U.S. Department of Education, Office of Special Education Programs. (2005). *IDEA data website* (http://www.ideadata.org/aboutThisSite.asp).

U.S. Surgeon General. (2000). *Mental health: A report of the surgeon general* (http://www.mentalhealth.org/specials).

Van Der Valk, J. C., Van Den Oord, E. J. C. G., Verhulst, F. C., & Boomsma, D. I. (2003). Genetic and environmental contributions to stability and change in children's internalizing and externalizing problems. *Journal of the American Academy of Child and Adolescent Psychiatry, 42*(10), 1212–1220.

Walker, H. M., Colvin, G., & Ramsey, E. (1995). *Antisocial behavior in school: Strategies and best practices.* New York: Brooks/Cole.

Walker, H. M., Zeller, R. W., Close, D. W., Webber, J., & Gresham, F. (1999). The present unwrapped: Change and challenge in the field of behavioral disorders. *Behavioral Disorders, 24*(4), 293–304.

Walker, J. S., Bruns, E. J., VanDenBerg, J. D., Rast, J., Osher, T. W., Koroloff, N., Miles, P., Adams, J., & National Wraparound Initiative Advisory Group. (2004). *Phases and activities of the wraparound process.* Portland, OR: Portland State University, Research and Training Center on Family Support and Children's

Mental Health, National Wraparound Initiative.

Walker, J. S., & Schutte, K. M. (2004). Practice and process in wraparound teamwork. *Journal of Emotional and Behavioral Disorders, 12,* 182–192.

Wehby, J. H., Lane, K. L., & Falk, K. B. (2003). Academic instruction for students with emotional and behavioral disorders. *Journal of Emotional and Behavioral Disorders, 11,* 194–197.

Wingenfeld, S. (2002). Assessment of behavioral and emotional difficulties in children and adolescents. *Peabody Journal of Education, 77*(2) 85–105.

Wright, D., & Torrey, G. K. (2001). A comparison of two peer-referenced assessment techniques with parent and teacher ratings of social skills and problem behaviors. *Behavior Disorders, 26,* 273–182.

Yeung, W. J., Linver, M. R., & Brooks-Gunn, J. (2002). How money matters for young children's development: Parental investment and family processes. *Child Development, 73*(6), 1861–1879.

Chapter 8

Alberto, P. A., & Troutman, A. C. (2003). *Applied behavior analysis for teachers* (6th ed.). Upper Saddle River, NJ: Merrill/Prentice Hall.

American Psychiatric Association. (2000). Diagnostic and statistical manual of mental disorders (4th ed., rev.). Washington, DC: Author.

Baren, M. (1994). *Hyperactivity and attention disorders in children.* San Ramon, CA: Health Information Network.

Barkley, R. A. (1998). *Attention-deficit hyperactivity disorder: A handbook for diagnosis and treatment.* New York: Guilford.

Barkley, R. A. (2000). *Taking charge of ADHD: The complete, authoritative guide for parents* (rev. ed.) New York: Guilford.

Barkley, R. A. (2003). Attention-deficit/hyper-activity disorder. In E. J. Mash & R. A. Barkley (Eds.), *Child psychopathology* (2nd ed., pp. 75–143). New York: Guilford.

Barry, T. D., Lyman, R. D., & Klinger, L. G. (2002). Academic underachievement and attention-deficit/hyperactivity disorder: The negative impact of symptom severity on school performance. *Journal of School Psychology, 40*(3), 259–283.

Biederman, J., Faraone, S. V., Mick, E., Spencer, T., Wilens, T., Kiely, K., et al. (1995). High risk for attention deficit hyperactivity disorder among children of parents with childhood onset of the disorder: A pilot study. *American Journal of Psychiatry, 152,* 431–435.

Biederman, J., Faraone, S., Milberger, S., Curtis, S., Chen, L., Marrs, A., et al. (1996). Predictors of persistence and remission of ADHD into adolescence: Results from a four-year prospective follow-up study. *Journal of the*

American Academy of Child and Adolescent Psychiatry, 35, 343–351.

Biederman, J., Monuteaux, M. C., Doyle, A. E., Seidman, L. J., Wilens, T. E., Ferrero, F., Morgan, C. L., & Faraone, S. V. (2004). Impact of executive function deficits and attention-deficit/hyperactivity disorder (ADHD) on academic outcomes in children. *Journal of Consulting and Clinical Psychology, 72*(5), 757–766.

BrainTrain. (2000). *Captain's log* [Computer Software]. Richmond, VA: Author.

Breton, J., Bergeron, L., Valla, J. P., Berthiaume, C., Gaudet, N., Lambert, J., et al. (1999). Quebec children mental health survey: Prevalence of DSM-III-R mental health disorders. *Journal of Child Psychology and Psychiatry, 40,* 375–384.

Broitman, M., Robb, A., & Stein, M. A. (1999). Paying attention to mood symptoms in children with AD/HD. In P. J. Accardo, T. A. Blondis, B. Y. Whitman, & M. A. Stein (Eds.), *Pediatric habilitation series: Vol. 10. Attention deficits and hyperactivity in children and adults: Diagnosis, treatment, management* (2nd rev. ed., pp. 325–344). New York: Marcel Dekker.

Brown, T. E. (2000). *Attention-deficit disorders and co-morbidities in children, adolescents, and adults.* Washington, DC: American Psychiatric Press.

Carbone, E. (2001). Arranging the classroom with an eye (and ear) to students with ADHD. *Teaching Exceptional Children, 34*(2), 72–81.

CHADD. (2005). *Educational rights for children with AD/HD.* CHADD Fact Sheet No. 4. Landover, MD: National Resource Center on AD/HD.

Cohen, D., & Leo, J. (2004). An update on ADHD neuroimaging research. *Journal of Mind and Behavior, 25*(2), 161–166.

Conners, C. K. (1997). *Conners' rating scales—revised technical manual.* North Tonawanda, NY: Multi-Health Systems.

Cook, E. H. (1999). Genetics of attention-deficit hyperactivity disorder. *Mental Retardation and Developmental Disabilities Research Reviews, 5*(3), 191–198.

Corkum, P., Tannock, R., & Moldofsky, H. (1998). Sleep disturbances in children with attention-deficit/hyperactivity disorder. *Journal of the American Academy of Child and Adolescent Psychiatry, 37,* 637–646.

Cramond, B. (1995). The coincidence of attention deficit hyperactivity disorder and creativity. *Attention Deficit Disorder Research-Based Decision Making Series 9508.* Washington, DC: Office of Educational Improvement. (ERIC Document Reproduction Service No. 388016).

Demaray, M. K., Elting, J., & Schaefer, K. (2003). Assessment of attention-deficit/hyperactivity disorder (AD/HD): A comparative evaluation of five, commonly used, published rating scales. *Psychology in the Schools, 40*(4), 341–361.

Demaray, M. K., Schaefer, K., & Delong, L. K. (2003). Attention-deficit/hyperactivity disorder (ADHD): A national survey of training and current assessment practices in the schools. *Psychology in the Schools, 40*(6), 583–597.

Dendy, C. A. Z. (1995). *Teenagers with ADD: A parent's guide.* Bethesda, MD: Woodbine House.

Dodson, W. W. (2002, Summer). Attention deficit-hyperactivity disorder (AD/HD): The basics and the controversies. *Understanding Our Gifted,* pp. 17–21.

dosReis, S., Owens, P. L., Puccia, K. B., & Leaf, P. J. (2004). Multimodal treatment for ADHD among youths in three Medicaid subgroups: Disabled, foster care, and low income. *Pychiatric Services, 55,* 1041–1048.

DuPaul, G. J., McGoey, K. E., Eckert, T. L., & VanBrakle, J. (2001). Preschool children with attention-deficit/hyperactivity disorder: Impairments in behavioral, social, and school functioning. *Journal of the American Academy of Child and Adolescent Psychiatry, 40,* 508–515.

Fletcher, J. M., Shaywitz, S. E., & Shaywitz, B. A. (1999). Co-morbidity of learning and attention disorders: Asperger but equal. *Pediatric Clinics of North America, 46,* 885–897.

Gordon, S. M., Tulak, F., & Troncale, J. (2004). Prevalence and characteristics of adolescent patients with co-occuring ADHD and substance dependence. *Journal of Addictive Diseases, 23*(4), 31–39.

Gresham, F. M., MacMillan, D. L., Bocian, K. M., Ward, S. L., & Forness, S. R. (1998). Comorbidity of hyperactivity-impulsivity-inattention and conduct problems: Risk factors in social, affective, and academic domains. *Journal of Abnormal Child Psychology, 26,* 393–406.

HaileMariam, A., Bradley-Johnson, S., & Johnson, C. M. (2002). Pediatricians' preferences for ADHD information from schools. *School Psychology Review, 31,* 94–105.

Harman, P. L. (2000, May/June). Collaboration instead of litigation. *Attention!, 6*(5), 27–29.

Harman, P. L., & Barkley, R. (2000). One-on-one with Russell Barkley. *Attention! 6*(4), 12–14.

Hinshaw, S. P., Zupan, B. A., Simmel, C., Nigg, J. T., & Melnick, S. (1997). Peer status in boys with attention-deficit/hyperactivity disorder: Predictions from overt and covert antisocial behavior, social isolation, and authoritative parenting beliefs. *Child Development, 68,* 880–896.

Hoover, D. W., & Milich, R. (1994). Effects of sugar ingestion expectancies on mother-child interactions. *Journal of Abnormal Child Psychology, 22,* 501–515.

Johnston, C., & Mash, E. J. (2001). Families of children with attention-deficit/hyperactivity disorder: Review and recommendations for future research. *Clinical Child and Family Psychology Review, 4,* 183–207.

Kaider, I., Wiener, J., & Tannock, R. (2003). The attributions of children with attention-deficit/hyperactivity disorder for their problem behaviors. *Journal of Attention Disorders, 6*(3), 99–109.

Kaplan, B. J., Crawford, S. G., Dewey, D. M., & Fisher, G. C. (2000). The IQs of children with ADHD are normally distributed. *Journal of Learning Disabilities, 33*(5), 425–432.

Kiersuk, T. J., Smith, A., & Cardillo, A. (1994). *Goal attainment scaling: Applications and measurement*. Hillsdale, NJ: Erlbaum.

Klassen, A. F., Miller, A., & Fine, S. (2004). Health-related quality of life in children and adolescents who have a diagnosis of attention-deficit/hyperactivity disorder. *Pediatrics, 114*(5), 1322–1323.

Kollins, S. H., Barkley, R. A., & DuPaul, G. J. (2001). Use and management of medications for children diagnosed with attention deficit hyperactivity disorder (ADHD). *Focus on Exceptional Children, 33*(5), 1–23.

Kourakis, I. E., Katachanakis, C. N., Vlahonikolis, I. G., & Paritsis, N. K. (2004). Examination of verbal memory and recall time in children with attention deficit hyperactivity disorder. *Developmental Neuropsychology, 26*(2), 565–570.

Kuntsi, J., & Stevenson, J. (1998). Testing psychological theories of hyperactivity within a twin study. *Behavior Genetics, 28*(6), 474.

Lahey, B. B., McBurnett, K., & Loeber, R. (2000). Are attention-deficit/hyperactivity disorder and oppositional defiant disorder developmental precursors to conduct disorder? In A. J. Sameroff, M. Lewis, & S. M. Miller (Eds.), *Handbook of developmental psychopathology* (2nd ed., pp. 431–446). New York: Kluwer.

Larsson, J. O., Larsson, H., & Lichtenstein, P. (2004). Genetic and environmental contributions to stability and change of ADHD symptoms between 8 and 13 years of age: A longitudinal twin study. *American Academy for Child and Adolescent Psychiatry, 43*(10), 1267–1275.

Lee, S. S., & Hinshaw, S. P. (2004). Severity of adolescent delinquency among boys with and without attention deficit hyperactivity disorder: Predictions from early antisocial behavior and peer status. *Journal of Clinical Child and Adolescent Psychology, 33*(4), 705–716.

LeFever, G. B., Villers, M. S., Morrow, A. L., & Vaughn, E. S. (2002). Parental perceptions of adverse educational outcomes among children diagnosed and treated for ADHD: A call for improved school/provider collaboration. *Psychology in the Schools, 39*(1), 63–71.

Leo, J. L., & Cohen, D. (2003). Broken brains or flawed studies? A critical review of ADHD neuroimaging studies. *Journal of Mind and Behavior, 24*, 29–56.

Locke, E. A., & Latham, G. P. (2002). Building a practically useful theory of goal setting and task motivation: A 35-year odyssey. *American Psychologist, 57*(9), 705–717.

McGoey, K. E., Eckert, T. L., & DuPaul, G. J. (2002). Early intervention for preschool-age children with ADHD: A literature review. *Journal of Emotional and Behavioral Disorders, 10*, 14–28.

Milberger, S., Biederman, J., Faraone, S. V., Chen, L., & Jones, J. (1997). Further evidence of an association between attention-deficit/hyperactivity disorder and cigarette smoking. Findings from a high-risk sample of siblings. *American Journal of Addiction, 6*, 205–217.

Miranda, A., & Presentacion, M. J. (2000). Efficacy of cognitive-behavioral therapy in the treatment of children with ADHD, with and without aggressiveness. *Psychology in the Schools, 37*, 169–182.

Mostofsky, S. H., Cooper, K. L., Kates, W. R., Denckla, M. B., & Kaufmann, W. E. (2002). Smaller prefrontal and premotor volumes in boys with attention-deficit/hyperactivity disorder. *Biological Psychiatry, 52*(8), 785–794.

MTA Cooperative Group. (1999a). A 14-month randomized clinical trial of treatment strategies for attention-deficit/hyperactivity disorder. *Archives of General Psychiatry, 56*, 1073–1086.

MTA Cooperative Group. (1999b). Moderators and mediators of treatment response for children with attention-deficit/hyperactivity disorder. *Archives of General Psychiatry, 56*, 1088–1096.

National Institute of Mental Health (NIMH). (2002, October 8). Brain shrinkage in AD/HD not caused by medications. *NIH News Release* (http://www.nimh.nih.gov/events/).

Nolan, E. E., Gadow, K. D., & Sprafkin, J. (2001). Teacher reports of DSM-IV ADHD, ODD, and CD symptoms in schoolchildren. *Journal of the American Academy of Child and Adolescent Psychiatry, 40*, 241–249.

Palmer, S. B., Wehmeyer, M. L., Gibson, K., & Agran, M. (2004). Promoting access to the general curriculum by teaching self-determination skills. *Exceptional Children, 70*, 427–439.

Parker, H. C. (1996). Adapt: Accommodations help students with attention deficit disorders. *ADD Warehouse Articles on ADD* (http://www.addwarehouse.com).

Play Attention. (2001). *Helping overcome learning difficulties: Play attention* (http://www.playattention.com).

Pliszka, S. R., Carlson, C. L., & Swanson, J. M. (1999). *ADHD with comorbid disorders: Clinical assessment and management*. New York: Guilford.

Roach, A. T., & Elliott, S. N. (2005). Goal attainment scaling: An efficient and effective approach to monitoring student progress. *Teaching Exceptional Children, 37*(4), 8–17.

Robison, L. M., Sclar, D. A., Skaer, T. L., & Galin, R. S. (1999). National trends in the prevalence of attention-deficit/hyperactivity disorder and the prescribing of methylphenidate among school-age children. *Clinical Pediatrics, 38*, 209–217.

Romano, E., Tremblay, R. E., Vitaro, F., Zoccolillo, M., & Pagani, L. (2001). Prevalence of psychiatric diagnoses and the role of perceived impairment: Findings from an adolescent community sample. *Journal of Child Psychology and Psychiatry, 42*, 451–462.

Sands, D. J., & Doll, E. (2005). Teaching goal setting and decision making to students with developmental disabilities. In M. L. Wehmeyer & M. Agran (Eds.), *Mental retardation and intellectual disabilities: Teaching students using innovative and research-based strategies*. Upper Saddle River, NJ: Merrill/Prentice Hall.

Sciutto, M. J., Nolfi, C. J., & Bluhm, C. (2004). Effects of child gender and symptom type on referrals for ADHD by elementary school teachers. *Journal of Emotional and Behavioral Disorders, 12*(4), 247–253.

Semrud-Clikeman, M., Steingard, R. J., Filipek, P., Biederman, J., Bekken, K., & Renshaw, P. F. (2000). Using MRI to examine brain-behavior relationships in males with attention deficit disorder with hyperactivity. *Journal of the American Academy of Child and Adolescent Psychiatry, 39*(4), 477–484.

Smith, S. (2002). *Applying cognitive behavioral strategies to social skills instruction*. Arlington, VA: ERIC/OSEP Digest.

Snider, V. E., Busch, T., & Arrowood, L. (2003). Teacher knowledge of stimulant medication and ADHD. *Remedial and Special Education, 24*(1), 1–16.

Solanto, M. V. (2002). Overlooked and undertreated? Inattentive AD/HD. *Attention! 9*(1), 28–31.

Sowell, E. R., Thompson, P. M., Welcome, S. E., Henkenius, A. L., Toga, A. W., & Peterson, B. S. (2003). Cortical abnormalities in children and adolescents with attention-deficit hyperactivity disorder. *Lancet, 362*, 1699–1707.

Spencer, T. J., Biederman, J., Wilens, T. E., & Faraone, S. (2002). Novel treatments for attention-deficit/hyperactivity disorder in children. *Journal of Clinical Psychiatry, 63*, 16–22.

Stanford, P., & Reeves, S. (2005). Assessment that drives instruction. *Teaching Exceptional Children, 37*(4), 18–23.

Stein, M. A., Efron, L. A., Schiff, W. B., & Glanzman, M. (2002). Attention deficits and hyperactivity. In M. L. Batshaw (Ed.), *Children with disabilities* (pp. 355–371). Baltimore: Brookes.

Stevens, J., Harman, J. S., & Kelleher, K. J. (2004). Ethnic and regional differences in primary care visits for attention-deficit hyperactivity disorder. *Journal of Developmental and Behavioral Pediatrics, 25*(5), 318–325.

Tannock, R., & Martinussen, R. (2001). Reconceptualizing ADHD. *Educational Leadership, 59*(3), 20–25.

Travis, P., Diehl, J., Trickel, K., & Webb, L. (1999, April). *Children with attention deficit disorder: The MDTP early intervention model*. Paper presented at the annual convention of the Council for Exceptional Children, Charlotte, NC.

Volkow, N. D., Fowler, J. S., Wang, G. J., Ding, Y., & Gatley, S. J. (2002). Role of dopamine in the therapeutic and reinforcing effects of methylphenidate in humans: Results from imaging studies. *European Neuropsychopharmacology, 12*(6), 557–566.

Walker, B. (2004). *The girls' guide to AD/HD*. Bethesda, MD: Woodbine House.

Wehmeyer, M. L., Palmer, S., Agran, M., Mithaug, D., & Martin, J. (2000). Promoting causal agency: The self-determined learning model of instruction. *Exceptional Children*, 66, 439–453.

Wehmeyer, M. L., & Shogren, K. (in press). Self-determination and learners with autism spectrum disorders. In R. Simpson & B. Myles (Eds.), *Educating children and youth with autism: Strategies for effective practice* (2nd ed.). Austin, TX: PRO-ED.

Weiler, M. D., Bernstein, J. H., Bellinger, D., & Waber, D. P. (2002). Information processing deficits in children with attention-deficit/hyperactivity disorder, inattentive type, and children with reading disability. *Journal of Learning Disabilities*, 35(5), 449–460.

Wells, R. D., Dahl, B. B., & Synder, D. (2000). Coping and compensatory strategies used by adults with attentional problems. *Attention!* 6(5), 22–24.

Whalen, C. K., Jamner, L. D., Henker, B., Delfino, J. M., & Lozano, J. M. (2002). The ADHD spectrum and everyday life: Experience sampling of adolescent moods, activities, smoking, and drinking. *Child Development*, 73(1), 209–227.

Willoughby, M. T., Curran, P. J., Costello, E. J., & Angold, A. (2000). Implications of early versus late onset of attention-deficit/hyperactivity disorder symptoms. *Journal of the American Academy of Child and Adolescent Psychiatry*, 39(12), 1512–1519.

Wolraich, M. L., Hannah, J. N., Pinnock, T. Y., Baumgaertel, A., & Brown, J. (1996). Comparison of diagnostic criteria for attention-deficit hyperactivity disorder in a country-wide sample. *Journal of the American Academy of Child and Adolescent Psychiatry*, 35, 319–324.

Chapter 9

Abbeduto, L. (2003). Language and communication in mental retardation. *International Review of Research in Mental Retardation* (Vol. 27). New York: Academic Press.

Agran, M., Blanchard, C., & Wehmeyer, M. L. (2000). Promoting transition goals and self-determination through student-directed learning: The self-determined learning model of instruction. *Education and Training in Mental Retardation and Developmental Disabilities*, 35, 351–364.

Agran, M., Snow, K., & Swaner, J. (1999). A survey of secondary level teachers' opinions on community-based instruction and inclusive education. *Journal of the Association for Persons with Severe Handicaps*, 24(1), 58–62.

American Association on Mental Retardation (AAMR). (2002). *Mental retardation: Definition, classification, and systems of supports* (10th ed.). Washington, DC: Author.

Bates, P. E., Quvo, T., Miner, C. A., & Korabek, C. A. (2001). Simulated and community-based instruction involving persons with mild and moderate mental retardation. *Research and Developmental Disabilities*, 22, 95–115.

Batshaw, M. L., & Shapiro, B. K. (2002). Mental retardation. In M. L. Batshaw (Ed.), *Children with disabilities* (5th ed., pp. 287–305). Baltimore: Brookes.

Bebko, J. M., & Luhaorg, H. (1998). The development of strategy use and metacognitive processing in mental retardation: Some sources of difficulty. In J. A. Burack, R. M. Hodapp, & E. Zigler (Eds.), *Handbook of mental retardation and development* (pp. 382–409). Cambridge, UK: Cambridge University Press.

Bebko, J. M., & McPherson, M. J. (1997). *Teaching mnemonic strategies as a functional skill to cognitively impaired students*. North York, ON: York University.

Belfiore, P., & Browder, D. (1992). The effects of self-monitoring on teacher's data-based decisions and on the progress of adults with mental retardation. *Education and Training in Mental Retardation*, 27, 60–67.

Blank, R. M. (2001). An overview of trends in social and economic well-being, by race. In N. J. Smelser, W. J. Wilson, & F. Mitchell (Eds.), *America becoming: Racial trends and their consequences* (Vol. 1, pp. 21–39). Washington, DC: National Academy Press.

Brady, N. C., & Warren, S. F. (2003). Language interventions for children with mental retardation. In L. Masters-Glidden & L. Abbeduto (Eds.), *Language and communication in mental retardation* (pp. 231–250). Boston: Academic Press.

Bray, N. W., Fletcher, K. L., & Turner, L. A. (1997). Cognitive competencies and strategy use in individuals with mental retardation. In W. E. MacLean, Jr. (Ed.), *Ellis' handbook of mental deficiency, psychological theory, and research* (3rd ed., pp. 197–217). Mahwah, NJ: Erlbaum.

Bray, N. W., Huffman, L. F., & Fletcher, K. L. (1999). Developmental and intellectual differences in self-report and strategy use. *Developmental Psychology*, 35(5), 1223–1236.

Browder, D., & Spooner, F. (2005). *Teaching reading, math, and science to students with significant cognitive disabilities*. Baltimore: Brookes.

Bryant, B. R., Bryant, D. P., & Chamberlain, S. (1999). Examination of gender and race factors in the assessment of adaptive behavior. In R. L. Schalock (Ed.), *Adaptive behavior and its measurement: Implications for the field of mental retardation* (pp. 141–160). Washington, DC: AAMR.

Carroll, D. (2001). Considering paraeducator training, roles, and responsibilities. *Council for Exceptional Children*, 34(2), 60–64.

Chapman, D. A., Scott, K. G., & Mason, C. A. (2002). Early risk factors for mental retardation: Role of maternal age and maternal education. *American Journal on Mental Retardation*, 107(1), 46–59.

Clark, G. M., & Patton, J. R. (1997). *Transition planning inventory*. Austin, TX: PRO-ED.

Clark, G. M., Patton, J. R., & Moulton, L. R. (2000). Informal assessments for transition planning. Austin, TX: PRO-ED.

Dalton, B., & Coyne, P. (2003). *Literacy by design*. Wakefield, MA: CAST.

Demchak, M., & Drinkwater, S. (1998). Assessing adaptive behavior. In H. B. Vance (Ed.), *Psychological assessment of children: Best practices for school and clinical settings* (pp. 297–322). New York: Wiley.

Denning, C. B., Chamberlain, J. A., & Polloway, E. A. (2000). An evaluation of state guidelines for mental retardation: Focus on definition and classification practices. *Education and Training in Mental Retardation and Developmental Disabilities*, 35(2), 226–232.

Ellis, N. R. (1970). Memory processes in retardates and normals. In N. R. Ellis (Ed.), *International review of research in mental retardation* (Vol. 4, pp. 1–32). New York: Academic Press.

Farlow, L., & Snell, M. (2005). Making the most of student performance data. In M. Wehmeyer & M. Argan (Eds.), *Empirically-validated strategies for teaching students with mental retardation and intellectual disabilities*. Upper Saddle River, NJ: Merril/Prentice Hall.

Feldman, M. A., & Walton-Allen, N. (1997). Effects of maternal mental retardation and poverty on intellectual, academic, and behavioral status of school-age children. *American Journal on Mental Retardation*, 101, 352–364.

Ferguson, D. L. (1995). The real challenge of inclusion: Confessions of a "rabid inclusionist." *Phi Delta Kappan*, 77, 281–287.

Fletcher, K. L., Huffman, L. F., & Bray, N. W. (2003). Effects of verbal and physical prompts on external strategy use in children with and without mild mental retardation. *American Journal on Mental Retardation*, 108(4), 245–256.

French, N. K. (2001). Supervising paraprofessionals: A survey of teacher practices. *Journal of Special Education*, 35(1), 41–53.

Fujiura, G. T. (2003). Continuum of intellectual disability: Demographic evidence for the "forgotten generation." *Mental Retardation* 41(6), 420–429.

Fujiura, G. T., & Yamaki, K. (2000). Trends in demography of childhood poverty and disability. *Exceptional Children*, 66, 187–199.

Giangreco, M. F., Edelman, S. W., Broer, S. M., & Doyle, M. B. (2001). Paraprofessional support of students with disabilities: Literature from the past decade. *Exceptional Children*, 68(1), 45–63.

Gordon, B., Saklofske, D. H., & Hildebrand, D. K. (1998). Assessing children with mental retardation. In H. B. Vance (Ed.), *Psychological assessment of children: Best practices for school and clinical settings* (2nd ed., pp. 454–481). New York: Wiley.

Hart, B., & Risley, T. R. (1995). *Meaningful differences in the everyday experience of young American children*. Baltimore: Brookes.

Horner, R. H., Dunlap, G., & Koegel, R. L. (Eds.). (1988). *Generalization and maintenance: Life-style changes in applied settings*. Baltimore: Brookes.

Katsiyannis, A., Zhang, D., & Archwamety, T. (2002). Placement and exit patterns for students with mental retardation: An analysis of national trends. *Education and Training in Mental Retardation and Developmental Disabilities, 37*(2), 134–145.

Kaufman, P., Kwon, J. Y., Klein, S., & Chapman, C. D. (2000). *Dropout rates in the United States: 1999*. Washington, DC: National Center for Educational Statistics.

Kluth, P. (2000). Community-referenced learning and the inclusive classroom [Electronic Version]. *Remedial and Special Education, 21*(1), 19–26.

Kochhar-Bryant, C., & Bassett, D. (2002). *Aligning transition and standards-based education: Issues and strategies*. Arlington, VA: Council for Exceptional Children.

Kraijer, D. (2000). Review of adaptive behavior studies in metally retarded persons with autism/pervasive developmental disorder. *Journal of Autism and Developmental Disorders, 30*(1), 39–47.

Lambert, N., Nihira, K., & Leland, H. (1993). *AAMR adaptive behavior scale—school* (2nd ed.). Austin, TX: PRO-ED.

Langone, J., Langone, C. A., & McLaughlin, P. J. (2000). Analyzing special educators' views on community-based instruction for students with mental retardation and developmental disabilities: Implications for teacher education. *Journal of Developmental and Physical Disabilities, 12*(1), 17–34.

Larson, S. A., Lakin, K. C., Anderson, L., Kwak, N., Lee, J. H., & Anderson, D. (2001). Prevalence of mental retardation and developmental disabilities: Estimates from the 1994/1995 National Health Interview Survey disability supplements. *American Journal on Mental Retardation, 106*, 231–252.

MacMillan, D. L. (1982). *Mental retardation in school and society* (2nd ed.). Glenview, IL: Scott, Foresman.

MacMillan, D. L., Siperstein, G. N., Gresham, F. M., & Bocian, K. M. (1997). Mild mental retardation: A concept that may have outlived its usefulness. *Psychology in Mental Retardation and Developmental Disabilities, 23*(1), 5–12.

Martin, J., Jorgensen, C. M., & Kelin, J. (1998). The promise of friendship for students with disabilities. In C. M. Jorgensen (Ed.), *Restructuring high schools for all students: Taking inclusion to the next level* (pp. 145–181). Baltimore: Brookes.

Mechling, L. C., & Gast, D. L. (2003). Multimedia instruction to teach grocery word associations and store locations: A study of generalization. *Education and Training in Developmental Disabilities, 38*, 62–76.

Mechling, L. C., Gast, D. L., & Langone, J. (2002). Computer-based video instruction to teach persons with moderate intellectual disabilities to read grocery aisle signs and locate items. *Journal of Special Education 35*(4), 224–240.

Morningstar, M., & Wehmeyer, M. L. (2005). The role of families in enhancing transition outcomes for youth with learning disabilities. In G. Blalock, P. Kohler, & J. Patton (Eds.), *Learning disabilities and transitions*. Austin, TX: PRO-ED.

Murphy, C. C., Boyle, C., Schendel, D., Decouflé, P., & Yeargin-Allsopp, M. (1998). Epidemiology of mental retardation in children. *Mental Retardation and Developmental Disabilities Research Reviews, 4*, 6–13.

National Research Council. (2002). *Minority students in special and gifted education*. Washington, DC: National Academy Press.

Palmer, S. B., Wehmeyer, M. L., Gibson, K., & Agran, M. (2004). Promoting access to the general curriculum by teaching self-determination skills. *Exceptional Children, 70*, 427–439.

Riggs, C. G., & Mueller, P. H. (2001). Employment and utilization of paraeducators in inclusive settings. *Journal of Special Education, 35*(1), 54–62.

Schonberg, R. L., & Tifft, C. J. (2002). Birth defects, prenatal diagnosis, and fetal therapy. In M. L. Batshaw (Ed.), *Children with disabilities* (5th ed., pp. 27–42). Baltimore: Brookes.

Snell, M., & Brown, F. (2001). *Instruction of students with severe disabilities* (5th ed.). Upper Saddle River, NJ: Merrill/Prentice Hall.

Stinnett, T. A., Fuqua, D. R., & Coombs, W. T. (1999). Construct validity of the AAMR adaptive behavior scale—school: 2. *School Psychology Review, 28*(1), 31–43.

Stokes, T. F., & Baer, D. M. (1977). An implicit technology of generalization. *Journal of Applied Behavior Analysis, 10*, 349–367.

Switzky, H. (Ed.). (2001). *Personality and motivational differences in persons with mental retardation*. Mahweh, NJ: Erlbaum.

Switzky, H. (2004). *Personality and motivational systems in mental retardation*. Boston: Elsevier.

Test, D., & Spooner, F. (2005). Community-based instructional support. In M. Wehmeyer & M. Agran (Eds.), *Empirically-validated strategies for teaching students with mental retardation and intellectual disabilities*. Upper Saddle River, NJ: Merrill/Prentice Hall.

Test, D. W., Mason, C., Hughes, C., Konrad, M., Neale, M., & Wood, W. M. (2004). Student involvement in individualized education program meetings. *Exceptional Children, 70*, 391–412.

Thoma, C., & Sax, C. (2002). *Transition assessment: Wise practices for quality lives*. Baltimore: Brookes.

Thurlow, M., & Bolt, S. (2001). *Empirical support for accommodations most often allowed in state policy* (Synthesis Report 41). Minneapolis: University of Minnesota, National Center on Educational Outcomes.

Turnbull, H. R., Turnbull, A. P., Wehmeyer, M. L., & Park, J. (2003). A quality of life framework for special education outcomes. *Remedial and Special Education, 24*, 67–74.

U.S. Department of Education. (1999). *To assure the free appropriate public education of all children with disabilities: Twenty-first annual report to Congress on the implementation of the Individuals with Disabilities Education Act*. Washington, DC: Author.

U.S. Department of Education. (2001). *To assure the free appropriate public education of all children with disabilities: Twenty-third annual report to Congress on the implementation of the Individuals with Disabilities Education Act*. Washington, DC: Author.

Warren, S. F., & Yoder, P. J. (1998). Facilitating the transition from preintentional to intentional communication. In A. M. Wetherby, S. Warren, & J. Reichle (Eds.), *Communication and language intervention series. Volume 7. Transitions in prelinguistic communication*. Baltimore: Brookes.

Wechsler, D. (1991). *Wechsler Intelligence Scale for Children III (WISC-III)*. San Antonio, TX: Psychological Corporation.

Wehmeyer, M. L. (2001). Self-determination and mental retardation. In L. M. Glidden (Ed.), *International review of research in mental retardation* (Vol. 24, pp. 1–48). San Diego: Academic Press.

Wehmeyer, M. L. (2003a). Defining mental retardation and ensuring access to the general curriculum. *Education and Training in Developmental Disabilities, 38*, 270–281.

Wehmeyer, M. L. (2003b). The impact of the disability on adolescent identity. In M. Sadowski (Ed.), *Adolescents at school: Perspectives on youth, identity, and education* (pp. 127–139). Cambridge, MA: Harvard Education Press.

Wehmeyer, M. L., Abery, B., Mithaug, D. E., & Stancliffe, R. J. (2003). *Theory in self-determination: Foundations for educational practice*. Springfield, IL: Thomas.

Wehmeyer, M. L., Agran, M., Palmer, S. B., & Mithaug, D. (1999). *A teacher's guide to implementing the self-determined learning model of instruction (adolescent version)*. Lawrence: University of Kansas, Beach Center.

Wehmeyer, M. L., & Palmer, S. B. (2003). Adult outcomes for students with cognitive disabilities three years after high school: The impact of self-determination. *Education and Training in Developmental Disabilities, 38*, 131–144.

Wehmeyer, M. L., Palmer, S. B., Agran, M., Mithaug, D. E., & Martin, J. (2000). Promoting causal agency: The self-determined learning model of instruction. *Exceptional Children, 66*(4), 439–453.

Wehmeyer, M. L., & Sailor, W. (2004). High school. In C. Kennedy & E. Horn (Eds.), *Including students with severe disabilities* (pp. 259–281). Boston: Allyn & Bacon.

Wehmeyer, M. L., Sands, D. J., Knowlton, H. E., & Kozleski, E. B. (2002). *Teaching students with mental retardation: Providing access to the general curriculum*. Baltimore: Brookes.

Wehmeyer, M. L., & Schwartz, M. (1997). Self-determination and positive adult outcomes: A

455

follow-up study of youth with mental retardation or learning disabilities. *Exceptional Children* (63), 245–255.

Widaman, K. F., & McGrew, K. S. (1996). The structure of adaptive behavior. In J. W. Jacobson & J. A. Mulick (Eds.), *Manual of diagnosis and professional practice in mental retardation* (pp. 97–110). Washington, DC: American Psychological Association.

Yeargin-Allsopp, M., Murphy, C. C., Cordero, J. F., Decoufle, P., & Hollowell, J. G. (1997). Reported biomedical causes and associated medical conditions for mental retardation among 10-year-old children, metropolitan Atlanta, 1985 to 1987. *Developmental Medicine and Child Neurology, 39*(3), 142–149.

Yoder, P. J., & Warren, S. F. (2001). Relative treatment effects of two prelinguistic communication interventions on language development in toddlers with developmental delays vary by maternal characteristics. *Journal of Speech, Language, and Hearing Research, 44*, 224–237.

Zigler, E. (2001). Looking back 40 years and still seeing the person with mental retardation as a whole person. In H. Switzky (Ed.), *Personality and motivational differences in persons with mental retardation* (pp. 3–56). Erlbaum, NJ: Mahwah.

Chapter 10

Abery, B., & McBride, M. (1998). Look and understand before you leap. *Impact, 11*(2), 2–26.

Agran, M., King-Sears, M., Wehmeyer, M. L., & Copeland, S. R. (2003). *Teachers' guides to inclusive practices: Student-directed learning strategies.* Baltimore: Brookes.

Bambara, L. M., Browder, D. M., & Koger, F. (2006). Home and community. In M. Snell & F. Brown (Eds.), *Instruction of students with severe disabilities* (6th ed., pp. 526–528). Upper Saddle River, NJ: Merrill/Prentice Hall.

Batshaw, M. L. (2002). *Children with disabilities* (5th ed.). Baltimore: Brookes.

Batshaw, M., & Shapiro, B. (2002). Mental retardation. In M. Batshaw (Ed.), *Children with disabilities* (5th ed., pp. 287–305). Baltimore: Brookes.

Baumgart, D., Brown, L., Pumpian, I., Nisbet, J., Ford, A., Sweet, M., et al. (1982). Principle of partial participation and individualized adaptations in educational programs for severely handicapped students. *Journal of the Association for Persons with Severe Disabilities, 7*, 17–27.

Bigge, J. L., Best, S. J., & Heller, K. W. (2001). *Teaching individuals with physical, health, or multiple disabilities* (4th ed.). Upper Saddle River, NJ: Merrill/Prentice Hall.

Browder, D. M., Ahlgrim-Delzell, L., Courtade-Little, G., & Snell, M. (2006). General curriculum access. In M. Snell & F. Brown (Eds.), *Instruction of students with severe*
disabilities (6th ed., pp. 489–525). Upper Saddle River, NJ: Merrill/Prentice Hall.

Brown, F., & Snell, M. E. (2006). Measurement, assessment, and evaluation. In M. Snell & F. Brown (Eds.), *Instruction of students with severe disabilities* (6th ed., pp. 170–205). Upper Saddle River, NJ: Merrill/Prentice Hall.

Brown, F., Snell, M. E., & Lehr, D. (2006). Meaningful assessment. In M. Snell & F. Brown (Eds.), *Instruction of students with severe disabilities* (6th ed., pp. 67–110). Upper Saddle River, NJ: Merrill/Prentice Hall.

Bui, Y. N., & Turnbull, A. (2003). East meets west: Analysis of person-centered planning in the context of Asian American values. *Education and Training in Mental Retardation and Developmental Disabilities, 28*(1), 18–31.

Burstein, J. R., Wright-Drechsel, M. L., & Wood, A. (1998). *Assistive technology.* Baltimore: Brookes.

Campbell, P. H. (2006). Addressing motor disabilities. In M. E. Snell & F. Brown (Eds.), *Instruction of students with severe disabilities* (6th ed., pp. 291–327). Upper Saddle River, NJ: Merrill/Prentice Hall.

Collins, B. C., Hendricks, T. B., Fetko, K., & Land, L. A. (2002). Student-2-student learning in inclusive classrooms. *Teaching Exceptional Children, 34*(4), 56–61.

Davies, D. M., Stock, S., & Wehmeyer, M. L. (2002a). Enhancing independent task performance for individuals with mental retardation through use of a handheld self-directed visual and audio prompting system. *Education and Training in Mental Retardation and Developmental Disabilities, 37*, 209–218.

Davies, D. M., Stock, S., & Wehmeyer, M. L. (2002b). Enhancing independent time management and personal scheduling for individuals with mental retardation through use of a palmtop visual and audio prompting system. *Mental Retardation, 40*, 358–365.

Downing, J. E. (2002). *Including students with severe and multiple disabilities in typical classrooms* (2nd ed.). Baltimore: Brookes.

Doyle, M. B. (2002). *The paraprofessional's guide to the inclusive classroom* (2nd ed.). Baltimore: Brookes.

Duffy, M. L., Jones, J., & Thomas, S. W. (1999). Using portfolios to foster independent thinking. *Intervention in School and Clinic, 35*, 34–37.

Engleman, M. D., Griffin, H. C., Griffin, L. W., & Maddox, J. I. (1999). A teacher's guide to communicating with students with deaf-blindness. *Teaching Exceptional Children, 31*(5), 64–70.

Eshilian, L., Falvey, M. A., Bove, C., Hibbard, M. J., Laiblin, J., Miller, C., et al. (2000). Restructuring to create a high school community of learners. In R. A. Villa & J. S. Thousand (Eds.), *Restructuring for caring and effective education* (pp. 402–427). Baltimore: Brookes.

Falvey, M. A., Eshilian, L., & Hibbard, J. (2000, April). Collaboration at Whittier High School. *TASH Newsletter, 26*, 8–9.

Falvey, M. A., Forest, M. S., Pearpoint, J., & Rosenberg, R. L. (2002). Building connections. In J. S. Thousand, R. A. Villa & A. I. Nevin (Eds.), *Creativity and collaborative learning* (2nd ed., pp. 29–54). Baltimore: Brookes.

Farlow, L. J., & Snell, M. E. (2006). Teaching self-care skills. In M. E. Snell & F. Brown (Eds.), *Instruction of students with severe disabilities* (6th ed., pp. 328–374). Upper Saddle River, NJ: Merrill/Prentice Hall.

Ferguson, D. L., & Baumgart, D. (1991). Partial participation revisited. *Journal of the Association for Persons with Severe Disabilities, 16*, 218–227.

Forney, P. E., & Wolff Heller, K. (2004). Sensorimotor development: Implications for the educational team. In F. P. Orelove, D. Sobsey, & R. K. Silberman (Eds.), *Educating children with multiple disabilities: A collaborative approach* (4th ed., pp. 193–247). Baltimore: Brookes.

Giangreco, M. F. (2006). Foundational concepts and practices for educating students with severe disabilities. In M. E. Snell & F. Brown (Eds.), *Instruction of students with severe disabilities* (6th ed., pp. 1–27). Upper Saddle River, NJ: Merrill/Prentice Hall.

Gilberts, G. H., Agran, M., Hughes, C., & Wehmeyer, M. (2001). The effects of peer delivered self-monitoring strategies on the participation of students with severe disabilities in general education classrooms. *Journal of the Association for Persons with Severe Handicaps, 26*(1), 25–36.

Glennen, S. L., & DeCoste, D. C. (1997). *The handbook of augmentative and alternative communication.* San Diego: Singular.

Guess, D., Roberts, S., & Rues, J. (2000). *Longitudinal analysis of state patterns and related variables among infants and children with significant disabilities.* Unpublished manuscript.

Hamre-Nietupski, S. (1993). How much time should be spent on skill instruction and friendship development? Preferences of parents of students with moderate and severe/profound disabilities. *Education and Training in Mental Retardation, 28*(3), 220–231.

Heller, K. W. (2000). *Meeting physical and health needs of children with disabilities: Teaching student participation and management.* Pacific Grove, CA: Brooks/Cole.

Holburn, S., & Vietze, P. M. (2002). *Person-centered planning: Research, practices, and future directions.* Baltimore: Brookes.

Hughes, C., Copeland, S. R., Guth, C., Rung, L. L., Hwang, B., Kleeb, G., et al. (2001). General education students' perspectives on their involvement in a high school peer buddy program. *Education and Training in Developmental Disabilities, 36*(4), 343–356.

Hughes, C., Rung, L. L., Wehmeyer, M. L., Agran, M., Copeland, S. R., & Hwang, B. (2000). Self-prompted communication book use to increase social interaction among high school students. *Journal of the Association for Persons with Severe Disabilities, 25*, 153–166.

Hunt, P., & Goetz, L. (1997). Research on inclusive educational programs, practices, and outcomes for students with severe disabilities. *Journal of Special Education, 31*, 3–29.

Kaiser, A. P., & Grim, J. C. (2006). Teaching functional communication skills. In M. E. Snell & F. Brown (Eds.), *Instruction of students with severe disabilities* (6th ed., pp. 447–488). Upper Saddle River, NJ: Merrill/Prentice Hall.

Kearnes, J. F., Burdge, M. D., & Kleinert, H. L. (2005). Alternate assessment and standards-based instruction: Practical strategies for teachers. In M. L. Wehmeyer & M. Agran (Eds.), *Empirically-validated practices for teaching students with mental retardation and intellectual disabilities.* Upper Saddle River, NJ: Merrill/Prentice Hall.

Kennedy, C. H., & Fisher, D. (2001). *Inclusive middle schools.* Baltimore: Brookes.

Kleinert, H. L., & Kearns, J. F. (2001). *Alternate assessment: Measuring outcomes and supports for students with disabilities.* Baltimore: Brookes.

Luckasson, R., Borthwick-Duffy, S., Buntinx, W. H. E., Coulter, D. L., Craig, E. M., Reeve, A., et al. (2002). *Mental retardation: Definition, classification, and systems of supports* (10th ed.). Washington, DC: American Association on Mental Retardation.

Martin, J., Marshall, L., Maxson, L., & Jerman, M. (1993). *Self-directed IEP: Teacher's manual.* Colorado Springs: University of Colorado at Colorado Springs, Center for Educational Research.

McDonnell, J. M., Mathot-Buckner, C., Thorson, N., & Fister, S. (2001). Supporting the inclusion of students with moderate and severe disabilities in junior high school general education classes: The effects of classwide peer tutoring, multi-element curriculum, and accommodations. *Education and Treatment of Children, 24*(2), 141–160.

Mount, B., & O'Brien, C. L. (2002). *Exploring new worlds for students with disabilities in transition from high school to adult life.* New York: Job Path.

Palmer, D. S., Fuller, K., Arora, T., & Nelson, M. (2001). Taking sides: Parent views on inclusion for their children with severe disabilities. *Council for Exceptional Children, 67*(4), 467–484.

Quenemoen, R., Thompson, S., & Thurlow, M. (2003). Measuring academic achievement of students with significant cognitive disabilities: Building understanding of alternate assessment scoring criteria (Synthesis Report 50). Minneapolis: University of Minnesota, National Center on Educational Outcomes (http://education.umn.edu/NCEO/OnlinePubs/Synthesis50.html).

Quist, R. W., & Lloyd, L. L. (1997). Principles and uses of technology. In L. L. Lloyd, D. Fuller, & H. Arvidson (Eds.), *Augmentative and alternative communication: A handbook of principles and practices.* Needham Heights, MA: Allyn & Bacon.

Riffel, L., Wehmeyer, M., Turnbull, A., Lattimore, J., Davies, D. K., Stock, S. E., et al. (in press). Promoting independent performance fo transition-related tasks using a palmtop PC based self-directed visual and auditory prompting system. *Journal of Special Education Technology.*

Rowland, C., & Schweigert, P. (2003). Cognitive skills and AAC. In D. R. Beukelman & J. Reichle (Series Eds.), J. C. Light, D. R. Beukelman, & J. Reichle (Vol. Eds.), *Augmentative and alternative communication series: Communicative competence for individuals who use AAC: From research to effective practice* (pp. 241–275). Baltimore: Brookes.

Ryndak, D. L., & Fisher, D. (Eds.). (2003). *The foundations of inclusive education: A compendium of articles on effective strategies to achieve inclusive education* (2nd ed.). Baltimore: TASH.

Sailor, W. (2002). Devolution, school/community/family partnerships, and inclusive education. In W. Sailor (Ed.), *Whole-school success and inclusive education: Building partnerships for learning, achievement, and accountability* (pp. 7–25). New York: Teachers College Press.

Schlosser, R. W. (2003). *The efficacy of augmentative and alternative communication: Toward evidence-based practice.* San Diego: Academic Press.

Silberman, R. K., Bruce, S. M., & Nelson, C. (2004). Children with sensory impairments. In F. P. Orelove, D. Sobsey, & R. K. Silberman (Eds.), *Educating children with multiple disabilities: A collaborative approach* (4th ed., pp. 425–527). Baltimore: Brookes.

Smith, M. G. (2000). Secondary teachers' perceptions toward inclusion of students with severe disabilities. *NASSP Bulletin, 84*(613), 54–60.

Snell, M. E., & Brown, F. (2006). Designing and implementing instructional programs. In M. Snell & F. Brown (Eds.), *Instruction of students with severe disabilities* (6th ed.). Upper Saddle River, NJ: Merrill/Prentice Hall.

Soodak, L. C., Erwin, E. J., Winton, P., Brotherson, M. J., Turnbull, A. P., Hanson, M. J., et al. (2002). Implementing inclusive early childhood education: A call for professional empowerment. *Topics in Early Childhood Special Education, 22*(2), 91–102.

Stephenson, J. R., & Dowrick, M. (2000). Parent priorities in communication intervention for young students with severe disabilities. *Education and Training in Mental Retardation and Developmental Disabilities, 35*(1), 25–35.

Stromme, P., & Hagberg, G. (2000). Aetiology in severe and mild mental retardation: A population based study of Norwegian children. *Developmental Medicine and Child Neurology, 42*, 76–86.

Szczepanski, M. (2004). Physical management in the classroom: Handling and positioning. In F. P. Orelove, D. Sobsey, & R. K. Silberman (Eds.), *Educating children with multiple disabilities: A collaborative approach* (4th ed., pp. 249–309). Baltimore: Brookes.

Thompson, B., Wegner, J. R., Wickham, D., & Ault, M. M. (1993). *Handbook for the inclusion of young children with severe disabilities: Strategies for implementing exemplary full inclusion programs.* Lawrence, KS: Learner Managed Designs.

Thompson, B., Wickham, D., Dhanks, P., Wegner, J. R., Ault, M. M., Reinertson, B., et al. (1991, Winter). Expanding the circle of inclusion: Integrating young children with severe and profound disabilities into Montessori programs. *Montessori Life*, 11–15.

Thompson, B., Wickham, D., Wegner, J. R., & Ault, M. M. (1996). All children should know joy: Inclusive family-centered services for young children with significant disabilities. In D. H. Lehr & F. Brown (Eds.), *People with disabilities who challenge the system* (pp. 23–56). Baltimore: Brookes.

Thousand, J. S., Rosenberg, R. L., Bishop, K. D., & Villa, R. A. (1997). The evolution of secondary inclusion. *Remedial and Special Education, 18*(5), 270–284, 306.

Thousand, J. S., Villa, R. A., & Nevin, A. I. (2002). *Creativity and collaborative learning: The practical guide to empowering students, teachers, and families* (2nd ed.). Baltimore: Brookes.

Turnbull, A. P., Turnbull, H. R., Erwin, E., & Soodak, L. (2006). *Families, professionals, and exceptionality: Positive outcomes through partnerships and trust* (5th ed.). Upper Saddle River, NJ: Merrill/Prentice Hall.

U.S. Department of Education, Office of Special Education Programs. (2005). *IDEA data website* (http://www.ideadata.org/aboutThisSite.asp).

Van der Klift, E., & Kunc, N. (1994). Beyond benevolence: Friendship and the politics of help. In J. S. Thousand, R. A. Villa, & A. I. Nevin (Eds.), *Creativity and collaborative learning: A practical guide to empowering students and teachers* (pp. 391–401). Baltimore: Brookes.

Ward, L. P., & McCune, S. K. (2002). The first weeks of life. In M. L. Batshaw (Ed.), *Children with disabilities* (5th ed., pp. 69–83). Baltimore: Brookes.

Wehmeyer, M. L., Smith, S. J., Palmer, S. B., Davies, D. K., & Stock, S. (2004). Technology use and people with mental retardation. In L. M. Glidden (Ed.), *International review of research in mental retardation.* San Diego: Academic Press.

Wilson, B. A. (1999). Peer tutoring in the context of cooperative learning: Including middle school students with moderate to severe disabilities in content area classes. *Dissertation Abstracts International Section A: Humanities and Social Sciences, 60*(1-A), 98.

Wolfe, P., & Hall, T. E. (2003). Making inclusion a reality for students with severe disabilities. *Teaching Exceptional Children, 35*(4), 56–60.

Zabala, J. S. (1995). *The SETT framework: Critical areas to consider when making informed assistive technology decisions.* Newton, MA: National Center to Improve Practice. (ERIC Document Reproduction Service No. ED381962).

Chapter 11

American Psychiatric Association. (2000). *Diagnostic and statistical manual of mental disorders* (4th ed., rev.). Washington, DC: Author.

Anzalone, M. E., & Williamson, G. G. (2000). *Sensory processing and motor performance in autism spectrum disorders* (Vol. 9). Baltimore: Brookes.

Apple Computer. (1994). *HyperCard* (Version 2.3.5) [Computer Software]. Cupertino, CA: Author.

Arick, J. R., Young, H. E., Falco, R. A., Loos, L. M., Krug, D. A., Gense, M. H., & Johnson, S. B. (2003). Designing an outcome study to monitor the progress of students with autism spectrum disorders. *Focus on Autism and Other Developmental Disabilities, 18,* 75–87.

Baer, D. M., Wolf, M. M., & Risley, T. R. (1968). Some current dimensions of applied behavior analysis. *Journal of Applied Behavior Analysis, 1,* 91–97.

Barnhill, G. P. (2001). What is Asperger syndrome? *Intervention in School and Clinic, 36*(5), 259–265.

Barnhill, G. P., & Myles, B. S. (2001). Attributional style and depression in adolescents with Asperger syndrome. *Journal of Positive Behavior Interventions, 3*(5), 175–182.

Baron-Cohen, S. (2001). Theory of mind and autism: A review. *International Review of Research in Mental Retardation, 23,* 169–184.

Baron-Cohen, S., Wheelwright, S., Lawson, J., Griffin, R., & Hill, J. (2002). The exact mind: Empathizing and systemizing in autism spectrum conditions. In U. Goswami (Ed.), *Blackwell handbook of childhood cognitive development* (pp. 491–508). Oxford: Blackwell.

Bristol, M., McIlvane, W. J., & Alexander, D. (1998). Autism research: Current context and future direction. *Mental Retardation and Developmental Disabilities Research Reviews, 4*(2), 61–64.

Brownell, M. D. (2000). *The use of musically adapted social stories to modify behaviors in students with autism: Four case studies.* Lawrence: University of Kansas.

Carpenter, M., & Tomasello, M. (2000). *Joint attention, cultural learning, and language, acquisition: Implications for children with autism* (Vol. 9). Baltimore: Brookes.

Carr, E. G., Dunlap, G., Horner, R. H., Koegel, R. L., Turnbull, A. P., Sailor, W., Anderson, J. L., Albin, R. W., Koegel, L. K., & Fox, L. (2002). Positive behavior support: Evolution of an applied science. *Journal of Positive Behavior Interventions, 4*(1), 4–16.

Carr, E. G., Horner, R. H., Turnbull, A. P., Marquis, J. G., Magito-McLaughlin, D., McAtee, M. L., Smith, C. E., Ryan, K. A., Ruef, M. B., & Doolabh, A. (1999). *Positive behavior support as an approach for dealing with problem behavior in people with developmental disabilities: A research synthesis.* Washington, DC: AAMR.

Carr, E. G., Levin, L., McConnachie, G., Carlson, J. I., Kemp, D. C., & Smith, C. E. (1994). *Communication-based intervention for problem behavior: A user's guide to producing positive change.* Baltimore: Brookes.

Chandler, L. K., & Dalquist, D. M. (2002). *Functional assessment strategies to present and remediate challenging behavior in school settings.* Upper Saddle River, NJ: Merrill/Prentice Hall.

Cheatham, S. K., Smith, J. D., Rucker, H. N., Polloway, E. A., & Lewis, G. W. (1995, September). Savant syndrome: Case studies, hypotheses, and implications for special education. *Education and Training in Mental Retardation,* pp. 243–253.

Corothers, D. E., & Taylor, R. L. (2004). Social cognitive processing in elementary school children with Asperger syndrome. *Education and Training in Developmental Disabilities, 39*(2), 177–187.

Courchesne, E. (2004). Brain development in autism: Early overgrowth followed by premature arrest of growth. *Mental Retardation and Developmental Disabilities, 10,* 106–111.

Crone, D. A., & Horner, R. H. (2003). *Building positive behavior support systems in schools.* New York: Guilford.

Dawson, G., & Watling, R. (2000). Interventions to facilitate auditory, visual, and motor integration in autism: A review of the evidence. *Journal of Autism and Developmental Disorders, 30*(5), 415–421.

Derby, K. M., Wacker, D. P., Sasso, G., Steege, M., Northup, J., Cigrand, K., & Asmus, J. (1992). Brief functional assessment techniques to evaluate aberrant behavior in an outpatient setting: A summary of 79 cases. *Journal of Applied Behavior Analysis, 25,* 713–721.

Didden, R., Duker, P. C., & Korzilius, H. (1997). Meta-analytic study on treatment effectiveness for problem behaviors with individuals who have mental retardation. *American Journal on Mental Retardation, 101,* 387–399.

Donnellan, A. M. (1999). Invented knowledge and autism: Highlighting our strengths and expanding the conversation. *Journal of the Association for Persons with Severe Handicaps, 24*(3), 230–236.

Dunlap, G., & Fox, L. (1999). A demonstration of behavioral support for young children with autism. *Journal of Positive Behavior Interventions, 1*(2), 77–87.

Dunlap, G., Newton, J. S., Fox, L., Benito, N., & Vaughn, B. (2001). Family involvement in functional assessment and positive behavior support. *Focus on Autism and Other Developmental Disabilities, 16*(4), 215–221.

Fombonne, E. (2003). Epidemiological surveys of autism and other pervasive developmental disorders: An update. *Journal of Autism and Developmental Disorders, 33*(4), 365–382.

Fox, L., Benito, N., & Dunlap, G. (2002). Early intervention with families of young children. In G. H. S. Singer, A. P. Turnbull, H. R. Turnbull, L. K. Irvin, & L. E. Powers (Eds.), *Families and positive behavior support: Addressing problem behavior in family contexts* (pp. 251–270). Baltimore: Brookes.

Fuchs, D., & Fuchs, L. S. (1986). Test procedure bias: A meta-analysis of examiner familiarity effects. *Review of Educational Research, 56,* 243–262.

Goldstein, H. (2003). Communication intervention for children with autism: A review of treatment efficacy. *Journal of Autism and Developmental Disorders, 32,* 373–396.

Grandin, T. (1997). A personal perspective on autism. In D. J. Cohen & F. R. Volkmar (Eds.), *Handbook of autism and pervasive developmental disorders* (2nd ed., pp. 1032–1042). New York: Wiley.

Gray, C. A. (1998). Social stories and comic strip conversations with students with Asperger syndrome and high-functioning autism. In E. Schopler, G. B. Mesibov, & L. J. Kunce (Eds.), *Asperger syndrome or high-functioning autism?* (pp. 167–198). New York: Plenum.

Gray, C., & White, A. L. (2002). *My social stories book.* Florence, KY: Taylor & Francis.

Handleman, J. S., & Harris, S. L. (2001). *Preschool education programs for children with autism.* Austin, TX: PRO-ED.

Hawken, L. S., & Horner, R. A. (2001). *Evaluation of a targeted group intervention within a schoolwide system of behavior support.* Unpublished manuscript.

Horner, R. H., Albin, R. W., Todd, A. W., & Sprague, J. (2006). Positive behavior support for individuals with disabilities. In M. E. Snell & F. Brown (Eds.), *Instruction of students with severe disabilities* (6th ed., pp. 206–250). Baltimore: Brookes.

Horner, R. H., Carr, E. G., Strain, P. S., Todd, A. W., & Reed, H. K. (2002). Problem behavior interventions for young children with autism: A research synthesis. *Journal of Autism and Developmental Disorders, 32,* 423–446.

Horner, R. H., Salentine, S. P., & Albin, R. (2003). *Self-assessment of contextual fit in schools.* Eugene: University of Oregon.

Howlin, P. (1982). Echolalic and spontaneous phrase speech in autistic children. *Journal of Child Psychology and Psychiatry, 23,* 281–293.

Iovannone, R., Dunlap, G., Huber, H., & Kincaid, D. (2003). Effective educational practices for students with autism spectrum disorders. *Focus on Austism and Other Developmental Disabilities, 18*(3), 150–165.

Iwata, B. A., Pace, G. M., Dorsey, M. F., Zarcone, J. R., Vollmer, T. R., Smith, R. G., Rodgers, T. A., Lerman, D. C., Shore, A. B., Mazaleski, J. L., Goh, H., Cowdery, G. E., Kalsher, M. J., McCosh, K. C., & Willis, K. D. (1994). The functions of self-injurious behavior: An experimental-epidemiological analysis. *Journal of Applied Behavior Analysis, 27,* 215–240.

Kelly, S. J., Macaruso, P., & Sokol, S. M. (1997). Mental calculations in an autistic savant: A case study. *Journal of Clinical and Experimental Neuropsychology, 19*(2), 172–184.

Kluth, P. (2003). *You're going to love this child: Teaching students with autism in the inclusive classroom.* Baltimore: Brookes.

Koegel, L. (2000). Interventions to facilitate communication in autism. *Journal of Autism and Developmental Disorders, 30,* 383–391.

Koegel, L. K., Koegel, R. L., & Smith, A. (1997). Variables related to differences in standardized test outcomes for children with autism. *Journal of Autism and Developmental Disorders, 27,* 233–243.

Krug, D. A., Arick, J. R., & Almond, P. (1993). *Autism screening instrument for educational planning—2.* Austin, TX: PRO-ED.

Leary, M. R., & Hill, D. A. (1996). Moving on: Autism and movement disturbance. *Mental Retardation, 34*(1), 39–53.

Lee, S. H., Amos, B. A., Gragoudas, S., Lee, Y., Shogren, K. A., Theoharis, R., & Wehmeyer, M. L. (2004). *Curriculum augmentation and adaptation strategies to promote access to the general curriculum for students with intellectual and developmental disabilities.* Unpublished paper.

Lewis, M. H., & Bodfish, J. W. (1998). Repetitive behavior disorders in autism. *Mental Retardation and Developmental Disabilities Research Reviews, 4*(2), 80–89.

Lewis, T. J., & Sugai, G. (1999). Effective behavior support: A systems approach to proactive school-wide management. *Focus on Exceptional Children, 31*(6), 1–24.

Lord, C. (1997). Diagnostic instruments in autism spectrum disorders. In D. J. Cohen & F. R. Volkman (Eds.), *Handbook of autism and pervasive developmental disorders* (2nd ed., pp. 460–482). New York: Wiley.

Lord, C., Pickles, A., McLennan, J., Rutter, M., Bergman, J., Folstein, S., Fombonne, E., Leboyer, M., & Minshew, N. (1997). Diagnosing autism: Analyses of data from the Autism Diagnostic Interview. *Journal of Austism and Developmental Disorders, 27*(5), 501–517.

Lord, C., & Risi, S. (2000). *Diagnosis of autism spectrum disorders in young children* (Vol. 9). Baltimore: Brookes.

Lord, C., Rutter, M., & Le Couteru, A. (1994). Autism diagnostic interview—revised: A revised version of a diagnostic interview for caregivers of individuals with possible pervasive developmental disorders. *Journal of Autism and Developmental Disorders, 24*(5), 659–685.

Lorimer, P. A., Simpson, R. L., Myles, B. S., & Ganz, J. B. (2002). The use of social stories as a preventative behavioral intervention in a home setting with a child with autism. *Journal of Positive Behavior Interventions, 4,* 53–60.

Lovass, O. I. (1977). *The autistic child: Language development through behavior modification.* New York: Irvington.

Mace, F. C., & Mauk, J. E. (1999). Biobehavioral diagnosis and treatment of self-injury. In A. Repp & R. H. Horner (Eds.), *Functional analysis of problem behavior: From effective assessment to effective support* (pp. 78–96). Belmont, CA: Wadsworth.

Marks, S. U., Shaw-Hegwer, J., Schrader, C., Longaker, T., Peters, I., Powers, F., & Levine, M. (2003). Instructional management of tips for teachers of students with autism spectrum disorders. *Teaching Exceptional Children, 35*(4), 50–55.

May, S., Ard, W., Todd, A. W., Horner, R., Sugai, G., Glasgow, A., & Sprague, J. R. (2003). *School-wide information system.* Eugene: University of Oregon.

Mayes, S. D., & Calhoun, S. L. (2003). Analysis of WISC-III, Stanford-Binet: IV, and academic achievement test scores in children with autism. *Journal of Autism and Developmental Disorders, 33*(3), 329–341.

McConnell, S. R. (2002). Interventions to facilitate social interaction for young children with autism: Review of available research and recommendations for educational intervention and future research. *Journal of Autism and Developmental Disorders, 32,* 351–372.

McGee, G. G., Morrier, M. J., & Daly, T. (1999). An incidental teaching approach to early intervention for toddlers with autism. *Journal of the Association for Persons with Severe Handicaps, 24*(3), 133–146.

Miller, L. K. (1999). The savant syndrome: Intellectual impairment and exceptional skill. *Psychological Bulletin, 125*(1), 31–46.

Myles, B. S., Barnhill, G. P., Hagiwara, T., Griswold, D. E., & Simpson, R. L. (2001). A synthesis of studies on the intellectual, academic, social/emotional and sensory characteristics of children and youth with Asperger syndrome. *Education and Training in Mental Retardation and Developmental Disabilities, 36*(3), 304–311.

Myles, B. S., Huggins, A., Rome-Lake, M., Hagiwara, T., Barnhill, G. P., & Griswold, D. E. (2003). Written language profile of children and youth with Asperger syndrome: From research to practice. *Education and Training in Developmental Disabilities, 38*(4), 362–369.

Myles, B. S., & Simpson, R. L. (2001). Understanding the hidden curriculum: An essential social skill for children and youth with Asperger syndrome. *Intervention in School and Clinic, 36*(5), 279–286.

Myles, B. S., & Simpson, R. (2003). *Asperger syndrome: A guide for educators and parents* (2nd ed.). Austin, TX: PRO-ED.

National Research Council. (2001). *Educating children with autism.* Washington, DC: National Academy Press.

Nettelbeck, T., & Young, R. (1996). Intelligence and savant syndrome: Is the whole greater than the sum of the fragments? *Intelligence, 22,* 49–68.

Nickel, R. E. (2000). Developmental delay and mental retardation. In R. E. Nickel & L. W. Desch (Eds.), *The physician's guide to caring for children with disabilities and chronic conditions* (pp. 99–140). Baltimore: Brookes.

O'Connor, N., Cowan, R., & Samella, K. (2000). Calendrical calculation and intelligence. *Intelligence, 28*(1), 31–48.

Orsmond, G. I., Krauss, M. W., & Seltzer, M. M. (2004). Peer relationships and social and recreational activities among adolescents and adults with autism. *Journal of Autism and Developmental Disorders, 34,* 245–256.

Ozonoff, S., Dawson, G., & McPartland, J. (2002). *A parent's guide to Asperger syndrome and high-functioning autism: How to meet the challenges and help your child thrive.* New York: Guilford.

Prater, C. D., & Zylstra, R. G. (2002). Autism: A medical primer. *American Family Physician, 66*(9), 1667–1680.

Prelock, P. A., Beatson, J., Bitner, B., Broder, C., & Ducker, A. (2003). Interdisciplinary assessment of young children with autism spectrum disorder. *Language, Speech, and Hearing Services in Schools, 34*(3), 194–202.

Prizant, B. M. (1983). Language acquisition and communicative behavior in autism: Toward an understanding of the "whole" of it. *Journal of Speech and Hearing Disorders, 48,* 296–307.

Prizant, B. M., & Rydell, P. J. (1984). Analysis of functions of delayed echolalia in autistic children. *Journal of Speech and Hearing Research, 27,* 183–192.

Prizant, B. M., Schuler, A. L., Wetherby, A., & Rydell, P. (1997). Enhancing language and communication development: Language approaches. In D. J. Cohen & F. R. Volkman (Eds.), *Handbook of autism and pervasive developmental disorders* (2nd ed., pp. 572–604). New York: Wiley.

Reese, R. M., Richman, D. M., Zarcone, J., & Zarcone, T. (2003). Individualizing functional assessments for children with autism: The contribution of perseverative behavior and sensory disturbances to disruptive behavior. *Focus on Autism and Other Developmental Disabilities, 18*(2), 89–94.

Robertson, K., Chamberlain, B., & Kasari, C. (2003). General education teachers' relationships with included students with autism. *Journal of Autism and Developmental Disorders, 33*(2), 123–130.

Rogers, M. F., & Myles, B. S. (2001). Using social stories and comic strip conversations to interpret social situations for an adolescent with Asperger syndrome. *Intervention in School and Clinic, 36*(5), 310–313.

Rogers, S. J. (2000). Interventions that facilitate socialization in children with autism. *Journal of Autism and Developmental Disorders, 30,* 399–409.

Ruble, L. A., & Dalrymple, N. J. (2002). Compass: A parent-teacher collaborative model for students with autism. *Focus on Autism and Other Developmental Disabilities, 17*(2), 76–83.

Ryan, A. L., Halsey, H. N., & Matthews, W. J. (2003). Using functional assessment to promote desirable student behavior in schools. *Teaching Exceptional Children, 35*(5), 8–15.

Rydell, P. J., & Prizant, B. M. (1995). Assessment and intervention strategies for children who use echolalia. In K. A. Quill (Ed.), *Teaching children with autism: Strategies to enhance communication and socialization* (pp. 105–132). New York: Delmar.

Safran, S. P., Safran, J. S., & Ellis, K. (2003). Intervention ABCs for children with Asperger syndrome. *Topics in Language Disorders, 23*(2), 154–165.

Saloviita, T., Ruusila, L., & Ruusila, U. (2000). Incidence of savant syndrome in Finland. *Perceptual and Motor Skills, 91,* 120–122.

Sansosti, F. J., Powell-Smith, K. A., & Kincaid, D. (2004). A research synthesis of social story interventions for children with autism spectrum disorders. *Focus on Autism and Other Developmental Disabilities, 19,* 194–204.

Simpson, R., & Myles, B. S. (in press). *Educating children and youth with autism: Strategies for effective practice* (2nd ed.). Austin, TX: PRO-ED.

Smith, T. (2001). Discrete trial training in the treatment of autism. *Focus on Autism and Other Developmental Disabilities, 16,* 86–92.

Smith, T., Green, A. D., & Wynn, J. W. (2000). Randomized trial of intensive early intervention for children with pervasive developmental disorder. *American Journal on Mental Retardation, 105*(4), 269–285.

Snell, M., & Janney, R. (2000). *Teachers' guides to inclusive practices: Social relationships and peer support.* Baltimore: Brookes.

Sugai, G., Horner, R. H., Dunlap, G., Hieneman, M., Lewis, T. J., Nelson, C. M., Scott, T., Liaupsin, C., Sailor, W., Turnbull, A. P., Turnbull, H. R., Wickham, D., Wilcox, B., & Ruef, M. (2000). Applying positive behavior support and functional behavioral assessment in schools. *Journal of Positive Behavior Interventions, 2*(3), 131–143.

Sugai, G., Lewis-Palmer, T., Todd, A. W., & Horner, R. (2001). *School-wide evaluation tool, version 2.0.* Eugene: University of Oregon, Educational and Community Supports.

Szarko, J. (2000). Familiar versus unfamiliar examiners: The effects on testing performance and behaviors of children with autism and related developmental disabilities. *Dissertation Abstracts International, 61/04,* p. 2247.

Tadevosyan-Leyfer, O., Dowd, M., Mankoski, R., Winklosky, B., Putnam, S., McGrath, L., Tager-Flusberg, H., & Folstein, S. E. (2003). A principal components analysis of the autism diagnostic interview—revised. *Journal of the American Academy of Child and Adolescent Psychiatry, 42*(7), 864–872.

Talay-Ongan, A., & Wood, K. (2000). Unusual sensory sensitivities in autism: A possible crossroads. *International Journal of Disability, Development, and Education, 47*(2), 201–212.

Tanguay, P. E. (2000). Pervasive developmental disorders: A 10-year review. *Journal of the American Academy of Child and Adolescent Psychiatry, 39*(9), 1079–1095.

Towbin, K. E., Mauk, J. E., & Batshaw, M. L. (2002). Pervasive developmental disorders. In M. L. Batshaw (Ed.), *Children with disabilities* (5th ed., pp. 365–387). Baltimore: Brookes.

Turnbull, A. P., Edmonson, H., Griggs, P., Wickham, D., Sailor, W., Freeman, R., Guess, D., Lassen, S., McCart, A., Park, J., Riffel, L., Turnbull, R., & Warren, J. (2002). A blueprint for schoolwide positive behavior support: Implementation of three components. *Council for Exceptional Children, 68*(3), 377–402.

Turnbull, A. P., & Ruef, M. (1996). Family perspectives on problem behavior. *Mental Retardation, 34,* 280–293.

Turnbull, A. P., & Ruef, M. (1997). Family perspectives on inclusive lifestyle issues for individuals with problem behavior. *Exceptional Children, 63,* 211–227.

Uberti, H. Z., Scruggs, T. E., & Mastropieri, M. A. (2003). Keywords make the difference! Mnemonic instruction in inclusive classrooms. *Teaching Exceptional Children, 35*(3), 56–61.

U.S. Department of Education, Office of Special Education Programs. (2005). *IDEA data website* (http://www.ideadata.org/aboutThisSite.asp).

Volkmar, F. R., Cicchetti, D. V., Dykens, E., Sparrow, S. S., Leckman, J. F., & Cohen, D. J. (1988). An evaluation of the autism behavior checklist. *Journal of Autism and Developmental Disorders, 18,* 81–97.

Volkmar, F. R., Klin, A., & Cohen, D. J. (1997). Diagnosis and classification of autism and related conditions: Consensus and issues. In D. J. Cohen & F. R. Volkmar (Eds.), *Handbook of autism and pervasive developmental disorders* (2nd ed., pp. 5–39). New York: Wiley.

Wadden, N. P., Bryson, S. E., & Rodger, R. S. (1991). A closer look at the autism behavior checklist: Discriminant validity and factor structure. *Journal of Autism and Developmental Disorders, 21,* 529–541.

Yeargin-Allsopp, M., Rice, C., Karapurkar, T., Doernberg, N., Boyle, C., & Murphy, C. (2003). Prevalence of autism in a US metropolitan area. *Journal of the American Medical Association, 289*(1), 49–55.

Chapter 12

Agnew, C. M., Nystul, M. S., & Conner, M. C. (1998). Seizure disorders: An alternative explanation for students' inattention. *Professional School Counseling, 2*(1), 54–60.

Aksu, I. (1990). Nature and prognosis of seizures in patients with cerebral palsy. *Developmental Medicine and Child Neurology, 32,* 661–668.

Aronson, S. S. (1995). Meeting the health needs of children with asthma. *Child Care Information Exchange, 101,* 59–60.

Austin, J. K., Huberty, T. J., Huster, G. A., & Dunn, D. W. (1999). Does academic achievement in children with epilepsy change over time? *Developmental Medicine and Child Neurology, 41*(7), 473–479.

Azcue, M., Zello, G., Levy, L., et al. (1996). Energy expenditure and body composition in children with spastic quadriplegic cerebral palsy. *Journal of Pediatrics, 129,* 870–876.

Berry, R. J., Li, Z., Erickson, J. D., Li, S., Moore, C. A., Wang, H., Mulinare, J., Zhao, P., Wong, L. Y. C., Gindler, J., Hong, S. X., & Correa, A. (1999). Prevention of neural-tube defects with folic acid in China. *New England Journal of Medicine, 341*(2), 1485–1490.

Bessell, A. G. (2001a). Children surviving cancer: Psychosocial adjustment, quality of life, and school experiences. *Exceptional Children. 67*(3), 345–359.

Bessell, A. G. (2001b, September). Educating children with chronic illness. *Exceptional Parent Magazine, 31*(9), 44.

Bigge, J. L., Best, S. J., & Heller, K. W. (2001). *Teaching individuals with physical, health, or multiple disabilities* (4th ed.). Upper Saddle River, NJ: Merrill/Prentice Hall.

Black, K. C., & Hynd, G. W. (1995). Epilepsy in the school aged child: Cognitive-behavioral characteristics and effects on academic performance. *School Psychology Quarterly, 10*(4), 345–358.

Cantu, C., & Buswell, D. J. (2003). Adapted PE: A vital contribution to health and well-being. *Exceptional Parent, 33*(10), 58–61.

Celano, M. P., & Geller, R. J. (1993). Learning, school performance, and children with asthma: How much at risk? *Journal of Learning Disabilities, 26*(1), 23–32.

Cole, J., & Swinth, Y. (2004). Comparison of the TouchFree switch to a physical switch: Children's abilities and preferences: A pilot study. *Journal of Special Education Technology, 19*(2), 19–30.

Committee on School Health. (2000). Home, hospital, and other non-school–based instruction for children and adolescents who are medically unable to attend school [Electronic Version]. *Pediatrics, 106*(5), 1154–1155.

Coster, W. J., Deeney, T. A., Haltiwanger, J. T., & Haley, S. M. (1998). *School function assessment.* San Antonio, TX: Psychological Corporation/ Therapy Skill Builders.

Coster, W. J., & Haltiwanger, J. T. (2004). Social-behavioral skills of elementary students with physical disabilities included in general education classrooms. *Remedial and Special Education, 25*(2), 95–103.

Coster, W. J., Mancini, M. C., & Ludlow, L. (1999). Factor structure of the school function assessment. *Educational and Psychological Measurement, 59*(4), 665–677.

Croen, L. A., Grether, J. K., Curry, C. J., & Nelson, K. B. (2001). Congenital abnormalities among children with cerebral palsy: More evidence of prenatal antecedents. *Journal of Pediatrics, 138,* 804–810.

DePaepe, P., Garrison-Kane, L., & Doelling, J. (2002). Supporting students with health needs in schools: An overview of selected health conditions. *Focus on Exceptional Children, 35*(1), 1–24.

Diette, G. B., Markson, L., Skinner, E. A., Nguyen, T. T. H., Algatt-Bergstrom, P., & Wu, A. W. (2000). Nocturnal asthma in children affects school attendance, school performance, and parents' work attendance. *Archives of Pediatric and Adolescent Medicine, 154*, 923–928.

Dunn, D. W., Austin, J. K., & Huster, G. A. (1999). Symptoms of depression in adolescents with epilepsy. *Journal of the American Academy of Child and Adolescent Psychiatry, 38*(9), 1132–1138.

Eisenberg, J. D. (2000). Chronic respiratory disorders. In R. E. Nickel & L. W. Desch (Eds.), *The physician's guide to caring for children with disabilities and chronic conditions* (pp. 617–639). Baltimore: Brookes.

Eriksson, K. J., & Koivikko, M. J. (1997). Prevalence, classification, and severity of epilepsy and epileptic syndromes in children. *Epilepsia, 38*, 1275–1282.

Friedrich, W. N., Lovejoy, M. C., Shaffer, J., Shurtleff, D. B., & Beilke, R. L. (1991). Cognitive-abilities and achievement status of children with myelomeningocele: A contemporary sample. *Journal of Pediatric Psychology, 16*(4), 423–428.

Frucht, M. M., Quigg, M., Schwaner, C., & Fountain, N. B. (2000). Distribution of seizure precipitants among epilepsy syndromes. *Epilepsia, 41*, 1534–1539.

Fuchs, L., & Fuchs, D. (2001). Computer applications to curriculum-based measurement. *Special Services in the Schools, 17*, 1–14.

Griffin, H. C., Fitch, C. L., & Griffin, L. W. (2002). Causes and interventions in the area of cerebral palsy. *Infants and Young Children, 14*(5), 18–23.

Hagberg, B., Hagberg, G., Olow, I., et al. (1996). The changing pattern of cerebral palsy in Sweden; VII: Prevalence and origin in the birth year period 1987–90. *Acta Paediatrica, 85*, 954–960.

Hauser, W. A. (1994). The prevalence and incidence of convulsive disorders in children. *Epilepsia, 35*, S1–S5.

Haynes, J. (2002). *California community colleges adapted physical education handbook.* Sacramento: California Community College System.

Heller, K. W. (2000). *Meeting physical and health needs of children with disabilities: Teaching student participation and management.* Pacific Grove, CA: Brooks/Cole.

Heller, K. W., Forney, P. E., Alberto, P. A., Schwartzman, M. N., & Goeckel, T. M. (2000). *Meeting physical and health needs of children with disabilities: Teaching student participation and management.* Belmont, CA: Wadsworth Thomson Learning.

Honein, M. A., Paulozzi, L. J., Mathews, T. J., Erickson, J. D., & Wong, L. Y. C. (2001). Impact of folic acid fortification of the U.S. food supply on the occurrence of neural tube defects. *Journal of the American Medical Association, 285*, 2981–2984.

Hwang, J. L., Davies, P. L., Taylor, M. P., & Gavin, W. J. (2002). Validation of school function assessment with elementary school children. *OTJR, 22*(2), 48–58.

Johnston, S. S. (2003). Making the most of single switch technology: A primer. *Journal of Special Education Technology, 18*(2), 47–50.

Jones, J. A., Wahlgren, D. R., Meltzer, S. B., Meltzer, E. O., Clark, N. M., & Hovell, M. F. (2001). Increasing asthma knowledge and changing home environments for Latino families with asthmatic children. *Patient Education and Counseling, 42*, 67–79.

Kliebenstein, M. A., & Broome, M. E. (2000). School re-entry for the child with chronic illness: Parent and school personnel perceptions. *Pediatric Nursing, 26*(6), 579–583.

Krahn, G. L. (2003). Survey of physician wellness practices with persons with disabilities. In RRTC Health and Wellness Consortium (Eds.), *Changing concepts of health and disability: State of the science conference and policy forum 2003* (pp. 47–51). Portland: Oregon Health and Sciences University.

Ladebauche, P., Nicholsi, R., Reece, S., Saucedo, K., Volicer, B., & Richards, T. (2001). Asthma in Head Start children: Prevalence, risk factors, and heath care utilization. *Pediatric Nursing, 27*, 396–399.

Lancioni, G. E., Singh, N. N., O'Reilly, M. F., Oliva, D., Baccani, S., & Canevaro, A. (2002). Using simple hand-movement responses with optic microswitches with two persons with multiple disabilities. *Research and Practice in Severe Disabilities, 27*, 276–279.

Lary, J. M., & Edmonds, L. D. (1996). Prevalence of spina bifida at birth: United States, 1983–1990: A comparison of two surveillance systems. *Morbidity and Mortality Weekly Report, 45*(SS-2), 15–27.

Liptak, G. S. (2002). Neural tube defects. In M. L. Batshaw (Ed.), *Children with disabilities* (5th ed., pp. 467–492). Baltimore: Brookes.

Lutkenhoff, M. (1999). *Children with spina bifida.* Bethesda, MD: Woodbine House.

Mannino, D. M., Homa, D. M., Akinbami, L. J., Moorman, J. E., Gwynn, C., & Redd, S. C. (2002). Surveillance for asthma—United States, 1980–1999. *Morbidity and Mortality Weekly Report, 51*(SS-1), 1–13.

McGill, T., & Vogtle, L. K. (2001). Driver's education for students with physical disabilities. *Exceptional Children, 67*, 455–466.

Meadows, M. (2003). Breathing better: Action plans keep asthma in check. *FDA Consumer, 37*(2), 20–27.

Mears, B. (2004). Adapted physical education and therapeutic recreation in schools. *Intervention in School and Clinic, 39*(4), 223–232.

Mitchell, W., & Flourie, T. (1999). Social and psychological aspects of epilepsy. *Exceptional Parent, 29*(10), 69–73.

National Heart, Lung, and Blood Institute. (1997). *National asthma education and prevention program expert panel report 2: Guidelines for the diagnosis and management of asthma.* Rockville, MD: National Institutes of Health.

Nickel, R. E. (2000). Cerebral palsy. In R. E. Nickel & L. W. Desch (Eds.), *The physician's guide to caring for children with disabilities and chronic conditions.* Baltimore: Brookes.

Pellegrino, L. (2002). Cerebral palsy. In M. L. Batshaw (Ed.), *Children with disabilities.* Baltimore: Brookes.

Powers, L. (2003). Health and wellness among persons with disability. In RRTC Health and Wellness Consortium (Eds.), *Changing concepts of health and disability: State of the science conference and policy forum 2003* (pp. 73–77). Portland: Oregon Health and Sciences University.

Putnam, M., Geenen, S., Powers, L. E., Saxton, M., Finney, S., & Dautel, P. (2003). Health and wellness: People with disabilities discuss barriers and facilitators to well being. *Journal of Rehabilitation, 69*(1), 37–45.

Reilly, S., Skuse, D., & Poblete, X. (1996). Prevalence of feeding problems and oral motor dysfunction in children with cerebral palsy: A community survey. *Journal of Pediatrics, 129*, 877–882.

Roberts, R. (2000). Seizure disorders. In R. E. Nickel & L. W. Desch (Eds.), *The physician's guide to caring for children with disabilities and chronic conditions.* Baltimore: Brookes.

Russell, C. L. (2004). Understanding nonverbal disorders in children with spina bifida. *Teaching Exceptional Children, 36*(4), 8–13.

Salam, M. T., Li, Y. F., Langholz, B., & Gilliland, F. D. (2004). Early-life environmental risk factors for asthma: Findings from the Children's Health Study. *Environmental Health Perspectives, 112*(6), 760–765.

Shinnar, S. (2000). Prognosis for epilepsy. *Exceptional Parent, 30*(12), 88–94.

Slezak, J. A., Persky, V. W., Kviz, F. J., Ramakrishnan, V., & Byers, C. (1998). Asthma prevalence and risk factors in selected Head Start sites in Chicago. *Asthma, 35*, 203–212.

Smith, K. (2004). *Token economies: A proactive intervention for the classroom.* Minneapolis: University of Minnesota, Institute for Community Integration.

Sotir, M., Yeatts, K., & Shy, C. (2003). Presence of asthma risk factors and environmental exposures related to upper respiratory infection–triggered wheezing in middle school–age children. *Environmental Health Perspectives, 111*(4), 657–662.

Stevenson, R. E., Allen, W. P., Pai, G. S., Best, R., Seaver, L. H., Dean, J., & Thompson, S. (2000). Decline in prevalence of neural tube defects in a high-risk region of the United States. *Pediatrics, 106*(4), 677–683.

Sullivan, N. A., Fulmer, D. L., & Zigmond, N. (2001). School: The normalizing factor for children with childhood leukemia. *Preventing School Failure, 46*(1), 4–14.

Taft, L. T. (1999). Accentuating the positive for children with cerebral palsy. *Exceptional Parent, 29*(3), 64–65.

Thies, K. (1999). Identifying the educational implications of chronic illness in school children. *Journal of School Health, 69*(10), 392–398.

Turnbull, H. R. (1976). Report of the Parents' Committee: Families in crisis, families at risk. In T. Tjossem (Ed.), *Intervention strategies for high risk infants and young children* (pp. 765–769). Baltimore: University Park Press.

Turner, G. R., & Levine, B. (2004). Disorders of executive functioning and self-awareness. In J. Ponsford (Ed.), *Cognitive and behavioral rehabilitation: From neurobiology to clinical practice* (pp. 224–268). New York: Guilford.

U.S. Department of Education, Office of Special Education Programs. (2005). *IDEA data website* (http://www.ideadata.org/aboutThisSite.asp).

Vogtle, L. K., Kern, D., & McCauley, A. (2000). Differences in the perception of social function between adolescents with and without disabilities. *Developmental Medicine and Child Neurology, 83,* 16–17.

Walders, N., McQuaid, E., & Dickstein, S. (2004). Asthma knowledge, awareness, and training: Among Head Start and early Head Start staff. *Journal of School Health, 74*(1), 32–34.

Wasserman, C. R., Shaw, G. M., Selvin, S., Gould, J. B., & Syme, S. L. (1998). Socioeconomic status, neighborhood social conditions, and neural tube defects. *American Journal of Public Health, 88*(11), 1674–1680.

Wehmeyer, M. L., Sands, D. J., Knowlton, H. E., & Kozleski, E. B. (2002). *Teaching students with mental retardation: Providing access to the general curriculum.* Baltimore: Brookes.

Weinstein, S. (2002). Epilepsy. In M. L. Batshaw (Ed.), *Children with disabilities* (5th ed.). Baltimore: Brookes.

Chapter 13

Agran, M., & Wehmeyer, M. (in press). Teaching problem solving to students with mental retardation. In M. Wehmeyer & M. Agran (Eds.), *Evidence-based practices for teaching students with mental retardation and intellectual disabilities.* Upper Saddle River, NJ: Merrill/Prentice Hall.

Anderson, V. A., Catroppa, C., Rosenfeld, J., Haritou, F., & Morse, S. A. (2000). Recovery of memory function following traumatic brain injury in pre-school children. *Brain injury, 14*(8), 679–692.

Andrews, T. K., Rose, F. D., & Johnson, D. A. (1998). Social and behavioral effects of traumatic brain injury in children. *Brain Injury, 12*(2), 133–138.

Arroyos-Jurado, E., Paulsen, J. S., Merrell, K. W., Lindgren, S. D., & Max, J. E. (2000). Traumatic brain injury in school-age children: Academic and social outcomes. *Journal of School Psychology, 38*(6), 571–587.

Bigler, E. D., Clark, E., & Farmer, J. E. (1997). *Childhood traumatic brain injury.* Austin, TX: PRO-ED.

Bloom, D. R., Levin, H. S., Ewing-Cobbs, L., Saunders, A., Song, J., Fletcher, J., et al. (2001).

Lifetime and novel psychiatric disorders after pediatric traumatic brain injury. *Journal of American Academy of Child and Adolescent Psychiatry, 40,* 572–579.

Bohnert, A. M., Parker, J. G., & Warschausky, S. A. (1997). Friendship and social adjustment of children following a traumatic brain injury: An exploratory investigation. *Developmental Neuropsychology, 13*(4), 477–486.

Brown, A. W., Leibson, C. L., Malec, J. F., Perkins, P. K., Diehl, N. N., & Larson, D. R. (2004). Long-term survival after traumatic brain injury: A population-based analysis. *Neuro Rehabilitation, 19,* 37–43.

Buyer, D. M. (1999). Neuropsychological assessment and schools. *Brain Injury Source, 3*(3), 18–20.

Cattelani, R., Lombardi, F., Brianti, R., & Mazzucchi, A. (1998). Traumatic brain injury in childhood: Intellectual, behavioural and social outcome into adulthood. *Brain Injury, 12*(4), 283–296.

Centers for Disease Control and Prevention (CDC). (1997). Traumatic brain injury— Colorado, Missouri, Oklahoma, and Utah, 1990–1993. *MMWR, 46*(1), 8–11.

Centers for Disease Control and Prevention (CDC). (1999). *Facts about concussion and brain injury.* Atlanta: Author.

Centers for Disease Control and Prevention (CDC). (2001). *National health statistics.* Atlanta: Author.

Chapman, S. B. (1998). Bridging the gap between research and education reintegration: Direct instruction on processing connected discourse. *Aphasiology, 12,* 1081–1088.

Clark, E. (1997). Children and adolescents with traumatic brain injury: Reintegration challenges in educational settings. In E. D. Bigler, E. Clark, & J. E. Farmer (Eds.), *Childhood traumatic brain injury: Diagnosis, assessment, and intervention* (pp. 191–211). Austin, TX: PRO-ED.

Clark, E., Russman, S., & Orme, S. F. (1999). Traumatic brain injury: Effects on school functioning and intervention strategies. *School Psychology Review, 28*(2), 242–250.

Cockrell, J. L., & Gregory, S. A. (1992). Audiological deficits in brain-injured children and adolescents. *Brain Injury, 6,* 261–266.

Cockrell, J. L., & Nickel, R. E. (2000). Traumatic brain injury. In R. E. Nickel & L. W. Desch (Eds.), *The physician's guide to caring for children with disabilites and chronic conditions* (pp. 513–527). Baltimore: Brookes.

Dalby, P. R., & Obrzut, J. E. (1991). Epidemiologic characteristics and sequelae of closed head-injured children and adolescents: A review. *Developmental Neuropsychology, 7*(1), 35–68.

D'Amato, R. C., & Rothlisberg, B. A. (1997). How education should respond to students with traumatic brain injury. In E. D. Bigler, E. Clark, & J. E. Farmer (Eds.), *Childhood traumatic brain injury* (pp. 213–237). Austin, TX: PRO-ED.

David, T. J. (1999). Shaken baby (shaken impact) syndrome: Non-accidental head injury in

infancy. *Journal of the Royal Society of Medicine, 92,* 556–561.

Daviss, W. B., Mooney, D., Racusin, R., Ford, J. D., Fleischer, A., & McHugo, G. J. (2000). Predicting posttraumatic stress after hospitalization for pediatric injury. *American Academy for Child and Adolescent Psychiatry, 39*(5), 576–583.

Dennis, M., Lockyer, L., Lazenby, A. L., Donnelly, R. E., Wilkinson, M., & Schoonheyt, W. (1999). Intelligence patterns among children with high-functioning autism, phenylketonuria, and childhood head injury. *Journal of Autism and Developmental Disorders, 29*(1), 5–17.

Donders, J. (1997). Sensitivity of the WISC-III to injury severity in children with traumatic head injury. *Assessment, 4*(1), 107–109.

Dykeman, B. F. (2003). School-based interventions for treating social adjustment difficulties in children with traumatic brain injury. *Journal of Instructional Psychology, 30*(3), 225–230.

Gil, A. M. (2003). Neurocognitive outcomes following pediatric brain injury: A developmental approach. *Journal of School Psychology, 41,* 337–353.

Gutentag, S. S., Naglieri, J. A., & Yeates, K. O. (1998). Performance of children with traumatic brain injury on the cognitive assessment system. *Assessment, 5*(3), 263–272.

Hall, T. (2002). *Explicit instruction: Effective classroom practices report.* Boston: National Center on Accessing the Curriculum.

Hammond, F. M., Grattan, K. D., Sasser, H., Corrigan, J. D. Rosenthal, M., Bushnik, T., & Shull, W. (2004). Five years after traumatic brain injury: A study of individual outcomes and predictors of change in function. *Neuro Rehabilitation, 19,* 25–35.

Hunt, P., Soto, G., Maier, J., Liboiron, N., & Bae, S. (2004). Collaborative teaming to support preschoolers with severe disabilities who are placed in general education early childhood programs. *Topics in Early Childhood Special Education, 24,* 123–142.

Janney, R. E., & Snell, M. E. (2000). *Teachers' guides to inclusive practices: Collaborative teaming.* Baltimore: Brookes.

Johnson, D. W., & Johnson, R. T. (1991). *Cooperation and competition: Theory and research.* Edina, MN: Interaction.

Johnson, D., Johnson, R., & Holubec, E. (1998). *Cooperation in the classroom.* Boston: Allyn & Bacon.

Kassam-Adams, N., & Winston, F. K. (2004). Predicting child PTSD: The relationship between acute stress disorder and PTSD in injured children. *American Academy for Child and Adolescent Psychiatry, 43*(4), 403–411.

Keyser-Marcus, L., Briel, L., Sherron-Targett, P., Yasuda, S., Johnson, S., & Wehmen, P. (2002). Enhancing the schooling of students with traumatic brain injury. *Teaching Exceptional Children, 38*(4), 62–67.

Koskinen, S. (1998). Quality of life 10 years after a very severe traumatic brain injury: The perspective of the injured and the closest relative. *Brain Injury, 12*(8), 631–648.

Langlois, J., & Gotsch, K. (2001). *Traumatic brain injury in the United States: Assessing outcomes in children.* Atlanta: Centers for Disease Control and Prevention (CDC), National Center for Injury Prevention and Control.

Lea, P. M. (2001). Traumatic brain injury: Developmental differences in glutamate receptor response and the impact on treatment. *Mental Retardation and Developmental-Disabilities Research Reviews, 7,* 235–248.

Max, J. E., Arndt, S., Castillo, C. A., Bokura, H., Robin, D. A., & Lindgren, S. D. (1998). Attention-deficit hyperactivity symptomatology after traumatic brain injury: A prospective study. *Journal of the American Academy of Child and Adolescent Psychiatry, 37*(8), 841–847.

Max, J. E., Robin, D. A., Lindgren, S. D., et al. (1997). Traumatic brain injury in children and adolescents: Psychiatric disorders at two years. *American Academy for Child and Adolescent Psychiatry, 36,* 1278–1285.

Michaud, L. F., Semel-Concepcion, J., Duhaime, A., & Lazar, M. R. (2002). Traumatic brain injury. In M. L. Batshaw (Ed.), *Children with disabilities* (5th ed., pp. 525–545). Baltimore: Brookes.

National Institutes of Health. (1998). Rehabilitation of persons with traumatic brain injury. *National Institutes of Health Consensus Statement, 16*(1), 1–41.

Nolet, V., & McLaughlin, M. (2000). *Accessing the general curriculum.* Thousand Oaks, CA: Corwin.

O'Neil-Pirozzi, T. M., Kendrick, H., Goldstein, R., & Glenn, M. (2004). Clinician influences on use of portable electronic memory devices in traumatic brain injury rehabilitation. *Brain Injury, 18,* 179–189.

Parente, R., Anderson-Parente, J., & Stapleton, M. (2001). The use of rhymes and mnemonics for teaching cognitive skills to persons with acquired brain injury. *Brain Injury Source, 5*(1), 16–19.

Ponsford, J., Willmott, C., Rothwell, A., Cameron, P., Ayton, G., Nelms, R., Curran, C., & Ng, K. T. (1999). Cognitive and behavioral outcomes following mild traumatic head injury in children. *Journal of Head Trauma Rehabilitation, 14,* 360–372.

Reece, R. M., & Sege, R. (2000). Childhood head injuries: Accidental or inflicted? *Archives of Pediatric and Adolescent Medicine, 154,* 11–15.

Semrud-Clikeman, M. (2001). *Traumatic brain injury in children and adolescents: Assessment and intervention.* New York: Guilford.

Suzman, K. B., Morris, R. D., Morris, M. K., & Milan, M. A. (1997). Cognitive behavioral remediation of problem solving deficits in children with acquired brain injury. *Journal of Behavioral Therapy and Experimental Psychiatry, 28,* 203–212.

Thousand, J., & Villa, R. (2000). Collaborative teaming: A powerful tool for school restructuring. In R. A. Villa & J. S. Thousand (Eds.), *Restructuring for caring and effective education: Piecing the puzzle together* (2nd ed. pp. 254–291). Baltimore: Brookes.

Thurman, D., Alverson, C., Dunn, K., Guerrero, J., & Sniezek, J. (1999). Traumatic brain injury in the United States: A public health perspective. *Journal of Head Trauma and Rehabilitation, 14*(6), 602–615.

Tyler, J. S., & Mira, M. P. (1999). *Traumatic brain injury in children and adolescents: A sourcebook for teachers and other school personnel.* Austin, TX: PRO-ED.

U.S. Department of Education, Office of Special Education Programs. (2005). *IDEA data website* (http://www.ideadata.org/aboutThis Site.asp).

Yeates, K. O., Luria, J., Bartkowski, H., Rusin, J., Martin, L., & Bigler, E. D. (1999). Postconcussive symptoms in children with mild closed head injuries. *Head Trauma Rehabilitation, 14*(4), 337–350.

Ylvisaker, M., & DeBonis, D. (2000). Executive function impairment in adolescence: TBI and ADHD. *Topics in Language Disorders, 20*(2), 29–57.

Ylvisaker, M., Hanks, R., & Johnson-Green, D. (2002). Perspectives on rehabilitation of individuals with cognitive impairment after brain injury: Rationale for reconsideration of theoretical paradigms. *Journal of Head Trauma Rehabilitation, 17*(3), 191–209.

Ylvisaker, M., Todia, B., Glang, A., Urbanczyk, B., Franklin, C., DePompei, R., et al. (2001). Educating students with TBI: Themes and recommendations. *Journal of Head Trauma Rehabilitation, 16*(1), 76.

Chapter 14

Batshaw, M. L. (2002). *Children with disabilities* (4th ed.). Baltimore: Brookes.

Block, M. H., & Okrand, M. (1983). Real-time closed-captioned television as an educational tool. *American Annals of the Deaf, 128*(5), 636–641.

Caldwell, D. C. (1973). Use of graded captions with instructional television for deaf learners. *American Annals of the Deaf, 118*(4), 500–507.

Clarke, B. R. (1983). Competence in communication for hearing impaired children: A conversation, activity, experience approach. *British Columbia Journal of Special Education, 7,* 15–27.

Commission on Education of the Deaf. (1988). *Toward equality: Education of the deaf.* Washington, DC: U.S. Government Printing Office.

Coryell, J., & Holcomb, T. K. (1997). The use of sign language and sign systems in facilitating language acquisition and communication of deaf students. *Language, Speech, and Hearing Services in Schools, 28,* 384–394.

Cummins, J. (1980). The entry and exit fallacy in bilingual education. *National Association for Bilingual Education, 4,* 25–60.

Cummins, J. (1992). Language proficiency, bilingualism, and academic achievement. In P. A. Richard-Amato & M. A. Snow (Eds.), *The multicultural classroom: Readings for content-area teachers* (pp. 16–26). Reading, MA: Addison-Wesley.

Delk, L., & Weidekamp, L. (2001). *Shared reading project: Evaluating implementation processes and family outcomes.* Washington, DC: Gallaudet University, Laurent Clerc National Deaf Education Center.

Easterbrooks, S. R., & Baker, S. (2002). *Language learning in children who are deaf and hard of hearing: Multiple pathways.* Boston: Allyn & Bacon.

Edwards, C. P., Gandini, L., & Forman, G. E. (Eds.). (1998). *The hundred languages of children: The Reggio Emilia approach—Advanced reflections* (2nd ed.). Greenwich, CT: Ablex.

Elliot, S. N., Kratochwill, T. R., & Schulte, A. G. (1998). The assessment accommodation checklist: Who, what, where, when, why, and how? *Teaching Exceptional Children, 3*(2), 10–14.

French, M. (1999). *Starting with assessment: A developmental approach to deaf children's literacy.* Washington, DC: Pre-College National Mission Programs.

Gallaudet Research Institute. (2002). *Literacy and deaf students* (http://gri.gallaudet.edu/literacy/).

Garay, S. (2003). Listening to the voices of deaf students essential transition issues. *Teaching Exceptional Children, 35*(4), 44–48.

Gerner de Garcia, B. (1995). ESL applications for Hispanic deaf students. *Bilingual Research Journal, 19,* 453-467.

Hanks, J., & Luckner, J. (2003). Job satisfaction: Perceptions of a national sample of teachers of students who are deaf or hard of hearing. *American Annals of the Deaf, 148*(1), 5–17.

Hyde, M., Power, D., & Cliffe, S. (1992). Teachers' communication with their deaf students: An Australian study. *Sign Language Studies, 75,* 159–166.

Kluwin, T. (1993). The cumulative effects of mainstreaming on the achievement of hearing impaired adolescents. *Exceptional Children, 60*(1), 73–81.

Lane, H., Hoffmeister, R., & Bahan, B. (1996). *A journey into the Deaf-world.* San Diego: Dawn Sign Press.

LaSasso, C. J., & Metzger, M. A. (1998). An alternative route for preparing deaf children for BiBi programs: The home language as L1 and cued speech for conveying traditionally-spoken languages. *Journal of Deaf Studies and Deaf Education, 3,* 265–289.

Marschark, M., Lang, H. G., & Albertini, J. A. (2002). *Educating deaf students: From research to practice.* New York: Oxford University Press.

Mayer, P., & Lowerbraun, S. (1990). Total communication use among elementary teachers of hearing-impaired children. *American Annals of the Deaf, 135,* 257–263.

Miller-Nomeland, M., & Gillespie, S. (1993). *Deaf studies curriculum guide.* Washington, DC: Gallaudet University, Pre-College Programs.

Moores, D. F. (2001). *Educating the deaf: Psychology, principles and practices* (5th ed.). Boston: Houghton Mifflin.

National agenda: Moving forward on achieving educational equality for deaf and hard of hearing students (April, 2005). (http://www.deafed.net).

National Center on Birth Defects and Developmental Disabilities. (2004). *Hearing loss* (http://www.cdc.gov/ncbddd).

National Institute on Deafness and Other Communication Disorders. (2000). Cochlear implants. *Health information: Hearing and balance* (http://www.nih.gov/nidcd/health/pubs_hb/coch.htm).

Nover, S., & Andrews, J. (1998). *Critical pedagogy in deaf education: Bilingual methodology and staff development* (Star Schools Project Grant No. R203A70030-97, Report No. 2). Santa Fe: New Mexico School for the Deaf.

Scheetz, N. A. (2004). *Psychosocial aspects of deafness*. Boston: Pearson Education.

Schleper, D. (1997). *Reading to deaf children: Learning from deaf adults*. Washington, DC: Pre-College National Mission Programs.

Spencer, P., & Meadow-Orlans, K. (1996). Play, language, and maternal responsiveness: A longitudinal study of deaf and hearing infants. *Child Development, 67,* 176–191.

Stewart, D. A., & Kluwin, T. N. (2001). *Teaching deaf and hard of hearing students: Content, strategies, and curriculum*. Needham Heights, MA: Allyn & Bacon.

Stuart, A., Harrison, D., & Simpson, P. (1991). The social and emotional development of a population of hearing-impaired children being educated in their local mainstream schools in Leicestershire, England. *Journal of the British Association of Teachers of the Deaf, 15*(5), 121–125.

Stuckless, E. R., Avery, J. C., & Hurwitz, T. A. (1989). *Educational interpreting for deaf students: Report of the National Task Force on Educational Interpreting*. Rochester, NY: Rochester Institute of Technology, National Technical Institute for the Deaf.

U.S. Department of Education. (1992). Deaf students education services: Policy guidance. *Federal Register, 57*(211). (October 30, 1992): 49274–49276.

U.S. Department of Education, Office of Special Education Programs. (2003). Individuals with Disabilities Education Act (IDEA) data (http://www.ideadata.org/).

Walker-Vann, C. (1998). Profiling Hispanic deaf students. *American Annals of the Deaf, 143,* 46–54.

Wolbers, K. A. (2002). Cultural factors and the achievement of black and Hispanic deaf students. *Multicultural Education, 10,* 43–52.

Woodward, J., & Allen, T. E. (1993). Sociolinguistic differences: U.S. teachers in residential schools and non-residential schools. *Sign Language Studies, 81,* 361–374.

Chapter 15

Allman, C. B. (2004). *Position paper: Use of extended time*. Louisville, KY: American Printing House for the Blind.

Anthony, T. L. (2000). Performing a functional low vision assessment. In F. M. D'Andrea & C. Farrenkopf (Eds.), *Looking to learn: Promoting literacy for students with low vision* (pp. 32–83). New York: AFB Press.

Anthony, T. L., Bleier, H., Fazzi, D. L., Kish, D., & Pogrund, R. L. (2002). Mobility focus: Developing early skills for orientation and mobility. In R. L. Pogrund & D. L. Fazzi (Eds.), *Early focus: Working with young children who are blind or visually impaired and their families* (2nd ed., pp. 326–404). New York: AFB Press.

Barclay, L. A. (2003). Preparation for assessment. In S. A. Goodman & S. H. Wittenstein (Eds.), *Collaborative assessment: Working with students who are blind or visually impaired, including those with additional disabilities* (pp. 37–70). New York: AFB Press.

Barraga, N. C., & Erin, J. N. (2001). *Visual impairments and learning* (4th ed.). Austin, TX: PRO-ED.

Bradley-Johnson, S. (1994). *Psychoeducational assessment of students who are visually impaired or blind*. Austin, TX: PRO-ED.

Caton, H., Pester, E., & Bradley, E. J. (1980). *Patterns: The primary braille reading program*. Louisville, KY: American Printing House for the Blind.

Corn, A. L., & Sacks, S. Z. (1994). The impact of non-driving on adults with visual impairments. *Journal of Visual Impairment and Blindness, 88*(1), 53–68.

Ferrell, K. A. (1996). Your child's development. In M. C. Holbrook (Ed.), *Children with visual impairments: A parent's guide* (pp. 73–96). Bethesda, MD: Woodbine House.

Ferrell, K. A (2000). Growth and development of young children. In M. C. Holbrook & A. J. Koenig (Eds.), *Foundations of education* (2nd ed.), *Volume I: History and theory of teaching children and youths with visual impairments* (pp. 111–134). New York: AFB Press.

Freeman, R. D., Goetz, E., Richards, D. P., & Groenveld, M. (1991). Defiers of negative prediction: A 14-year follow-up study of legally blind children. *Journal of Visual Impairment and Blindness, 85*(9), 365–370.

Harrell, L. (1992). *Children's vision concerns look beyond the eyes!* Placerville, CA: L. Harrell Productions.

Hatlen, P. H. (1996). The core curriculum for blind and visually impaired students, including those with additional disabilities. *RE:view, 28*(1), 25–32.

Hatlen, P. H., & Curry, S. A. (1987). In support of specialized programs for blind and visually impaired children: The impact of vision loss on learning. *Journal of Visual Impairment and Blindness, 81*(1), 7–13.

Huebner, K. M. (2000). Visual impairment. In M. C. Holbrook & A. J. Koenig (Eds.), *Foundations of education (2nd ed.), Volume I: History and theory of teaching children and youths with visual impairments* (pp. 55–76). New York: AFB Press.

Kirchner, C., & Diament, S. (1999). Estimates of the number of visually impaired students, their teachers, and orientation and mobility specialists. *Journal of Visual Impairment and Blindness, 93*(9), 600–606.

Koenig, A. J., & Farrenkopf, C. (1997). Essential experiences to undergird the early development of literacy. *Journal of Visual Impairment and Blindness, 91*(1), 14–24.

Koenig, A. J., & Holbrook, M. C. (1993). *Learning media assessment of students with visual impairments: A resource guide for teachers*. Austin, TX: Texas School for the Blind and Visually Impaired.

Koenig, A. J., & Holbrook, M. C. (2000). Planning instruction in unique skills. In A. J. Koenig & M. C. Holbrook (Eds.), *Foundations of education (2nd ed.), Volume II: Instructional strategies for teaching children and youths with visual impairments* (pp. 196–221). New York: AFB Press.

Koestler, F. A. (1976). *The unseen minority: A social history of blindness in the United States*. New York: McKay.

Lewis, S., & Allman, C. B. (2000). Educational programming. In M. C. Holbrook & A. J. Koenig (Eds.), *Foundations of education (2nd ed.), Volume I: History and theory of teaching children and youths with visual impairments* (pp. 218–259). New York: AFB Press.

Lewis, S., & Russo, R. (1977). Educational assessment for students who have visual impairments with other disabilities. In S. Z. Sacks & R. K. Silberman (Eds.), *Educating students who have visual impairments with other disabilities* (pp. 39–71). Baltimore: Brookes.

Liefert, F. (2003). Introduction to visual impairment. In S. A. Goodman & S. H. Wittenstein (Eds.), *Collaborative assessment: Working with students who are blind or visually impaired, including those with additional disabilities* (pp. 1–22). New York: AFB Press.

Lowenfeld, B. (1973). Psychological considerations. In B. Lowenfeld (Ed.), *The visually handicapped child in school* (pp. 27–60). New York: Day.

Lueck, A. H. (2004). Comprehensive low vision care. In A. H. Lueck (Ed.), *Functional vision: A practitioner's guide to evaluation and intervention* (pp. 3–24). Alexandria, VA: Association for Education and Rehabilitation of the Blind and Visually Impaired.

Lussenhop, K., & Corn, A. L. (2002). Comparative studies of the reading performance of students with low vision. *RE:view, 34*(2), 57–69.

Milian, M. (2000). Multicultural issues. In M. C. Holbrook & A. J. Koenig (Eds.), *Foundations of education (2nd ed.), Volume I: History and theory of teaching children and youths with visual impairments* (pp. 197–217). New York: AFB Press.

Nelson, K. A., & Dimitrova, E. (1993). Severe visual impairment in the United States and in each state. *Journal of Visual Impairment and Blindness*, 87(3), 80–85.

Pogrund, R. L. (2002). Refocus: Setting the stage for working with young children who are blind or visually impaired. In R. L. Pogrund & D. L. Fazzi (Eds.), *Early focus: Working with young children who are blind or visually impaired and their families* (2nd ed., pp. 1–15). New York: AFB Press.

Pugh, G. S., & Erin, J. (Eds.), (1999). *Blind and visually impaired students: Educational service guidelines*. Watertown, MA: Perkins School for the Blind.

Sacks, S. Z., & Silberman, R. K. (2000). Social skills. In A. J. Koenig & M. C. Holbrook (Eds.), *Foundations of education (2nd ed.), Volume II: Instructional strategies for teaching children and youths with visual impairments* (pp. 616–652). New York: AFB Press.

Scott, E. P., Jan, J. E., & Freeman, R. D. (1995). *Can't your child see? A guide for parents of visually impaired children* (3rd ed.). Austin, TX: PRO-ED.

Silberman, R. K. (2000). Children and youth with visual impairments and other exceptionalities. In M. C. Holbrook & A. J. Koening (Eds.). *Foundations of education (2nd ed.), Volume I: History and theory of teaching children and youths with visual impairments* (pp. 173–196). New York: AFB Press.

Simons, B., & Lapolice, D. J. (2000). Working effectively with a low vision clinic. In F. M. D'Andrea & C. Farrenkopf (Eds.), *Looking to learn: Promoting literacy for students with low vision* (pp. 84–116). New York: AFB Press.

U.S. Department of Education. (2002). *Twenty-fourth annual report to Congress on the implementation of the Individuals with Disabilities Education Act*. Washington, DC: Author.

U.S. Department of Education, Office of Special Education Programs. (2005). *IDEA data website* (http://www.ideadata.org/aboutThisSite.asp).

Wolffe, K. (2000). Career education. In A. J. Koenig & M. C. Holbrook (Eds.), *Foundations of education (2nd ed.), Volume II: Instructional strategies for teaching children and youths with visual impairments* (pp. 679–719). New York: AFB Press.

Wolffe, K. E., Sacks, S. Z., & Thomas, K. L. (2000). *Focused on: Importance and need for social skills*. New York: AFB Press.

Young, L. (1997). Adding positive experiences with dogs to the curriculum. *RE:view*, 29(2), 55–61.

Chapter 16

Amabile, T. M. (1990). Within you, without you: Towards a social psychology of creativity, and beyond. In M. A. Runco & R. S. Albert (Eds.), *Theories of creativity* (pp. 61–91). Newbury Park, CA: Sage.

Andrade, H. G. (2000). Using rubrics to promote thinking and learning. *Educational Leadership*, 57(5), 13–18.

Baker, E. L. (1996). Introduction to theme issue in educational assessment. *Journal of Educational Research*, 89, 194–196.

Baldwin, A. Y., & Vialle, W. (1999). *The many faces of giftedness: Lifting the masks*. Belmont, CA: Wadsworth.

Bean, S. N., & Karnes, F. A. (2001). Developing leadership potential of gifted students. In F. A. Karnes & S. M. Bean (Eds.), *Methods and materials for teaching the gifted*. Waco, TX: Prufrock.

Betts, G., & Kercher, J. (1999). *Autonomous learner model: Optimizing ability*. Greeley, CO: ALPS.

Bloom, B. S. (Ed.). (1956). *Handbook 1: Cognitive domain*. New York: McKay.

Castellano, J. A. (2003). The "browning" of American schools: Identifying and educating gifted Hispanic students. In J. A. Castellano (Ed.), *Special populations in gifted education: Working with diverse gifted learners* (pp. 29–44). Boston: Allyn & Bacon.

Clark, B. (2002). *Growing up gifted: Developing the potential of children at home and at school*. Upper Saddle River, NJ: Merrill/Prentice Hall.

Council of State Directors of Programs for the Gifted and National Association for Gifted Children. (2003). *State of the states: Gifted and talented education report 2001–2002*. Washington, DC: Author.

Davis, G. A. (2003). Identifying creative students, teaching for creative growth. In N. Colangelo & G. A. Davis (Eds.), *Handbook of gifted education* (3rd ed.). Boston: Allyn & Bacon.

Dickson, K. (2003). Gifted education and African American learners: An equity perspecitve. In J. A. Castellano (Ed.), *Special populations in gifted education: Working with diverse gifted learners* (pp. 45–64). Boston: Allyn & Bacon.

Doman, G., & Doman, J. (1994). *How to multiply your baby's intelligence* (2nd ed.). New York: Avery.

Elkind, D. (1981). *The hurried child: Growing up too fast, too soon*. Reading, MA: Addison-Wesley.

Feldhusen, J. F. (2003). Precocity and acceleration. *Gifted Education International*, 17, 55–58.

Fishkin, A. S., Cramond, B., & Olszewski-Kubilius, P. (2001). *Investigating creativity in youth: Research and methods*. Cresskill, NJ: Hampton.

Ford, D. Y., & Grantham, T. C. (2003). Providing access for culturally diverse gifted students: From deficit to dynamic thinking. *Theory into Practice*, 42(3), 217–225.

Gallagher, J. J. (2002). Gifted education in the 21st century. *Gifted Education International*, 16, 100–110.

Gardner, H. (1983). *Frames of mind: The theory of multiple intelligences*. New York: Basic Books.

Gardner, H. (1993a). *Creating minds*. New York: Basic Books.

Gardner, H. (1993b). *Multiple intelligences: The theory in practice*. New York: Basic Books.

Gardner, H. (1999). *Intelligence reframed: Multiple intelligences for the 21st century*. New York: Basic Books.

Gardner, H., & Hatch, T. (1989). Multiple intelligences go to school: Educational implications of the theory of multiple intelligences. *Educational Researcher*, 18(8), 4–9.

Goleman, D. (1995). *Emotional intelligence*. New York: McGraw-Hill.

Grantham, T. C. (2003). Increasing black student enrollment in gifted programs: An exploration of the Pulaski County special school district's advocacy efforts. *Gifted Child Quarterly*, 47(1), 46–65.

Greenwood, S. D. (2003). Contracting revisited: Lessons learned in literacy differentiation. *Journal of Adolescent and Adult Literacy*, 46, 338–350.

Guastello, S. J. (2002). *Managing emergent phenomena*. Mahwah, NJ: Erlbaum.

Guilford, J. P. (1967). *The nature of human intelligence*. New York: McGraw-Hill.

Henderson, L. M., & Ebner, F. F. (1997). The biological basis for early intervention with gifted children. *Peabody Journal of Education*, 72, 59–80.

Hodge, K. A., & Kemp, C. R. (2000). Exploring the nature of giftedness in preschool children. *Journal for the Education of the Gifted*, 24, 46–73.

Hughes, C. E., & Murawski, W. A. (2001). Lessons from another field: Applying coteaching strategies to gifted education. *Gifted Child Quarterly*, 45(3), 195–204.

Jolly, J., & Kettler, T. (2004). Authentic assessment of leadership in problem-solving groups. *Gifted Child Today*, 27(1), 32–39.

Kapusnick, R. A., & Hauslein, C. M. (2001). The "silver cup" of differentiated instruction. *Kappa Delta Pi Record*, 37, 156–159.

Karolyi, C. V., Ramos-Ford, V., & Gardner, H. (2003). Multiple intelligences: A perspective on giftedness. In N. Colangelo & G. A. Davis (Eds.), *Handbook of gifted education* (3rd ed., pp. 100–112). Boston: Allyn & Bacon.

Maker, C. J. (1993). Creativity, intelligence and problem solving: A definition and design for cross-cultural research and measurement related to giftedness. *Gifted Education International*, 9, 68–77.

Maker, C. J. (2001). DISCOVER: Assessing and developing problem solving. *Gifted Education International*, 15, 232–251.

Mayer, J. D., Perkins, D. M., Caruso, D. R., & Salovey, P. (2001). Emotional intelligence and giftedness. *Roeper Review*, 23, 131–137.

Melber, L. H. (2003). Partnerships in science learning: Museum outreach and elementary gifted education. *Gifted Child Quarterly*, 47(4), 251–258.

Miller, L. S. (2000). *Minority high academic achievement patterns and their implication for the gifted and talented education community*. Unpublished manuscript.

References

Moon, T. R., Brighton, C. M., & Callahan, C. M. (2003). State standardized testing programs: Friend or foe of gifted education? *Roeper Review, 25*(2), 49–60.

Morelock, M., & Feldman, D. (1997). High IQ children, extreme precocity and savant syndrome. In N. C. G. Davis (Ed.), *Handbook of gifted education* (pp. 382–397). Boston: Allyn & Bacon.

Mumford, M. D. (1998). Creative thought: Structure, components, and educational implications. *Roeper Review, 21*(1), 14–19.

Nakamura, J., & Csikszentmihalyi, M. (2001). Catalytic creativity: The case of Linus Pauling. *American Psychologist, 56,* 337–341.

National Research Council, Division of Behavior and Social Sciences and Education. (2002). *Minority students in special and gifted education.* Washington, DC: National Academy Press.

Neihart, M., Reis, S. M., Robinson, N. M., & Moon, S. M. (2002). *The social and emotional development of gifted children: What do we know?* Waco, TX: Prufrock.

Nevo, B. (1994). Definitions, ideologies, and hypotheses in gifted education. *Gifted Child Quarterly, 38*(4), 184–186.

Noble, T. (2004). Integrating the revised Bloom's taxonomy with multiple intelligences: A planning tool for curriculum differentiation. *Teachers College Record, 106*(1), 193–211.

Olszewski-Kubilius, P., & Turner, D. (2002). Gender differences among elementary school-aged gifted students in achievement, perceptions of ability, and subject preference. *Journal for the Education of the Gifted, 25*(3), 233–268.

Pettig, K. L. (2000). On the road to differentiated practice. *Educational Leadership, 58*(1), 14–18.

Pfeiffer, S. I. (2003). Challenges and opportunities for students who are gifted: What the experts say. *Gifted Child Quarterly, 47*(2), 161–169.

Piirto, J. (1998). *Understanding those who create.* Scottsdale, AZ: Gifted Psychology.

Public Law 103–382, Title XIV. (1988). Jacob K. Javits Gifted and Talented Students Education Act.

Purcell, J. (1992). Programs for the gifted in a state without a mandate: An "endangered species"? *Roeper Review, 15,* 93–95.

Reis, S. M. (1998). *Work left undone: Choices and compromises of talented females.* Mansfield Center, CT: Creative Learning Press.

Reis, S. M., & McCoach, D. B. (2002). Underachievement in gifted students. In S. R. M. Neihart, N. M. Robins, & S. M. Moon (Eds.), *The social and emotional development of gifted children: What do we know?* (pp. 81–92) Waco, TX: Prufrock Press.

Reis, S. M., & Renzulli, J. S. (2004). Current research on the social and emotional development of gifted and talented students: Good news and future possibilities. *Psychology in the Schools, 41*(1), 119.

Renzulli, J. S. (2002). Expanding the conception of giftedness to include co-cognitive traits to promote social capital. *Phi Delta Kappan, 84*(1), 33–58.

Renzulli, J. S., & Reis, S. M. (2003). The schoolwide enrichment model: Developing creative and productive giftedness. In N. Colangelo & G. A. Davis (Eds.), *Handbook of gifted education* (3rd ed., pp. 184–203). Boston: Allyn & Bacon.

Rizza, M. G. & Gentry, M. (2001). A legacy of promise: Reflections, suggestions, and directions from contemporary leaders in the field of gifted education. *Teacher Education, 36*(3), 167–184.

Roach, A. A., Wyman, L. T., Brookes, H., Chavez, C., Heath, S. B., & Valdes, G. (1999). Leadership giftedness: Models revisited. *Gifted Child Quarterly, 43*(1), 13–24.

Robinson, N. M. (2003). Two wrongs do not make a right: Sacrificing the needs of gifted students does not solve society's unsolved problems. *Journal for the Education of the Gifted, 26*(4), 251–273.

Salovey, P., & Mayer, J. (1990). Emotional intelligence. *Imagination, Cognition, and Personality, 9,* 185–211.

Sarouphim, K. M. (1999). Discovering multiple intelligences through a performance-based assessment: Consistency with independent ratings. *Exceptional Children, 65*(2), 151–161.

Sarouphim, K. M. (2001). DISCOVER: Concurrent validity, gender differences, and identification of minority students. *Gifted Child Quarterly, 45*(2), 130–138.

Schiever, S., & Maker, C. J. (2003). In N. Colangelo & G. A. Davis (Eds.), *Handbook of gifted education* (3rd ed., pp. 444–452). Boston: Allyn & Bacon.

Schuler, P. (2002). Perfectionism in gifted children and adolescents. In M. Neihart, S. Reis, N. M. Robinson, & S. M. Moon (Eds.), *The social and emotional development of gifted children: What do we know?* Waco, TX: Prufrock.

Seeley, K. (2003). High risk gifted learners. In N. Colangelo & G. A. Davis (Eds.), *Handbook of gifted education* (3rd ed., pp. 444–452). Boston: Allyn & Bacon.

Shaunessy, E. (2003). State policies regarding gifted education. *Gifted Child Today, 26*(3), 16–21.

Silverman, L. K. (1998). Through the lens of giftedness. *Roeper Review, 20*(3), 204–210.

Sony Pictures. (2000). *Finding Forrester.* Culver City, CA: Author.

Stamps, L. S. (2004). The effectiveness of curriculum compacting in first grade classrooms. *Roeper Review, 27*(1), 31–41.

Stephens, K. R., & Karnes, F. (2000). State definitions for the gifted and talented revisited. *Exceptional Children, 66*(2), 219–238.

Sternberg, R. J. (1985). *Beyond IQ: A triarchic theory of human intelligence.* New York: Cambridge University Press.

Swiatek, M. A., & Lupkowski-Shoplik, A. (2000). Gender differences in academic attitudes among gifted elementary school students. *Journal for the Education of the Gifted, 23,* 360–377.

Torrance, E. P. (1964). *Rewarding creative behavior.* Upper Saddle River, NJ: Merrill/Prentice Hall.

Torrance, E. P. (1966a). *Thinking creatively with pictures.* Bensenville, IL: Scholastic Testing Service.

Torrance, E. P. (1966b). *Thinking creatively with words.* Bensenville, IL: Scholastic Testing Service.

Torrance, E. P. (1984). Some products of 25 years of creativity research. *Educational Perspectives, 22*(3), 3–8.

Torrance, E. P. (1990). Torrance test of creative thinking: Norms-technical manual figural (streamlined) forms A & B. Bensenville, IL: Scholastic Testing Service.

Torrance, E. P., & Wu, T. H. (1981). A comparative longitudinal study of the adult creative achievements of elementary school children identified as highly intelligent and as highly creative. *Creative Child and Adult Quarterly, 6,* 71–76.

Uresti, R., Goertz, J., & Bernal, E. M. (2002). Maximizing achievement for potentially gifted and talented and regular minority students in a primary classroom. *Roeper Review, 25,* 27–31.

Wallace, M. (1999/2000). Nurturing noncomformists. *Educational Leadership, 57*(4), 44–46.

White, B. Y., & Fredericksen, J. R. (1998). Inquiry, modeling, and metacognition: Making science accessible to all students. *Cognition and Instruction, 16*(1), 3–118.

Name Index

Subject Index